Microsoft

Microsoft® Excel® 2010

Step by Step

Curtis Frye

PUBLISHED BY
Microsoft Press
A Division of Microsoft Corporation
One Microsoft Way
Redmond, Washington 98052-6399

Library of Congress Control Number: 2010924442

Printed and bound in the United States of America.

1 2 3 4 5 6 7 8 9 WCT 5 4 3 2 1 0

A CIP catalogue record for this book is available from the British Library.

Microsoft Press books are available through booksellers and distributors worldwide. For further information about international editions, contact your local Microsoft Corporation office or contact Microsoft Press International directly at fax (425) 936-7329. Visit our Web site at www.microsoft.com/mspress. Send comments to mspinput@microsoft.com.

Acquisitions Editor: Juliana Aldous
Developmental Editor: Devon Musgrave
Project Editor: Valerie Woolley
Editorial Production: Online Training Solutions, Inc.
Technical Reviewer: Bob Dean; Technical Review services provided by Content Master, a member of CM Group, Ltd.

Body Part No. X16-88507

Contents

Acknowledgments

Creating a book is a time-consuming (sometimes all-consuming) process, but working within an established relationship makes everything go much more smoothly. In that light, I'd like to thank Juliana Aldous Atkinson and Devon Musgrave from Microsoft Press for bringing me back for another tilt at the windmill. I've been lucky to work with Microsoft Press for the past nine years, and always enjoy working with Valerie Woolley, who oversaw this project for Microsoft Press.

I'd also like to thank Kathy Krause and Marlene Lambert of OTSI. Kathy provided able project oversight and a thorough copy edit, while Marlene managed the production process. Bob Dean did a great job with the technical edit, Elisabeth Van Every brought everything together as the book's compositor, and Jaime Odell completed the project with a careful proofread. I hope I get the chance to work with all of them again.

Introducing Microsoft Excel 2010

For those of you who are upgrading to Microsoft Excel 2010 from an earlier version of the program, this introduction summarizes the new features in Excel 2010. One of the first things you'll notice about Excel 2010 is that the program incorporates the ribbon, which was introduced in Excel 2007. If you used Excel 2003 or an earlier version of Excel, you'll need to spend only a little bit of time working with the new user interface to bring yourself back up to your usual proficiency.

Managing Excel Files and Settings in the Backstage View

If you used Excel 2007, you'll immediately notice one significant change: the Microsoft Office button, located at the top left corner of the program window in Excel 2007, has been replaced by the File tab. After releasing the 2007 Microsoft Office System, the Office User Experience team re-examined the programs' user interfaces to determine how they could be improved. During this process, they discovered that it was possible to divide user tasks into two categories: "in" tasks, such as formatting and formula creation, which affect the contents of the workbook directly, and "out" tasks, such as saving and printing, which could be considered workbook management tasks.

When the User Experience and Excel teams focused on the Excel 2007 user interface, they discovered that several workbook management tasks were sprinkled among the ribbon tabs that contained content-related tasks. The Excel team moved all of the workbook management tasks to the File tab, which users can click to display these commands in the new Backstage view.

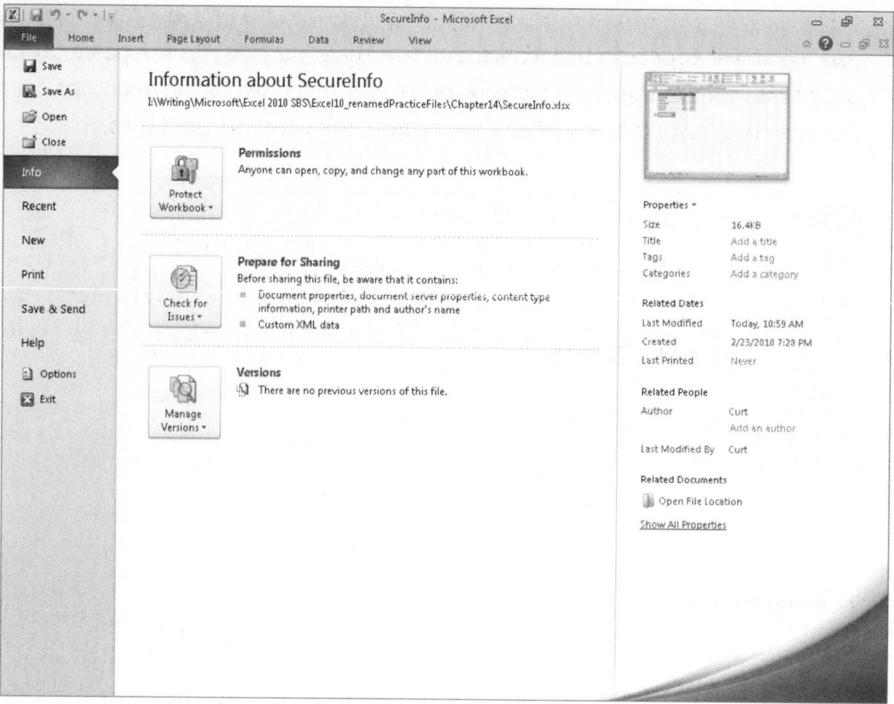

Previewing Data by Using Paste Preview

One of the most common tasks undertaken by Excel users involves cutting or copying a worksheet's contents, such as text or numbers, and pasting that data into either the same workbook or a separate Office document. Users have always been able to paste data from the Microsoft Office Clipboard and control which formatting elements were pasted into the destination; however, in versions prior to Excel 2010, you had to select a paste option, observe the results, and (often) undo the paste and try another option until you found the option that produced the desired result.

In Excel 2010, you can take advantage of the new Paste Preview capability to see how your data will appear in the worksheet before you commit to the paste. By pointing to any of the icons in the Paste Options palette, you can switch between options to discover the one that makes your pasted data appear the way you want it to.

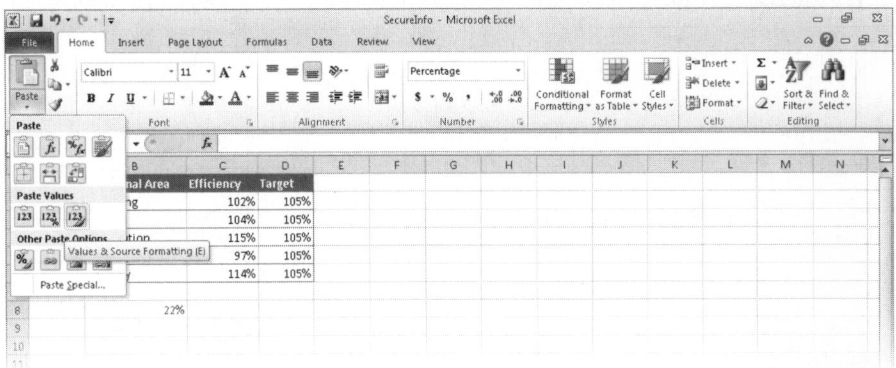

Troubleshooting The appearance of buttons and groups on the ribbon changes depending on the width of the program window. For information about changing the appearance of the ribbon to match our screen images, see "Modifying the Display of the Ribbon" at the beginning of this book.

Customizing the Excel 2010 User Interface

When the Office User Experience team designed the ribbon interface for Excel 2007, they allowed users to modify the program window by adding and removing commands on the Quick Access Toolbar. In Excel 2010, you can still modify the Quick Access Toolbar, but you also have many more options for changing the ribbon interface. You can hide or display built-in ribbon tabs, change the order of built-in ribbon tabs, add custom groups to a ribbon tab, and create custom ribbon tabs which, in turn, can contain custom groups. These custom groups provide easy access to existing ribbon commands as well as custom commands that run macros stored in the workbook.

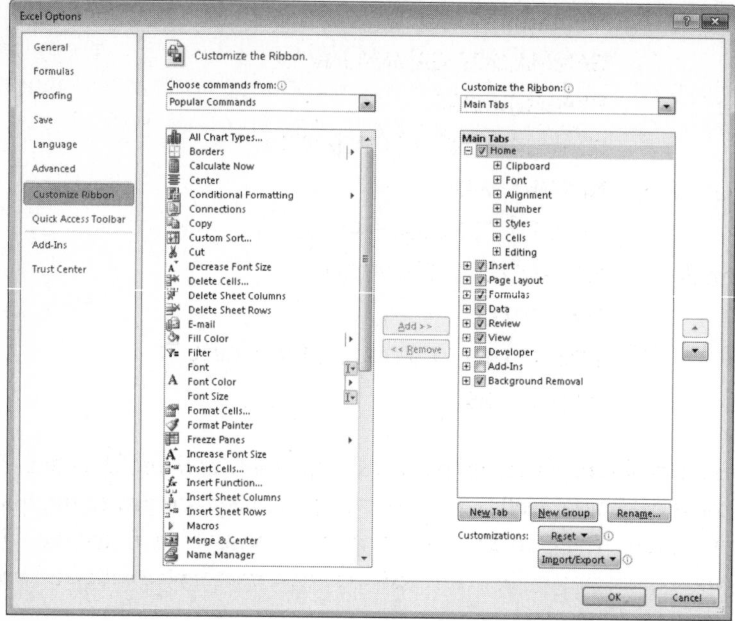

Summarizing Data by Using More Accurate Functions

In earlier versions of Excel, the program contained statistical, scientific, engineering, and financial functions that would return inaccurate results in some relatively rare circumstances. For Excel 2010, the Excel programming team identified the functions that returned inaccurate results and collaborated with academic and industry analysts to improve the functions' accuracy.

The Excel team also changed the naming conventions used to identify the program's functions. This change is most noticeable with regard to the program's statistical functions. The table below lists the statistical distribution functions that have been improved in Excel 2010.

Distribution	Functions
Beta	BETA.DIST, BETA.INV
Binomial	BINOM.DIST, BINOM.INV
Chi squared	CHISQ.DIST, CHISQ.DIST.RT, CHISQ.INV, CHISQ.INV.RT
Exponential	EXPON.DIST
F	F.DIST, F.DIST.RT, F.INV, F.INV.RT

Distribution	Functions
Gamma	GAMMA.DIST, GAMMA.INV
Hypergeometric	HYPGEOM.DIST
Lognormal	LOGNORM.DIST, LOGNORM.INV
Negative Binomial	NEGBINOM.DIST
Normal	NORM.DIST, NORM.INV
Standard Normal	NORM.S.DIST, NORMS.INV
Poisson	POISSON.DIST
Student's t	T.DIST, T.DIST.RT, T.DIST.2T, T.INV, T.INV.2T
Weibull	WEIBULL.DIST

Excel 2010 also contains more accurate statistical summary and test functions. The following table lists those functions, as well as the new naming convention that distinguishes between new and old functions. The Excel programming team chose to retain the older functions to ensure that workbooks created in Excel 2010 would be compatible with workbooks created in previous versions of the program.

Function name	Description
CEILING.PRECISE	Consistent with mathematical definition; rounds up towards positive infinity regardless of sign of number being rounded
FLOOR.PRECISE	Consistent with mathematical definition; rounds down towards negative infinity regardless of sign of number being rounded
CONFIDENCE.NORM	Name for existing CONFIDENCE function that is internally consistent with naming of other confidence function
CONFIDENCE.T	Consistent definition with industry best practice;. confidence function assuming a Student's t distribution
COVARIANCE.P	Name for existing COVAR function that is internally consistent with naming of other covariance function
COVARIANCE.S	Internally consistent name with other functions that act on a population or a sample
MODE.MULT	Consistent with user expectations; returns multiple modes for a range
MODE.SNGL	Name for existing MODE function that is internally consistent with naming of other mode function
PERCENTILE.EXC	Consistent with industry best practices, assuming percentile is a value between 0 and 1, exclusive
PERCENTILE.INC	Name for existing PERCENTILE function that is internally consistent with naming of other percentile function

Function name	Description
PERCENTRANK.EXC	Consistent with industry best practices; assuming percentile is a value between 0 and 1, exclusive
PERCENTRANK.INC	Name for existing PERCENTRANK function that is internally consistent with naming of other PERCENTRANK function
QUARTILE.EXC	Consistent with industry best practices, assuming percentile is a value between 0 and 1, exclusive
QUARTILE.INC	Name for existing QUARTILE function that is internally consistent with naming of other quartile function
RANK.AVG	Consistent with industry best practices, returning the average rank when there is a tie
RANK.EQ	Name for existing RANK function that is internally consistent with naming of other rank function
STDEV.P	Name for existing STDEVP function that is internally consistent with naming of other standard deviation function
STDEV.S	Name for existing STDEV function that is internally consistent with naming of other standard deviation function
VAR.P	Name for existing VARP function that is internally consistent with naming of other variance function
VAR.S	Name for existing VAR function that is internally consistent with naming of other variance function
CHISQ.TEST	Name for existing CHITEST function that is internally consistent with naming of other hypothesis test functions
F.TEST	Name for existing FTEST function that is internally consistent with naming of other hypothesis functions
T.TEST	Name for existing TTEST function that is internally consistent with naming of other hypothesis functions
Z.TEST	Name for existing ZTEST function that is internally consistent with naming of other hypothesis functions

It is possible in Excel 2010 to create formulas by using the older functions. The Excel team assigned these functions to a new group called Compatibility Functions. These older functions appear at the bottom of the Formula AutoComplete list, but they are marked with a different icon than the newer functions. Additionally, the tooltip that appears when you point to the older function's name indicates that the function is included for backward compatibility only.

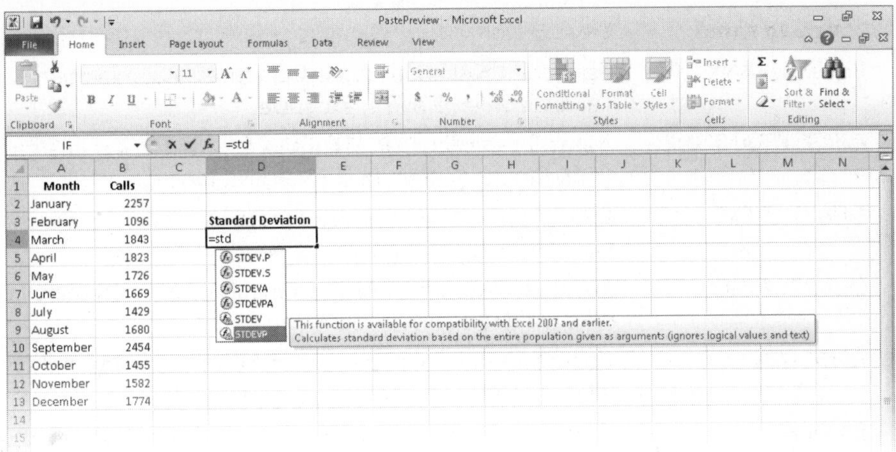

When a user saves a workbook that contains functions that are new in Excel 2010 to an older format, the Compatibility Checker flags the functions and indicates that they will return a #NAME? error when the workbook is opened in Excel 2007 or earlier versions.

Summarizing Data by Using Sparklines

In his book *Beautiful Evidence*, Edward Tufte describes sparklines as "intense, simple, wordlike graphics." In Excel 2010, sparklines take the form of small charts that summarize data in a single cell. These small but powerful additions to Excel 2010 enhance the program's reporting and summary capabilities.

Adding a sparkline to a summary worksheet provides context for a single value, such as an average or total, displayed in the worksheet. Excel 2010 includes three types of sparklines: line, column, and win/loss. A line sparkline is a line chart that displays a data trend over time. A column sparkline summarizes data by category, such as sales by product type or by month. Finally, a win/loss sparkline indicates whether the points in a data series are positive, zero, or negative.

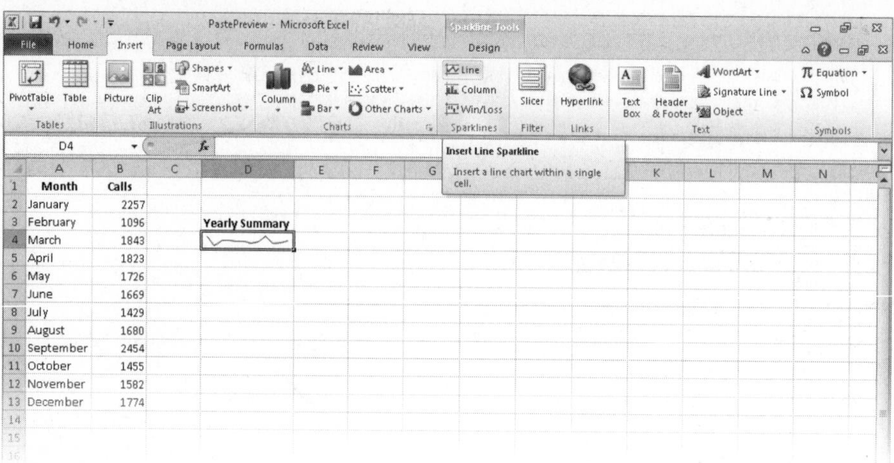

Filtering PivotTable Data by Using Slicers

With PivotTables, users can summarize large data sets efficiently, such as by rearranging values dynamically to emphasize different aspects of the data. It's often useful to be able to limit the data that appears in a PivotTable, so the Excel team included the functionality for users to filter PivotTables. The PivotTable indicates that a filter is present for a particular data column, but it doesn't indicate which items are currently displayed or hidden by the filter.

Slicers, which are new in Excel 2010, visually indicate which values appear in a PivotTable and which are hidden. They are particularly useful when presenting data to an audience that contains visual thinkers who might not be skilled at working with numerical values. For example, a corporate analyst could use a Slicer to indicate which months are displayed in a PivotTable that summarizes monthly package volumes.

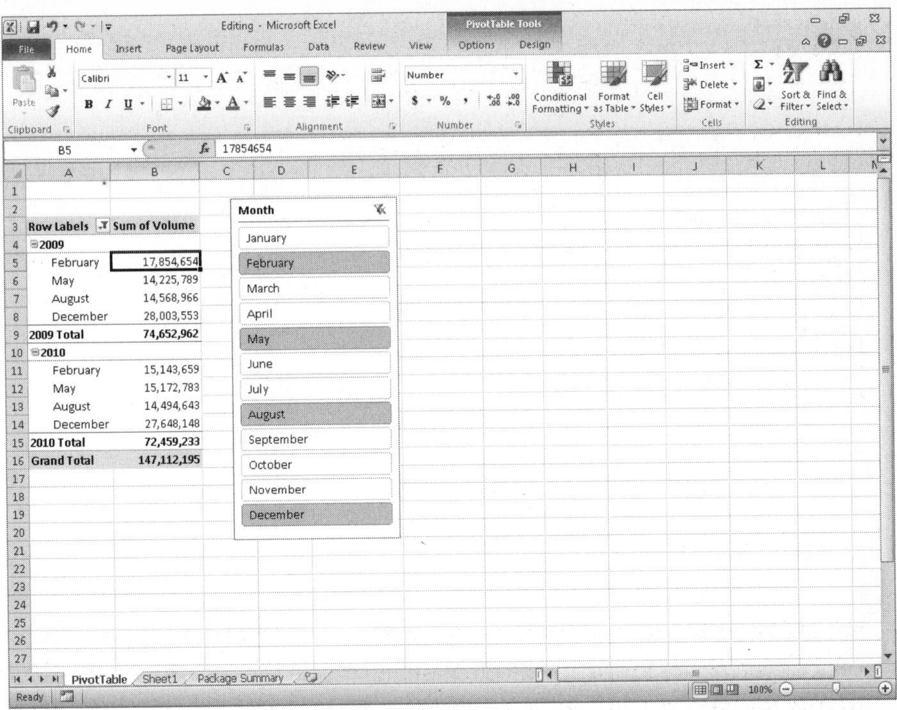

Filtering PivotTable Data by Using Search Filters

Excel 2007 introduced several new ways to filter PivotTables. Excel 2010 extends these filtering capabilities by introducing search filters. With a search filter, you begin typing a sequence of characters that occur in the term (or terms) by which you want to filter. As you type in these characters, the PivotTable field's filter list displays only those terms that reflect the values entered into the search filter box.

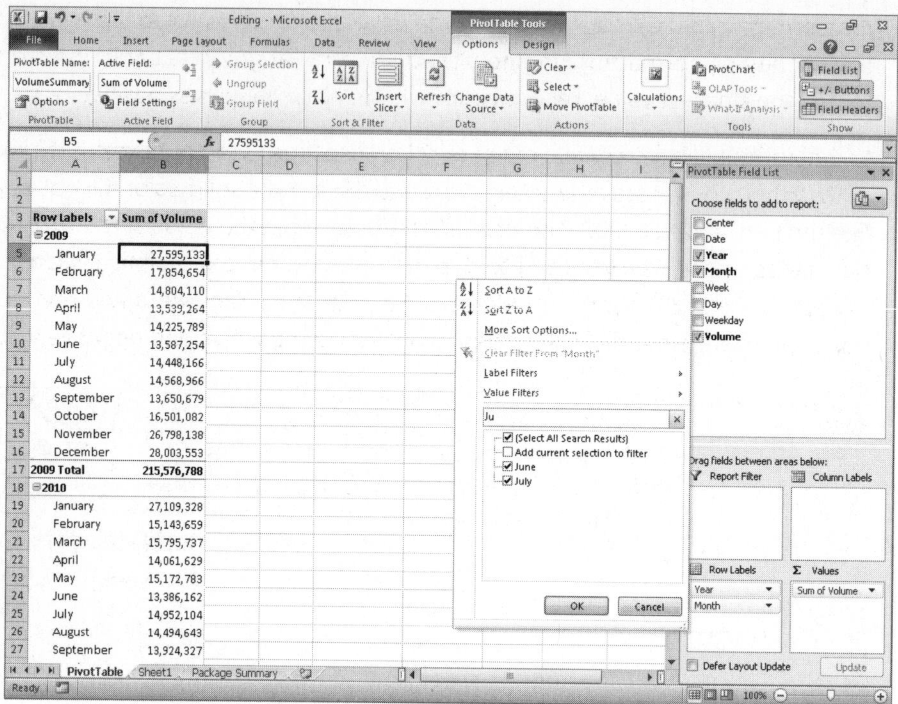

Visualizing Data by Using Improved Conditional Formats

In Excel 2007, the Excel programming team greatly improved the user's ability to change a cell's format based on the cell's contents. One new conditional format, data bars, indicated a cell's relative value by the length of the bar within the cell that contained the value. The cell in the range that contained the smallest value displayed a zero-length bar, and the cell that contained the largest value displayed a bar that spanned the entire cell width.

The default behavior of the Excel 2010 data bars has been changed so that bar length is calculated in comparison to a baseline value, such as zero. If you prefer, you can display values based on the Excel 2007 method or change the comparison value to something other than zero. Data bars in Excel 2010 also differ from those in Excel 2007 in that they display negative values in a different color than the positive values. In addition, data bars representing negative values extend to the left of the baseline, not to the right. In Excel 2007, the conditional formatting engine placed the zero-length data bar in the cell that contained the smallest value, regardless of whether that value was positive or negative.

You have much more control over your data bars' formatting in Excel 2010 than in Excel 2007. When you create a data bar in Excel 2010, it has a solid color fill, not a gradient fill like the bars in Excel 2007. The gradient fill meant that the color of the Excel 2007 data bars faded as the bar extended to the right, making the cells' relative values harder to discern. In Excel 2010 you can select a solid or gradient fill style, apply borders to data bars, and change the fill and border colors for both positive and negative values.

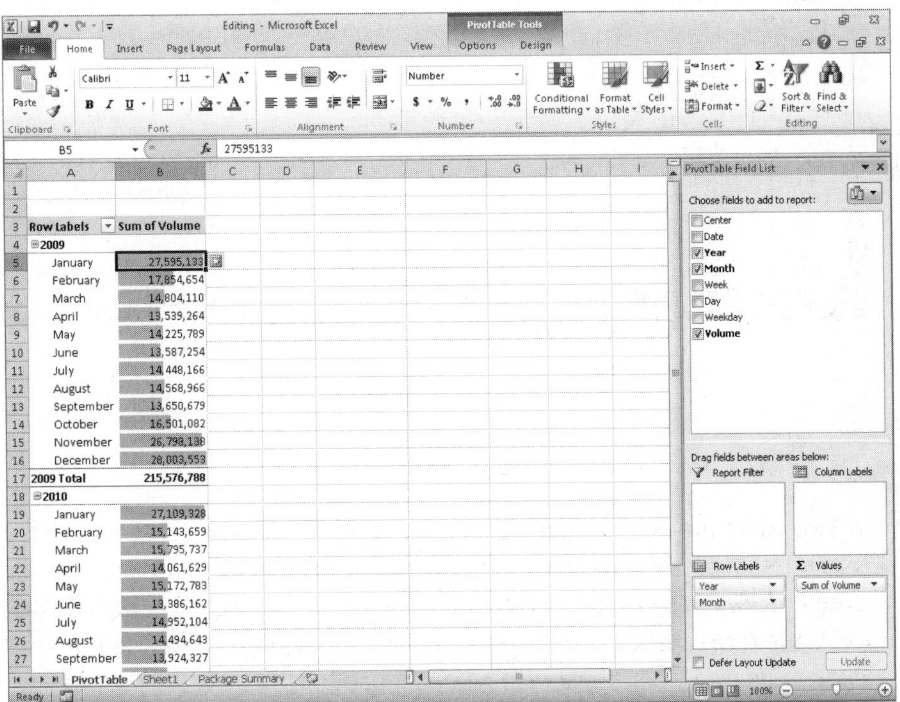

Another conditional format introduced in Excel 2007, icon sets, displayed an icon selected from a set of three, four, or five icons based on a cell's value. In Excel 2007, users were limited to using the icons within each set and had no ability to create their own sets. In Excel 2010, you can create custom icon sets from the icons included in the program and, if you prefer, define conditions that, when met, display no icon in the cell.

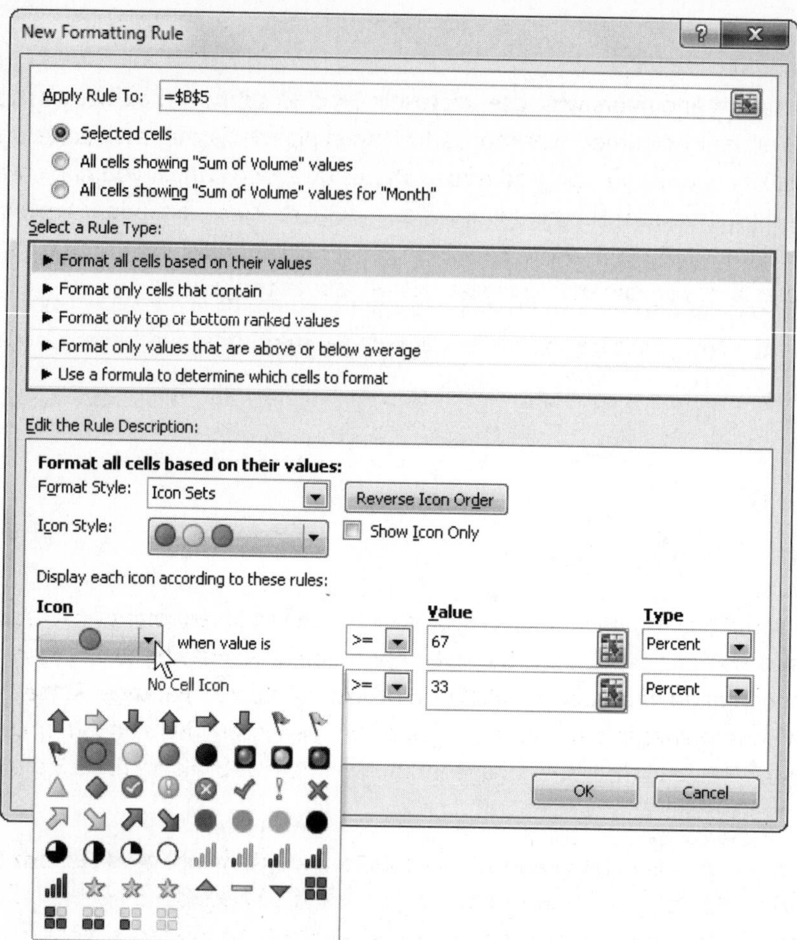

Finally, with Excel 2010 you can create conditional formats that refer to values on worksheets other than the sheet that contains the cell you're formatting. In previous versions of Excel, users had to create conditional formats that referred to values on the same worksheet.

Creating and Displaying Math Equations

Scientists and engineers who use Microsoft Excel to support their work often want to include equations in their workbooks to help explain how they arrived at their results. Excel 2010 includes an updated equation designer with which you can create any equation you require. The new editor has several common equations built in, such as the quadratic formula and the Pythagorean theorem, but it also contains numerous templates that you can use to create custom equations quickly.

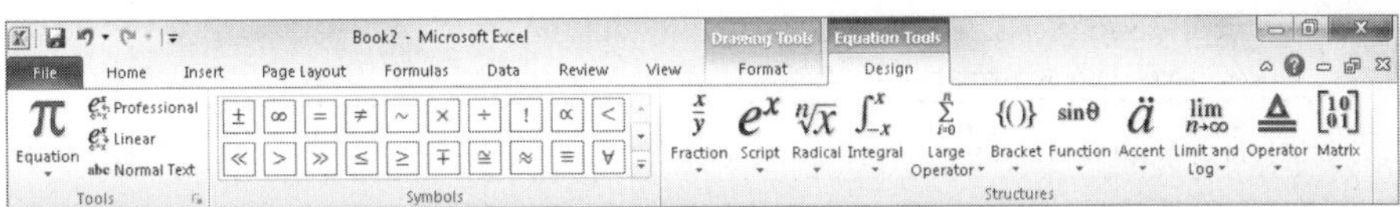

Editing Pictures within Excel 2010

When you present data in an Excel workbook, you can insert images into your worksheets to illustrate aspects of your data. For example, a shipping company could display a scanned image of a tracking label or a properly prepared package. Rather than having to edit your images in a separate program and then insert them into your Excel 2010 workbook, you can insert the image and then modify it by using the editing tools built into Excel 2010.

One very helpful capability that is new in Excel 2010 is the ability to remove the background elements of an image. Removing an image's background enables you to create a composite image in which the foreground elements are placed in front of another background. For example, you could focus on a flower's bloom and remove most of the leaves and stem from the photo. After you isolate the foreground image, you can place the bloom in front of another background.

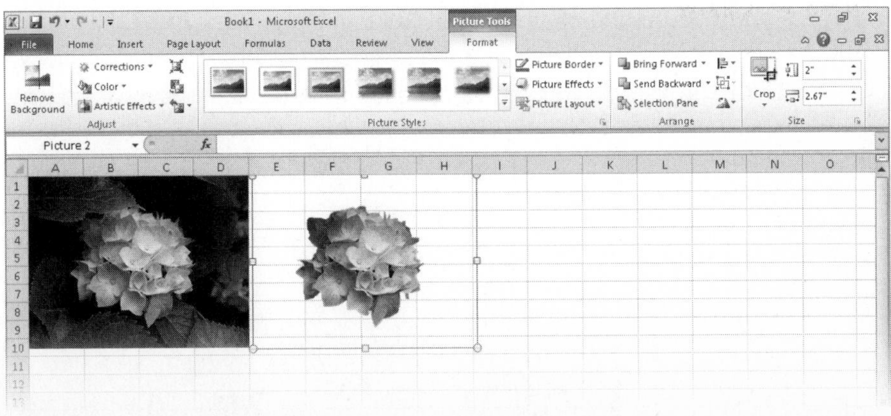

Managing Large Worksheets by Using the 64-bit Version of Excel 2010

Some Excel 2010 users, such as business analysts and scientists, will need to manipulate extremely large data sets. In some cases, these data sets won't fit into the more than one million rows available in a standard Excel 2010 worksheet. To meet the needs of these users, the Excel product team developed the 64-bit version of Excel 2010. The 64-bit version takes advantage of the greater amount of random access memory (RAM) available in newer computers. As a result of its ability to use more RAM than the standard 32-bit version of Excel 2010, users of the 64-bit version can store hundreds of millions of rows of data in a worksheet. In addition, the 64-bit version takes advantage of multicore processors to manage its larger data collections efficiently.

All of the techniques described in *Microsoft Excel 2010 Step by Step* apply to both the 32-bit and 64-bit versions of the program.

Summarizing Large Data Sets by Using the PowerPivot (Project Gemini) Add-In

As businesses collect and maintain increasingly large data sets, the need to analyze that data efficiently grows in importance. More powerful computers offer some performance improvements, but even the fastest computer takes a long time to process huge data sets when using traditional data-handling procedures. A new add-in, PowerPivot for Excel 2010, uses enhanced data management techniques to store the data in a computer's memory, rather than forcing the Excel program to read the data from a hard disk. Reading data from a computer's memory instead of a hard disk speeds up the data analysis and display operations substantially. Tasks that might have taken minutes to complete in Excel 2010 without the PowerPivot add-in now take seconds.

PowerPivot relies on the Microsoft SQL Server Analysis Services engine to produce its results, so discussion of it is outside the scope of this book. If you would like to learn more about PowerPivot, you can visit the team's blog at blogs.msdn.com/powerpivot/.

Accessing Your Data from Almost Anywhere by Using the Excel Web App and Excel Mobile 2010

As the workforce becomes increasingly mobile, information workers need to access their Excel 2010 data as they move around the world. To enable these mobile use scenarios, the Excel product team developed the Excel Web App and Excel Mobile 2010. The Excel Web App provides a high-fidelity experience that is very similar to the experience of using the Excel 2010 desktop application. In addition, you can collaborate with other users in real time. The Excel Web App identifies which changes were made by which users and enables you to decide which changes to keep and which to reject.

You can use the Excel Web App in Windows Internet Explorer 7 or 8, Safari 4, and Firefox 3.5.

With Excel Mobile 2010, you can access and, in some cases, manipulate your data by using a Windows Phone or other mobile device. If you have a Windows Phone running Windows Mobile 6.5, you can use Excel Mobile 2010 to view and edit your Excel 2010 workbooks. If you have another mobile device that provides access to the Web, you can use your device's built-in Web browser to view your files.

A full discussion of the Excel Web App and Excel Mobile 2010 are beyond the scope of this book.

Modifying the Display of the Ribbon

The goal of the Microsoft Office working environment is to make working with Office documents, including Microsoft Word documents, Excel workbooks, PowerPoint presentations, Outlook e-mail messages, and Access database tables, as intuitive as possible. You work with an Office document and its contents by giving commands to the program in which the document is open. All Office 2010 programs organize commands on a horizontal bar called the *ribbon*, which appears across the top of each program window whether or not there is an active document.

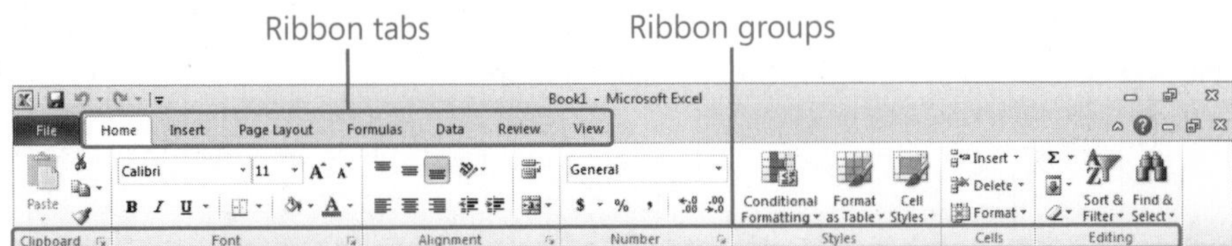

Commands are organized on task-specific tabs of the ribbon, and in feature-specific groups on each tab. Commands generally take the form of buttons and lists. Some appear in galleries. Some groups have related dialog boxes or task panes that contain additional commands.

Throughout this book, we discuss the commands and ribbon elements associated with the program feature being discussed. In this topic, we discuss the general appearance of the ribbon, things that affect its appearance, and ways of locating commands that aren't visible on compact views of the ribbon.

Tip Some older commands no longer appear on the ribbon, but are still available in the program. You can make these commands available by adding them to the Quick Access Toolbar. For more information, see "Customizing the Excel 2010 Program Window" in Chapter 1, "Setting Up a Workbook."

Dynamic Ribbon Elements

The ribbon is dynamic, meaning that the appearance of commands on the ribbon changes as the width of the ribbon changes. A command might be displayed on the ribbon in the form of a large button, a small button, a small labeled button, or a list entry. As the width of the ribbon decreases, the size, shape, and presence of buttons on the ribbon adapt to the available space.

For example, when sufficient horizontal space is available, the buttons on the Review tab of the Word program window are spread out and you're able to see more of the commands available in each group.

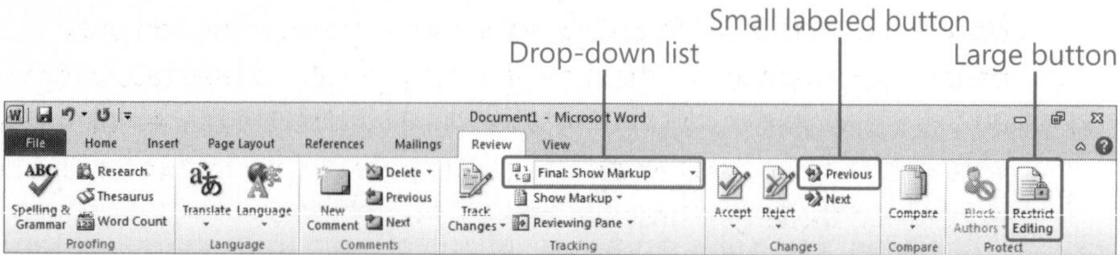

If you decrease the width of the ribbon, small button labels disappear and entire groups of buttons hide under one button that represents the group. Click the group button to display a list of the commands available in that group.

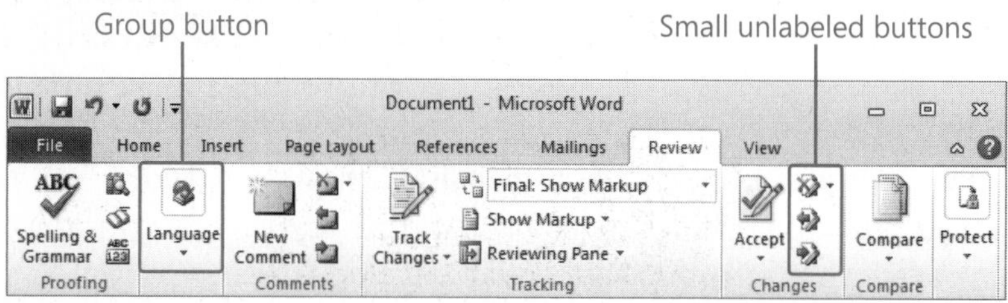

When the window becomes too narrow to display all the groups, a scroll arrow appears at its right end. Click the scroll arrow to display hidden groups.

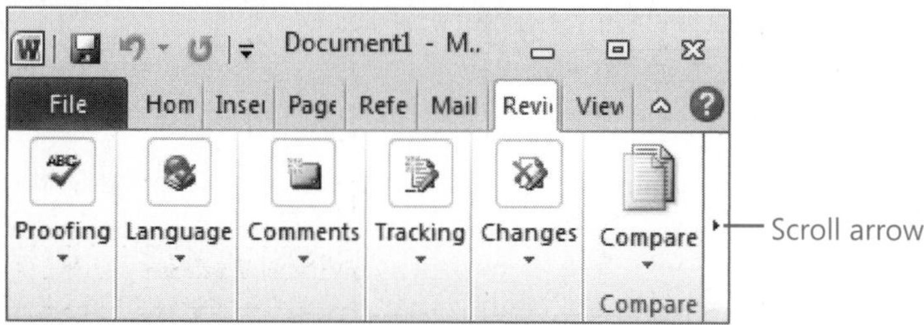

Changing the Width of the Ribbon

The width of the ribbon is dependent on the horizontal space available to it, which depends on these three factors:

- **The width of the program window** Maximizing the program window provides the most space for ribbon elements. You can resize the program window by clicking the button in its upper-right corner or by dragging the border of a non-maximized window.

Tip On a computer running Windows 7, you can maximize the program window by dragging its title bar to the top of the screen.

- Your screen resolution Screen resolution is the size of your screen display expressed as pixels wide × pixels high. The greater the screen resolution, the greater the amount of information that will fit on one screen. Your screen resolution options are dependent on your monitor. At the time of writing, possible screen resolutions range from 800 × 600 to 2048 × 1152. In the case of the ribbon, the greater the number of pixels wide (the first number), the greater the number of buttons that can be shown on the ribbon, and the larger those buttons can be.

  On a computer running Windows 7, you can change your screen resolution from the Screen Resolution window of Control Panel. You set the resolution by dragging the pointer on the slider.

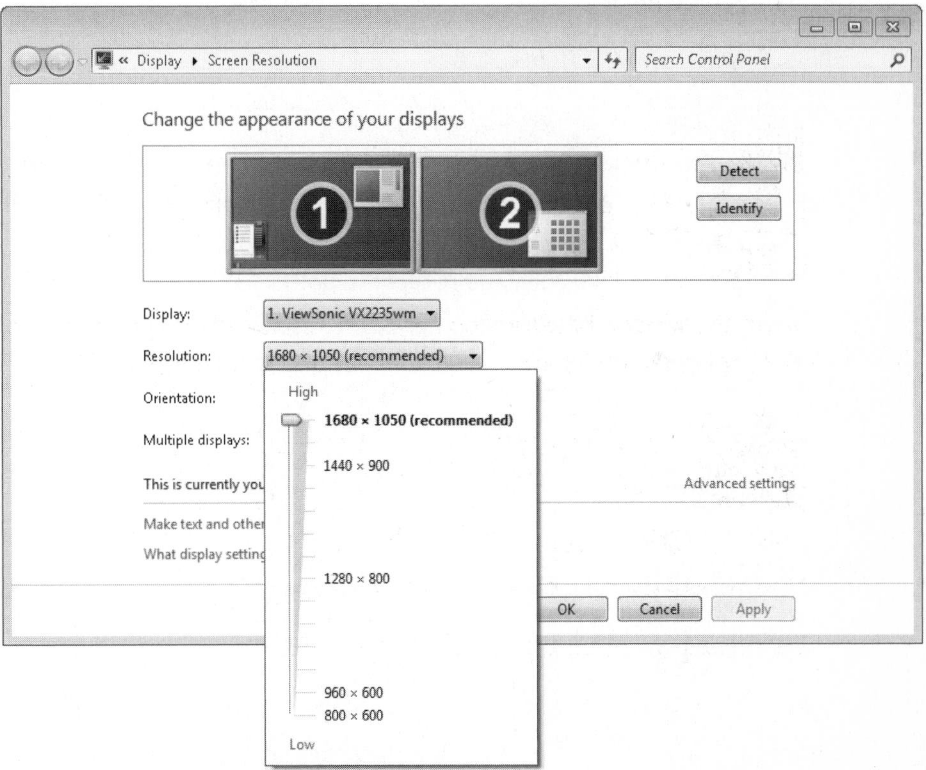

- The density of your screen display You might not be aware that you can change the magnification of everything that appears on your screen by changing the screen magnification setting in Windows. Setting your screen magnification to 125% makes text and user interface elements larger on screen. This increases the legibility of information, but means that less fits onto each screen.

On a computer running Windows 7, you can change the screen magnification from the Display window of Control Panel. You can choose one of the standard display magnification options, or create another by setting a custom text size.

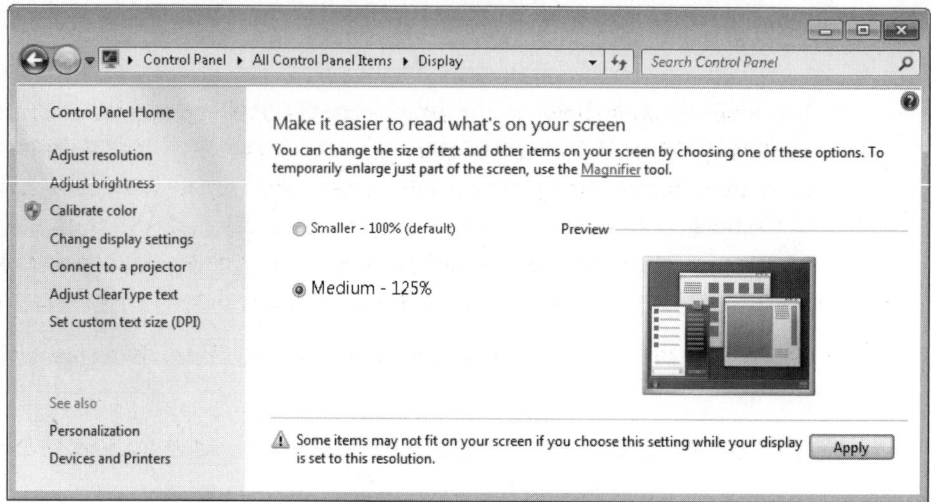

The screen magnification is directly related to the density of the text elements on screen, which is expressed in dots per inch (dpi) or points per inch (ppi). (The terms are interchangeable, and in fact are both used in the Windows dialog box in which you change the setting.) The greater the dpi, the larger the text and user interface elements appear on screen. By default, Windows displays text and screen elements at 96 dpi. Choosing the Medium - 125% display setting changes the dpi of text and screen elements to 120 dpi. You can choose a custom setting of up to 500% magnification, or 480 dpi, in the Custom DPI Setting dialog box. The list allows you to choose a magnification of up to 200%.You can choose a greater magnification by dragging across the ruler from left to right.

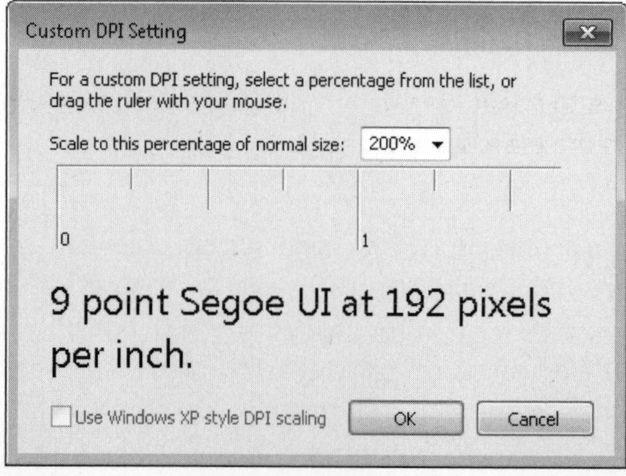

See Also For more information about display settings, refer to *Windows 7 Step by Step* (Microsoft Press, 2009), *Windows Vista Step by Step* (Microsoft Press, 2006), or *Windows XP Step by Step* (Microsoft Press, 2002) by Joan Lambert Preppernau and Joyce Cox.

Adapting Exercise Steps

The screen images shown in the exercises in this book were captured at a screen resolution of 1024 × 768, at 100% magnification, and the default text size (96 dpi). If any of your settings are different, the ribbon on your screen might not look the same as the one shown in the book. For example, you might see more or fewer buttons in each of the groups, the buttons you see might be represented by larger or smaller icons than those shown, or the group might be represented by a button that you click to display the group's commands.

When we instruct you to give a command from the ribbon in an exercise, we do it in this format:

- On the **Insert** tab, in the **Illustrations** group, click the **Chart** button.

If the command is in a list, we give the instruction in this format:

- On the **Page Layout** tab, in the **Page Setup** group, click the **Breaks** button and then, in the list, click **Page**.

The first time we instruct you to click a specific button in each exercise, we display an image of the button in the page margin to the left of the exercise step.

If differences between your display settings and ours cause a button on your screen to look different from the one shown in the book, you can easily adapt the steps to locate the command. First, click the specified tab. Then locate the specified group. If a group has been collapsed into a group list or group button, click the list or button to display the group's commands. Finally, look for a button that features the same icon in a larger or smaller size than that shown in the book. If necessary, point to buttons in the group to display their names in ScreenTips.

If you prefer not to have to adapt the steps, set up your screen to match ours while you read and work through the exercises in the book.

Features and Conventions of This Book

This book has been designed to lead you step by step through all the tasks you're most likely to want to perform in Microsoft Excel 2010. If you start at the beginning and work your way through all the exercises, you'll gain enough proficiency to be able to create and work with all the common types of Excel workbooks. However, each topic is self contained. If you've worked with a previous version of Excel, or if you completed all the exercises and later need help remembering how to perform a procedure, the following features of this book will help you locate specific information:

- **Detailed table of contents** Search the listing of the topics and sidebars within each chapter.
- **Chapter thumb tabs** Easily locate the beginning of the chapter you want.
- **Topic-specific running heads** Within a chapter, quickly locate the topic you want by looking at the running heads at the top of odd-numbered pages.
- **Glossary** Look up the meaning of a word or the definition of a concept.
- **Detailed index** Look up specific tasks and features in the index, which has been carefully crafted with the reader in mind.

You can save time when reading this book by understanding how the *Step by Step* series shows exercise instructions, keys to press, buttons to click, and other information.

Convention	Meaning
SET UP	This paragraph preceding a step-by-step exercise indicates the practice files that you will use when working through the exercise. It also indicates any requirements you should attend to or actions you should take before beginning the exercise.
CLEAN UP	This paragraph following a step-by-step exercise provides instructions for saving and closing open files or programs before moving on to another topic. It also suggests ways to reverse any changes you made to your computer while working through the exercise.
1 2	Blue numbered steps guide you through hands-on exercises in each topic.
1 2	Black numbered steps guide you through procedures in sidebars and expository text.
See Also	This paragraph directs you to more information about a topic in this book or elsewhere.
Troubleshooting	This paragraph alerts you to a common problem and provides guidance for fixing it.
Tip	This paragraph provides a helpful hint or shortcut that makes working through a task easier.
Important	This paragraph points out information that you need to know to complete a procedure.
Keyboard Shortcut	This paragraph provides information about an available keyboard shortcut for the preceding task.
Ctrl+B	A plus sign (+) between two keys means that you must press those keys at the same time. For example, "Press Ctrl+B" means that you should hold down the Ctrl key while you press the B key.
	Pictures of buttons appear in the margin the first time the button is used in a chapter.
Black bold	In exercises that begin with SET UP information, the names of program elements, such as buttons, commands, windows, and dialog boxes, as well as files, folders, or text that you interact with in the steps, are shown in black, bold type.
Blue bold	In exercises that begin with SET UP information, text that you should type is shown in blue bold type.

Using the Practice Files

Before you can complete the exercises in this book, you need to copy the book's practice files to your computer. These practice files, and other information, can be downloaded from the book's detail page, located at:

go.microsoft.com/fwlink/?LinkId=191751

Display the detail page in your Web browser and follow the instructions for downloading the files.

Important The Microsoft Excel 2010 program is not available from this Web site. You should purchase and install that program before using this book.

The following table lists the practice files for this book.

Chapter	File
Chapter 1: Setting Up a Workbook	ExceptionSummary_start.xlsx ExceptionTracking_start.xlsx MisroutedPackages_start.xlsx PackageCounts_start.xlsx RouteVolume_start.xlsx
Chapter 2: Working with Data and Excel Tables	2010Q1ShipmentsByCategory_start.xlsx AverageDeliveries_start.xlsx DriverSortTimes_start.xlsx Series_start.xlsx ServiceLevels_start.xlsx
Chapter 3: Performing Calculations on Data	ConveyerBid_start.xlsx ITExpenses_start.xlsx PackagingCosts_start.xlsx VehicleMiles_start.xlsx

(continued)

Chapter	File
Chapter 4: Changing Workbook Appearance	CallCenter_start.xlsx Dashboard_start.xlsx ExecutiveSearch_start.xlsx HourlyExceptions_start.xlsx HourlyTracking_start.xlsx phone.jpg texture.jpg VehicleMileSummary_start.xlsx
Chapter 5: Focusing on Specific Data by Using Filters	Credit_start.xlsx ForFollowUp_start.xlsx PackageExceptions_start.xlsx
Chapter 6: Reordering and Summarizing Data	GroupByQuarter_start.xlsx ShipmentLog_start.xlsx ShippingSummary_start.xlsx
Chapter 7: Combining Data from Multiple Sources	Consolidate_start.xlsx DailyCallSummary_start.xlsx FebruaryCalls_start.xlsx FleetOperatingCosts_start.xlsx JanuaryCalls_start.xlsx OperatingExpenseDashboard_start.xlsx
Chapter 8: Analyzing Alternative Data Sets	2DayScenario_start.xlsx AdBuy_start.xlsx DriverSortTimes_start.xlsx MultipleScenarios_start.xlsx TargetValues_start.xlsx
Chapter 9: Creating Dynamic Lists by Using PivotTables	Creating_start.txt Creating_start.xlsx Editing_start.xlsx Focusing_start.xlsx Formatting_start.xlsx

Chapter	File
Chapter 10: Creating Charts and Graphics	FutureVolumes_start.xlsx OrgChart_start.xlsx RevenueAnalysis_start.xlsx RevenueSummary_start.xlsx Shapes_start.xlsx VolumebyCenter_start.xlsx YearlyPackageVolume_start.xlsx
Chapter 11: Printing	ConsolidatedMessenger.png CorporateRevenue_start.xlsx HourlyPickups_start.xlsx PickupsByHour_start.xlsx RevenueByCustomer_start.xlsx SummaryByCustomer_start.xlsx
Chapter 12: Automating Repetitive Tasks by Using Macros	PerformanceDashboard_start.xlsm RunOnOpen_start.xlsm VolumeHighlights_start.xlsm YearlySalesSummary_start.xlsx
Chapter 13: Working with Other Microsoft Office Programs	2010YearlyRevenueSummary_start.pptx Hyperlink_start.xlsx LevelDescriptions_start.xlsx RevenueByServiceLevel_start.xlsx RevenueChart_start.xlsx RevenueSummary_start.pptx SummaryPresentation_start.xlsx
Chapter 14: Collaborating with Colleagues	CostProjections_start.xlsx ProjectionChangeTracking_start.xlsx ProjectionsForComment_start.xlsx ProjectionsSigned_start.xlsx SecureInfo_start.xlsx ShipmentSummary_start.xlsx

Getting Help

Every effort has been made to ensure the accuracy of this book. If you do run into problems, please contact the sources listed in the following topics.

Getting Help with This Book

If your question or issue concerns the content of this book or its practice files, please first consult the book's errata page, which can be accessed at:

go.microsoft.com/fwlink/?LinkId=191751

This page provides information about known errors and corrections to the book. If you do not find your answer on the errata page, send your question or comment to Microsoft Press Technical Support at:

mspinput@microsoft.com

Getting Help with Excel 2010

If your question is about Microsoft Excel 2010, and not about the content of this book, your first recourse is the Excel Help system. This system is a combination of tools and files stored on your computer when you installed Excel and, if your computer is connected to the Internet, information available from Office.com. You can find general or specific Help information in the following ways:

- To find out about an item on the screen, you can display a ScreenTip. For example, to display a ScreenTip for a button, point to the button without clicking it. The ScreenTip gives the button's name, the associated keyboard shortcut if there is one, and unless you specify otherwise, a description of what the button does when you click it.
- In the Excel program window, you can click the Microsoft Excel Help button (a question mark in a blue circle) at the right end of the ribbon to display the Excel Help window.
- After opening a dialog box, you can click the Help button (also a question mark) at the right end of the dialog box title bar to display the Excel Help window. Sometimes, topics related to the functions of that dialog box are already identified in the window.

To practice getting help, you can work through the following exercise.

SET UP You don't need any practice files to complete this exercise. Start Excel, and then follow the steps.

1. At the right end of the ribbon, click the **Microsoft Excel Help** button.

   The Excel Help window opens.

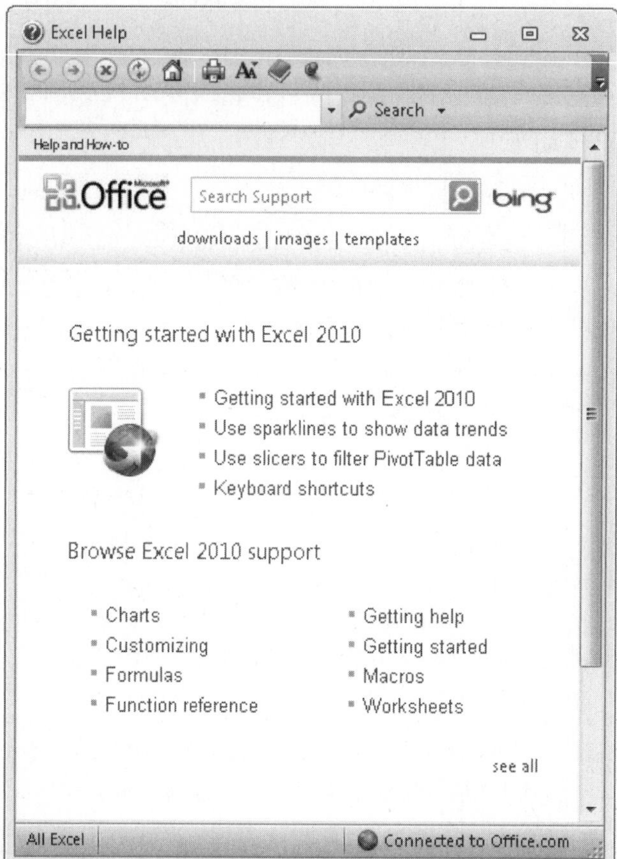

   If you are connected to the Internet, clicking any of the buttons below the Microsoft Office banner (Downloads, Images, and Templates) takes you to a corresponding page of the Office Web site.

   Tip You can maximize the window or adjust its size by dragging the handle in the lower-right corner. You can change the size of the font by clicking the Change Font Size button on the toolbar.

2. Below the bulleted list under **Browse Excel 2010 support**, click **see all**.

   The window changes to display a list of help topics.

3. In the list of topics, click **Activating Excel**.

   Excel Help displays a list of topics related to activating Microsoft Office programs. You can click any topic to display the corresponding information.

4. On the toolbar, click the **Show Table of Contents** button.

   The window expands to accommodate two panes. The Table Of Contents task pane appears on the left, organized by category, like the table of contents in a book. If you're connected to the Internet, Excel displays categories, topics, and training available from the Office Online Web site as well as those stored on your computer. Clicking any category (represented by a book icon) displays that category's topics (represented by help icons).

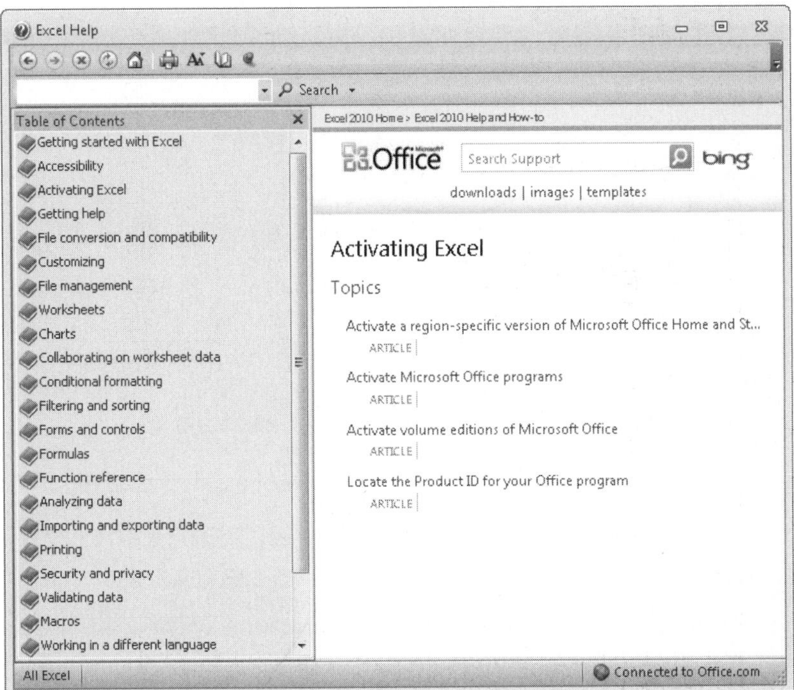

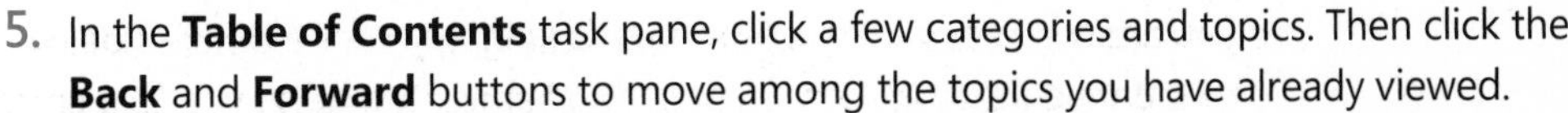

5. In the **Table of Contents** task pane, click a few categories and topics. Then click the **Back** and **Forward** buttons to move among the topics you have already viewed.

6. At the right end of the **Table of Contents** title bar, click the **Close** button.

7. At the top of the **Excel Help** window, click the **Type words to search for** box, type **saving**, and then press the Enter key.

   The Excel Help window displays topics related to the word you typed. Next and Back buttons appear to make it easier to search for the topic you want.

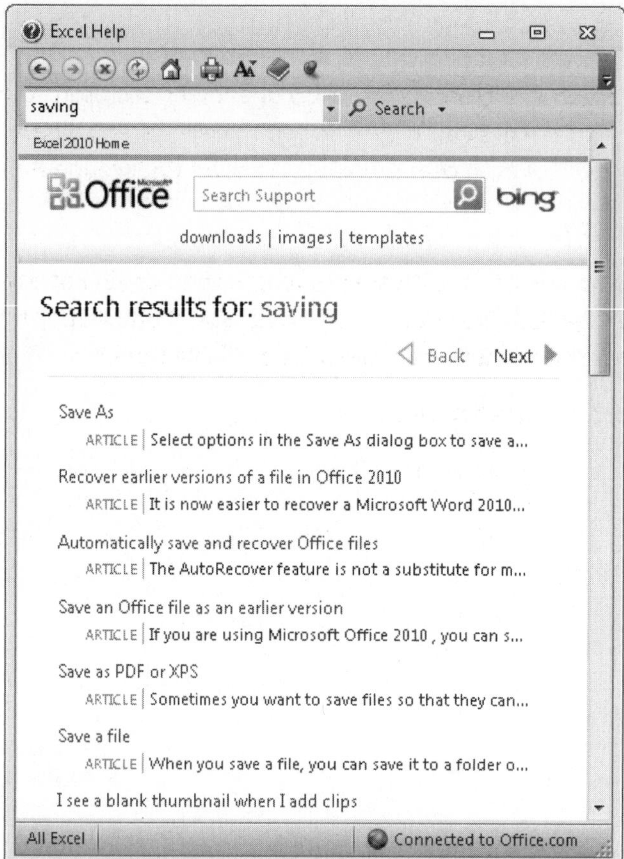

8. In the results list, click the **Recover earlier versions of a file in Office 2010** topic.

   The selected topic appears in the Excel Help window.

9. Below the title at the top of the topic, click **Show All**.

   Excel displays any hidden auxiliary information available in the topic and changes the Show All button to Hide All. You can jump to related information by clicking hyperlinks identified by blue text.

   Tip You can click the Print button on the toolbar to print a topic. Only the displayed information is printed.

CLEAN UP Click the Close button at the right end of the Excel Help window.

More Information

If your question is about Microsoft Excel 2010 or another Microsoft software product and you cannot find the answer in the product's Help system, please search the appropriate product solution center or the Microsoft Knowledge Base at:

support.microsoft.com

In the United States, Microsoft software product support issues not covered by the Microsoft Knowledge Base are addressed by Microsoft Product Support Services. Location-specific software support options are available from:

support.microsoft.com/gp/selfoverview/

Chapter at a Glance

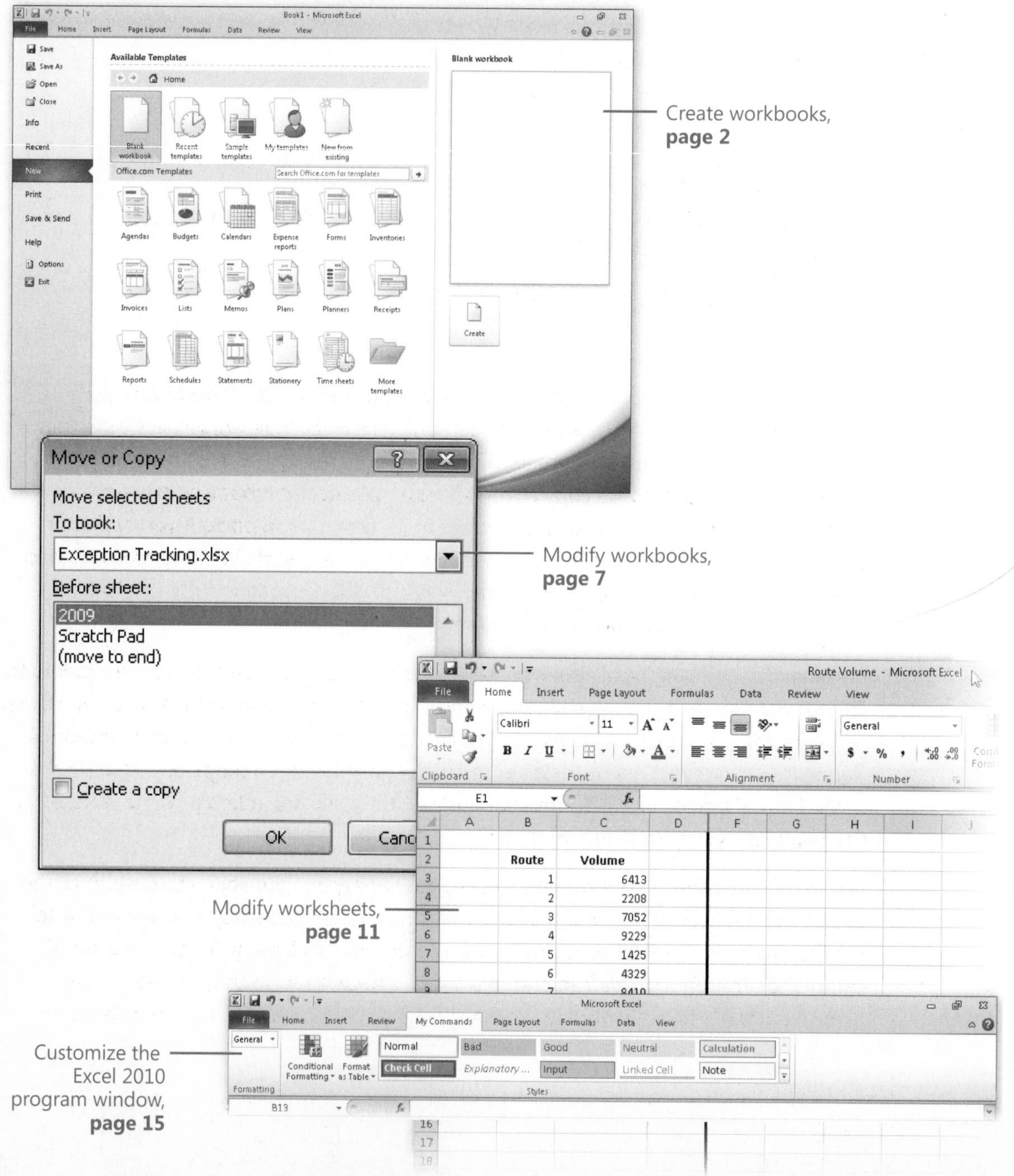

1 Setting Up a Workbook

In this chapter, you will learn how to

- ✔ Create workbooks.
- ✔ Modify workbooks.
- ✔ Modify worksheets.
- ✔ Customize the Excel 2010 program window.

When you start Microsoft Excel 2010, the program presents a blank workbook that contains three worksheets. You can add or delete worksheets, hide worksheets within the workbook without deleting them, and change the order of your worksheets within the workbook. You can also copy a worksheet to another workbook or move the worksheet without leaving a copy of the worksheet in the first workbook. If you and your colleagues work with a large number of documents, you can define property values to make your workbooks easier to find when you and your colleagues attempt to locate them by using the Windows search facility.

Another way to make Excel easier to use is by customizing the Excel program window to fit your work style. If you have several workbooks open at the same time, you can move between the workbook windows quickly. However, if you switch between workbooks frequently, you might find it easier to resize the workbooks so they don't take up the entire Excel window. If you do this, you just need to click the title bar of the workbook you want to modify to switch to it.

The Microsoft Office User Experience team has enhanced your ability to customize the Excel user interface. If you find that you use a command frequently, you can add it to the Quick Access Toolbar so it's never more than one click away. If you use a set of commands frequently, you can create a custom ribbon tab so they appear in one place. You can also hide, display, or change the order of the tabs on the ribbon.

In this chapter, you'll learn how to create and modify workbooks, create and modify worksheets, make your workbooks easier to find, and customize the Excel 2010 program window.

> **Practice Files** Before you can complete the exercises in this chapter, you need to copy the book's practice files to your computer. The practice files you'll use to complete the exercises in this chapter are in the Chapter01 practice file folder. A complete list of practice files is provided in "Using the Practice Files" at the beginning of this book.

Creating Workbooks

Every time you want to gather and store data that isn't closely related to any of your other existing data, you should create a new workbook. The default new workbook in Excel has three worksheets, although you can add more worksheets or delete existing worksheets if you want. Creating a new workbook is a straightforward process—you just click the File tab, click New, identify the type of workbook you want, and click the Create button.

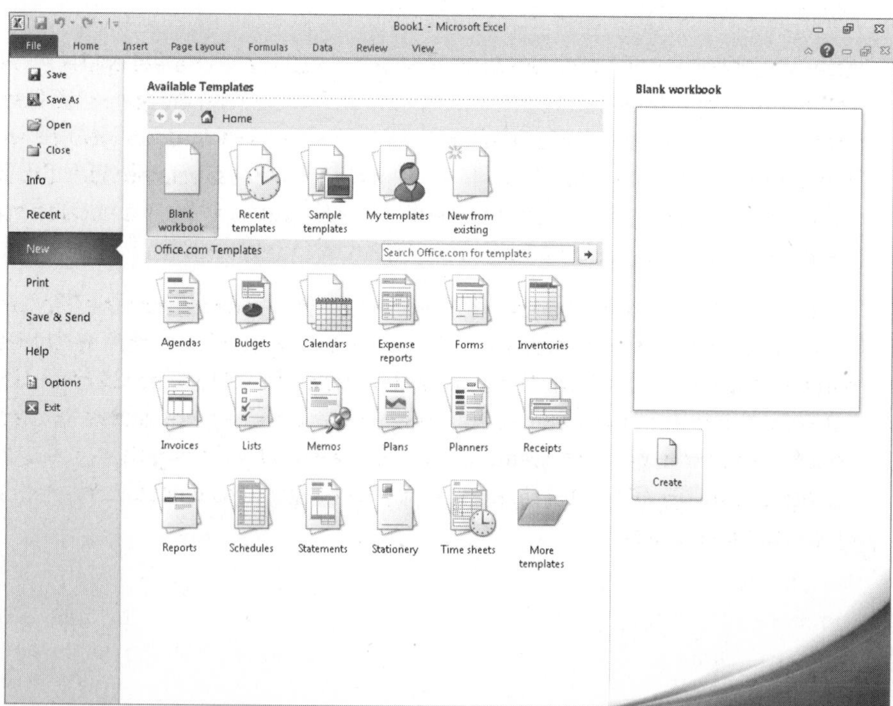

When you start Excel, the program displays a new, blank workbook; you can begin to type data into the worksheet's cells or open an existing workbook. In this book's exercises, you'll work with workbooks created for Consolidated Messenger, a fictional global shipping company. After you make changes to a workbook, you should save it to preserve your work.

Tip Readers frequently ask, "How often should I save my files?" It is good practice to save your changes every half hour or even every five minutes, but the best time to save a file is whenever you make a change that you would hate to have to make again.

When you save a file, you overwrite the previous copy of the file. If you have made changes that you want to save, but you also want to keep a copy of the file as it was when you saved it previously, you can use the Save As command to specify a name for the new file.

You also can use the controls in the Save As dialog box to specify a different format for the new file and a different location in which to save the new version of the file. For example, Lori Penor, the chief operating officer of Consolidated Messenger, might want to save an Excel file that tracks consulting expenses as an Excel 2003 file if she needs to share the file with a consulting firm that uses Excel 2003.

After you create a file, you can add information to make the file easier to find when you use the Windows search facility to search for it. Each category of information, or property, stores specific information about your file. In Windows, you can search for files based on the file's author or title, or by keywords associated with the file. A file tracking the postal code destinations of all packages sent from a vendor might have the keywords *postal*, *destination*, and *origin* associated with it.

To set values for your workbook's built-in properties, you can click the File tab, click Info, click Properties, and then click Show Document Panel to display the Document Properties panel just below the ribbon. The standard version of the Document Properties panel has fields for the file's author, title, subject, keywords, category, and status, and any comments about the file. You can also create custom properties by clicking the arrow located just to the right of the Document Properties label, and clicking Advanced Properties to display the Properties dialog box.

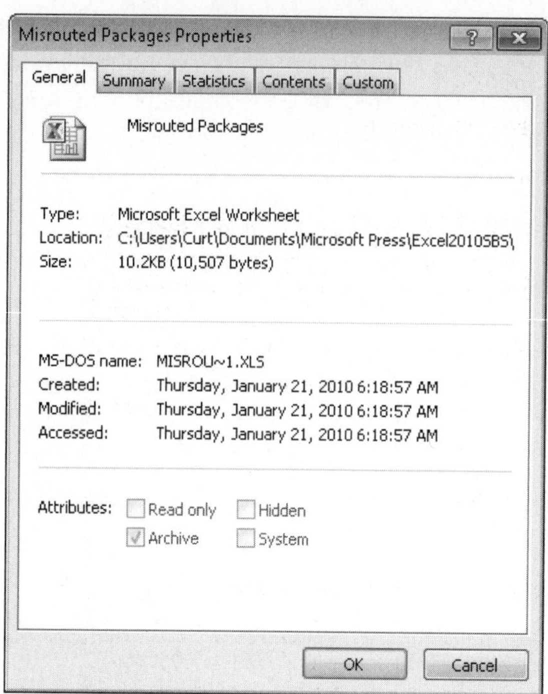

On the Custom page of the Properties dialog box, you can click one of the existing custom categories or create your own by typing a new property name in the Name field, clicking the Type arrow and selecting a data type (for example, Text, Date, Number, or Yes/No), selecting or typing a value in the Value field, and then clicking Add. If you want to delete an existing custom property, point to the Properties list, click the property you want to get rid of, and click Delete. After you finish making your changes, click the OK button. To hide the Document Properties panel, click the Close button in the upper-right corner of the panel.

In this exercise, you'll create a new workbook, save the workbook with a new name, assign values to the workbook's standard properties, and create a custom property.

SET UP You need the ExceptionSummary_start workbook located in your Chapter01 practice file folder to complete this exercise. Start Excel, and open the ExceptionSummary_start workbook. Then follow the steps.

1. Click the **File** tab, and then click **Close**.

   The ExceptionSummary_start workbook closes.

2. Click the **File** tab, and then click **New**.

   The New Workbook page of the Backstage view appears.

3. Click **Blank Workbook**, and then click **Create**.

   A new, blank workbook opens.

4. Click the **File** tab, and then click **Save As**.

   The Save As dialog box opens.

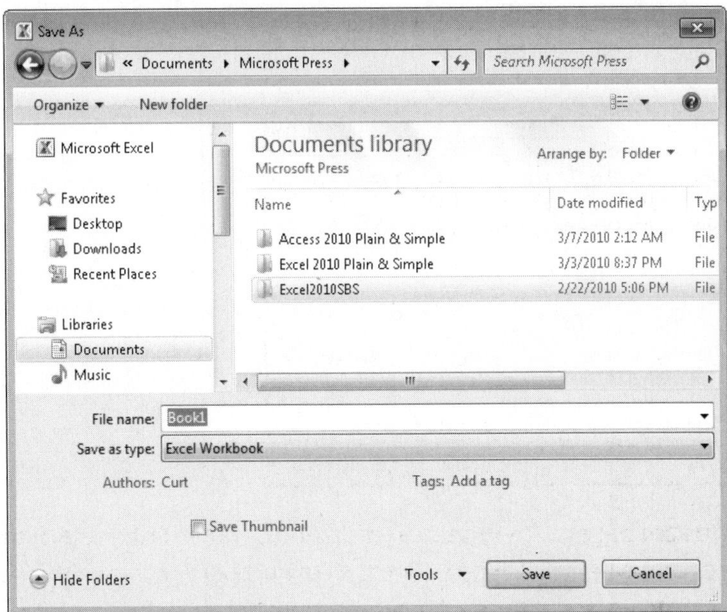

5. Use the navigation controls to display the **Chapter01** folder. In the **File name** field, type **Exceptions 2010**.

6. Click the **Save** button.

   Excel 2010 saves your work, and the Save As dialog box closes.

7. Click the **File** tab, click **Info**, click **Properties**, and then click **Show Document Panel**.

   The Document Properties panel opens.

8. In the **Keywords** field, type **exceptions, regional, percentage**.
9. In the **Category** field, type **performance**.
10. Click the arrow at the right end of the Document Properties button, and then click **Advanced Properties**.

    The Exceptions 2010 Properties dialog box opens.

11. Click the **Custom** tab.

    The Custom page is displayed.

12. In the **Name** field, type **Performance**.
13. In the **Value** field, type **Exceptions**.

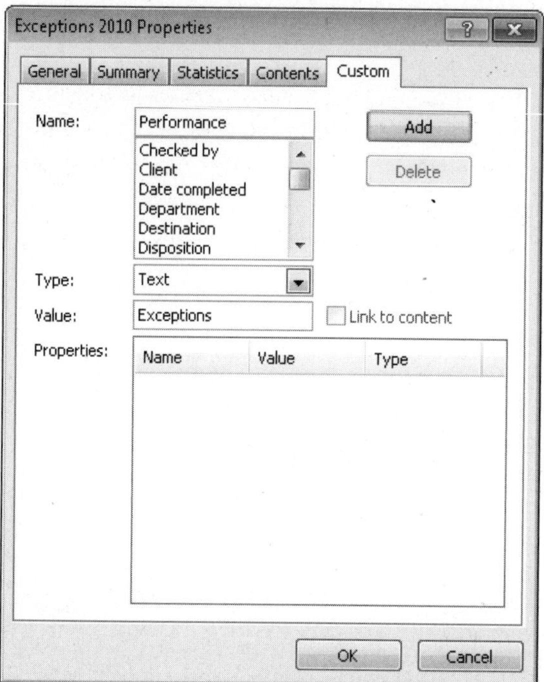

14. Click the **Add** button, and then click **OK**.

    The Exceptions 2010 Properties dialog box closes.

15. On the Quick Access Toolbar, click the **Save** button to save your work.

    Keyboard Shortcut Press Ctrl+S to save a workbook.

    See Also To see a complete list of keyboard shortcuts, see "Keyboard Shortcuts" at the end of this book.

CLEAN UP Close the Exceptions 2010 workbook.

Modifying Workbooks

Most of the time, you create a workbook to record information about a particular activity, such as the number of packages that a regional distribution center handles or the average time a driver takes to complete all deliveries on a route. Each worksheet within that workbook should represent a subdivision of that activity. To display a particular worksheet, just click the worksheet's tab on the tab bar (just below the grid of cells).

In the case of Consolidated Messenger, the workbook used to track daily package volumes could have a separate worksheet for each regional distribution center. New Excel workbooks contain three worksheets; because Consolidated Messenger uses nine regional distribution centers, you would need to create six new ones. To create a new worksheet, click the Insert Worksheet button at the right edge of the tab bar.

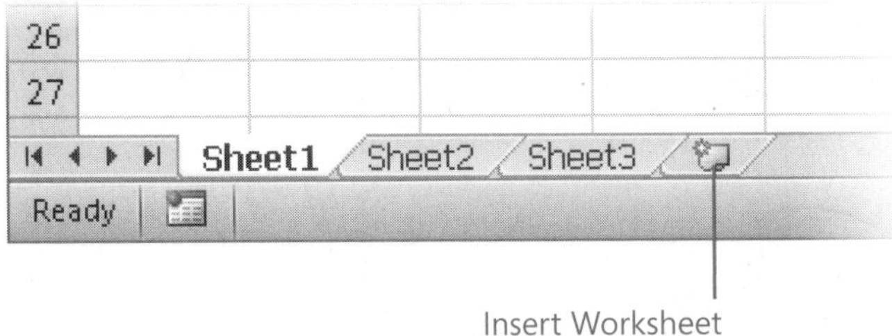

When you create a worksheet, Excel assigns it a generic name such as Sheet4, Sheet5, or Sheet6. After you decide what type of data you want to store on a worksheet, you should change the default worksheet name to something more descriptive. For example, you could change the name of Sheet1 in the regional distribution center tracking workbook to *Northeast*. When you want to change a worksheet's name, double-click the worksheet's tab on the tab bar to highlight the worksheet name, type the new name, and press Enter.

Another way to work with more than one worksheet is to copy a worksheet from another workbook to the current workbook. One circumstance in which you might consider copying worksheets to the current workbook is if you have a list of your current employees in another workbook. You can copy worksheets from another workbook by right-clicking the tab of the sheet you want to copy and, on the shortcut menu, clicking Move Or Copy to display the Move Or Copy dialog box.

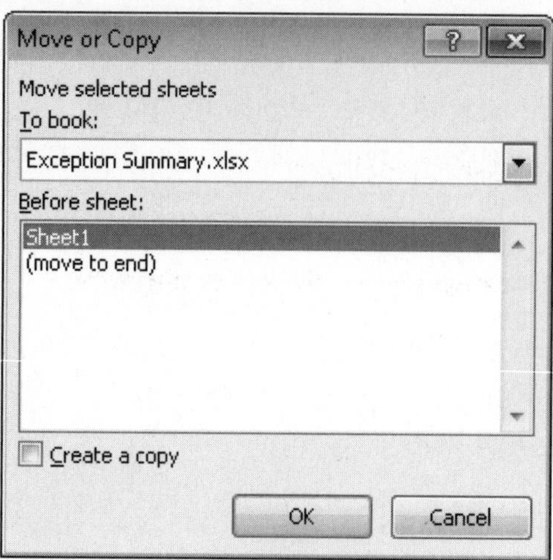

Tip Selecting the Create A Copy check box leaves the copied worksheet in its original workbook, whereas clearing the check box causes Excel to delete the worksheet from its original workbook.

After the worksheet is in the target workbook, you can change the worksheets' order to make the data easier to locate within the workbook. To change a worksheet's location in the workbook, you drag its sheet tab to the desired location on the tab bar. If you want to remove a worksheet from the tab bar without deleting the worksheet, you can do so by right-clicking the worksheet's tab on the tab bar and clicking Hide on the context menu. When you want Excel to redisplay the worksheet, right-click any visible sheet tab and then click Unhide. In the Unhide dialog box, click the name of the sheet you want to display, and click OK.

To differentiate a worksheet from others, or to visually indicate groups or categories of worksheets in a multiple-worksheet workbook, you can easily change the color of a worksheet tab. To do so, right-click the tab, point to Tab Color, and then click the color you want.

Tip If you copy a worksheet to another workbook, and the destination workbook has the same Office Theme applied as the active workbook, the worksheet retains its tab color. If the destination workbook has another theme applied, the worksheet's tab color changes to reflect that theme. For more information on Office themes, see Chapter 4, "Changing Workbook Appearance."

If you determine that you no longer need a particular worksheet, such as one you created to store some figures temporarily, you can delete the worksheet quickly. To do so, right-click its sheet tab, and then click Delete.

In this exercise, you'll insert and rename a worksheet, change a worksheet's position in a workbook, hide and unhide a worksheet, copy a worksheet to another workbook, change a worksheet's tab color, and delete a worksheet.

SET UP You need the ExceptionTracking_start workbook located in your Chapter01 practice file folder to complete this exercise. Open the ExceptionTracking_start file, and save it as *ExceptionTracking*. Then follow the steps.

1. On the tab bar, click the **Insert Worksheet** button.

   A new worksheet is displayed.

2. Right-click the new worksheet's sheet tab, and then click **Rename**.

   Excel highlights the new worksheet's name.

3. Type **2010**, and then press Enter.
4. On the tab bar, double-click the **Sheet1** sheet tab.

   Excel highlights the worksheet's name.

5. Type **2009**, and then press Enter.
6. Right-click the **2009** sheet tab, point to **Tab Color**, and then, in the **Standard Colors** area of the color palette, click the green square.

   Excel changes the 2009 sheet tab to green.

7. On the tab bar, drag the **2010** sheet tab to the left of the **Scratch Pad** sheet tab.
8. Right-click the **2010** sheet tab, and then click **Hide**.

   Excel hides the 2010 worksheet.

9. Right-click the **2009** sheet tab, and then click **Move or Copy**.

   The Move Or Copy dialog box opens.

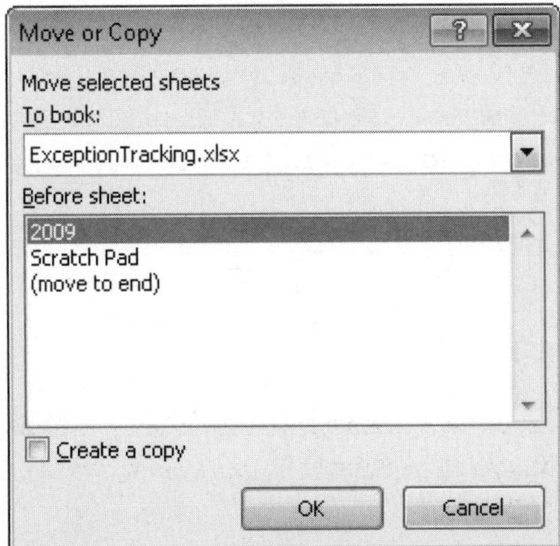

10. Click the **To book** arrow, and then in the list, click **(new book)**.
11. Select the **Create a copy** check box.

12. Click **OK**.

    A new workbook opens, containing only the worksheet you copied into it.

13. On the Quick Access Toolbar, click **Save**.

    The Save As dialog box opens.

14. In the **File name** field, type **2009 Archive**, and then press Enter.

    Excel saves the workbook, and the Save As dialog box closes.

15. On the **View** tab, click the **Switch Windows** button, and then click **ExceptionTracking**.

    The ExceptionTracking workbook is displayed.

16. On the tab bar, right-click the **Scratch Pad** sheet tab, and then click **Delete**. In the dialog box that opens, click **Delete** to confirm the operation.

    The Scratch Pad worksheet is deleted.

17. Right-click the **2009** sheet tab, and then click **Unhide**.

    The Unhide dialog box opens.

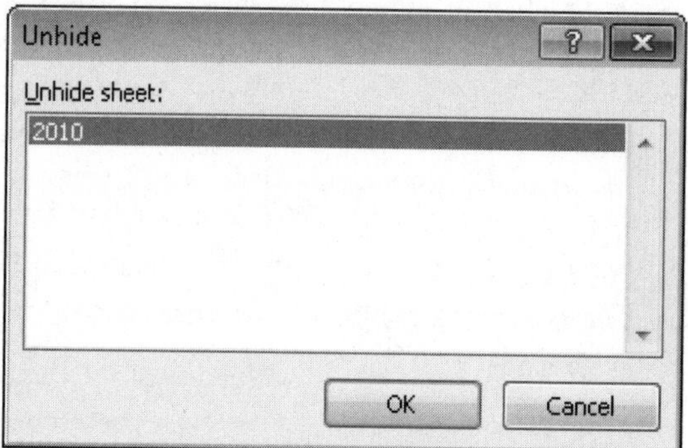

18. Click **2010,** and then click **OK**.

    The Unhide dialog box closes, and the 2010 worksheet is displayed in the workbook.

CLEAN UP Save and close the ExceptionTracking workbook and the 2009 Archive workbook.

Modifying Worksheets

After you put up the signposts that make your data easy to find, you can take other steps to make the data in your workbooks easier to work with. For example, you can change the width of a column or the height of a row in a worksheet by dragging the column's right border or the row's bottom border to the desired position. Increasing a column's width or a row's height increases the space between cell contents, making your data easier to read and work with.

Tip You can apply the same change to more than one row or column by selecting the rows or columns you want to change and then dragging the border of one of the selected rows or columns to the desired location. When you release the mouse button, all the selected rows or columns change to the new height or width.

Modifying column width and row height can make a workbook's contents easier to work with, but you can also insert a row or column between cells that contain data to make your data easier to read. Adding space between the edge of a worksheet and cells that contain data, or perhaps between a label and the data to which it refers, makes the workbook's contents less crowded. You insert rows by clicking a cell and clicking the Home tab on the ribbon. Then, in the Cells group, in the Insert list, click Insert Sheet Rows. Excel inserts a row above the row that contains the active cell. You insert a column in much the same way, by choosing Insert Sheet Columns from the Insert list. When you do this, Excel inserts a column to the left of the active cell.

When you insert a row, column, or cell in a worksheet that has had formatting applied, the Insert Options button appears. Clicking the Insert Options button displays a list of choices you can make about how the inserted row or column should be formatted. The following table summarizes your options.

Option	Action
Format Same As Above	Applies the formatting of the row above the inserted row to the new row
Format Same As Below	Applies the formatting of the row below the inserted row to the new row
Format Same As Left	Applies the formatting of the column to the left of the inserted column to the new column
Format Same As Right	Applies the formatting of the column to the right of the inserted column to the new column
Clear Formatting	Applies the default format to the new row or column

If you want to delete a row or column, right-click the row or column head and then, on the shortcut menu that appears, click Delete. You can temporarily hide rows or columns by selecting those rows or columns and then, on the Home tab, in the Cells group, clicking the Format button, pointing to Hide & Unhide, and then clicking either Hide Rows or Hide Columns. The rows or columns you selected disappear, but they aren't gone for good, as they would be if you'd used Delete. Instead, they have just been removed from the display until you call them back. To return the hidden rows to the display, select the row or column headers on either side of the hidden rows or columns. Then, on the Home tab, in the Cells group, click the Format button, point to Hide & Unhide, and then click either Unhide Rows or Unhide Columns.

Important If you hide the first row or column in a worksheet, you must click the Select All button in the upper-left corner of the worksheet (above the first row header and to the left of the first column header) or press Ctrl+A to select the entire worksheet. Then, on the Home tab, in the Cells group, click Format, point to Hide & Unhide, and then click either Unhide Rows or Unhide Columns to make the hidden data visible again.

Just as you can insert rows or columns, you can insert individual cells into a worksheet. To insert a cell, click the cell that is currently in the position where you want the new cell to appear. On the Home tab, in the Cells group, in the Insert list, click Insert Cells to display the Insert dialog box. In the Insert dialog box, you can choose whether to shift the cells surrounding the inserted cell down (if your data is arranged as a column) or to the right (if your data is arranged as a row). When you click OK, the new cell appears, and the contents of affected cells shift down or to the right, as appropriate. In a similar vein, if you want to delete a block of cells, select the cells, and on the Home tab, in the Cells group, in the Delete list, click Delete Cells to display the Delete dialog box—complete with options that enable you to choose how to shift the position of the cells around the deleted cells.

Tip The Insert dialog box also includes options you can click to insert a new row or column; the Delete dialog box has similar options for deleting an entire row or column.

If you want to move the data in a group of cells to another location in your worksheet, select the cells you want to move and use the mouse pointer to point to the selection's border. When the pointer changes to a four-pointed arrow, you can drag the selected cells to the desired location on the worksheet. If the destination cells contain data, Excel displays a dialog box asking whether you want to overwrite the destination cells' contents. If you want to replace the existing values, click OK. If you don't want to overwrite the existing values, click Cancel and insert the required number of cells to accommodate the data you want to move.

In this exercise, you'll insert a column and row into a worksheet, specify insert options, hide a column, insert a cell into a worksheet, delete a cell from a worksheet, and move a group of cells within the worksheet.

SET UP You need the RouteVolume_start workbook located in your Chapter01 practice file folder to complete this exercise. Open the RouteVolume_start workbook, and save it as *RouteVolume*. Then follow the steps.

1. On the **May 12** worksheet, select cell **A1**.

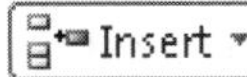

2. On the **Home** tab, in the **Cells** group, click the **Insert** arrow, and then in the list, click **Insert Sheet Columns**.

   A new column A appears.

3. In the **Insert** list, click **Insert Sheet Rows**.

   A new row 1 appears.

4. Click the **Insert Options** button that appears below the lower-right corner of the selected cell, and then click **Clear Formatting**.

   Excel removes the formatting from the new row 1.

5. Right-click the column header of column E, and then click **Hide**.

   Column E disappears.

	A	B	C	D	F	G	H	I
1								
2		Route	Volume					
3		1	6413					
4		2	2208					
5		3	7052					
6		4	9229					
7		5	1425					
8		6	4329					
9		7	8410					
10		8	8785					
11		9	5812					
12		10	1112					

6. On the tab bar, click the **May 13** sheet tab.

   The worksheet named *May 13* appears.

7. Click cell **B6**.

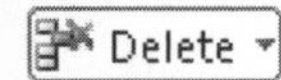

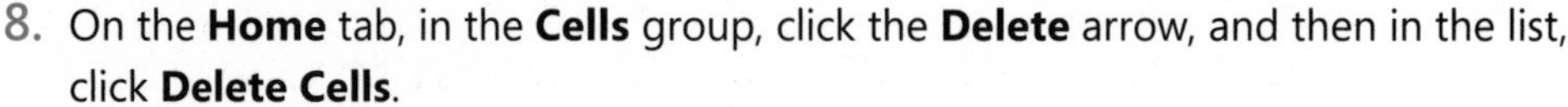

8. On the **Home** tab, in the **Cells** group, click the **Delete** arrow, and then in the list, click **Delete Cells**.

   The Delete dialog box opens.

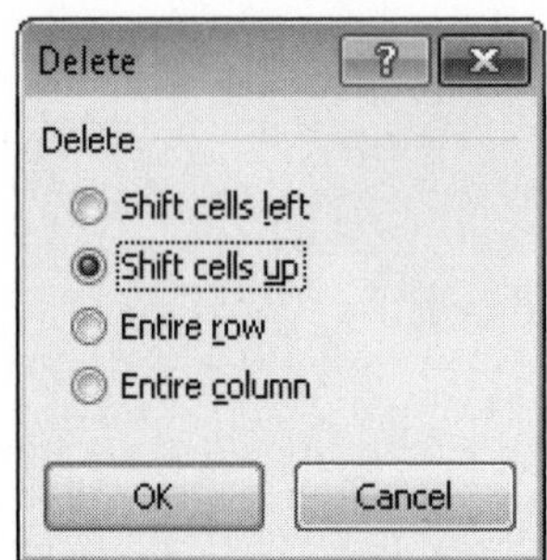

9. If necessary, click **Shift cells up**, and then click **OK**.

   The Delete dialog box closes and Excel deletes cell B6, moving the cells below it up to fill in the gap.

10. Click cell **C6**.

11. In the **Cells** group, in the **Insert** list, click **Insert Cells**.

    The Insert dialog box opens.

12. If necessary, click **Shift cells down**, and then click **OK**.

    The Insert dialog box closes, and Excel creates a new cell C6, moving cells C6:C11 down to accommodate the inserted cell.

13. In cell **C6**, type **4499**, and then press Enter.

14. Select cells **E13:F13**.

15. Point to the border of the selected cells. When your mouse pointer changes to a four-pointed arrow, drag the selected cells to cells **B13:C13**.

    The dragged cells replace cells B13:C13.

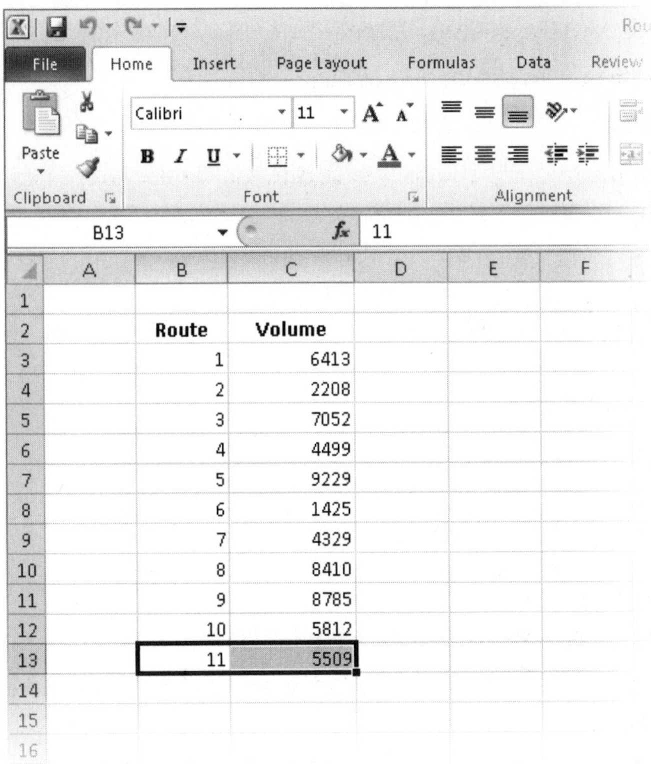

CLEAN UP Save the RouteVolume workbook, and then close it.

Customizing the Excel 2010 Program Window

How you use Excel 2010 depends on your personal working style and the type of data collections you manage. The Excel product team interviews customers, observes how differing organizations use the program, and sets up the user interface so that many users won't need to change it to work effectively. If you do want to change the Excel program window, including the user interface, you can. You can change how Excel displays your worksheets; zoom in on worksheet data; add frequently used commands to the Quick Access Toolbar; hide, display, and reorder ribbon tabs; and create custom tabs to make groups of commands readily accessible.

Zooming In on a Worksheet

One way to make Excel easier to work with is to change the program's zoom level. Just as you can "zoom in" with a camera to increase the size of an object in the camera's viewer, you can use the zoom setting to change the size of objects within the Excel 2010 program window. For example, if Peter Villadsen, the Consolidated Messenger European Distribution Center Manager, displayed a worksheet that summarized his distribution center's package volume by month, he could click the View tab and then, in the Zoom group, click the Zoom button to display the Zoom dialog box. The Zoom dialog box contains controls that he can use to select a preset magnification level or to type in a custom magnification level. He could also use the Zoom control in the lower-right corner of the Excel 2010 window.

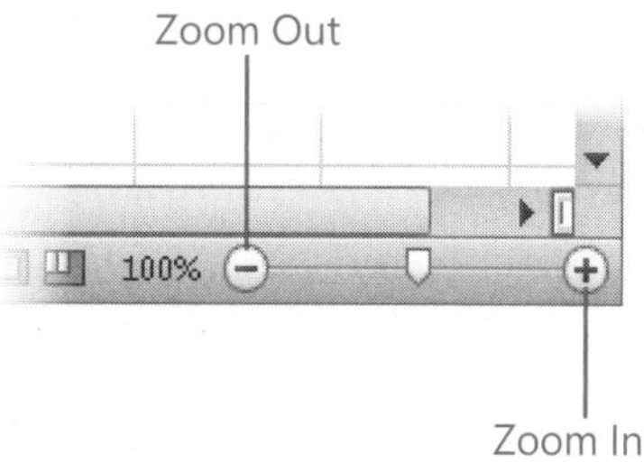

Clicking the Zoom In control increases the size of items in the program window by 10 percent, whereas clicking the Zoom Out control decreases the size of items in the program window by 10 percent. If you want more fine-grained control of your zoom level, you can use the slider control to select a specific zoom level or click the magnification level indicator, which indicates the zoom percentage, and use the Zoom dialog box to set a custom magnification level.

The Zoom group on the View tab also contains the Zoom To Selection button, which fills the program window with the contents of any selected cells, up to the program's maximum zoom level of 400 percent.

Tip The minimum zoom level in Excel 2010 is 10 percent.

Arranging Multiple Workbook Windows

As you work with Excel, you will probably need to have more than one workbook open at a time. For example, you could open a workbook that contains customer contact information and copy it into another workbook to be used as the source data for a mass mailing you create in Microsoft Word 2010. When you have multiple workbooks open simultaneously, you can switch between them by clicking the View tab and then, in the Window group, clicking the Switch Windows button and clicking the name of the workbook you want to view.

You can arrange your workbooks within the Excel window so that most of the active workbook is shown but the others are easily accessible. To do so, click the View tab and then, in the Window group, click the Arrange All button. Then, in the Arrange Windows dialog box, click Cascade.

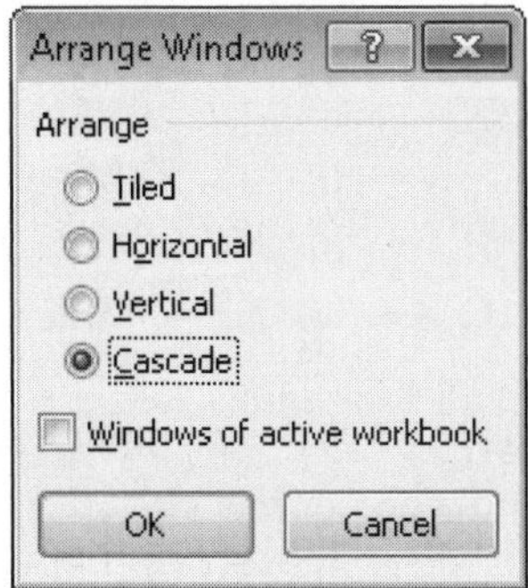

Many Excel 2010 workbooks contain formulas on one worksheet that derive their value from data on another worksheet, which means you need to change between two worksheets every time you want to see how modifying your data changes the formula's result. However, an easier way to approach this is to display two copies of the same workbook simultaneously, displaying the worksheet that contains the data in the original window and displaying the worksheet with the formula in the new window. When you change the data in either copy of the workbook, Excel updates the other copy. To display two copies of the same workbook, open the desired workbook and then, in the View tab's Window group, click New Window. Excel opens a second copy of the workbook. To display the workbooks side by side, on the View tab, in the Window group, click Arrange All. Then, in the Arrange Windows dialog box, click Vertical and then click OK.

If the original workbook's name is *Exception Summary*, Excel 2010 displays the name *Exception Summary:1* on the original workbook's title bar and *Exception Summary:2* on the second workbook's title bar.

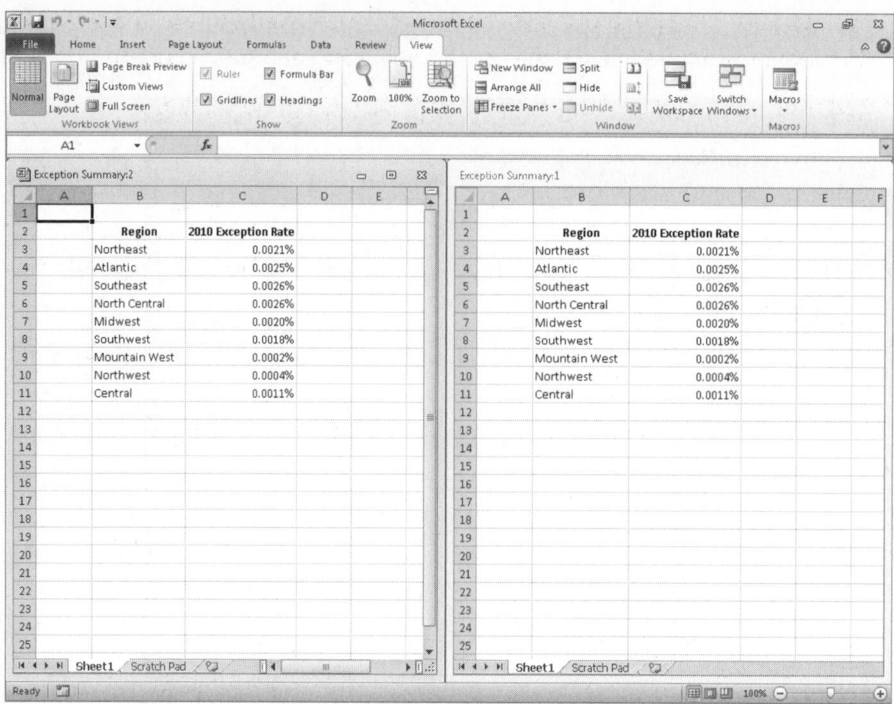

Troubleshooting The appearance of buttons and groups on the ribbon changes depending on the width of the program window. For information about changing the appearance of the ribbon to match our images, see "Modifying the Display of the Ribbon" at the beginning of this book.

Adding Buttons to the Quick Access Toolbar

As you continue to work with Excel 2010, you might discover that you use certain commands much more frequently than others. If your workbooks draw data from external sources, for example, you might find yourself displaying the Data tab and then, in the Connections group, clicking the Refresh All button much more often than the program's designers might have expected. You can make any button accessible with one click by adding the button to the Quick Access Toolbar, located just above the ribbon in the upper-left corner of the Excel program window.

To add a button to the Quick Access Toolbar, click the File tab, and then click Options. In the Excel Options dialog box, display the Customize The Quick Access Toolbar page. This Options page contains two panes. The pane on the left lists all of the controls that are available within a given category, and the pane on the right lists the controls currently displayed on the Quick Access Toolbar. To add a command to the Quick Access Toolbar, display the Customize The Quick Access Toolbar page of the Options dialog box. Then, in the Choose Commands From list, click the category that contains the control you want to add. Excel 2010 displays the available commands in the box below the Choose Commands From field. Click the control you want, and then click the Add button.

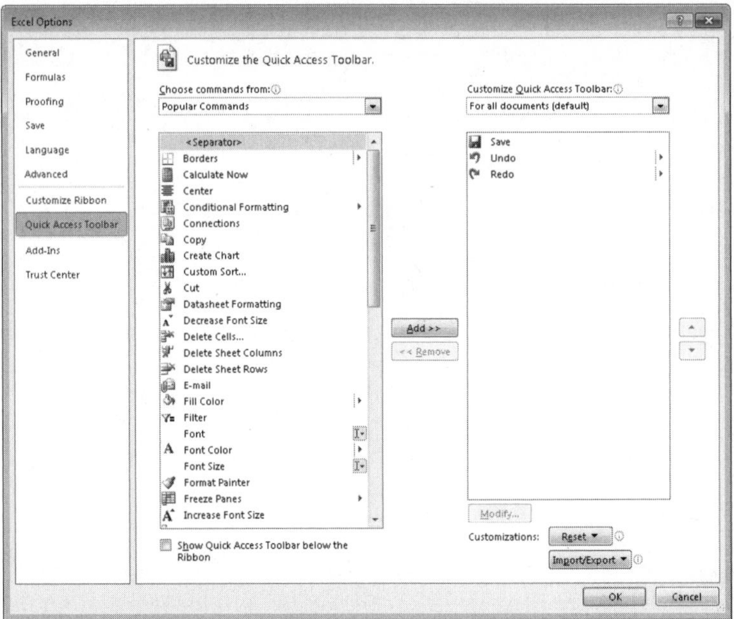

You can change a button's position on the Quick Access Toolbar by clicking its name in the right pane and then clicking either the Move Up or Move Down button at the right edge of the dialog box. To remove a button from the Quick Access Toolbar, click the button's name in the right pane, and then click the Remove button. When you're done making your changes, click the OK button. If you prefer not to save your changes, click the Cancel button. If you saved your changes but want to return the Quick Access Toolbar to its original state, click the Reset button and then click either Reset Only Quick Access Toolbar, which removes any changes you made to the Quick Access Toolbar, or Reset All Customizations, which returns the entire ribbon interface to its original state.

You can also choose whether your Quick Access Toolbar changes affect all your workbooks or just the active workbook. To control how Excel applies your change, in the Customize Quick Access Toolbar list, click either For All Documents to apply the change to all of your workbooks or For Workbook to apply the change to the active workbook only.

If you'd like to export your Quick Access Toolbar customizations to a file that can be used to apply those changes to another Excel 2010 installation, click the Import/Export button and then click Export All Customizations. Use the controls in the dialog box that opens to save your file. When you're ready to apply saved customizations to Excel, click the Import/Export button, click Import Customization File, select the file in the File Open dialog box, and click Open.

Customizing the Ribbon

Excel 2010 enhances your ability to customize the entire ribbon by enabling you to hide and display ribbon tabs, reorder tabs displayed on the ribbon, customize existing tabs (including tool tabs, which appear when specific items are selected), and to create custom tabs.

To begin customizing the ribbon, click the File tab and then click Options. In the Excel Options dialog box, click Customize Ribbon to display the Customize The Ribbon page.

To select which tabs appear in the tabs pane on the right side of the screen, click the Customize The Ribbon field's arrow and then click either Main Tabs, which displays the tabs that can appear on the standard ribbon; Tool Tabs, which displays the tabs that appear when you click an item such as a drawing object or PivotTable; or All Tabs.

Tip The procedures taught in this section apply to both the main tabs and the tool tabs.

Each ribbon tab's name has a check box next to it. If a tab's box is selected, then that tab appears on the ribbon. You can hide a tab by clearing the check box and bring it back by selecting the check box. You can also change the order in which the tabs are displayed on the ribbon. To do so, click the name of the tab you want to move and then click the Move Up or Move Down arrows to reposition the selected tab.

Just as you can change the order of the tabs on the ribbon, with Excel 2010, you can change the order in which groups of commands appear on a tab. For example, the Page Layout tab contains five groups: Themes, Page Setup, Scale To Fit, Sheet Options, and Arrange. If you use the Themes group less frequently than the other groups, you could move the group to the right end of the tab by clicking the group's name and then clicking the Move Down arrow button until the group appears in the desired position.

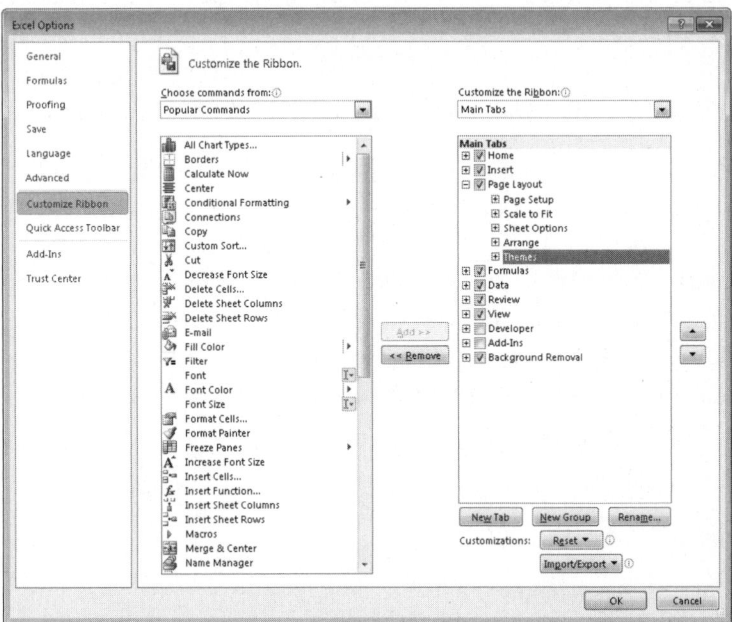

To remove a group from a built-in ribbon tab, click the name of the group in the right pane and click the Remove button. If you remove a group from a built-in tab and later decide you want to put it back on the tab, display the tab in the right pane. Then, click the Choose Commands From field's arrow and click Main Tabs. With the tab displayed, in the left pane, click the expand control (which looks like a plus sign) next to the name of the tab that contains the group you want to add back. You can now click the name of the group in the left pane and click the Add button to put the group back on the selected ribbon tab.

The built-in ribbon tabs are designed efficiently, so adding new command groups might crowd the other items on the tab and make those controls harder to find. Rather than adding controls to an existing ribbon tab, you can create a custom tab and then add groups and commands to it. To create a custom ribbon tab, click the New Tab button on the Customize The Ribbon page of the Excel Options dialog box. When you do, a new tab named New Tab (Custom), which contains a group named New Group (Custom), appears in the tab list.

You can add an existing group to your new ribbon tab by clicking the Choose Commands From field's arrow, selecting a collection of commands, clicking the group you want to add, and then clicking the Add button. You can also add individual commands to your ribbon tab by clicking a command in the command list and clicking the Add button. To add a command to your tab's custom group, click the new group in the right tab list, click the command in the left list, and then click the Add button. If you want to add another custom group to your new tab, click the new tab, or any of the groups within that tab, and then click New Group.

Tip You can change the order of the groups and commands on your custom ribbon tabs by using the techniques described earlier in this section.

The New Tab (Custom) name doesn't tell you anything about the commands on your new ribbon tab, so you can rename it to reflect its contents. To rename any tab on the ribbon, display the Customize The Ribbon page of the Excel Options dialog box, click the tab you want to modify, and then click the Rename button. Type the tab's new name in the Rename dialog box, and click OK. To rename any group on the ribbon, click the name of the group, and then click Rename. When you do, a different version of the Rename dialog box appears. Click the symbol that you want to use to represent the group on the ribbon, type a new name for the group in the Display Name box, and click OK.

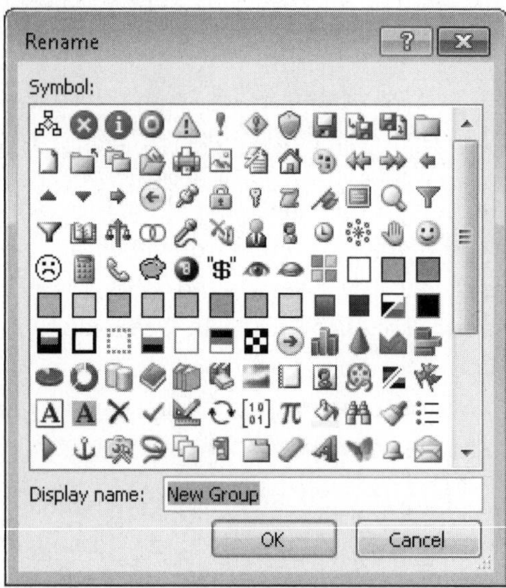

If you'd like to export your ribbon customizations to a file that can be used to apply those changes to another Excel 2010 installation, click the Import/Export button and then click Export All Customizations. Use the controls in the dialog box that opens to save your file. When you're ready to apply saved customizations to Excel, click the Import/Export button, click Import Customization File, select the file in the File Open dialog box, and click Open.

When you're done customizing the ribbon, click the OK button to save your changes or click Cancel to keep the user interface as it was before you started this round of changes. You can also change a ribbon tab, or the entire ribbon, back to the state it was in when you installed Excel. To restore a single ribbon tab, click the tab you want to restore, click the Reset button, and then click Reset Only Selected Ribbon Tab. To restore the entire ribbon, including the Quick Access Toolbar, click the Reset button and then click Reset All Customizations.

Maximizing Usable Space in the Program Window

You can increase the amount of space available inside the program window by hiding the ribbon, the formula bar, or the row and column labels.

To hide the ribbon, double-click the active tab label. The tab labels remain visible at the top of the program window, but the tab content is hidden. To temporarily redisplay the ribbon, click the tab label you want. Then click any button on the tab, or click away from the tab, to rehide it. To permanently redisplay the ribbon, double-click any tab label.

Keyboard Shortcut Press Ctrl+F1 to hide and unhide the ribbon.

To hide the formula bar, clear the Formula Bar check box in the Show/Hide group on the View tab. To hide the row and column labels, clear the Headings check box in the Show/Hide group on the View tab.

In this exercise, you'll change your worksheet's zoom level, zoom in to emphasize a selected cell range, switch between multiple open workbooks, cascade multiple open workbooks within the Excel program window, add a button to the Quick Access Toolbar, and customize the ribbon.

SET UP You need the PackageCounts_start and MisroutedPackages_start workbooks located in your Chapter01 practice file folder to complete this exercise. Open the PackageCounts_start and MisroutedPackages_start workbooks, and name them as *PackageCounts* and *MisroutedPackages*, respectively. Then follow the steps.

1. In the **MisroutedPackages** workbook, in the lower-right corner of the Excel 2010 window, click the **Zoom In** control five times.

   The worksheet's zoom level changes to 150%.

2. Select cells **B2:C11**.

3. On the **View** tab, in the **Zoom** group, click the **Zoom to Selection** button.

   Excel displays the selected cells so they fill the program window.

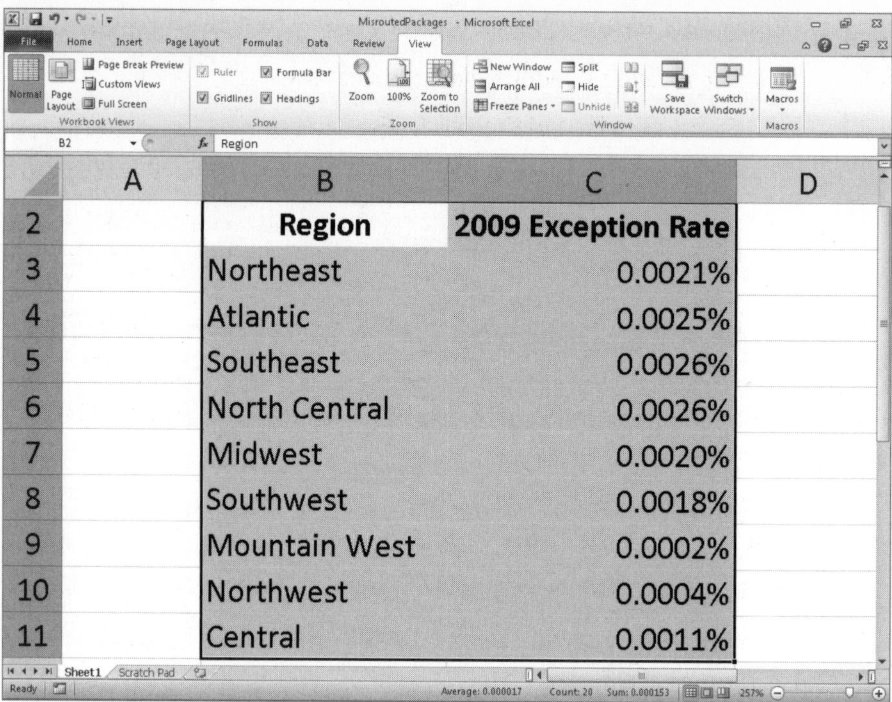

4. On the **View** tab, in the **Zoom** group, click the **Zoom** button.

   The Zoom dialog box opens.

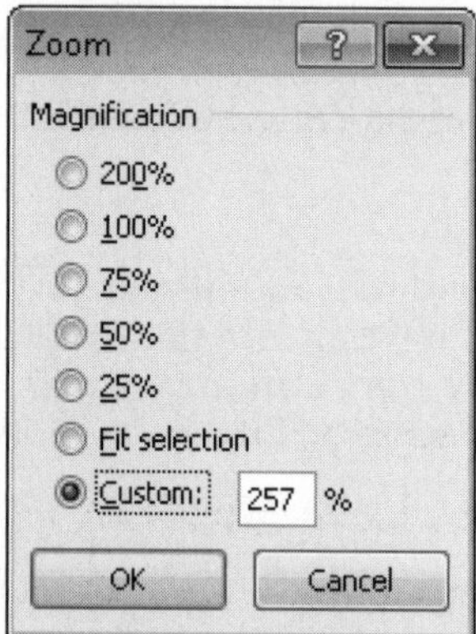

5. Click **100%**, and then click **OK**.

   The worksheet returns to its default zoom level.

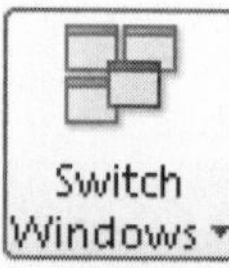

6. On the **View** tab, in the **Window** group, click the **Switch Windows** button, and then click **PackageCounts**.

   The PackageCounts workbook opens.

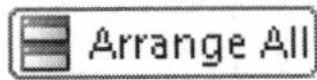

7. On the **View** tab, in the **Window** group, click the **Arrange All** button.

   The Arrange Windows dialog box opens.

8. Click **Cascade**, and then click **OK**.

   Excel cascades the open workbook windows within the program window.

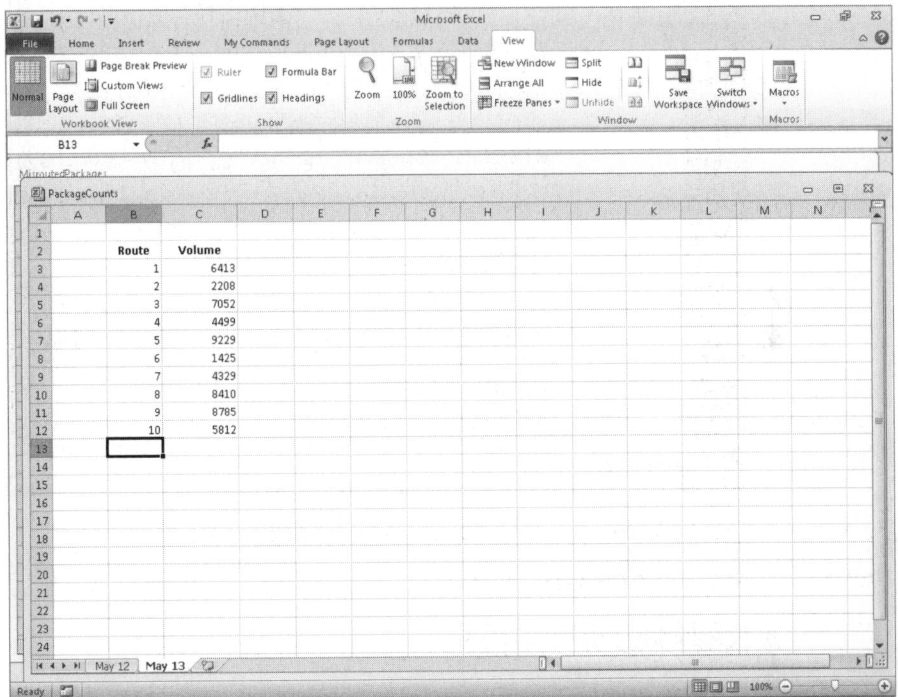

9. Click the **File** tab, and then click **Options**.

   The Excel Options dialog box opens.

10. Click **Quick Access Toolbar**.

    The Customize The Quick Access Toolbar page opens.

11. Click the **Choose commands from** arrow, and then in the list, click **Review Tab**.

    The commands in the Review Tab category appear in the command list.

12. Click the **Spelling** command, and then click **Add**.

    Excel adds the Spelling command to the Quick Access Toolbar.

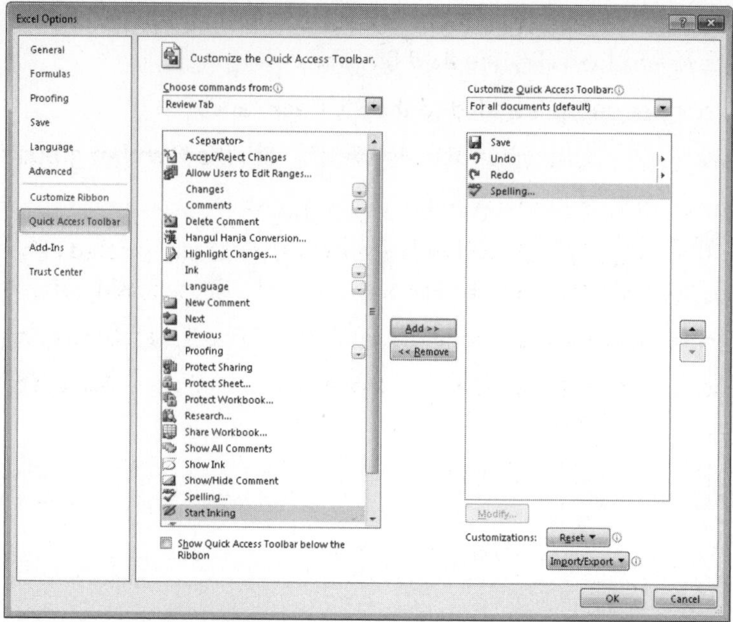

13. Click **Customize Ribbon**.

    The Customize The Ribbon page of the Excel Options dialog box appears.

14. If necessary, click the **Customize the Ribbon** box's arrow and click **Main Tabs**. In the right tab list, click the **Review** tab and then click the **Move Up** button three times.

    Excel moves the Review tab between the Insert and Page Layout tabs.

15. Click the **New Tab** button.

    A tab named New Tab (Custom) appears below the most recently active tab in the Main Tabs list.

16. Click the **New Tab (Custom)** tab name, click the **Rename** button, type **My Commands** in the **Display Name** box, and click **OK**.

    The new tab's name changes to My Commands.

17. Click the **New Group (Custom)** group's name and then click the **Rename** button. In the **Rename** dialog box, click the icon that looks like a paint palette (second row, fourth from the right). Then, in the **Display name** box, type **Formatting**, and click **OK**.

    The new group's name changes to Formatting.

18. In the right tab list, click the **My Commands** tab name. Then, on the left side of the dialog box, click the **Choose Commands From** box's arrow and click **Main Tabs**.

    The Main Tabs group of ribbon tabs appears in the left tab list.

19. In the left tab list, click the **Home** tab's expand control, click the **Styles** group's name, and then click the **Add** button.

    The Styles group is added to the My Commands tab.

20. In the left tab list, under the **Home** tab, click the **Number** group's expand control.

    The commands in the Number group appear.

21. In the right tab list, click the **Formatting** group you created earlier. Then, in the left tab list, click the **Number Format** item and click the **Add** button.

    Excel 2010 adds the Number Format item to the Formatting custom group.

22. Click **OK** to save your ribbon customizations, and then click the **My Commands** tab on the ribbon.

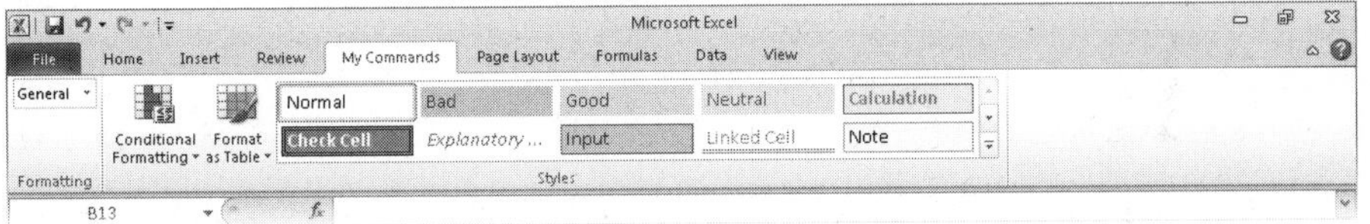

Important The remaining exercises in this book assume you are using Excel 2010 as it was installed on your computer. After you complete this exercise, you should reset the ribbon to its original configuration so the instructions in the remaining exercises in the book are consistent with your copy of Excel.

CLEAN UP Save and close all open workbooks. If you are not continuing directly to the next chapter, exit Excel.

Key Points

- Save your work whenever you do something you'd hate to have to do again.
- Assigning values to a workbook's properties makes it easier to find your workbook using the Windows search facility.
- Be sure to give your worksheets descriptive names.
- If you want to use a worksheet's data in another workbook, you can send a copy of the worksheet to that other workbook without deleting the original worksheet.
- You can delete a worksheet you no longer need, but you can also hide a worksheet in the workbook. When you need the data on the worksheet, you can unhide it.
- You can save yourself a lot of bothersome cutting and pasting by inserting and deleting worksheet cells, columns, and rows.
- Customize your Excel 2010 program window by changing how it displays your workbooks, zooming in on data, adding frequently used buttons to the Quick Access Toolbar, and rearranging or customizing the ribbon to meet your needs.

Chapter at a Glance

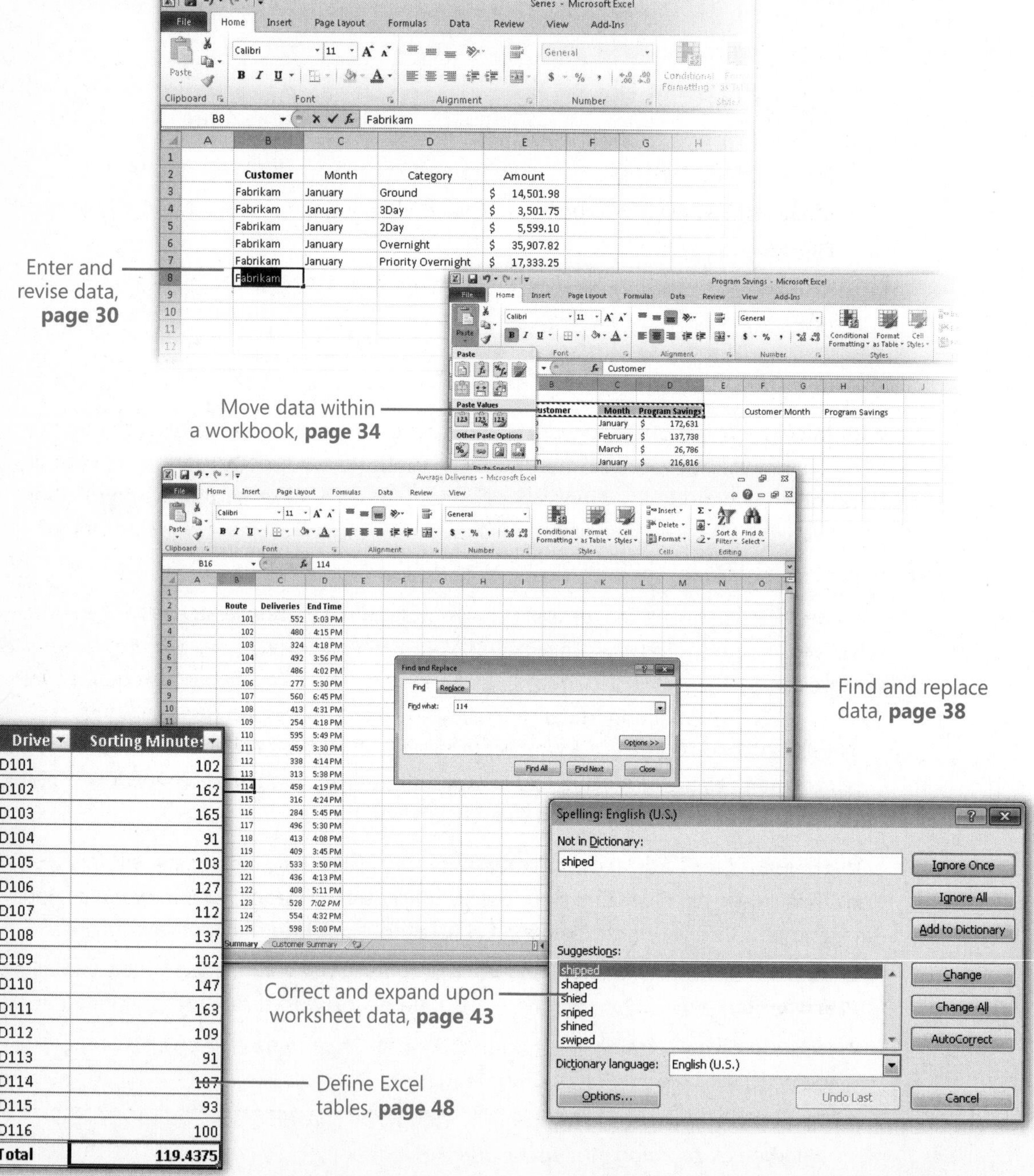

2 Working with Data and Excel Tables

In this chapter, you will learn how to

- ✔ Enter and revise data.
- ✔ Move data within a workbook.
- ✔ Find and replace data.
- ✔ Correct and expand upon worksheet data.
- ✔ Define Excel tables.

With Microsoft Excel 2010, you can visualize and present information effectively by using charts, graphics, and formatting, but the data is the most important part of any workbook. By learning to enter data efficiently, you will make fewer data entry errors and give yourself more time to analyze your data so you can make decisions about your organization's performance and direction.

Excel provides a wide variety of tools you can use to enter and manage worksheet data effectively. For example, you can organize your data into Excel tables, which enables you to store and analyze your data quickly and efficiently. Also, you can enter a data series quickly, repeat one or more values, and control how Excel formats cells, columns, and rows moved from one part of a worksheet to another with a minimum of effort. With Excel, you can check the spelling of worksheet text, look up alternative words by using the Thesaurus, and translate words to foreign languages.

In this chapter, you'll learn how to enter and revise Excel data, move data within a workbook, find and replace existing data, use proofing and reference tools to enhance your data, and organize your data by using Excel tables.

Practice Files Before you can complete the exercises in this chapter, you need to copy the book's practice files to your computer. The practice files you'll use to complete the exercises in this chapter are in the Chapter02 practice file folder. A complete list of practice files is provided in "Using the Practice Files" at the beginning of this book.

Entering and Revising Data

After you create a workbook, you can begin entering data. The simplest way to enter data is to click a cell and type a value. This method works very well when you're entering a few pieces of data, but it is less than ideal when you're entering long sequences or series of values. For example, Craig Dewar, the VP of Marketing for Consolidated Messenger, might want to create a worksheet listing the monthly program savings that large customers can realize if they sign exclusive delivery contracts with Consolidated Messenger. To record those numbers, he would need to create a worksheet tracking each customer's monthly program savings.

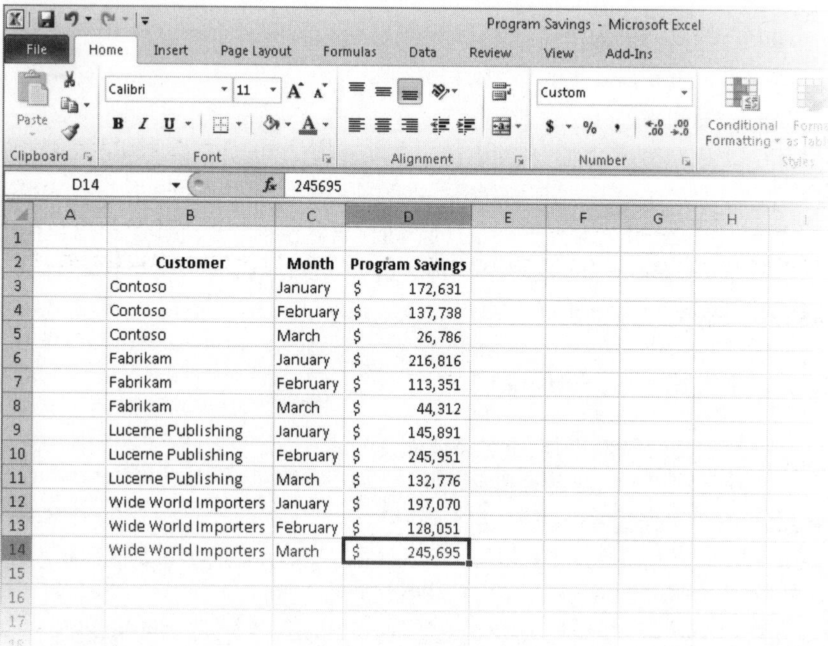

	A	B	C	D
1				
2		**Customer**	**Month**	**Program Savings**
3		Contoso	January	$ 172,631
4		Contoso	February	$ 137,738
5		Contoso	March	$ 26,786
6		Fabrikam	January	$ 216,816
7		Fabrikam	February	$ 113,351
8		Fabrikam	March	$ 44,312
9		Lucerne Publishing	January	$ 145,891
10		Lucerne Publishing	February	$ 245,951
11		Lucerne Publishing	March	$ 132,776
12		Wide World Importers	January	$ 197,070
13		Wide World Importers	February	$ 128,051
14		Wide World Importers	March	$ 245,695

Repeatedly entering the sequence January, February, March, and so on can be handled by copying and pasting the first occurrence of the sequence, but there's an easier way to do it: use AutoFill. With AutoFill, you enter the first element in a recognized series, click and hold the mouse button down on the fill handle at the lower-right corner of the cell, and drag the fill handle until the series extends far enough to accommodate your data. Using a similar tool, FillSeries, you can enter two values in a series and use the fill handle to extend the series in your worksheet. For example, if you want to create a series starting at 2 and increasing by 2, you can put 2 in the first cell and 4 in the second cell, select both cells, and then use the fill handle to extend the series to your desired end value.

You do have some control over how Excel extends the values in a series when you drag the fill handle. For example, if you drag the fill handle up (or to the left), Excel extends the series to include previous values. If you type *January* in a cell and then drag that cell's fill handle up (or to the left), Excel places *December* in the first cell, *November* in the second cell, and so on.

Another way to control how Excel extends a data series is by holding down the Ctrl key while you drag the fill handle. For example, if you select a cell that contains the value *January* and then drag the fill handle down, Excel extends the series by placing *February* in the next cell, *March* in the cell after that, and so on. If you hold down the Ctrl key while you drag the fill handle, however, Excel repeats the value *January* in each cell you add to the series.

Tip Be sure to experiment with how the fill handle extends your series and how pressing the Ctrl key changes that behavior. Using the fill handle can save you a lot of time entering data.

Other data entry techniques you'll use in this section are AutoComplete, which detects when a value you're entering is similar to previously entered values; Pick From Drop-Down List, from which you can choose a value from among the existing values in a column; and Ctrl+Enter, which you can use to enter a value in multiple cells simultaneously.

Troubleshooting If an AutoComplete suggestion doesn't appear as you begin typing a cell value, the option might be turned off. To turn on AutoComplete, click the File tab, and then click Options. In the Excel Options dialog box, display the Advanced page. In the Editing Options area of the page, select the Enable AutoComplete For Cell Values check box, and then click OK.

The following table summarizes these data entry techniques.

Method	Action
AutoFill	Enter the first value in a recognized series and use the fill handle to extend the series.
FillSeries	Enter the first two values in a series and use the fill handle to extend the series.
AutoComplete	Type the first few letters in a cell, and if a similar value exists in the same column, Excel suggests the existing value.
Pick From Drop-Down List	Right-click a cell, and then click Pick From Drop-Down List. A list of existing values in the cell's column is displayed. Click the value you want to enter into the cell.
Ctrl+Enter	Select a range of cells, each of which you want to contain the same data, type the data in the active cell, and press Ctrl+Enter.

Another handy feature in Excel is the AutoFill Options button that appears next to data you add to a worksheet by using the fill handle.

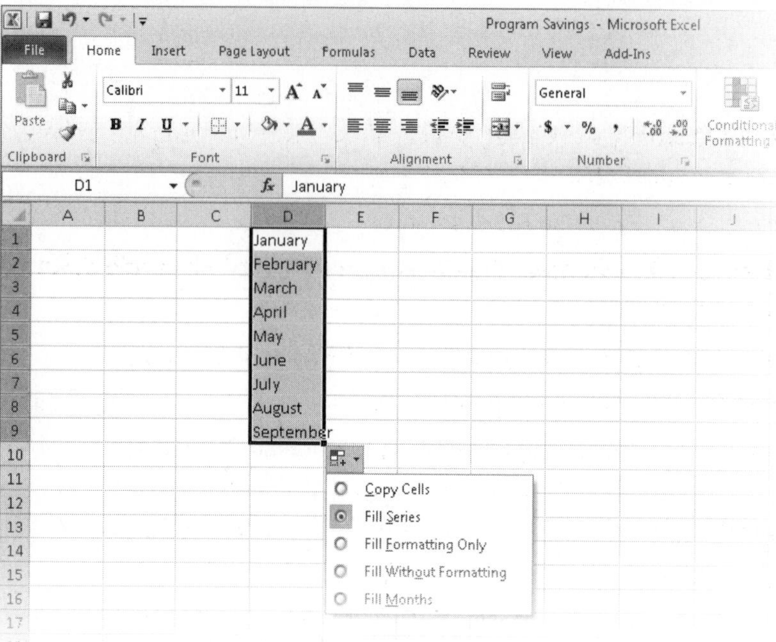

Clicking the AutoFill Options button displays a list of actions Excel can take regarding the cells affected by your fill operation. The options in the list are summarized in the following table.

Option	Action
Copy Cells	This copies the contents of the selected cells to the cells indicated by the fill operation.
Fill Series	This action fills the cells indicated by the fill operation with the next items in the series.
Fill Formatting Only	This copies the format of the selected cell to the cells indicated by the fill operation, but does not place any values in the target cells.
Fill Without Formatting	This action fills the cells indicated by the fill operation with the next items in the series, but ignores any formatting applied to the source cells.
Fill Days, Weekdays, and so on	The appearance of this option changes according to the series you extend. For example, if you extend the values *Wed*, *Thu*, and *Fri*, Excel presents two options, Fill Days and Fill Weekdays, and you can select which one you intended. If you do not use a recognized sequence, this option does not appear.

In this exercise, you'll enter data by using multiple methods and control how Excel formats an extended data series.

SET UP You need the Series_start workbook located in your Chapter02 practice file folder to complete this exercise. Start Excel, open the Series_start workbook, and save it as *Series*. Then follow the steps.

1. On the **Monthly** worksheet, select cell **B3**, and then drag the fill handle down until it covers cells **B3:B7**.

   Excel repeats the value *Fabrikam* in cells B4:B7.

2. Select cell **C3**, hold down the Ctrl key, and drag the fill handle down until it covers cells **C3:C7**.

   Excel repeats the value *January* in cells C4:C7.

3. Select cell **B8**, and then type the letter **F**.

   Excel displays the characters *abrikam* in reverse colors.

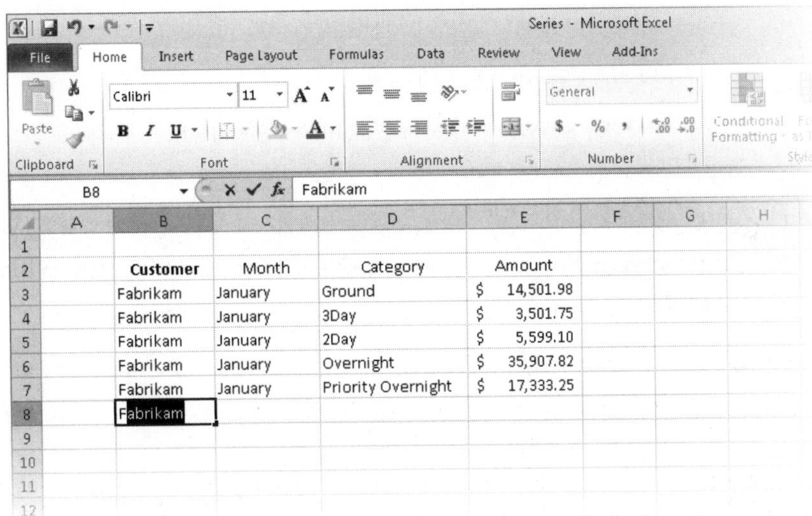

4. Press Tab to accept the value *Fabrikam* for the cell.

5. In cell **C8**, type **February**.

6. Right-click cell **D8**, and then click **Pick From Drop-down List**.

   A list of values in column D appears below cell D8.

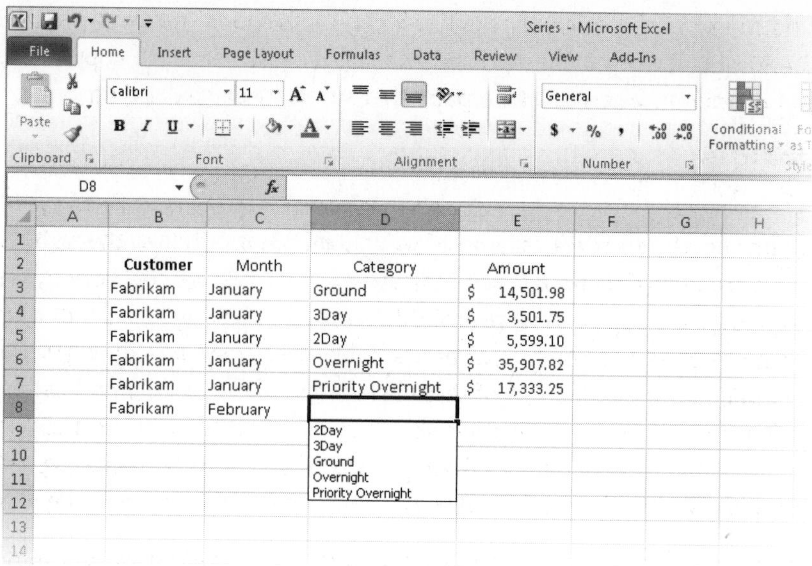

7. From the list, click **2Day**.

   The value *2Day* appears in cell D8.

8. In cell **E8**, type **11802.14**, and then press Tab or Enter.

   The value *$11,802.14* appears in cell E8.

9. Select cell **B2**, and then drag the fill handle so that it covers cells **C2:E2**.

   Excel replaces the values in cells C2:E2 with the value *Customer.*

10. Click the **AutoFill Options** button, and then click **Fill Formatting Only**.

    Excel restores the original values in cells C2:E2 but applies the formatting of cell B2 to those cells.

CLEAN UP Save the Series workbook, and then close it.

Moving Data Within a Workbook

You can move to a specific cell in lots of ways, but the most direct method is to click the desired cell. The cell you click will be outlined in black, and its contents, if any, will appear in the formula bar. When a cell is outlined, it is the active cell, meaning that you can modify its contents. You use a similar method to select multiple cells (referred to as a cell range)—just click the first cell in the range, hold down the left mouse button, and drag the mouse pointer over the remaining cells you want to select. After you select the cell or cells you want to work with, you can cut, copy, delete, or change the format of the contents of the cell or cells. For instance, Gregory Weber, the Northwest Distribution Center Manager for Consolidated Messenger, might want to copy the cells that contain a set of column labels to a new page that summarizes similar data.

Important If you select a group of cells, the first cell you click is designated as the active cell.

You're not limited to selecting cells individually or as part of a range. For example, you might need to move a column of price data one column to the right to make room for a column of headings that indicate to which service category (ground, three-day express, two-day express, overnight, or priority overnight) a set of numbers belongs. To move an entire column (or entire columns) of data at a time, you click the column's header, located at the top of the worksheet. Clicking a column header highlights every cell in that column and enables you to copy or cut the column and paste it elsewhere in the workbook. Similarly, clicking a row's header highlights every cell in that row, enabling you to copy or cut the row and paste it elsewhere in the workbook.

When you copy a cell, cell range, row, or column, Excel copies the cells' contents and formatting. In previous versions of Excel, you would paste the cut or copied items and then click the Paste Options button to select which aspects of the cut or copied cells to paste into the target cells. The problem with using the Paste Options button was that there was no way to tell what your pasted data would look like until you completed the paste operation. If you didn't like the way the pasted data looked, you had to click the Paste Options button again and try another option.

With the new Paste Live Preview capability in Excel, you can see what your pasted data will look like without forcing you to commit to the paste operation. To preview your data using Paste Live Preview, cut or copy worksheet data and then, on the Home tab of the ribbon, in the Clipboard group, click the Paste button's arrow to display the Paste gallery, and point to one of the icons. When you do, Excel displays a preview of how your data will appear if you click that paste option.

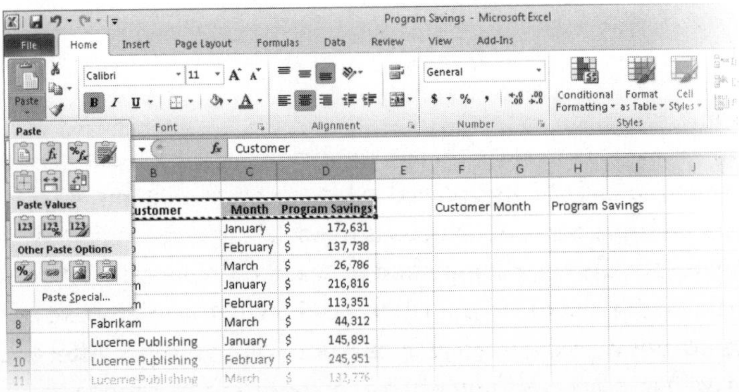

If you position your mouse pointer over one icon in the Paste gallery and then move it over another icon without clicking, Excel will update the preview to reflect the new option. Depending on the cells' contents, two or more of the paste options might lead to the same result.

Troubleshooting If pointing to an icon in the Paste gallery doesn't result in a live preview, that option might be turned off. To turn Paste Live Preview on, click the File tab and click Options to display the Excel Options dialog box. Click General, select the Enable Live Preview check box, and click OK.

After you click an icon to complete the paste operation, Excel displays the Paste Options button next to the pasted cells. Clicking the Paste Options button displays the Paste Options palette as well, but pointing to one of those icons doesn't generate a preview. If you want to display Paste Live Preview again, you will need to press Ctrl+Z to undo the paste operation and, if necessary, cut or copy the data again to use the icons in the Home tab's Clipboard group.

Troubleshooting If the Paste Options button doesn't appear, you can turn the feature on by clicking the File tab and then clicking Options to display the Excel Options dialog box. In the Excel Options dialog box, display the Advanced page and then, in the Cut, Copy, And Paste area, select the Show Paste Options Buttons When Content Is Pasted check box. Click OK to close the dialog box and save your setting.

After cutting or copying data to the Clipboard, you can access additional paste options from the Paste gallery and from the Paste Special dialog box, which you display by clicking Paste Special at the bottom of the Paste gallery.

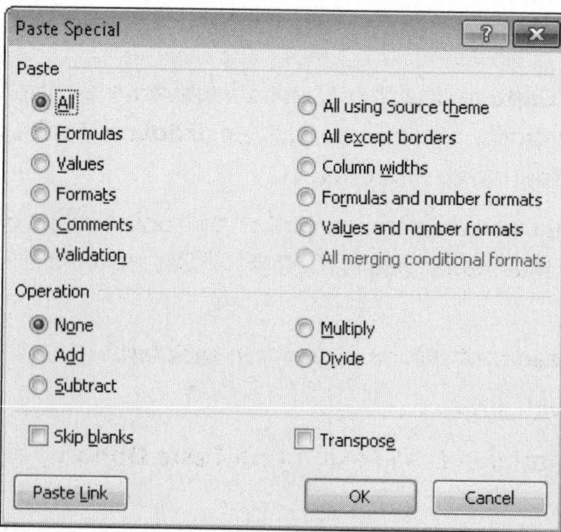

In the Paste Special dialog box, you can specify the aspect of the Clipboard contents you want to paste, restricting the pasted data to values, formats, comments, or one of several other options. You can perform mathematical operations involving the cut or copied data and the existing data in the cells you paste the content into. You can transpose data—change rows to columns and columns to rows—when you paste it, by clicking Transpose in the Paste gallery or by selecting the Transpose check box in the Paste Special dialog box.

In this exercise, you'll copy a set of data headers to another worksheet, move a column of data within a worksheet, and use Paste Live Preview to control the appearance of copied data.

SET UP You need the 2010Q1ShipmentsByCategory_start workbook located in your Chapter02 practice file folder to complete this exercise. Open the 2010Q1ShipmentsByCategory_start workbook, and save it as *2010Q1ShipmentsByCategory*. Then follow the steps.

1. On the **Count** worksheet, select cells **B2:D2**.

2. On the **Home** tab, in the **Clipboard** group, click the **Copy** button.

   Excel copies the contents of cells B2:D2 to the Clipboard.

   Keyboard Shortcut Press Ctrl+C to copy worksheet contents to the Clipboard.

   See Also To see a complete list of keyboard shortcuts, see "Keyboard Shortcuts" at the end of this book.

3. On the tab bar, click the **Sales** tab to display that worksheet.
4. Select cell **B2**.

5. On the **Home** tab, in the **Clipboard** group, click the **Paste** button's arrow, point to the first icon in the **Paste** group, and then click the **Keep Source Formatting** icon (the final icon in the first row of the **Paste** gallery.)

   Excel displays how the data would look if you pasted the copied values without formatting, and then pastes the header values into cells B2:D2, retaining the original cells' formatting.

6. Right-click the column header of column **I**, and then click **Cut**.

   Excel outlines column I with a marquee.

7. Right-click the header of column **E**, and then, under **Paste Options**, click **Paste**.

Excel pastes the contents of column I into column E.

Keyboard Shortcut Press Ctrl+V to paste worksheet contents exactly as they appear in the original cell.

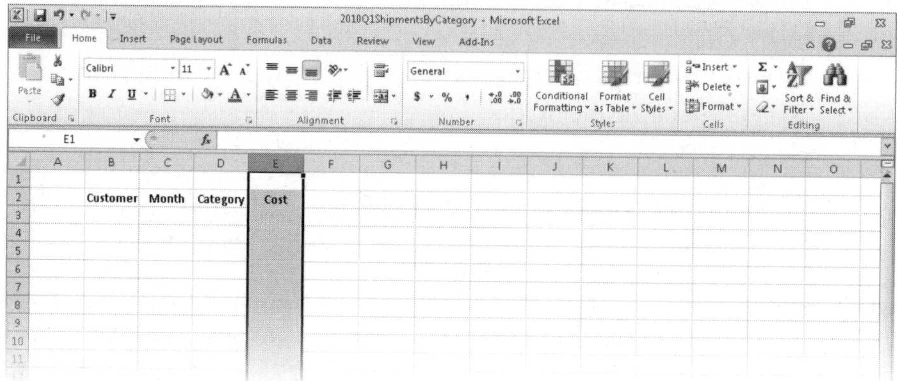

Troubleshooting The appearance of buttons and groups on the ribbon changes depending on the width of the program window. For information about changing the appearance of the ribbon to match our screen images, see "Modifying the Display of the Ribbon" at the beginning of this book.

CLEAN UP Save the 2010Q1ShipmentsByCategory workbook, and then close it.

Finding and Replacing Data

Excel worksheets can hold more than one million rows of data, so in large data collections it's unlikely that you would have the time to move through a worksheet one row at a time to locate the data you want to find. You can locate specific data in an Excel worksheet by using the Find And Replace dialog box, which has two pages (one named *Find*, the other named *Replace*) that you can use to search for cells that contain particular values. Using the controls on the Find page identifies cells that contain the data you specify; using the controls on the Replace page, you can substitute one value for another. For example, if one of Consolidated Messenger's customers changes its company name, you can change every instance of the old name to the new name by using the Replace functionality.

When you need more control over the data that you find and replace, for instance, if you want to find cells in which the entire cell value matches the value you're searching for, you can click the Options button to expand the Find And Replace dialog box.

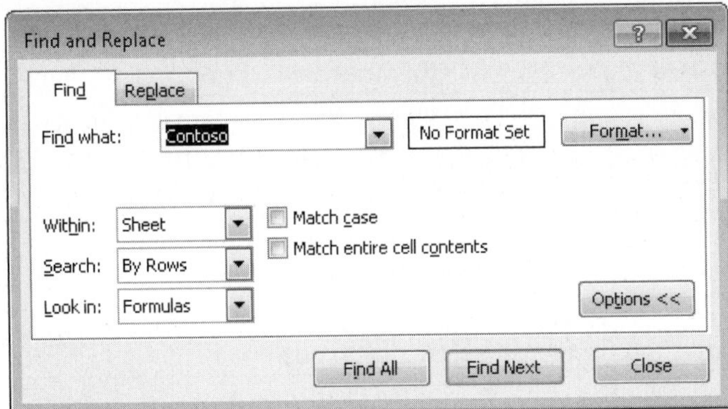

One way you can use the extra options in the Find And Replace dialog box is to use a specific format to identify data that requires review. As an example, Consolidated Messenger VP of Marketing Craig Dewar could make corporate sales plans based on a projected budget for the next year and mark his trial figures using a specific format. After the executive board finalizes the numbers, he could use the Find Format capability in the Find And Replace dialog box to locate the old values and change them by hand.

The following table summarizes the Find And Replace dialog box controls' functions.

Control	Function
Find What field	Contains the value you want to find or replace
Find All button	Selects every cell that contains the value in the Find What field
Find Next button	Selects the next cell that contains the value in the Find What field
Replace With field	Contains the value to overwrite the value in the Find What field
Replace All button	Replaces every instance of the value in the Find What field with the value in the Replace With field
Replace button	Replaces the highlighted occurrence of the value in the Find What field and highlights the next cell that contains that value
Options button	Expands the Find And Replace dialog box to display additional capabilities
Format button	Displays the Find Format dialog box, which you can use to specify the format of values to be found or values to be replaced
Within box	Enables you to select whether to search the active worksheet or the entire workbook

(continued)

Control	Function
Search box	Enables you to select whether to search by rows or by columns
Look In box	Enables you to select whether to search cell formulas or values
Match Case check box	When checked, requires that all matches have the same capitalization as the text in the Find What field (for example, *cat* doesn't match *Cat*)
Match Entire Cell Contents check box	Requires that the cell contain exactly the same value as in the Find What field (for example, *Cat* doesn't match *Catherine*)
Close button	Closes the Find And Replace dialog box

To change a value by hand, select the cell, and then either type a new value in the cell or, in the formula bar, select the value you want to replace and type the new value. You can also double-click a cell and edit its contents within the cell.

In this exercise, you'll find a specific value in a worksheet, replace every occurrence of a company name in a worksheet, and find a cell with a particular formatting.

SET UP You need the AverageDeliveries_start workbook located in your Chapter02 practice file folder to complete this exercise. Open the AverageDeliveries_start workbook, and save it as *AverageDeliveries*. Then follow the steps.

1. If necessary, click the **Time Summary** sheet tab.

   The Time Summary worksheet is displayed.

2. On the **Home** tab, in the **Editing** group, click **Find & Select**, and then click **Find**.

   The Find And Replace dialog box opens with the Find tab displayed.

   Keyboard Shortcut Press Ctrl+F to display the Find tab of the Find And Replace dialog box.

3. In the **Find what** field, type **114**.
4. Click **Find Next**.

Excel highlights cell B16, which contains the value *114*.

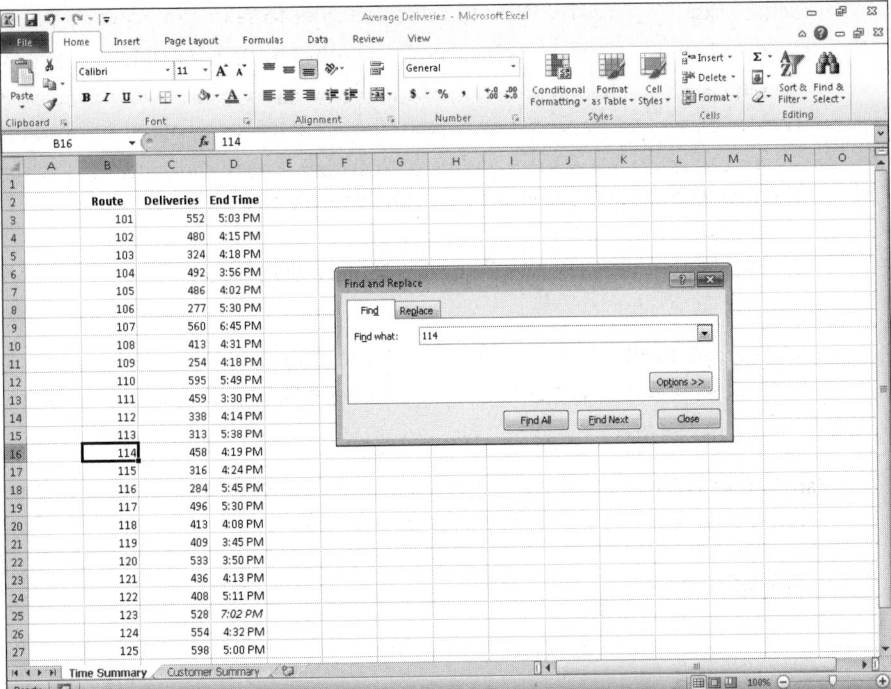

5. Delete the value in the **Find what** field, and then click the **Options** button.

   The Find And Replace dialog box expands to display additional search options.

6. Click **Format**.

   The Find Format dialog box opens.

7. Click the **Font** tab.

   The Font page is displayed.

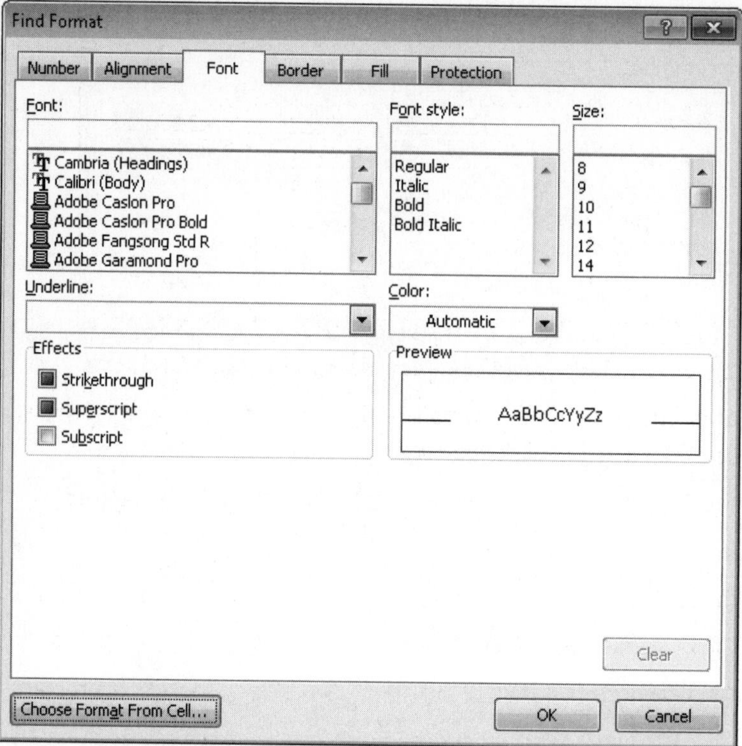

8. In the **Font style** list, click **Italic**.
9. Click **OK**.

   The Find Format dialog box closes.
10. Click **Find Next**.

    Excel highlights cell D25.
11. Click **Close**.

    The Find And Replace dialog box closes.
12. On the tab bar, click the **Customer Summary** sheet tab.

    The Customer Summary worksheet is displayed.
13. On the **Home** tab, in the **Editing** group, click **Find & Select**, and then click **Replace**.

    The Find And Replace dialog box opens with the Replace tab displayed.

    Keyboard Shortcut Press Ctrl+H to display the Replace tab of the Find And Replace dialog box.

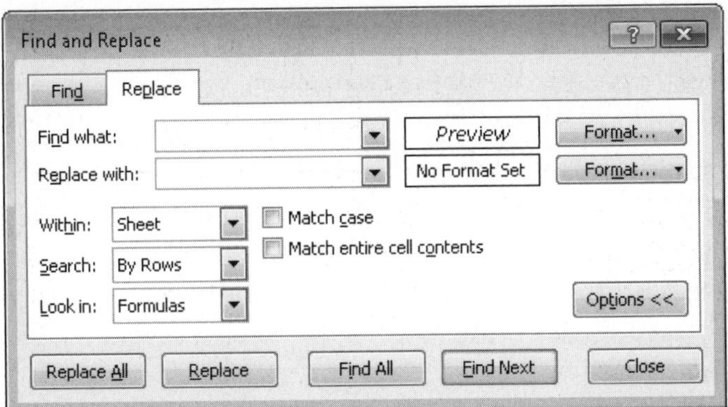

14. Click the **Format** arrow to the right of the **Find what** field, and then in the list, click **Clear Find Format**.

    The format displayed next to the Find What field disappears.

15. In the **Find what** field, type **Contoso**.
16. In the **Replace with** field, type **Northwind Traders**.
17. Click **Replace All**.

    A message box appears, indicating that Excel made three replacements.

18. Click **OK** to close the message box.
19. Click **Close**.

    The Find And Replace dialog box closes.

CLEAN UP Save the AverageDeliveries workbook, and then close it.

Correcting and Expanding Upon Worksheet Data

After you enter your data, you should take the time to check and correct it. You do need to verify visually that each piece of numeric data is correct, but you can make sure that your worksheet's text is spelled correctly by using the Excel spelling checker. When the spelling checker encounters a word it doesn't recognize, it highlights the word and offers suggestions representing its best guess of the correct word. You can then edit the word directly, pick the proper word from the list of suggestions, or have the spelling checker ignore the misspelling. You can also use the spelling checker to add new words to a custom dictionary so that Excel will recognize them later, saving you time by not requiring you to identify the words as correct every time they occur in your worksheets.

Tip After you make a change in a workbook, you can usually remove the change as long as you haven't closed the workbook. To undo a change, click the Undo button on the Quick Access Toolbar. If you decide you want to keep a change, you can use the Redo command to restore it.

If you're not sure of your word choice, or if you use a word that is almost but not quite right for your intended meaning, you can check for alternative words by using the Thesaurus. Several other research tools are also available, such as the Bing search engine and the Microsoft Encarta dictionary, to which you can refer as you create your workbooks. To display those tools, on the Review tab, in the Proofing group, click Research to display the Research task pane.

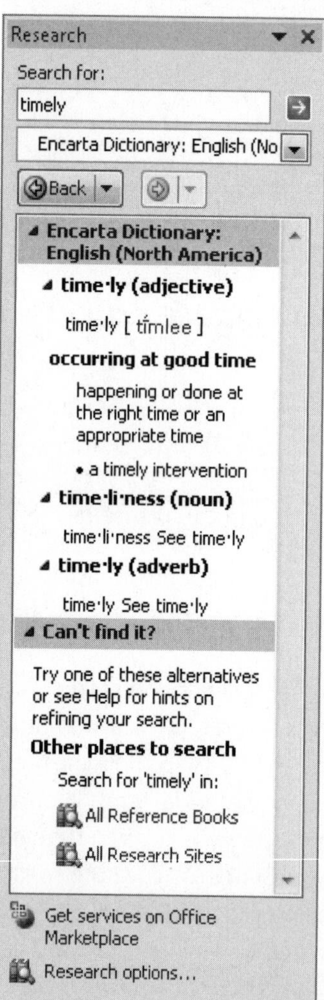

Finally, if you want to translate a word from one language to another, you can do so by selecting the cell that contains the value you want to translate, displaying the Review tab, and then, in the Language group, clicking Translate. The Research task pane opens (or changes if it's already open) and displays controls you can use to select the original and destination languages.

Important Excel translates a sentence by using word substitutions, which means that the translation routine doesn't always pick the best word for a given context. The translated sentence might not capture your exact meaning.

In this exercise, you'll check a worksheet's spelling, add two new terms to a dictionary, search for an alternative word by using the Thesaurus, and translate a word from English into French.

SET UP You need the ServiceLevels_start workbook located in your Chapter02 practice file folder to complete this exercise. Open the ServiceLevels_start workbook, and save it as *ServiceLevels*. Then follow the steps.

1. On the **Review** tab, in the **Proofing** group, click **Spelling**.

   The Spelling dialog box opens with the first misspelled word in the worksheet displayed in the Not In Dictionary field.

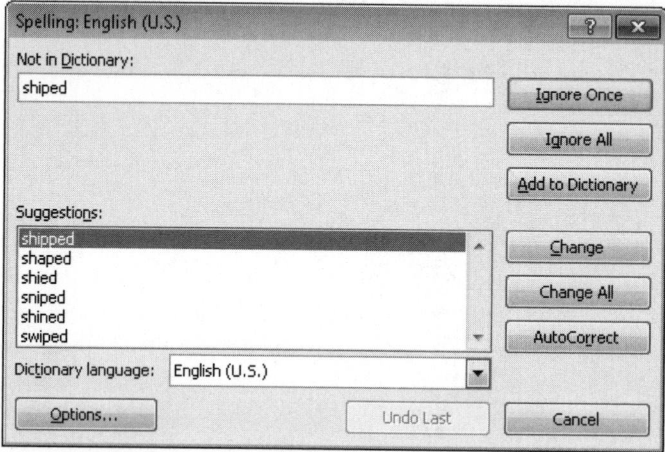

2. Verify that the word *shipped* is highlighted in the **Suggestions** pane, and then click **Change**.

   Excel corrects the word and displays the next questioned word: *withn*.

3. Click **Change**.

   Excel corrects the word and displays the next questioned word: *TwoDay*.

4. Click **Add to Dictionary**.

   Excel adds the word to the dictionary and displays the next questioned word: *ThreeDay*.

5. Click **Add to Dictionary**.

   Excel adds the word to the dictionary.

6. If necessary, click **Close** to close the Spelling dialog box.

   The Spelling dialog box closes, and a message box appears, indicating that the spelling check is complete for the worksheet.

7. Click **OK** to close the message box.
8. Click cell **B6**.

9. On the **Review** tab, in the **Proofing** group, click **Thesaurus**.

   The Research task pane opens and displays a list of synonyms for the word *Overnight*.

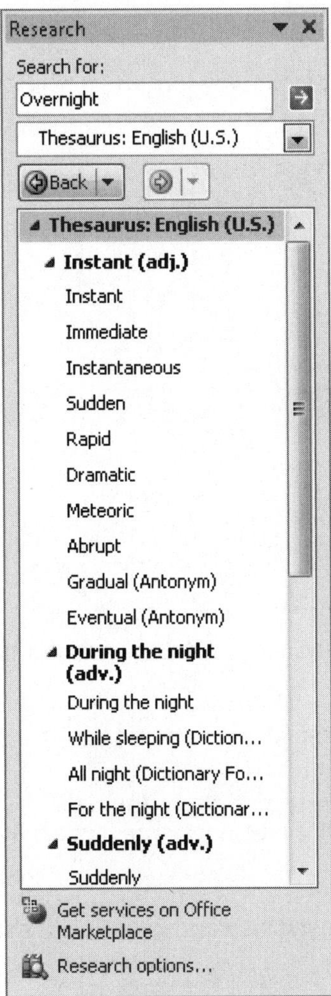

10. On the **Review** tab, in the **Language** group, click **Translate**.

    The Research task pane displays the translation tools.

11. If necessary, in the **From** list, click **English (U.S.).**
12. In the **To** list, click **French (France).**

    The Research task pane displays French words that mean *overnight*.

CLEAN UP Save the ServiceLevels workbook, and then close it.

Defining Excel Tables

With Exel, you've always been able to manage lists of data effectively, enabling you to sort your worksheet data based on the values in one or more columns, limit the data displayed by using criteria (for example, show only those routes with fewer than 100 stops), and create formulas that summarize the values in visible (that is, unfiltered) cells. In Excel 2007, the Excel product team extended your ability to manage your data by introducing Excel tables. Excel 2010 offers you the same capability.

Customer	Month	Program Savings
Contoso	January	$ 172,631
Contoso	February	$ 137,738
Contoso	March	$ 26,786
Fabrikam	January	$ 216,816
Fabrikam	February	$ 113,351
Fabrikam	March	$ 44,312
Lucerne Publishing	January	$ 145,891
Lucerne Publishing	February	$ 245,951
Lucerne Publishing	March	$ 132,776
Wide World Importers	January	$ 197,070
Wide World Importers	February	$ 128,051
Wide World Importers	March	$ 245,695

To create an Excel table, type a series of column headers in adjacent cells, and then type a row of data below the headers. Click any header or data cell into which you just typed, and then, on the Home tab, in the Styles group, click Format As Table. Then, from the gallery that opens, click the style you want to apply to the table. When the Format As Table dialog box opens, verify that the cells in the Where Is The Data For Your Table? field reflect your current selection and that the My Table Has Headers check box is selected, and then click OK.

Excel can also create an Excel table from an existing cell range as long as the range has no blank rows or columns within the data and there is no extraneous data in cells immediately below or next to the list. To create the Excel table, click any cell in the range and then, on the Home tab, in the Styles group, click the Format As Table button and select a table style. If your existing data has formatting applied to it, that formatting remains applied to those cells when you create the Excel table. If you want Excel to replace the existing formatting with the Excel table's formatting, right-click the table style you want to apply and then click Apply And Clear Formatting.

When you want to add data to an Excel table, click the rightmost cell in the bottom row of the Excel table and press the Tab key to create a new row. You can also select a cell in the row immediately below the last row in the table or a cell in the column immediately to the right of the table and type a value into the cell. After you enter the value and move out of the cell, the AutoCorrect Options action button appears. If you didn't mean to include the data in the Excel table, you can click Undo Table AutoExpansion to exclude the cells from the Excel table. If you never want Excel to include adjacent data in an Excel table again, click Stop Automatically Expanding Tables.

Tip To stop Table AutoExpansion before it starts, click the File tab, and then click Options. In the Excel Options dialog box, click Proofing, and then click the AutoCorrect Options button to display the AutoCorrect dialog box. Click the AutoFormat As You Type tab, clear the Include New Rows And Columns In Table check box, and then click OK twice.

You can add rows and columns to an Excel table, or remove them from an Excel table without deleting the cells' contents, by dragging the resize handle at the Excel table's lower-right corner. If your Excel table's headers contain a recognizable series of values (such as *Region1*, *Region2*, and *Region3*), and you drag the resize handle to create a fourth column, Excel creates the column with the label *Region4*—the next value in the series.

Excel tables often contain data you can summarize by calculating a sum or average, or by finding the maximum or minimum value in a column. To summarize one or more columns of data, you can add a Total row to your Excel table.

Customer	Month	Program Savings	
Contoso	January	$	172,631
Contoso	February	$	137,738
Contoso	March	$	26,786
Fabrikam	January	$	216,816
Fabrikam	February	$	113,351
Fabrikam	March	$	44,312
Lucerne Publishing	January	$	145,891
Lucerne Publishing	February	$	245,951
Lucerne Publishing	March	$	132,776
Wide World Importers	January	$	197,070
Wide World Importers	February	$	128,051
Wide World Importers	March	$	245,695
Total		**$**	**1,807,068**

When you add the Total row, Excel creates a formula that summarizes the values in the rightmost Excel table column. To change that summary operation, or to add a summary operation to any other cell in the Total row, click the cell, click the arrow that appears, and then click the summary operation you want to apply. Clicking the More Functions menu item displays the Insert Function dialog box, from which you can select any of the functions available in Excel.

Much as it does when you create a new worksheet, Excel gives your Excel tables generic names such as *Table1* and *Table2*. You can change an Excel table's name to something easier to recognize by clicking any cell in the table, clicking the Design contextual tab, and then, in the Properties group, editing the value in the Table Name box. Changing an Excel table name might not seem important, but it helps make formulas that summarize Excel table data much easier to understand. You should make a habit of renaming your Excel tables so you can recognize the data they contain.

See Also For more information about using the Insert Function dialog box and about referring to tables in formulas, see "Creating Formulas to Calculate Values" in Chapter 3, "Performing Calculations on Data."

If for any reason you want to convert your Excel table back to a normal range of cells, click any cell in the Excel table and then, on the Design contextual tab, in the Tools group, click Convert To Range. When Excel displays a message box asking if you're sure you want to convert the table to a range, click OK.

In this exercise, you'll create an Excel table from existing data, add data to an Excel table, add a Total row, change the Total row's summary operation, and rename the Excel table.

SET UP You need the DriverSortTimes_start workbook located in your Chapter02 practice file folder to complete this exercise. Open the DriverSortTimes_start workbook, and save it as *DriverSortTimes*. Then follow the steps.

1. Select cell **B2**.

2. On the **Home** tab, in the **Styles** group, click **Format as Table**, and then select a table style.

   The Format As Table dialog box opens.

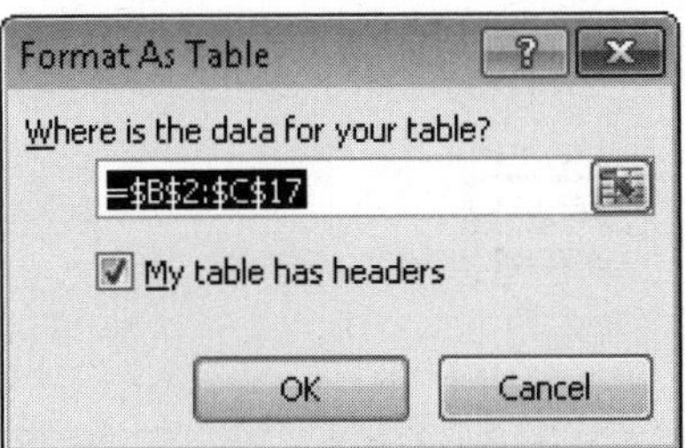

3. Verify that the range *=$B$2:$C$17* is displayed in the **Where is the data for your table?** field and that the **My table has headers** check box is selected, and then click **OK**.

   Excel creates an Excel table from your data and displays the Design contextual tab.

4. In cell **B18**, type **D116**, press Tab, type **100** in cell **C18**, and then press Enter.

   Excel includes the data in your Excel table.

5. Select a cell in the table. Then on the **Design** contextual tab, in the **Table Style Options** group, select the **Total Row** check box.

   A Total row appears at the bottom of your Excel table.

6. Select cell **C19**, click the arrow that appears at the right edge of the cell, and then click **Average**.

   Excel changes the summary operation to Average.

Drive	Sorting Minutes
D101	102
D102	162
D103	165
D104	91
D105	103
D106	127
D107	112
D108	137
D109	102
D110	147
D111	163
D112	109
D113	91
D114	107
D115	93
D116	100
Total	**119.4375**

7. On the **Design** contextual tab, in the **Properties** group, type the value **SortTimes** in the **Table Name** field, and then press Enter.

   Excel renames your Excel table.

8. On the Quick Access Toolbar, click the **Save** button to save your work.

CLEAN UP Close the DriverSortTimes workbook. If you are not continuing directly to the next chapter, exit Excel.

Key Points

- You can enter a series of data quickly by typing one or more values in adjacent cells, selecting the cells, and then dragging the fill handle. To change how dragging the fill handle extends a data series, hold down the Ctrl key.
- Dragging a fill handle displays the Auto Fill Options button, which you can use to specify whether to copy the selected cells' values, extend a recognized series, or apply the selected cells' formatting to the new cells.
- With Excel, you can enter data by using a list, AutoComplete, or Ctrl+Enter. You should experiment with these techniques and use the one that best fits your circumstances.
- When you copy (or cut) and paste cells, columns, or rows, you can use the new Paste Live Preview capability to preview how your data will appear before you commit to the paste operation.
- After you paste cells, rows, or columns into your worksheet, Excel displays the Paste Options action button. You can use its controls to change which aspects of the cut or copied elements Excel applies to the pasted elements.
- By using the options in the Paste Special dialog box, you can paste only specific aspects of cut or copied data, perform mathematical operations, transpose data, or delete blank cells when pasting.
- You can find and replace data within a worksheet by searching for specific values or by searching for cells that have a particular format applied.
- Excel provides a variety of powerful proofing and research tools, enabling you to check your workbook's spelling, find alternative words by using the Thesaurus, and translate words between languages.
- With Excel tables, you can organize and summarize your data effectively.

Chapter at a Glance

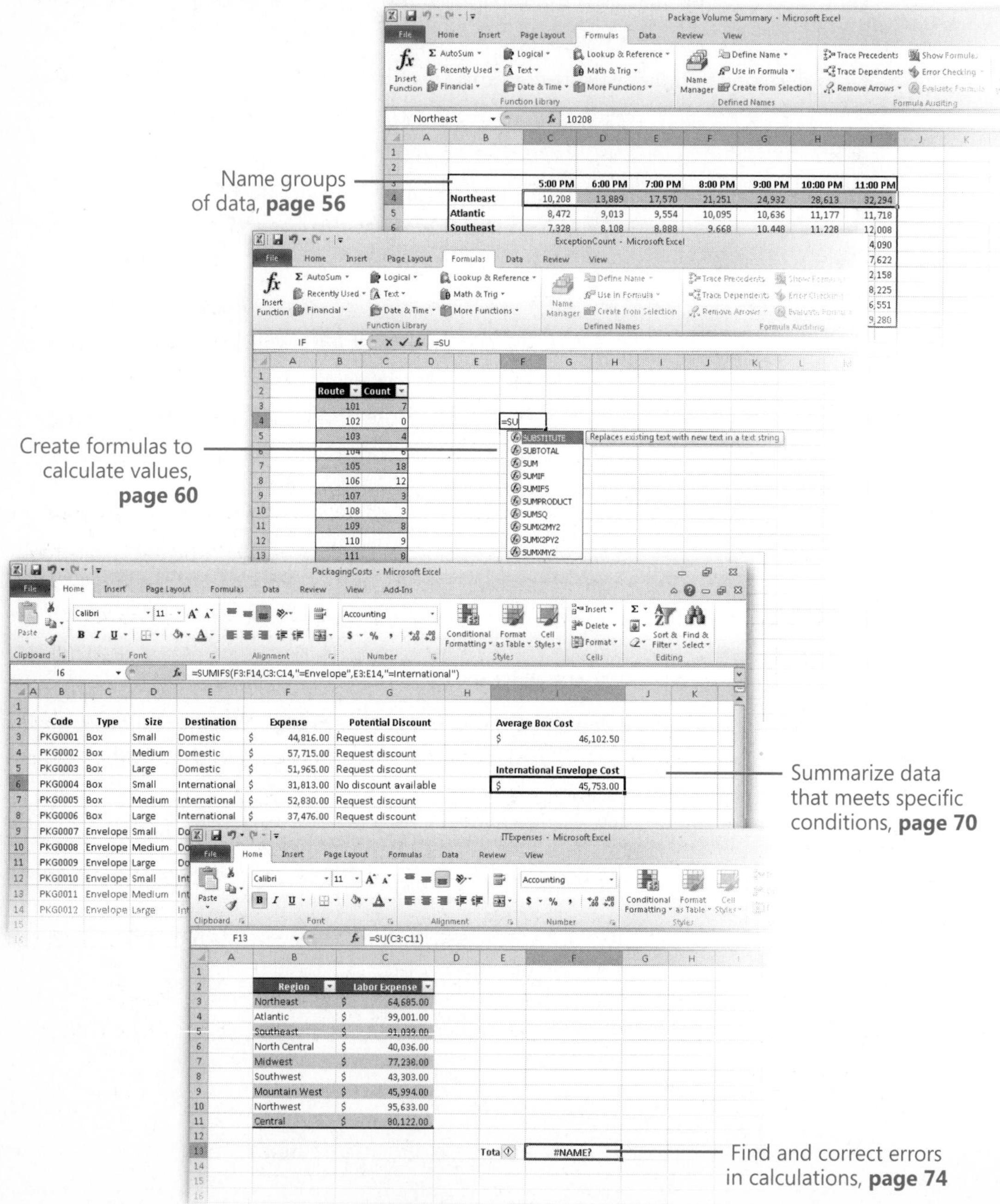

3 Performing Calculations on Data

In this chapter, you will learn how to

- ✔ Name groups of data.
- ✔ Create formulas to calculate values.
- ✔ Summarize data that meets specific conditions.
- ✔ Find and correct errors in calculations.

Microsoft Excel 2010 workbooks give you a handy place to store and organize your data, but you can also do a lot more with your data in Excel. One important task you can perform is to calculate totals for the values in a series of related cells. You can also use Excel to discover other information about the data you select, such as the maximum or minimum value in a group of cells. By finding the maximum or minimum value in a group, you can identify your best salesperson, product categories you might need to pay more attention to, or suppliers that consistently give you the best deal. Regardless of your bookkeeping needs, Excel gives you the ability to find the information you want. And if you make an error, you can find the cause and correct it quickly.

Many times, you can't access the information you want without referencing more than one cell, and it's also often true that you'll use the data in the same group of cells for more than one calculation. Excel makes it easy to reference a number of cells at once, enabling you to define your calculations quickly.

In this chapter, you'll learn how to streamline references to groups of data on your worksheets and how to create and correct formulas that summarize an organization's business operations.

> **Practice Files** Before you can complete the exercises in this chapter, you need to copy the book's practice files to your computer. The practice files you'll use to complete the exercises in this chapter are in the Chapter03 practice file folder. A complete list of practice files is provided in "Using the Practice Files" at the beginning of this book.

Naming Groups of Data

When you work with large amounts of data, it's often useful to identify groups of cells that contain related data. For example, you can create a worksheet in which cells C4:I4 hold the number of packages Consolidated Messenger's Northeast processing facility handled from 5:00 P.M. to 12:00 A.M. on the previous day.

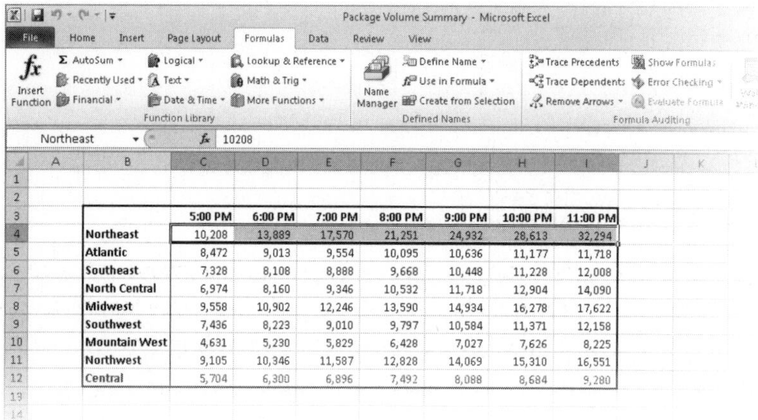

	5:00 PM	6:00 PM	7:00 PM	8:00 PM	9:00 PM	10:00 PM	11:00 PM
Northeast	10,208	13,889	17,570	21,251	24,932	28,613	32,294
Atlantic	8,472	9,013	9,554	10,095	10,636	11,177	11,718
Southeast	7,328	8,108	8,888	9,668	10,448	11,228	12,008
North Central	6,974	8,160	9,346	10,532	11,718	12,904	14,090
Midwest	9,558	10,902	12,246	13,590	14,934	16,278	17,622
Southwest	7,436	8,223	9,010	9,797	10,584	11,371	12,158
Mountain West	4,631	5,230	5,829	6,428	7,027	7,626	8,225
Northwest	9,105	10,346	11,587	12,828	14,069	15,310	16,551
Central	5,704	6,300	6,896	7,492	8,088	8,684	9,280

Instead of specifying the cells individually every time you want to use the data they contain, you can define those cells as a range (also called a *named range*). For example, you can group the items from the cells described in the preceding paragraph into a range named *NortheastPreviousDay*. Whenever you want to use the contents of that range in a calculation, you can simply use the name of the range instead of specifying each cell individually.

Tip Yes, you could just name the range *Northeast*, but if you use the range's values in a formula in another worksheet, the more descriptive range name tells you and your colleagues exactly what data is used in the calculation.

To create a named range, select the cells you want to include in your range, click the Formulas tab, and then, in the Defined Names group, click Define Name to display the New Name dialog box. In the New Name dialog box, type a name in the Name field, verify that the cells you selected appear in the Refers To field, and then click OK. You can also add a comment about the range in the Comment field and select whether you want to make the name available for formulas in the entire workbook or just on an individual worksheet.

If the cells you want to define as a named range have labels in a row or column that's part of the cell group, you can use those labels as the names of the named ranges. For example, if your data appears in worksheet cells B4:I12 and the values in column B are the row labels, you can make each row its own named range. To create a series of named ranges from a group of cells, select all of the data cells, including the labels, display the Formulas tab and then, in the Defined Names group, click Create From Selection to display the Create Names From Selection dialog box. In the Create Names From Selection dialog box, select the check box that represents the labels' position in the selected range, and then click OK.

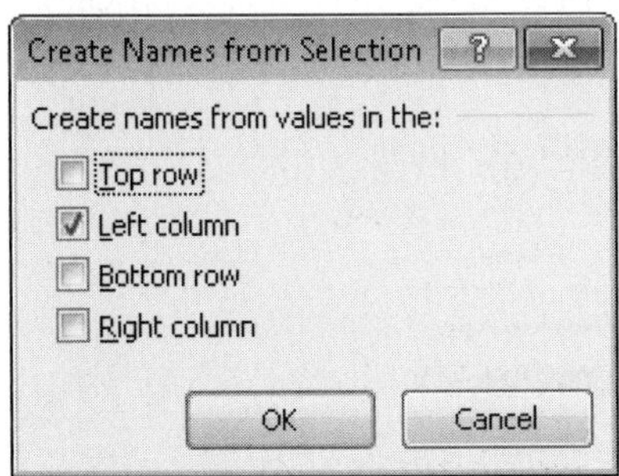

A final way to create a named range is to select the cells you want in the range, click in the Name box next to the formula box, and then type the name for the range. You can display the ranges available in a workbook by clicking the Name arrow.

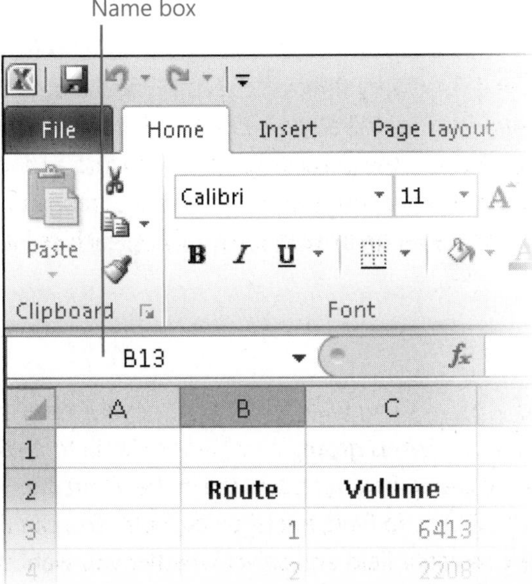

To manage the named ranges in a workbook, display the Formulas tab, and then, in the Defined Names group, click Name Manager to display the Name Manager dialog box.

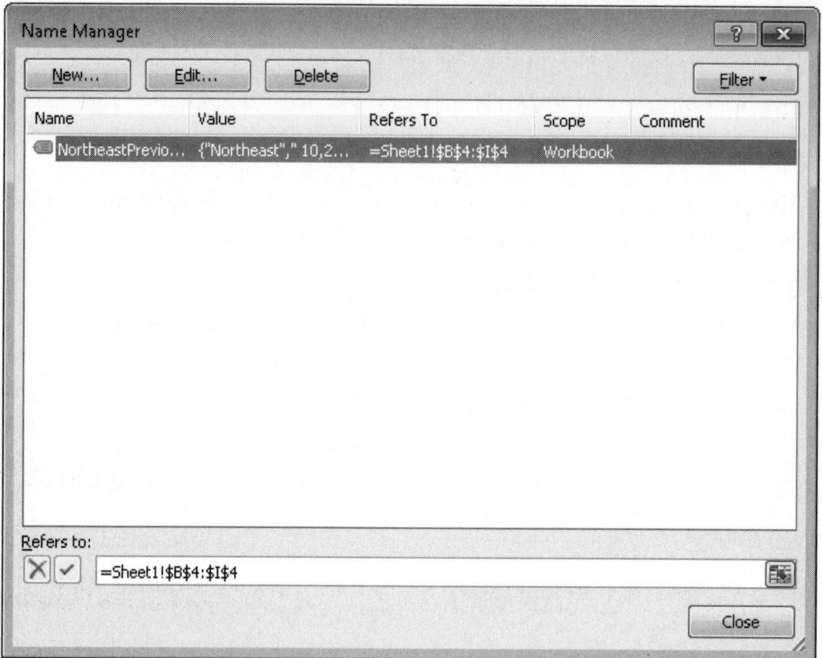

When you click a named range, Excel displays the cells it encompasses in the Refers To field. Clicking the Edit button displays the Edit Name dialog box, which is a version of the New Name dialog box, enabling you to change a named range's definition; for example, by adding a column. You can also use the controls in the Name Manager dialog box to delete a named range (the range, not the data) by clicking it, clicking the Delete button, and then clicking OK in the confirmation dialog box that opens.

Tip If your workbook contains a lot of named ranges, you can click the Filter button in the Name Manager dialog box and select a criterion to limit the names displayed in the Name Manager dialog box.

In this exercise, you'll create named ranges to streamline references to groups of cells.

SET UP You need the VehicleMiles_start workbook located in your Chapter03 practice file folder to complete this exercise. Start Excel, open the VehicleMiles_start workbook, and save it as *VehicleMiles*. Then follow the steps.

1. Select cells **C4:G4**.

   You are intentionally leaving cell H4 out of this selection. You will edit the named range later in this exercise.

2. In the **Name** box at the left end of the formula bar, type **V101LastWeek**, and then press Enter.

   Excel creates a named range named *V101LastWeek*.

3. On the **Formulas** tab, in the **Defined Names** group, click **Name Manager**.

   The Name Manager dialog box opens.

4. Click the **V101LastWeek** name.

   The cell range to which the V101LastWeek name refers appears in the Refers To box at the bottom of the Name Manager dialog box.

5. Edit the cell range in the **Refers to** box to **=MilesLastWeek!$C$4:$H$4** (change the *G* to an *H*), and then click the check mark button to the left of the box to finalize the update.

   Excel changes the named range's definition.

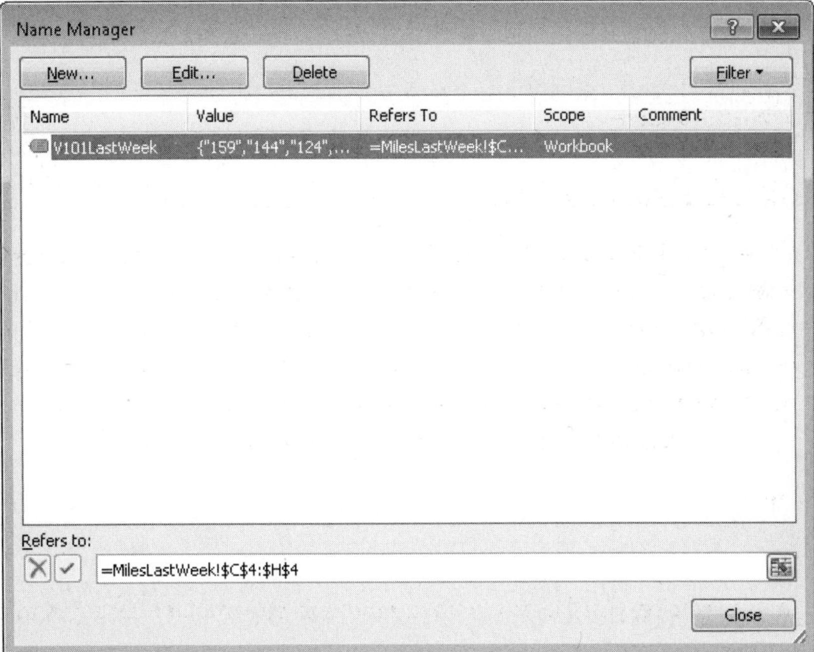

6. Click **Close**.

   The Name Manager dialog box closes.

7. Select the cell range **C5:H5**.

8. On the **Formulas** tab, in the **Defined Names** group, click **Define Name**.

The New Name dialog box opens.

9. In the **Name** field, type **V102LastWeek**.
10. Verify that the definition in the **Refers to** field is **=MilesLastWeek!$C$5:$H$5**.
11. Click **OK**.

Excel creates the name and closes the New Name dialog box.

CLEAN UP Save the VehicleMiles workbook, and then close it.

Creating Formulas to Calculate Values

After you add your data to a worksheet and define ranges to simplify data references, you can create a formula, which is an expression that performs calculations on your data. For example, you can calculate the total cost of a customer's shipments, figure the average number of packages for all Wednesdays in the month of January, or find the highest and lowest daily package volumes for a week, month, or year.

To write an Excel formula, you begin the cell's contents with an equal (=) sign; when Excel sees it, it knows that the expression following it should be interpreted as a calculation, not text. After the equal sign, type the formula. For example, you can find the sum of the numbers in cells C2 and C3 by using the formula *=C2+C3*. After you have entered a formula into a cell, you can revise it by clicking the cell and then editing the formula in the formula box. For example, you can change the preceding formula to *=C3-C2*, which calculates the difference between the contents of cells C2 and C3.

Troubleshooting If Excel treats your formula as text, make sure that you haven't accidentally put a space before the equal sign. Remember, the equal sign must be the first character!

Typing the cell references for 15 or 20 cells in a calculation would be tedious, but Excel makes it easy to enter complex calculations. To create a new calculation, click the Formulas tab, and then in the Function Library group, click Insert Function. The Insert Function dialog box opens, with a list of functions, or predefined formulas, from which you can choose.

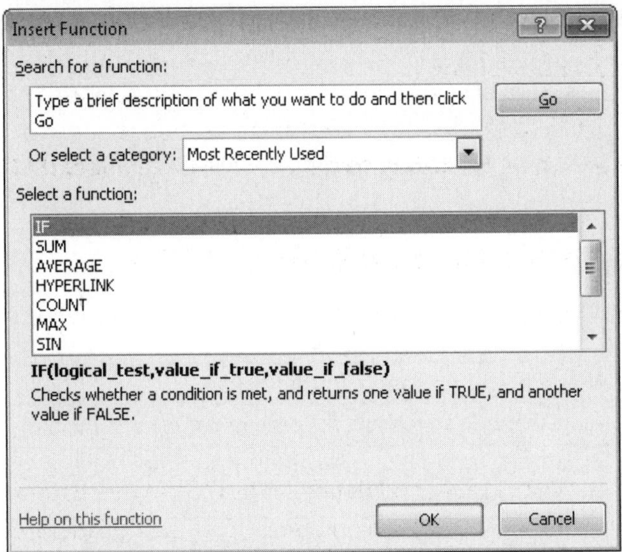

The following table describes some of the most useful functions in the list.

Function	Description
SUM	Finds the sum of the numbers in the specified cells
AVERAGE	Finds the average of the numbers in the specified cells
COUNT	Finds the number of entries in the specified cells
MAX	Finds the largest value in the specified cells
MIN	Finds the smallest value in the specified cells

Two other functions you might use are the *NOW* and *PMT* functions. The *NOW* function displays the time Excel updated the workbook's formulas, so the value will change every time the workbook recalculates. The proper form for this function is *=NOW()*. To update the value to the current date and time, just press the F9 key or display the Formulas tab and then, in the Calculation group, click the Calculate Now button. You could, for example, use the *NOW* function to calculate the elapsed time from when you started a process to the present time.

The *PMT* function is a bit more complex. It calculates payments due on a loan, assuming a constant interest rate and constant payments. To perform its calculations, the *PMT* function requires an interest rate, the number of payments, and the starting balance. The elements to be entered into the function are called *arguments* and must be entered in a certain order. That order is written as *PMT(rate, nper, pv, fv, type)*. The following table summarizes the arguments in the *PMT* function.

Argument	Description
rate	The interest rate, to be divided by 12 for a loan with monthly payments, by 4 for quarterly payments, and so on
nper	The total number of payments for the loan
pv	The amount loaned (*pv* is short for *present value*, or principal)
fv	The amount to be left over at the end of the payment cycle (usually left blank, which indicates 0)
type	0 or 1, indicating whether payments are made at the beginning or at the end of the month (usually left blank, which indicates 0, or the end of the month)

If Consolidated Messenger wanted to borrow $2,000,000 at a 6 percent interest rate and pay the loan back over 24 months, you could use the *PMT* function to figure out the monthly payments. In this case, the function would be written *=PMT(6%/12, 24, 2000000)*, which calculates a monthly payment of $88,641.22.

You can also use the names of any ranges you defined to supply values for a formula. For example, if the named range NortheastLastDay refers to cells C4:I4, you can calculate the average of cells C4:I4 with the formula *=AVERAGE(NortheastLastDay)*. With Excel, you can add functions, named ranges, and table references to your formulas more efficiently by using the Formula AutoComplete capability. Just as AutoComplete offers to fill in a cell's text value when Excel recognizes that the value you're typing matches a previous entry, Formula AutoComplete offers to help you fill in a function, named range, or table reference while you create a formula.

As an example, consider a worksheet that contains a two-column Excel table named *Exceptions*. The first column is labeled *Route*; the second is labeled *Count*.

Route	Count
101	7
102	0
103	4
104	6
105	18
106	12
107	3
108	3
109	8
110	9
111	8
112	18
113	12
114	16
115	12
116	9
117	10
118	6
119	10
120	4

You refer to a table by typing the table name, followed by the column or row name in square brackets. For example, the table reference *Exceptions[Count]* would refer to the Count column in the Exceptions table.

To create a formula that finds the total number of exceptions by using the *SUM* function, you begin by typing *=SU*. When you type the letter *S*, Formula AutoComplete lists functions that begin with the letter *S*; when you type the letter *U*, Excel narrows the list down to the functions that start with the letters *SU*.

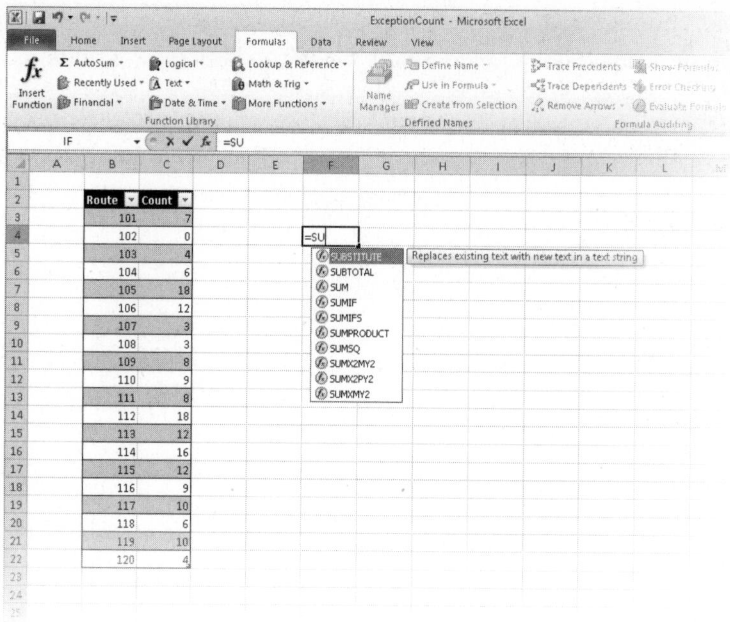

To add the *SUM* function (followed by an opening parenthesis) to the formula, click *SUM* and then press Tab. To begin adding the table reference, type the letter *E*. Excel displays a list of available functions, tables, and named ranges that start with the letter *E*. Click Exceptions, and press Tab to add the table reference to the formula. Then, because you want to summarize the values in the table's Count column, type a left square bracket and then, in the list of available table items, click Count. To finish creating the formula, type a right square bracket followed by a right parenthesis to create the formula *=SUM(Exceptions[Count])*.

If you want to include a series of contiguous cells in a formula, but you haven't defined the cells as a named range, you can click the first cell in the range and drag to the last cell. If the cells aren't contiguous, hold down the Ctrl key and select all of the cells to be included. In both cases, when you release the mouse button, the references of the cells you selected appear in the formula.

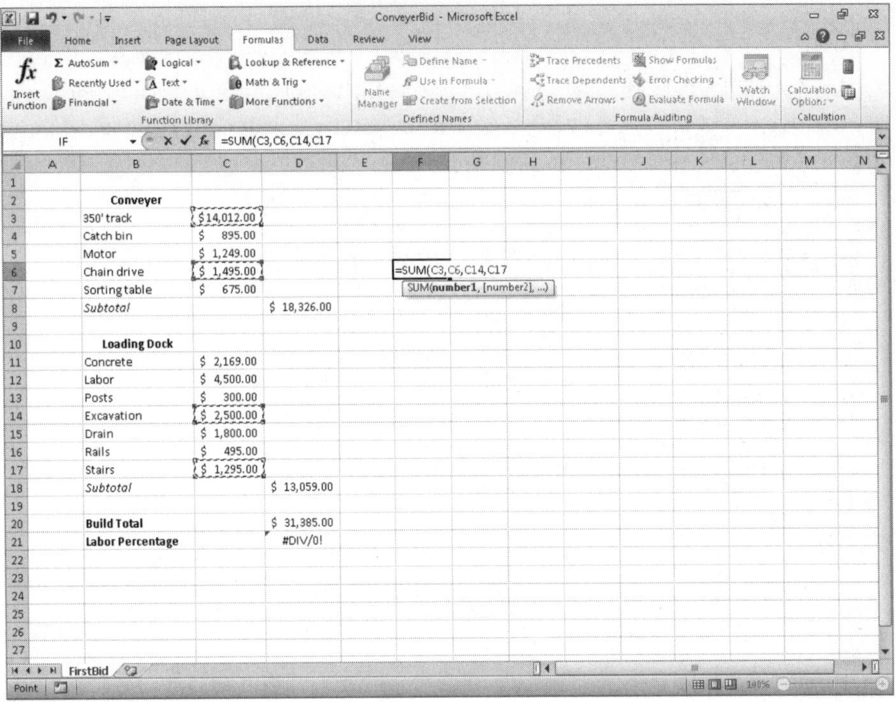

Troubleshooting The appearance of buttons and groups on the ribbon changes depending on the width of the program window. For information about changing the appearance of the ribbon to match our screen images, see "Modifying the Display of the Ribbon" at the beginning of this book.

After you create a formula, you can copy it and paste it into another cell. When you do, Excel tries to change the formula so that it works in the new cells. For instance, suppose you have a worksheet where cell D8 contains the formula *=SUM(C2:C6)*. Clicking cell D8, copying the cell's contents, and then pasting the result into cell D16 writes *=SUM(C10:C14)* into cell D16. Excel has reinterpreted the formula so that it fits the surrounding cells! Excel knows it can reinterpret the cells used in the formula because the formula uses a relative reference, or a reference that can change if the formula is copied to another cell. Relative references are written with just the cell row and column (for example, *C14*).

Relative references are useful when you summarize rows of data and want to use the same formula for each row. As an example, suppose you have a worksheet with two columns of data, labeled *SalePrice* and *Rate*, and you want to calculate your sales representative's commission by multiplying the two values in a row. To calculate the commission for the first sale, you would type the formula *=B4*C4* in cell D4.

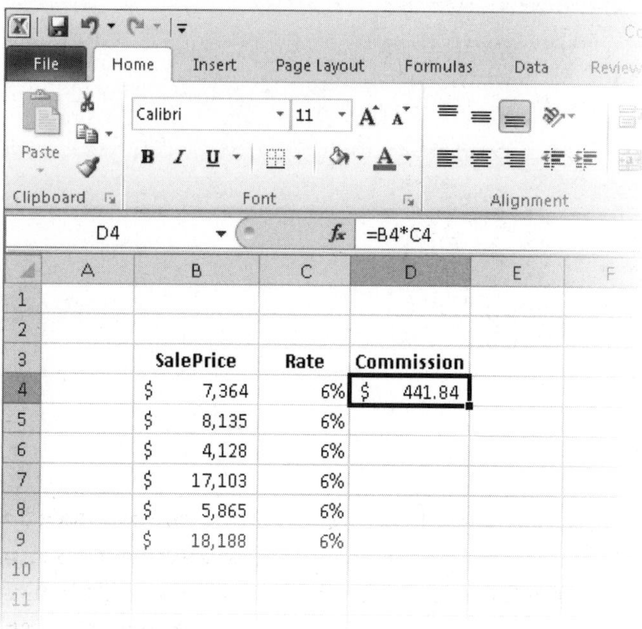

Selecting cell D4 and dragging the fill handle until it covers cells D4:D9 copies the formula from cell D4 into each of the other cells. Because you created the formula using relative references, Excel updates each cell's formula to reflect its position relative to the starting cell (in this case, cell D4.) The formula in cell D9, for example, is *=B9*C9*.

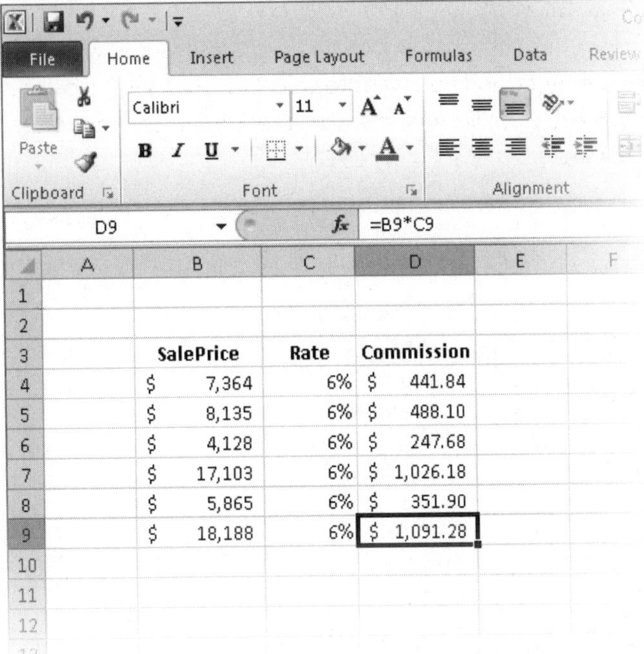

SalePrice	Rate	Commission
$ 7,364	6%	$ 441.84
$ 8,135	6%	$ 488.10
$ 4,128	6%	$ 247.68
$ 17,103	6%	$ 1,026.18
$ 5,865	6%	$ 351.90
$ 18,188	6%	$ 1,091.28

You can use a similar technique when you add a formula to an Excel table column. If the sale price and rate data were in an Excel table and you created the formula *=B4*C4* in cell D4, Excel would apply the formula to every other cell in the column. Because you used relative references in the formula, the formulas would change to reflect each cell's distance from the original cell.

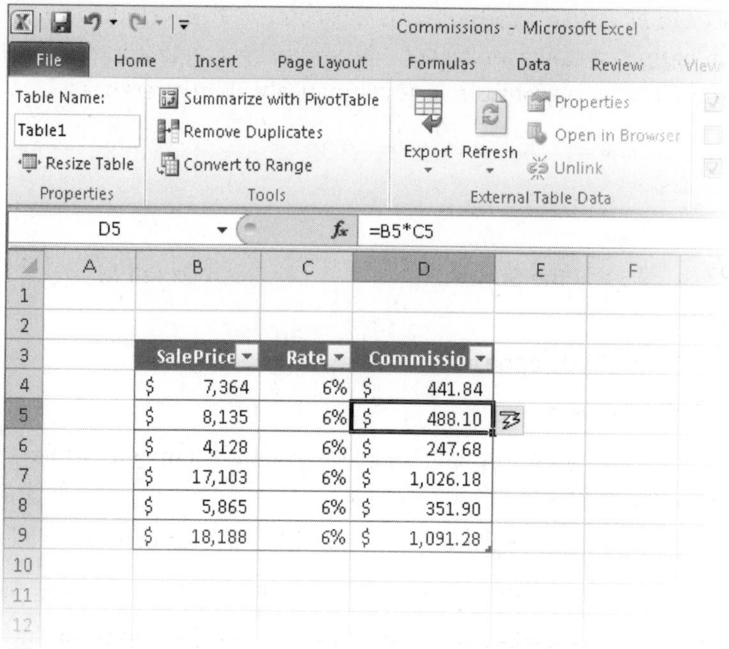

If you want a cell reference to remain constant when the formula using it is copied to another cell, you can use an absolute reference. To write a cell reference as an absolute reference, type $ before the row letter and the column number. For example, if you want the formula in cell D16 to show the sum of values in cells C10 through C14 regardless of the cell into which it is pasted, you can write the formula as *=SUM($C$10:$C$14)*.

Tip Another way to ensure your cell references don't change when you copy the formula to another cell is to click the cell that contains the formula, copy the formula's text in the formula bar, press the Esc key to exit cut-and-copy mode, click the cell where you want to paste the formula, and press Ctrl+V. Excel doesn't change the cell references when you copy your formula to another cell in this manner.

One quick way to change a cell reference from relative to absolute is to select the cell reference in the formula box and then press F4. Pressing F4 cycles a cell reference through the four possible types of references:

- Relative columns and rows (for example, C4)
- Absolute columns and rows (for example, $C$4)
- Relative columns and absolute rows (for example, C$4)
- Absolute columns and relative rows (for example, $C4)

In this exercise, you'll create a formula manually, revise it to include additional cells, create a formula that contains an Excel table reference, create a formula with relative references, and change the formula so it contains absolute references.

SET UP You need the ITExpenses_start workbook located in your Chapter03 practice file folder to complete this exercise. Open the ITExpenses_start workbook, and save it as *ITExpenses*. Then follow the steps.

1. If necessary, display the **Summary** worksheet. Then, in cell **F9**, type =C4, and press Enter.

   The value *$385,671.00* appears in cell F9.

2. Select cell **F9** and type =SU.

   Excel erases the existing formula, and Formula AutoComplete displays a list of possible functions to use in the formula.

3. In the **Formula AutoComplete** list, click **SUM**, and then press Tab.

   Excel changes the contents of the formula bar to *=SUM(*.

4. Select the cell range **C3:C8**, type a right parenthesis ( )) to make the formula bar's contents *=SUM(C3:C8)*, and then press Enter.

   The value *$2,562,966.00* appears in cell F9.

5. In cell **F10**, type =SUM(C4:C5), and then press Enter.

6. Select cell **F10**, and then in the formula box, select the cell reference **C4**, and press F4.

   Excel changes the cell reference to *$C$4*.

7. In the formula box, select the cell reference **C5**, press F4, and then press Enter.

   Excel changes the cell reference to *$C$5*.

8. On the tab bar, click the **JuneLabor** sheet tab.

   The JuneLabor worksheet opens.

9. In cell **F13**, type =SUM(J.

   Excel displays JuneSummary, the name of the table in the JuneLabor worksheet.

10. Press Tab.

    Excel extends the formula to read *=SUM(JuneSummary*.

11. Type [, and then in the **Formula AutoComplete** list, click **Labor Expense**, and press Tab.

    Excel extends the formula to read *=SUM(JuneSummary[Labor Expense.*

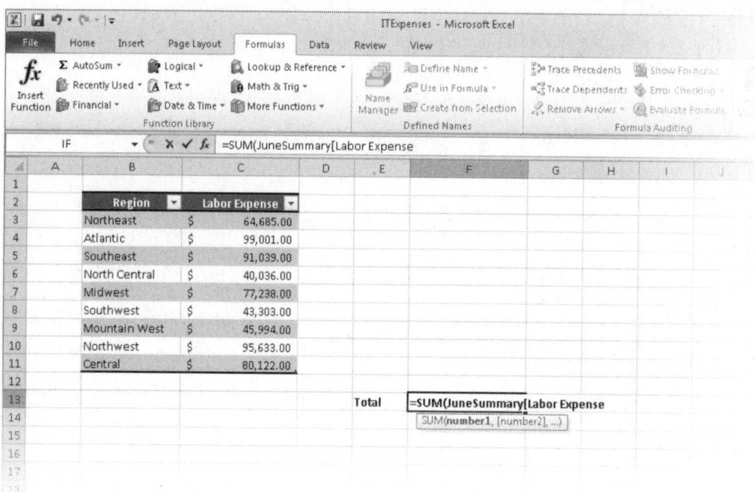

12. Type]) to complete the formula, and then press Enter.

    The value *$637,051.00* appears in cell F13.

CLEAN UP Save the ITExpenses workbook, and then close it.

Summarizing Data That Meets Specific Conditions

Another use for formulas is to display messages when certain conditions are met. For instance, Consolidated Messenger's VP of Marketing, Craig Dewar, might have agreed to examine the rates charged to corporate customers who were billed for more than $100,000 during a calendar year. This kind of formula is called a *conditional formula*; one way to create a conditional formula in Excel is to use the *IF* function. To create a conditional formula, you click the cell to hold the formula and open the Insert Function dialog box. From within the dialog box, click *IF* in the list of available functions, and then click OK. When you do, the Function Arguments dialog box opens.

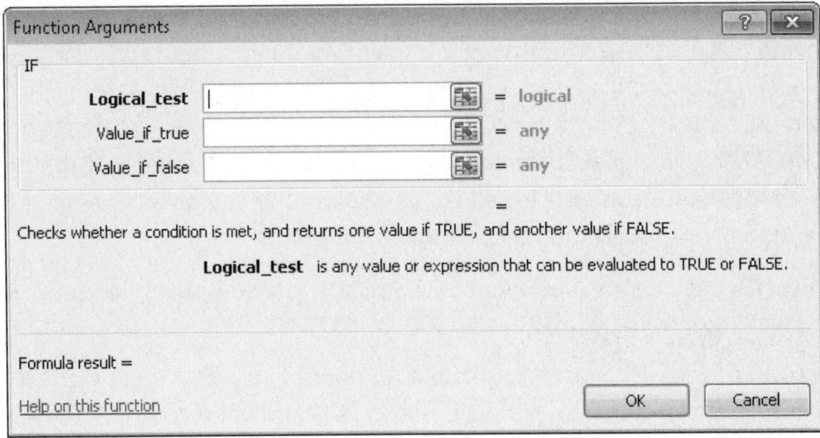

When you work with an *IF* function, the Function Arguments dialog box has three boxes: Logical_test, Value_if_true, and Value_if_false. The Logical_test box holds the condition you want to check. If the customer's year-to-date shipping bill appears in cell G8, the expression would be *G8>100000*.

Now you need to have Excel display messages that indicate whether Craig Dewar should evaluate the account for a possible rate adjustment. To have Excel print a message from an *IF* function, you enclose the message in quotes in the Value_if_true or Value_if_false box. In this case, you would type *"High-volume shipper—evaluate for rate decrease."* in the Value_if_true box and *"Does not qualify at this time."* in the Value_if_false box.

Excel also includes several other conditional functions you can use to summarize your data, shown in the following table.

Function	Description
AVERAGEIF	Finds the average of values within a cell range that meet a given criterion
AVERAGEIFS	Finds the average of values within a cell range that meet multiple criteria
COUNT	Counts the number of cells in a range that contain a numerical value
COUNTA	Counts the number of cells in a range that are not empty
COUNTBLANK	Counts the number of cells in a range that are empty
COUNTIF	Counts the number of cells in a range that meet a given criterion
COUNTIFS	Counts the number of cells in a range that meet multiple criteria
IFERROR	Displays one value if a formula results in an error and another if it doesn't
SUMIF	Finds the sum of values in a range that meet a single criterion
SUMIFS	Finds the sum of values in a range that meet multiple criteria

You can use the *IFERROR* function to display a custom error message, instead of relying on the default Excel error messages to explain what happened. For example, you could use an *IFERROR* formula when looking up the CustomerID value from cell G8 in the Customers table by using the *VLOOKUP* function. One way to create such a formula is *=IFERROR(VLOOKUP(G8,Customers,2,false),"Customer not found")*. If the function finds a match for the CustomerID in cell G8, it displays the customer's name; if it doesn't find a match, it displays the text *Customer not found*.

See Also For more information about the VLOOKUP function, see "Looking Up Information in a Worksheet" in Chapter 6, "Reordering and Summarizing Data."

Just as the *COUNTIF* function counts the number of cells that meet a criterion and the *SUMIF* function finds the total of values in cells that meet a criterion, the *AVERAGEIF* function finds the average of values in cells that meet a criterion. To create a formula using the *AVERAGEIF* function, you define the range to be examined for the criterion, the criterion, and, if required, the range from which to draw the values. As an example, consider a worksheet that lists each customer's ID number, name, state, and total monthly shipping bill.

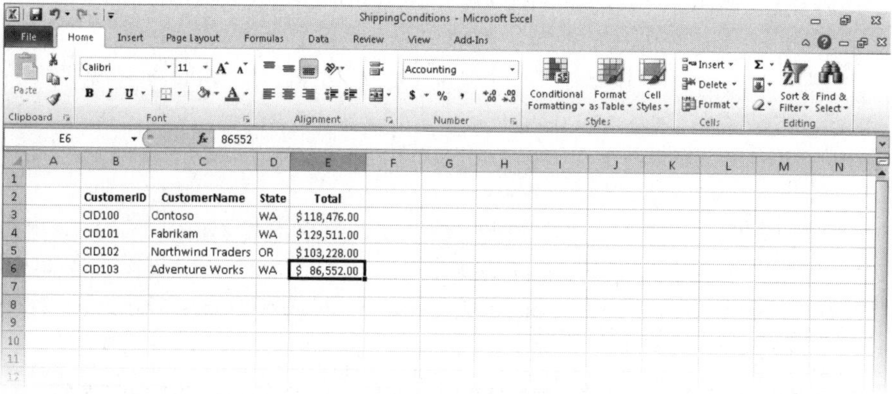

If you want to find the average order of customers from the state of Washington (abbreviated in the worksheet as WA), you can create the formula *=AVERAGEIF(D3:D6, "WA", E3:E6)*.

The *AVERAGEIFS*, *SUMIFS*, and *COUNTIFS* functions extend the capabilities of the *AVERAGEIF*, *SUMIF*, and *COUNTIF* functions to allow for multiple criteria. If you want to find the sum of all orders of at least $100,000 placed by companies in Washington, you can create the formula *=SUMIFS(E3:E6, D3:D6, "=WA", E3:E6, ">=100000")*.

The *AVERAGEIFS* and *SUMIFS* functions start with a data range that contains values that the formula summarizes; you then list the data ranges and the criteria to apply to that range. In generic terms, the syntax runs *=AVERAGEIFS(data_range, criteria_range1, criteria1[,criteria_range2, criteria2...])*. The part of the syntax in square brackets (which aren't used when you create the formula) is optional, so an *AVERAGEIFS* or *SUMIFS* formula that contains a single criterion will work. The *COUNTIFS* function, which doesn't perform any calculations, doesn't need a data range—you just provide the criteria ranges and criteria. For example, you could find the number of customers from Washington who were billed at least $100,000 by using the formula *=COUNTIFS(D3:D6, "=WA", E3:E6, ">=100000")*.

In this exercise, you'll create a conditional formula that displays a message if a condition is true, find the average of worksheet values that meet one criterion, and find the sum of worksheet values that meet two criteria.

SET UP You need the PackagingCosts_start workbook located in your Chapter03 practice file folder to complete this exercise. Open the PackagingCosts_start workbook, and save it as *PackagingCosts*. Then follow the steps.

1. In cell **G3**, type the formula **=IF(F3>=35000, "Request discount", "No discount available")**, and press Enter.

   Excel accepts the formula, which displays *Request discount* if the value in cell F3 is at least 35,000 and displays *No discount available* if not. The value *Request discount* appears in cell G3.

2. Click cell **G3**, and drag the fill handle down until it covers cell **G14**.

   Excel copies the formula in cell G3 to cells G4:G14, adjusting the formula to reflect the cells' addresses. The results of the copied formulas appear in cells G4:G14.

3. In cell **I3**, type the formula **=AVERAGEIF(C3:C14, "=Box", F3:F14)**, and press Enter.

   The value *$46,102.50*, which represents the average cost per category of boxes, appears in cell I3.

4. In cell **I6**, type **=SUMIFS(F3:F14, C3:C14, "=Envelope", E3:E14, "=International")**.

   The value *$45,753.00*, which represents the total cost of all envelopes used for international shipments, appears in cell I6.

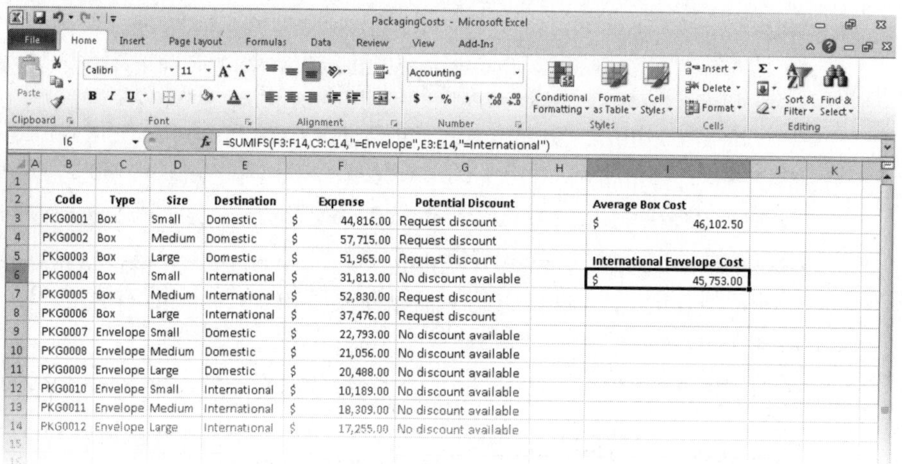

CLEAN UP Save the PackagingCosts workbook, and then close it.

Finding and Correcting Errors in Calculations

Including calculations in a worksheet gives you valuable answers to questions about your data. As is always true, however, it is possible for errors to creep into your formulas. With Excel, you can find the source of errors in your formulas by identifying the cells used in a given calculation and describing any errors that have occurred. The process of examining a worksheet for errors is referred to as *auditing*.

Excel identifies errors in several ways. The first way is to display an error code in the cell holding the formula generating the error.

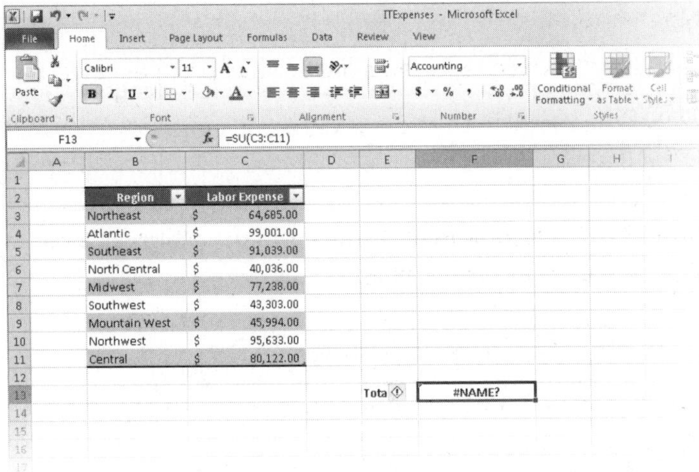

When a cell with an erroneous formula is the active cell, an Error button is displayed next to it. Pointing to the Error button causes it to display an arrow on the button's right edge. Clicking the arrow displays a menu with options that provide information about the error and offer to help you fix it.

The following table lists the most common error codes and what they mean.

Error code	Description
#####	The column isn't wide enough to display the value.
#VALUE!	The formula has the wrong type of argument (such as text in a cell where a numerical value is required).
#NAME?	The formula contains text that Excel doesn't recognize (such as an unknown named range).
#REF!	The formula refers to a cell that doesn't exist (which can happen whenever cells are deleted).
#DIV/0!	The formula attempts to divide by zero.

Another technique you can use to find the source of formula errors is to ensure that the appropriate cells are providing values for the formula. For example, you might want to calculate the total number of deliveries for a service level, but you could accidentally create a formula referring to the service levels' names instead of their package quantities. You can identify the source of an error by having Excel trace a cell's *precedents*, which are the cells with values used in the active cell's formula. To do so, click the Formulas tab, and then in the Formula Auditing group, click Trace Precedents. When you do, Excel identifies those cells by drawing a blue tracer arrow from the precedents to the active cell.

You can also audit your worksheet by identifying cells with formulas that use a value from a given cell. For example, you might use one region's daily package total in a formula that calculates the average number of packages delivered for all regions on a given day. Cells that use another cell's value in their calculations are known as *dependents*, meaning that they depend on the value in the other cell to derive their own value. As with tracing precedents, you can click the Formulas tab, and then in the Formula Auditing group, click Trace Dependents to have Excel draw blue arrows from the active cell to those cells that have calculations based on that value.

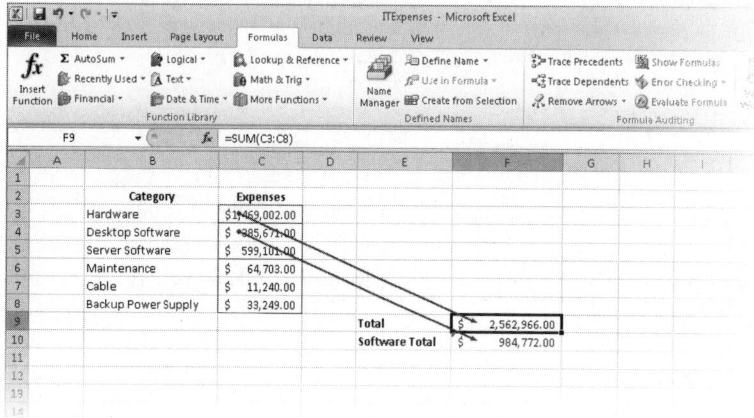

If the cells identified by the tracer arrows aren't the correct cells, you can hide the arrows and correct the formula. To hide the tracer arrows on a worksheet, display the Formulas tab, and then in the Formula Auditing group, click Remove Arrows.

If you prefer to have the elements of a formula error presented as text in a dialog box, you can use the Error Checking dialog box to view the error and the formula in the cell in which the error occurs. To display the Error Checking dialog box, display the Formulas tab, and then in the Formula Auditing group, click the Error Checking button. You can use the controls in the Error Checking dialog box to move through the formula one step at a time, to choose to ignore the error, or to move to the next or the previous error. If you click the Options button in the dialog box, you can also use the controls in the Excel Options dialog box to change how Excel determines what is an error and what isn't.

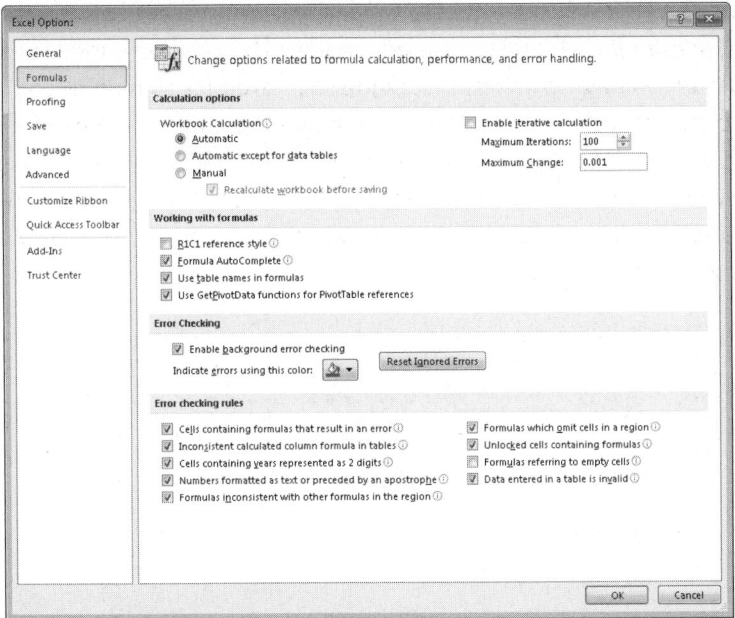

Tip You can have the Error Checking tool ignore formulas that don't use every cell in a region (such as a row or column). If you clear the Formulas That Omit Cells In A Region check box, you can create formulas that don't add up every value in a row or column (or rectangle) without Excel marking them as an error.

For times when you just want to display the results of each step of a formula and don't need the full power of the Error Checking tool, you can use the Evaluate Formula dialog box to move through each element of the formula. To display the Evaluate Formula dialog box, you display the Formulas tab and then, in the Formula Auditing group, click the Evaluate Formula button. The Evaluate Formula dialog box is much more useful for examining formulas that don't produce an error but aren't generating the result you expect.

Finally, you can monitor the value in a cell regardless of where in your workbook you are by opening a Watch Window that displays the value in the cell. For example, if one of your formulas uses values from cells in other worksheets or even other workbooks, you can set a watch on the cell that contains the formula and then change the values in the other cells. To set a watch, click the cell you want to monitor, and then on the Formulas tab, in the Formula Auditing group, click Watch Window. Click Add Watch to have Excel monitor the selected cell.

As soon as you type in the new value, the Watch Window displays the new result of the formula. When you're done watching the formula, select the watch, click Delete Watch, and close the Watch Window.

In this exercise, you'll use the formula-auditing capabilities in Excel to identify and correct errors in a formula.

SET UP You need the ConveyerBid_start workbook located in your Chapter03 practice file folder to complete this exercise. Open the ConveyerBid_start workbook, and save it as *ConveyerBid*. Then follow the steps.

1. Click cell **D20**.

2. On the **Formulas** tab, in the **Formula Auditing** group, click **Watch Window**.

   The Watch Window opens.

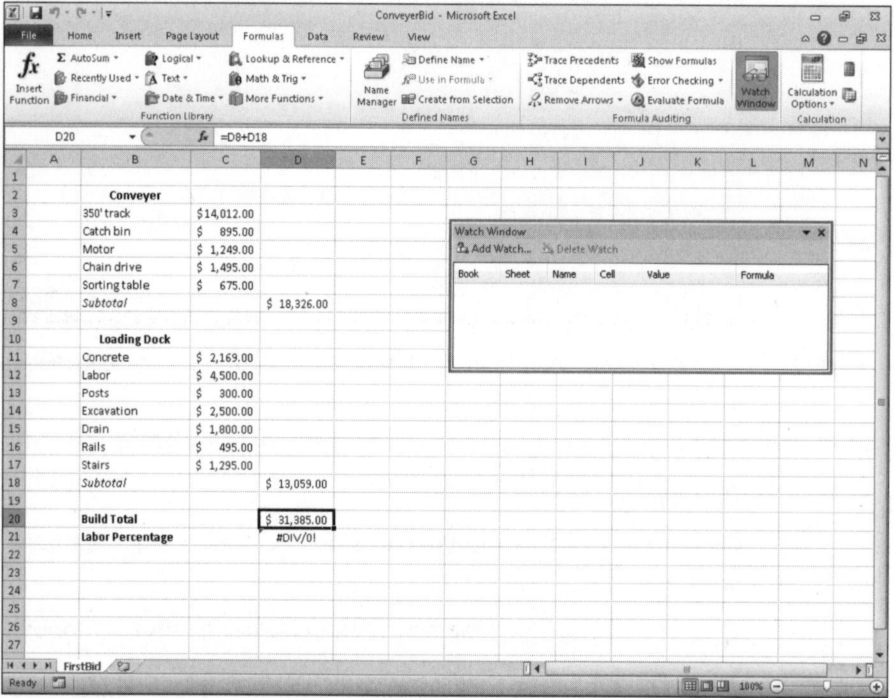

3. Click **Add Watch**, and then in the **Add Watch** dialog box, click **Add**.

   Cell D20 appears in the Watch Window.

4. Click cell **D8**.

   =SUM(C3:C7) appears in the formula bar.

5. On the **Formulas** tab, in the **Formula Auditing** group, click the **Trace Precedents** button.

   A blue arrow begins at the cell range C3:C7 and points to cell D8, indicating that the cells in the range C3:C7 provide the values for the formula in cell D8.

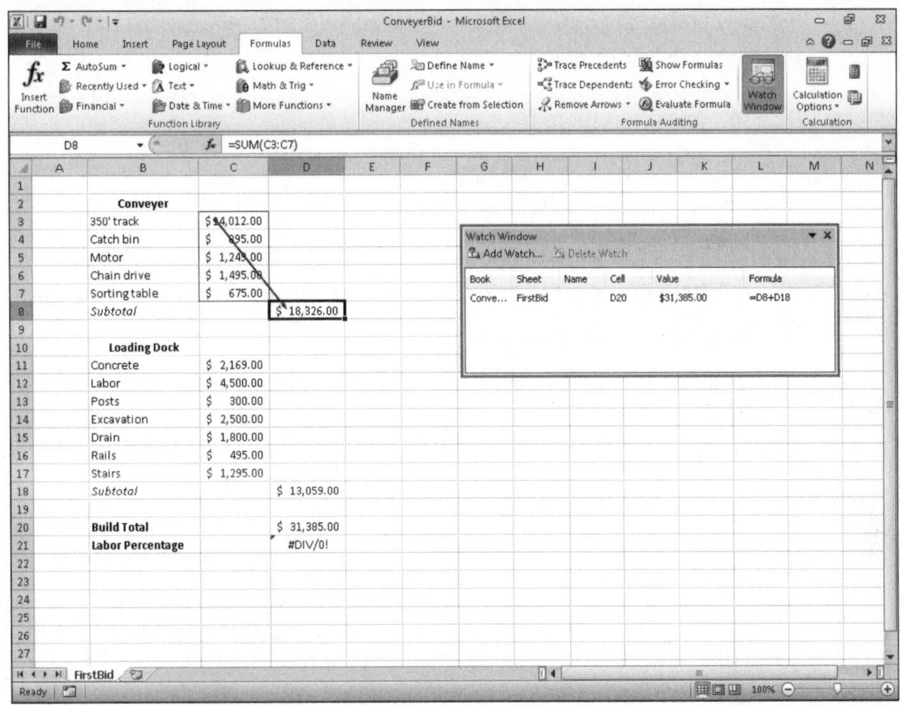

6. On the **Formulas** tab, in the **Formula Auditing** group, click the **Remove Arrows** button.

   The arrow disappears.

7. Click cell **A1**.

8. On the **Formulas** tab, in the **Formula Auditing** group, click the **Error Checking** button.

   The Error Checking dialog box opens, displaying the error found in cell D1.

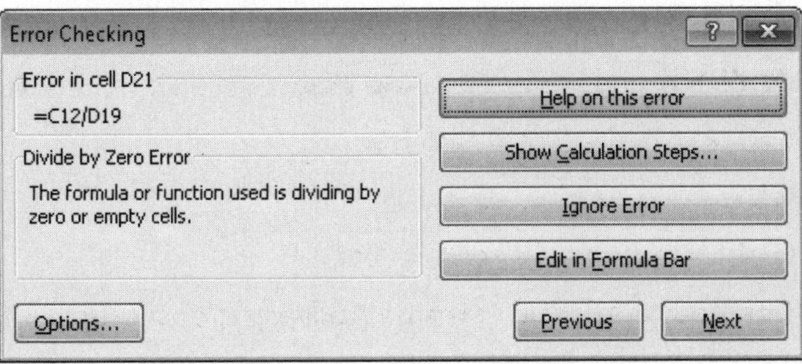

9. Click **Next**.

   Excel displays a message box indicating that there are no more errors in the worksheet.

10. Click **OK**.

    The message box and the Error Checking dialog box close.

11. On the **Formulas** tab, in the **Formula Auditing** group, click the **Error Checking** arrow, and then in the list, click **Trace Error**.

    Blue arrows appear, pointing to cell D21 from cells C12 and D19. These arrows indicate that using the values (or lack of values, in this case) in the indicated cells generates the error in cell D21.

12. On the **Formulas** tab, in the **Formula Auditing** group, click **Remove Arrows**.

    The arrows disappear.

13. In the formula box, delete the existing formula, type **=C12/D20**, and press Enter.

    The value *14%* appears in cell D21.

14. Click cell **D21**.

15. On the **Formulas** tab, in the **Formula Auditing** group, click the **Evaluate Formula** button.

    Evaluate Formula

    The Evaluate Formula dialog box opens, with the formula from cell D21 displayed.

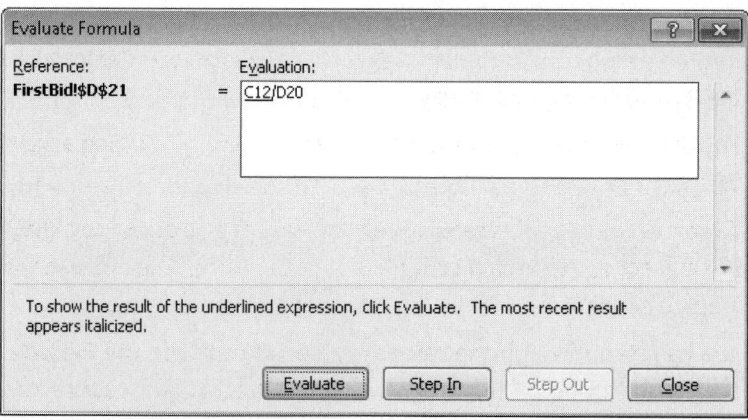

16. Click **Evaluate** three times to step through the formula's elements, and then click **Close**.

    The Evaluate Formula dialog box closes.

17. In the **Watch Window**, click the watch in the list.
18. Click **Delete Watch**.

    The watch disappears.
19. On the **Formulas** tab, in the **Formula Auditing** group, click **Watch Window**.

    The Watch Window closes.

CLEAN UP Save the ConveyerBid workbook, and then close it. If you are not continuing directly to the next chapter, exit Excel.

Key Points

- You can add a group of cells to a formula by typing the formula, and then at the spot in the formula in which you want to name the cells, selecting the cells by using the mouse.
- By creating named ranges, you can refer to entire blocks of cells with a single term, saving you lots of time and effort. You can use a similar technique with table data, referring to an entire table or one or more table columns.
- When you write a formula, be sure you use absolute referencing ($A$1) if you want the formula to remain the same when it's copied from one cell to another, or use relative referencing (A1) if you want the formula to change to reflect its new position in the worksheet.
- Instead of typing a formula from scratch, you can use the Insert Function dialog box to help you on your way.
- You can monitor how the value in a cell changes by adding a watch to the Watch Window.
- To see which formulas refer to the values in the selected cell, use Trace Dependents; if you want to see which cells provide values for the formula in the active cell, use Trace Precedents.
- You can step through the calculations of a formula in the Evaluate Formula dialog box or go through a more rigorous error-checking procedure by using the Error Checking tool.

Chapter at a Glance

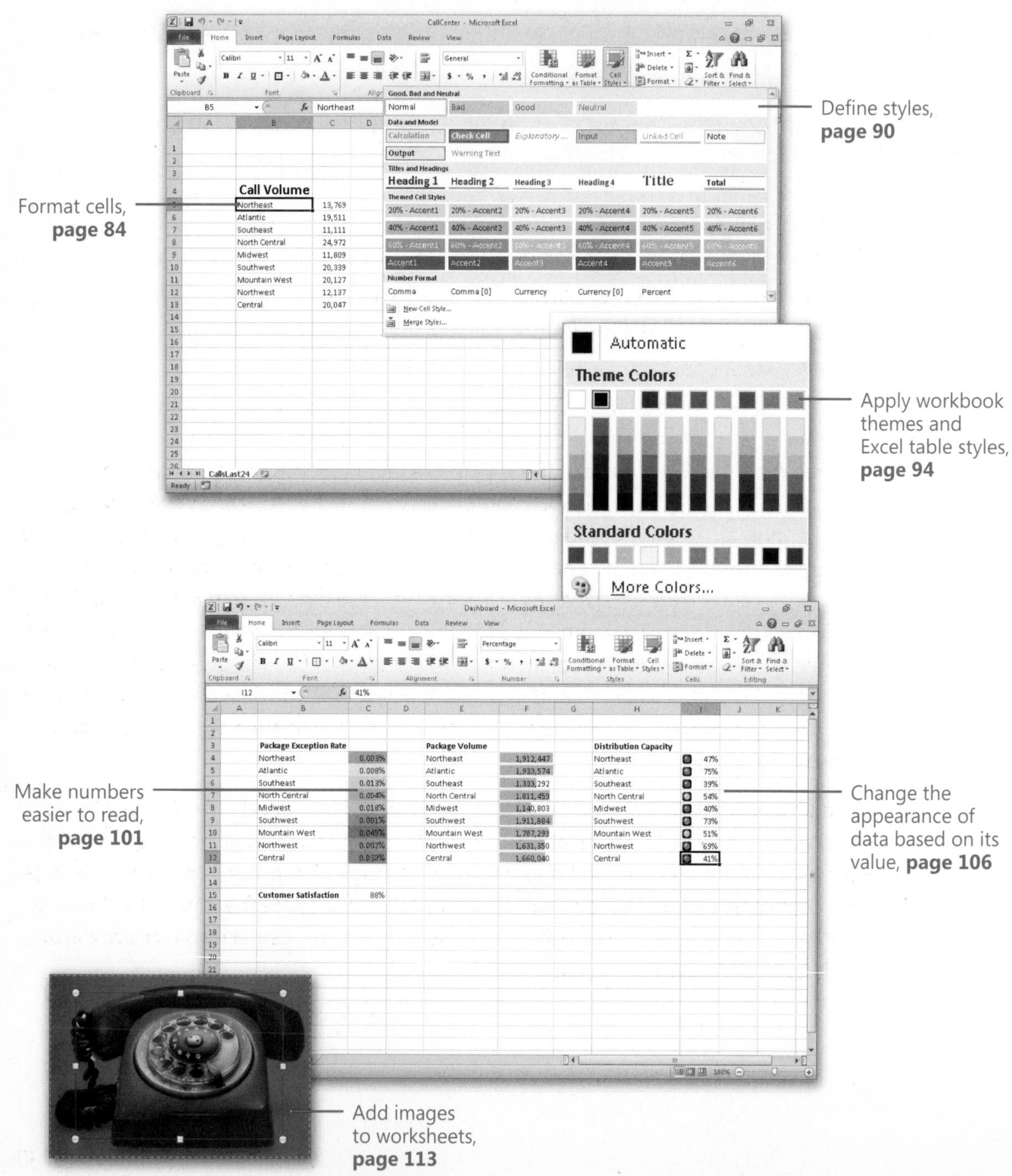
Define styles, page 90
Format cells, page 84
Apply workbook themes and Excel table styles, page 94
Make numbers easier to read, page 101
Change the appearance of data based on its value, page 106
Add images to worksheets, page 113

4 Changing Workbook Appearance

In this chapter, you will learn how to

- ✔ Format cells.
- ✔ Define styles.
- ✔ Apply workbook themes and Excel table styles.
- ✔ Make numbers easier to read.
- ✔ Change the appearance of data based on its value.
- ✔ Add images to worksheets.

Entering data into a workbook efficiently saves you time, but you must also ensure that your data is easy to read. Microsoft Excel 2010 gives you a wide variety of ways to make your data easier to understand; for example, you can change the font, character size, or color used to present a cell's contents. Changing how data appears on a worksheet helps set the contents of a cell apart from the contents of surrounding cells. The simplest example of that concept is a data label. If a column on your worksheet contains a list of days, you can easily set apart a label (for example, *Day*) by presenting it in bold type that's noticeably larger than the type used to present the data to which it refers. To save time, you can define a number of custom formats and then apply them quickly to the desired cells.

You might also want to specially format a cell's contents to reflect the value in that cell. For example, Lori Penor, the chief operating officer of Consolidated Messenger, might want to create a worksheet that displays the percentage of improperly delivered packages from each regional distribution center. If that percentage exceeds a threshold, she could have Excel display a red traffic light icon, indicating that the center's performance is out of tolerance and requires attention.

In this chapter, you'll learn how to change the appearance of data, apply existing formats to data, make numbers easier to read, change data's appearance based on its value, and add images to worksheets.

> **Practice Files** Before you can complete the exercises in this chapter, you need to copy the book's practice files to your computer. The practice files you'll use to complete the exercises in this chapter are in the Chapter04 practice file folder. A complete list of practice files is provided in "Using the Practice Files" at the beginning of this book.

Formatting Cells

Excel spreadsheets can hold and process lots of data, but when you manage numerous spreadsheets it can be hard to remember from a worksheet's title exactly what data is kept in that worksheet. Data labels give you and your colleagues information about data in a worksheet, but it's important to format the labels so that they stand out visually. To make your data labels or any other data stand out, you can change the format of the cells that hold your data.

	A	B	C	D	E	F
1						
2						
3						
4		**Call Volume**				
5		Northeast	13,769			
6		Atlantic	19,511			
7		Southeast	11,111			
8		North Central	24,972			
9		Midwest	11,809			
10		Southwest	20,339			
11		Mountain West	20,127			
12		Northwest	12,137			
13		Central	20,047			
14						
15						
16						
17						

Most of the tools you need to change a cell's format can be found on the Home tab. You can apply the formatting represented on a button by selecting the cells you want to apply the style to and then clicking that button. If you want to set your data labels apart by making them appear bold, click the Bold button. If you have already made a cell's contents bold, selecting the cell and clicking the Bold button will remove the formatting.

Tip Deleting a cell's contents doesn't delete the cell's formatting. To delete a selected cell's formatting, on the Home tab, in the Editing group, click the Clear button (which looks like an eraser), and then click Clear Formats. Clicking Clear All from the same list will remove the cell's contents and formatting.

Buttons in the Home tab's Font group that give you choices, such as Font Color, have an arrow at the right edge of the button. Clicking the arrow displays a list of options accessible for that button, such as the fonts available on your system or the colors you can assign to a cell.

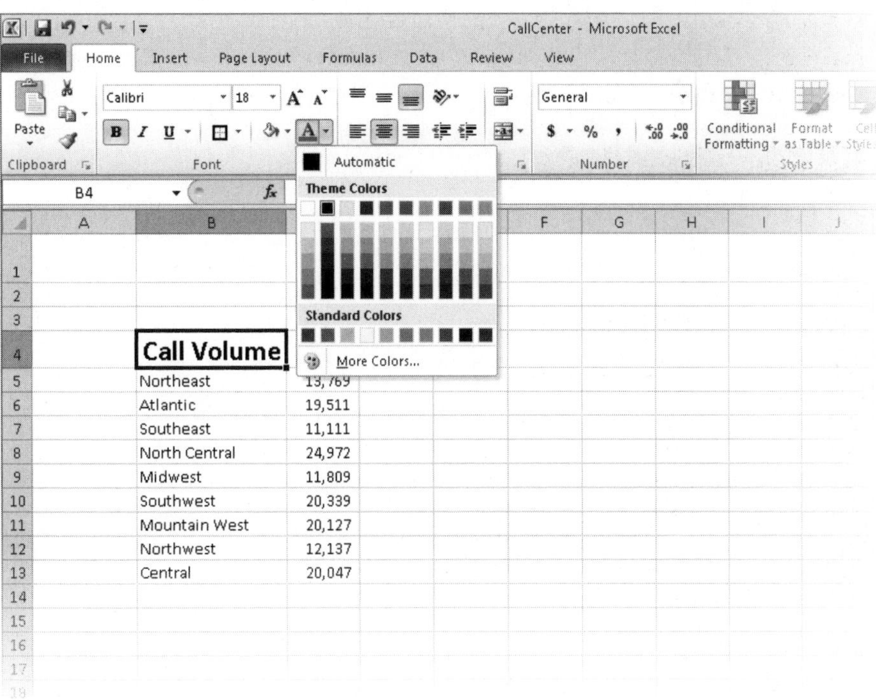

Another way you can make a cell stand apart from its neighbors is to add a border around the cell. To place a border around one or more cells, select the cells, and then choose the border type you want by selecting from the Border list in the Font group. Excel does provide more options: To display the full range of border types and styles, in the Border list, click More Borders. The Border page of the Format Cells dialog box contains the full range of tools you can use to define your cells' borders.

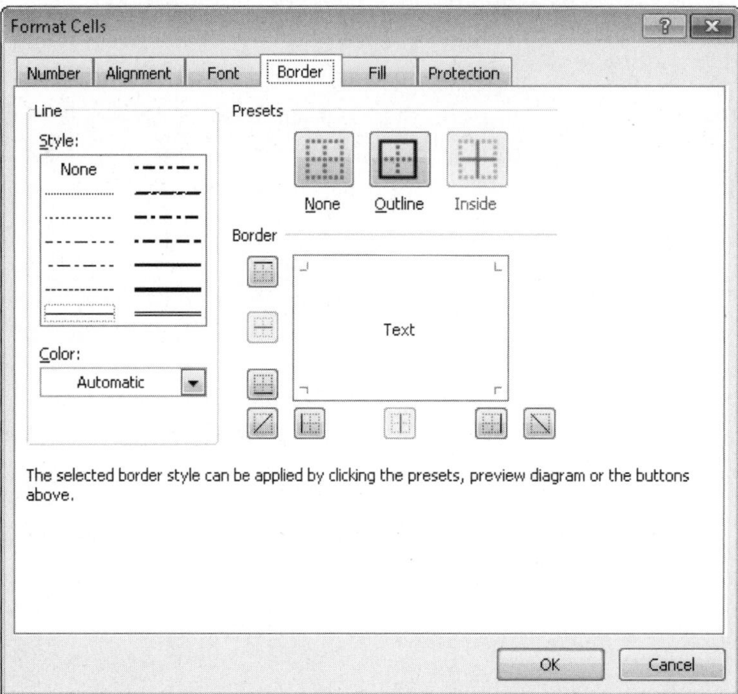

You can also make a group of cells stand apart from its neighbors by changing its shading, which is the color that fills the cells. On a worksheet that tracks total package volume for the past month, Lori Penor could change the fill color of the cells holding her data labels to make the labels stand out even more than by changing the labels' text formatting.

Tip You can display the most commonly used formatting controls by right-clicking a selected range. When you do, a Mini Toolbar containing a subset of the Home tab formatting tools appears above the shortcut menu.

If you want to change the attributes of every cell in a row or column, you can click the header of the row or column you want to modify and then select your desired format.

One task you can't perform by using the tools on the Home tab is to change the standard font for a workbook, which is used in the Name box and on the formula bar. The standard font when you install Excel is Calibri, a simple font that is easy to read on a computer screen and on the printed page. If you want to choose another font, click the File tab, and then click Options. On the General page of the Excel Options dialog box, set the values in the Use This Font and Font Size list boxes to pick your new display font.

Important The new standard font doesn't take effect until you exit Excel and restart the program.

In this exercise, you'll emphasize a worksheet's title by changing the format of cell data, adding a border to a cell range, and then changing a cell range's fill color. After those tasks are complete, you'll change the default font for the workbook.

SET UP You need the VehicleMileSummary_start workbook located in your Chapter04 practice file folder to complete this exercise. Start Excel, open the VehicleMileSummary_start workbook, and save it as *VehicleMileSummary*. Then follow the steps.

1. Click cell **D2**.

2. On the **Home** tab, in the **Font** group, click the **Bold** button.

   Excel displays the cell's contents in bold type.

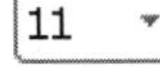

3. In the **Font** group, click the **Font Size** arrow, and then in the list, click **18**.

   Excel increases the size of the text in cell D2.

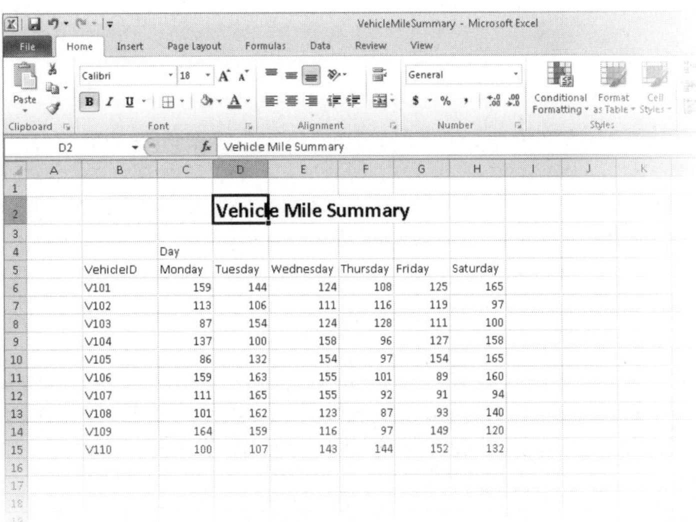

4. Click cell **B5**, hold down the Ctrl key, and click cell **C4** to select the non-contiguous cells.
5. On the **Home** tab, in the **Font** group, click the **Bold** button.

   Excel displays the cells' contents in bold type.
6. Select the cell ranges **B6:B15** and **C5:H5**.
7. In the **Font** group, click the **Italic** button.

   Excel displays the cells' contents in italic type.

Vehicle Mile Summary

	Day					
VehicleID	*Monday*	*Tuesday*	*Wednesday*	*Thursday*	*Friday*	*Saturday*
V101	159	144	124	108	125	165
V102	113	106	111	116	119	97
V103	87	154	124	128	111	100
V104	137	100	158	96	127	158
V105	86	132	154	97	154	165
V106	159	163	155	101	89	160
V107	111	165	155	92	91	94
V108	101	162	123	87	93	140
V109	164	159	116	97	149	120
V110	100	107	143	144	152	132

8. Select the cell range **C6:H15**.

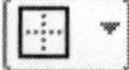

9. In the **Font** group, click the **Border** arrow, and then in the list, click **Outside Borders**.

   Excel places a border around the outside edge of the selected cells.
10. Select the cell range **B4:H15**.
11. In the **Border** list, click **Thick Box Border**.

    Excel places a thick border around the outside edge of the selected cells.
12. Select the cell ranges **B4:B15** and **C4:H5**.

13. In the **Font** group, click the **Fill Color** arrow, and then in the **Standard Colors** area of the color palette, click the yellow button.

    Excel changes the selected cells' background color to yellow.

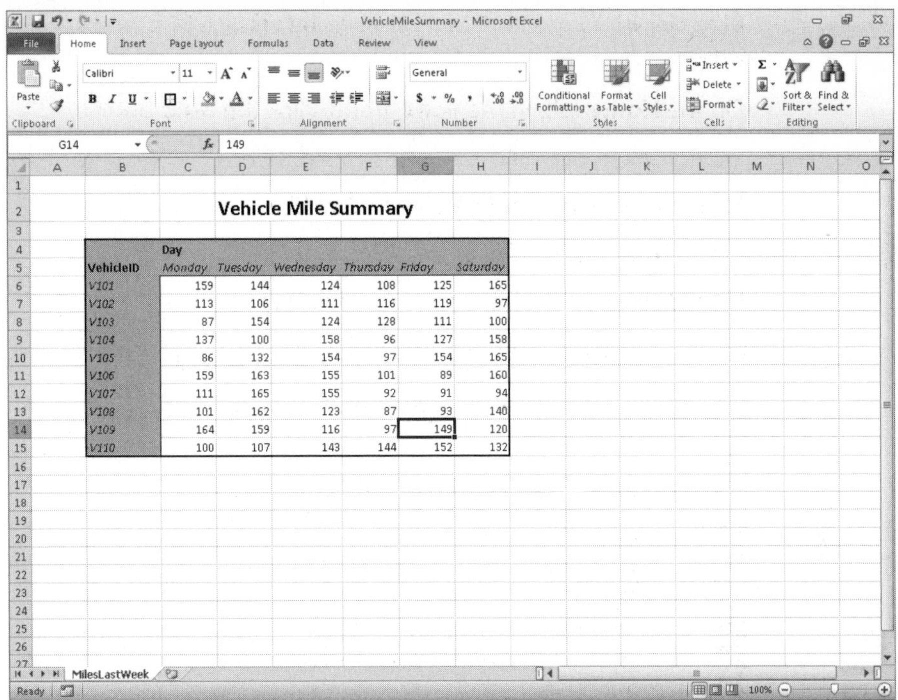

Troubleshooting The appearance of buttons and groups on the ribbon changes depending on the width of the program window. For information about changing the appearance of the ribbon to match our screen images, see "Modifying the Display of the Ribbon" at the beginning of this book.

14. Click the **File** tab, and then click **Options**.

    The Excel Options dialog box opens.

15. If necessary, click **General** to display the **General** page.

16. In the **When creating new workbooks** area, in the **Use this font** list, click **Verdana**.

    Verdana appears in the Use This Font field.

17. Click **Cancel**.

    The Excel Options dialog box closes without saving your change.

CLEAN UP Save the VehicleMileSummary workbook, and then close it.

Defining Styles

As you work with Excel, you will probably develop preferred formats for data labels, titles, and other worksheet elements. Instead of adding a format's characteristics one element at a time to the target cells, you can have Excel store the format and recall it as needed. You can find the predefined formats by displaying the Home tab, and then in the Styles group, clicking Cell Styles.

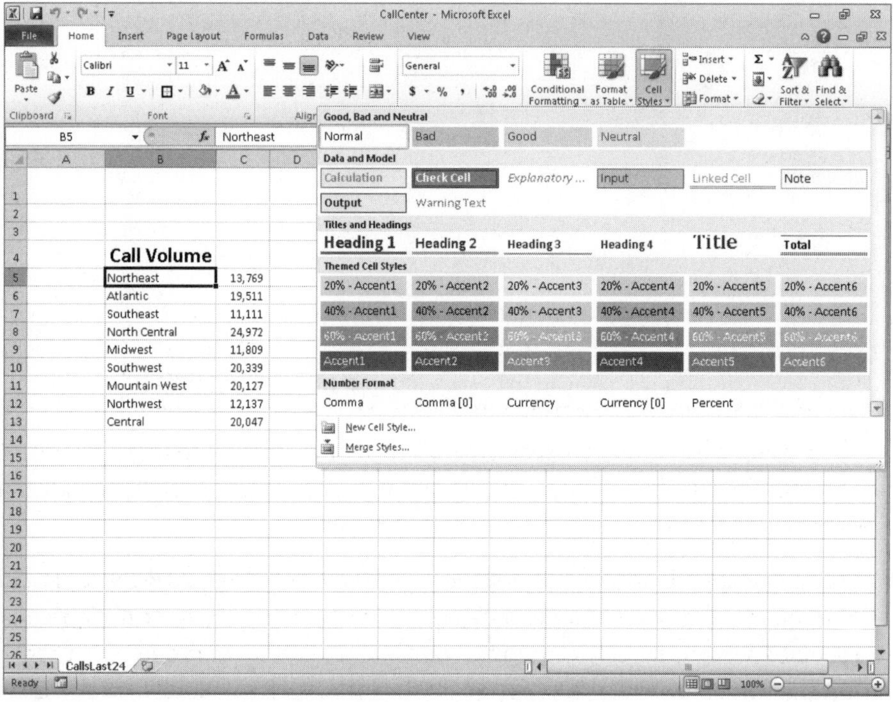

Clicking a style from the Cell Styles gallery applies the style to the selected cells, but Excel also displays a live preview of a format when you point to it. If none of the existing styles is what you want, you can create your own style by clicking New Cell Style at the bottom of the gallery to display the Style dialog box. In the Style dialog box, type the name of your new style in the Style Name field, and then click Format. The Format Cells dialog box opens.

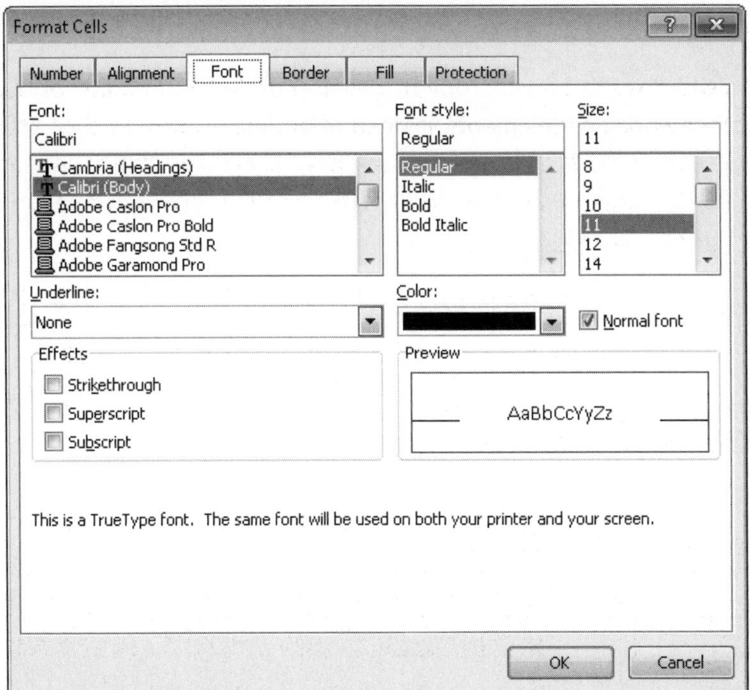

After you set the characteristics of your new style, click OK to make your style available in the Cell Styles gallery. If you ever want to delete a custom style, display the Cell Styles gallery, right-click the style, and then click Delete.

The Style dialog box is quite versatile, but it's overkill if all you want to do is apply formatting changes you made to a cell to the contents of another cell. To do so, use the Format Painter button, found in the Home tab's Clipboard group. Just click the cell that has the format you want to copy, click the Format Painter button, and select the target cells to have Excel apply the copied format to the target range.

Tip If you want to apply the same formatting to multiple cells by using the Format Painter button, double-click the Format Painter button and then click the cells to which you want to apply the formatting. When you're done applying the formatting, press the Esc key.

In this exercise, you'll create a style and apply the new style to a data label.

SET UP You need the HourlyExceptions_start workbook located in your Chapter04 practice file folder to complete this exercise. Open the HourlyExceptions_start workbook, and save it as *HourlyExceptions*. Then follow the steps.

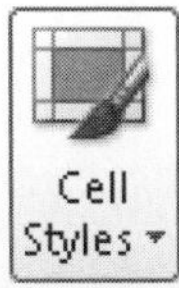

1. On the **Home** tab, in the **Styles** group, click **Cell Styles**, and then click **New Cell Style**.

   The Style dialog box opens.

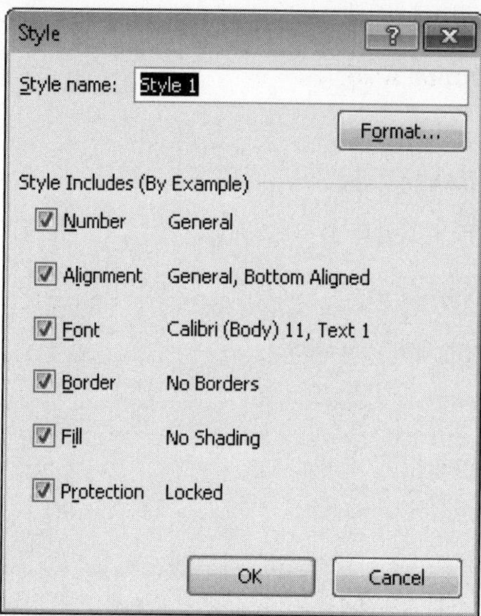

2. In the **Style name** field, type **Crosstab Column Heading**.
3. Click the **Format** button.

   The Format Cells dialog box opens.
4. Click the **Alignment** tab.

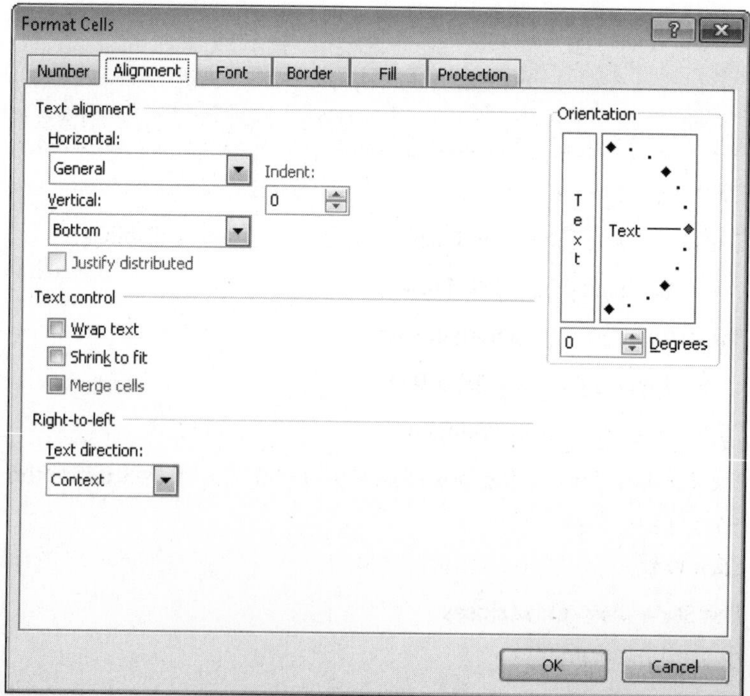

5. In the **Horizontal** list, click **Center**.

   Center appears in the Horizontal field.

6. Click the **Font** tab.
7. In the **Font style** list, click **Italic**.

   The text in the Preview pane appears in italicized text.

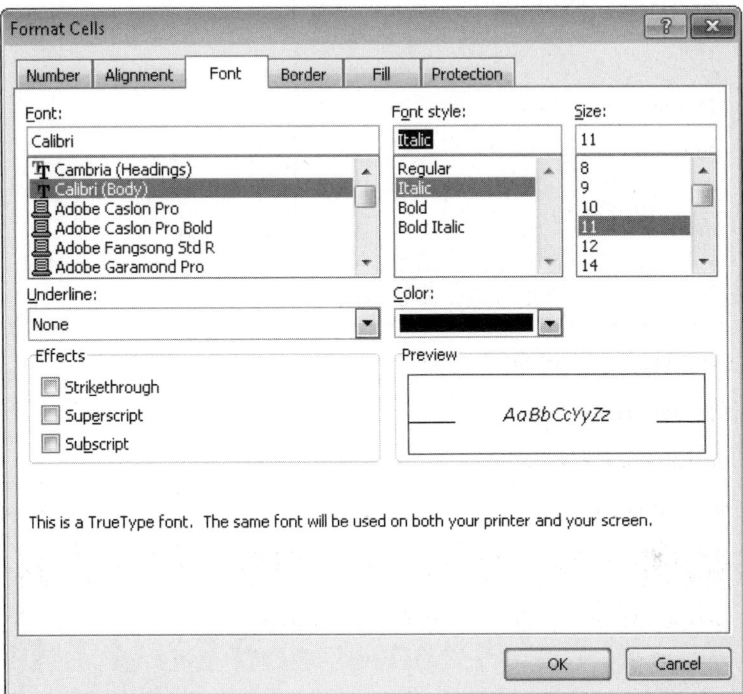

8. Click the **Number** tab.

   The Number page of the Format Cells dialog box is displayed.

9. In the **Category** list, click **Time**.

   The available time formats appear.

10. In the **Type** pane, click **1:30 PM**.
11. Click **OK** to save your changes.

    The Format Cells dialog box closes, and your new style's definition appears in the Style dialog box.

12. Click **OK**.

    The Style dialog box closes.

13. Select cells **C4:N4**.

14. On the **Home** tab, in the **Styles** group, click **Cell Styles**.

    Your new style appears at the top of the gallery, in the Custom group.

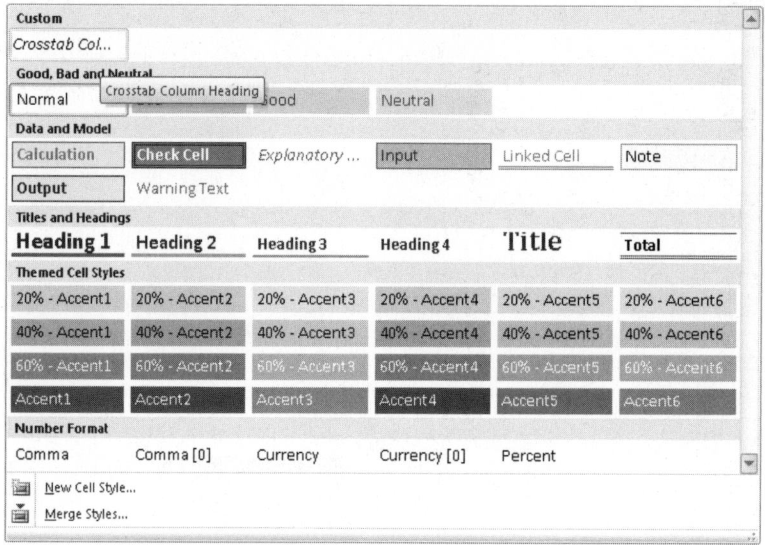

15. Click the **Crosstab Column Heading** style.

    Excel applies your new style to the selected cells.

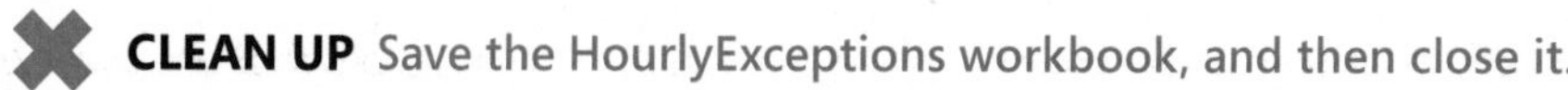

CLEAN UP Save the HourlyExceptions workbook, and then close it.

Applying Workbook Themes and Excel Table Styles

Microsoft Office 2010 includes powerful design tools that enable you to create attractive, professional documents quickly. The Excel product team implemented the new design capabilities by defining workbook themes and Excel table styles. A theme is a way to specify the fonts, colors, and graphic effects that appear in a workbook. Excel comes with many themes installed.

To apply an existing workbook theme, display the Page Layout tab. Then, in the Themes group, click Themes, and click the theme you want to apply to your workbook. By default, Excel applies the Office theme to your workbooks.

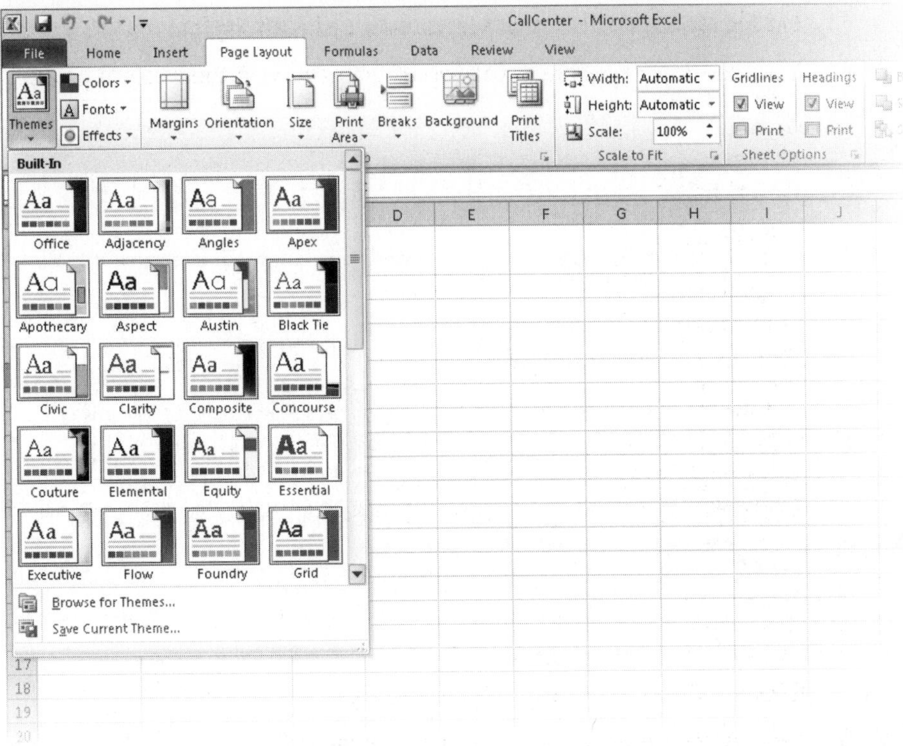

When you want to format a workbook element, Excel displays colors that are available within the active theme. For example, selecting a worksheet cell and then clicking the Font Color button's arrow displays a palette of colors you can use. The theme colors appear in the top segment of the color palette—the standard colors and the More Colors link, which displays the Colors dialog box, appear at the bottom of the palette. If you format workbook elements using colors from the Theme Colors area of the color palette, applying a different theme changes that object's colors.

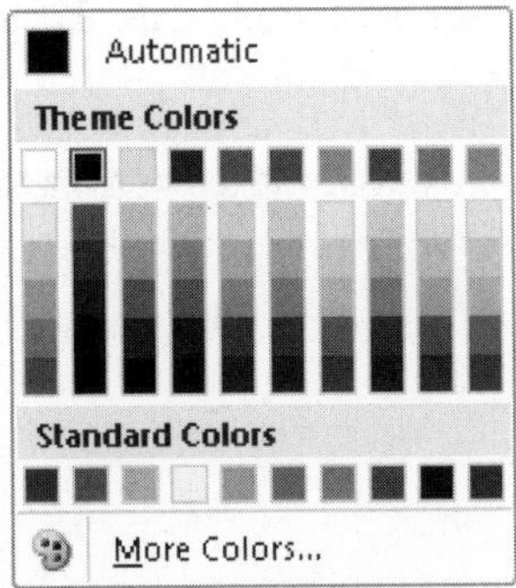

You can change a theme's colors, fonts, and graphic effects by displaying the Page Layout tab and then, in the Themes group, selecting new values from the Colors, Fonts, and Effects lists. To save your changes as a new theme, display the Page Layout tab, and in the Themes group, click Themes, and then click Save Current Theme. Use the controls in the Save Current Theme dialog box that opens to record your theme for later use. Later, when you click the Themes button, your custom theme will appear at the top of the gallery.

Tip When you save a theme, you save it as an Office Theme file. You can apply the theme to other Office 2010 documents as well.

Just as you can define and apply themes to entire workbooks, you can apply and define Excel table styles. You select an Excel table's initial style when you create it; to create a new style, display the Home tab, and in the Styles group, click Format As Table. In the Format As Table gallery, click New Table Style to display the New Table Quick Style dialog box.

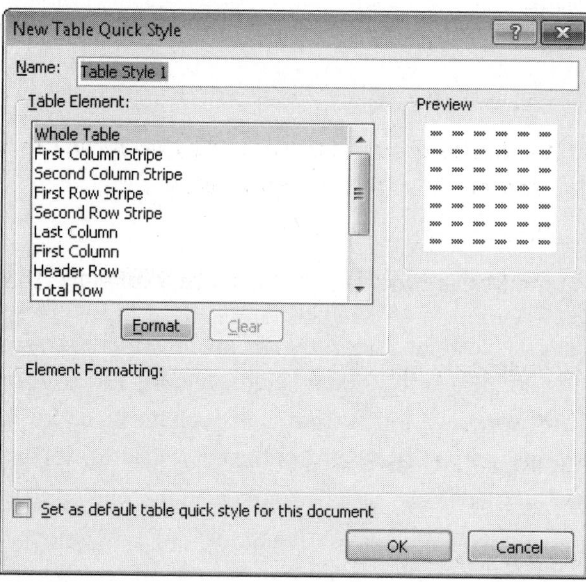

Type a name for the new style, select the first table element you want to format, and then click Format to display the Format Cells dialog box. Define the element's formatting, and then click OK. When the New Table Quick Style dialog box reopens, its Preview pane displays the overall table style and the Element Formatting area describes the selected element's appearance. Also, in the Table Element list, Excel displays the element's name in bold to indicate it has been changed. To make the new style the default for new Excel tables created in the current workbook, select the Set As Default Table Quick Style For This Document check box. When you click OK, Excel saves the new table style.

Tip To remove formatting from a table element, click the name of the table element and then click the Clear button.

In this exercise, you'll create a new workbook theme, change a workbook's theme, create a new table style, and apply the new style to an Excel table.

SET UP You need the HourlyTracking_start workbook located in your Chapter04 practice file folder to complete this exercise. Open the HourlyTracking_start workbook, and save it as *HourlyTracking*. Then follow the steps.

1. If necessary, click any cell in the Excel table.

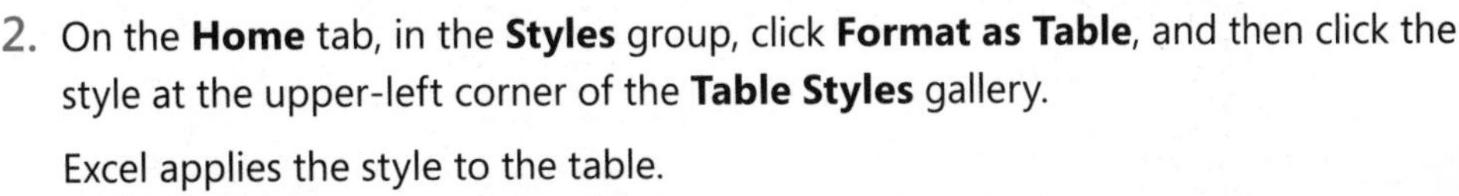

2. On the **Home** tab, in the **Styles** group, click **Format as Table**, and then click the style at the upper-left corner of the **Table Styles** gallery.

   Excel applies the style to the table.

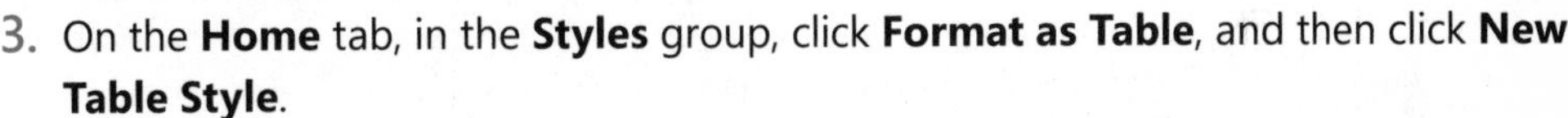

3. On the **Home** tab, in the **Styles** group, click **Format as Table**, and then click **New Table Style**.

   The New Table Quick Style dialog box opens.
4. In the **Name** field, type **Exception Default**.
5. In the **Table Element** list, click **Header Row**.
6. Click **Format**.

   The Format Cells dialog box opens.

7. Click the **Fill** tab.

   The Fill page is displayed.

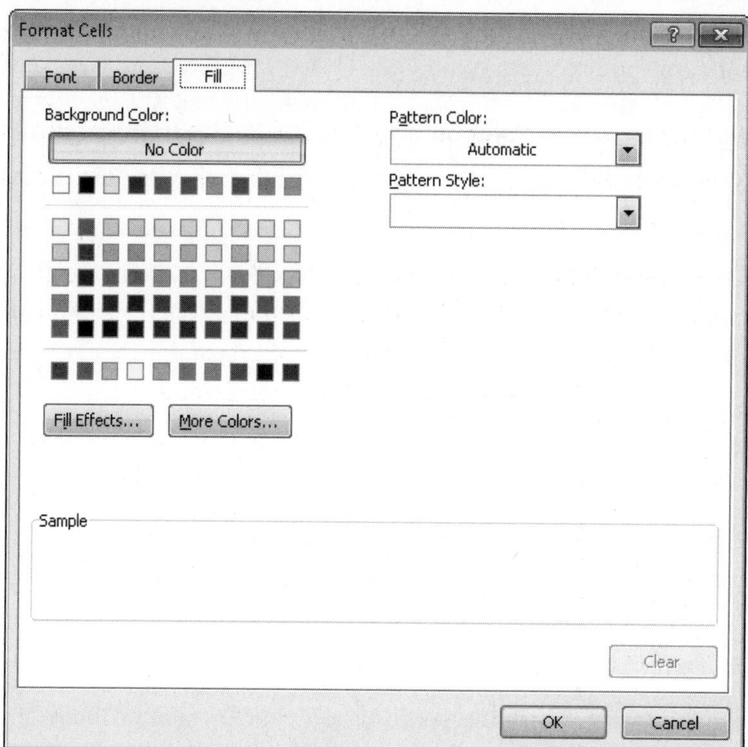

8. In the first row of color squares, just below the **No Color** button, click the third square from the left.

   The new background color appears in the Sample pane of the dialog box.

9. Click **OK**.

The Format Cells dialog box closes. When the New Table Quick Style dialog box reopens, the Header Row table element appears in bold, and the Preview pane's header row is shaded.

10. In the **Table Element** list, click **Second Row Stripe**, and then click **Format**.

    The Format Cells dialog box opens.

11. Just below the **No Color** button, click the third square from the left again.

    The new background color appears in the Sample pane of the dialog box.

12. Click **OK**.

    The Format Cells dialog box closes. When the New Table Quick Style dialog box reopens, the Second Row Stripe table element appears in bold, and every second row is shaded in the Preview pane.

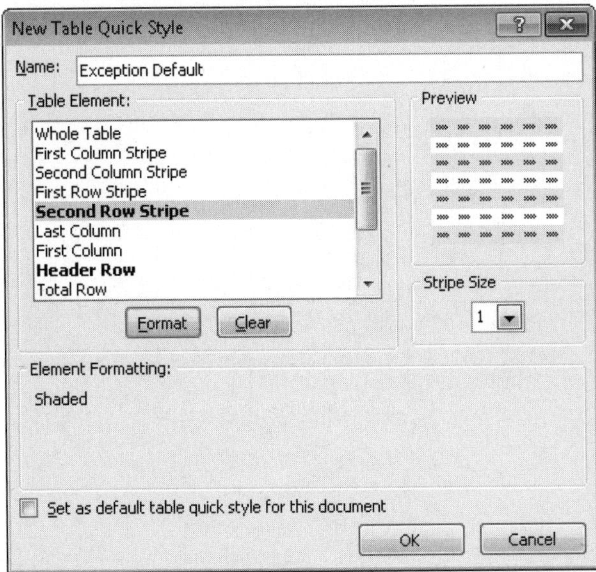

13. Click **OK**.

    The New Table Quick Style dialog box closes.

14. On the **Home** tab, in the **Styles** group, click **Format as Table**. In the gallery, in the **Custom** area, click the new format.

    Excel applies the new format.

15. On the **Page Layout** tab, in the **Themes** group, click the **Fonts** arrow, and then in the list, click **Verdana**.

    Excel changes the theme's font to Verdana (which is part of the Aspect font set).

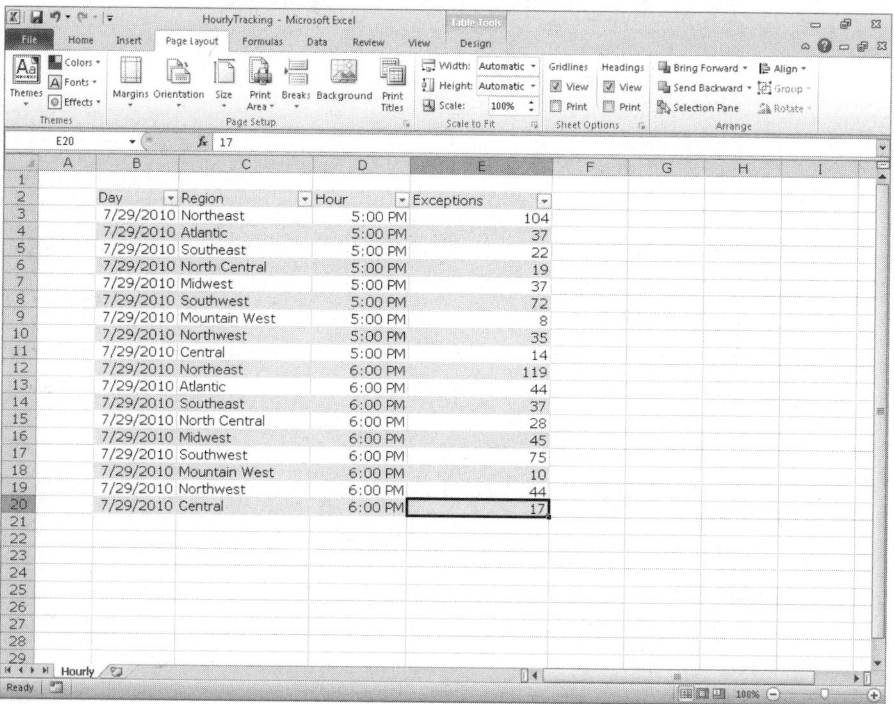

16. In the **Themes** group, click the **Themes** button, and then click **Save Current Theme**.

    The Save Current Theme dialog box opens.

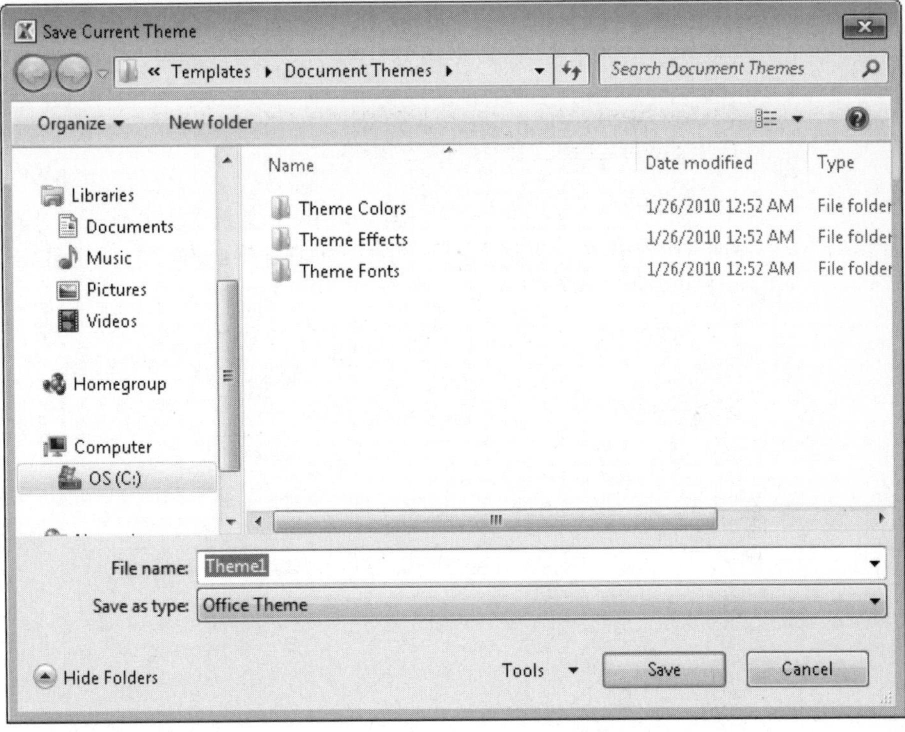

17. In the **File name** field, type **Verdana Office**, and then click **Save**.

    Excel saves your theme.

18. In the **Themes** group, click the **Themes** button, and then click **Origin**.

    Excel applies the new theme to your workbook.

CLEAN UP Save the HourlyTracking workbook, and then close it.

Making Numbers Easier to Read

Changing the format of the cells in your worksheet can make your data much easier to read, both by setting data labels apart from the actual data and by adding borders to define the boundaries between labels and data even more clearly. Of course, using formatting options to change the font and appearance of a cell's contents doesn't help with idiosyncratic data types such as dates, phone numbers, or currency values.

As an example, consider U.S. phone numbers. These numbers are 10 digits long and have a 3-digit area code, a 3-digit exchange, and a 4-digit line number written in the form (###) ###-####. Although it's certainly possible to type a phone number with the expected formatting in a cell, it's much simpler to type a sequence of 10 digits and have Excel change the data's appearance.

You can tell Excel to expect a phone number in a cell by opening the Format Cells dialog box to the Number page and displaying the formats available for the Special category.

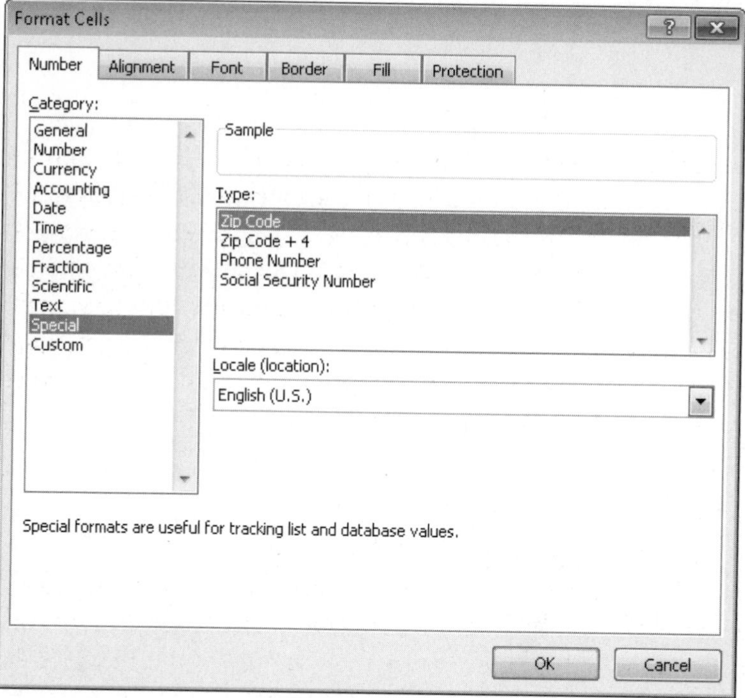

Clicking Phone Number in the Type list tells Excel to format 10-digit numbers in the standard phone number format. You can see this in operation if you compare the contents of the active cell and the contents of the formula box for a cell with the Phone Number formatting.

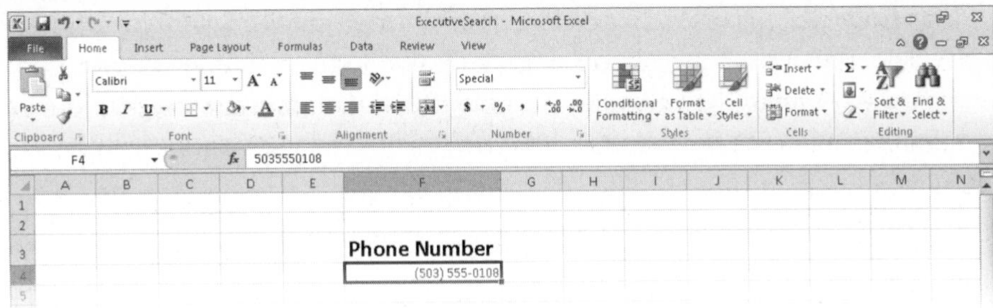

Troubleshooting If you type a 9-digit number in a field that expects a phone number, you won't see an error message; instead, you'll see a 2-digit area code. For example, the number 425550012 would be displayed as (42) 555-0012. An 11-digit number would be displayed with a 4-digit area code. If the phone number doesn't look right, you probably left out a digit or included an extra one, so you should make sure your entry is correct.

Just as you can instruct Excel to expect a phone number in a cell, you can also have it expect a date or a currency amount. You can make those changes from the Format Cells dialog box by choosing either the Date category or the Currency category. The Date category enables you to pick the format for the date (and determine whether the date's appearance changes due to the Locale setting of the operating system on the computer viewing the workbook). In a similar vein, selecting the Currency category displays controls to set the number of places after the decimal point, the currency symbol to use, and the way in which Excel should display negative numbers.

Tip The Excel user interface enables you to make the most common format changes by displaying the Home tab of the ribbon and then, in the Number group, either clicking a button representing a built-in format or selecting a format from the Number Format list.

You can also create a custom numeric format to add a word or phrase to a number in a cell. For example, you can add the phrase *per month* to a cell with a formula that calculates average monthly sales for a year to ensure that you and your colleagues will recognize the figure as a monthly average. To create a custom number format, click the Home tab, and then click the Number dialog box launcher (found at the bottom right corner of the Number group on the ribbon) to display the Format Cells dialog box. Then, if necessary, click the Number tab.

In the Category list, click Custom to display the available custom number formats in the Type list. You can then click the base format you want and modify it in the Type box. For example, clicking the 0.00 format causes Excel to format any number in a cell with two digits to the right of the decimal point.

Tip The zeros in the format indicate that the position in the format can accept any number as a valid value.

To customize the format, click in the Type box and add any symbols or text you want to the format. For example, typing a dollar ($) sign to the left of the existing format and then typing *"per month"* (including quote marks) to the right of the existing format causes the number 1500 to be displayed as *$1500.00 per month*.

Important You need to enclose any text to be displayed as part of the format in quotes so that Excel recognizes the text as a string to be displayed in the cell.

In this exercise, you'll assign date, phone number, and currency formats to ranges of cells.

SET UP You need the ExecutiveSearch_start workbook located in your Chapter04 practice file folder to complete this exercise. Open the ExecutiveSearch_start workbook, and save it as *ExecutiveSearch*. Then follow the steps.

1. Click cell **A3**.
2. On the **Home** tab, click the **Font** dialog box launcher.

   The Format Cells dialog box opens.
3. If necessary, click the **Number** tab.
4. In the **Category** list, click **Date**.

   The Type list appears with a list of date formats.

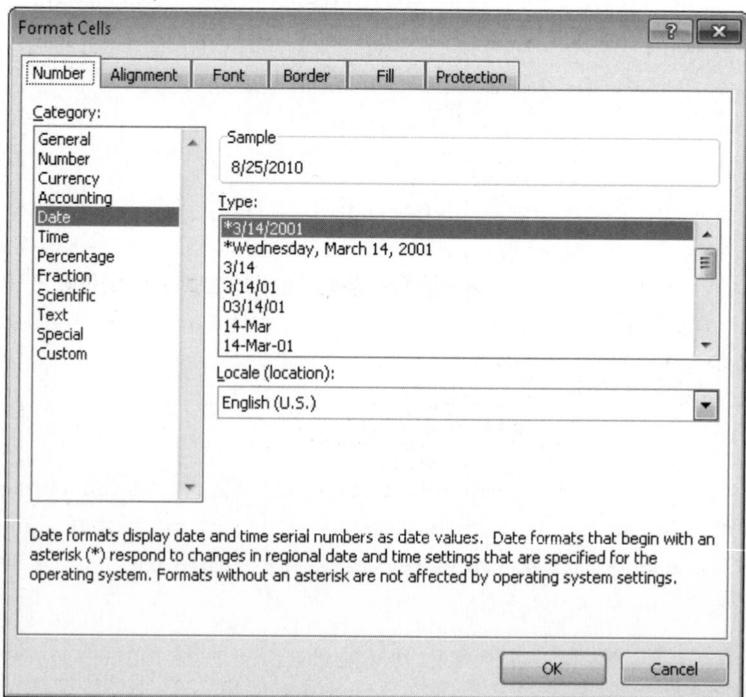

5. In the **Type** list, click **3/14/01**.

6. Click **OK** to assign the chosen format to the cell.

   Excel displays the contents of cell A3 to reflect the new format.

7. Click cell **G3**.

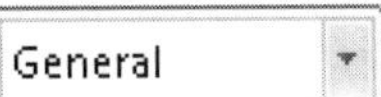

8. On the **Home** tab, in the **Number** group, click the **Number Format** button's down arrow and then click **More Number Formats**.

9. If necessary, click the **Number** tab in the **Format Cells** dialog box.

10. In the **Category** list, click **Special**.

    The Type list appears with a list of special formats.

11. In the **Type** list, click **Phone Number**, and then click **OK**.

    Excel displays the contents of the cell as (425) 555-0102, matching the format you selected, and the Format Cells dialog box closes.

12. Click cell **H3**.

13. Click the **Font** dialog box launcher.

14. If necessary, click the **Number** tab in the **Format Cells** dialog box.

15. In the **Category** list, click **Custom**.

    The contents of the Type list are updated to reflect your choice.

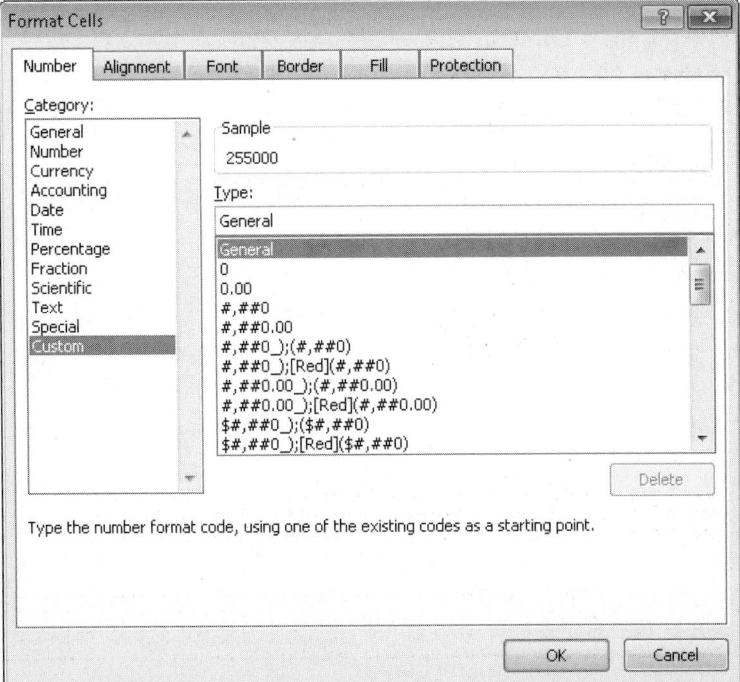

16. In the **Type** list, click the **#,##0** item.

    #,##0 appears in the Type box.

17. In the **Type** box, click to the left of the existing format, and type **$**. Then click to the right of the format, and type **" before bonuses"** (note the space after the opening quote).

18. Click **OK** to close the dialog box.

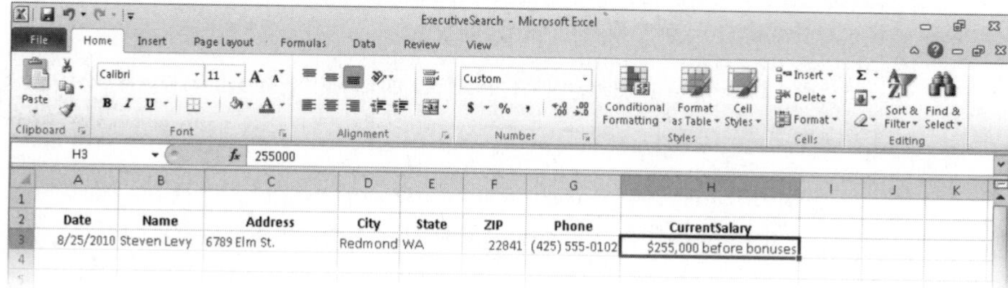

CLEAN UP Save the ExecutiveSearch workbook, and then close it.

Changing the Appearance of Data Based on Its Value

Recording package volumes, vehicle miles, and other business data in a worksheet enables you to make important decisions about your operations. And as you saw earlier in this chapter, you can change the appearance of data labels and the worksheet itself to make interpreting your data easier.

Another way you can make your data easier to interpret is to have Excel change the appearance of your data based on its value. These formats are called conditional formats because the data must meet certain conditions, defined in conditional formatting rules, to have a format applied to it. For example, if chief operating officer Lori Penor wanted to highlight any Thursdays with higher-than-average weekday package volumes, she could define a conditional format that tests the value in the cell recording total sales and changes the format of the cell's contents when the condition is met.

To create a conditional format, you select the cells to which you want to apply the format, display the Home tab, and then in the Styles group, click Conditional Formatting to display a menu of possible conditional formats. In Excel, you can define conditional formats that change how the program displays data in cells that contain values above or below the average values of the related cells, that contain values near the top or bottom of the value range, or that contain values duplicated elsewhere in the selected range.

When you select which kind of condition to create, Excel displays a dialog box that contains fields and controls you can use to define your rule. To display all of the rules for the selected cells, display the Home tab, and then in the Styles group, click Conditional Formatting. On the menu, click Manage Rules to display the Conditional Formatting Rules Manager.

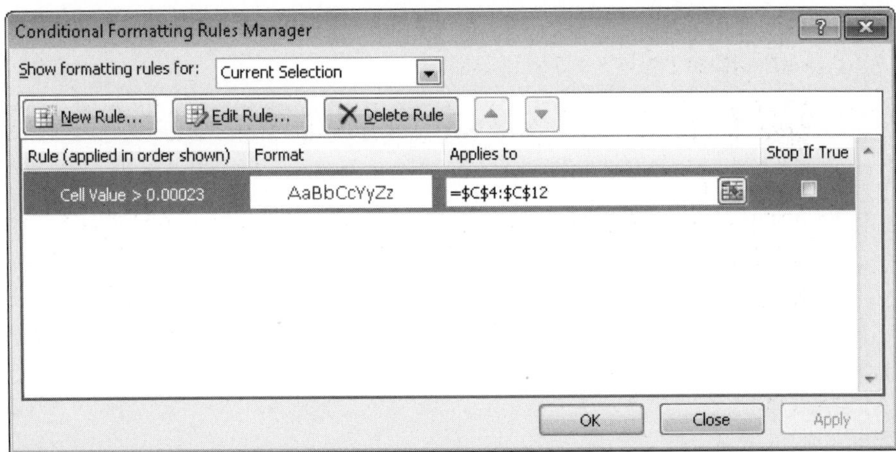

The Conditional Formatting Rules Manager enables you to control your conditional formats in the following ways:

- Create a new rule by clicking the New Rule button.
- Change a rule by clicking the rule and then clicking the Edit Rule button.
- Remove a rule by clicking the rule and then clicking the Delete Rule button.
- Move a rule up or down in the order by clicking the rule and then clicking the Move Up button or Move Down button.
- Control whether Excel continues evaluating conditional formats after it finds a rule to apply by selecting or clearing a rule's Stop If True check box.
- Save any new rules and close the Conditional Formatting Rules Manager by clicking OK.
- Save any new rules without closing the Conditional Formatting Rules Manager by clicking Apply.
- Discard any unsaved changes by clicking Cancel.

Tip Clicking the New Rule button in the Conditional Formatting Rules Manager opens the New Formatting Rule dialog box. The commands in the New Formatting Rule dialog box duplicate the options displayed when you click the Conditional Formatting button in the Styles group on the Home tab.

After you create a rule, you can change the format applied if the rule is true by clicking the rule and then clicking the Edit Rule button to display the Edit Formatting Rule dialog box. In that dialog box, click the Format button to display the Format Cells dialog box. After you define your format, click OK to display the rule.

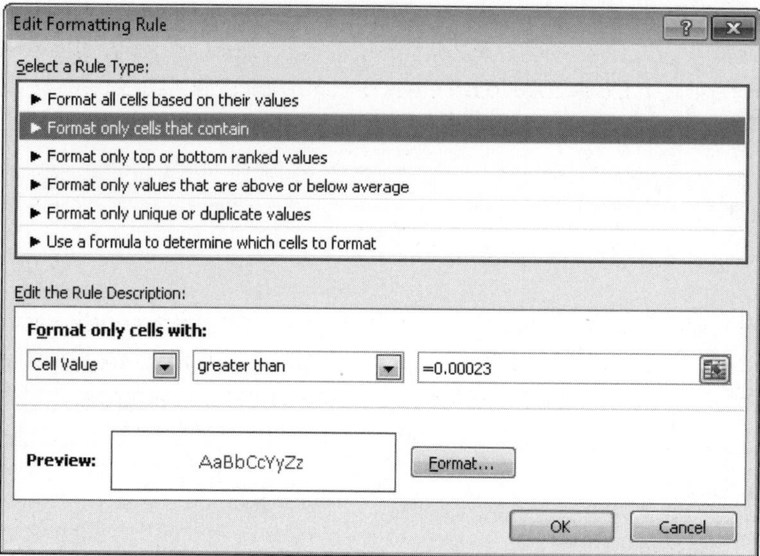

Important Excel doesn't check to make sure that your conditions are logically consistent, so you need to be sure that you plan and enter your conditions correctly.

Excel also enables you to create three other types of conditional formats: data bars, color scales, and icon sets. Data bars summarize the relative magnitude of values in a cell range by extending a band of color across the cell.

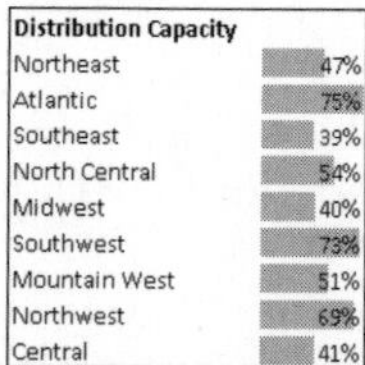

Distribution Capacity	
Northeast	47%
Atlantic	75%
Southeast	39%
North Central	54%
Midwest	40%
Southwest	73%
Mountain West	51%
Northwest	69%
Central	41%

You can create two types of data bars in Excel 2010: solid fill and gradient fill. When data bars were introduced in Excel 2007, they filled cells with a color band that decreased in intensity as it moved across the cell. This gradient fill pattern made it a bit difficult to determine the relative length of two data bars because the end points weren't as distinct as they would have been if the bars were a solid color. Excel 2010 enables you to choose between a solid fill pattern, which makes the right edge of the bars easier to discern, and a gradient fill, which you can use if you share your workbook with colleagues who use Excel 2007.

Excel also draws data bars differently than was done in Excel 2007. Excel 2007 drew a very short data bar for the lowest value in a range and a very long data bar for the highest value. The problem was that similar values could be represented by data bars of very different lengths if there wasn't much variance among the values in the conditionally formatted range. In Excel 2010, data bars compare values based on their distance from zero, so similar values are summarized using data bars of similar lengths.

Tip Excel 2010 data bars summarize negative values by using bars that extend to the left of a baseline that the program draws in a cell. You can control how your data bars summarize negative values by clicking the Negative Value And Axis button, which can be accessed from either the New Formatting Rule dialog box or the Edit Formatting Rule dialog box.

Color scales compare the relative magnitude of values in a cell range by applying colors from a two-color or three-color set to your cells. The intensity of a cell's color reflects the value's tendency toward the top or bottom of the values in the range.

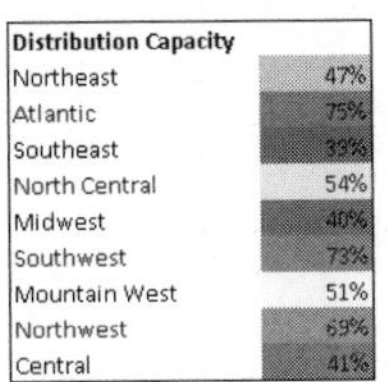

Distribution Capacity	
Northeast	47%
Atlantic	75%
Southeast	39%
North Central	54%
Midwest	40%
Southwest	73%
Mountain West	51%
Northwest	69%
Central	41%

Icon sets are collections of three, four, or five images that Excel displays when certain rules are met.

Distribution Capacity	
Northeast	47%
Atlantic	75%
Southeast	39%
North Central	54%
Midwest	40%
Southwest	73%
Mountain West	51%
Northwest	69%
Central	41%

When icon sets were introduced in Excel 2007, you could apply an icon set as a whole, but you couldn't create custom icon sets or choose to have Excel 2007 display no icon if the value in a cell met a criterion. In Excel 2010, you can display any icon from any set for any criterion or display no icon.

When you click a color scale or icon set in the Conditional Formatting Rules Manager and then click the Edit Rule button, you can control when Excel applies a color or icon to your data.

Important Be sure to not include cells that contain summary formulas in your conditionally formatted ranges. The values, which could be much higher or lower than your regular cell data, could throw off your comparisons.

In this exercise, you'll create a series of conditional formats to change the appearance of data in worksheet cells displaying the package volume and delivery exception rates of a regional distribution center.

SET UP You need the Dashboard_start workbook located in your Chapter04 practice file folder to complete this exercise. Open the Dashboard_start workbook, and save it as *Dashboard*. Then follow the steps.

1. Select cells **C4:C12**.

2. On the **Home** tab, in the **Styles** group, click **Conditional Formatting**. On the menu, point to **Color Scales**, and then in the top row of the palette, click the second pattern from the left.

   Excel formats the selected range.

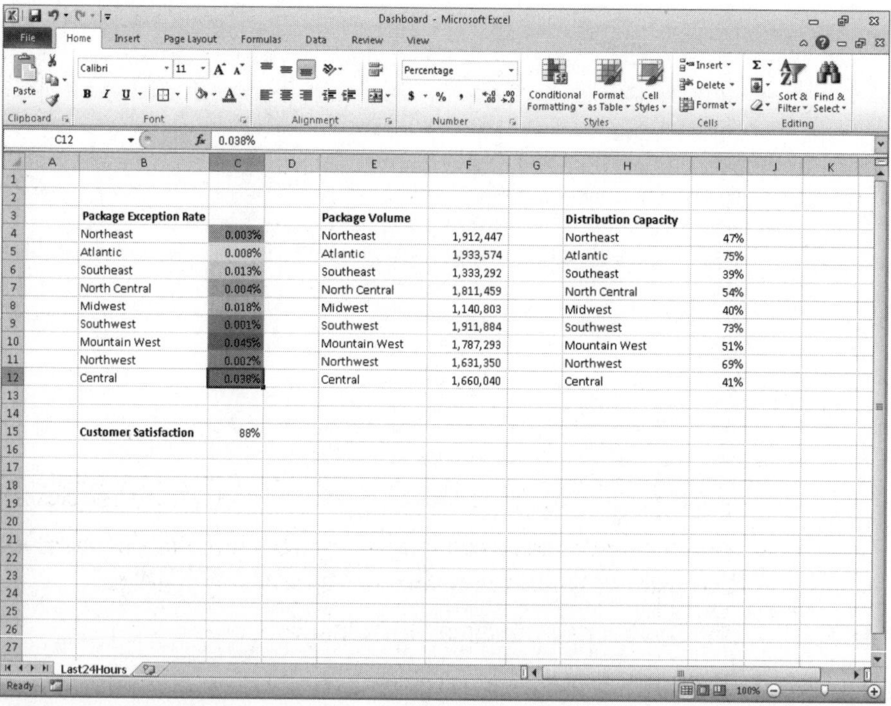

3. Select cells **F4:F12**.

4. On the **Home** tab, in the **Styles** group, click **Conditional Formatting**. On the menu, point to **Data Bars**, and then, in the **Solid Fill** group, click the orange data bar format.

   Excel formats the selected range.

5. Select cells **I4:I12**.

6. On the **Home** tab, in the **Styles** group, click **Conditional Formatting**. On the menu, point to **Icon Sets**, and then in the left column of the list of formats, click the three traffic lights with black borders.

   Excel formats the selected cells.

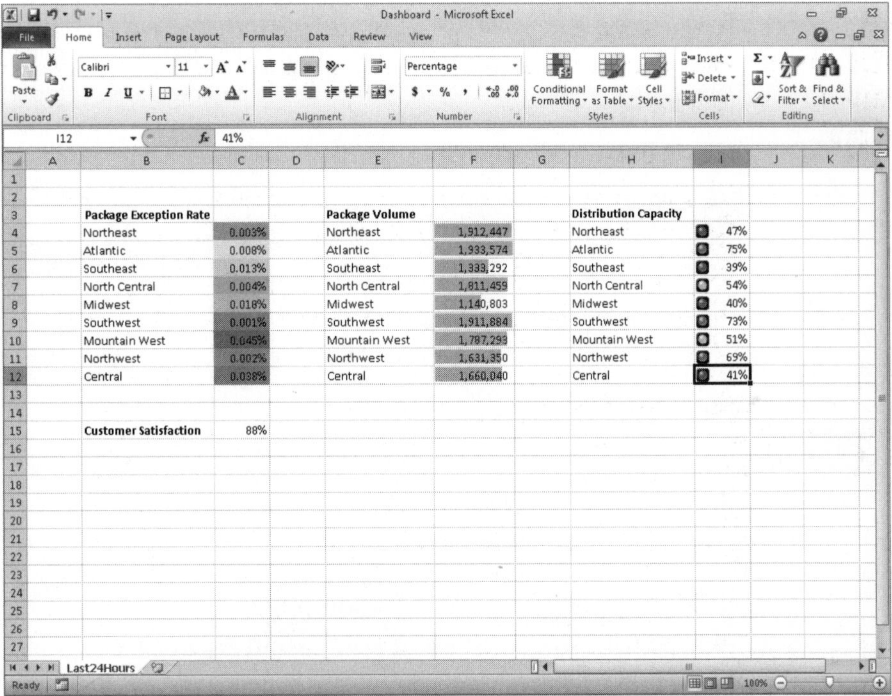

7. With the range **I4:I12** still selected, on the **Home** tab, in the **Styles** group, click **Conditional Formatting**, and then click **Manage Rules**.

   The Conditional Formatting Rules Manager opens.

8. Click the **Icon Set** rule, and then click **Edit Rule**.

   The Edit Formatting Rule dialog box opens.

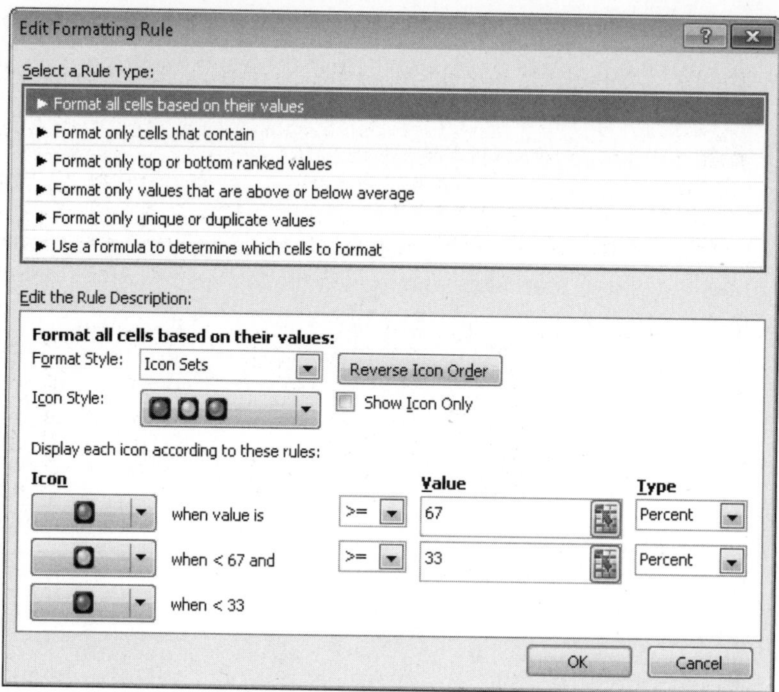

9. Click the **Reverse Icon Order** button.

   Excel reconfigures the rules so the red light icon is at the top and the green light icon is at the bottom.

10. In the red light icon's row, in the **Type** list, click **Number**.
11. In the red light icon's **Value** field, type **0.7**.
12. In the yellow light icon's row, in the **Type** list, click **Number**.
13. In the yellow light icon **Value** field, type **0.5**.
14. Click **OK** twice to close the **Edit Formatting Rule** dialog box and the **Conditional Formatting Rules Manager**.

    Excel formats the selected cell range.

15. Click cell **C15**.
16. On the **Home** tab, in the **Styles** group, click **Conditional Formatting**. On the menu, point to **Highlight Cells Rules**, and then click **Less Than**.

    The Less Than dialog box opens.

17. In the left field, type **96%**.
18. In the **With** list, click **Red text**.

19. Click **OK**.

    The Less Than dialog box closes, and Excel displays the text in cell C15 in red.

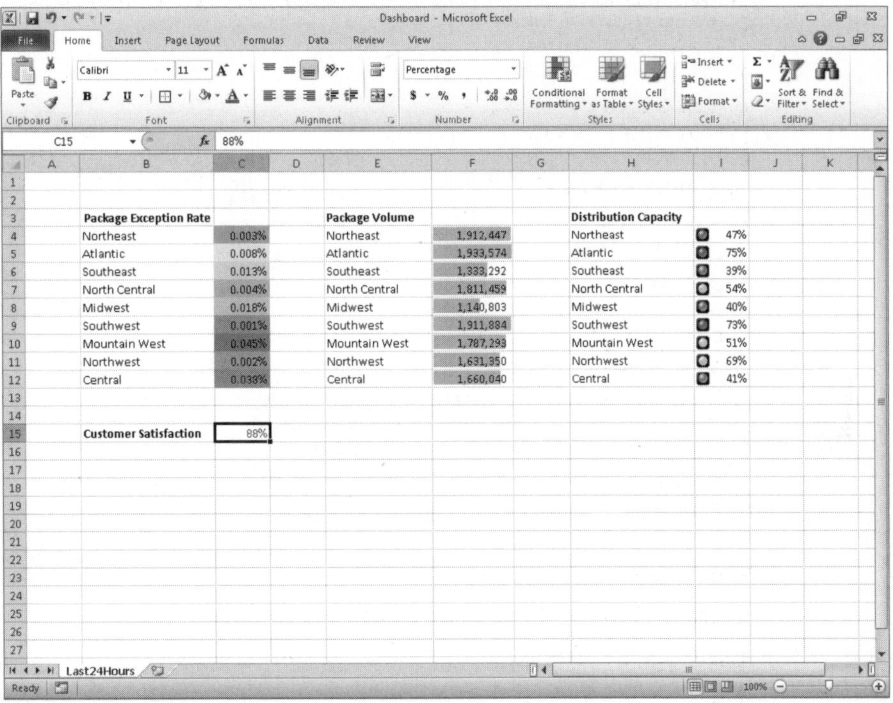

 **CLEAN UP** Save the Dashboard workbook, and then close it.

Adding Images to Worksheets

Establishing a strong corporate identity helps customers remember your organization as well as the products and services you offer. Setting aside the obvious need for sound management, two important physical attributes of a strong retail business are a well-conceived shop space and an eye-catching, easy-to-remember logo. After you or your graphic artist has created a logo, you should add the logo to all your documents, especially any that might be seen by your customers. Not only does the logo mark the documents as coming from your company but it also serves as an advertisement, encouraging anyone who sees your worksheets to call or visit your company.

One way to add a picture to a worksheet is to display the Insert tab, and then in the Illustrations group, click Picture. Clicking Picture displays the Insert Picture dialog box, from which you can locate the picture you want to add from your hard disk. When you insert a picture, the Picture Tools Format contextual tab appears on the ribbon. You can use the tools on the Format contextual tab to change the picture's contrast, brightness, and other attributes. With the controls in the Picture Styles group, you can place a border around the picture, change the picture's shape, or change a picture's effects (such as shadow, reflection, or three-dimensional effects). Other tools, found in the Arrange and Size groups, enable you to rotate, reposition, and resize the picture.

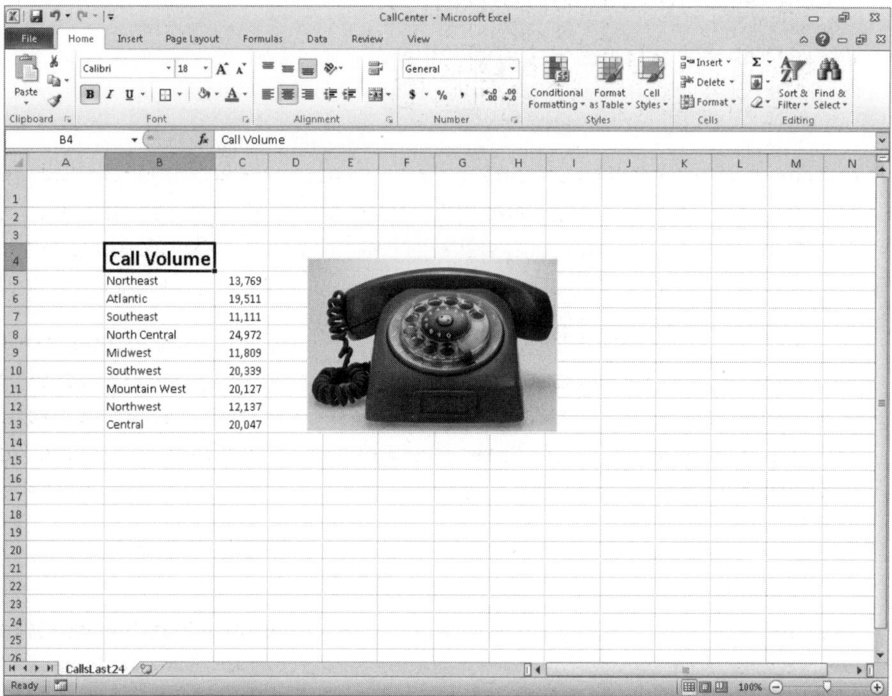

You can also resize a picture by clicking it and then dragging one of the handles that appears on the graphic. If you accidentally resize a graphic by dragging a handle, just click the Undo button to remove your change.

Excel 2010 includes a new built-in capability that you can use to remove the background of an image you insert into a workbook. To do so, click the image and then, on the Format contextual tab of the ribbon, in the Adjust group, click Remove Background. When you do, Excel attempts to identify the foreground and background of the image.

You can drag the handles on the inner square of the background removal tool to change how the tool analyzes the image. When you have adjusted the outline to identify the elements of the image you want to keep, click the Keep Changes button on the Background Removal contextual tab of the ribbon to complete the operation.

If you want to generate a repeating image in the background of a worksheet to form a tiled pattern behind your worksheet's data, you can display the Page Layout tab, and then in the Page Setup group, click Background. In the Sheet Background dialog box, click the image that you want to serve as the background pattern for your worksheet, and click OK.

Tip To remove a background image from a worksheet, display the Page Layout tab, and then in the Page Setup group, click Delete Background.

To achieve a watermark-type effect with words displayed behind the worksheet data, save the watermark information as an image, and then use the image as the sheet background; you could also insert the image in the header or footer, and then resize or scale it to position the watermark information where you want it.

In this exercise, you'll add an image to an existing worksheet, change its location on the worksheet, reduce the size of the image, and then set another image as a repeating background for the worksheet.

SET UP You need the CallCenter_start workbook and the phone and texture images located in your Chapter04 practice file folder to complete this exercise. Open the CallCenter_start workbook, and save it as *CallCenter*. Then follow the steps.

1. On the **Insert** tab, in the **Illustrations** group, click **Picture**.

   The Insert Picture dialog box opens.

2. Navigate to the **Chapter04** practice file folder, and then double-click the **phone** image file.

   The image appears on your worksheet.

3. On the **Format** contextual tab, in the **Adjust** group, click **Remove Background**.

   Excel attempts to separate the image's foreground from its background.

4. Drag the handles at the upper-left and bottom-right corners of the outline until the entire phone, including the cord, is within the frame.

5. On the **Background Removal** tab, click **Keep Changes**.

   Excel removes the highlighted image elements.

6. Move the image to the upper-left corner of the worksheet, click and hold the handle at the lower-right corner of the image, and drag it up and to the left until the image no longer obscures the **Call Volume** label.

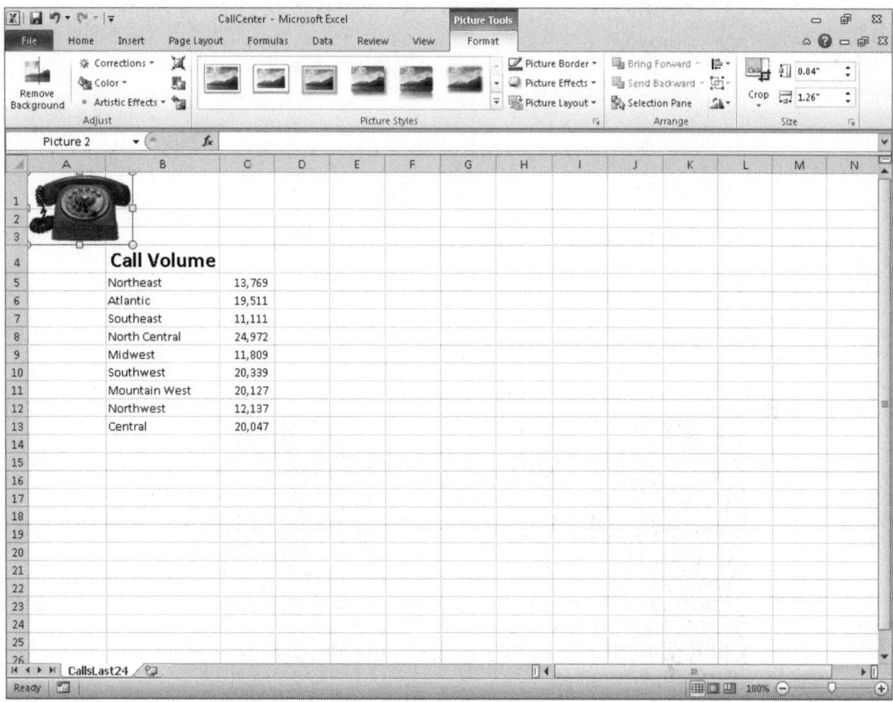

7. On the **Page Layout** tab, in the **Page Setup** group, click **Background**.

   The Sheet Background dialog box opens.

8. Navigate to the **Chapter04** practice file folder, and then double-click the **texture** image file.

   Excel repeats the image to form a background pattern.

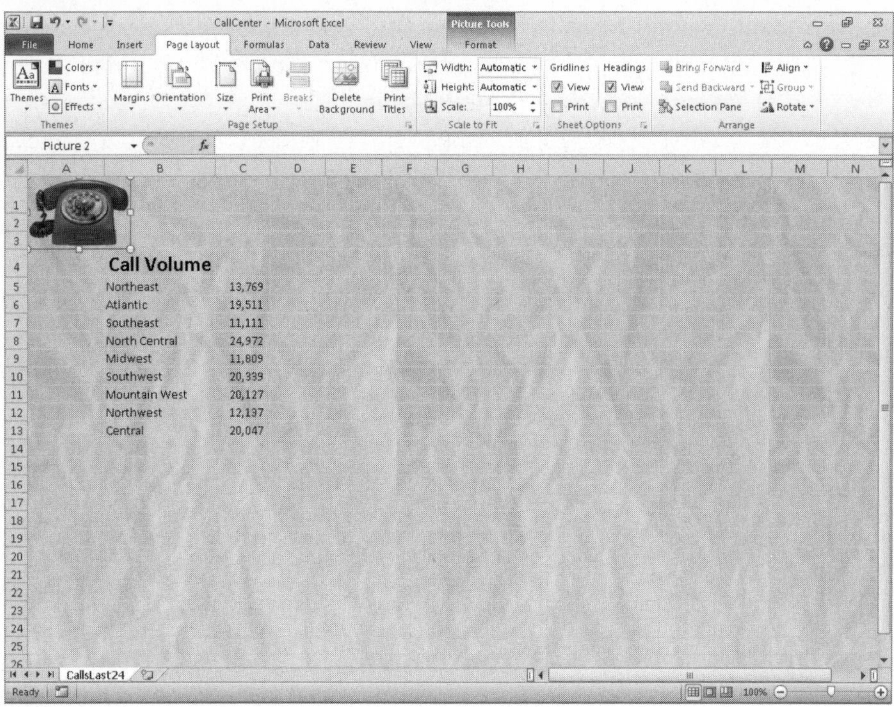

9. On the **Page Layout** tab, in the **Page Setup** group, click **Delete Background**.

   Excel removes the background image.

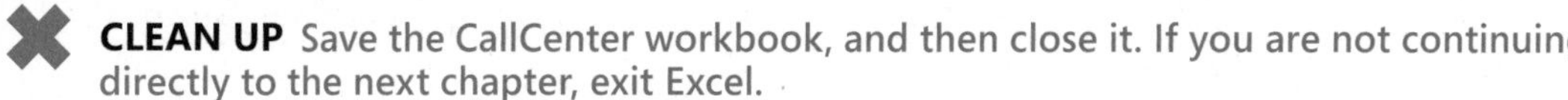

CLEAN UP Save the CallCenter workbook, and then close it. If you are not continuing directly to the next chapter, exit Excel.

Key Points

- If you don't like the default font in which Excel displays your data, you can change it.
- You can use cell formatting, including borders, alignment, and fill colors, to emphasize certain cells in your worksheets. This emphasis is particularly useful for making column and row labels stand out from the data.
- Excel comes with a number of existing styles that enable you to change the appearance of individual cells. You can also create new styles to make formatting your workbooks easier.
- If you want to apply the formatting from one cell to another cell, use the Format Painter to copy the format quickly.
- There are quite a few built-in document themes and Excel table formats you can apply to groups of cells. If you see one you like, use it and save yourself lots of formatting time.
- Conditional formats enable you to set rules so that Excel changes the appearance of a cell's contents based on its value.
- Adding images can make your worksheets more visually appealing and make your data easier to understand. Excel 2010 greatly enhances your ability to manage your images without leaving Excel.

Chapter at a Glance

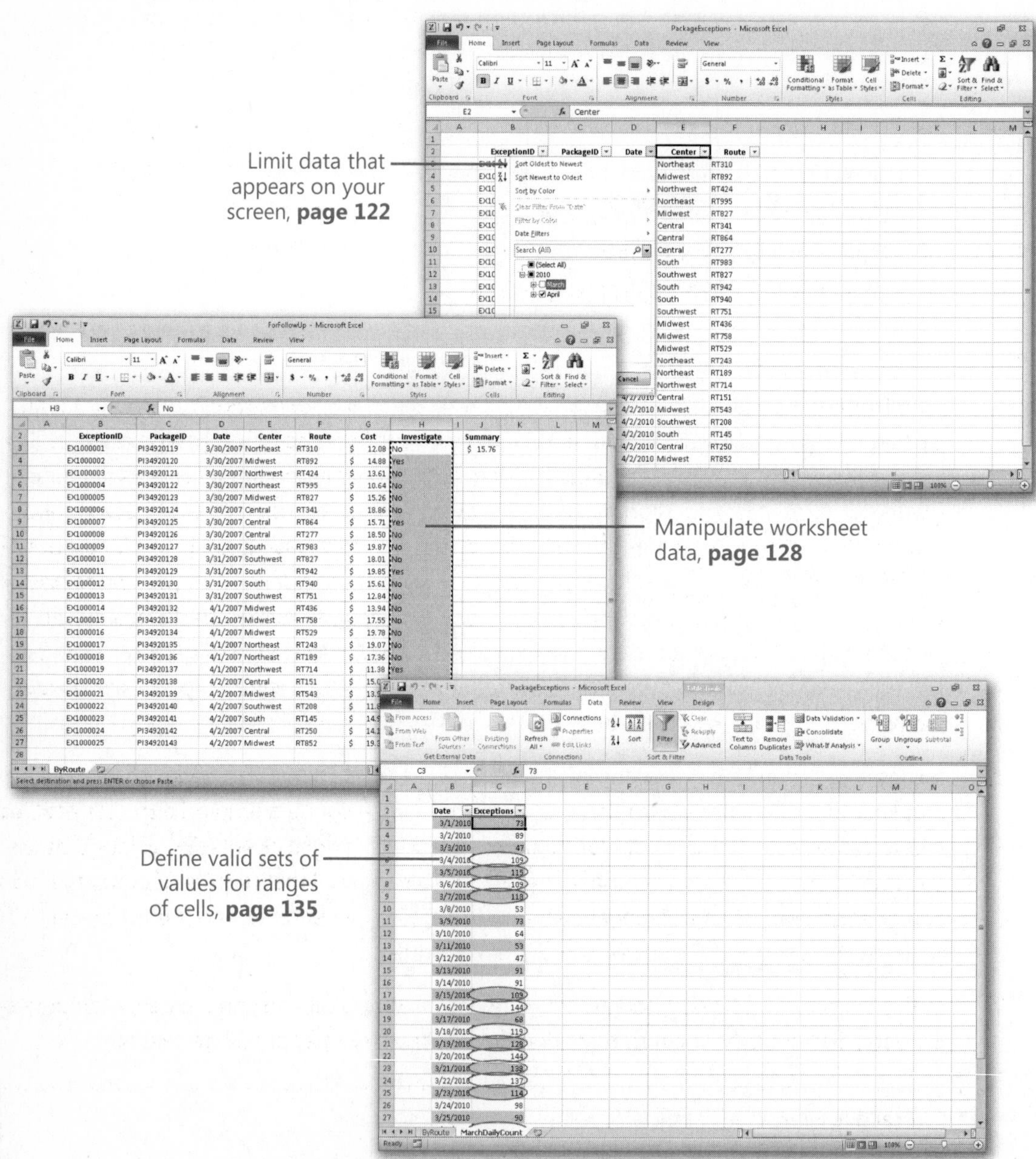

5 Focusing on Specific Data by Using Filters

In this chapter, you will learn how to

- ✔ Limit data that appears on your screen.
- ✔ Manipulate worksheet data.
- ✔ Define valid sets of values for ranges of cells.

With Microsoft Excel 2010, you can manage huge data collections, but storing more than 1 million rows of data doesn't help you make business decisions unless you have the ability to focus on the most important data in a worksheet. Focusing on the most relevant data in a worksheet facilitates decision making, whether that data represents the 10 busiest days in a month or revenue streams that you might need to reevaluate. Excel offers a number of powerful and flexible tools with which you can limit the data displayed in your worksheet. When your worksheet displays the subset of data you need to make a decision, you can perform calculations on that data. You can discover what percentage of monthly revenue was earned in the 10 best days in the month, find your total revenue for particular days of the week, or locate the slowest business day of the month.

Just as you can limit the data displayed by your worksheets, you can create validation rules that limit the data entered into them as well. Setting rules for data entered into cells enables you to catch many of the most common data entry errors, such as entering values that are too small or too large, or attempting to enter a word in a cell that requires a number. If you add a validation rule to worksheet cells after data has been entered into them, you can circle any invalid data so that you know what to correct.

In this chapter, you'll learn how to limit the data that appears on your screen, manipulate list data, and create validation rules that limit data entry to appropriate values.

Practice Files Before you can complete the exercises in this chapter, you need to copy the book's practice files to your computer. The practice files you'll use to complete the exercises in this chapter are in the Chapter05 practice file folder. A complete list of practice files is provided in "Using the Practice Files" at the beginning of this book.

Limiting Data That Appears on Your Screen

Excel spreadsheets can hold as much data as you need them to, but you might not want to work with all the data in a worksheet at the same time. For example, you might want to see the revenue figures for your company during the first third, second third, and final third of a month. You can limit the data shown on a worksheet by creating a filter, which is a rule that selects rows to be shown in a worksheet.

To create a filter, you click the cell in the data you want to filter and then, on the Home tab, in the Editing group, click Sort & Filter and then click Filter. When you do, Excel displays a filter arrow at the right edge of the top cell in each column of the data. The arrow indicates that the Excel AutoFilter capability is active.

Important When you turn on filtering, Excel treats the cells in the active cell's column as a range. To ensure that the filtering works properly, you should always have a label at the top of the column you want to filter. If you don't, Excel treats the first value in the list as the label and doesn't include it in the list of values by which you can filter the data.

Clicking the filter arrow displays a menu of filtering options and a list of the unique values in the column. The first few commands in the list are sorting commands, followed by the Clear Filter command and then the Filter By Color command. The next command that appears on the list depends on the type of data in the column. For example, if the column contains a set of dates, the command will be Date Filters. Clicking the command displays a list of commands specific to that data type.

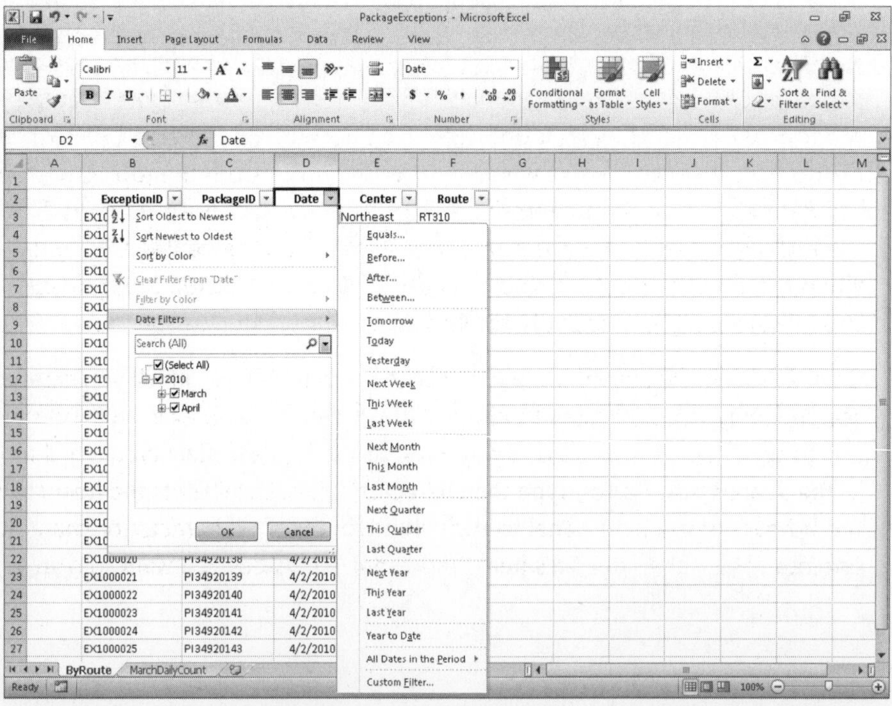

Troubleshooting The appearance of buttons and groups on the ribbon changes depending on the width of the program window. For information about changing the appearance of the ribbon to match our screen images, see "Modifying the Display of the Ribbon" at the beginning of this book.

Tip When a column contains several types of data, the filter command becomes Number Filters.

When you click a filtering option, Excel displays a dialog box in which you can define the filter's criteria. As an example, you could create a filter that displays only dates after 3/31/2010.

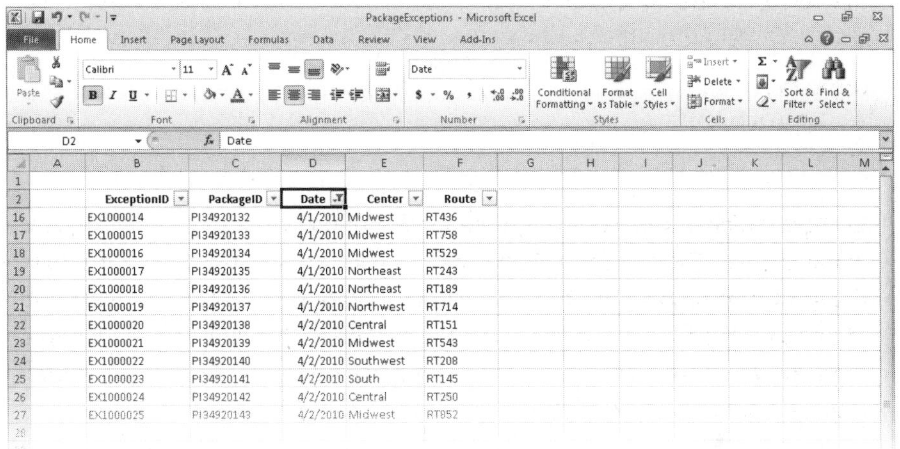

If you want to see the highest or lowest values in a data column, you can create a Top 10 filter. Choosing the Top 10 command from the menu doesn't just limit the display to the top 10 values. Instead, it opens the Top 10 AutoFilter dialog box. From within this dialog box, you can choose whether to show values from the top or bottom of the list, define the number of items you want to see, and choose whether the number in the middle box indicates the number of items or the percentage of items to be shown when the filter is applied. Using the Top 10 AutoFilter dialog box, you can find your top 10 salespeople or identify the top 5 percent of your customers.

Excel 2010 includes a new capability called the *search filter*, which you can use to type a search string that Excel uses to identify which items to display in an Excel table or a data list. To use a search filter, click a column's filter arrow and start typing a character string in the Search box. As you type the character string, Excel limits the items displayed at the bottom of the filter panel to those that contain the character or characters you've entered. When the filter list's items represent the values you want to display, click OK.

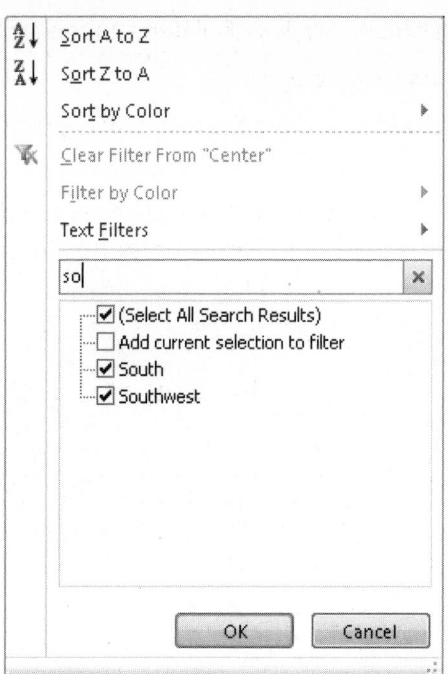

When you point to Text Filters and then click Custom Filter, you can define a rule that Excel uses to decide which rows to show after the filter is applied. For instance, you can create a rule that determines that only days with package volumes of less than 100,000 should be shown in your worksheet. With those results in front of you, you might be able to determine whether the weather or another factor resulted in slower business on those days.

Excel indicates that a column has a filter applied by changing the appearance of the column's filter arrow to include an icon that looks like a funnel. After you finish examining your data by using a filter, you can remove the filter by clicking the column's filter arrow and then clicking Clear Filter. To turn off filtering entirely and remove the filter arrows, display the Home tab and then, in the Editing group, click Sort & Filter and then click Filter.

In this exercise, you'll filter worksheet data by using a series of AutoFilter commands, create a filter showing the five days with the highest delivery exception counts in a month, create a search filter, and create a custom filter.

SET UP You need the PackageExceptions_start workbook located in your Chapter05 practice file folder to complete this exercise. Start Excel, open the PackageExceptions_start workbook, and save it as *PackageExceptions*. Then follow the steps.

1. On the **ByRoute** worksheet, click any cell in the cell range **B2:F27**.

2. On the **Home** tab, in the **Editing** group, click **Sort & Filter**, and then click **Filter**.

   A filter arrow appears in each column's header cell.

3. Click the **Date** column filter arrow and then, from the menu that appears, clear the **March** check box.

   Excel removes the check from the March check box and changes the state of the Select All and 2010 check boxes to indicate that some items within those categories have been filtered.

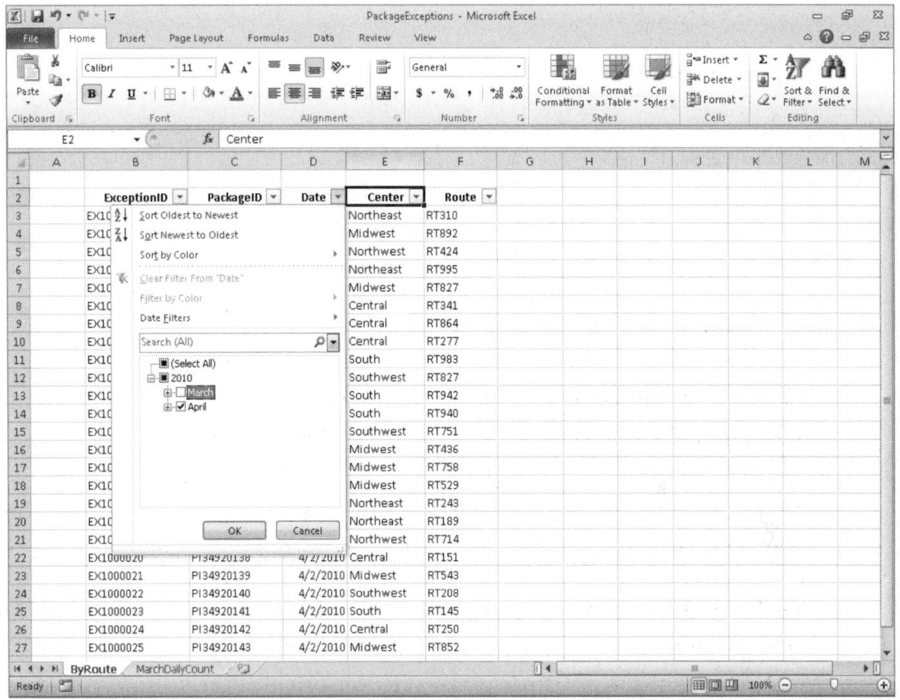

4. Click **OK**.

   Excel hides all rows that contain a date from the month of March.

5. Click the **Center** column filter arrow and then, from the menu that appears, clear the **Select All** check box.

   Excel clears all the check boxes in the list.

6. Select the **Midwest** check box, and then click **OK**.

   Excel displays only those exceptions that occurred in the Midwest distribution center during the month of April.

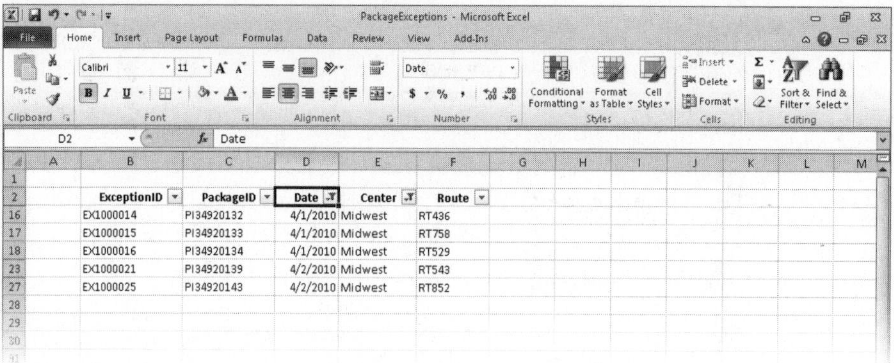

7. On the **Home** tab, in the **Editing** group, click **Sort & Filter**, and then click **Clear**.

   Excel clears all active filters but leaves the filter arrows in place.

8. Click the **Route** column header's filter arrow, and then type **RT9** in the **Search** box.

   The filter list displays only those routes with an identifier that includes the characters *RT9*.

9. Click **OK**.

   Excel applies the filter, displaying exceptions that occurred on routes with identifiers that contain the string *RT9*.

10. Click the **MarchDailyCount** sheet tab.

    The MarchDailyCount worksheet appears.

11. Click any cell in the Excel table.

12. Click the **Exceptions** column filter arrow, point to **Number Filters**, and then click **Top 10**.

    The Top 10 AutoFilter dialog box opens.

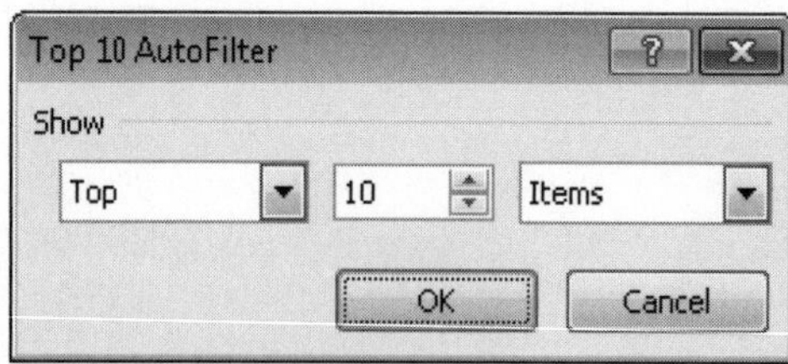

13. In the middle field, type **5**.

14. Click **OK**.

    Excel displays the table rows that contain the five highest values in the Exceptions column.

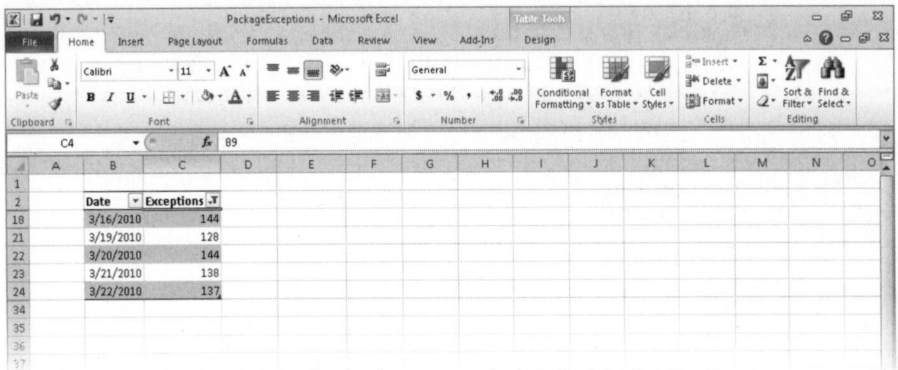

15. Click the **Exceptions** column filter arrow, and then click **Clear Filter from "Exceptions"**.

    Excel removes the filter.

16. Click the **Date** column filter arrow, point to **Date Filters**, and then click **Custom Filter**.

    The Custom AutoFilter dialog box opens.

17. In the upper-left list, click **is after or equal to**.
18. In the upper-right list, click **3/8/2010**.
19. In the lower-left list, click **is before or equal to**.
20. In the lower-right list, click **3/14/2010**.
21. Click **OK**.

    Because you left the And option selected, Excel displays all table rows that contain a date from 3/8/2010 to 3/14/2010, inclusive.

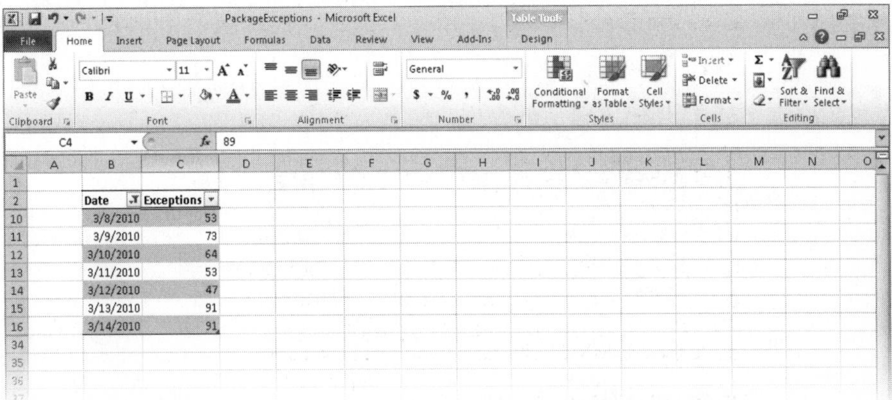

22. On the Quick Access Toolbar, click the **Undo** button to remove your filter.

    Excel restores the table to its unfiltered state.

CLEAN UP Save the PackageExceptions workbook, and then close it.

Manipulating Worksheet Data

Excel offers a wide range of tools you can use to summarize worksheet data. This section shows you how to select rows at random using the *RAND* and *RANDBETWEEN* functions, how to summarize worksheet data using the *SUBTOTAL* and *AGGREGATE* functions, and how to display a list of unique values within a data set.

Selecting List Rows at Random

In addition to filtering the data that is stored in your Excel worksheets, you can choose rows at random from a list. Selecting rows randomly is useful for choosing which customers will receive a special offer, deciding which days of the month to audit, or picking prize winners at an employee party.

To choose rows randomly, you can use the *RAND* function, which generates a random value between 0 and 1, and compare the value it returns with a test value included in the formula. As an example, suppose Consolidated Messenger wanted to offer approximately 30 percent of its customers a discount on their next shipment. A formula that returns a *TRUE* value 30 percent of the time would be *RAND<=0.3*; that is, whenever the random value was between 0 and 0.3, the result would be *TRUE*. You could use this formula to select each row in a list with a probability of 30 percent. A formula that displayed *TRUE* when the value was equal to or less than 30 percent, and *FALSE* otherwise, would be *=IF(RAND()<=0.3,"True","False")*.

If you recalculate this formula 10 times, it's very unlikely that you would see exactly three *TRUE* results and seven *FALSE* results. Just as flipping a coin can result in the same result 10 times in a row by chance, so can the *RAND* function's results appear to be off if you only recalculate it a few times. However, if you were to recalculate the function 10 thousand times, it is extremely likely that the number of *TRUE* results would be very close to 30 percent.

Tip Because the *RAND* function is a volatile function (it recalculates its results every time you update the worksheet), you should copy the cells that contain the *RAND* function in a formula and paste the formulas' values back into their original cells. To do so, select the cells that contain the *RAND* formulas and press Ctrl+C to copy the cell's contents. Then, on the Home tab, in the Clipboard group, in the Paste list, click Paste Values to replace the formula with its current result. If you don't replace the formulas with their results, you will never have a permanent record of which rows were selected.

The *RANDBETWEEN* function generates a random whole number within a defined range. For example, the formula *=RANDBETWEEN(1,100)* would generate a random integer value from 1 to 100, inclusive. The *RANDBETWEEN* function is very useful for creating sample data collections for presentations. Before the *RANDBETWEEN* function was introduced, you had to create formulas that added, subtracted, multiplied, and divided the results of the *RAND* function, which are always decimal values between 0 and 1, to create your data.

Summarizing Worksheets with Hidden and Filtered Rows

The ability to analyze the data that's most vital to your current needs is important, but there are some limitations to how you can summarize your filtered data by using functions such as *SUM* and *AVERAGE*. One limitation is that any formulas you create that include the *SUM* and *AVERAGE* functions don't change their calculations if some of the rows used in the formula are hidden by the filter.

Excel provides two ways to summarize just the visible cells in a filtered data list. The first method is to use AutoCalculate. To use AutoCalculate, you select the cells you want to summarize. When you do, Excel displays the average of values in the cells, the sum of the values in the cells, and the number of visible cells (the count) in the selection. You'll find the display on the status bar at the lower edge of the Excel window.

When you use AutoCalculate, you aren't limited to finding the sum, average, and count of the selected cells. To display the other functions you can use, right-click the status bar and select the function you want from the shortcut menu. If a check mark appears next to a function's name, that function's result appears on the status bar. Clicking a checked function name removes that function from the status bar.

AutoCalculate is great for finding a quick total or average for filtered cells, but it doesn't make the result available in the worksheet. Formulas such as *=SUM(C3:C26)* always consider every cell in the range, regardless of whether you hide a cell's row by right-clicking the row's header and then clicking Hide, so you need to create a formula by using either the *SUBTOTAL* function or the *AGGREGATE* function (which is new in Excel 2010) to summarize just those values that are visible in your worksheet. The *SUBTOTAL* function enables you to summarize every value in a range or summarize only those values in rows you haven't manually hidden. The *SUBTOTAL* function has this syntax: *SUBTOTAL(function_num, ref1, ref2, ...)*. The *function_num* argument holds the number of the operation you want to use to summarize your data. (The operation numbers are summarized in a table later in this section.) The *ref1*, *ref2*, and further arguments represent up to 29 ranges to include in the calculation.

As an example, assume you have a worksheet where you hid rows 20-26 manually. In this case, the formula *=SUBTOTAL(9, C3:C26, E3:E26, G3:G26)* would find the sum of all values in the ranges C3:C26, E3:E26, and G3:G26, regardless of whether that range contained any hidden rows. The formula *=SUBTOTAL(109, C3:C26, E3:E26, G3:G26)* would find the sum of all values in cells C3:C19, E3:E19, and G3:G19, ignoring the values in the manually hidden rows.

Important Be sure to place your *SUBTOTAL* formula in a row that is even with or above the headers in the range you're filtering. If you don't, your filter might hide the formula's result!

The following table lists the summary operations available for the *SUBTOTAL* formula. Excel displays the available summary operations as part of the Formula AutoComplete functionality, so you don't need to remember the operation numbers or look them up in the Help system.

Operation number (includes hidden values)	Operation number (ignores values in manually hidden rows)	Function	Description
1	101	*AVERAGE*	Returns the average of the values in the range
2	102	*COUNT*	Counts the cells in the range that contain a number
3	103	*COUNTA*	Counts the nonblank cells in the range
4	104	*MAX*	Returns the largest (maximum) value in the range
5	105	*MIN*	Returns the smallest (minimum) value in the range
6	106	*PRODUCT*	Returns the result of multiplying all numbers in the range
7	107	*STDEV.S*	Calculates the standard deviation of values in the range by examining a sample of the values
8	108	*STDEV.P*	Calculates the standard deviation of the values in the range by using all the values
9	109	*SUM*	Returns the result of adding all numbers in the range together
10	110	*VAR.S*	Calculates the variance of values in the range by examining a sample of the values
11	111	*VAR.P*	Calculates the variance of the values in the range by using all of the values

As the previous table shows, the *SUBTOTAL* function has two sets of operations. The first set (operations 1-11) represents operations that include hidden values in their summary, and the second set (operations 101-111) represents operations that summarize only values visible in the worksheet. Operations 1-11 summarize all cells in a range, regardless of whether the range contains any manually hidden rows. By contrast, the operations 101-111 ignore any values in manually hidden rows. What the *SUBTOTAL* function doesn't do, however, is change its result to reflect rows hidden by using a filter.

The new *AGGREGATE* function extends the capabilities of the *SUBTOTAL* function. With it, you can select from a broader range of functions and use another argument to determine which, if any, values to ignore in the calculation. *AGGREGATE* has two possible syntaxes, depending on the summary operation you select. The first syntax is *=AGGREGATE(function_num, options, ref1…)*, which is similar to the syntax of the *SUBTOTAL* function. The other possible syntax, *=AGGREGATE(function_num, options, array, [k])*, is used to create *AGGREGATE* functions that use the *LARGE, SMALL, PERCENTILE.INC, QUARTILE.INC, PERCENTILE.EXC*, and *QUARTILE.EXC* operations.

The following table summarizes the summary operations available for use in the *AGGREGATE* function.

Number	Function	Description
1	*AVERAGE*	Returns the average of the values in the range.
2	*COUNT*	Counts the cells in the range that contain a number.
3	*COUNTA*	Counts the nonblank cells in the range.
4	*MAX*	Returns the largest (maximum) value in the range.
5	*MIN*	Returns the smallest (minimum) value in the range.
6	*PRODUCT*	Returns the result of multiplying all numbers in the range.
7	*STDEV.S*	Calculates the standard deviation of values in the range by examining a sample of the values.
8	*STDEV.P*	Calculates the standard deviation of the values in the range by using all the values.
9	*SUM*	Returns the result of adding all numbers in the range together.
10	*VAR.S*	Calculates the variance of values in the range by examining a sample of the values.
11	*VAR.P*	Calculates the variance of the values in the range by using all of the values.
12	*MEDIAN*	Returns the value in the middle of a group of values.
13	*MODE.SNGL*	Returns the most frequently occurring number from a group of numbers.
14	*LARGE*	Returns the *k*-th largest value in a data set; *k* is specified using the last function argument. If *k* is left blank, Excel returns the largest value.

(continued)

Number	Function	Description
15	*SMALL*	Returns the *k*-th smallest value in a data set; *k* is specified using the last function argument. If *k* is left blank, Excel returns the smallest value.
16	*PERCENTILE.INC*	Returns the *k*-th percentile of values in a range, where *k* is a value from 0 to 1, inclusive.
17	*QUARTILE.INC*	Returns the quartile value of a data set, based on a percentage from 0 to 1, inclusive.
18	*PERCENTILE.EXC*	Returns the *k*-th percentile of values in a range, where *k* is a value from 0 to 1, exclusive.
19	*QUARTILE.EXC*	Returns the quartile value of a data set, based on a percentage from 0 to 1, exclusive.

The second argument, *options*, enables you to select which items the *AGGREGATE* function should ignore. These items can include hidden rows, errors, and *SUBTOTAL* and *AGGREGATE* functions. The following table summarizes the values available for the options argument and the effect they have on the function's results.

Number	Description
0	Ignore nested *SUBTOTAL* and *AGGREGATE* functions
1	Ignore hidden rows and nested *SUBTOTAL* and *AGGREGATE* functions
2	Ignore error values and nested *SUBTOTAL* and *AGGREGATE* functions
3	Ignore hidden rows, error values, and nested *SUBTOTAL* and *AGGREGATE* functions
4	Ignore nothing
5	Ignore hidden rows
6	Ignore error values
7	Ignore hidden rows and error values

Finding Unique Values Within a Data Set

Summarizing numerical values can provide valuable information that helps you run your business. It can also be helpful to know how many different values appear within a column. For example, you might want to display all of the countries in which Consolidated Messenger has customers. If you want to display a list of the unique values in a column, click any cell in the data set, display the Data tab and then, in the Sort & Filter group, click Advanced to display the Advanced Filter dialog box.

In the List Range field, type the reference of the cell range you want to examine for unique values, select the Unique Records Only check box, and then click OK to have Excel display the row that contains the first occurrence of each value in the column.

Important Excel treats the first cell in the data range as a header cell, so it doesn't consider the cell as it builds the list of unique values. Be sure to include the header cell in your data range!

In this exercise, you'll select random rows from a list of exceptions to identify package delivery misadventures to investigate, create an *AGGREGATE* formula to summarize the visible cells in a filtered worksheet, and find the unique values in one column of data.

SET UP You need the ForFollowUp_start workbook located in your Chapter05 practice file folder to complete this exercise. Open the ForFollowUp_start workbook, and save it as *ForFollowUp*. Then follow the steps.

1. Select cells **G3:G27**.

   The average of the values in the selected cells, the number of cells selected, and the total of the values in the selected cells appear in the AutoCalculate area of the status bar.

2. In cell **J3**, enter the formula **=AGGREGATE(1,1,G3:G27)**.

   The value *$15.76* appears in cell J3.

3. On the **Data** tab, in the **Sort & Filter** group, click **Advanced**.

   The Advanced Filter dialog box opens.

4. In the **List range** field, type **E2:E27**.

5. Select the **Unique records only** check box, and then click **OK**.

   Excel displays the rows that contain the first occurrence of each different value in the selected range.

Tip Remember that you must include cell E2, the header cell, in the List Range field so that the filter doesn't display two occurrences of Northeast in the unique values list. To see what happens when you don't include the header cell, try changing the range in the List Range field to E3:E27, selecting the Unique Records Only check box, and clicking OK.

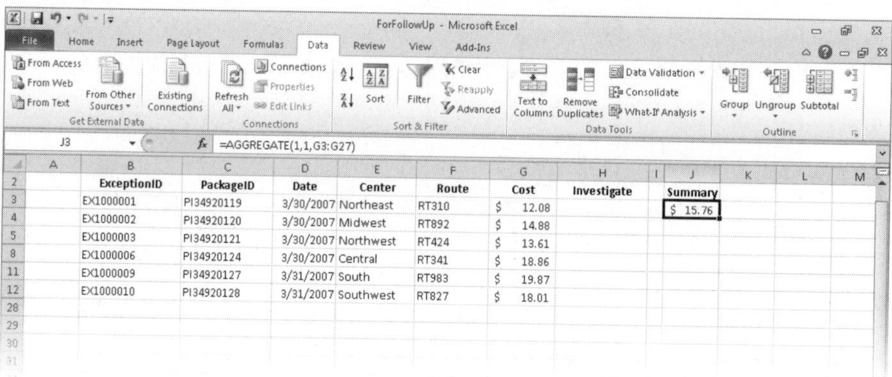

6. On the **Data** tab, in the **Sort & Filter** group, click **Clear**.

   Excel removes the filter.

7. In cell **H3**, type the formula **=IF(RAND()<0.15,"Yes","No")**, and press Enter.

   A value of *Yes* or *No* appears in cell H3, depending on the *RAND* function result.

8. Select cell **H3**, and then drag the fill handle down until it covers cell **H27**.

   Excel copies the formula into every cell in the range H3:H27.

9. With the range **H3:H27** still selected, on the **Home** tab, in the **Clipboard** group, click the **Copy** button.

   Excel copies the cell range's contents to the Microsoft Office Clipboard.

10. Click the **Paste** arrow, and then in the **Paste** gallery that appears, click the first icon in the **Paste Values** group.

    Excel replaces the cells' formulas with the formulas' current results.

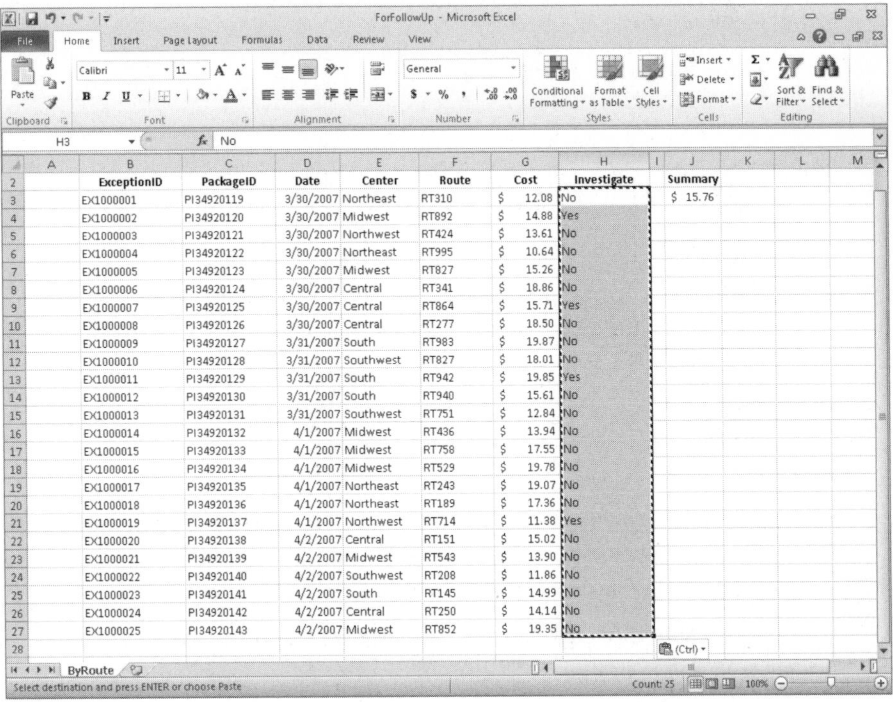

 **CLEAN UP** Save the ForFollowUp workbook, and then close it.

Defining Valid Sets of Values for Ranges of Cells

Part of creating efficient and easy-to-use worksheets is to do what you can to ensure the data entered into your worksheets is as accurate as possible. Although it isn't possible to catch every typographical or transcription error, you can set up a validation rule to make sure that the data entered into a cell meets certain standards.

To create a validation rule, display the Data tab on the ribbon and then, in the Data Tools group, click the Data Validation button to open the Data Validation dialog box. You can use the controls in the Data Validation dialog box to define the type of data that Excel should allow in the cell and then, depending on the data type you choose, to set the conditions data must meet to be accepted in the cell. For example, you can set the conditions so that Excel knows to look for a whole number value between 1000 and 2000.

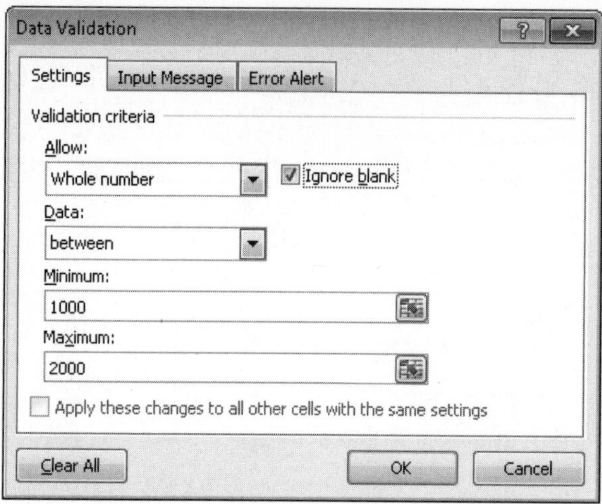

Setting accurate validation rules can help you and your colleagues avoid entering a customer's name in the cell designated to hold the phone number or setting a credit limit above a certain level. To require a user to enter a numeric value in a cell, display the Settings page of the Data Validation dialog box, and, depending on your needs, choose either Whole Number or Decimal from the Allow list.

If you want to set the same validation rule for a group of cells, you can do so by selecting the cells to which you want to apply the rule (such as a column in which you enter the credit limit of customers of Consolidated Messenger) and setting the rule by using the Data Validation dialog box. One important fact you should keep in mind is that, with Excel, you can create validation rules for cells in which you have already entered data. Excel doesn't tell you whether any of those cells contain data that violates your rule at the moment you create the rule, but you can find out by having Excel circle any worksheet cells containing data that violates the cell's validation rule. To do so, display the Data tab and then, in the Data Tools group, click the Data Validation arrow. On the menu, click the Circle Invalid Data button to circle cells with invalid data.

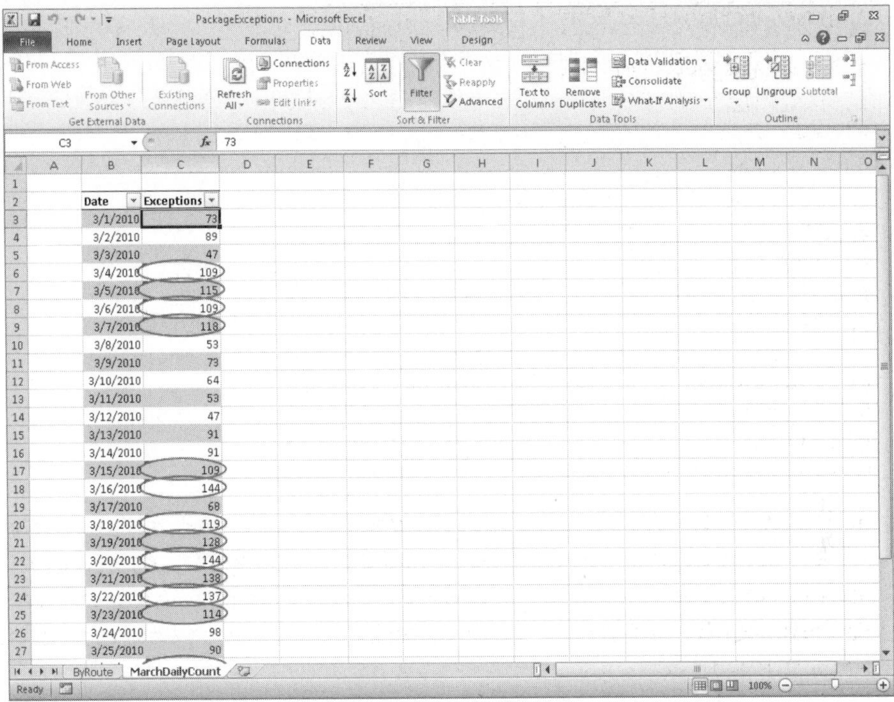

When you're ready to hide the circles, in the Data Validation list, click Clear Validation Circles.

Of course, it's frustrating if you want to enter data into a cell and, when a message box appears that tells you the data you tried to enter isn't acceptable, you aren't given the rules you need to follow. With Excel, you can create a message that tells the user which values are expected before the data is entered and then, if the conditions aren't met, reiterate the conditions in a custom error message.

You can turn off data validation in a cell by displaying the Settings page of the Data Validation dialog box and clicking the Clear All button in the lower-left corner of the dialog box.

In this exercise, you'll create a data validation rule limiting the credit line of Consolidated Messenger customers to $25,000, add an input message mentioning the limitation, and then create an error message if someone enters a value greater than $25,000. After you create your rule and messages, you'll test them.

SET UP You need the Credit_start workbook located in your Chapter05 practice file folder to complete this exercise. Open the Credit_start workbook, and save it as *Credit*. Then follow the steps.

1. Select the cell range **J4:J7**.

   Cell J7 is currently blank, but you will add a value to it later in this exercise.

2. On the **Data** tab, in the **Data Tools** group, click **Data Validation**.

   The Data Validation dialog box opens and displays the Settings page.

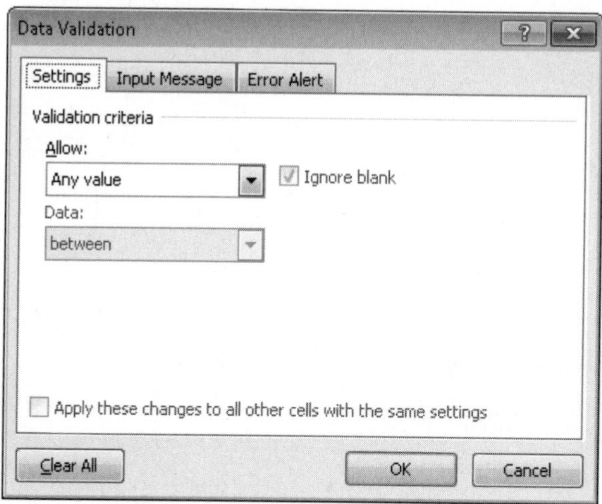

3. In the **Allow** list, click **Whole Number**.

   Boxes labeled Minimum and Maximum appear below the Data box.

4. In the **Data** list, click **less than or equal to**.

   The Minimum box disappears.

5. In the **Maximum** box, type **25000**.
6. Clear the **Ignore blank** check box.
7. Click the **Input Message** tab.

   The Input Message page is displayed.

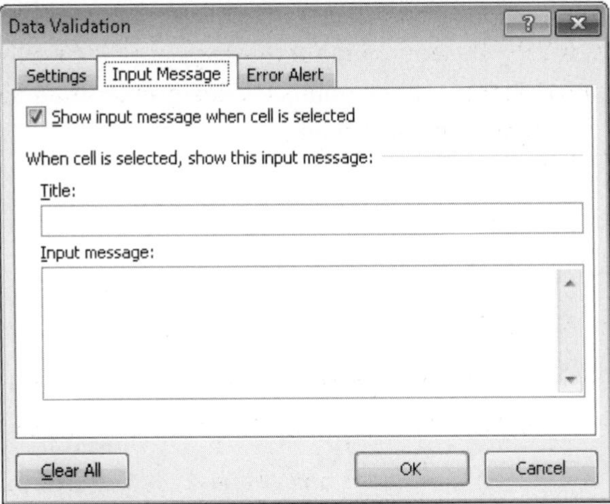

8. In the **Title** box, type **Enter Limit**.
9. In the **Input Message** box, type **Please enter the customer's credit limit, omitting the dollar sign and any commas**.
10. Click the **Error Alert** tab.

    The Error Alert page is displayed.
11. In the **Style** list, click **Stop**.

    The icon that appears on your message box changes to the Stop icon.

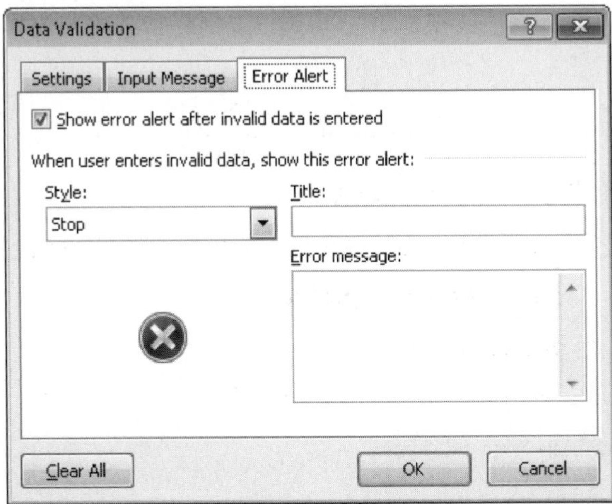

12. In the **Title** box, type **Error**, and then click **OK**.
13. Click cell **J7**.

    A ScreenTip with the title *Enter Limit* and the text *Please enter the customer's credit limit, omitting the dollar sign and any commas* appears near cell J7.

14. Type **25001**, and press Enter.

    A stop box with the title Error opens. Leaving the Error Message box blank in step 12 causes Excel to use its default message.

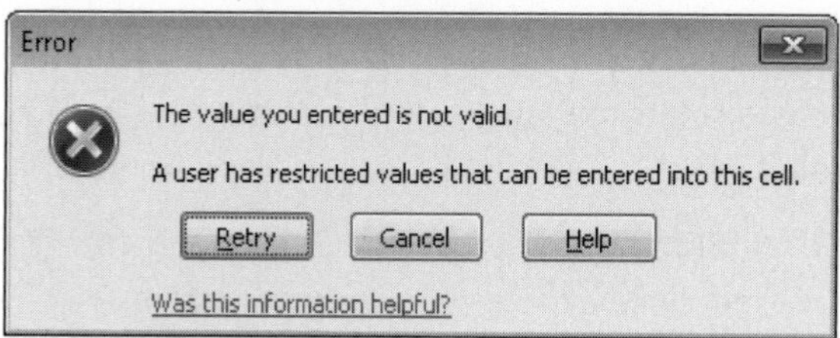

15. Click **Cancel**.

    The error box closes.

    Important Clicking Retry enables you to edit the bad value, whereas clicking Cancel deletes the entry.

16. Click cell **J7**.

    Cell J7 becomes the active cell, and the ScreenTip reappears.

17. Type **25000**, and press Enter.

    Excel accepts your input.

18. On the **Data** tab, in the **Data Tools** group, click the **Data Validation** arrow and then, in the list, click **Circle Invalid Data**.

    A red circle appears around the value in cell J4.

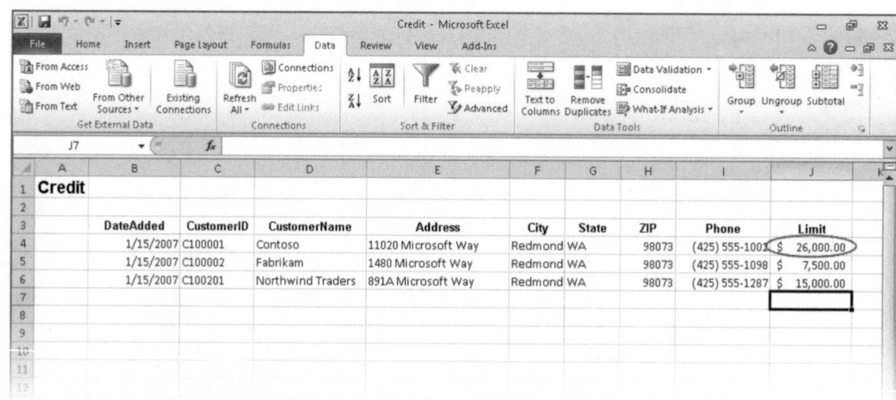

19. In the **Data Validation** list, click **Clear Validation Circles**.

    The red circle around the value in cell K4 disappears.

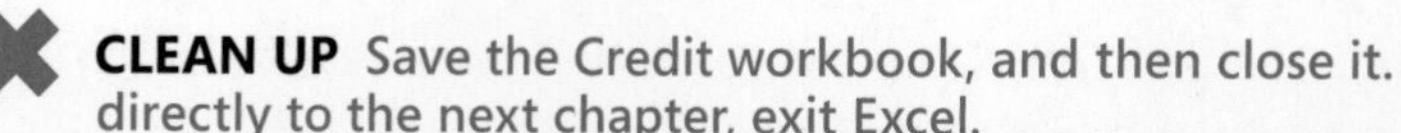

CLEAN UP Save the Credit workbook, and then close it. If you are not continuing directly to the next chapter, exit Excel.

Key Points

- A number of filters are defined in Excel. (You might find the one you want is already available.)
- Filtering an Excel worksheet based on values in a single column is easy to do, but you can create a custom filter to limit your data based on the values in more than one column as well.
- With the new search filter capability in Excel 2010, you can limit the data in your worksheets based on characters the terms contain.
- Don't forget that you can get a running total (or an average, or any one of several other summary operations) for the values in a group of cells. Just select the cells and look on the status bar: the result will be there.
- Use data validation techniques to improve the accuracy of data entered into your worksheets and to identify data that doesn't meet the guidelines you set.

Chapter at a Glance

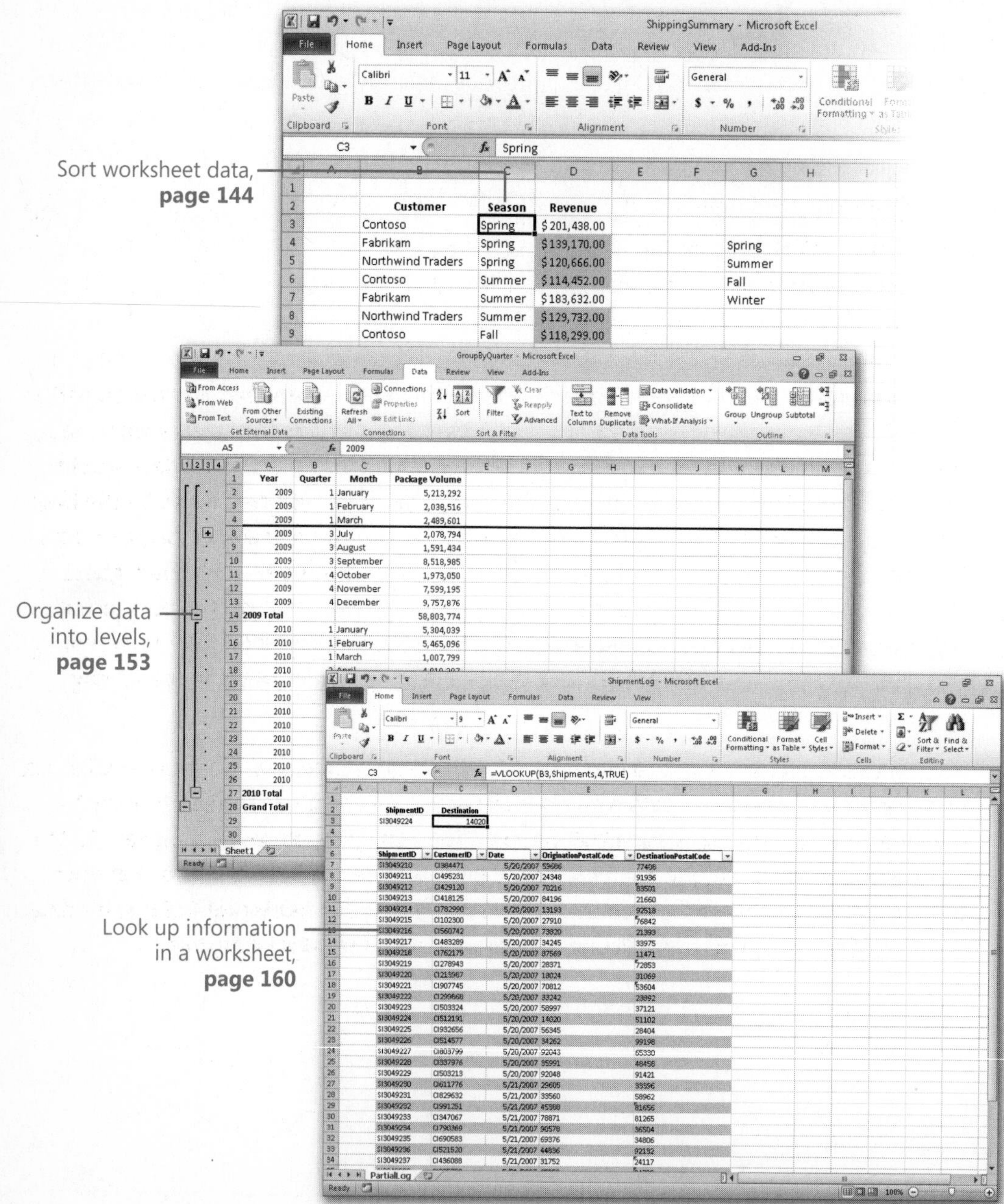

6 Reordering and Summarizing Data

In this chapter, you will learn how to

- ✔ Sort worksheet data.
- ✔ Organize data into levels.
- ✔ Look up information in a worksheet.

Most of the time, when you enter data in a Microsoft Excel worksheet, you will enter it in chronological order. For example, you could enter hourly shipment data in a worksheet, starting with the first hour of the day and ending with the last hour. The data would naturally be displayed in the order you entered it, but that might not always be the best arrangement to answer your questions. For instance, you might want to sort your data so that the top row in your worksheet shows the day of the month with the highest package volume, with subsequent rows displaying the remaining days in decreasing order of package volumes handled. You can also sort based on the contents of more than one column. A good example is sorting package handling data by week, day, and then hour of the day.

After you have sorted your data into the desired order with Excel, you can find partial totals, or subtotals, for groups of cells within a given range. Yes, you can create formulas to find the sum, average, or standard deviation of data in a cell range, but you can do the same thing much more quickly by having Excel calculate the total for rows that have the same value in one of their columns. For example, if your worksheet holds sales data for a list of services, you can calculate subtotals for each product category.

When you calculate subtotals in a worksheet, Excel creates an outline that marks the cell ranges used in each subtotal. For example, if the first 10 rows of a worksheet contain overnight shipping data, and the second 10 rows contain second-day shipping data, Excel divides the rows into two units. You can use the markers on the worksheet to hide or display the rows used to calculate a subtotal; in this case, you can hide all the rows that contain overnight shipping data, hide all the rows that contain second-day shipping data, hide both, or show both.

Excel also has a capability you might expect to find only in a database program—in Excel, you can type a value in a cell and have Excel look in a named range to find a corresponding value. For instance, you can have a two-column named range with one column displaying customer identification numbers and the second column displaying the name of the company assigned each number. By using a *VLOOKUP* formula that references the named range, you can let colleagues using your workbook type a customer identification number in a cell and have the name of the corresponding company appear in the cell with the formula.

In this chapter, you'll learn how to sort your data using one or more criteria, calculate subtotals, organize your data into levels, and look up information in a worksheet.

> **Practice Files** Before you can complete the exercises in this chapter, you need to copy the book's practice files to your computer. The practice files you'll use to complete the exercises in this chapter are in the Chapter06 practice file folder. A complete list of practice files is provided in "Using the Practice Files" at the beginning of this book.

Sorting Worksheet Data

Although Excel makes it easy to enter your business data and to manage it after you've saved it in a worksheet, unsorted data will rarely answer every question you want to ask it. For example, you might want to discover which of your services generates the most profits, which service costs the most for you to provide, and so on. You can discover that information by sorting your data.

When you sort data in a worksheet, you rearrange the worksheet rows based on the contents of cells in a particular column or set of columns. For instance, you can sort a worksheet to find your highest-revenue services.

You can sort a group of rows in a worksheet in a number of ways, but the first step is to identify the column that will provide the values by which the rows should be sorted. In the revenue example, you could find the highest revenue totals by sorting on the cells in the Revenue column. First you would select the cells in the Revenue column and display the Home tab. Then, in the Editing group, in the Sort & Filter list, click Sort Largest

To Smallest. Clicking Sort Largest To Smallest makes Excel put the row with the highest value in the Revenue column at the top of the worksheet and continue down to the lowest value.

Service	Revenue
Overnight	$ 1,598,643
3Day	$ 1,000,142
Ground	$ 994,775
2Day	$ 745,600
Priority Overnight	$ 502,991

If you want to sort the rows in the opposite order, from the lowest revenue to the highest, select the cells in the Revenue column and then, in the Sort & Filter list, click Sort Smallest To Largest.

Tip The exact set of values that appears in the Sort & Filter list changes to reflect the data in your column. If your column contains numerical values, you'll see the options Sort Largest To Smallest, Sort Smallest To Largest, and Custom List. If your column contains text values, the options will be Sort A To Z (ascending order), Sort Z To A (descending order), and Custom List. And if your column contains dates, you'll see Sort Newest To Oldest, Sort Oldest To Newest, and Custom List.

The Sort Smallest To Largest and Sort Largest To Smallest options enable you to sort rows in a worksheet quickly, but you can use them only to sort the worksheet based on the contents of one column, even though you might want to sort by two columns. For example, you might want to order the worksheet rows by service category and then by total so that you can see the customers that use each service category most frequently. You can sort rows in a worksheet by the contents of more than one column by using the Sort dialog box, in which you can pick any number of columns to use as sort criteria and choose whether to sort the rows in ascending or descending order.

To display the Sort dialog box, click Custom Sort in the Sort & Filter list.

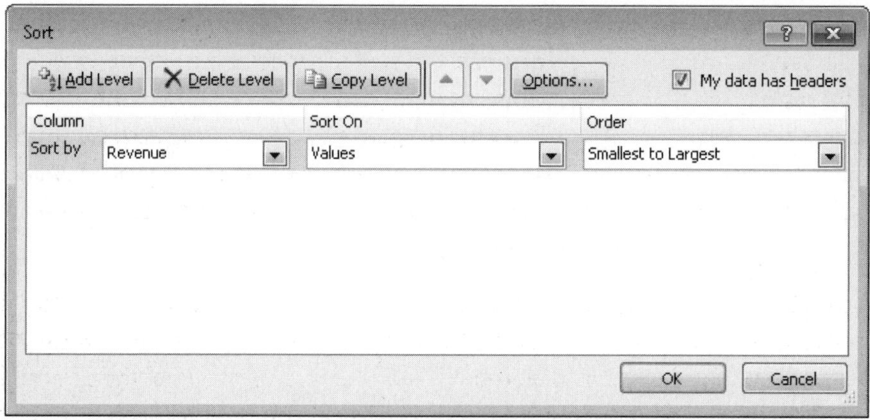

If your data has a header row, select the My Data Has Headers check box so the column headers will appear in the Sort By list. After you identify the column by which you want to sort, the Sort On list enables you to select whether you want to sort by a cell's value (the default), a cell's fill color, a cell's font color, or an icon displayed in the cell.

See Also For more information about creating conditional formats that change a cell's formatting or display icon to reflect the cell's value, see "Changing the Appearance of Data Based on Its Value" in Chapter 4, "Changing Workbook Appearance."

Finally, from the Order list, you can select how you want Excel to sort the column values. As with the Sort & Filter button's list, the exact values that appear in the Order list change to reflect the data you want to sort.

Adding, moving, copying, and deleting sorting levels are a matter of clicking the appropriate button in the Sort dialog box. To add a second level to your sort, click the Add Level button.

Tip In Excel 2003 and earlier versions of the program, you could define a maximum of three sorting levels. You can create up to 64 sorting levels in Excel 2010.

To delete a level, click the level in the list, and then click Delete Level. Clicking the Copy Level button enables you to put all the settings from one rule into another, saving you some work if you need to change only one item. The Move Up and Move Down buttons, which display an upward-pointing arrow and a downward-pointing arrow, respectively, enable you to change a sorting level's position in the order. Finally, clicking the Options button displays the Sort Options dialog box, which you can use to make a sorting level case sensitive and to change the orientation of the sort.

The default setting for Excel is to sort numbers according to their values and to sort words in alphabetical order, but that pattern doesn't work for some sets of values. One example in which sorting a list of values in alphabetical order would yield incorrect results is the months of the year. In an "alphabetical" calendar, April is the first month and September is the last! Fortunately, Excel recognizes a number of special lists, such as days of the week and months of the year. You can have Excel sort the contents of a worksheet based on values in a known list; if needed, you can create your own list of values. For example, the default lists of weekdays in Excel start with Sunday. If you keep your business records based on a Monday–Sunday week, you can create a new list with Monday as the first day and Sunday as the last.

To create a new list, type the list of values you want to use as your list into a contiguous cell range, select the cells, click the File tab, and then click Options. On the Advanced page of the Excel Options dialog box, in the General group near the bottom of the page, click the Edit Custom Lists button to display the Custom Lists dialog box.

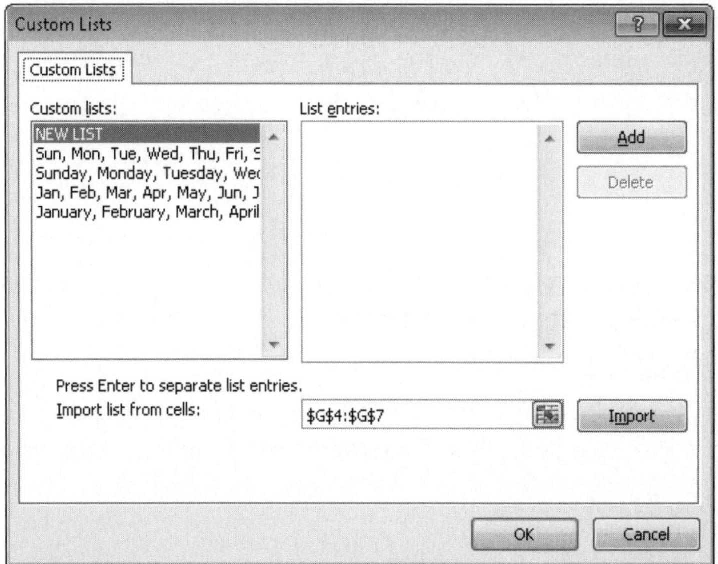

The selected cell range's reference appears in the Import List From Cells field. To record your list, click the Import button.

If you prefer, you can type the list in the List Entries box, to the right of the Custom Lists box.

Tip Another benefit of creating a custom list is that dragging the fill handle of a list cell that contains a value causes Excel to extend the series for you. For example, if you create the list *Spring, Summer, Fall, Winter*, then type Summer in a cell and drag the cell's fill handle, Excel extends the series as *Fall, Winter, Spring, Summer, Fall*, and so on.

To use a custom list as a sorting criterion, display the Sort dialog box, click the rule's Order arrow, click Custom List, and select your list from the dialog box that opens.

Tip In Excel 2003 and earlier, your custom list had to be the primary sorting criterion. In Excel 2010 and Excel 2007, you can use your custom list as any criterion.

In this exercise, you'll sort worksheet data, sort by multiple criteria, change the order in which sorting criteria are applied, sort data by using a custom list, and sort data by color.

SET UP You need the ShippingSummary_start workbook located in your Chapter06 practice file folder to complete this exercise. Start Excel, open the ShippingSummary_start workbook, and save it as *ShippingSummary*. Then follow the steps.

1. Click cell **C3**.

2. On the **Home** tab, in the **Editing** group, click the **Sort & Filter** button and then, in the list, click **Sort A to Z**.

   Excel sorts the data by season, with the seasons listed in alphabetical order.

3. In the **Sort & Filter** list, click **Custom Sort**.

   The Sort dialog box opens and displays the parameters of the sort you just applied.

4. If it's not already selected, select the **My data has headers** check box.
5. In the **Column** list, click **Customer**. If necessary, in the **Sort On** list, click **Values**; then in the **Order** list, click **A to Z**.
6. Click **Add Level**.

   A new Then By sorting level appears.

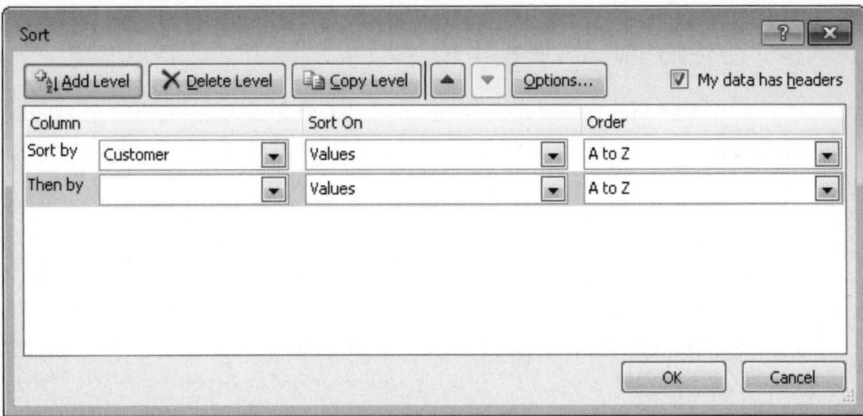

7. In the new **Column** list, click **Revenue**.
8. In the new **Order** list, click **Largest to Smallest**.
9. Click **OK**.

   Excel closes the Sort dialog box and sorts the data list.

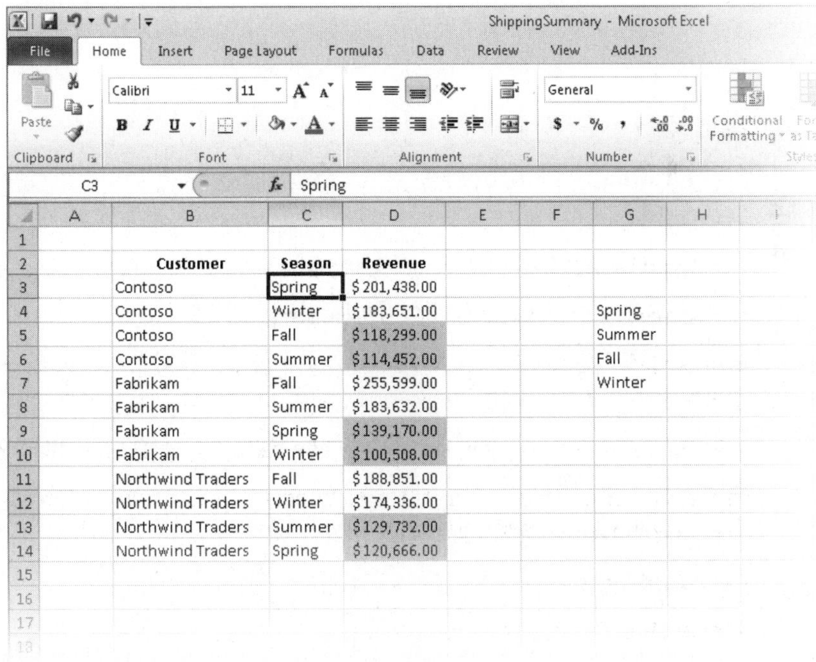

10. In the **Sort & Filter** list, click **Custom Sort**.

    The Sort dialog box opens.

11. Click **Then by**.

    Excel highlights the Revenue sorting rule.

12. Click the **Move Up** button.

    Excel moves the Revenue sorting rule above the Customer sorting rule.

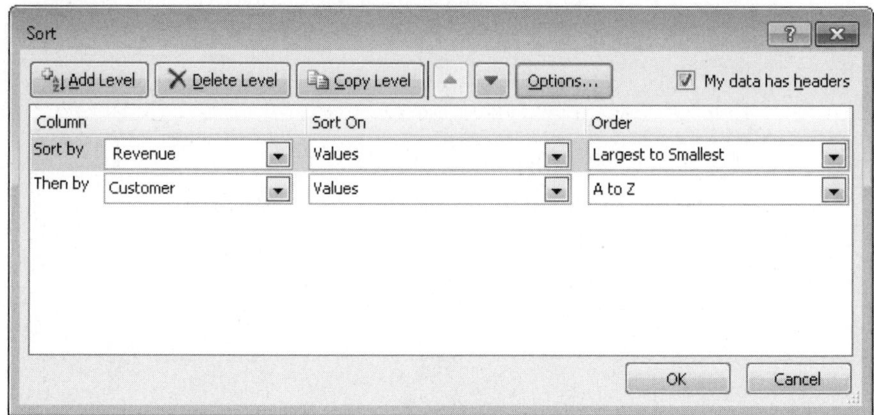

13. Click **OK**.

    Excel closes the Sort dialog box and sorts the data list.

14. Select cells **G4:G7**, click the **File** tab, and then click **Options**.

    The Excel Options dialog box opens.

15. On the **Advanced** page, in the **General** group toward the bottom of the page, click **Edit Custom Lists**.

    The Custom Lists dialog box opens.

16. Verify that the cell range **$G$4:$G$7** appears in the **Import list from cells** field, and then click **Import**.

    The new list appears in the Custom Lists pane.

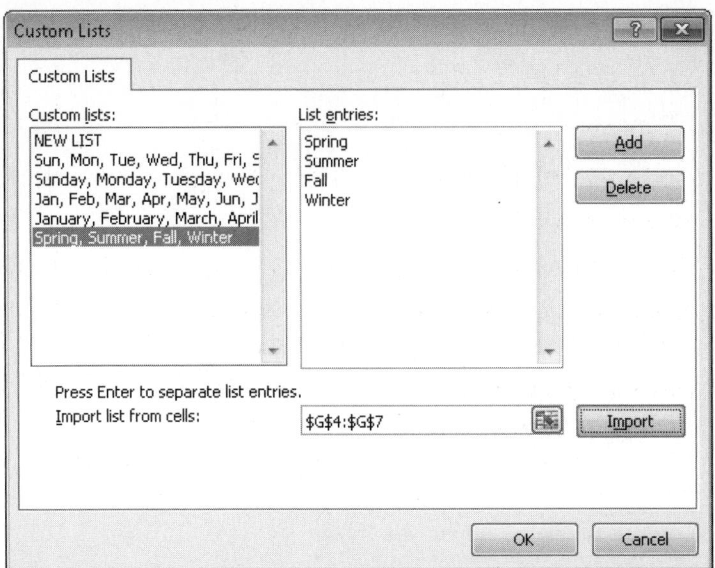

17. Click **OK** twice to close the **Custom Lists** dialog box and the **Excel Options** dialog box.
18. Click cell **C3**.
19. On the **Home** tab, in the **Editing** group, click **Sort & Filter**, and then click **Custom Sort**.

    The Sort dialog box opens, displaying the sorting operation you defined earlier.
20. Click the rule in the **Sort by** row, and then click **Delete Level**.

    The sorting rule disappears.
21. If necessary, in the new **Sort by** row, in the **Column** list, click **Season**.
22. In the same row, in the **Order** list, click **Custom List**.

    The Custom Lists dialog box opens.
23. In the **Custom lists** pane, click the sequence **Spring, Summer, Fall, Winter**.
24. Click **OK** twice to close the **Custom Lists** dialog box and the **Sort** dialog box.

    Excel sorts the data list.

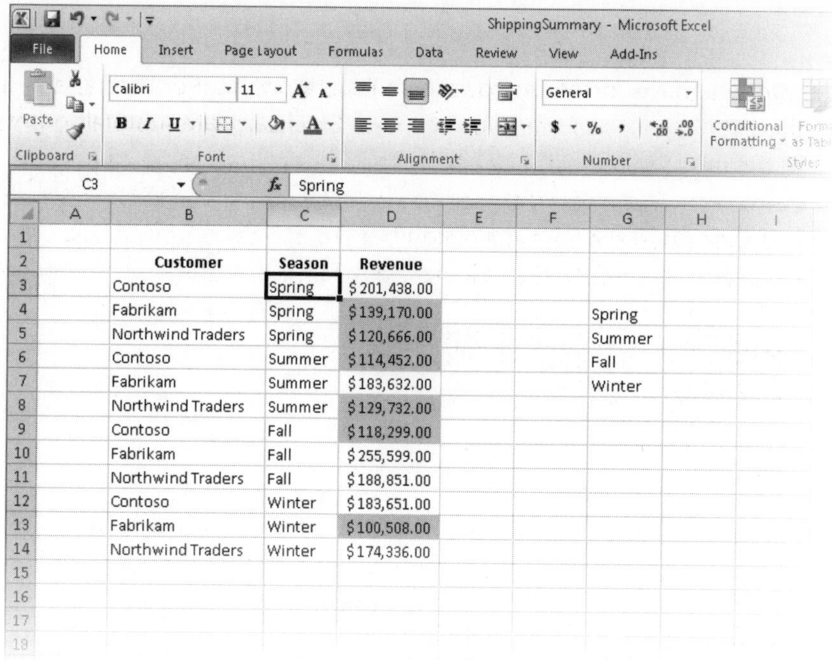

25. Click cell **C3**. Then on the **Home** tab, in the **Editing** group, click **Sort & Filter**, and click **Custom Sort.**

    The Sort dialog box opens.

26. In the **Sort by** row, in the **Column** list, click **Revenue**.
27. In the **Sort on** list, click **Cell Color**.
28. In the new list control that appears in the **Sort by** row, click **On Bottom** to have Excel put the Revenue cells that have no cell color on the bottom.
29. Click **OK**.

    Excel sorts the data list.

CLEAN UP Save the ShippingSummary workbook, and then close it.

Organizing Data into Levels

After you have sorted the rows in an Excel worksheet or entered the data so that it doesn't need to be sorted, you can have Excel calculate subtotals or totals for a portion of the data. In a worksheet with sales data for three different product categories, for example, you can sort the products by category, select all the cells that contain data, and then open the Subtotal dialog box. To open the Subtotal dialog box, display the Data tab and then, in the Outline group, click Subtotal.

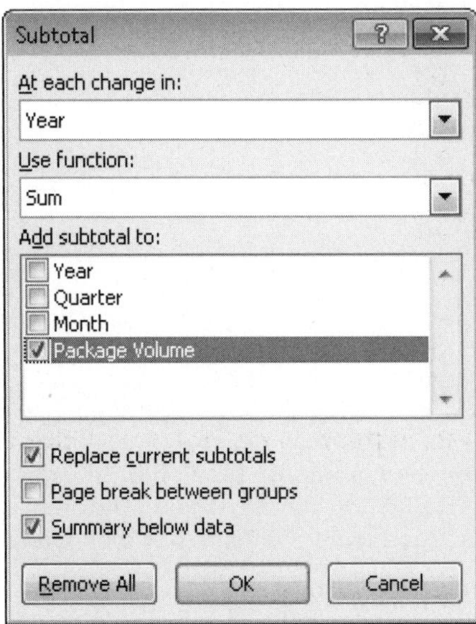

In the Subtotal dialog box, you can choose the column on which to base your subtotals (such as every change of value in the Week column), the summary calculation you want to perform, and the column or columns with values to be summarized. After you define your subtotals, they appear in your worksheet.

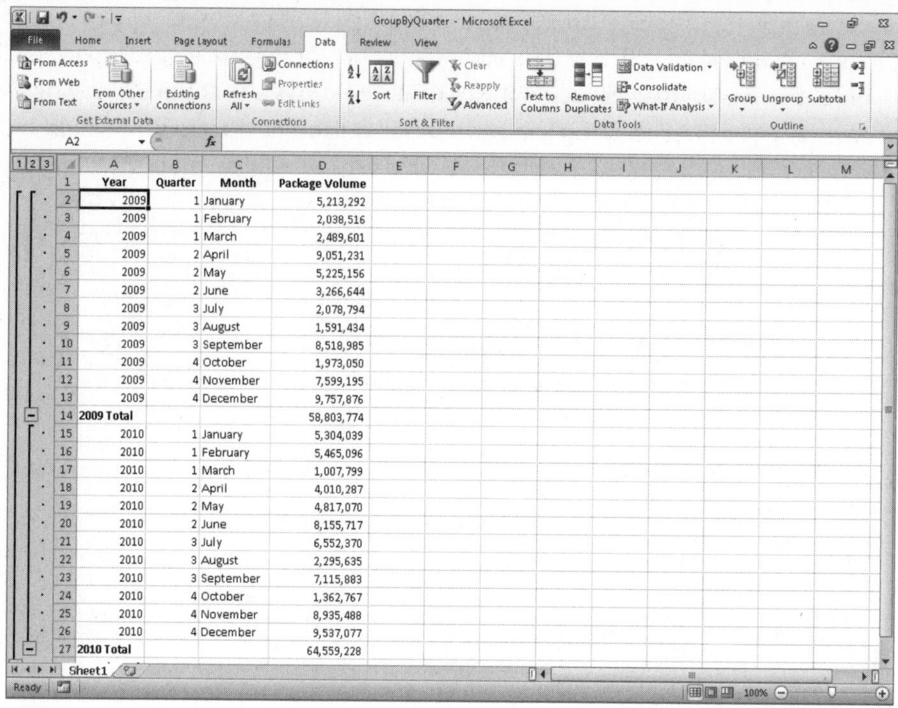

GroupByQuarter - Microsoft Excel
File
Home
Insert
Page Layout
Formulas
Data
Review
View
From Access
From Web
From Text
From Other Sources
Existing Connections
Refresh All
Connections
Properties
Edit Links
Sort
Filter
Clear
Reapply
Advanced
Text to Columns
Remove Duplicates
Data Validation
Consolidate
What-If Analysis
Group
Ungroup
Subtotal
Get External Data
Connections
Sort & Filter
Data Tools
Outline
A2
Year Quarter Month Package Volume
2009 1 January 5,213,292
2009 1 February 2,038,516
2009 1 March 2,489,601
2009 2 April 9,051,231
2009 2 May 5,225,156
2009 2 June 3,266,644
2009 3 July 2,078,794
2009 3 August 1,591,434
2009 3 September 8,518,985
2009 4 October 1,973,050
2009 4 November 7,599,195
2009 4 December 9,757,876
2009 Total 58,803,774
2010 1 January 5,304,039
2010 1 February 5,465,096
2010 1 March 1,007,799
2010 2 April 4,010,287
2010 2 May 4,817,070
2010 2 June 8,155,717
2010 3 July 6,552,370
2010 3 August 2,295,635
2010 3 September 7,115,883
2010 4 October 1,362,767
2010 4 November 8,935,488
2010 4 December 9,537,077
2010 Total 64,559,228
Sheet1
Ready
100%

Troubleshooting The appearance of buttons and groups on the ribbon changes depending on the width of the program window. For information about changing the appearance of the ribbon to match our screen images, see "Modifying the Display of the Ribbon" at the beginning of this book.

When you add subtotals to a worksheet, Excel also defines groups based on the rows used to calculate a subtotal. The groupings form an outline of your worksheet based on the criteria you used to create the subtotals. For example, all the rows representing months in the year 2009 could be in one group, rows representing months in 2010 in another, and so on. The outline area at the left of your worksheet holds controls you can use to hide or display groups of rows in your worksheet.

Three types of controls can appear in the outline area: Hide Detail buttons, Show Detail buttons, and level buttons. The Hide Detail button beside a group can be clicked to hide the rows in that group. In a worksheet that has a subtotal group consisting of rows 2 through 13, clicking the Hide Detail button next to row 14 would hide rows 2 through 13 but leave the row holding the subtotal for that group, row 14, visible.

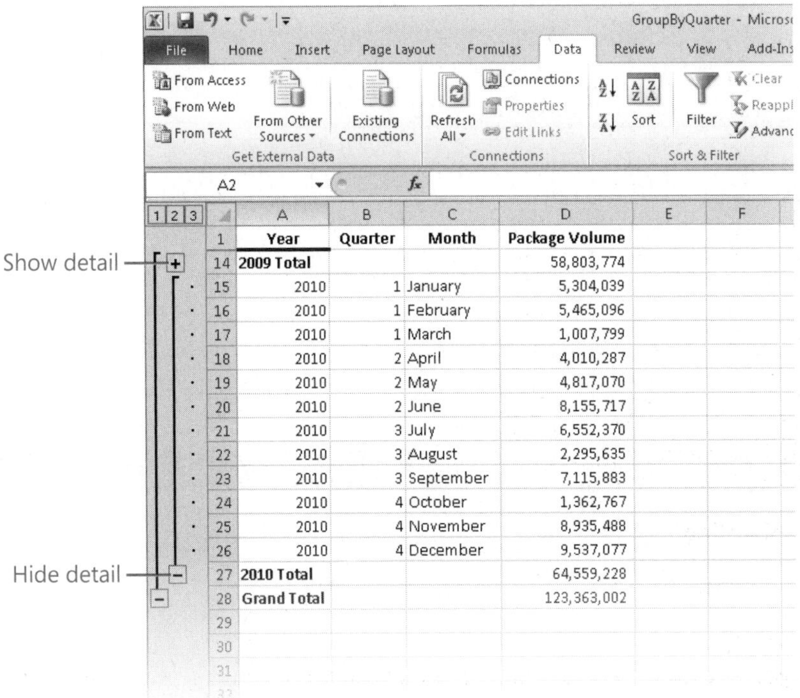

	A	B	C	D
1	Year	Quarter	Month	Package Volume
14	2009 Total			58,803,774
15	2010	1	January	5,304,039
16	2010	1	February	5,465,096
17	2010	1	March	1,007,799
18	2010	2	April	4,010,287
19	2010	2	May	4,817,070
20	2010	2	June	8,155,717
21	2010	3	July	6,552,370
22	2010	3	August	2,295,635
23	2010	3	September	7,115,883
24	2010	4	October	1,362,767
25	2010	4	November	8,935,488
26	2010	4	December	9,537,077
27	2010 Total			64,559,228
28	Grand Total			123,363,002

When you hide a group of rows, the button displayed next to the group changes to a Show Detail button. Clicking a group's Show Detail button restores the rows in the group to the worksheet.

The level buttons are the other buttons in the outline area of a worksheet with subtotals. Each button represents a level of organization in a worksheet; clicking a level button hides all levels of detail below that of the button you clicked. The following table describes the data contained at each level of a worksheet with three levels of organization.

Level	Description
1	Grand total
2	Subtotals for each group
3	Individual rows in the worksheet

Clicking the Level 2 button in the worksheet would hide the rows with data on, for example, each month's revenue but would leave the row that contains the grand total (Level 1) and all rows that contain the subtotal for each year (Level 2) visible in the worksheet.

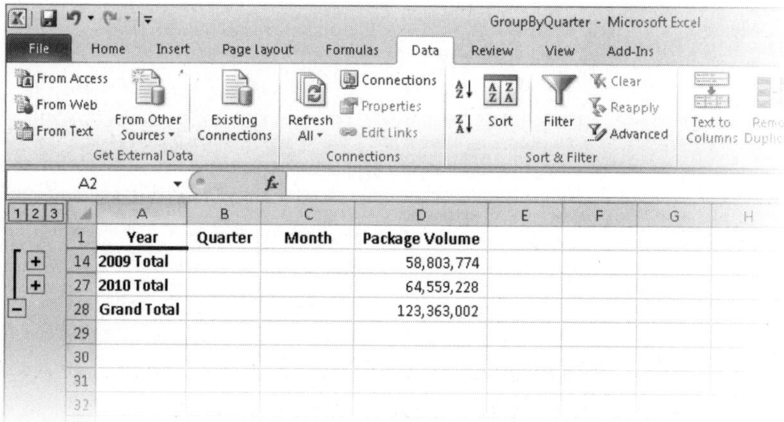

If you like, you can add levels of detail to the outline that Excel creates. For example, you might want to be able to hide revenues from January and February, which you know are traditionally strong months. To create a new outline group within an existing group, select the rows you want to group; on the Data tab, in the Outline group, point to Group, and then click Group.

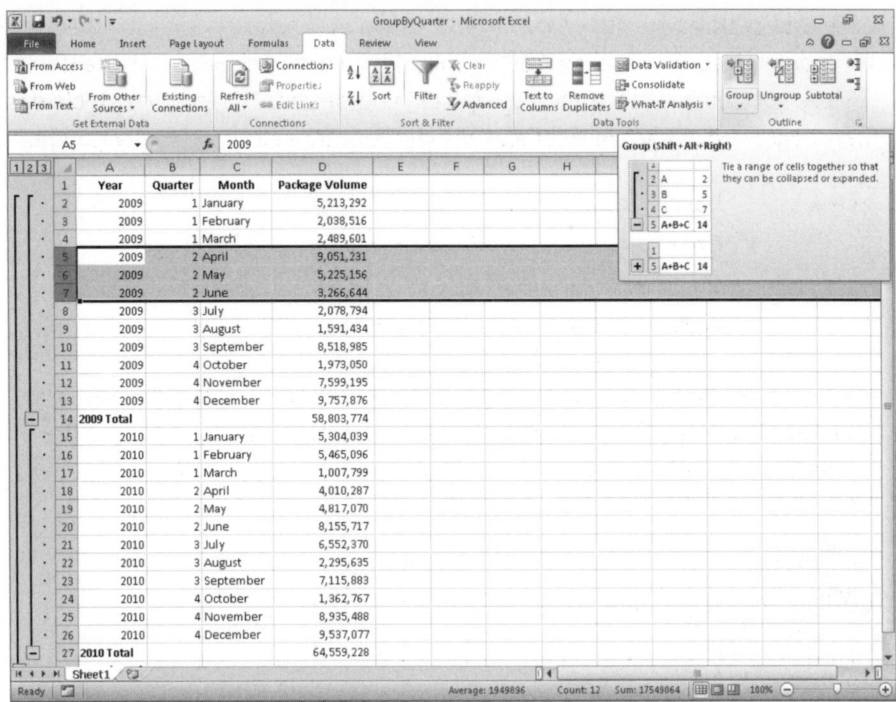

You can remove a group by selecting the rows in the group and then, in the Outline group, clicking Ungroup.

Tip If you want to remove all subtotals from a worksheet, open the Subtotal dialog box, and click the Remove All button.

In this exercise, you'll add subtotals to a worksheet and then use the outline that appears to show and hide different groups of data in your worksheet.

SET UP You need the GroupByQuarter_start workbook located in your Chapter06 practice file folder to complete this exercise. Open the GroupByQuarter_start workbook, and save it as *GroupByQuarter*. Then follow the steps.

1. Click any cell in the data list.

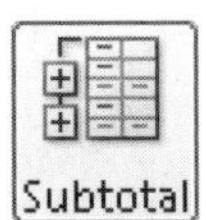

2. On the **Data** tab, in the **Outline** group, click **Subtotal**.

   The Subtotal dialog box opens with the default options to add a subtotal at every change in the Year column, to return the sum of the values in the subtotaled rows, and to add a row with the subtotal of values in the Package Volume column below the final selected row.

3. Click **OK**.

   The Subtotal dialog box closes. New rows appear with subtotals for package volume during each year represented in the worksheet. The new rows are numbered 14 and 27. A row with the grand total of all rows also appears; that row is row 28. A new area with outline bars and group-level indicators appears to the left of column A.

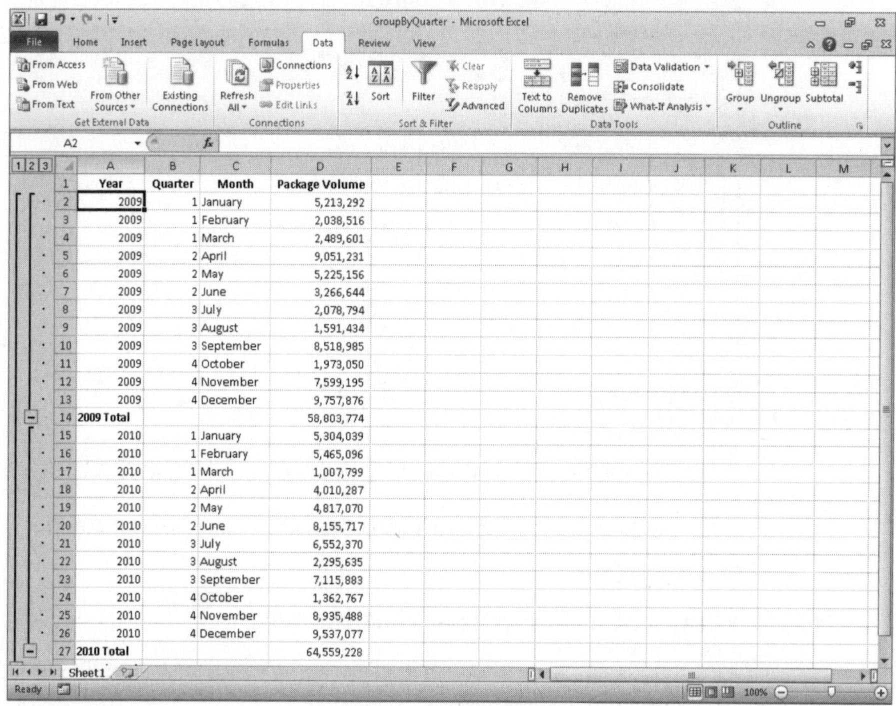

	A	B	C	D
1	Year	Quarter	Month	Package Volume
2	2009	1	January	5,213,292
3	2009	1	February	2,038,516
4	2009	1	March	2,489,601
5	2009	2	April	9,051,231
6	2009	2	May	5,225,156
7	2009	2	June	3,266,644
8	2009	3	July	2,078,794
9	2009	3	August	1,591,434
10	2009	3	September	8,518,985
11	2009	4	October	1,973,050
12	2009	4	November	7,599,195
13	2009	4	December	9,757,876
14	2009 Total			58,803,774
15	2010	1	January	5,304,039
16	2010	1	February	5,465,096
17	2010	1	March	1,007,799
18	2010	2	April	4,010,287
19	2010	2	May	4,817,070
20	2010	2	June	8,155,717
21	2010	3	July	6,552,370
22	2010	3	August	2,295,635
23	2010	3	September	7,115,883
24	2010	4	October	1,362,767
25	2010	4	November	8,935,488
26	2010	4	December	9,537,077
27	2010 Total			64,559,228

4. Click the row heading of row **5**, and drag to the row heading of row **7**.

   Rows 5 through 7 are selected.

5. On the **Data** tab, in the **Outline** group, click **Group**.

   Rows 5 through 7 are made into a new group. An outline bar appears on a new level in the outline area, and a corresponding Level 4 button appears at the top of the outline area.

6. In the outline area, click the **Hide Detail** button next to row **8**.

   Rows 5 through 7 are hidden, and the Hide Detail button you clicked changes to a Show Detail button.

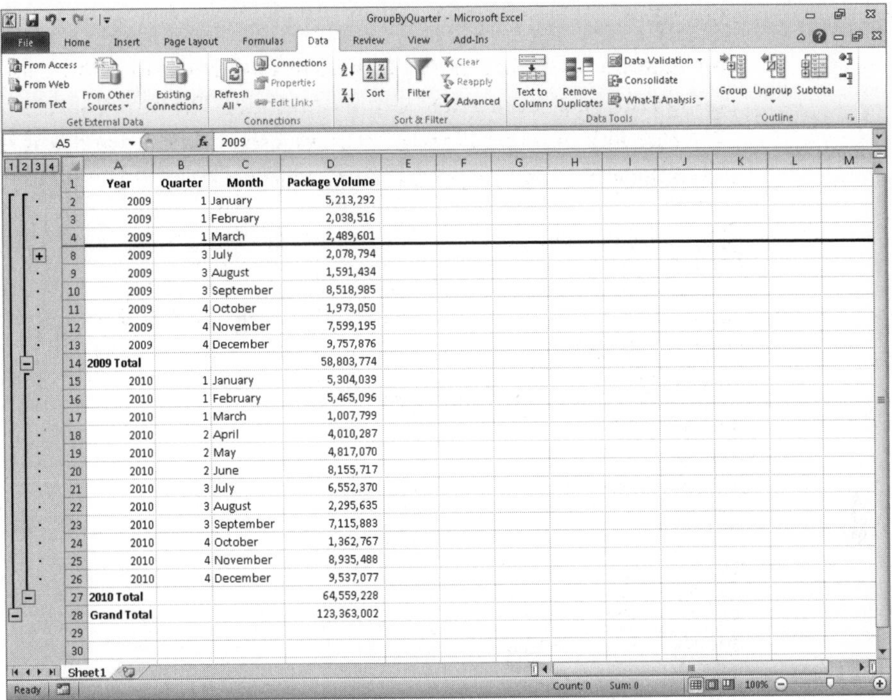

	A	B	C	D
1	Year	Quarter	Month	Package Volume
2	2009	1	January	5,213,292
3	2009	1	February	2,038,516
4	2009	1	March	2,489,601
8	2009	3	July	2,078,794
9	2009	3	August	1,591,434
10	2009	3	September	8,518,985
11	2009	4	October	1,973,050
12	2009	4	November	7,599,195
13	2009	4	December	9,757,876
14	2009 Total			58,803,774
15	2010	1	January	5,304,039
16	2010	1	February	5,465,096
17	2010	1	March	1,007,799
18	2010	2	April	4,010,287
19	2010	2	May	4,817,070
20	2010	2	June	8,155,717
21	2010	3	July	6,552,370
22	2010	3	August	2,295,635
23	2010	3	September	7,115,883
24	2010	4	October	1,362,767
25	2010	4	November	8,935,488
26	2010	4	December	9,537,077
27	2010 Total			64,559,228
28	Grand Total			123,363,002

7. In the outline area, click the **Show Detail** button next to row **8**.

   Rows 5 through 7 reappear.

8. In the outline area, click the **Level 1** button.

   All rows except row 1 with the column headings and row 28 with the grand total are hidden.

9. In the outline area, click the **Level 2** button.

   The rows with the subtotal for each year appear.

10. In the outline area, click the **Level 3** button.

    All rows except rows 5 through 7 appear.

11. In the outline area, click the **Level 4** button.

    Rows 5 through 7 reappear.

CLEAN UP Save the GroupByQuarter workbook, and then close it.

Looking Up Information in a Worksheet

Whenever you create a worksheet that holds information about a list of distinct items, such as products offered for sale by a company, you should ensure that at least one column in the list contains a unique value that distinguishes that row (and the item the row represents) from every other row in the list. Assigning each row a column that contains a unique value means that you can associate data in one list with data in another list. For example, if you assign every customer a unique identification number, you can store a customer's contact information in one worksheet and all orders for that customer in another worksheet. You can then associate the customer's orders and contact information without writing the contact information in a worksheet every time the customer places an order.

In the case of shipments handled by Consolidated Messenger, the column that contains those unique values, also known as the primary key column, is the ShipmentID column.

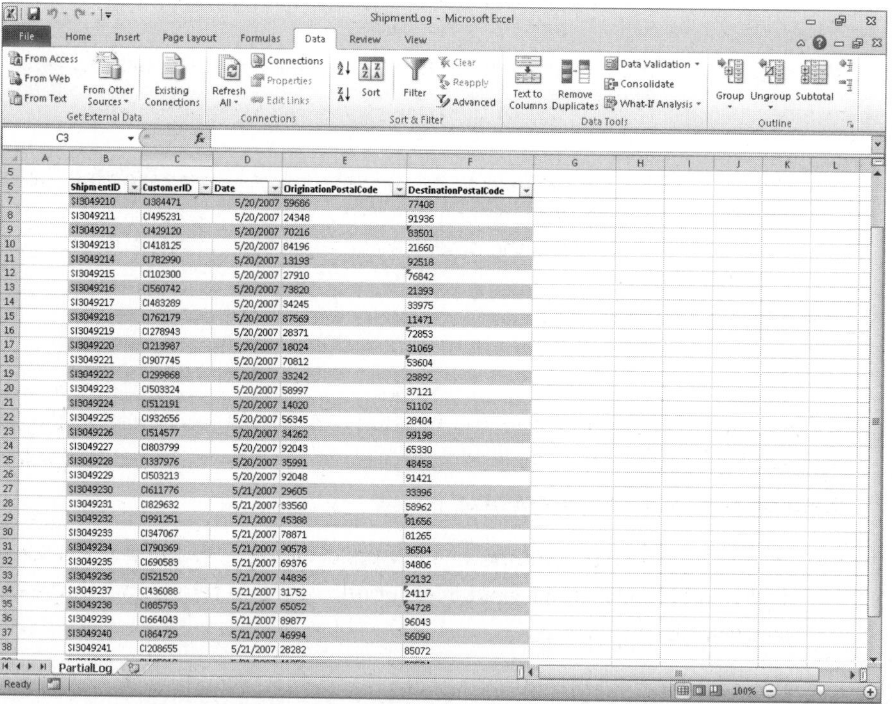

If you know a shipment's ShipmentID, it's no trouble to look through a list of 20 or 30 items to find a particular shipment. If, however, you have a list of many thousands of shipments, looking through the list to find one would take quite a bit of time. Instead, you can use the *VLOOKUP* function to let your colleagues type a ShipmentID in a cell and have the corresponding details appear in another cell.

The *VLOOKUP* function finds a value in the leftmost column of a named range, such as a table, and then returns the value from the specified cell to the right of the cell with the found value. A properly formed *VLOOKUP* function has four arguments (data that is passed to the function), as shown in the following definition: *=VLOOKUP(lookup_value, table_array, col_index_num, range_lookup).*

The following table summarizes the values Excel expects for each of these arguments.

Argument	**Expected value**
lookup_value	The value to be found in the first column of the named range specified by the *table_array* argument. The *lookup_value* argument can be a value, a cell reference, or a text string.
table_array	The multicolumn range or name of the range or data table to be searched.
col_index_num	The number of the column in the named range with the value to be returned.
range_lookup	A *TRUE* or *FALSE* value, indicating whether the function should find an approximate match (*TRUE*) or an exact match (*FALSE*) for the *lookup_value*. If left blank, the default value for this argument is *TRUE*.

Important When *range_lookup* is left blank or set to *TRUE*, for *VLOOKUP* to work properly the rows in the named range specified in the *table_array* argument must be sorted in ascending order based on the values in the leftmost column of the named range.

The *VLOOKUP* function works a bit differently depending on whether the *range_lookup* argument is set to *TRUE* or *FALSE*. The following list summarizes how the function works based on the value of *range_lookup*:

- If the *range_lookup* argument is left blank or set to *TRUE*, and *VLOOKUP* doesn't find an exact match for *lookup_value*, the function returns the largest value that is less than *lookup_value*.
- If the *range_lookup* argument is left blank or set to *TRUE*, and *lookup_value* is smaller than the smallest value in the named range, an *#N/A* error is returned.

- If the *range_lookup* argument is left blank or set to *TRUE*, and *lookup_value* is larger than all values in the named range, the largest value in the named range is returned.
- If the *range_lookup* argument is set to *FALSE*, and *VLOOKUP* doesn't find an exact match for *lookup_value*, the function returns an *#N/A* error.

As an example of a *VLOOKUP* function, consider the following data, which shows an Excel table with its headers in row 2 and the first column in column B of the worksheet.

CustomerID	Customer
CI01	Fabrikam
CI02	Northwind Traders
CI03	Tailspin Toys
CI04	Contoso

If the *=VLOOKUP (E3, Table1, 2, TRUE)* formula is used, when you type *CI02* in cell E3 and press Enter, the *VLOOKUP* function searches the first column of the table, finds an exact match, and returns the value *Northwind Traders* to cell F3.

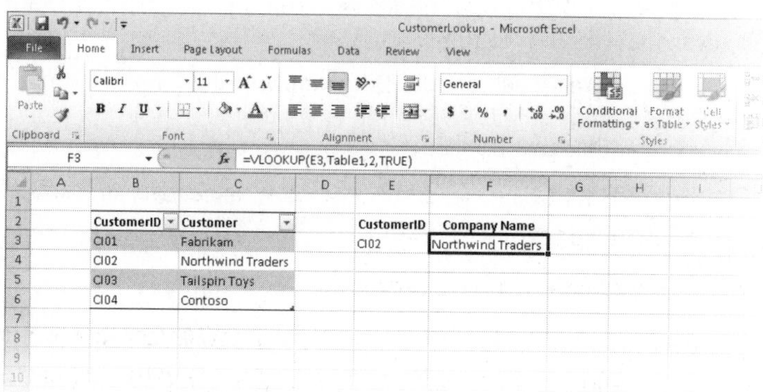

Tip The relatedHLOOKUP function matches a value in a column of the first row of a table and returns the value in the specified row number of the same column. The letter "H" in the *HLOOKUP* function name refers to the horizontal layout of the data, just as the "V" in the *VLOOKUP* function name refers to the data's vertical layout. For more information on using the *HLOOKUP* function, click the Excel Help button, type *HLOOKUP* in the search terms box, and then click Search.

Important Be sure to give the cell in which you type the *VLOOKUP* formula the same format as the data you want the formula to display. For example, if you create a *VLOOKUP* formula in cell G14 that finds a date, you must apply a date cell format to cell G14 for the result of the formula to display properly.

In this exercise, you'll create a *VLOOKUP* function to return the destination postal code of deliveries with ShipmentIDs typed in a specific cell.

SET UP You need the ShipmentLog_start workbook located in your Chapter06 practice file folder to complete this exercise. Open the ShipmentLog_start workbook, and save it as *ShipmentLog*. Then follow the steps.

1. In cell **C3**, type the formula **=VLOOKUP(B3, Shipments, 5, FALSE)**.

   Cell B3, which the formula uses to look up values in the Shipments table, is blank, so the *#N/A* error code appears in cell C3.

2. In cell **B3**, type **SI3049224**, and press Enter.

   The value *51102* appears in cell C3.

3. In cell **C3**, edit the formula so that it reads **=VLOOKUP(B3, Shipments, 2, FALSE)**.

   The formula now finds its target value in table column 2 (the CustomerID column), so the value *CI512191* appears in cell C3.

4. In cell **C3**, edit the formula so that it reads **=VLOOKUP(B3, Shipments, 4, TRUE)**.

   Changing the last argument to *TRUE* enables the *VLOOKUP* formula to find an approximate match for the ShipmentID in cell B3, whereas changing the column to *4* means the formula gets its result from the OriginationPostalCode column. The value *14020* appears in cell C3.

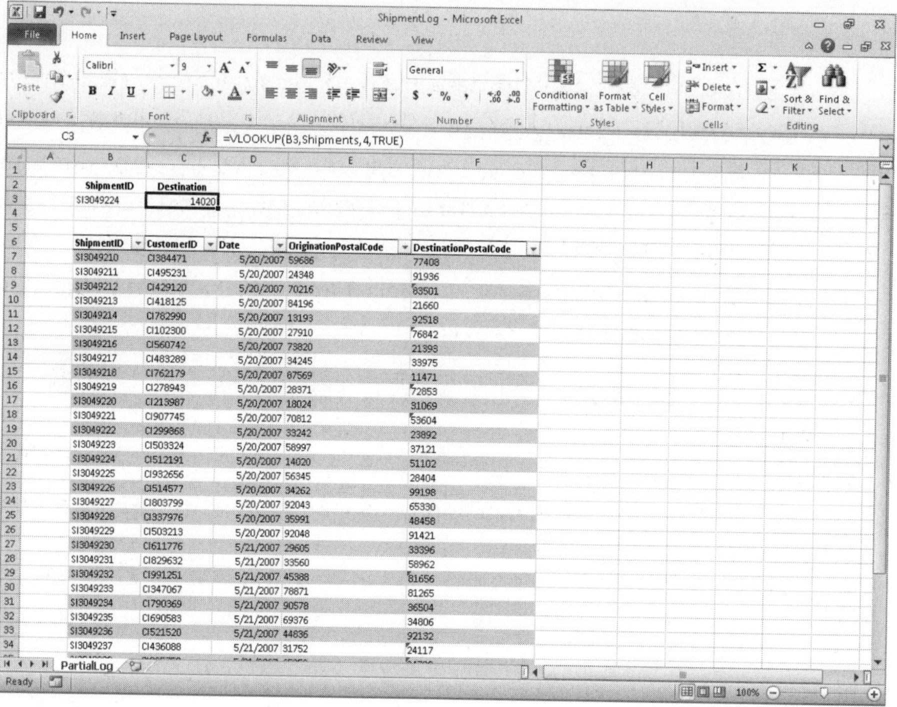

5. In cell **B3**, type **SI3049209**.

   The value in cell B3 is smaller than the smallest value in the Shipments table's first column, so the *VLOOKUP* formula displays the *#N/A* error code in cell C3.

6. In cell **B3**, type **SI3049245**.

   The ShipmentID typed into cell B3 is greater than the last value in the table's first column, so the *VLOOKUP* formula displays the last value in the target column (in this case, the fourth column). Therefore, the value *44493* appears in cell C3.

CLEAN UP Save the ShipmentLog workbook, and then close it. If you are not continuing directly to the next chapter, exit Excel.

Key Points

- You can rearrange the data in a worksheet quickly by clicking either the Sort Ascending or Sort Descending button in the Sort & Filter group on the Data tab.
- Don't forget that you can sort the rows in a worksheet by using orders other than alphabetical or numerical. For example, you can sort a series of days based on their order in the week or by cell color.
- If none of the existing sort orders (days, weekdays, and so on) meets your needs, you can create your own custom sort order.
- You can divide the data in your worksheet into levels and find a subtotal for each level.
- Creating subtotals enables you to show or hide groups of data in your worksheets.
- Use the *VLOOKUP* function to look up a value in one column of data and return a value from another column in the same row.

Chapter at a Glance

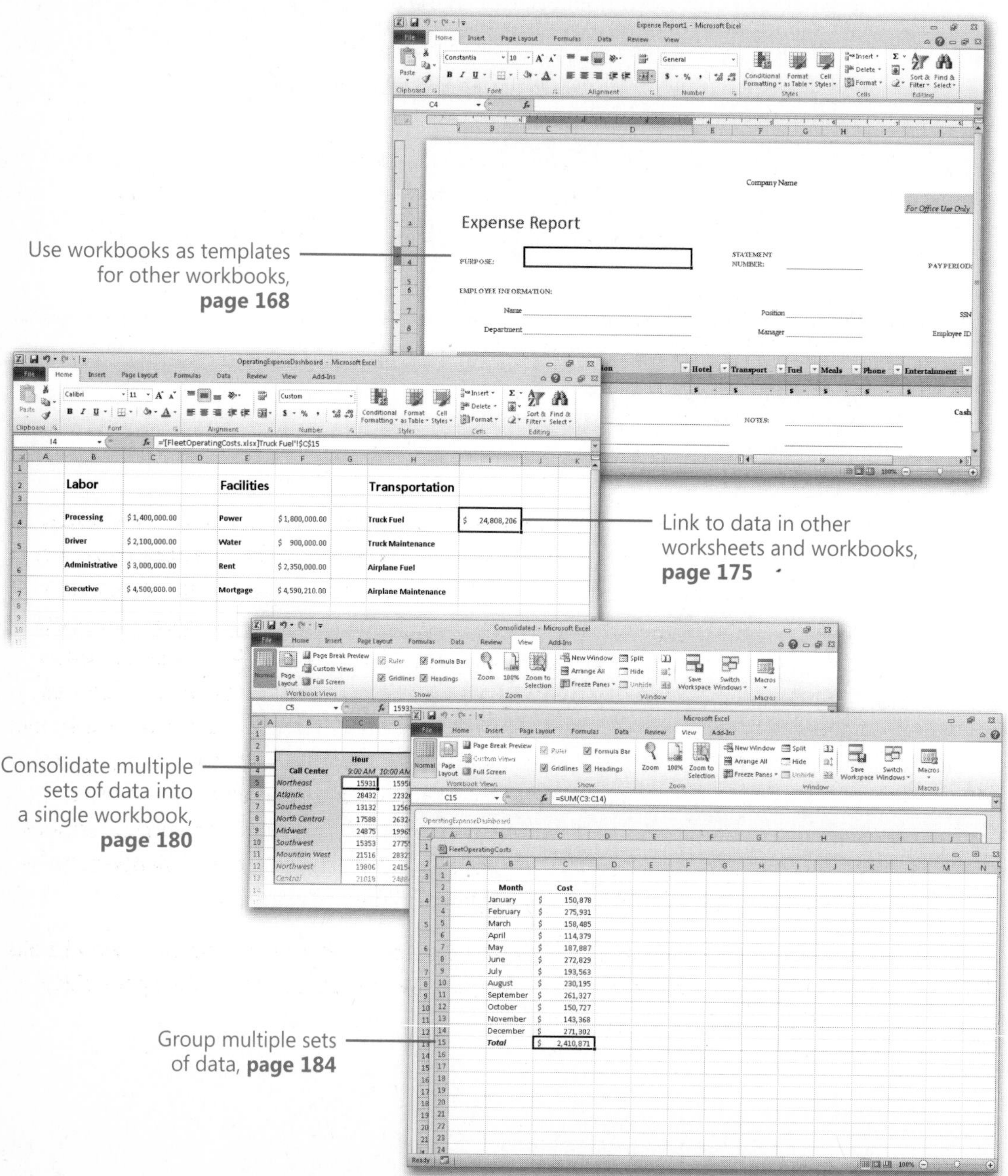

Use workbooks as templates for other workbooks, **page 168**

Link to data in other worksheets and workbooks, **page 175**

Consolidate multiple sets of data into a single workbook, **page 180**

Group multiple sets of data, **page 184**

7 Combining Data from Multiple Sources

In this chapter, you will learn how to

- ✔ Use workbooks as templates for other workbooks.
- ✔ Link to data in other worksheets and workbooks.
- ✔ Consolidate multiple sets of data into a single workbook.
- ✔ Group multiple sets of data.

Microsoft Excel 2010 gives you a wide range of tools with which to format, summarize, and present your data. After you have created a workbook to hold data about a particular subject, you can create as many worksheets as you need to make that data easier to find within your workbook. For example, you can create a workbook to store sales data for a year, with each worksheet representing a month in that year. To ensure that every year's workbook has a similar appearance, you can create a workbook with the desired characteristics (such as more than the standard number of worksheets, custom worksheet formatting, or a particular color for the workbook's sheet tabs) and save it as a pattern, or *template*, for similar workbooks you will create in the future. The benefit of ensuring that all your sales data worksheets have the same layout is that you and your colleagues immediately know where to look for specific totals. You can use that knowledge to summarize, or consolidate, that data into a single worksheet.

If you work with the same set of workbooks repeatedly, you can group those workbooks in a special type of Excel file called a *workspace*. When you open the workspace, Excel knows to open the files you included in that workspace.

A consequence of organizing your data into different workbooks and worksheets is that you need ways to manage, combine, and summarize data from more than one Excel document. You can always copy data from one worksheet to another, but if the original value were to change, that change would not be reflected in the cell range to which you copied the data. Rather than remembering which cells you need to update when a value changes, you can create a link to the original cell. That way, Excel will update the value for you whenever you open the workbook. If multiple worksheets hold related values, you can use links to summarize those values in a single worksheet.

In this chapter, you'll learn how to use a workbook as a template for other workbooks, work with more than one set of data, link to data in other workbooks, summarize multiple sets of data, and group multiple workbooks.

Practice Files Before you can complete the exercises in this chapter, you need to copy the book's practice files to your computer. The practice files you'll use to complete the exercises in this chapter are in the Chapter07 practice file folder. A complete list of practice files is provided in "Using the Practice Files" at the beginning of this book.

Using Workbooks as Templates for Other Workbooks

After you decide on the type of data you want to store in a workbook and what that workbook should look like, you probably want to be able to create similar workbooks without adding all of the formatting and formulas again. For example, you might have established a design for your monthly sales-tracking workbook.

When you have settled on a design for your workbooks, you can save one of the workbooks as a template for similar workbooks you will create in the future. You can leave the workbook's labels to aid data entry, but you should remove any existing data from a workbook that you save as a template, both to avoid data entry errors and to remove any confusion as to whether the workbook is a template. You can also remove any worksheets you and your colleagues won't need by right-clicking the tab of an unneeded worksheet and, on the shortcut menu that appears, clicking Delete.

If you want your template workbook to have more than the standard number of worksheets (such as 12 worksheets to track shipments for a year, by month), you can add worksheets by clicking the Insert Worksheet button that appears to the right of the existing worksheet tabs.

To create a template from an existing workbook, save the model workbook as an Excel template file (a file with an .xltx extension), which is a file format you can choose from the Save As Type list in the Save As dialog box. If you ever want to change the template, you can open it like a standard workbook and make your changes. When you have completed your work, save the file by clicking the Save button on the Quick Access Toolbar—it will still be a template.

Tip You can also save your Excel 2010 workbook either as an Excel 97–2003 template (.xlt) or as a macro-enabled Excel 2010 workbook template (.xltm). For information on using macros in Excel 2010 workbooks, see "Introducing Macros" in Chapter 12, "Automating Repetitive Tasks by Using Macros."

After you save a workbook as a template, you can use it as a model for new workbooks. To create a workbook from a template in Excel, click the File tab to display the Backstage view, and then click New.

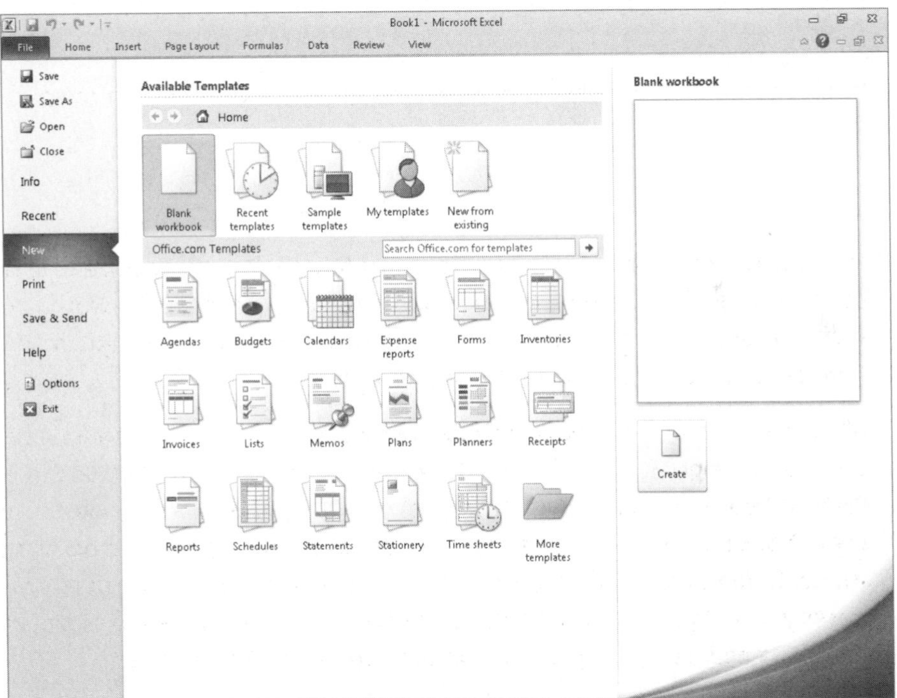

When you click New in the Backstage view, the top of the middle pane displays the blank workbook template, templates you have used recently, sample templates, and templates you created. Below that list is a set of template categories available through the Office.com Web site and a search box you can use to locate helpful templates on Office.com.

Tip When you display the New page of the Backstage view, you can also find templates and other tools related to your job functions by clicking the More Templates folder at the bottom of the Office.com Templates area of the page.

From the list of available templates, you can double-click the template you want to use as the model for your workbook. Excel creates a new workbook (an .xlsx workbook file, not an .xlst template file) with the template's formatting and contents in place.

In addition to creating a workbook template, you can create a template to add as a worksheet within an existing workbook. To create a worksheet template, design the worksheet you want to use as a template, delete all the other worksheets in that workbook, and save the single-sheet workbook as a template. You can then add a worksheet based on that template to your workbook by right-clicking a sheet tab and then clicking Insert to display the Insert dialog box.

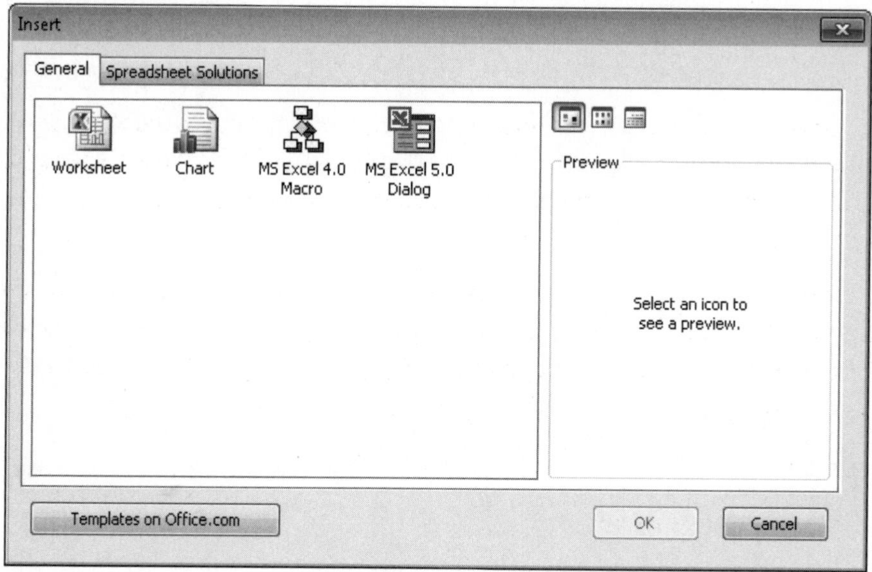

The Insert dialog box splits its contents into two pages. The General page contains icons you can click to insert a blank worksheet, a chart sheet, and any worksheet templates you have created.

Tip The other two options on the General page, MS Excel 4.0 Macro and MS Excel 5.0 Dialog, are there to help users integrate older Excel spreadsheet solutions into Excel 2010.

The Spreadsheet Solutions page contains a set of useful templates for a variety of financial and personal tasks.

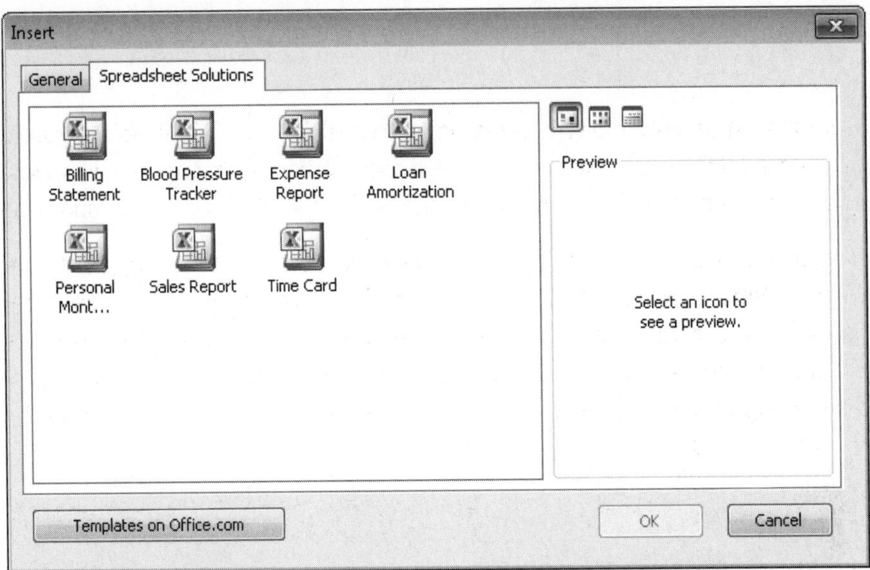

To add a spreadsheet from the Insert dialog box to your workbook, click the desired template, and then click OK. When you click a template, a preview of that template's contents appears in the preview pane, so you can verify you've selected the template you want.

In this exercise, you'll create a workbook from an existing template, save a template to track hourly call volumes to each regional center, save another version of the file as a worksheet template, and insert a worksheet based on that template into a new workbook.

SET UP You need the DailyCallSummary_start workbook located in your Chapter07 practice file folder to complete this exercise. Start Excel, open the DailyCallSummary_start workbook, and save it as *DailyCallSummary*. Then follow the steps.

1. Click the **File** tab, and then click **Save As**.

   The Save As dialog box opens.

2. In the **Save as type** list, click **Excel Template**.

   Excel displays the default Microsoft Office template folder.

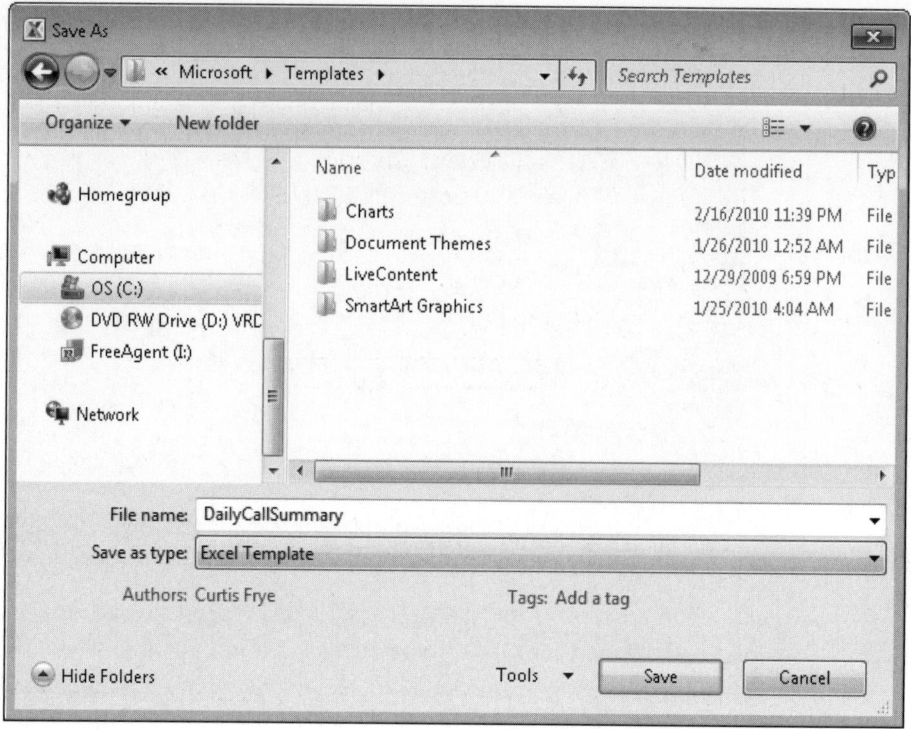

3. Click **Save**.

   Excel saves the workbook as a template and closes the Save As dialog box.

4. Click the **File** tab, and then click **Close**.

   Excel closes the DailyCallSummary workbook.

5. Click the **File** tab, and then click **New**.

   The New Workbook dialog box opens.

6. In the **Available Templates** list, click **Sample Templates**.

   The Sample Templates gallery appears.

7. Click **Expense Report**, and then click **Create**.

   Excel creates a workbook based on the selected template.

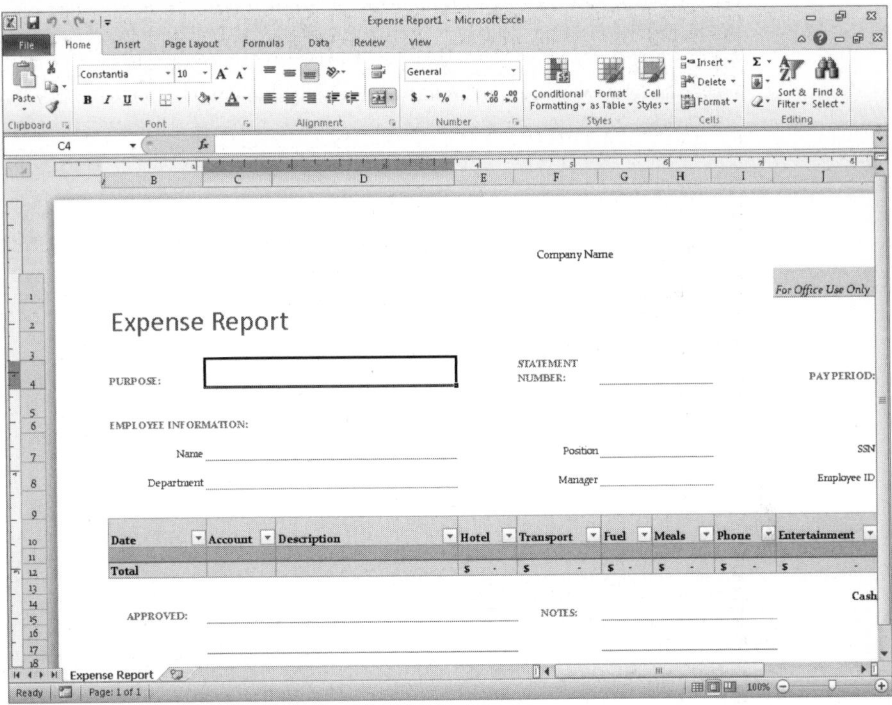

Troubleshooting The appearance of buttons and groups on the ribbon changes depending on the width of the program window. For information about changing the appearance of the ribbon to match our screen images, see "Modifying the Display of the Ribbon" at the beginning of this book.

8. On the Quick Access Toolbar, click the **Save** button.

   The Save As dialog box opens.

9. In the **File name** box, type **ExpenseReport**. Use the dialog box controls to browse to the **Chapter07** folder, and then click **Save**.

   Excel saves your workbook.

10. Click the **File** tab to display the Backstage view, click **Recent**, and then, in the **Recent Workbooks** list, click the **DailyCallSummary** workbook file (not the template).

    The DailyCallSummary file is displayed.

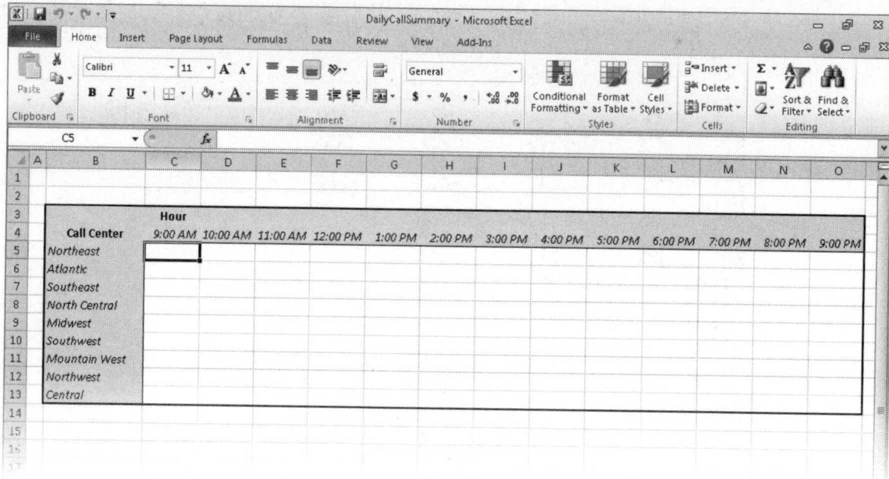

11. Right-click the **Sheet2** sheet tab, and then click **Delete**.

    Excel deletes the worksheet, leaving one worksheet in the workbook.

12. Click the **File** tab, and then click **Save As**.

    The Save As dialog box opens.

13. In the **File name** box, type DailyCallWorksheet.
14. If necessary, in the **Save as type** list, click **Excel Template**.
15. Click **Save**.

    Excel saves your template.

16. Click the **File** tab, and then click **Close**.

    Excel closes the template.

17. Click the **File** tab, and then click **New**.

    The New Workbook dialog box opens.

18. Click **Blank Workbook**, and then click **Create**.

    A blank workbook is displayed.

19. Right-click any sheet tab, and then click **Insert**.

    The Insert dialog box opens.

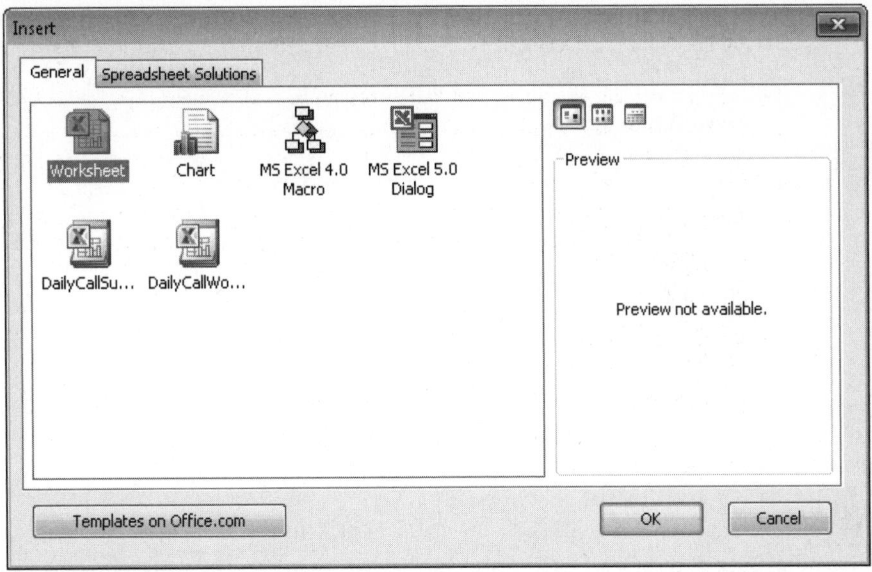

20. On the **General** page, click **DailyCallWorksheet**, and then click **OK**.

    Excel creates a new worksheet based on the template.

21. On the Quick Access Toolbar, click the **Save** button.

    The Save As dialog box opens.

22. In the **File name** box, type **CurrentCallSummary**. Use the dialog box controls to browse to the **Chapter07** folder, and then click **Save**.

    Excel saves your workbook.

CLEAN UP Close the CurrentCallSummary workbook.

Linking to Data in Other Worksheets and Workbooks

Copying and pasting data from one workbook to another is a quick and easy way to gather related data in one place, but there is a substantial limitation: If the data from the original cell changes, the change is not reflected in the cell to which the data was copied. In other words, copying and pasting a cell's contents doesn't create a relationship between the original cell and the target cell.

You can ensure that the data in the target cell reflects any changes in the original cell by creating a link between the two cells. Instead of entering a value into the target cell by typing or pasting, you create a formula that identifies the source from which Excel will derive the target cell's value and updates the value when it changes in the source cell.

To create a link between cells, open both the workbook that contains the cell from which you want to pull the value and the workbook with the target cell. Then click the target cell and type an equal sign, signifying that you want to create a formula. After you type the equal sign, activate the workbook with the cell from which you want to derive the value, click that cell, and then press the Enter key.

When you switch back to the workbook with the target cell, you see that Excel has filled in the formula with a reference to the cell you clicked.

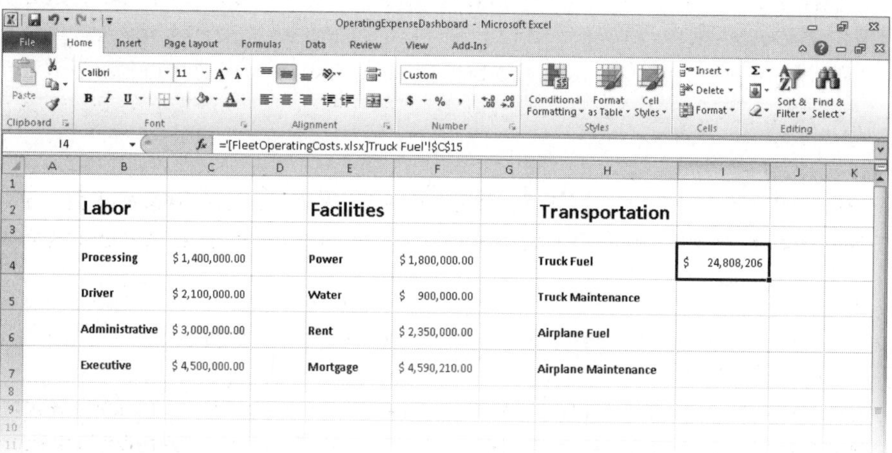

For example, the reference *='[FleetOperatingCosts.xlsx]Truck Fuel'!$C$15* gives three pieces of information: the workbook, the worksheet, and the cell you clicked in the worksheet. The first element of the reference, the name of the workbook, is enclosed in square brackets; the end of the second element (the worksheet) is marked with an exclamation point; and the third element, the cell reference, has a dollar sign before both the row and the column identifier. The single quotes around the workbook name and worksheet name are there to account for the space in the Truck Fuel worksheet's name. This type of reference is known as a *3-D* reference, reflecting the three dimensions (workbook, worksheet, and cell range) that you need to point to a group of cells in another workbook.

Tip For references to cells in the same workbook, the workbook information is omitted. Likewise, references to cells in the same worksheet don't use a worksheet identifier.

You can also link to cells in an Excel table. Such links include the workbook name, worksheet name, name of the Excel table, and row and column references of the cell to which you've linked. Creating a link to the Cost column's cell in a table's Totals row, for example, results in a reference such as *='FleetOperatingCosts.xlsx'!Truck Maintenance[[#Totals],[Cost]]*.

Important Hiding or displaying a table's Totals row affects any links to a cell in that row. Hiding the Totals row causes references to that row to display a *#REF!* error message.

Whenever you open a workbook containing a link to another document, Excel tries to update the information in linked cells. If the program can't find the source, as would happen if a workbook or worksheet is deleted or renamed, an alert box appears to indicate that there is a broken link. At that point, you can click the Update button and then the Edit Links button to open the Edit Links dialog box and find which link is broken. After you identify the broken link, you can close the Edit Links dialog box, click the cell containing the broken link, and create a new link to the desired data.

If you type a link and you make an error, a *#REF!* error message appears in the cell that contains the link. To fix the link, click the cell, delete its contents, and then either retype the link or create it with the point-and-click method described earlier in this section.

Tip Excel tracks workbook changes, such as when you change a workbook's name, very well. Unless you delete a worksheet or workbook, or move a workbook to a new folder, odds are good that Excel can update your link references automatically to reflect the change.

In this exercise, you'll create a link to another workbook, make the link's reference invalid, use the Edit Links dialog box to break the link, and then re-create the link correctly.

SET UP You need the OperatingExpenseDashboard_start and FleetOperatingCosts_start workbooks located in your Chapter07 practice file folder to complete this exercise. Open the OperatingExpenseDashboard_start and FleetOperatingCosts_start workbooks, and save them as *OperatingExpenseDashboard* and *FleetOperatingCosts*, respectively. Then follow the steps.

1. In the **OperatingExpenseDashboard** workbook, in cell **I6**, type =, but do not press Enter.

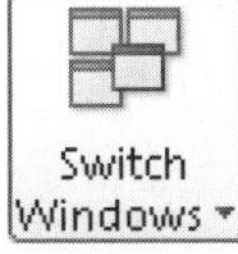

2. On the **View** tab, in the **Window** group, click **Switch Windows** and then, in the list, click **FleetOperatingCosts**.

   The FleetOperatingCosts workbook is displayed.

3. If necessary, click the **Plane Repair** sheet tab to display the Plane Repair worksheet, and then click cell **C15**.

   Excel sets the cell's formula to *='[FleetOperatingCosts.xlsx]Plane Repair'!$C$15*.

4. Press Enter.

   Excel displays the OperatingExpenseDashboard workbook; the value *$2,410,871* appears in cell I6.

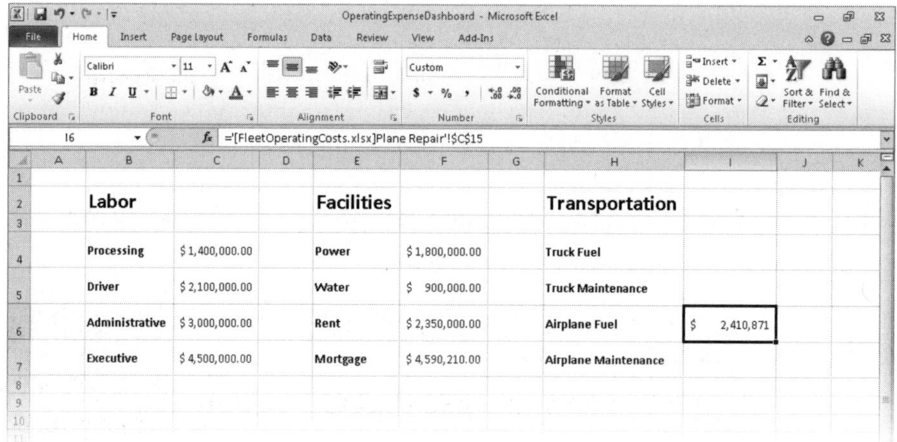

Tip Yes, cell C15 on the Plane Repair worksheet contains the wrong total for the Airplane Fuel category; that's why you replace it later in this exercise.

5. In the **Switch Windows** list, click **FleetOperatingCosts**.

   The FleetOperatingCosts workbook is displayed.

6. Right-click the **Plane Repair** sheet tab, and then click **Delete**. In the message box that appears, click **Delete** to confirm that you want to delete the worksheet.

   Excel deletes the Plane Repair worksheet.

7. In the **Switch Windows** list, click **OperatingExpenseDashboard**.

   The OperatingExpenseDashboard workbook is displayed, showing a #REF! error in cell I6.

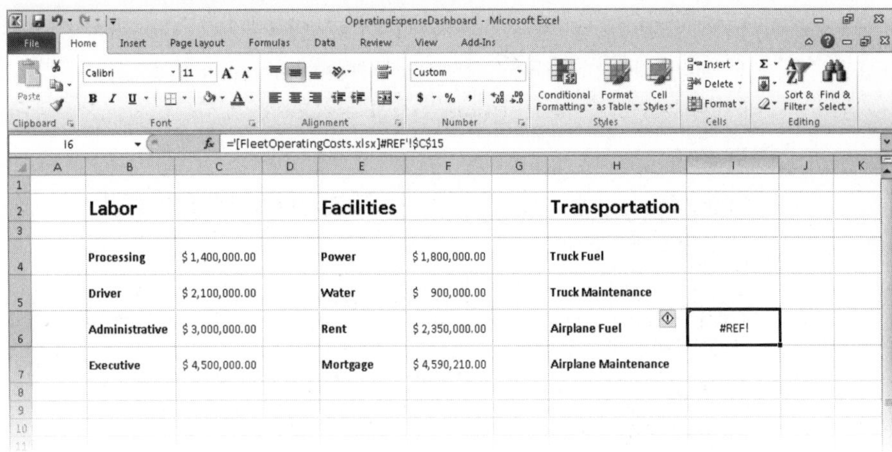

Edit Links

8. On the **Data** tab, in the **Connections** group, click **Edit Links**.

   The Edit Links dialog box opens.

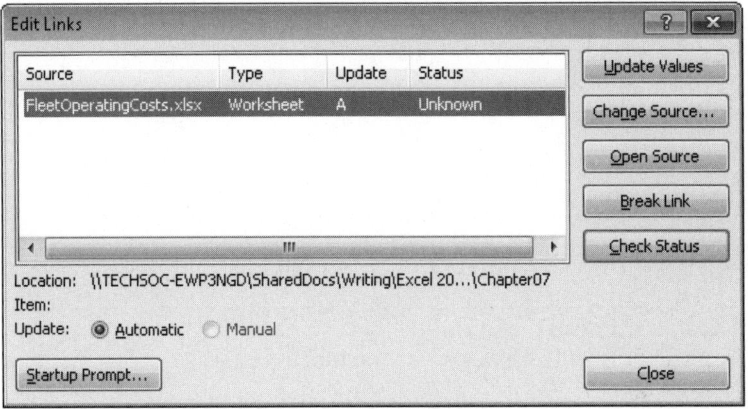

9. Click **Break Link**.

   Excel displays a warning box asking if you're sure you want to break the link.

10. Click **Break Links**.

    The warning box closes, and Excel removes the link from the workbook.

11. Click **Close**.

    The Edit Links dialog box closes.

12. In cell **I6**, type =, but do not press Enter.
13. In the **Switch Windows** list, click **FleetOperatingCosts**.

    The FleetOperatingCosts workbook is displayed.
14. Click the **Plane Fuel** sheet tab.

    The Plane Fuel worksheet is displayed.
15. Click cell **C15**, and then press Enter.

    Excel displays the OperatingExpenseDashboard workbook with the value *$52,466,303* in cell I6.

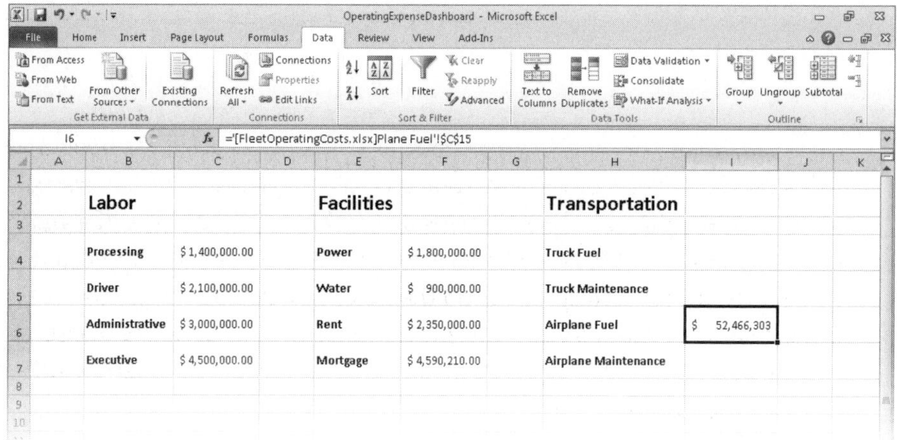

CLEAN UP Save the OperatingExpenseDashboard and FleetOperatingCosts workbooks, and then close them.

Consolidating Multiple Sets of Data into a Single Workbook

When you create a series of worksheets that contain similar data, perhaps by using a template, you build a consistent set of workbooks in which data is stored in a predictable place. For example, consider a workbook template that uses cell C5 to record the number of calls received from 9:00 A.M. to 10:00 P.M. by the Northeast distribution center.

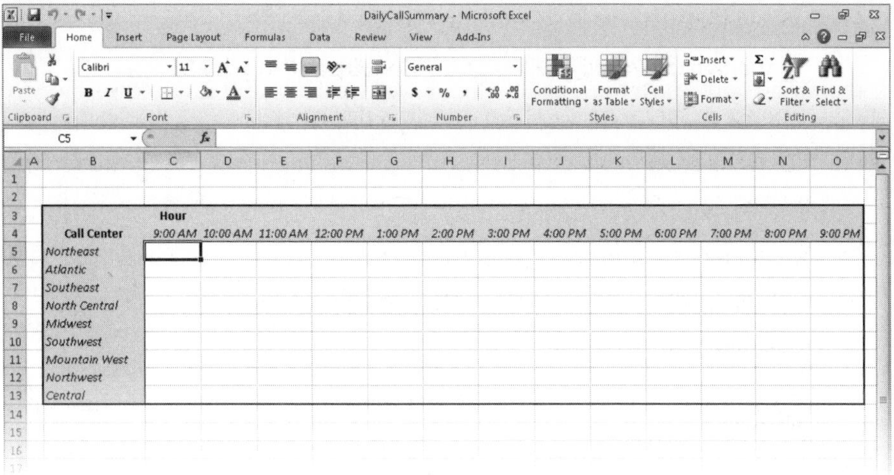

Using links to bring data from one worksheet to another gives you a great deal of power to combine data from several sources into a single resource. For example, you can create a worksheet that lists the total revenue just for certain months of a year, use links to draw the values from the worksheets in which the sales were recorded, and then create a formula to perform calculations on the data. However, for large worksheets with hundreds of cells filled with data, creating links from every cell is a time-consuming process. Also, to calculate a sum or an average for the data, you would need to include links to cells in every workbook.

Fortunately, there is an easier way to combine data from multiple worksheets in a single worksheet. This process, called *data consolidation*, enables you to define ranges of cells from multiple worksheets and have Excel summarize the data. You define these ranges in the Consolidate dialog box.

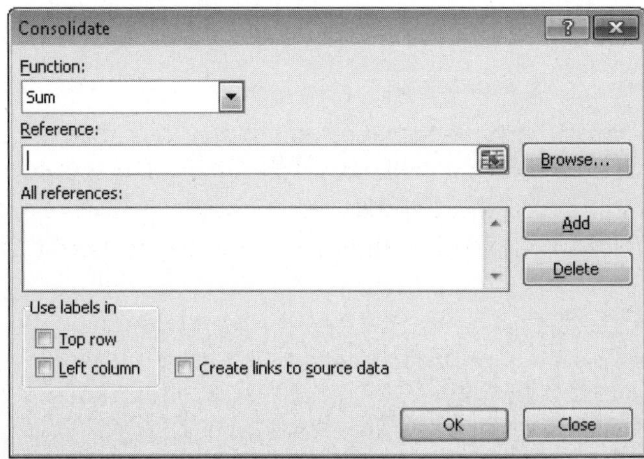

After you open the dialog box, you move to the worksheet that contains the first cell range you want to include in your summary. When you select the cells, the 3-D reference for the range appears in the Consolidate dialog box. Clicking Add stores the reference. You can then choose the other cell ranges that contain data you want to include in the summary, or you can remove a range from the calculation by clicking the range and then clicking Delete.

Cells that are in the same relative position in the ranges have their contents summarized together. When you consolidate the ranges, the cell in the upper-left corner of one range is added to the cell in the upper-left corner of every other range, even if those ranges are in different areas of the worksheet. After you choose the ranges to be used in your summary, you can choose the calculation to perform on the data (sum, average, and so on). When you're done selecting ranges to use in the calculation, click OK to have Excel summarize the data on your target worksheet.

Important You can define only one data consolidation summary per workbook.

In this exercise, you'll define a data consolidation range consisting of ranges from two other workbooks. You'll then add the contents of the ranges and show the results in a worksheet.

SET UP You need the Consolidate_start, JanuaryCalls_start, and FebruaryCalls_start workbooks located in your Chapter07 practice file folder to complete this exercise. Open the Consolidate_start, JanuaryCalls_start, and FebruaryCalls_start workbooks, and save them as *Consolidate*, *JanuaryCalls*, and *FebruaryCalls*, respectively. Then follow the steps.

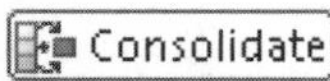

1. In the **Consolidate** workbook, on the **Data** tab, in the **Data Tools** group, click **Consolidate**.

   The Consolidate dialog box opens.

2. Click the **Collapse Dialog** button at the right edge of the **Reference** field.

   The Consolidate dialog box contracts.

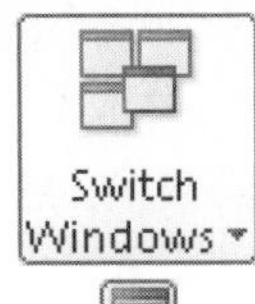

3. On the **View** tab, in the **Window** group, click **Switch Windows** and then, in the list, click **JanuaryCalls**.

   The JanuaryCalls workbook is displayed.

4. Select the cell range **C5:O13**, and then click the **Expand Dialog** button.

   The Consolidate dialog box is restored to its full size.

5. Click **Add**.

   The range you selected appears in the All References pane.

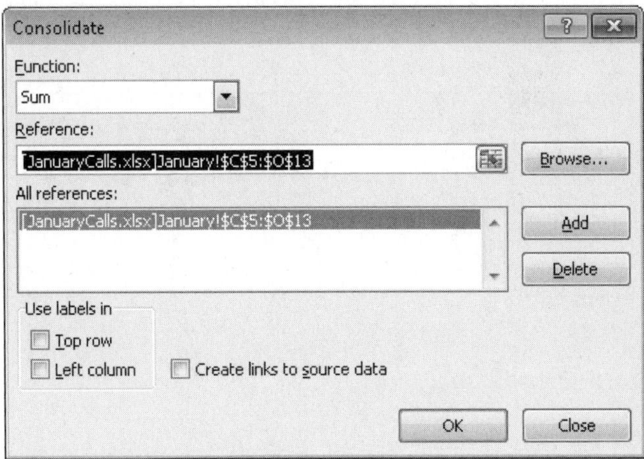

6. Click the **Collapse Dialog** button at the right edge of the **Reference** field.

   The Consolidate dialog box contracts.

7. In the **Switch Windows** list, click **FebruaryCalls**.

   The FebruaryCalls workbook is displayed.

8. Select the cell range **C5:O13**, and then click the **Expand Dialog** button.

   The Consolidate dialog box is restored to its full size.

9. Click **Add**.

   The range *'[FebruaryCalls.xlsx]February'!$C$5:$O$13* appears in the All References pane.

10. Click **OK**.

    Excel consolidates the JanuaryCalls and FebruaryCalls workbook data into the range C5:O13 in the Consolidate workbook. You didn't change the *SUM* operation in the Function box, so the values in the Consolidate workbook are the sum of the other workbooks' values.

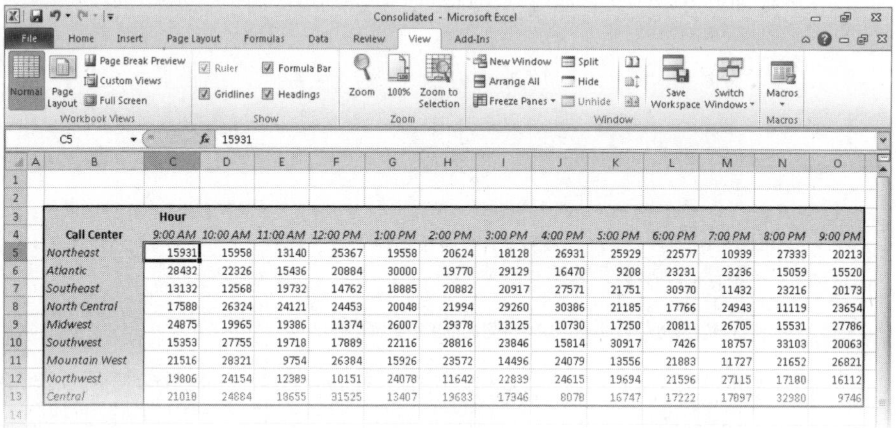

Call Center	Hour 9:00 AM	10:00 AM	11:00 AM	12:00 PM	1:00 PM	2:00 PM	3:00 PM	4:00 PM	5:00 PM	6:00 PM	7:00 PM	8:00 PM	9:00 PM
Northeast	15931	15958	13140	25367	19558	20624	18128	26931	25929	22577	10939	27333	20213
Atlantic	28432	22326	15436	20884	30000	19770	29129	16470	9208	23231	23236	15059	15520
Southeast	13132	12568	19732	14762	18885	20882	20917	27571	21751	30970	11432	23216	20173
North Central	17588	26324	24121	24453	20048	21994	29260	30386	21185	17766	24943	11119	23654
Midwest	24875	19965	19386	11374	26007	29378	13125	10730	17250	20811	26705	15531	27786
Southwest	15353	27755	19718	17889	22116	28816	23846	15814	30917	7426	18757	33103	20063
Mountain West	21516	28321	9754	26384	15926	23572	14496	24079	13556	21883	11727	21652	26821
Northwest	19806	24154	12389	10151	24078	11642	22839	24615	19694	21596	27115	17180	16112
Central	21018	24884	18655	31525	13407	13683	17346	8078	16747	17222	17897	32980	9746

CLEAN UP Save the Consolidate, JanuaryCalls, and FebruaryCalls workbooks, and then close them.

Grouping Multiple Sets of Data

When you work with Excel for a while, you'll find that you often open a number of the same workbooks at the same time. For instance, Lori Penor, the chief operating officer of Consolidated Messenger, might always pull up a workbook that tracks labor costs at the same time she opens the package volume summary workbook. She can open the workbooks individually through the Open dialog box, but she can also group the files so that she has the option of opening them all simultaneously.

If you want to open a set of files simultaneously, you can define them as part of a workspace, which uses one file name to reference several workbooks. To define a workspace, you open the files you want to include and then open the Save Workspace dialog box.

Clicking Save in the Save Workspace dialog box saves references to all the Excel files that are currently open. Whenever you open the workspace you create, all the files that were open when you defined the workspace are displayed. Including a file in a workspace doesn't remove it from general circulation; you can still open it by itself.

In this exercise, you'll save a workspace that consists of two workbooks, close the included files, and then test the workspace by opening it from the Open dialog box.

SET UP You need the OperatingExpenseDashboard and FleetOperatingCosts workbooks you created in the second exercise in this chapter to complete this exercise. If you did not complete that exercise, you should do so now. Open the OperatingExpenseDashboard and FleetOperatingCosts workbooks. Then follow the steps.

1. In either workbook, on the **View** tab, in the **Window** group, click **Save Workspace**.

   The Save Workspace dialog box opens.

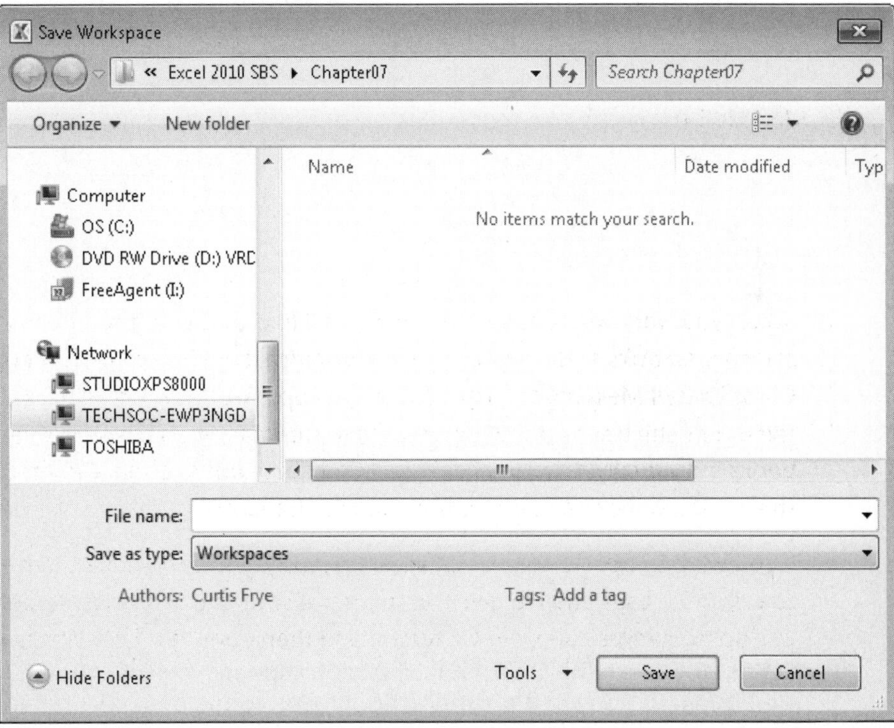

2. In the **File name** field, type **Expenses**.
3. Click **Save**.

   Excel saves your workspace and closes the Save Workspace dialog box.
4. Click the **File** tab, and then click **Close**.

   Excel closes the active workbook.
5. Click the **File** tab, and then click **Close**.

   Excel closes the second workbook.
6. Click the **File** tab and (if necessary), click **Recent**. In the **Recent Workbooks** list, click **Expenses.xlw**.

   Excel opens the OperatingExpenseDashboard and FleetOperatingCosts workbooks.

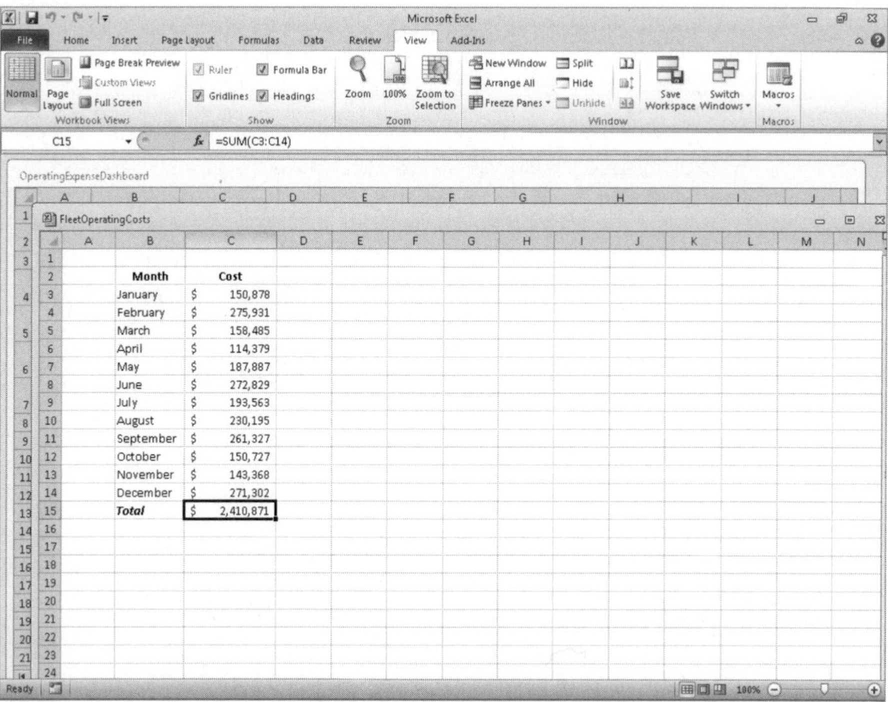

CLEAN UP Close the OperatingExpenseDashboard and FleetOperatingCosts workbooks. If you are not continuing directly to the next chapter, exit Excel.

Key Points

- If you create a lot of workbooks with the same layout and design, saving a workbook with the common elements (and no data) will save you time when you create similar workbooks in the future.
- You can use data in other worksheets or workbooks in your formulas. You make the link by clicking the cell, which creates a 3-D reference to that cell.
- When you create a link to a cell in a table's Totals row, hiding the Totals row causes Excel to display a #REF! error in the cell where you created the link.
- If you always work on a group of workbooks at the same time, create a workspace so that you can open them all at once.

Chapter at a Glance

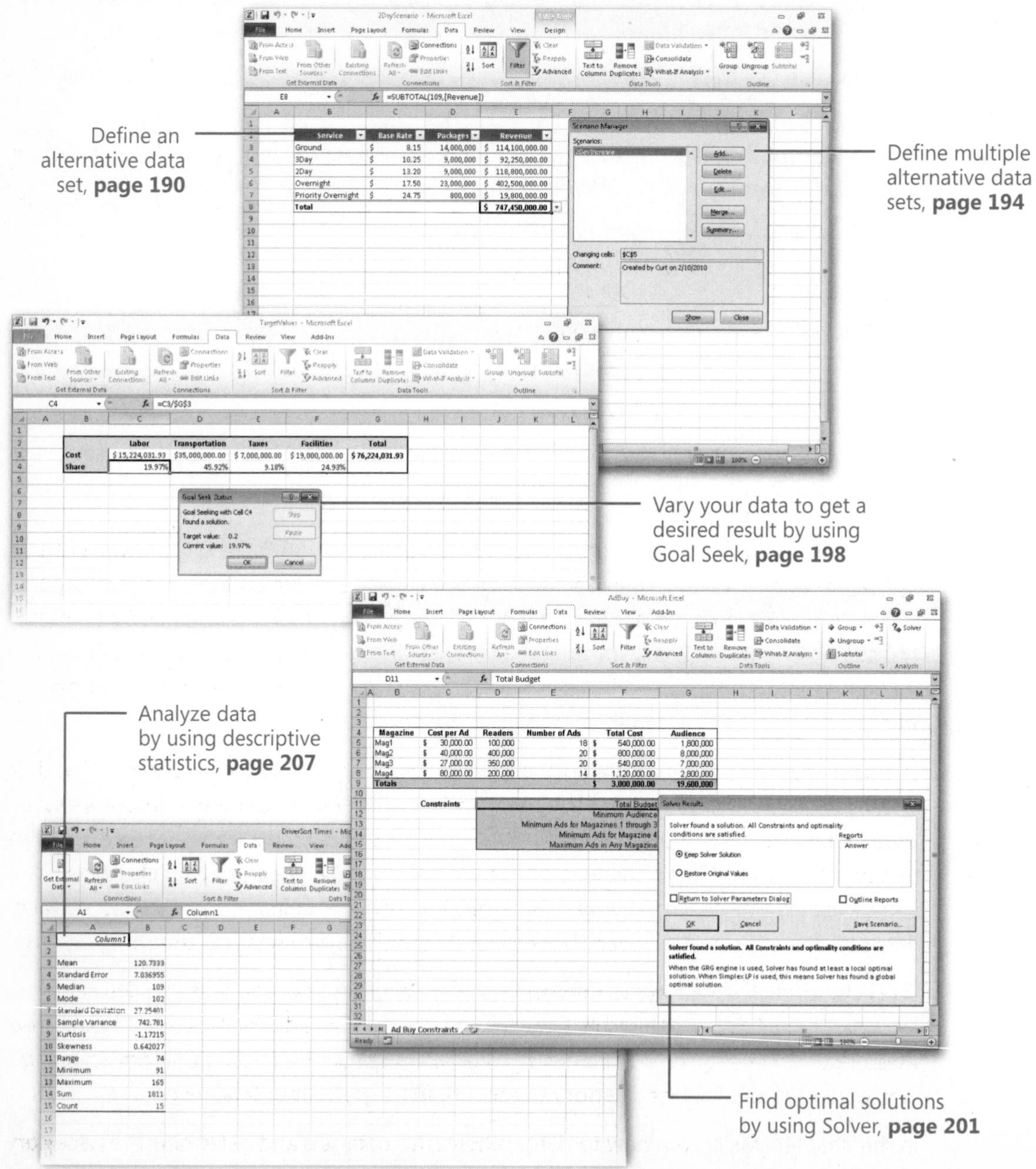
Define an alternative data set, **page 190**
Define multiple alternative data sets, **page 194**
Vary your data to get a desired result by using Goal Seek, **page 198**
Analyze data by using descriptive statistics, **page 207**
Find optimal solutions by using Solver, **page 201**

8 Analyzing Alternative Data Sets

In this chapter, you will learn how to

- ✔ Define an alternative data set.
- ✔ Define multiple alternative data sets.
- ✔ Vary your data to get a desired result by using Goal Seek.
- ✔ Find optimal solutions by using Solver.
- ✔ Analyze data by using descriptive statistics.

When you store data in a Microsoft Excel 2010 workbook, you can use that data, either by itself or as part of a calculation, to discover important information about your organization. When you track total sales on a time basis, you can find your best and worst sales periods and correlate them with outside events. For businesses such as Consolidated Messenger, package volume increases dramatically during the holidays as customers ship gifts to friends and family members.

The data in your orksheets is great for answering the question, "What happened?" The data is less useful for answering "what-if" questions, such as, "How much money would we save if we reduced our labor to 20 percent of our total costs?" You can always save an alternative version of a workbook and create formulas that calculate the effects of your changes, but you can do the same thing in your existing workbooks by defining one or more alternative data sets and switching between the original data and the new sets you create.

Excel also provides the tools to determine the input values that would be required for a formula to produce a given result. For example, the chief operating officer of Consolidated Messenger, Lori Penor, could find out to what level the revenues from three-day shipping would need to rise for that category to account for 25 percent of total revenue.

In this chapter, you'll learn how to define alternative data sets and determine the necessary inputs to make a calculation produce a particular result.

Practice Files Before you can complete the exercises in this chapter, you need to copy the book's practice files to your computer. The practice files you'll use to complete the exercises in this chapter are in the Chapter08 practice file folder. A complete list of practice files is provided in "Using the Practice Files" at the beginning of this book.

Defining an Alternative Data Set

When you save data in an Excel worksheet, you create a record that reflects the characteristics of an event or object. That data could represent the number of deliveries in an hour on a particular day, the price of a new delivery option, or the percentage of total revenue accounted for by a delivery option. After the data is in place, you can create formulas to generate totals, find averages, and sort the rows in a worksheet based on the contents of one or more columns. However, if you want to perform a what-if analysis or explore the impact that changes in your data would have on any of the calculations in your workbooks, you need to change your data.

The problem with manipulating data that reflects an event or item is that when you change any data to affect a calculation you run the risk of destroying the original data if you accidentally save your changes. You can avoid ruining your original data by creating a duplicate workbook and making your changes to it, but you can also create alternative data sets, or scenarios, within an existing workbook.

When you create a scenario, you give Excel alternative values for a list of cells in a worksheet. You can use the Scenario Manager to add, delete, and edit scenarios.

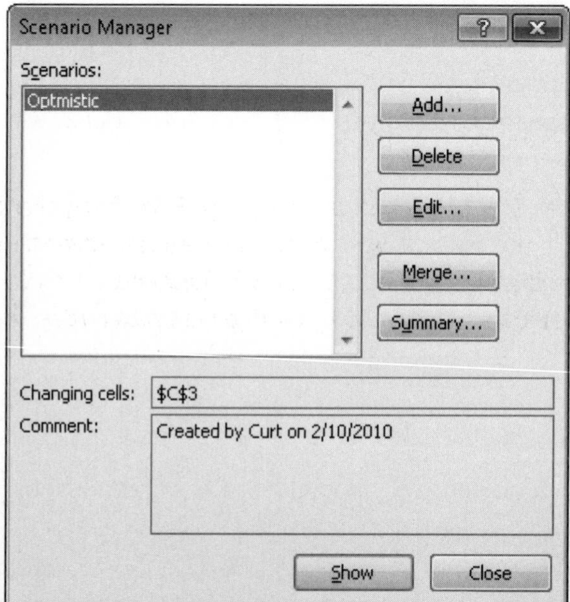

Clicking the Add button displays the Add Scenario dialog box.

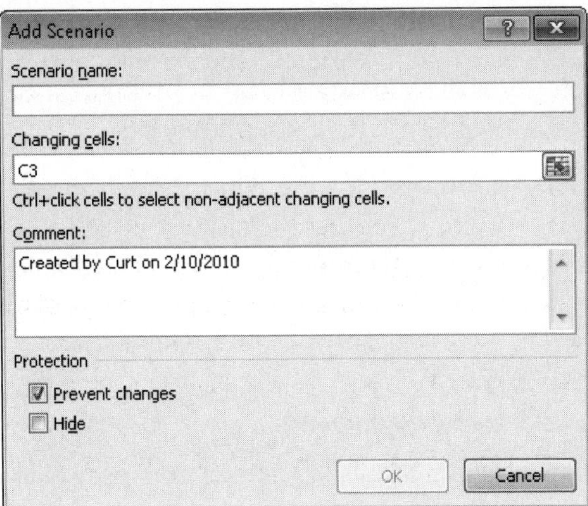

From within this dialog box, you can name the scenario and identify the cells for which you want to define alternative values. After you click OK, a new dialog box opens with spaces for you to type the new values.

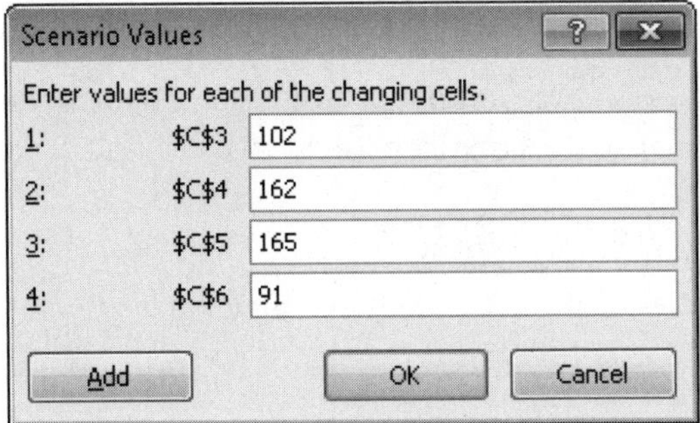

Clicking OK returns you to the Scenario Manager dialog box. From there, clicking the Show button replaces the values in the original worksheet with the alternative values you just defined in the scenario. Any formulas referencing cells with changed values will recalculate their results. You can then remove the scenario by clicking the Undo button on the Quick Access Toolbar.

Important If you save and close a workbook while a scenario is in effect, those values become the default values for the cells changed by the scenario! You should seriously consider creating a scenario that contains the original values of the cells you change or creating a scenario summary worksheet (a topic covered in the next section).

In this exercise, you'll create a scenario to measure the projected impact on total revenue of a rate increase on two-day shipping.

SET UP You need the 2DayScenario_start workbook located in your Chapter08 practice file folder to complete this exercise. Start Excel, open the 2DayScenario_start workbook, and save it as *2DayScenario*. Then follow the steps.

1. On the **Data** tab, in the **Data Tools** group, click **What-If Analysis** and then, in the list, click **Scenario Manager**.

   The Scenario Manager dialog box opens.
2. Click **Add**.

   The Add Scenario dialog box opens.
3. In the **Scenario name** field, type **2DayIncrease**.

4. At the right edge of the **Changing cells** field, click the **Collapse Dialog** button so the worksheet contents are visible.

   The Add Scenario dialog box collapses.

5. In the worksheet, click cell **C5** and then, in the **Add Scenario** dialog box, click the **Expand Dialog** button.

   $C$5 appears in the Changing Cells field, and the dialog box title changes to Edit Scenario.

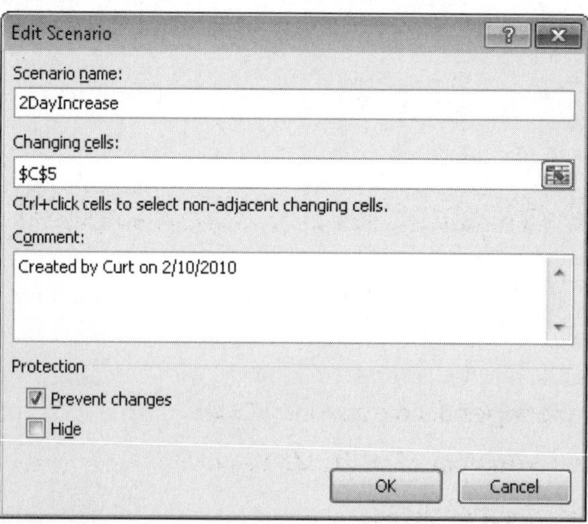

6. Click **OK**.

   The Scenario Values dialog box opens.

7. In the value field, type **13.2**, and then click **OK**.

   The Scenario Values dialog box closes, and the Scenario Manager is displayed again.

8. If necessary, drag the **Scenario Manager** dialog box to another location on the screen so that you can view the entire table.

9. In the **Scenario Manager** dialog box, click **Show**.

   Excel applies the scenario, changing the value in cell C5 to *$13.20*, which in turn increases the value in cell E8 to *$747,450,000.00*.

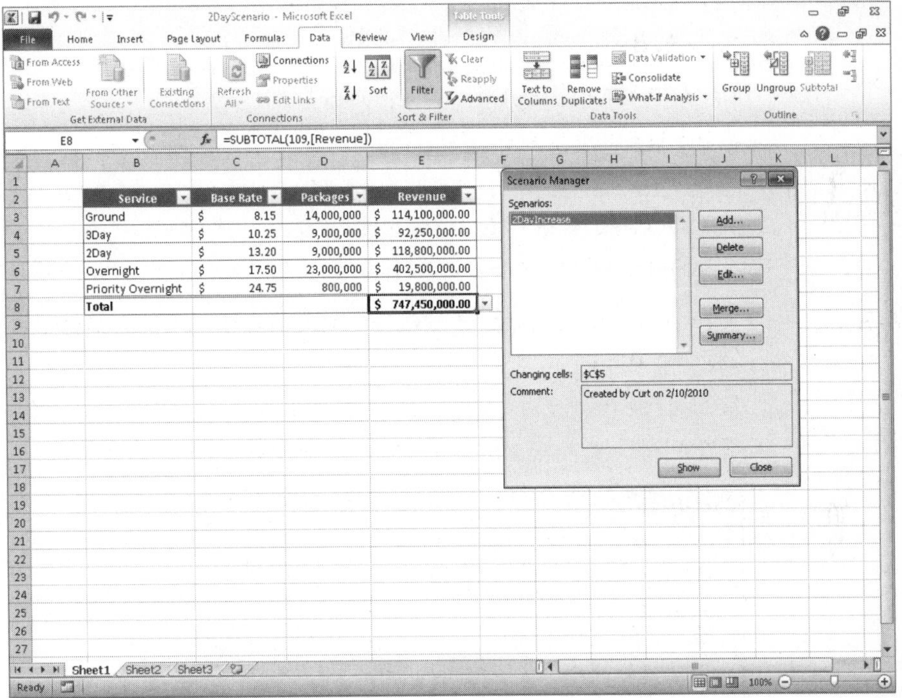

Troubleshooting The appearance of buttons and groups on the ribbon changes depending on the width of the program window. For information about changing the appearance of the ribbon to match our screen images, see "Modifying the Display of the Ribbon" at the beginning of this book.

10. In the **Scenario Manager** dialog box, click **Close**.

11. On the Quick Access Toolbar, click the **Undo** button.

    Excel removes the effect of the scenario.

CLEAN UP Save the 2DayScenario workbook, and then close it.

Defining Multiple Alternative Data Sets

One great feature of Excel scenarios is that you're not limited to creating one alternative data set—you can create as many scenarios as you like and apply them by using the Scenario Manager. To apply more than one scenario by using the Scenario Manager, click the name of the first scenario you want to display, click the Show button, and then do the same for any subsequent scenarios. The values you defined as part of those scenarios will appear in your worksheet, and Excel will update any calculations involving the changed cells.

Tip If you apply a scenario to a worksheet and then apply another scenario to the same worksheet, both sets of changes appear. If multiple scenarios change the same cell, the cell will contain the value in the most recently applied scenario.

Applying multiple scenarios alters the values in your worksheets. You can see how those changes affect your formulas, but Excel also gives you a way to view the results of all your scenarios in a single, separate worksheet. To create a worksheet in your current workbook that summarizes the changes caused by your scenarios, open the Scenario Manager, and then click the Summary button. When you do, the Scenario Summary dialog box opens.

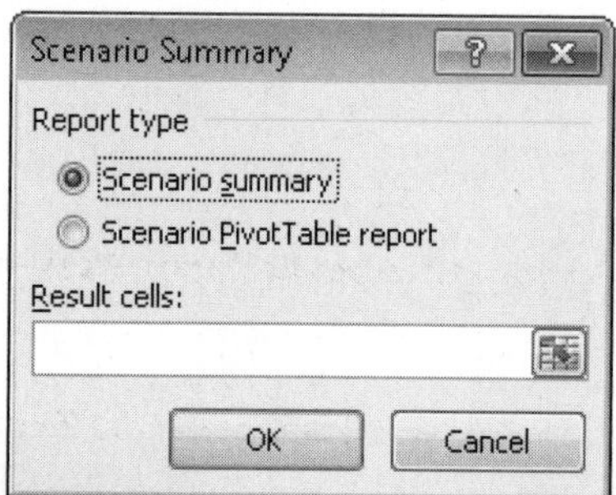

From within the dialog box, you can choose the type of summary worksheet you want to create and the cells you want to display in the summary worksheet. To choose the cells to display in the summary, click the Collapse Dialog button in the box, select the cells you want to display, and then expand the dialog box. After you verify that the range in the box represents the cells you want to have included on the summary sheet, click OK to create the new worksheet.

It's a good idea to create an "undo" scenario named *Normal* that holds the original values of the cells you're going to change before they're changed in other scenarios. For example, if you create a scenario named *High Fuel Costs* that changes the sales figures in three cells, your Normal scenario restores those cells to their original values. That way, even if you accidentally modify your worksheet, you can apply the Normal scenario and not have to reconstruct the worksheet from scratch.

Tip Each scenario can change a maximum of 32 cells, so you might need to create more than one scenario to ensure that you can restore a worksheet.

In this exercise, you'll create scenarios to represent projected revenue increases from two rate changes, view the scenarios, and then summarize the scenario results in a new worksheet.

SET UP You need the MultipleScenarios_start workbook located in your Chapter08 practice file folder to complete this exercise. Open the MultipleScenarios_start workbook, and save it as *MultipleScenarios*. Then follow the steps.

1. On the **Data** tab, in the **Data Tools** group, click **What-If Analysis** and then, in the list, click **Scenario Manager**.

   The Scenario Manager dialog box opens.
2. Click **Add**.

   The Add Scenario dialog box opens.
3. In the **Scenario name** field, type **3DayIncrease**.

4. At the right edge of the **Changing cells** field, click the **Collapse Dialog** button.

   The Add Scenario dialog box collapses.

5. In the worksheet, click cell **C4** and then, in the dialog box, click the **Expand Dialog** button.

   $C$4 appears in the Changing Cells field, and the dialog box title changes to Edit Scenario.
6. Click **OK**.

   The Scenario Values dialog box opens.
7. In the value field, type **11.50**.

8. Click **OK**.

   The Scenario Values dialog box closes, and the Scenario Manager is displayed again.

9. Click **Add**.

   The Add Scenario dialog box opens.

10. In the **Scenario name** field, type **Ground and Overnight Increase**.

11. At the right edge of the **Changing cells** field, click the **Collapse Dialog** button.

    The Add Scenario dialog box collapses.

12. Click cell **C3**, hold down the Ctrl key, and click cell **C6**. Then click the **Expand Dialog** button.

    $C$3,$C$6 appears in the Changing Cells field, and the dialog box title changes to Edit Scenario.

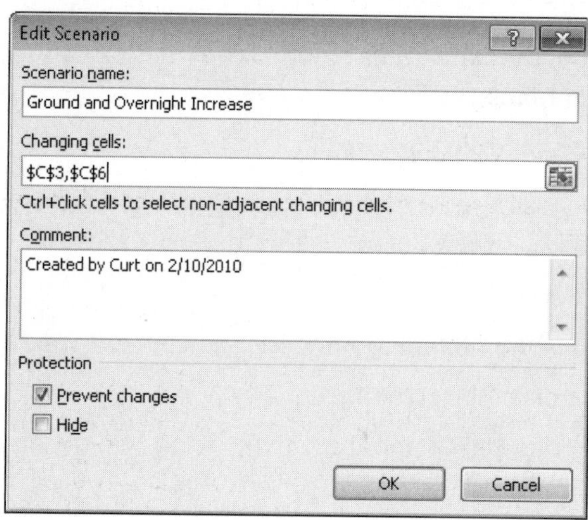

13. Click **OK**.

    The Scenario Values dialog box opens.

14. In the **$C$3** field, type **10.15**.

15. In the **$C$6** field, type **18.5**.

16. Click **OK**.

    The Scenario Values dialog box closes, and the Scenario Manager dialog box is displayed again.

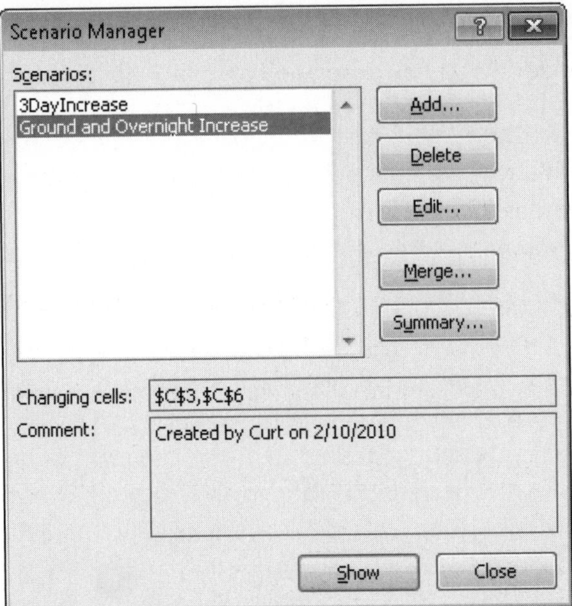

17. Click **Summary**.

    The Scenario Summary dialog box opens.

18. Verify that the **Scenario summary** option is selected and that cell **E8** appears in the **Result cells** field.

19. Click **OK**.

    Excel creates a Scenario Summary worksheet.

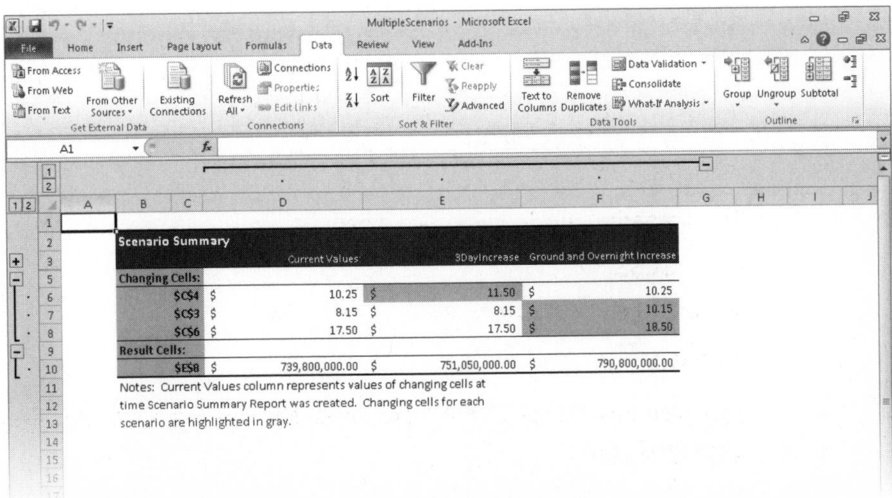

 **CLEAN UP** Save the MultipleScenarios workbook, and then close it.

Varying Your Data to Get a Desired Result by Using Goal Seek

When you run an organization, you must track how every element performs, both in absolute terms and in relation to other parts of the organization. Just as you might want to reward your employees for maintaining a perfect safety record and keeping down your insurance rates, you might also want to stop carrying products you cannot sell.

When you plan how you want to grow your business, you should have specific goals in mind for each department or product category. For example, Lori Penor of Consolidated Messenger might have the goal of reducing the firm's labor costs by 20 percent as compared to the previous year. Finding the labor amount that represents a 20-percent decrease is simple, but expressing goals in other ways can make finding the solution more challenging. Instead of decreasing labor costs 20 percent over the previous year, Lori might want to decrease labor costs so they represent no more than 20 percent of the company's total outlay.

As an example, consider a worksheet that holds cost figures for Consolidated Messenger's operations and uses those figures to calculate both total costs and the share each category has of that total.

	A	B	C	D	E	F	G	H
1								
2			Labor	Transportation	Taxes	Facilities	Total	
3		Cost	$ 18,000,382.00	$35,000,000.00	$ 7,000,000.00	$ 19,000,000.00	**$ 79,000,382.00**	
4		Share	22.79%	44.30%	8.86%	24.05%		
5								

Important In the worksheet, the values in the Share row are displayed as percentages, but the underlying values are decimals. For example, Excel represents *0.3064* as *30.64%*.

Although it would certainly be possible to figure the target number that would make labor costs represent 20 percent of the total, there is an easier way to do it in Excel: Goal Seek. To use Goal Seek, you display the Data tab and then, in the Data Tools group, click What-If Analysis. On the menu that is displayed, click Goal Seek to open the Goal Seek dialog box.

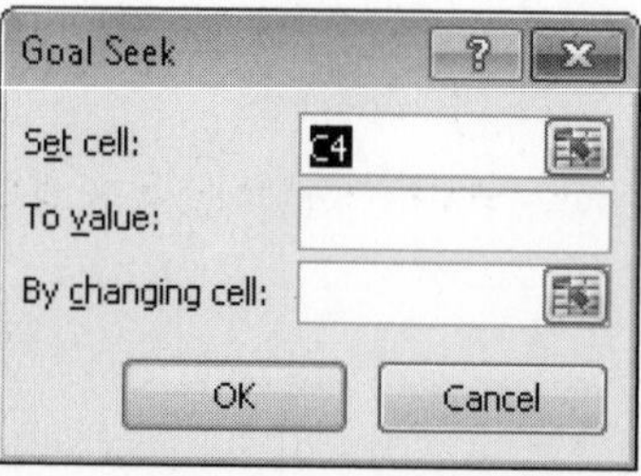

Important If you save a workbook with the results of a Goal Seek calculation in place, you will overwrite the values in your workbook.

In the dialog box, you identify the cell with the target value; in this example, it is cell C4, which has the percentage of costs accounted for by the Labor category. The To Value field has the target value (.2, which is equivalent to 20 percent), and the By Changing Cell field identifies the cell with the value Excel should change to generate the target value of 20 percent in cell C4. In this example, the cell to be changed is C3.

Clicking OK tells Excel to find a solution for the goal you set. When Excel finishes its work, the new values appear in the designated cells, and the Goal Seek Status dialog box opens.

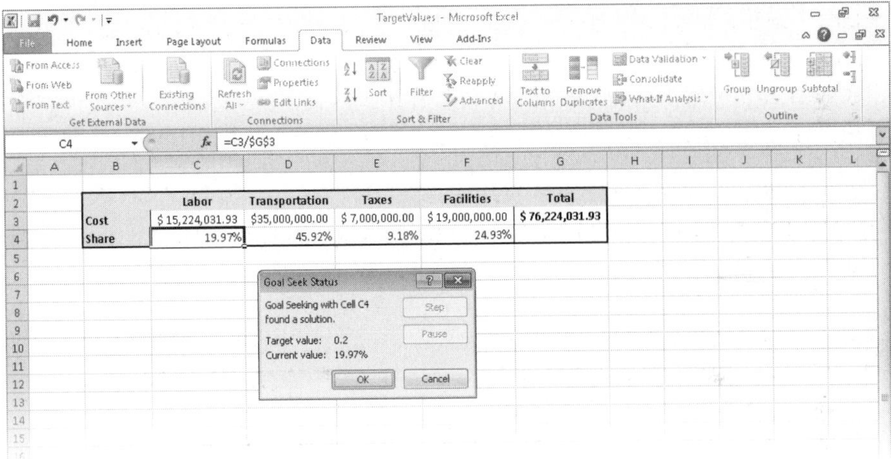

Tip Goal Seek finds the closest solution it can without exceeding the target value. In this case, the closest percentage it could find was 19.97 percent.

In this exercise, you'll use Goal Seek to determine how much you need to decrease transportation costs so those costs make up no more than 40 percent of Consolidated Messenger's operating costs.

SET UP You need the TargetValues_start workbook located in your Chapter08 practice file folder to complete this exercise. Open the TargetValues_start workbook, and save it as *TargetValues*. Then follow the steps.

1. On the **Data** tab, in the **Data Tools** group, click **What-If Analysis** and then, in the list, click **Goal Seek**.

The Goal Seek dialog box opens.

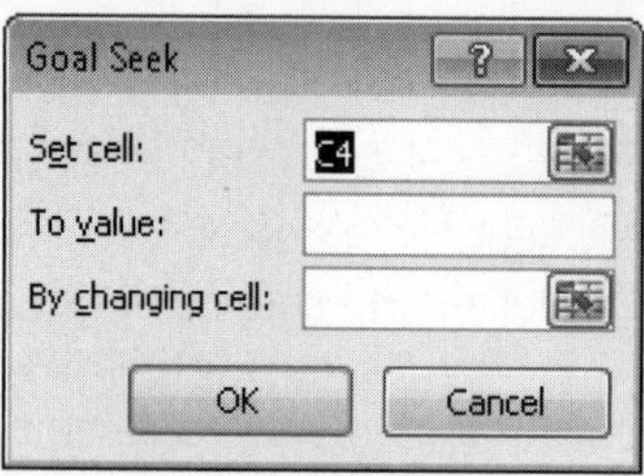

2. In the **Set cell** field, type **D4**.
3. In the **To value** field, type **.4**.
4. In the **By changing cell** field, type **D3**.
5. Click **OK**.

   Excel displays the solution in both the worksheet and the Goal Seek Status dialog box.

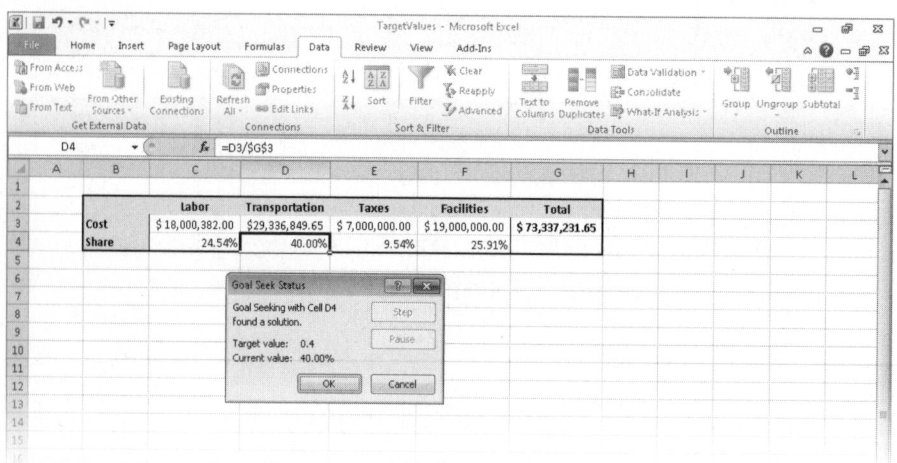

6. Click **Cancel**.

   Excel closes the Goal Seek Status dialog box without saving the new worksheet values.

CLEAN UP Save the TargetValues workbook, and then close it.

Finding Optimal Solutions by Using Solver

Goal Seek is a great tool for finding out how much you need to change a single input value to generate a desired result from a formula, but it's of no help if you want to find the best mix of several input values. For example, marketing vice president Craig Dewar might want to advertise in four national magazines to drive customers to Consolidated Messenger's Web site, but he might not know the best mix of ads to reach the greatest number of readers. He asked the publishers for ad pricing and readership numbers, which he recorded in a spreadsheet, along with the minimum number of ads per publication (three) and the minimum number of times he wants the ad to be seen (10,000,000). Because one of the magazines has a high percentage of corporate executive readers, Craig does want to take out at least four ads in that publication, despite its relatively low readership. The goal of the ad campaign is for the ads to be seen as many times as possible without costing the company more than the $3,000,000 budget.

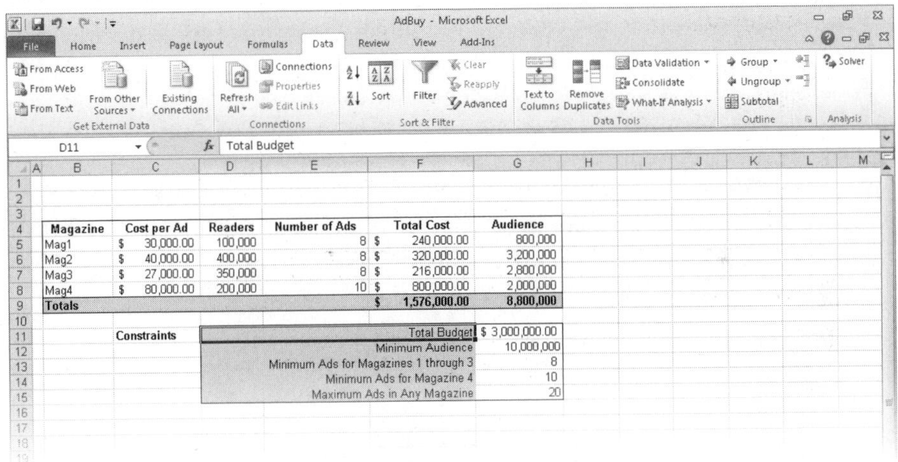

Tip It helps to spell out every aspect of your problem so that you can identify the cells you want Solver to use in its calculations.

If you performed a complete installation when you installed Excel on your computer, you see the Solver button on the Data tab in the Analysis group. If not, you need to install the Solver Add-In. To do so, click the File tab, and then click Options. In the Excel Options dialog box, click Add-Ins to display the Add-Ins page. At the bottom of the dialog box, in the Manage list, click Excel Add-Ins, and then click Go to display the Add-Ins dialog box. Select the Solver Add-in check box and click OK to install Solver.

Tip You might be prompted for the Microsoft Office system installation CD. If so, put the CD in your CD drive, and click OK.

After the installation is complete, Solver appears on the Data tab, in the Analysis group. Clicking Solver displays the Solver Parameters dialog box.

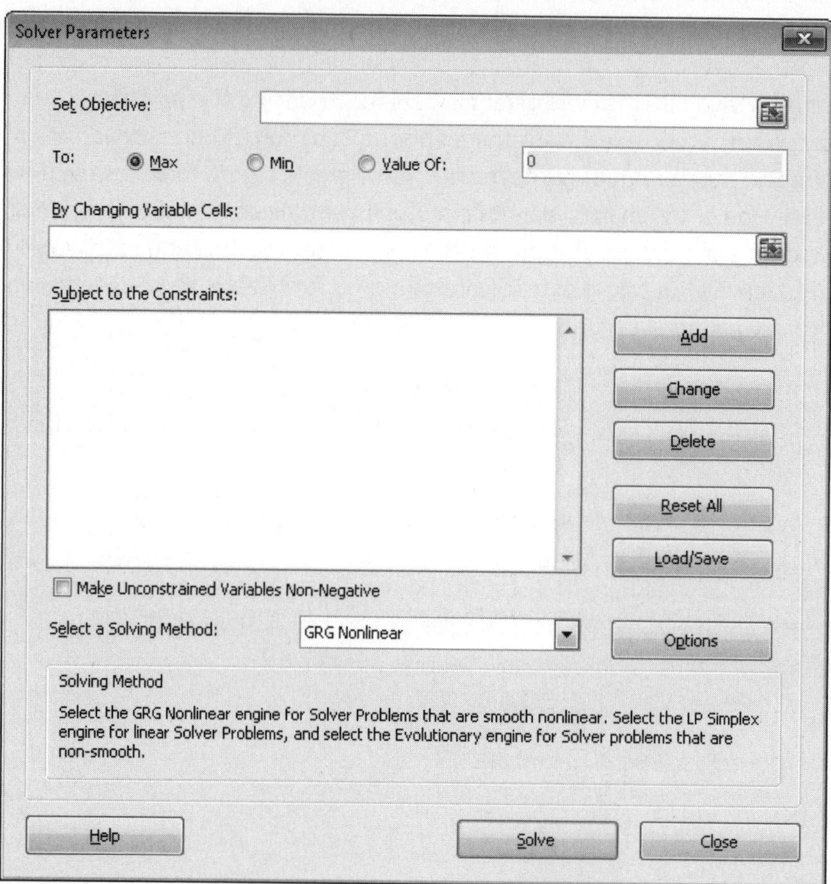

The first step of setting up your Solver problem is to identify the cell that contains the summary formula you want to establish as your objective. To identify that cell, click in the Set Objective box, click the target cell in the worksheet, and then select the option representing whether you want to minimize the cell's value, maximize the cell's value, or make the cell take on a specific value. Next, you click in the By Changing Variable Cells box and select the cells Solver should vary to change the value in the objective cell. Finally, you can create constraints that will set the limits for the values Solver can use. To do so, click Add to open the Add Constraint dialog box.

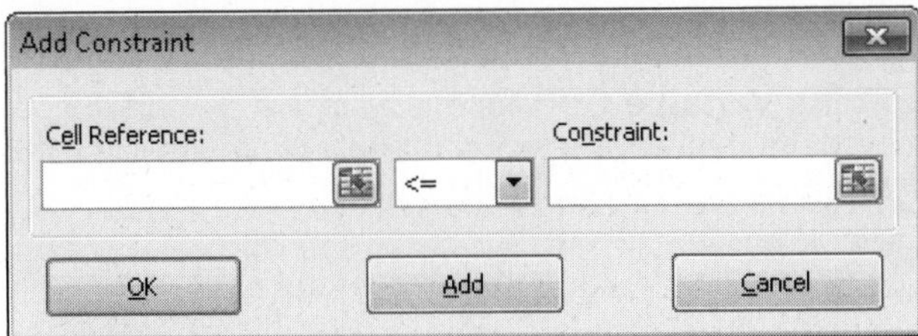

You add constraints to the Solver problem by selecting the cells to which you want to apply the constraint, selecting the comparison operation (such as less than or equal to, greater than or equal to, or must be an integer), and clicking in the Constraint box to select the cell with the value of the constraint. You could also type a value in the Constraint box, but referring to a cell makes it possible for you to change the constraint later without opening Solver.

Tip After you run Solver, you can use the commands in the Solver Results dialog box to save the results as changes to your worksheet or create a scenario based on the changed data.

In this exercise, you'll use Solver to determine the best mix of ads given the following constraints:

- You want to maximize the number of people who see the ads.
- You must buy at least 8 ads in 3 magazines and at least 10 in the fourth.
- You can't buy part of an ad (that is, all numbers must be integers).
- You can buy no more than 20 ads in any one magazine.
- You must reach at least 10,000,000 people.
- Your ad budget is $3,000,000.

SET UP You need the AdBuy_start workbook located in your Chapter08 practice file folder to complete this exercise. Open the AdBuy_start workbook, and save it as *AdBuy*. Then follow the steps.

1. If the **Solver** button doesn't appear in the **Analysis** group on the **Data** tab, follow the instructions from earlier in this section to install it.

2. In the **Analysis** group on the **Data** tab, click **Solver**.

   The Solver Parameters dialog box opens.

3. Click in the **Set Objective** box, and then click cell **G9**.

   $G$9 appears in the Set Objective field.

4. Click **Max**.
5. Click in the **By Changing Variable Cells** field, and select cells **E5:E8**.

   $E$5:$E$8 appears in the By Changing Variable Cells field.

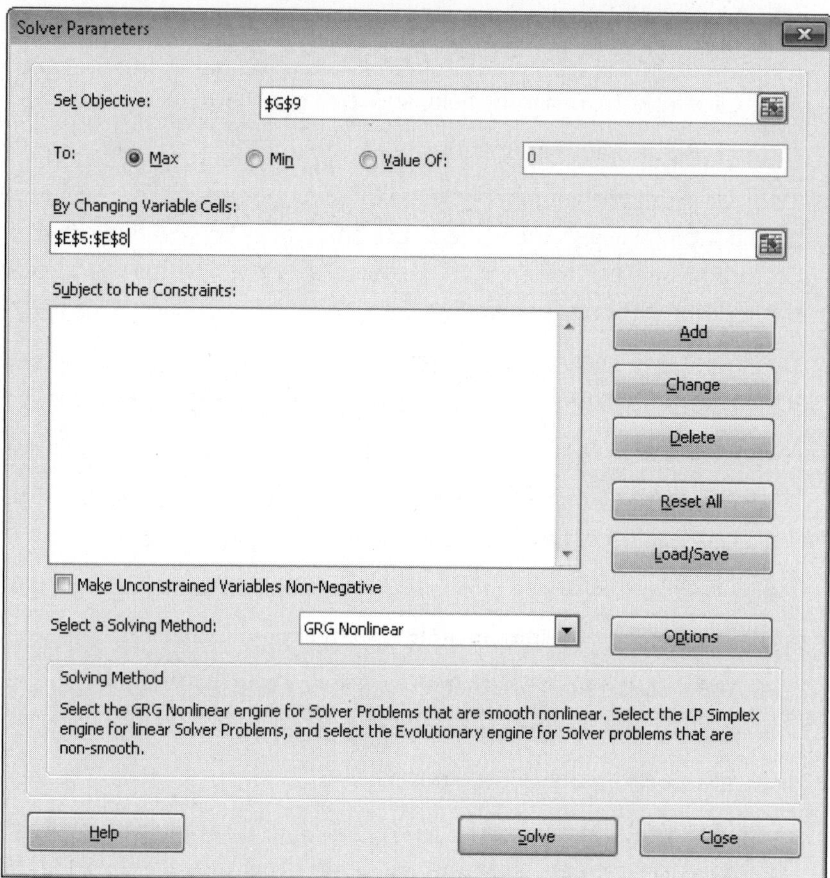

6. Click **Add**.

   The Add Constraint dialog box opens.
7. Select cells **E5:E8**.

   $E$5:$E$8 appears in the Cell Reference field.

8. In the operator list, click **int**. Then click **Add**.

   Excel adds the constraint to the Solver problem, and the Add Constraint dialog box clears to accept the next constraint.

9. Click cell **F9**.

   =$F$9 appears in the Cell Reference field.

10. Click in the **Constraint** field, and then click cell **G11**.

    =$G$11 appears in the Constraint field.

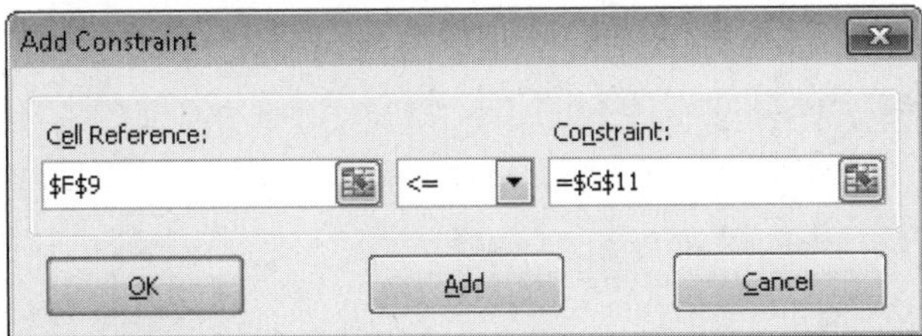

11. Click **Add**.

    Excel adds the constraint to the Solver problem, and the Add Constraint dialog box clears to accept the next constraint.

12. Click cell **G9**.

    $G$9 appears in the Cell Reference field.

13. In the operator list, click **>=**.

14. Click in the **Constraint** field, and then click cell **G12**.

    =$G$12 appears in the Constraint field.

15. Click **Add**.

    Excel adds the constraint to the Solver problem, and the Add Constraint dialog box clears to accept the next constraint.

16. Select cells **E5:E7**.

    $E$5:$E$7 appears in the Cell Reference field.

17. In the operator list, click **>=**.

18. Click in the **Constraint** field, and then click cell **G13**.

=$G$13 appears in the Constraint field.

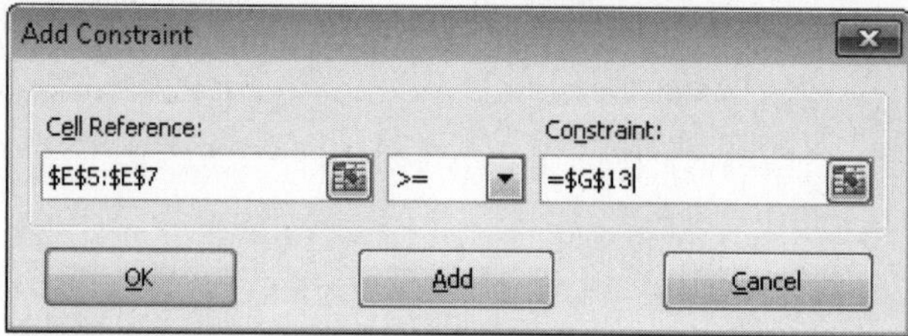

19. Click **Add**.

    Excel adds the constraint to the Solver problem, and the Add Constraint dialog box clears to accept the next constraint.

20. Click cell **E8**.

    $E$8 appears in the Cell Reference field.

21. In the operator list, click **>=**.
22. Click in the **Constraint** field, and then click cell **G14**.

    =$G$14 appears in the Constraint field.

23. Click **Add**.

    Excel adds the constraint to the Solver problem, and the Add Constraint dialog box clears to accept the next constraint.

24. Select cells **E5:E8**.

    $E$5:$E$8 appears in the Cell Reference field.

25. Verify that the **<=** operator appears in the operator field, click in the **Constraint** field, and then click cell **G15**.

    =$G$15 appears in the Constraint field.

26. Click **OK**.

    Excel adds the constraint to the Solver problem and closes the Add Constraint dialog box, and the Solver Parameters dialog box opens again.

27. Click **Solve**.

    The Solver Results dialog box opens, indicating that Solver found a solution. The result is displayed in the body of the worksheet.

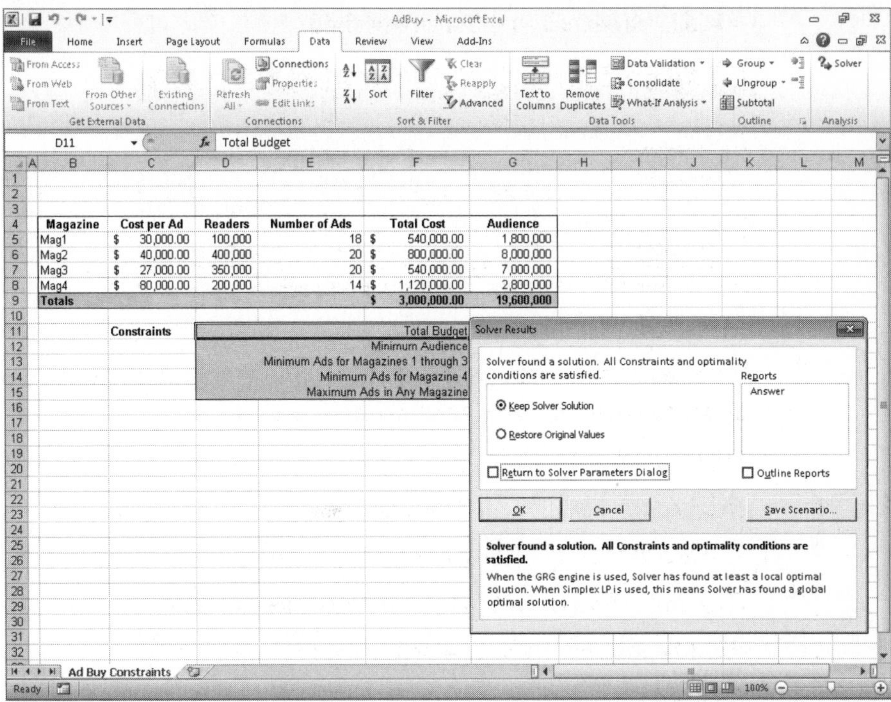

28. Click **Cancel**.

    The Solver Results dialog box closes.

CLEAN UP Save the AdBuy workbook, and then close it.

Analyzing Data by Using Descriptive Statistics

Experienced business people can tell a lot about numbers just by looking at them to see if they "look right." That is, the sales figures are about where they're supposed to be for a particular hour, day, or month; the average seems about right; and sales have increased from year to year. When you need more than an informal assessment, however, you can use the tools in the Analysis ToolPak.

If you don't see the Data Analysis item in the Analysis group on the Data tab, you can install it. To do so, click the File tab, and then click Options. In the Excel Options dialog box, click Add-Ins to display the Add-Ins page. At the bottom of the dialog box, in the Manage list, click Excel Add-Ins, and then click Go to display the Add-Ins dialog box. Select the Analysis ToolPak check box and click OK.

Tip You might be prompted for the Microsoft Office system installation CD. If so, put the CD in your CD drive, and click OK.

After the installation is complete, the Data Analysis item appears in the Analysis group on the Data tab.

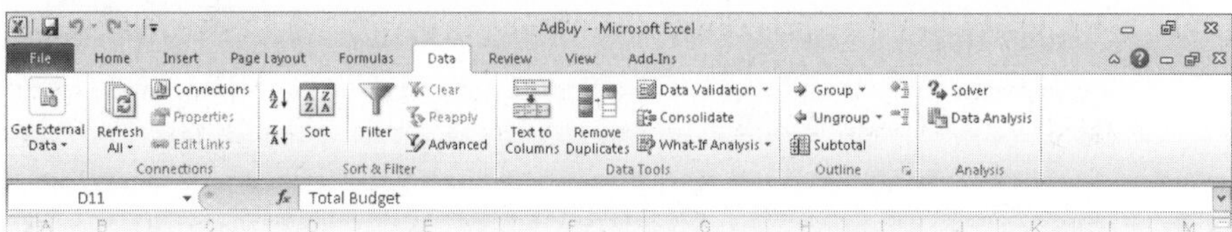

You then click the item representing the type of data analysis you want to perform, click OK, and use the commands in the resulting dialog box to analyze your data.

In this exercise, you'll use the Analysis ToolPak to generate descriptive statistics of driver sorting time data.

SET UP You need the DriverSortTimes_start workbook located in your Chapter08 practice file folder to complete this exercise. Open the DriverSortTimes_start workbook, and save it as *DriverSortTimes*. Then follow the steps.

1. On the **Data** tab, in the **Analysis** group, click **Data Analysis**.

   The Data Analysis dialog box opens.

2. Click **Descriptive Statistics**, and then click **OK**.

   The Descriptive Statistics dialog box opens.

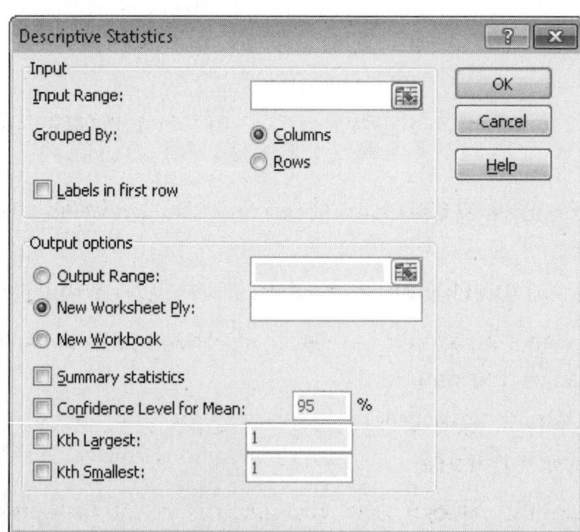

3. Click in the **Input Range** field, and then select cells **C3:C17**.

   $C$3:$C$17 appears in the Input Range field.

4. Select the **Summary statistics** check box.
5. Click **OK**.

   A new worksheet that contains summary statistics about the selected data appears.

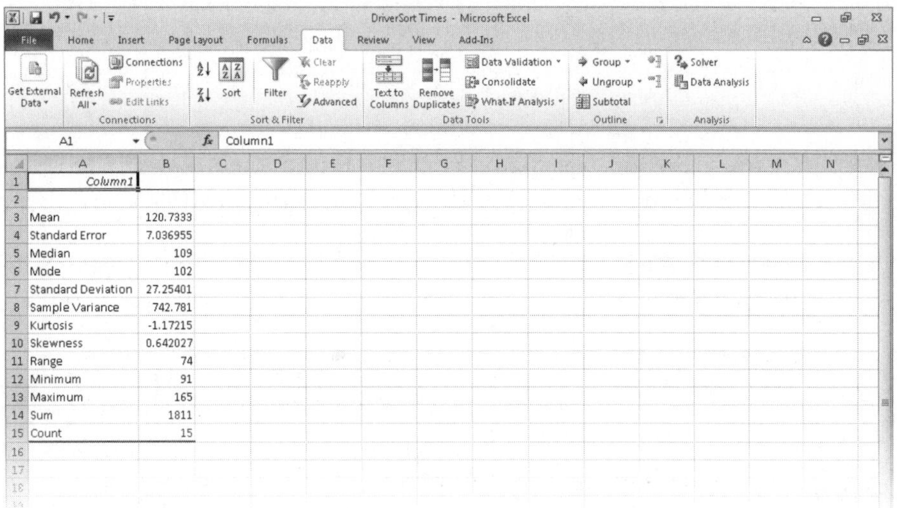

CLEAN UP Save the DriverSortTimes workbook, and then close it. If you're not continuing directly to the next chapter, exit Excel.

Key Points

- Scenarios enable you to describe many potential business cases within a single workbook.
- It's usually a good idea to create a "normal" scenario that enables you to reset your worksheet.
- Remember that you can change up to 32 cells in a scenario, but no more.
- You can summarize your scenarios on a new worksheet to compare how each scenario approaches the data.
- Use Goal Seek to determine what value you need in a single cell to generate the desired result from a formula.
- If you want to vary the values in more than one cell to find the optimal mix of inputs for a calculation, use the Solver Add-In.
- Advanced statistical tools are available in the Analysis ToolPak—use them to examine your data thoroughly.

Chapter at a Glance

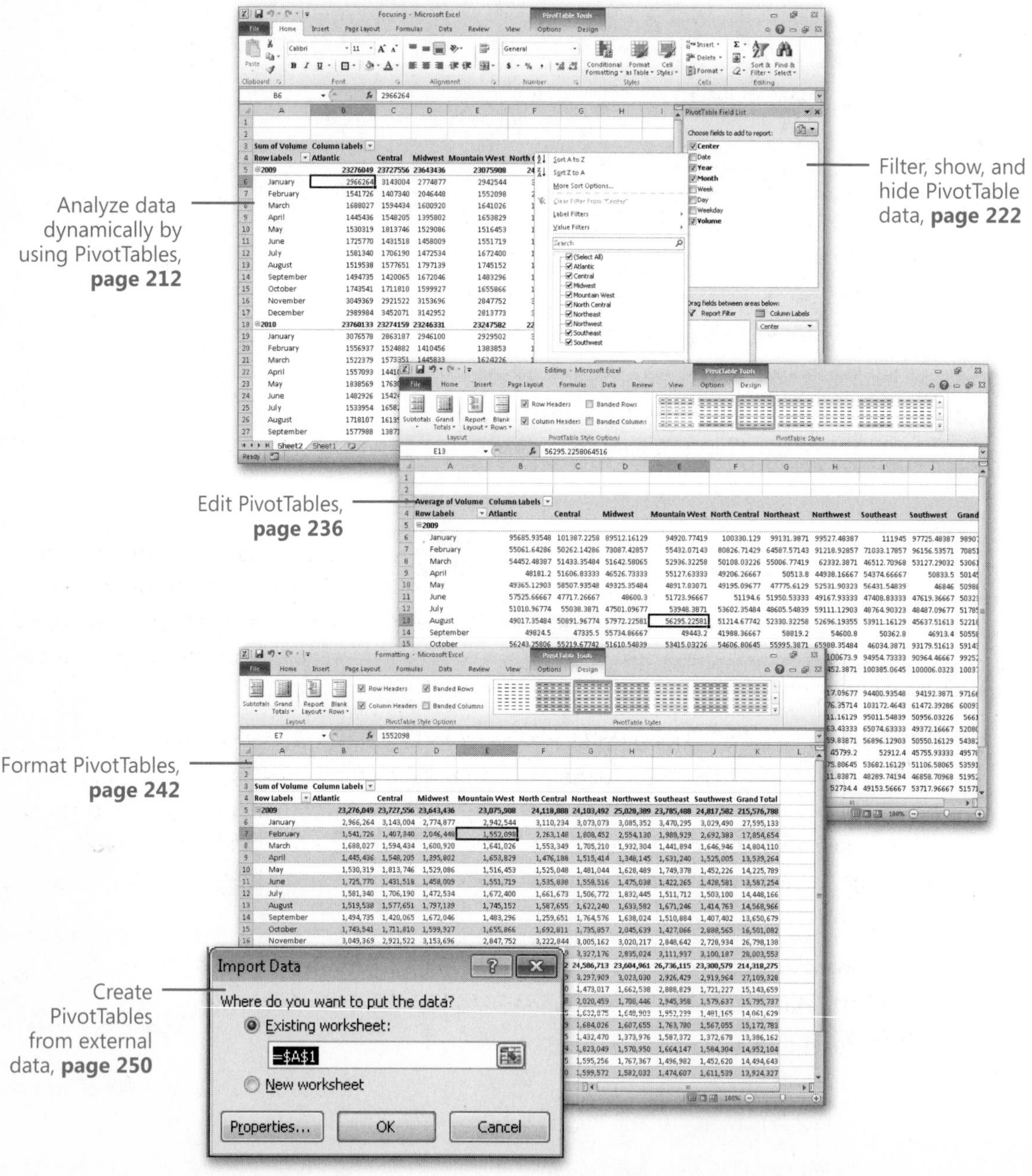

9 Creating Dynamic Worksheets by Using PivotTables

In this chapter, you will learn how to

- ✔ Analyze data dynamically by using PivotTables.
- ✔ Filter, show, and hide PivotTable data.
- ✔ Edit PivotTables.
- ✔ Format PivotTables.
- ✔ Create PivotTables from external data.

When you create Microsoft Excel 2010 worksheets, you must consider how you want the data to appear when you show it to your colleagues. You can change the formatting of your data to emphasize the contents of specific cells, sort and filter your worksheets based on the contents of specific columns, or hide rows containing data that isn't relevant to the point you're trying to make.

One limitation of the standard Excel worksheet is that you can't easily change how the data is organized on the page. For example, in a worksheet in which each column represents an hour in the day, each row represents a day in a month, and the body of the worksheet contains the total sales for every hourly period of the month, you can't change the worksheet quickly so that it displays only sales on Tuesdays during the afternoon.

There is an Excel tool with which you can create worksheets that can be sorted, filtered, and rearranged dynamically to emphasize different aspects of your data. That tool is the PivotTable.

In this chapter, you'll learn how to create and edit PivotTables from an existing worksheet, focus your PivotTable data using filters and Slicers, format PivotTables, and create a PivotTable with data imported from a text file.

Practice Files Before you can complete the exercises in this chapter, you need to copy the book's practice files to your computer. The practice files you'll use to complete the exercises in this chapter are in the Chapter09 practice file folder. A complete list of practice files is provided in "Using the Practice Files" at the beginning of this book.

Analyzing Data Dynamically by Using PivotTables

With Excel worksheets you can gather and present important data, but the standard worksheet can't be changed from its original configuration easily. As an example, consider a worksheet that records monthly package volumes for each of nine distribution centers in the United States.

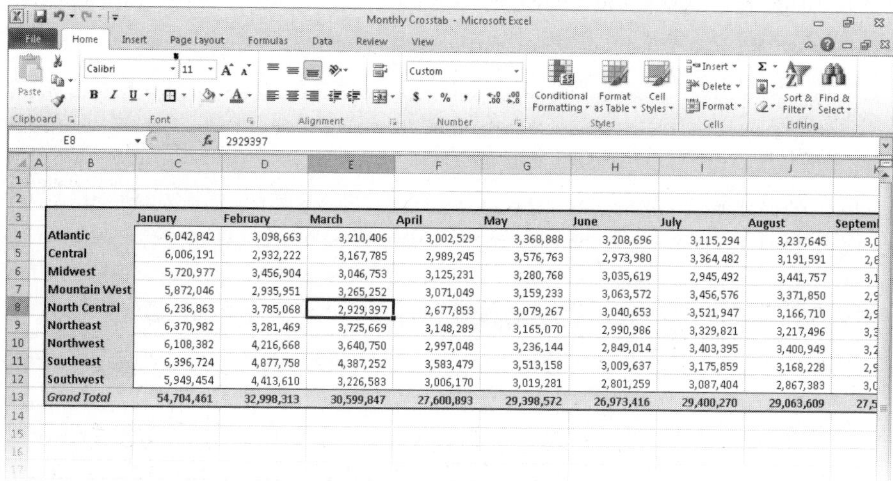

Troubleshooting The appearance of buttons and groups on the ribbon changes depending on the width of the program window. For information about changing the appearance of the ribbon to match our screen images, see "Modifying the Display of the Ribbon" at the beginning of this book.

The data in the worksheet is organized so that each row represents a distribution center and each column represents a month of the year. When presented in this arrangement, the monthly totals for all centers and the yearly total for each distribution center are given equal billing: neither set of totals stands out.

Such a neutral presentation of your data is versatile, but it has limitations. First, although you can use sorting and filtering to restrict the rows or columns shown, it's difficult to change the worksheet's organization. For example, in this worksheet, you can't easily reorganize the contents of your worksheet so that the months are assigned to the rows and the distribution centers are assigned to the columns.

The Excel tool to reorganize and redisplay your data dynamically is the PivotTable. You can create a PivotTable, or dynamic worksheet, that enables you to reorganize and filter your data on the fly. For instance, you can create a PivotTable with the same layout as the worksheet described previously, which emphasizes totals by month, and then change the PivotTable layout to have the rows represent the months of the year and the columns represent the distribution centers. The new layout emphasizes the totals by regional distribution center.

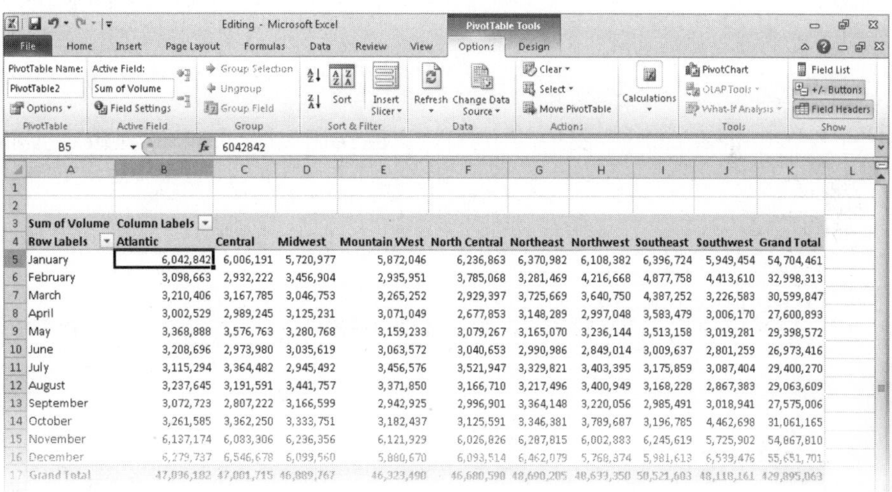

Sum of Volume	Column Labels									
Row Labels	Atlantic	Central	Midwest	Mountain West	North Central	Northeast	Northwest	Southeast	Southwest	Grand Total
January	6,042,842	6,006,191	5,720,977	5,872,046	6,236,863	6,370,982	6,108,382	6,396,724	5,949,454	54,704,461
February	3,098,663	2,932,222	3,456,904	2,935,951	3,785,068	3,281,469	4,216,668	4,877,758	4,413,610	32,998,313
March	3,210,406	3,167,785	3,046,753	3,265,252	2,929,397	3,725,669	3,640,750	4,387,252	3,226,583	30,599,847
April	3,002,529	2,989,245	3,125,231	3,071,049	2,677,853	3,148,289	2,997,048	3,583,479	3,006,170	27,600,893
May	3,368,888	3,576,763	3,280,768	3,159,233	3,079,267	3,165,070	3,236,144	3,513,158	3,019,281	29,398,572
June	3,208,696	2,973,980	3,035,619	3,063,572	3,040,653	2,990,986	2,849,014	3,009,637	2,801,259	26,973,416
July	3,115,294	3,364,482	2,945,492	3,456,576	3,521,947	3,329,821	3,403,395	3,175,859	3,087,404	29,400,270
August	3,237,645	3,191,591	3,441,757	3,371,850	3,166,710	3,217,496	3,400,949	3,168,228	2,867,383	29,063,609
September	3,072,723	2,807,222	3,166,599	2,942,925	2,996,901	3,364,148	3,220,056	2,985,491	3,018,941	27,575,006
October	3,261,585	3,362,250	3,333,751	3,182,437	3,125,591	3,346,381	3,789,687	3,196,785	4,462,698	31,061,165
November	6,137,174	6,083,306	6,236,356	6,121,929	6,026,826	6,287,815	6,002,883	6,245,619	5,725,902	54,867,810
December	6,279,737	6,546,678	6,099,560	5,880,670	6,093,514	6,462,079	5,768,374	5,981,613	6,539,476	55,651,701
Grand Total	47,036,182	47,001,715	46,889,767	46,323,490	46,680,590	48,690,205	48,633,350	50,521,603	48,118,161	429,895,063

To create a PivotTable, you must have your data collected in a list. Excel tables mesh perfectly with PivotTable dynamic views; not only do Excel tables have a well-defined column and row structure, but the ability to refer to an Excel table by its name also greatly simplifies PivotTable creation and management.

In the Excel table used to create the distribution PivotTable, each row of the table contains a value representing the distribution center, date, month, week, weekday, day, and volume for every day of the years 2009 and 2010.

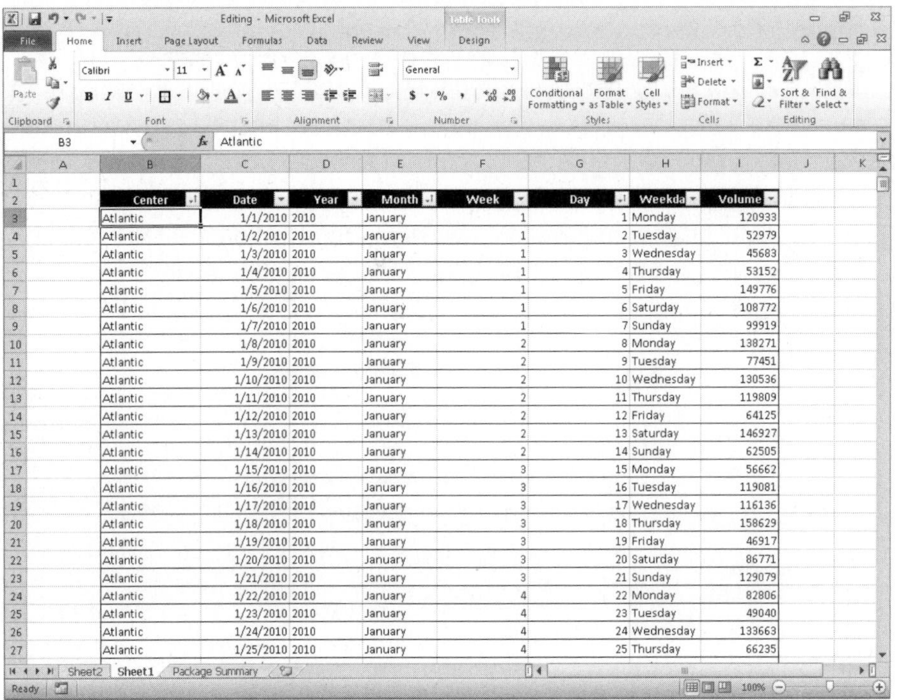

Center	Date	Year	Month	Week	Day	Weekda	Volume
Atlantic	1/1/2010	2010	January	1	1	Monday	120933
Atlantic	1/2/2010	2010	January	1	2	Tuesday	52979
Atlantic	1/3/2010	2010	January	1	3	Wednesday	45683
Atlantic	1/4/2010	2010	January	1	4	Thursday	53152
Atlantic	1/5/2010	2010	January	1	5	Friday	149776
Atlantic	1/6/2010	2010	January	1	6	Saturday	108772
Atlantic	1/7/2010	2010	January	1	7	Sunday	99919
Atlantic	1/8/2010	2010	January	2	8	Monday	138271
Atlantic	1/9/2010	2010	January	2	9	Tuesday	77451
Atlantic	1/10/2010	2010	January	2	10	Wednesday	130536
Atlantic	1/11/2010	2010	January	2	11	Thursday	119809
Atlantic	1/12/2010	2010	January	2	12	Friday	64125
Atlantic	1/13/2010	2010	January	2	13	Saturday	146927
Atlantic	1/14/2010	2010	January	2	14	Sunday	62505
Atlantic	1/15/2010	2010	January	3	15	Monday	56662
Atlantic	1/16/2010	2010	January	3	16	Tuesday	119081
Atlantic	1/17/2010	2010	January	3	17	Wednesday	116136
Atlantic	1/18/2010	2010	January	3	18	Thursday	158629
Atlantic	1/19/2010	2010	January	3	19	Friday	46917
Atlantic	1/20/2010	2010	January	3	20	Saturday	86771
Atlantic	1/21/2010	2010	January	3	21	Sunday	129079
Atlantic	1/22/2010	2010	January	4	22	Monday	82806
Atlantic	1/23/2010	2010	January	4	23	Tuesday	49040
Atlantic	1/24/2010	2010	January	4	24	Wednesday	133663
Atlantic	1/25/2010	2010	January	4	25	Thursday	66235

Excel needs that data when it creates the PivotTable so that it can maintain relationships among the data. If you want to filter your PivotTable so that it shows all package volumes on Thursdays in January, for example, Excel must be able to identify January 11 as a Thursday.

After you create an Excel table, you can click any cell in the table, display the Insert tab and then, in the Tables group, click PivotTable to open the Create PivotTable dialog box.

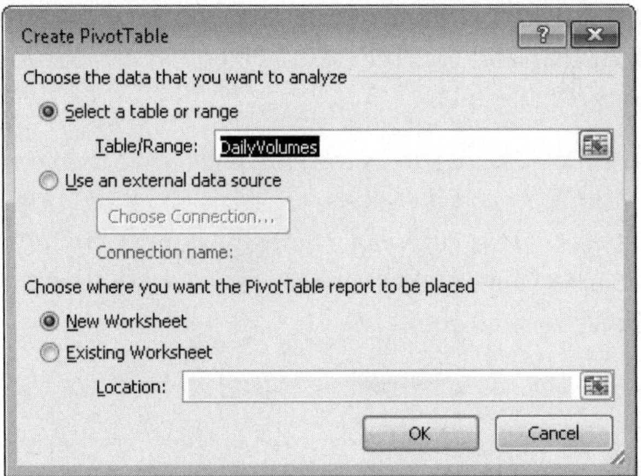

In this dialog box, you verify the data source for your PivotTable and whether you want to create a PivotTable on a new worksheet or an existing worksheet. After you click OK, Excel displays a new or existing worksheet and displays the PivotTable Field List task pane.

Tip You should always place your PivotTable on its own worksheet to avoid cluttering the display.

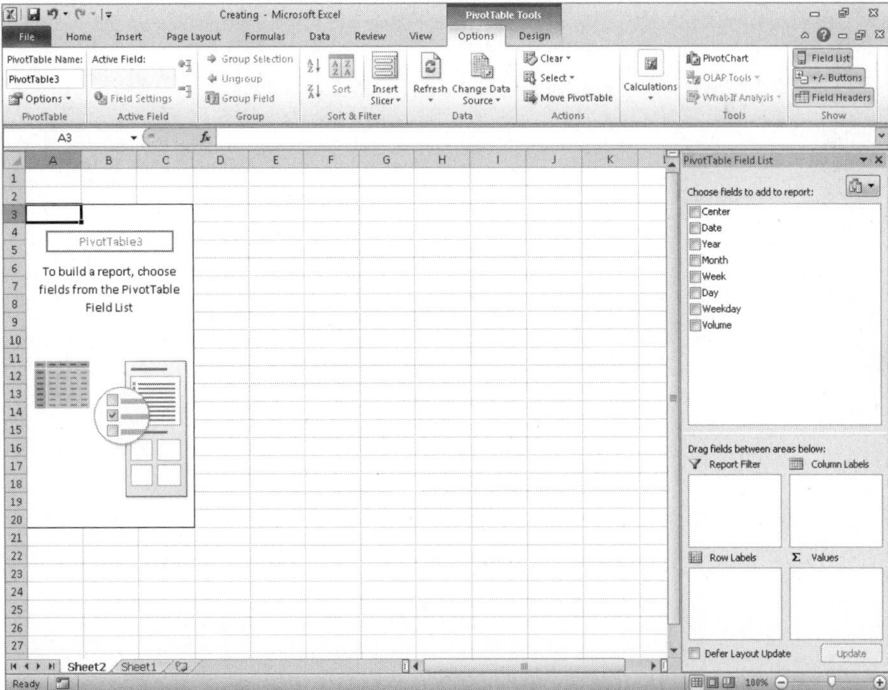

If the PivotTable Field List task pane isn't visible, you can display it by clicking any cell in the PivotTable to display the PivotTable Tools contextual tabs. On the Options contextual tab, in the Show/Hide group, click Field List.

To assign a field, or column of data, to an area of the PivotTable, drag the field header from the Choose Fields To Add To Report area at the top of the PivotTable Field List task pane to the Drag Fields Between Areas Below area at the bottom of the task pane. For example, if you drag the Volume field header to the Values area, the PivotTable displays the total of all entries in the Volume column.

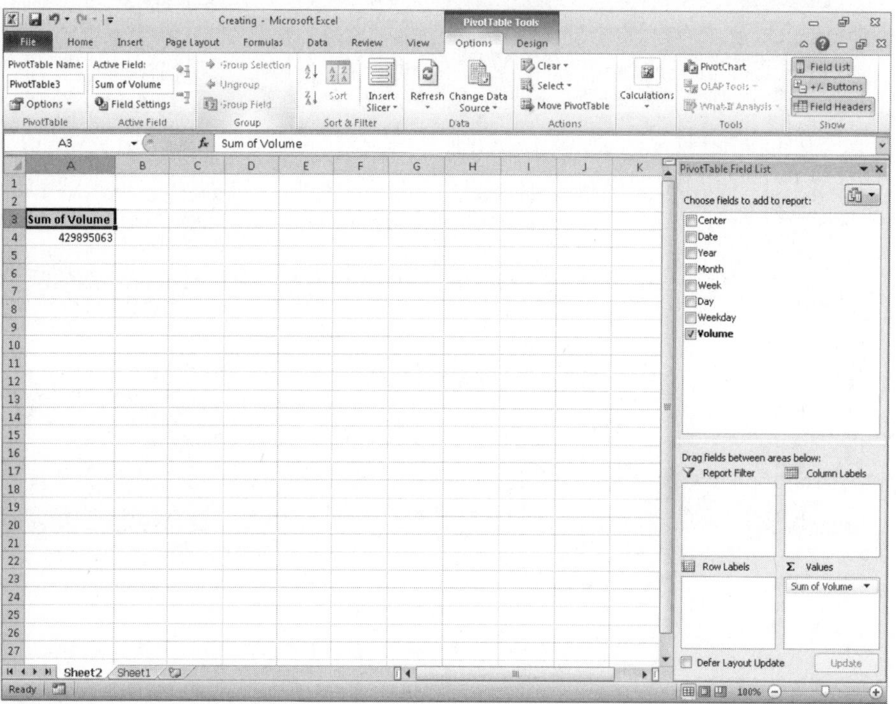

It's important to note that the order in which you enter the fields in the Row Labels and Column Labels areas affects how Excel organizes the data in your PivotTable. As an example, consider a PivotTable that groups the PivotTable rows by distribution center and then by month.

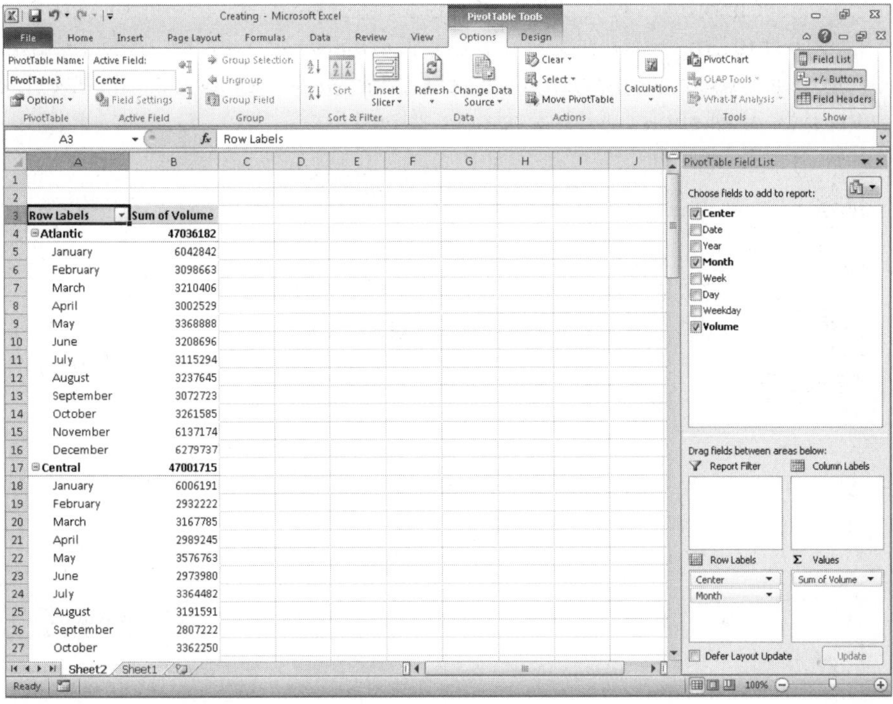

The same PivotTable data could also be organized by month and then by distribution center.

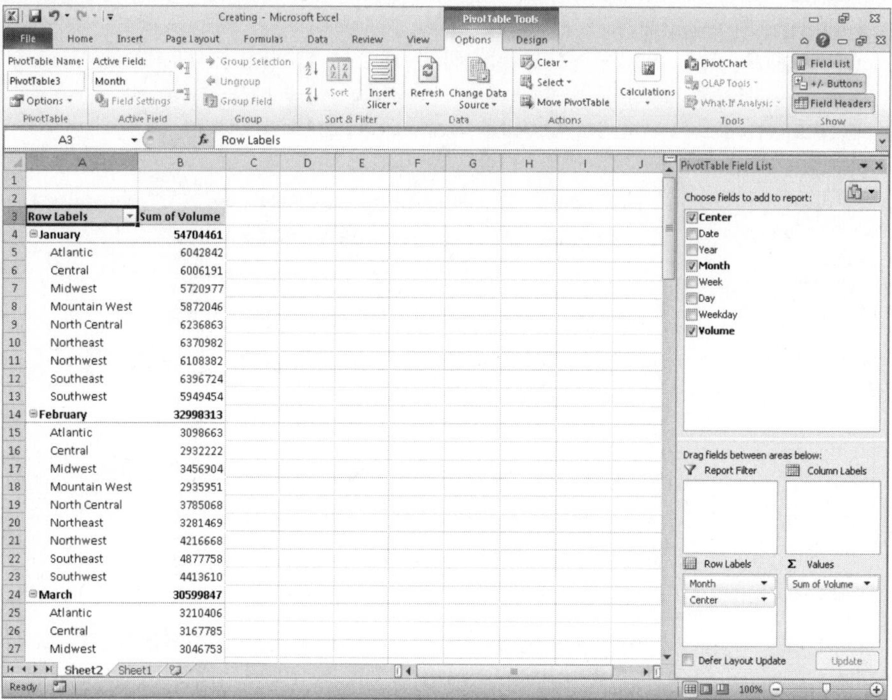

In the preceding examples, all the field headers are in the Row Labels area. If you drag the Center header from the Row Labels area to the Column Labels area, the PivotTable reorganizes (pivots) its data to form a different configuration.

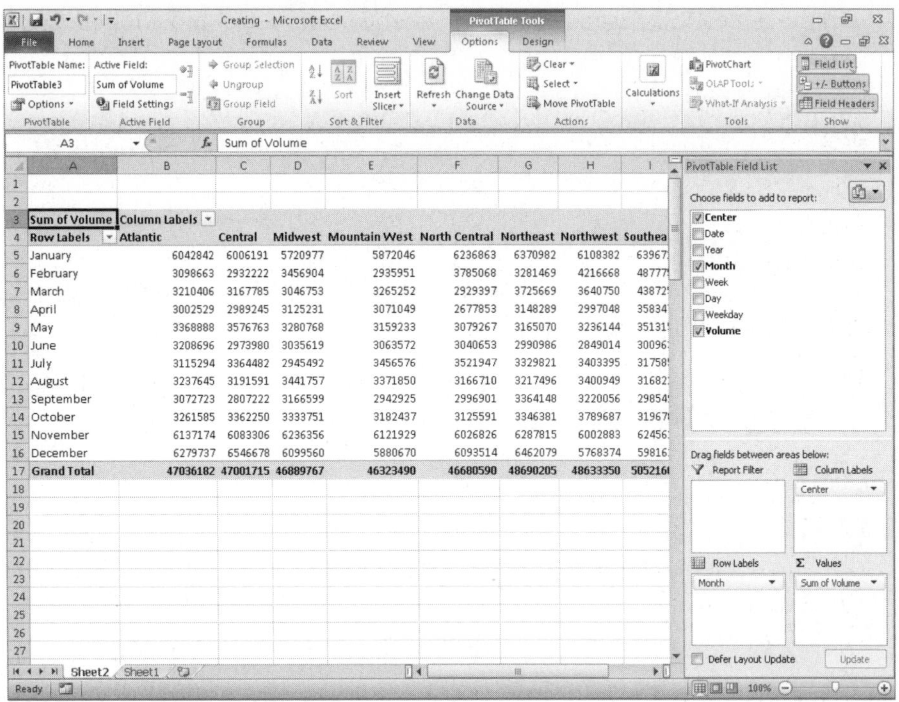

To pivot a PivotTable, you drag a field header to a new position in the PivotTable Field List task pane. As you drag a field within the task pane, Excel displays a blue line in the interior of the target area so you know where the field will appear when you release the left mouse button. If your data set is large or if you based your PivotTable on a data collection on another computer, it might take some time for Excel to reorganize the PivotTable after a pivot. You can have Excel delay redrawing the PivotTable by selecting the Defer Layout Update check box in the lower-left corner of the PivotTable Field List task pane. When you're ready for Excel to display the reorganized PivotTable, click Update.

If you expect your PivotTable source data to change, such as when you link to an external database that records shipments or labor hours, you should ensure that your PivotTable summarizes all the available data. To do that, you can refresh the PivotTable connection to its data source. If Excel detects new data in the source table, it updates the PivotTable contents accordingly. To refresh your PivotTable, click any cell in the PivotTable and then, on the Options contextual tab, in the Data group, click Refresh.

In this exercise, you'll create a PivotTable by using data from a table, add fields to the PivotTable, and then pivot the PivotTable.

SET UP You need the Creating_start workbook located in your Chapter09 practice file folder to complete this exercise. Start Excel, open the Creating_start workbook, and save it as *Creating*. Then follow the steps.

1. Click any cell in the Excel table.

2. On the **Insert** tab, in the **Tables** group, click the **PivotTable** button (not the arrow).

   The Create PivotTable dialog box opens.

3. Verify that the **DailyVolumes** table name appears in the **Table/Range** field and that the **New Worksheet** option is selected.

4. Click **OK**.

   Excel creates a PivotTable on a new worksheet.

5. In the **PivotTable Field List** task pane, drag the **Center** field header to the **Row Labels** area.

   Excel adds the Center field values to the PivotTable row area.

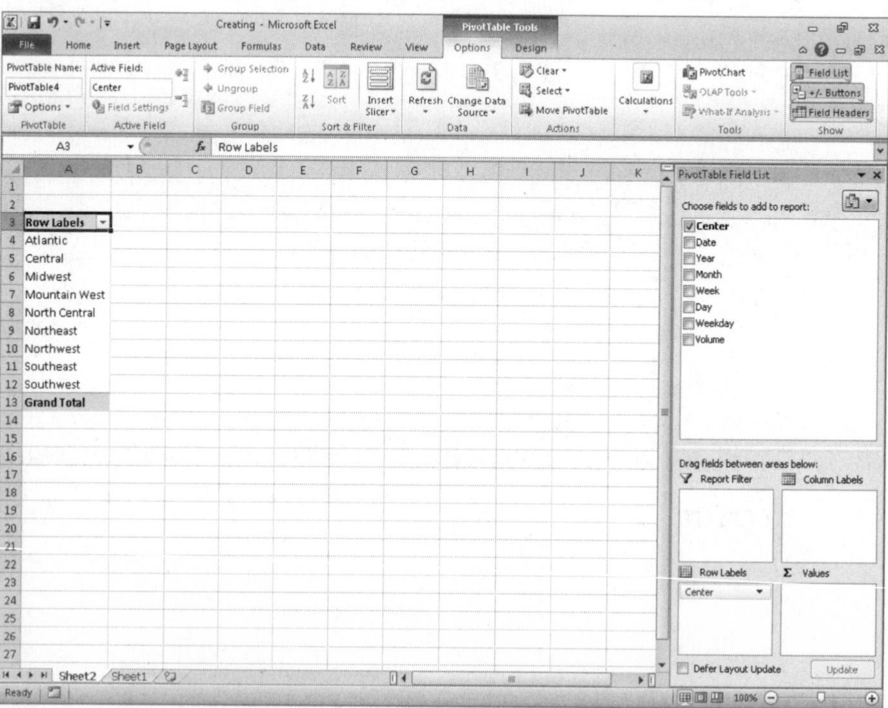

6. In the **PivotTable Field List** task pane, drag the **Year** field header to the **Column Labels** area.

   Excel adds the Year field values to the PivotTable column area.

7. In the **PivotTable Field List** task pane, drag the **Volume** field header to the **Values** area.

   Excel fills in the body of the PivotTable with the Volume field values.

8. In the **PivotTable Field List** task pane, in the **Column Labels** area, drag the **Year** field header to the **Row Labels** area, and drop it beneath the **Center** field header.

   Excel changes the PivotTable to reflect the new organization.

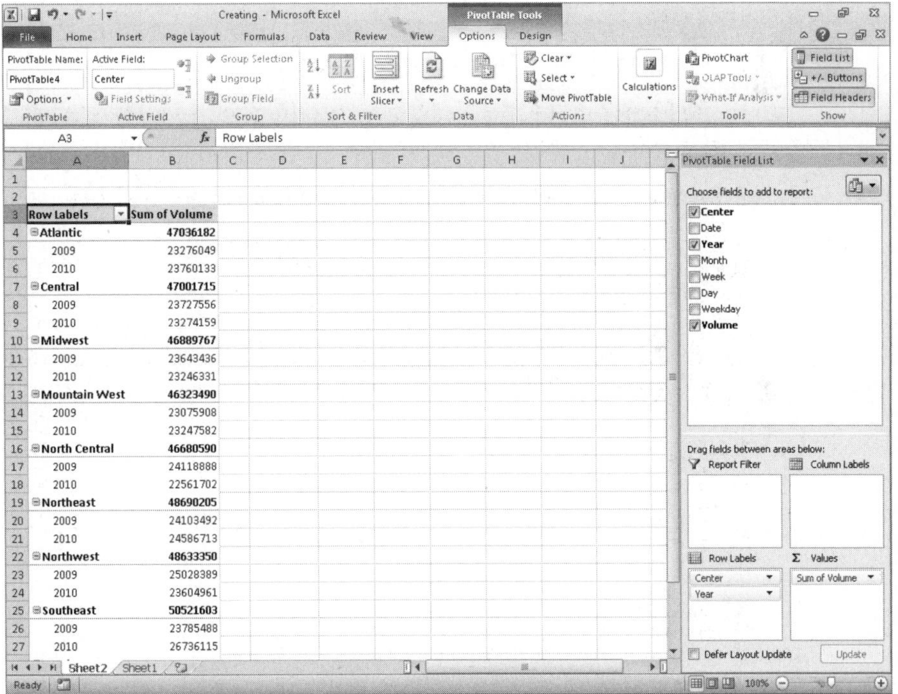

 **CLEAN UP** Save the Creating workbook, and then close it.

Filtering, Showing, and Hiding PivotTable Data

PivotTables often summarize huge data sets in a relatively small worksheet. The more details you can capture and write to a table, the more flexibility you have in analyzing the data. As an example, consider all the details captured in a table in which each row contains a value representing the distribution center, date, month, week, weekday, day, and volume for every day of the year.

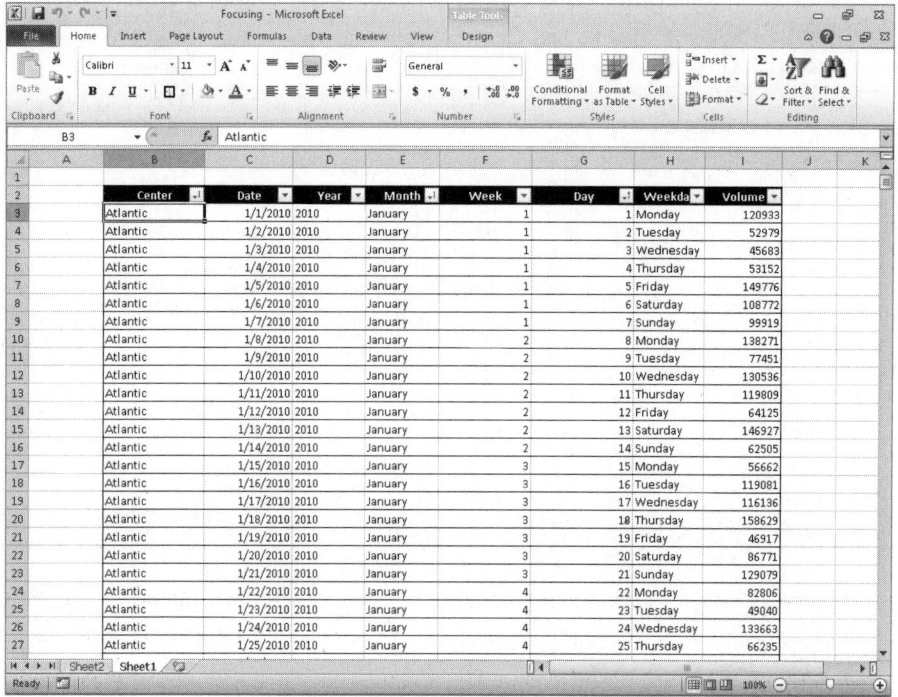

Center	Date	Year	Month	Week	Day	Weekda	Volume
Atlantic	1/1/2010	2010	January	1	1	Monday	120933
Atlantic	1/2/2010	2010	January	1	2	Tuesday	52979
Atlantic	1/3/2010	2010	January	1	3	Wednesday	45683
Atlantic	1/4/2010	2010	January	1	4	Thursday	53152
Atlantic	1/5/2010	2010	January	1	5	Friday	149776
Atlantic	1/6/2010	2010	January	1	6	Saturday	108772
Atlantic	1/7/2010	2010	January	1	7	Sunday	99919
Atlantic	1/8/2010	2010	January	2	8	Monday	138271
Atlantic	1/9/2010	2010	January	2	9	Tuesday	77451
Atlantic	1/10/2010	2010	January	2	10	Wednesday	130536
Atlantic	1/11/2010	2010	January	2	11	Thursday	119809
Atlantic	1/12/2010	2010	January	2	12	Friday	64125
Atlantic	1/13/2010	2010	January	2	13	Saturday	146927
Atlantic	1/14/2010	2010	January	2	14	Sunday	62505
Atlantic	1/15/2010	2010	January	3	15	Monday	56662
Atlantic	1/16/2010	2010	January	3	16	Tuesday	119081
Atlantic	1/17/2010	2010	January	3	17	Wednesday	116136
Atlantic	1/18/2010	2010	January	3	18	Thursday	158629
Atlantic	1/19/2010	2010	January	3	19	Friday	46917
Atlantic	1/20/2010	2010	January	3	20	Saturday	86771
Atlantic	1/21/2010	2010	January	3	21	Sunday	129079
Atlantic	1/22/2010	2010	January	4	22	Monday	82806
Atlantic	1/23/2010	2010	January	4	23	Tuesday	49040
Atlantic	1/24/2010	2010	January	4	24	Wednesday	133663
Atlantic	1/25/2010	2010	January	4	25	Thursday	66235

Each column, in turn, contains numerous values: there are nine distribution centers, data from two years, 12 months in a year, seven weekdays, and as many as five weeks and 31 days in a month. Just as you can filter the data that appears in an Excel table or other data collection, you can filter the data displayed in a PivotTable by selecting which values you want the PivotTable to include.

See Also For more information on filtering an Excel table, see "Limiting Data That Appears on Your Screen" in Chapter 5, "Focusing on Specific Data by Using Filters."

To filter a PivotTable based on a field's contents, click the field's header in the Choose Fields To Add To Report area of the PivotTable Field List task pane. When you do, Excel displays a menu of sorting and filtering options.

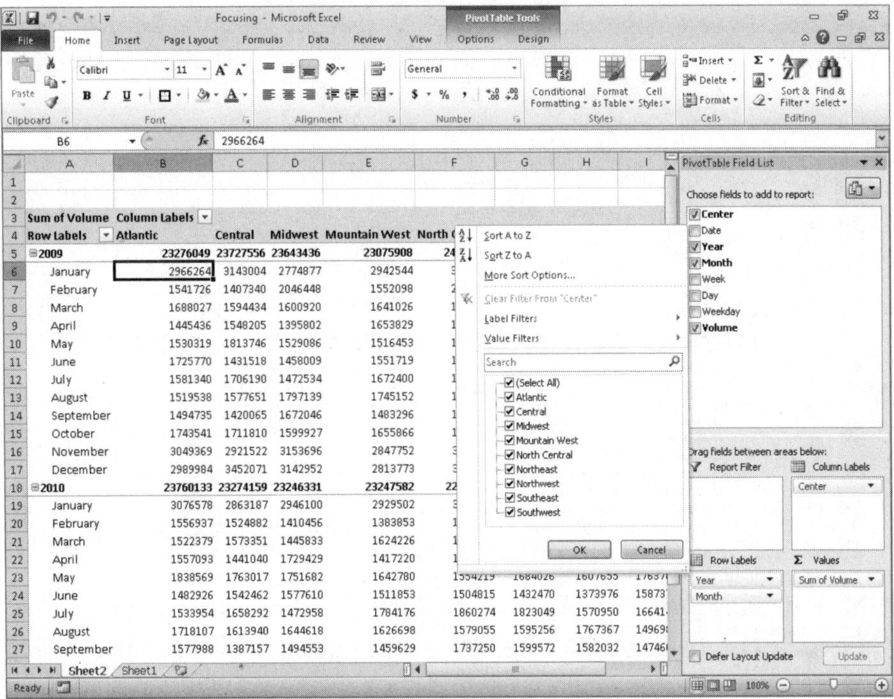

The PivotTable displays several sorting options, commands for different categories of filters, and a list of items that appear in the field you want to filter. Every list item has a check box next to it. Items with a check mark in the box are currently displayed in the PivotTable, and items without a check mark are hidden.

The first entry at the top of the item list is the Select All check box. The Select All check box can have one of three states: displaying a check mark, displaying a black square, or empty. If the Select All check box contains a check mark, then the PivotTable displays every item in the list. If the Select All check box is empty, then no filter items are selected. Finally, if the Select All check box contains a black square, it means that some, but not all, of the items in the list are displayed. Selecting only the Northwest check box, for example, leads to a PivotTable configuration in which only the data for the Northwest center is displayed.

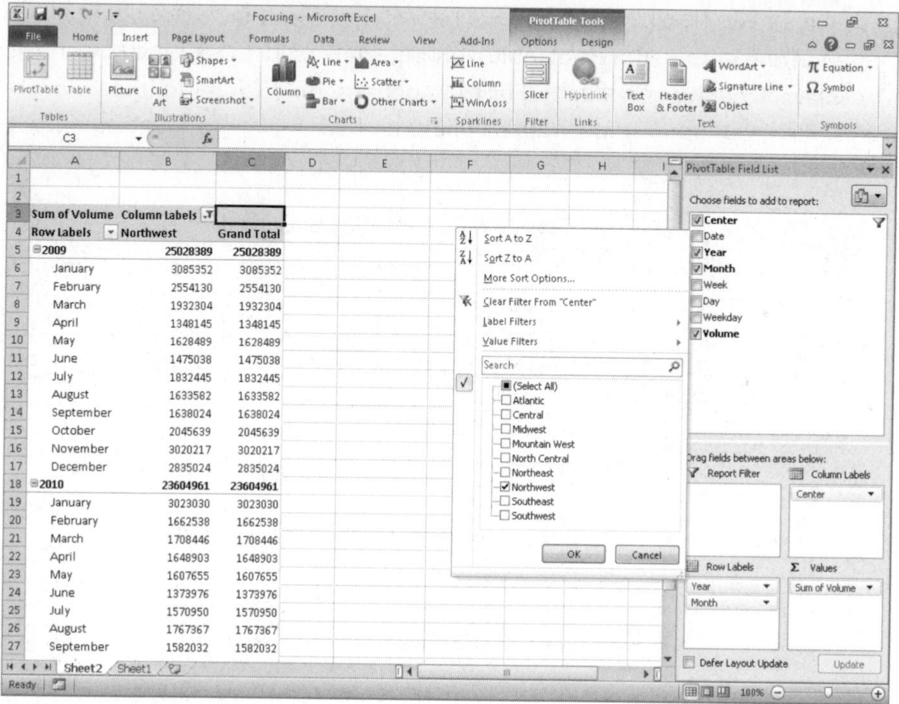

If you'd rather display as much PivotTable data as possible, you can hide the PivotTable Field List task pane and filter the PivotTable by using the filter arrows on the Row Labels and Column Labels headers within the body of the PivotTable. Clicking either of those headers enables you to select a field by which you can filter; you can then define the filter by using the same controls you see when you click a field header in the PivotTable Field List task pane.

Excel indicates that a PivotTable has filters applied by placing a filter indicator next to the Column Labels or Row Labels header, as appropriate, and the filtered field name in the PivotTable Field List task pane.

So far, all the fields by which we've filtered the PivotTable have changed the organization of the data in the PivotTable. Adding some fields to a PivotTable, however, might create unwanted complexity. For example, you might want to filter a PivotTable by weekday, but adding the Weekday field to the body of the PivotTable expands the table unnecessarily.

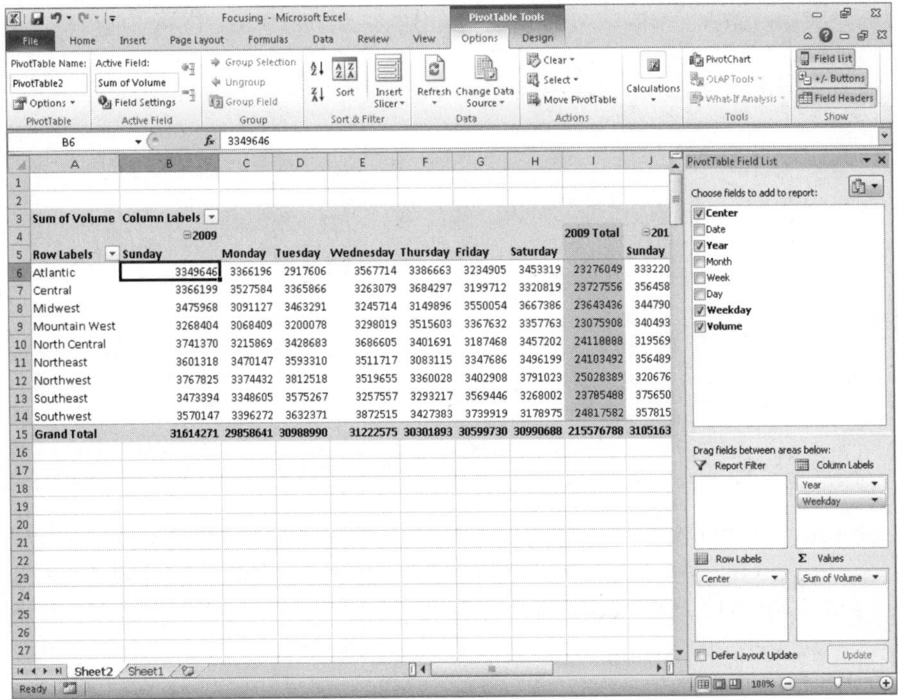

Instead of adding the Weekday field to the Row Labels or Column Labels area, you can drag the field to the Report Filter area near the bottom of the PivotTable Field List task pane. Doing so leaves the body of the PivotTable unchanged, but adds a new area above the PivotTable in its worksheet.

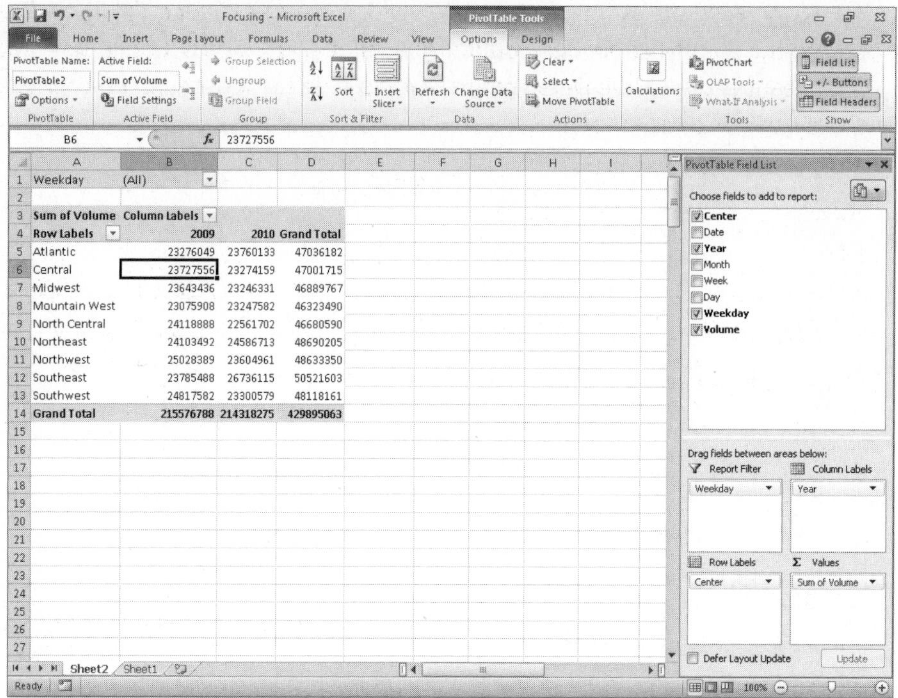

Tip In Excel 2003 and earlier versions, this area was called the Page Field area.

When you click the filter arrow of a field in the Report Filter area, Excel displays a list of the values in the field. When you click the filter arrow, you can choose to filter by one value at a time. If you'd like to filter your PivotTable by more than one value, you can do so by selecting the Select Multiple Items check box.

If your PivotTable has more than one field in the Row Labels area, you can filter values in a PivotTable by hiding and collapsing levels of detail within the report. To do that, you click the Hide Detail control (which looks like a box with a minus sign in it) or the Show Detail control (which looks like a box with a plus sign in it) next to a header.

For example, you might have your data divided by year; clicking the Show Detail control next to the 2009 year header would display that year's details. Conversely, clicking the 2010 year header's Hide Detail control would hide the individual months' values and display only the year's total.

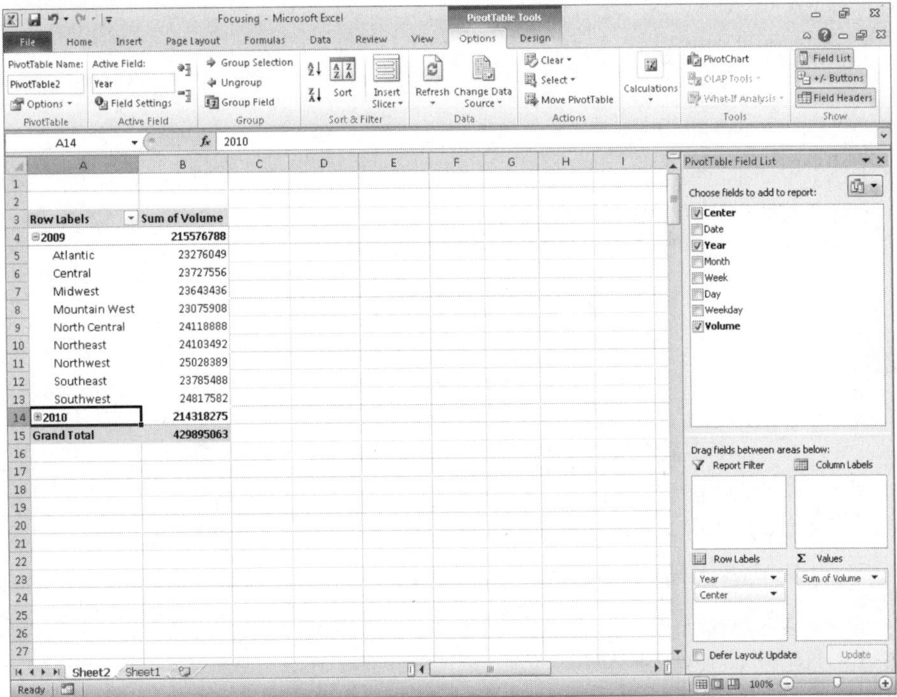

Excel 2010 provides two new ways for you to filter PivotTables: search filters and Slicers. With a search filter, you can type in a series of characters for Excel to filter that field's values. To create a search filter, click a field's filter arrow and type the character string for which you want to search in the filter menu's Search box.

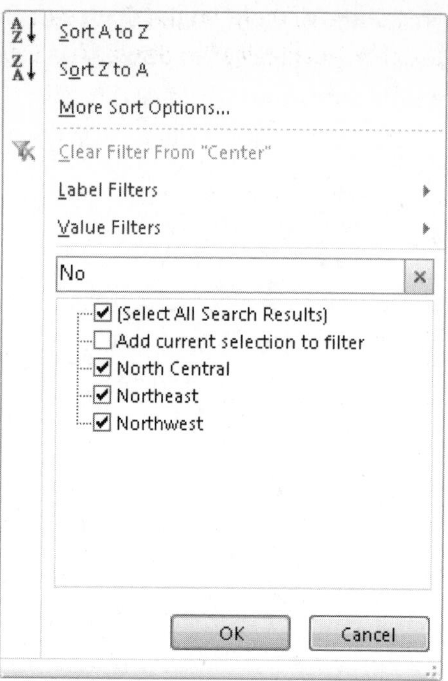

For example, if the PivotTable's Center field contains the values Atlantic, Central, Midwest, Mountain West, North Central, Northeast, Northwest, Southeast, and Southwest, typing the character string "No" limits the values to *North Central*, *Northeast*, and *Northwest*.

Tip Search filters look for the character string you specify anywhere within a field's value, not just at the start of the value. In the previous example, the search filter string "cen" would return both *Central* and *North Central*.

In versions of Excel prior to Excel 2010, the only visual indication that you had applied a filter to a field was the indicator added to a field's filter arrow. The indicator told users that there was an active filter applied to that field but provided no information on which values were displayed and which were hidden. In Excel 2010, Slicers provide a visual indication of which items are currently displayed or hidden in a PivotTable.

To create a Slicer, click any cell in a PivotTable and then, on the Options contextual tab of the ribbon, in the Sort & Filter group, click Insert Slicer to display the Insert Slicers dialog box.

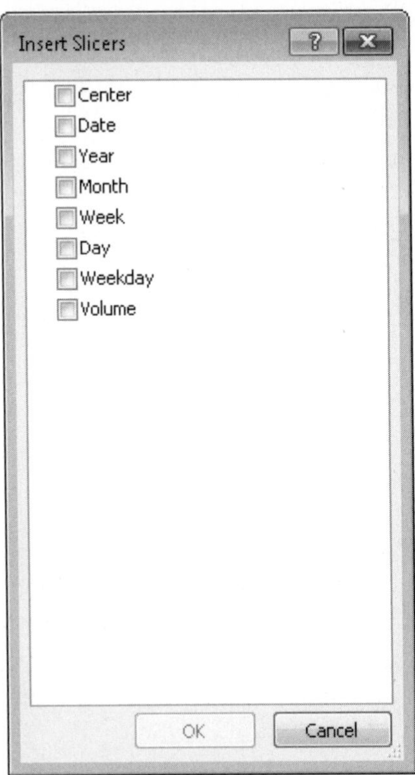

Select the check box next to the fields for which you want to create a Slicer, and click OK. When you do, Excel 2010 displays a Slicer for each field you identified.

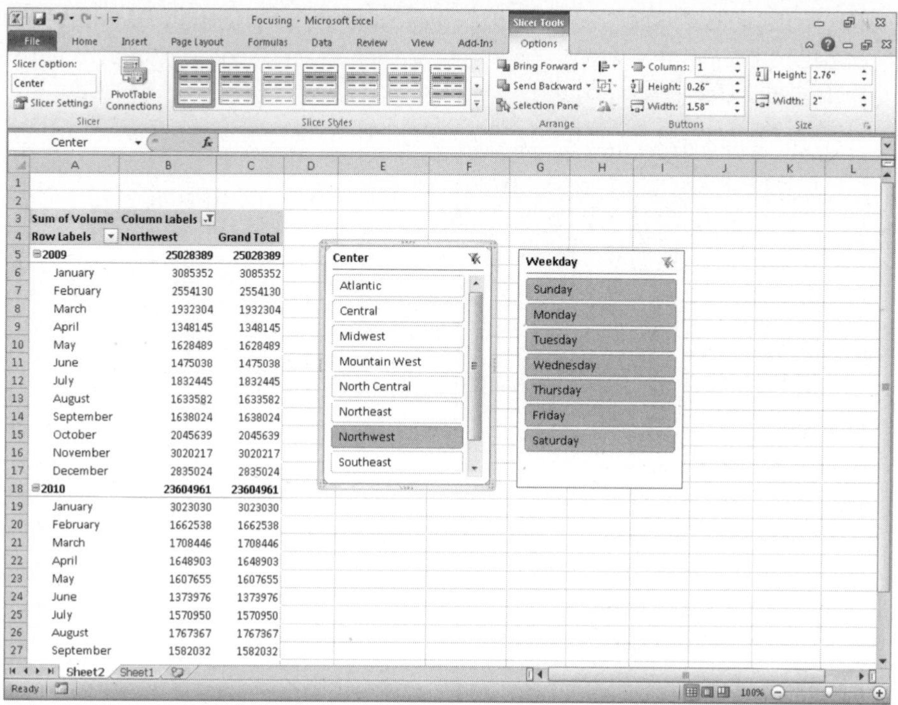

Tip If you have already applied a filter to the field for which you display a Slicer, the Slicer reflects the filter's result.

A Slicer displays the values within the PivotTable field you identified. Any value displayed in color (or gray if you select a gray-and-white color scheme) appears within the PivotTable. Values displayed in light gray or white do not appear in the PivotTable.

Clicking an item in a Slicer changes that item's state—if a value is currently displayed in a PivotTable, clicking it hides it. If it's hidden, clicking its value in the Slicer displays it in the PivotTable. As with other objects in an Excel 2010 workbook, you can use the Shift and Ctrl keys to help define your selections. For example, suppose you create a Slicer for the Month field while every month is displayed.

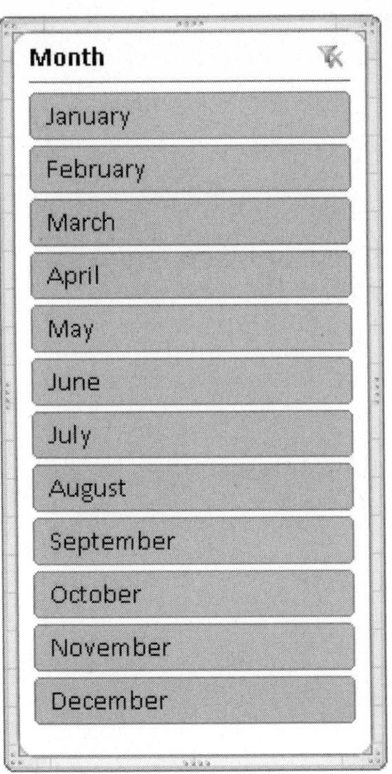

If you want to hide every month except January, February, and March, you click the January item to hide every month except January. Then hold down the Shift key and click March to have Excel 2010 display just the data for the months of January, February, and March. You can then add another month, such as July, to the filter by holding down the Ctrl key and clicking July in the Slicer.

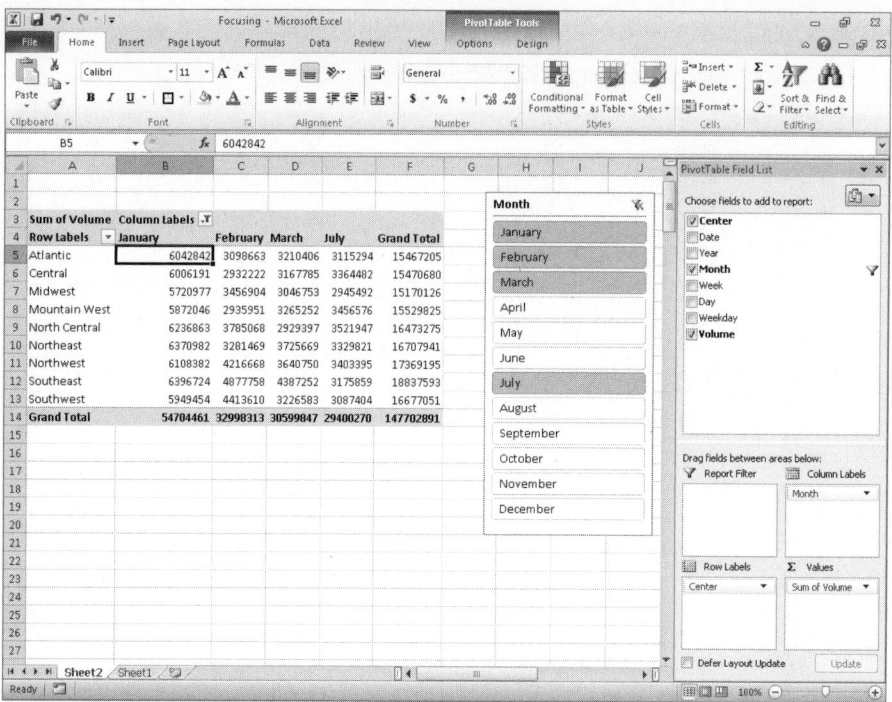

To use a Slicer to remove a filter, click the Clear Filter button in the upper-right corner of the Slicer. If you want to resize a Slicer, you can do so by dragging the resize handle in the lower-right corner of the Slicer. To hide the Slicer, right-click it and then click the menu command that starts with the word "Remove." For example, the Month field's menu command would be Remove Month.

Tip You can change a Slicer's formatting by clicking the Slicer and then, on the Slicer Tools Options contextual tab on the ribbon, clicking a style in the Slicer Styles gallery.

In this exercise, you'll focus the data displayed in a PivotTable by creating a filter, by filtering a PivotTable based on the contents of a field in the Report Filters area, by showing and hiding levels of detail within the body of the PivotTable, by using the Search box, and by using Slicers.

SET UP You need the Focusing_start workbook located in your Chapter09 practice file folder to complete this exercise. Open the Focusing_start workbook, and save it as *Focusing*. Then follow the steps.

1. On the **Sheet2** worksheet, click any cell in the PivotTable.
2. In the **PivotTable Field List** task pane's **Choose fields to add to report** area, click the **Center** field header, click the **Center** field filter arrow, and then clear the **(Select All)** check box.

Excel clears all the check boxes in the filter menu.

3. Select the **Northwest** check box, and then click **OK**.

   Excel filters the PivotTable.

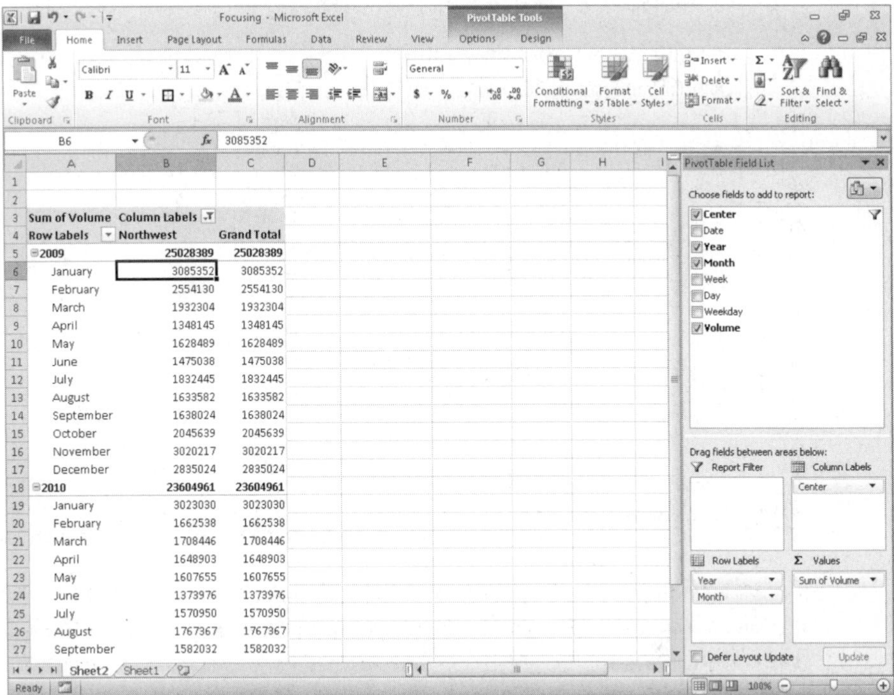

4. On the Quick Access Toolbar, click the **Undo** button.

   Excel removes the filter.

5. In the **PivotTable Field List** task pane, drag the **Weekday** field header from the **Choose fields to add to report** area to the **Report Filter** area in the **Drag fields between areas below** area.

6. In the **PivotTable Field List** task pane, click the **Close** button.

   The PivotTable Field List task pane closes.

7. In the body of the worksheet, click the **Weekday** filter arrow, and then, if necessary, select the **Select Multiple Items** check box.

   Excel adds check boxes beside the items in the Weekday field filter list.

8. Clear the **All** check box.

   Excel clears each check box in the list.

9. Select the **Tuesday** and **Thursday** check boxes, and then click **OK**.

   Excel filters the PivotTable, summarizing only those values from Tuesdays and Thursdays.

10. In cell A5, click the **Hide Detail** button.

    Excel collapses rows that contain data from the year 2009, leaving only the subtotal row that summarizes that year's data.

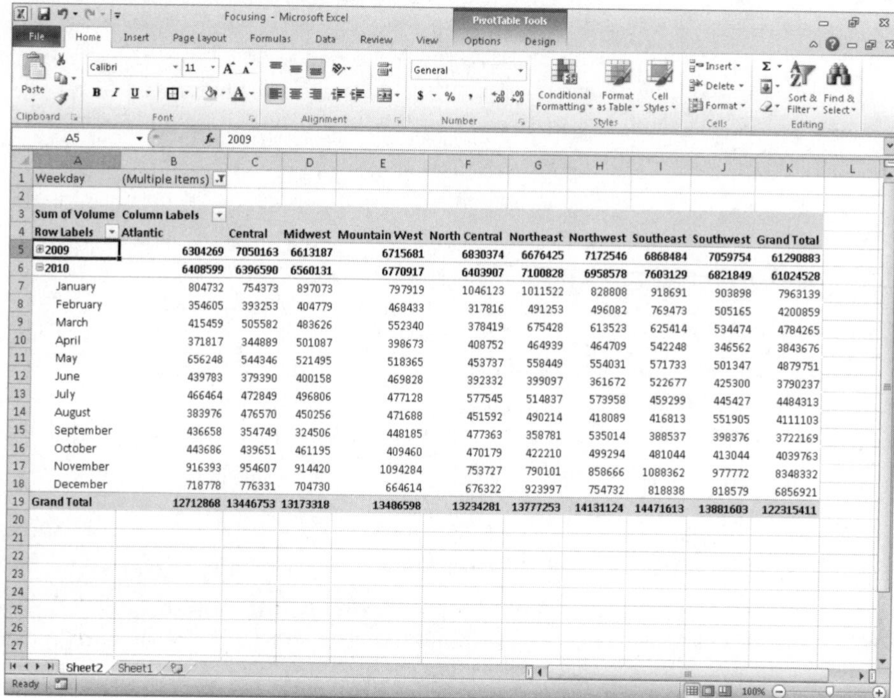

Weekday	(Multiple Items)									
Sum of Volume	Column Labels									
Row Labels	Atlantic	Central	Midwest	Mountain West	North Central	Northeast	Northwest	Southeast	Southwest	Grand Total
2009	**6304269**	**7050163**	**6613187**	**6715681**	**6830374**	**6676425**	**7172546**	**6868484**	**7059754**	**61290883**
2010	**6408599**	**6396590**	**6560131**	**6770917**	**6403907**	**7100828**	**6958578**	**7603129**	**6821849**	**61024528**
January	804732	754373	897073	797919	1046123	1011522	828808	918691	903898	7963139
February	354605	393253	404779	468433	317816	491253	496082	769473	505165	4200859
March	415459	505582	483626	552340	378419	675428	613523	625414	534474	4784265
April	371817	344889	501087	398673	408752	464939	464709	542248	346562	3843676
May	656248	544346	521495	518365	453737	558449	554031	571733	501347	4879751
June	439783	379390	400158	469828	392332	399097	361672	522677	425300	3790237
July	466464	472849	496806	477128	577545	514837	573958	459299	445427	4484313
August	383976	476570	450256	471688	451592	490214	418089	416813	551905	4111103
September	436658	354749	324506	448185	477363	358781	535014	388537	398376	3722169
October	443686	439651	461195	409460	470179	422210	499294	481044	413044	4039763
November	916393	954607	914420	1094284	753727	790101	858666	1088362	977772	8348332
December	718778	776331	704730	664614	676322	923997	754732	818838	818579	6856921
Grand Total	**12712868**	**13446753**	**13173318**	**13486598**	**13234281**	**13777253**	**14131124**	**14471613**	**13881603**	**122315411**

11. In cell **A5**, click the **Show Detail** button.

    Excel redisplays the collapsed rows.

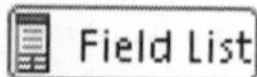

12. On the ribbon, click the **Options** contextual tab, and then, in the **Show** group, click **Field List**.

    The PivotTable Field List task pane opens.

13. In the **PivotTable Field List** task pane, click the **Month** field header arrow.

    The filter menu opens.

14. In the **Search** box, type **Ju**.

    Excel displays the months June and July in the filter list.

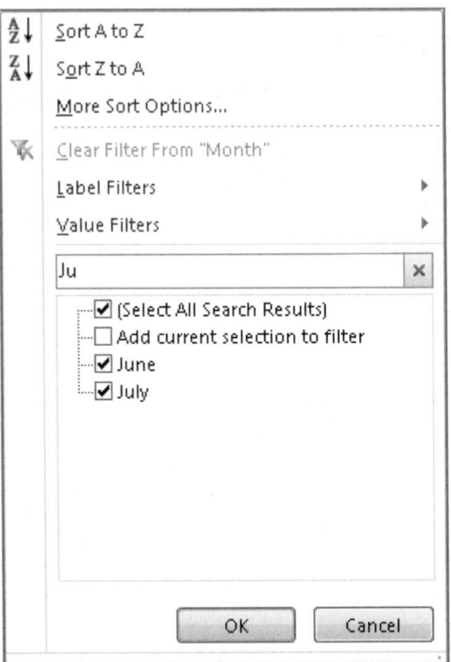

15. Click **OK**.

    Excel applies the filter.

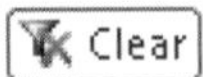

16. On the **Options** contextual tab of the ribbon, in the **Actions** group, click the **Clear** button, and then click **Clear Filters**.

    Excel clears all filters from the PivotTable.

17. On the **Options** contextual tab of the ribbon, in the **Sort & Filter** group, click **Insert Slicer**.

    The Insert Slicers dialog box opens.

18. In the **Insert Slicers** dialog box, select the **Center** check box, and then click **OK**.

    A Slicer for the Center field appears.

19. Click the **Atlantic** item.

    Excel filters the PivotTable so only results for the Atlantic center appear.

20. In the Slicer, click **Midwest**, and then, while holding down the Ctrl key, click **Mountain West** and then **Northwest**.

    Excel filters the PivotTable so it displays results for the Midwest, Mountain West, and Northwest centers.

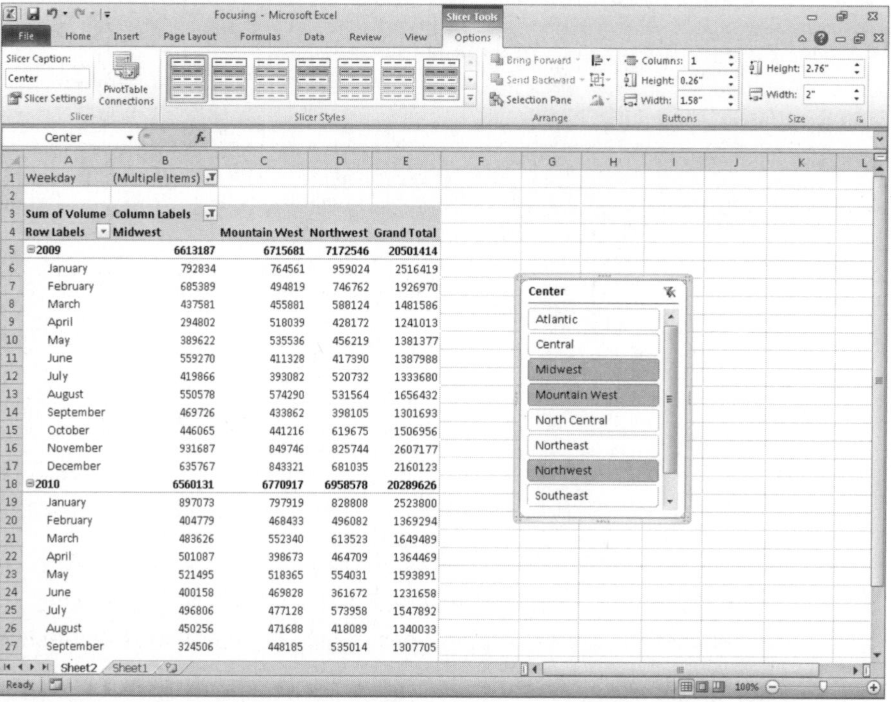

Sum of Volume	Column Labels			
Row Labels	Midwest	Mountain West	Northwest	Grand Total
2009	6613187	6715681	7172546	20501414
January	792834	764561	959024	2516419
February	685389	494819	746762	1926970
March	437581	455881	588124	1481586
April	294802	518039	428172	1241013
May	389622	535536	456219	1381377
June	559270	411328	417390	1387988
July	419866	393082	520732	1333680
August	550578	574290	531564	1656432
September	469726	433862	398105	1301693
October	446065	441216	619675	1506956
November	931687	849746	825744	2607177
December	635767	843321	681035	2160123
2010	6560131	6770917	6958578	20289626
January	897073	797919	828808	2523800
February	404779	468433	496082	1369294
March	483626	552340	613523	1649489
April	501087	398673	464709	1364469
May	521495	518365	554031	1593891
June	400158	469828	361672	1231658
July	496806	477128	573958	1547892
August	450256	471688	418089	1340033
September	324506	448185	535014	1307705

21. In the upper-right corner of the Slicer, click the **Clear Filter** button.

    Excel removes the filter from the Center field.

22. Right-click the Slicer, and then click **Remove "Center"**.

    Excel closes the Slicer.

CLEAN UP Save the Focusing workbook, and then close it.

Editing PivotTables

After you create a PivotTable, you can rename it, edit it to control how it summarizes your data, and use the PivotTable cell data in a formula. As an example, consider a PivotTable named *PivotTable2* that summarizes package volumes for every Consolidated Messengers regional distribution hub.

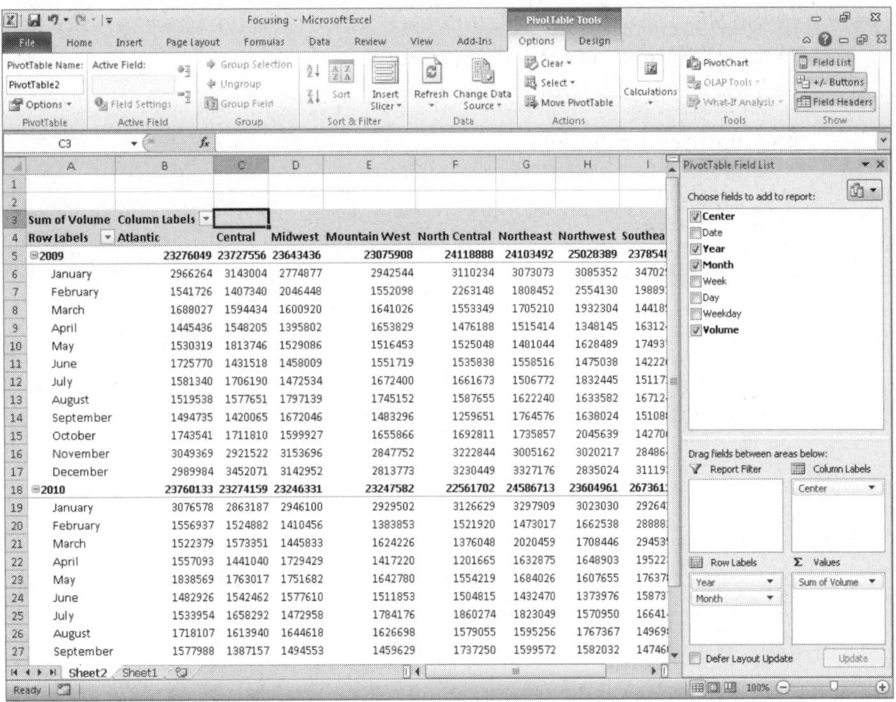

Excel displays the PivotTable name on the Options contextual tab, in the PivotTable Options group. The name *PivotTable2* doesn't help you or your colleagues understand the data the PivotTable contains, particularly if you use the PivotTable data in a formula on another worksheet. To give your PivotTable a more descriptive name, click any cell in the PivotTable and then, on the Options contextual tab, in the PivotTable Options group, type the new name in the PivotTable Name field.

When you create a PivotTable with at least one field in the Row Labels area and one field in the Column Labels area of the PivotTable Field List task pane, Excel adds a grand total row and column to summarize your data. You can control how and where these summary rows and columns appear by clicking any PivotTable cell and then, on the Design contextual tab, in the Layout group, clicking either the Subtotals or Grand Totals button and selecting the desired layout.

After you create a PivotTable, Excel determines the best way to summarize the data in the column you assign to the Values area. For numeric data, for example, Excel uses the *SUM* function. If you want to change a PivotTable summary function, right-click any data cell in the PivotTable values area, point to Summarize Values By, and then click the desired operation. If you want to use a function other than those listed, click More Options to display the Value Field Settings dialog box. On the Summarize Values By page of the dialog box, you can choose the summary operation you want to use.

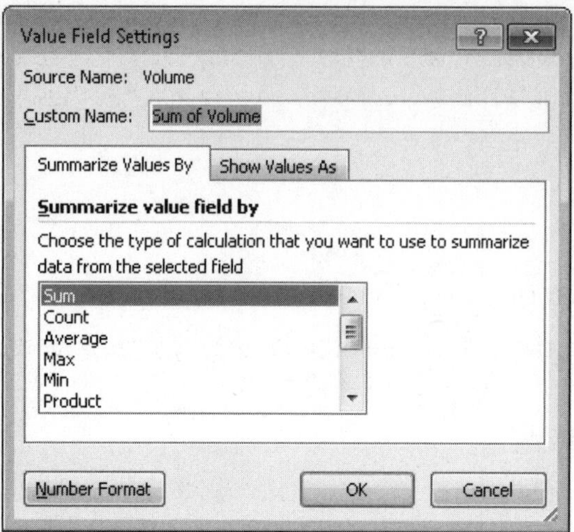

You can also change how the PivotTable displays the data in the Values area. On the Show Values As page of the Value Field Settings dialog box, you can select whether to display each cell's percentage contribution to its column's total, its row's total, or its contribution to the total of all values displayed in the PivotTable.

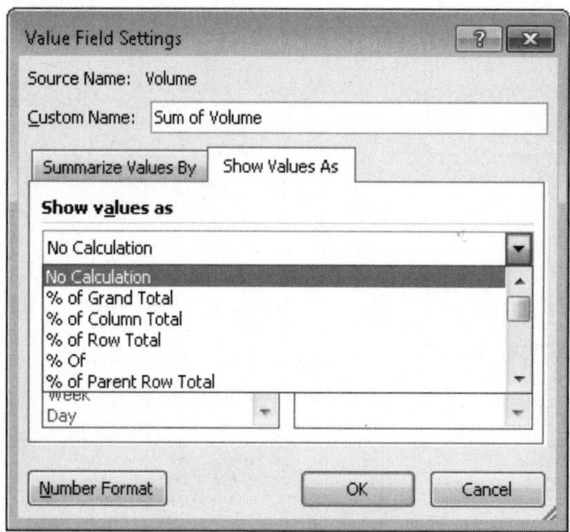

If you want, you can create a formula that incorporates a value from a PivotTable cell. To do so, you click the cell where you want to create the formula, type an equal sign, and then click the cell in the PivotTable that contains the data you want to appear in the other cell. A *GETPIVOTDATA* formula appears in the formula box of the worksheet that contains the PivotTable. When you press Enter, Excel creates the *GETPIVOTDATA* formula and displays the contents of the PivotTable cell in the target cell.

In this exercise, you'll rename a PivotTable, specify whether subtotal and grand total rows will appear, change the PivotTable summary function, display each cell's contribution to its row's total, and create a formula that incorporates a value in a PivotTable cell.

SET UP You need the Editing_start workbook located in your Chapter09 practice file folder to complete this exercise. Open the Editing_start workbook, and save it as *Editing*. Then follow the steps.

1. On the **Sheet2** worksheet, click any cell in the PivotTable.
2. On the **Options** contextual tab, in the **PivotTable** group, in the **PivotTable Name** field, type **VolumeSummary** and press **Enter**.

   Excel renames the PivotTable.

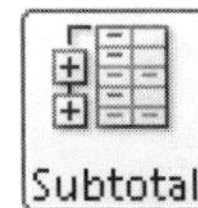

3. On the **Design** contextual tab, in the **Layout** group, click **Subtotals**, and then click **Do Not Show Subtotals**.

   Excel removes the subtotal rows from the PivotTable.

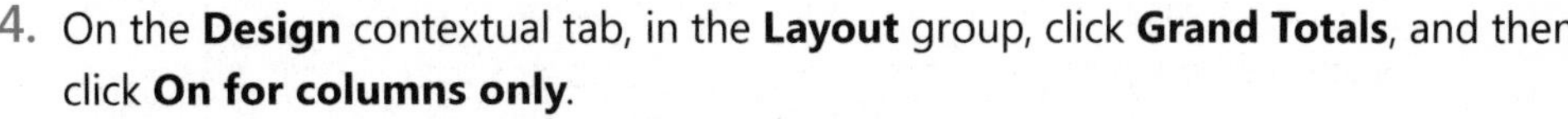

4. On the **Design** contextual tab, in the **Layout** group, click **Grand Totals**, and then click **On for columns only**.

   Excel removes the cells that calculate each row's grand total.

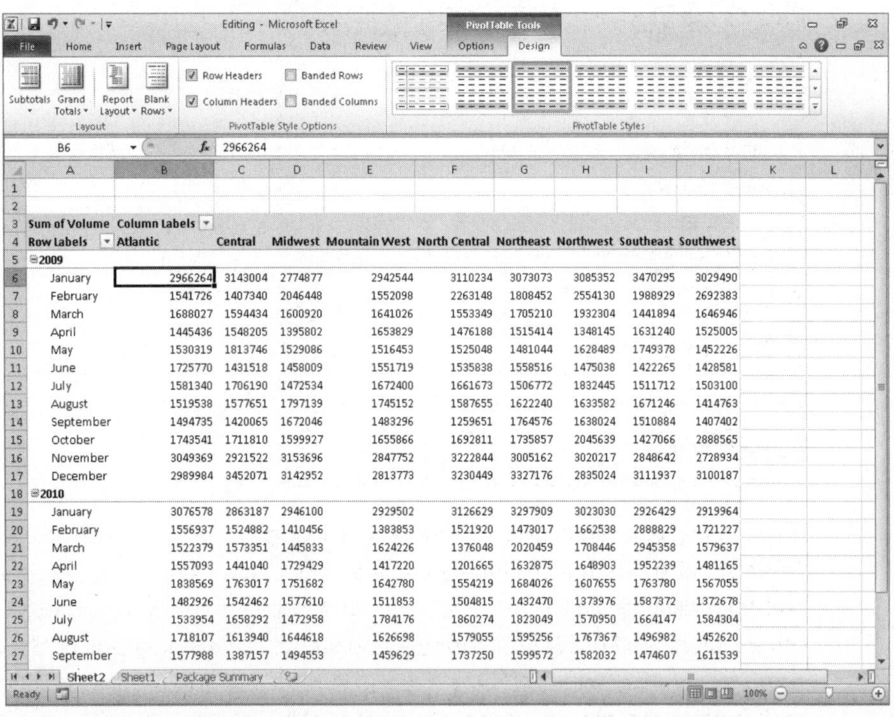

Sum of Volume	Column Labels								
Row Labels	Atlantic	Central	Midwest	Mountain West	North Central	Northeast	Northwest	Southeast	Southwest
2009									
January	2966264	3143004	2774877	2942544	3110234	3073073	3085352	3470295	3029490
February	1541726	1407340	2046448	1552098	2263148	1808452	2554130	1988929	2692383
March	1688027	1594434	1600920	1641026	1553349	1705210	1932304	1441894	1646946
April	1445436	1548205	1395802	1653829	1476188	1515414	1348145	1631240	1525005
May	1530319	1813746	1529086	1516453	1525048	1481044	1628489	1749378	1452226
June	1725770	1431518	1458009	1551719	1535838	1558516	1475038	1422265	1428581
July	1581340	1706190	1472534	1672400	1661673	1506772	1832445	1511712	1503100
August	1519538	1577651	1797139	1745152	1587655	1622240	1633582	1671246	1414763
September	1494735	1420065	1672046	1483296	1259651	1764576	1638024	1510884	1407402
October	1743541	1711810	1599927	1655866	1692811	1735857	2045639	1427066	2888565
November	3049369	2921522	3153696	2847752	3222844	3005162	3020217	2848642	2728934
December	2989984	3452071	3142952	2813773	3230449	3327176	2835024	3111937	3100187
2010									
January	3076578	2863187	2946100	2929502	3126629	3297909	3023030	2926429	2919964
February	1556937	1524882	1410456	1383853	1521920	1473017	1662538	2888829	1721227
March	1522379	1573351	1445833	1624226	1376048	2020459	1708446	2945358	1579637
April	1557093	1441040	1729429	1417220	1201665	1632875	1648903	1952239	1481165
May	1838569	1763017	1751682	1642780	1554219	1684026	1607655	1763780	1567055
June	1482926	1542462	1577610	1511853	1504815	1432470	1373976	1587372	1372678
July	1533954	1658292	1472958	1784176	1860274	1823049	1570950	1664147	1584304
August	1718107	1613940	1644618	1626698	1579055	1595256	1767367	1496982	1452620
September	1577988	1387157	1494553	1459629	1737250	1599572	1582032	1474607	1611539

5. On the Quick Access Toolbar, click the **Undo** button.

   Excel reverses the last change.

6. Right-click any data cell in the PivotTable, point to **Summarize Values By**, and then click **Average**.

   Excel changes the Value field summary operation.

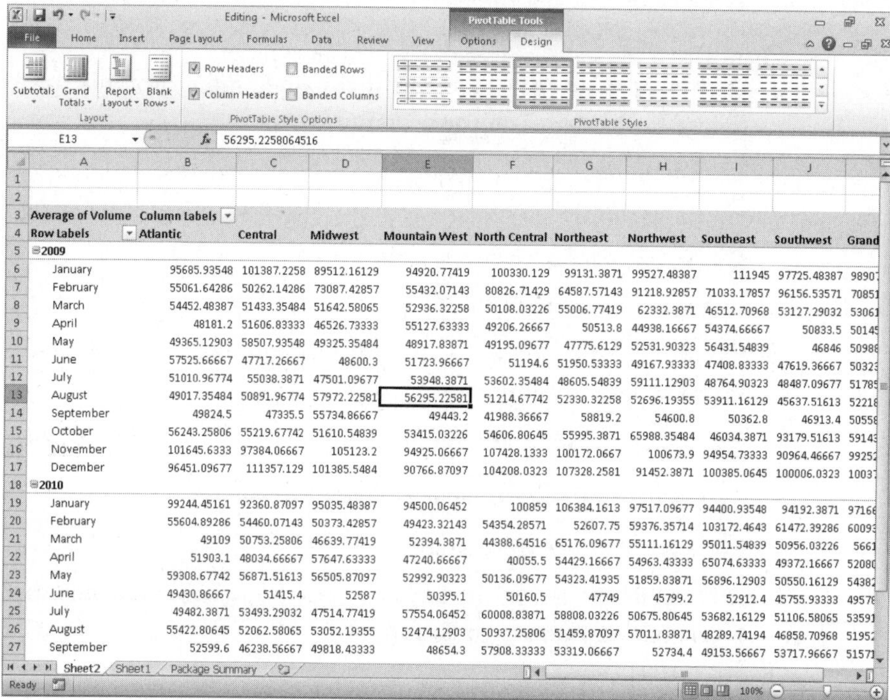

Average of Volume	Column Labels									
Row Labels	Atlantic	Central	Midwest	Mountain West	North Central	Northeast	Northwest	Southeast	Southwest	Grand
⊟2009										
January	95685.93548	101387.2258	89512.16129	94920.77419	100330.129	99131.3871	99527.48387	111945	97725.48387	9890
February	55061.64286	50262.14286	73087.42857	55432.07143	80826.71429	64587.57143	91218.92857	71033.17857	96156.53571	70851
March	54452.48387	51433.35484	51642.58065	52936.32258	50108.03226	55006.77419	62332.3871	46512.70968	53127.29032	53061
April	48181.2	51606.83333	46526.73333	55127.63333	49206.26667	50513.8	44938.16667	54374.66667	50833.5	5014
May	49365.12903	58507.93548	49325.35484	48917.83871	49195.09677	47775.6129	52531.90323	56431.54839	46846	50988
June	57525.66667	47717.26667	48600.3	51723.96667	51194.6	51950.53333	49167.93333	47408.83333	47619.36667	5032
July	51010.96774	55038.3871	47501.09677	53948.3871	53602.35484	48605.54839	59111.12903	48764.90323	48487.09677	51785
August	49017.35484	50891.96774	57972.22581	56295.22581	51214.67742	52330.32258	52696.19355	53911.16129	45637.51613	52218
September	49824.5	47335.5	55734.86667	49443.2	41988.36667	58819.2	54600.8	50362.8	46913.4	50558
October	56243.25806	55219.67742	51610.54839	53415.03226	54606.80645	55995.3871	65988.35484	46034.3871	93179.51613	5914
November	101645.6333	97384.06667	105123.2	94925.06667	107428.1333	100172.0667	100673.9	94954.73333	90964.46667	9925
December	96451.09677	111357.129	101385.5484	90766.87097	104208.0323	107328.2581	91452.3871	100385.0645	100006.0323	1003
⊟2010										
January	99244.45161	92360.87097	95035.48387	94500.06452	100859	106384.1613	97517.09677	94400.93548	94192.3871	9716
February	55604.89286	54460.07143	50373.42857	49423.32143	54354.28571	52607.75	59376.35714	103172.4643	61472.39286	6009
March	49109	50753.25806	46639.77419	52394.3871	44388.64516	65176.09677	55111.16129	95011.54839	50956.03226	5661
April	51903.1	48034.66667	57647.63333	47240.66667	40055.5	54429.16667	54963.43333	65074.63333	49372.16667	5208
May	59308.67742	56871.51613	56505.87097	52992.90323	50136.09677	54323.41935	51859.83871	56896.12903	50550.16129	5438
June	49430.86667	51415.4	52587	50395.1	50160.5	47749	45799.2	52912.4	45755.93333	4957
July	49482.3871	53493.29032	47514.77419	57554.06452	60008.83871	58808.03226	50675.80645	53682.16129	51106.58065	5359
August	55422.80645	52062.58065	53052.19355	52474.12903	50937.25806	51459.87097	57011.83871	48289.74194	46858.70968	5195
September	52599.6	46238.56667	49818.43333	48654.3	57908.33333	53319.06667	52734.4	49153.56667	53717.96667	5157

7. On the Quick Access Toolbar, click the **Undo** button.

   Excel reverses the last change.

8. Right-click any data cell in the PivotTable, and then click **Value Field Settings**.

   The Value Field Settings dialog box opens.

9. Click the **Show Values As** tab.

   The Show Values As page appears.

10. In the **Show Values As** list, click **% of Row Total**.

11. Click **OK**.

    Excel changes how it calculates the values in the PivotTable.

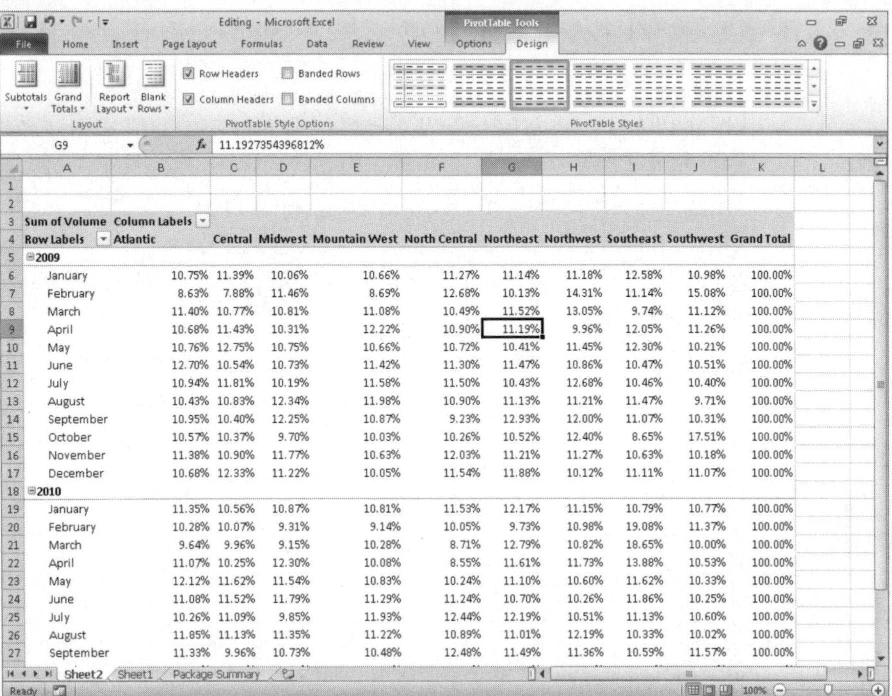

Sum of Volume	Column Labels									
Row Labels	Atlantic	Central	Midwest	Mountain West	North Central	Northeast	Northwest	Southeast	Southwest	Grand Total
2009										
January	10.75%	11.39%	10.06%	10.66%	11.27%	11.14%	11.18%	12.58%	10.98%	100.00%
February	8.63%	7.88%	11.46%	8.69%	12.68%	10.13%	14.31%	11.14%	15.08%	100.00%
March	11.40%	10.77%	10.81%	11.08%	10.49%	11.52%	13.05%	9.74%	11.12%	100.00%
April	10.68%	11.43%	10.31%	12.22%	10.90%	11.19%	9.96%	12.05%	11.26%	100.00%
May	10.76%	12.75%	10.75%	10.66%	10.72%	10.41%	11.45%	12.30%	10.21%	100.00%
June	12.70%	10.54%	10.73%	11.42%	11.30%	11.47%	10.86%	10.47%	10.51%	100.00%
July	10.94%	11.81%	10.19%	11.58%	11.50%	10.43%	12.68%	10.46%	10.40%	100.00%
August	10.43%	10.83%	12.34%	11.98%	10.90%	11.13%	11.21%	11.47%	9.71%	100.00%
September	10.95%	10.40%	12.25%	10.87%	9.23%	12.93%	12.00%	11.07%	10.31%	100.00%
October	10.57%	10.37%	9.70%	10.03%	10.26%	10.52%	12.40%	8.65%	17.51%	100.00%
November	11.38%	10.90%	11.77%	10.63%	12.03%	11.21%	11.27%	10.63%	10.18%	100.00%
December	10.68%	12.33%	11.22%	10.05%	11.54%	11.88%	10.12%	11.11%	11.07%	100.00%
2010										
January	11.35%	10.56%	10.87%	10.81%	11.53%	12.17%	11.15%	10.79%	10.77%	100.00%
February	10.28%	10.07%	9.31%	9.14%	10.05%	9.73%	10.98%	19.08%	11.37%	100.00%
March	9.64%	9.96%	9.15%	10.28%	8.71%	12.79%	10.82%	18.65%	10.00%	100.00%
April	11.07%	10.25%	12.30%	10.08%	8.55%	11.61%	11.73%	13.88%	10.53%	100.00%
May	12.12%	11.62%	11.54%	10.83%	10.24%	11.10%	10.60%	11.62%	10.33%	100.00%
June	11.08%	11.52%	11.79%	11.29%	11.24%	10.70%	10.26%	11.86%	10.25%	100.00%
July	10.26%	11.09%	9.85%	11.93%	12.44%	12.19%	10.51%	11.13%	10.60%	100.00%
August	11.85%	11.13%	11.35%	11.22%	10.89%	11.01%	12.19%	10.33%	10.02%	100.00%
September	11.33%	9.96%	10.73%	10.48%	12.48%	11.49%	11.36%	10.59%	11.57%	100.00%

12. On the Quick Access Toolbar, click the **Undo** button.

    Excel reverses the last change.

13. On the **Design** tab, in the **Layout** group, click **Subtotals**, and then click **Show All Subtotals at Bottom of Group**.

    Excel displays subtotals in the workbook.

14. Click the **Package Summary** sheet tab.

    The Package Summary worksheet appears.

15. In cell **C4**, type =, but do not press Enter.
16. Click the **PivotTable** sheet tab.

    The PivotTable worksheet appears.

17. Click cell **K32**, and then press Enter.

    Excel creates the formula *=GETPIVOTDATA("Volume",PivotTable!$A$3,"Year",2010)* in cell C4.

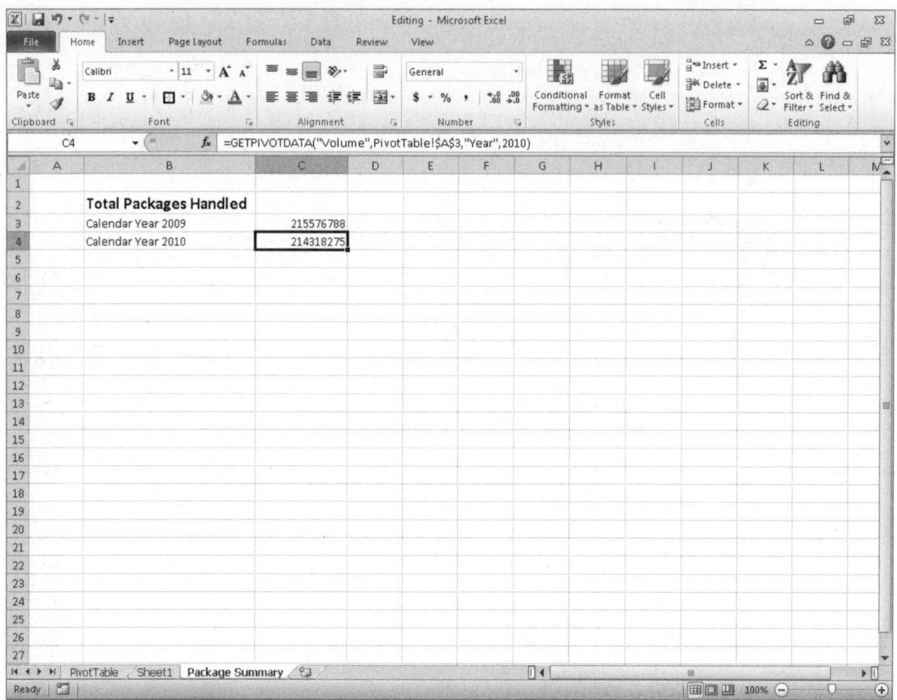

 **CLEAN UP** Save the Focusing workbook, and then close it.

Formatting PivotTables

PivotTables are the ideal tools for summarizing and examining large data tables, even those containing more than 10,000 or even 100,000 rows. Even though PivotTables often end up as compact summaries, you should do everything you can to make your data more comprehensible. One way to improve your data's readability is to apply a number format to the PivotTable Values field. To apply a number format to a field, right-click any cell in the field, and then click Number Format to display the Format Cells dialog box. Select or define the format you want to apply, and then click OK to enact the change.

See Also For more information on selecting and defining cell formats by using the Format Cells dialog box, see "Formatting Cells" in Chapter 4, "Changing Workbook Appearance."

Analysts often use PivotTables to summarize and examine organizational data with an eye to making important decisions about the company. For example, chief operating officer Lori Penor might examine monthly package volumes handled by Consolidated Messenger and notice that there's a surge in package volume during the winter months in the United States.

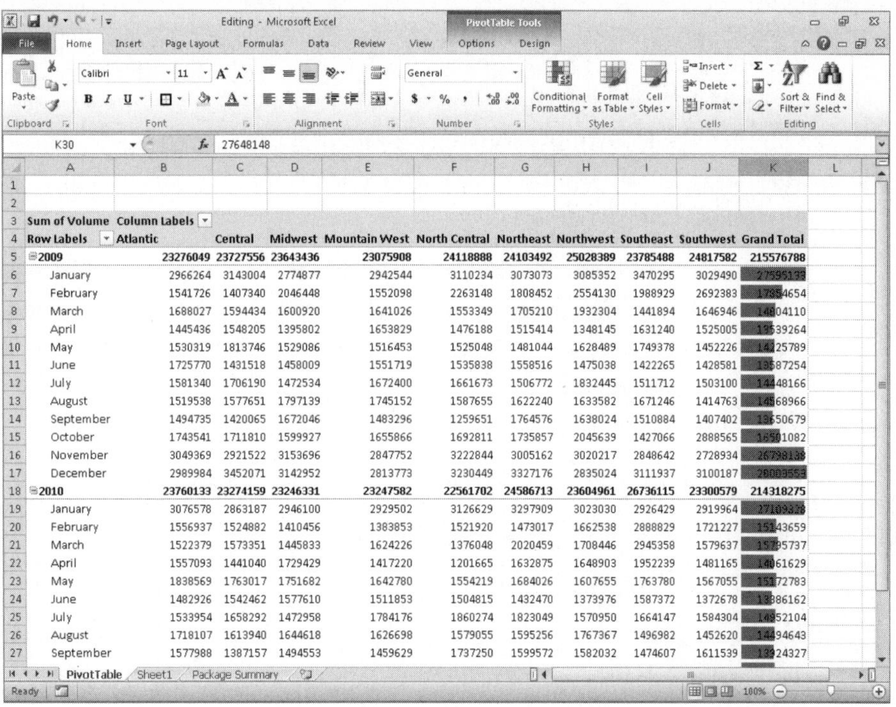

Sum of Volume	Column Labels									
Row Labels	Atlantic	Central	Midwest	Mountain West	North Central	Northeast	Northwest	Southeast	Southwest	Grand Total
2009	**23276049**	**23727556**	**23643436**	**23075908**	**24118888**	**24103492**	**25028389**	**23785488**	**24817582**	**215576788**
January	2966264	3143004	2774877	2942544	3110234	3073073	3085352	3470295	3029490	[illegible]
February	1541726	1407340	2046448	1552098	2263148	1808452	2554130	1988929	2692383	17854654
March	1688027	1594434	1600920	1641026	1553349	1705210	1932304	1441894	1646946	14804110
April	1445436	1548205	1395802	1653829	1476188	1515414	1348145	1631240	1525005	13539264
May	1530319	1813746	1529086	1516453	1525048	1481044	1628489	1749378	1452226	14225789
June	1725770	1431518	1458009	1551719	1535838	1558516	1475038	1422265	1428581	13587254
July	1581340	1706190	1472534	1672400	1661673	1506772	1832445	1511712	1503100	14448166
August	1519538	1577651	1797139	1745152	1587655	1622240	1633582	1671246	1414763	14568966
September	1494735	1420065	1672046	1483296	1259651	1764576	1638024	1510884	1407402	13650679
October	1743541	1711810	1599927	1655866	1692811	1735857	2045639	1427066	2888565	16501082
November	3049369	2921522	3153696	2847752	3222844	3005162	3020217	2848642	2728934	[illegible]
December	2989984	3452071	3142952	2813773	3230449	3327176	2835024	3111937	3100187	[illegible]
2010	**23760133**	**23274159**	**23246331**	**23247582**	**22561702**	**24586713**	**23604961**	**26736115**	**23300579**	**214318275**
January	3076578	2863187	2946100	2929502	3126629	3297909	3023030	2926429	2919964	[illegible]
February	1556937	1524882	1410456	1383853	1521920	1473017	1662538	2888829	1721227	15143659
March	1522379	1573351	1445833	1624226	1376048	2020459	1708446	2945358	1579637	15795737
April	1557093	1441040	1729429	1417220	1201665	1632875	1648903	1952239	1481165	14061629
May	1838569	1763017	1751682	1642780	1554219	1684026	1607655	1763780	1567055	15172783
June	1482926	1542462	1577610	1511853	1504815	1432470	1373976	1587372	1372678	13386162
July	1533954	1658292	1472958	1784176	1860274	1823049	1570950	1664147	1584304	14952104
August	1718107	1613940	1644618	1626698	1579055	1595256	1767367	1496982	1452620	14494643
September	1577988	1387157	1494553	1459629	1737250	1599572	1582032	1474607	1611539	13924327

Excel extends the capabilities of your PivotTables by enabling you to apply a conditional format to the PivotTable cells. What's more, you can select whether to apply the conditional format to every cell in the Values area, to every cell at the same level as the selected cell (that is, a regular data cell, a subtotal cell, or a grand total cell) or to every cell that contains or draws its values from the selected cell's field (such as the Volume field in the previous example).

To apply a conditional format to a PivotTable field, click a cell in the Values area. On the Home tab, in the Styles group, click Conditional Formatting, and then create the desired conditional format. After you do, Excel displays a Formatting Options action button, which offers three options for applying the conditional format:

- **Selected Cells** Applies the conditional format to the selected cells only
- **All Cells Showing Sum of field_name Values** Applies the conditional format to every cell in the data area, regardless of whether the cell is in the data area, a subtotal row or column, or a grand total row or column
- **All Cells Showing Sum of field_name Values for Fields** Applies the conditional format to every cell at the same level (for example, data cell, subtotal, or grand total) as the selected cells

See Also For more information on creating conditional formats, see "Changing the Appearance of Data Based on Its Value" in Chapter 4, "Changing Workbook Appearance."

In Excel, you can take full advantage of the Microsoft Office system enhanced formatting capabilities to apply existing formats to your PivotTables. Just as you can create Excel table formats, you can also create your own PivotTable formats to match your organization's desired color scheme.

To apply a PivotTable style, click any cell in the PivotTable and then, on the Design contextual tab, in the PivotTable Styles group, click the gallery item representing the style you want to apply. If you want to create your own PivotTable style, click the More button in the PivotTable Styles gallery (in the lower-right corner of the gallery), and then click New PivotTable Style to display the New PivotTable Quick Style dialog box.

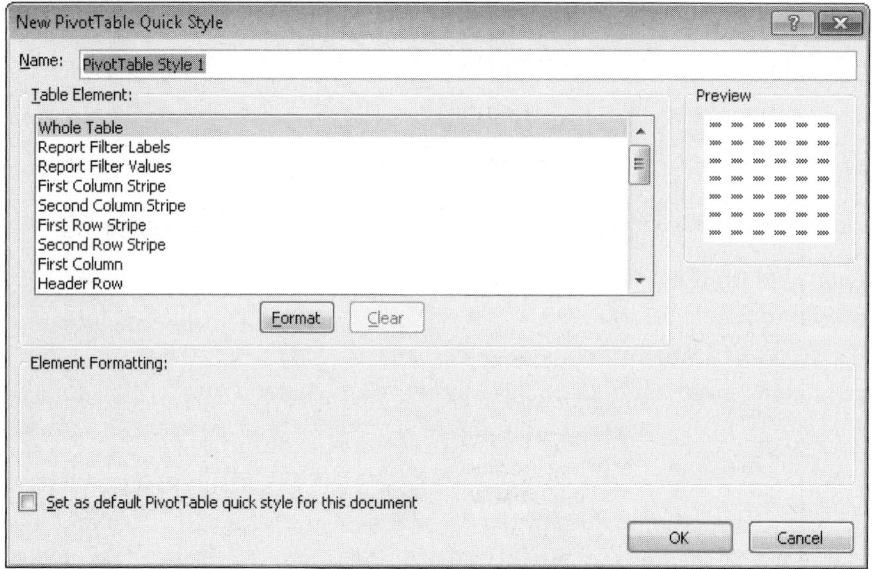

Type a name for the style in the Name field, click the first table element you want to customize, and then click Format. Use the controls in the Format Cells dialog box to change the element's appearance. After you click OK to close the Format Cells dialog box, the New PivotTable Quick Style dialog box Preview pane displays the style's appearance. If you want Excel to use the style by default, select the Set As Default PivotTable Quick Style For This Document check box. After you finish creating your formats, click OK to close the New PivotTable Quick Style dialog box and save your style.

The Design contextual tab contains many other tools you can use to format your PivotTable, but one of the most useful is the Banded Columns check box, which you can find in the PivotTable Style Options group. If you select a PivotTable style that offers banded rows as an option, selecting the Banded Rows check box turns banding on. If you prefer not to have Excel band the rows in your PivotTable, clearing the check box turns banding off.

In this exercise, you'll apply a number format to a PivotTable values field, apply a PivotTable style, create your own PivotTable style, give your PivotTable banded rows, and apply a conditional format to a PivotTable.

SET UP You need the Formatting_start workbook located in your Chapter09 practice file folder to complete this exercise. Open the Formatting_start workbook, and save it as *Formatting*. Then follow the steps.

1. On the **Sheet2** worksheet, right-click any data cell, and then click **Number Format**.

   The Format Cells dialog box opens.

2. In the **Category** list, click **Number**.

   The Number page is displayed.

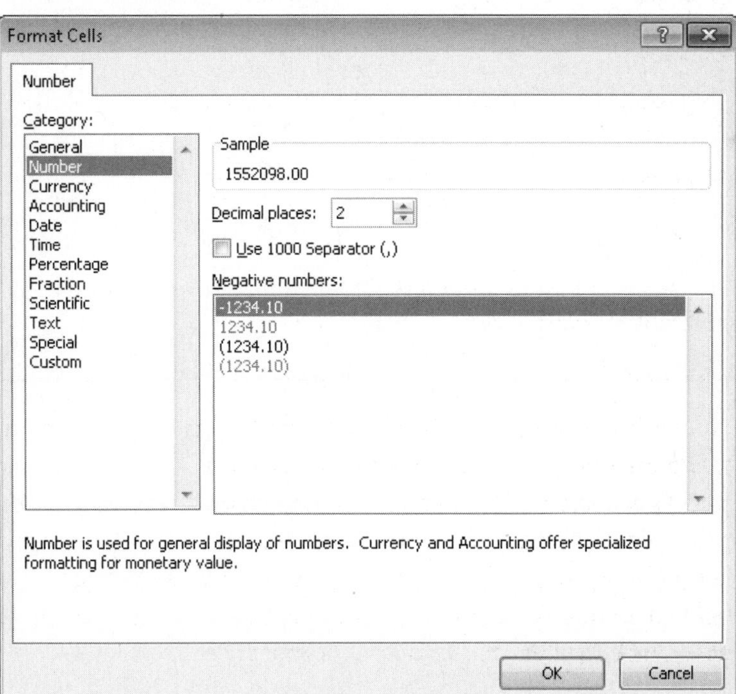

3. In the **Decimal places** field, type **0**.
4. Select the **Use 1000 Separator (,)** check box.
5. Click **OK**.

   Excel reformats your PivotTable data.

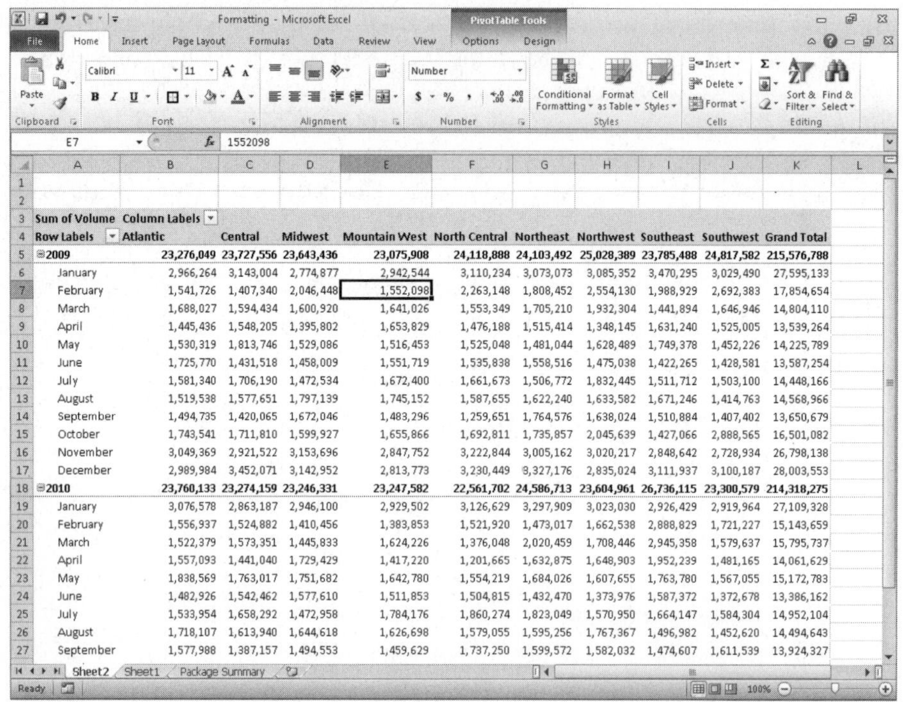

6. If necessary, on the **Design** contextual tab, in the **PivotTable Style Options** group, select the **Banded Rows** check box.

7. On the **Design** contextual tab, in the **PivotTable Styles** group, click the **More** button. Then, in the top row of the gallery, click the third style from the left. (When you point to it, Excel displays a ScreenTip that reads **Pivot Style Light 2**.)

Excel applies the PivotTable style.

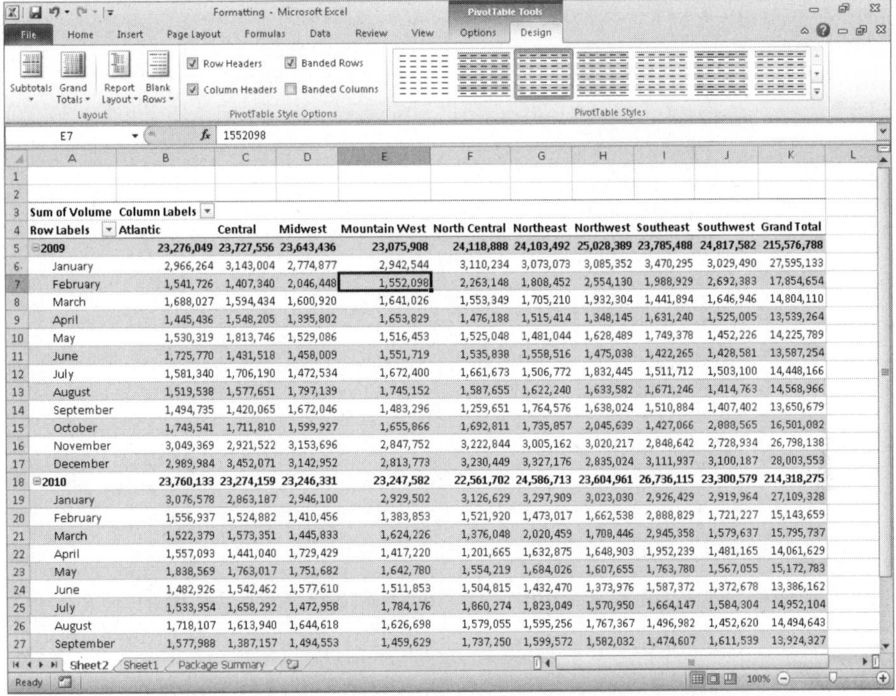

Sum of Volume	Column Labels									
Row Labels	Atlantic	Central	Midwest	Mountain West	North Central	Northeast	Northwest	Southeast	Southwest	Grand Total
2009	**23,276,049**	**23,727,556**	**23,643,436**	**23,075,908**	**24,118,888**	**24,103,492**	**25,028,389**	**23,785,488**	**24,817,582**	**215,576,788**
January	2,966,264	3,143,004	2,774,877	2,942,544	3,110,234	3,073,073	3,085,352	3,470,295	3,029,490	27,595,133
February	1,541,726	1,407,340	2,046,448	1,552,098	2,263,148	1,808,452	2,554,130	1,988,929	2,692,383	17,854,654
March	1,688,027	1,594,434	1,600,920	1,641,026	1,553,349	1,705,210	1,932,304	1,441,894	1,646,946	14,804,110
April	1,445,436	1,548,205	1,395,802	1,653,829	1,476,188	1,515,414	1,348,145	1,631,240	1,525,005	13,539,264
May	1,530,319	1,813,746	1,529,086	1,516,453	1,525,048	1,481,044	1,628,489	1,749,378	1,452,226	14,225,789
June	1,725,770	1,431,518	1,458,009	1,551,719	1,535,838	1,558,516	1,475,038	1,422,265	1,428,581	13,587,254
July	1,581,340	1,706,190	1,472,534	1,672,400	1,661,673	1,506,772	1,832,445	1,511,712	1,503,100	14,448,166
August	1,519,538	1,577,651	1,797,139	1,745,152	1,587,655	1,622,240	1,633,582	1,671,246	1,414,763	14,568,966
September	1,494,735	1,420,065	1,672,046	1,483,296	1,259,651	1,764,576	1,638,024	1,510,884	1,407,402	13,650,679
October	1,743,541	1,711,810	1,599,927	1,655,866	1,692,811	1,735,857	2,045,639	1,427,066	2,888,565	16,501,082
November	3,049,369	2,921,522	3,153,696	2,847,752	3,222,844	3,005,162	3,020,217	2,848,642	2,728,934	26,798,138
December	2,989,984	3,452,071	3,142,952	2,813,773	3,230,449	3,327,176	2,835,024	3,111,937	3,100,187	28,003,553
2010	**23,760,133**	**23,274,159**	**23,246,331**	**23,247,582**	**22,561,702**	**24,586,713**	**23,604,961**	**26,736,115**	**23,300,579**	**214,318,275**
January	3,076,578	2,863,187	2,946,100	2,929,502	3,126,629	3,297,909	3,023,030	2,926,429	2,919,964	27,109,328
February	1,556,937	1,524,882	1,410,456	1,383,853	1,521,920	1,473,017	1,662,538	2,888,829	1,721,227	15,143,659
March	1,522,379	1,573,351	1,445,833	1,624,226	1,376,048	2,020,459	1,708,446	2,945,358	1,579,637	15,795,737
April	1,557,093	1,441,040	1,729,429	1,417,220	1,201,665	1,632,875	1,648,903	1,952,239	1,481,165	14,061,629
May	1,838,569	1,763,017	1,751,682	1,642,780	1,554,219	1,684,026	1,607,655	1,763,780	1,567,055	15,172,783
June	1,482,926	1,542,462	1,577,610	1,511,853	1,504,815	1,432,470	1,373,976	1,587,372	1,372,678	13,386,162
July	1,533,954	1,658,292	1,472,958	1,784,176	1,860,274	1,823,049	1,570,950	1,664,147	1,584,304	14,952,104
August	1,718,107	1,613,940	1,644,618	1,626,698	1,579,055	1,595,256	1,767,367	1,496,982	1,452,620	14,494,643
September	1,577,988	1,387,157	1,494,553	1,459,629	1,737,250	1,599,572	1,582,032	1,474,607	1,611,539	13,924,327

8. In the lower-right corner of the **PivotTable Styles** gallery, click the **More** button.

   The gallery expands.

9. Click **New PivotTable Style**.

   The New PivotTable Quick Style dialog box opens.

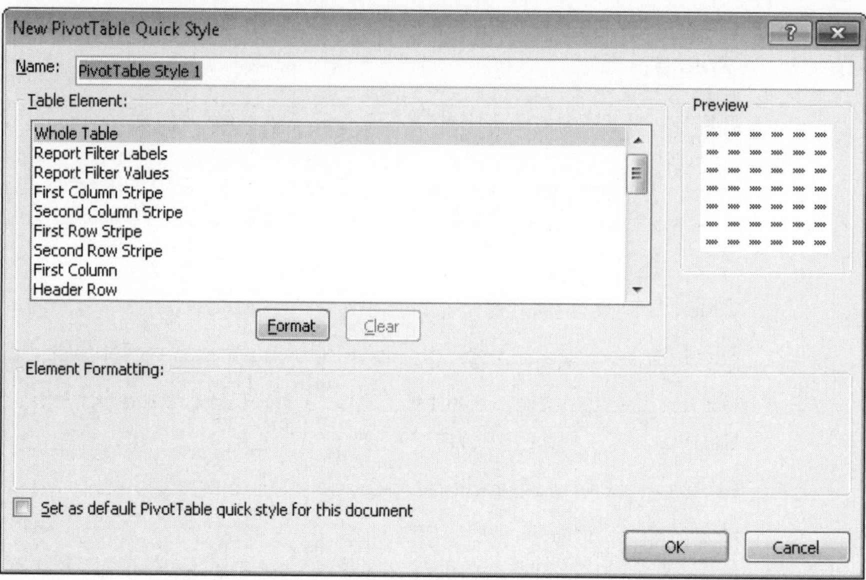

10. In the **Name** field, type **Custom Style 1**.
11. In the **Table Element** list, click **Header Row**, and then click **Format**.

    The Format Cells dialog box opens.
12. On the **Font** page, in the **Color** list, click the white square.
13. On the **Border** page, in the **Presets** area, click **Outline**.
14. On the **Fill** page, in the **Background Color** area, click the purple square at the lower-right corner of the color palette.
15. Click **OK**.

    The Format Cells dialog box closes, and the style change appears in the Preview pane of the New PivotTable Quick Style dialog box.
16. In the **Table Element** list, click **Second Row Stripe**, and then click **Format**.

    The Format Cells dialog box opens.
17. On the **Fill** page, in the middle part of the **Background Color** area, click the eighth square in the second row (it's a light, dusty purple).
18. Click **OK** twice.

The Format Cells dialog box closes, and your format appears in the PivotTable Styles gallery.

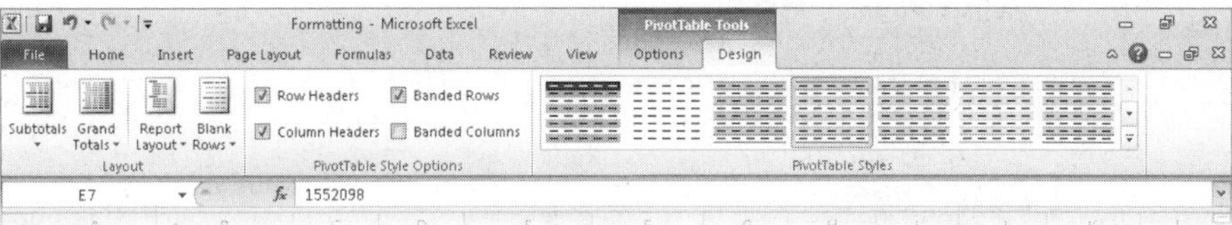

19. Click the new style.

    Excel formats your PivotTable using your custom PivotTable style.

20. On the **Design** contextual tab, in the **PivotTable Style Options** group, clear the **Banded Rows** check box.

    Excel removes the banding from your PivotTable and from the preview of the custom style.

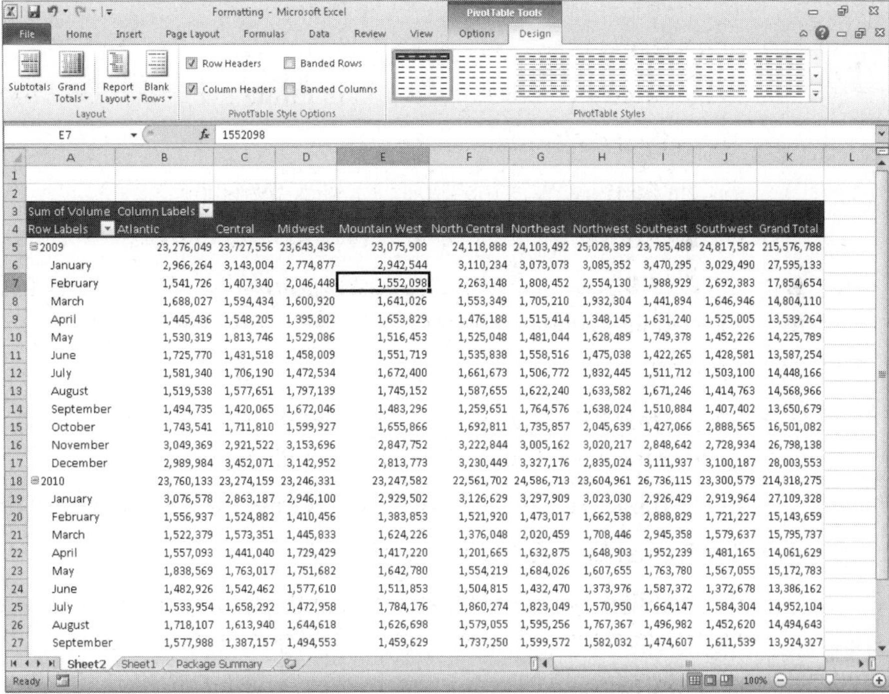

Sum of Volume Row Labels	Column Labels Atlantic	Central	Midwest	Mountain West	North Central	Northeast	Northwest	Southeast	Southwest	Grand Total
2009	23,276,049	23,727,556	23,643,436	23,075,908	24,118,888	24,103,492	25,028,389	23,785,488	24,817,582	215,576,788
January	2,966,264	3,143,004	2,774,877	2,942,544	3,110,234	3,073,073	3,085,352	3,470,295	3,029,490	27,595,133
February	1,541,726	1,407,340	2,046,448	1,552,098	2,263,148	1,808,452	2,554,130	1,988,929	2,692,383	17,854,654
March	1,688,027	1,594,434	1,600,920	1,641,026	1,553,349	1,705,210	1,932,304	1,441,894	1,646,946	14,804,110
April	1,445,436	1,548,205	1,395,802	1,653,829	1,476,188	1,515,414	1,348,145	1,631,240	1,525,005	13,539,264
May	1,530,319	1,813,746	1,529,086	1,516,453	1,525,048	1,481,044	1,628,489	1,749,378	1,452,226	14,225,789
June	1,725,770	1,431,518	1,458,009	1,551,719	1,535,838	1,558,516	1,475,038	1,422,265	1,428,581	13,587,254
July	1,581,340	1,706,190	1,472,534	1,672,400	1,661,673	1,506,772	1,832,445	1,511,712	1,503,100	14,448,166
August	1,519,538	1,577,651	1,797,139	1,745,152	1,587,655	1,622,240	1,633,582	1,671,246	1,414,763	14,568,966
September	1,494,735	1,420,065	1,672,046	1,483,296	1,259,651	1,764,576	1,638,024	1,510,884	1,407,402	13,650,679
October	1,743,541	1,711,810	1,599,927	1,655,866	1,692,811	1,735,857	2,045,639	1,427,066	2,888,565	16,501,082
November	3,049,369	2,921,522	3,153,696	2,847,752	3,222,844	3,005,162	3,020,217	2,848,642	2,728,934	26,798,138
December	2,989,984	3,452,071	3,142,952	2,813,773	3,230,449	3,327,176	2,835,024	3,111,937	3,100,187	28,003,553
2010	23,760,133	23,274,159	23,246,331	23,247,582	22,561,702	24,586,713	23,604,961	26,736,115	23,300,579	214,318,275
January	3,076,578	2,863,187	2,946,100	2,929,502	3,126,629	3,297,909	3,023,030	2,926,429	2,919,964	27,109,328
February	1,556,937	1,524,882	1,410,456	1,383,853	1,521,920	1,473,017	1,662,538	2,888,829	1,721,227	15,143,659
March	1,522,379	1,573,351	1,445,833	1,624,226	1,376,048	2,020,459	1,708,446	2,945,358	1,579,637	15,795,737
April	1,557,093	1,441,040	1,729,429	1,417,220	1,201,665	1,632,875	1,648,903	1,952,239	1,481,165	14,061,629
May	1,838,569	1,763,017	1,751,682	1,642,780	1,554,219	1,684,026	1,607,655	1,763,780	1,567,055	15,172,783
June	1,482,926	1,542,462	1,577,610	1,511,853	1,504,815	1,432,470	1,373,976	1,587,372	1,372,678	13,386,162
July	1,533,954	1,658,292	1,472,958	1,784,176	1,860,274	1,823,049	1,570,950	1,664,147	1,584,304	14,952,104
August	1,718,107	1,613,940	1,644,618	1,626,698	1,579,055	1,595,256	1,767,367	1,496,982	1,452,620	14,494,643
September	1,577,988	1,387,157	1,494,553	1,459,629	1,737,250	1,599,572	1,582,032	1,474,607	1,611,539	13,924,327

21. Select the cell ranges **K6:K17** and **K19:K30**.

22. On the **Home** tab, in the **Styles** group, click **Conditional Formatting**, point to **Color Scales**, and in the top row, click the second three-color scale from the left.

    Excel applies the conditional format to the selected cells.

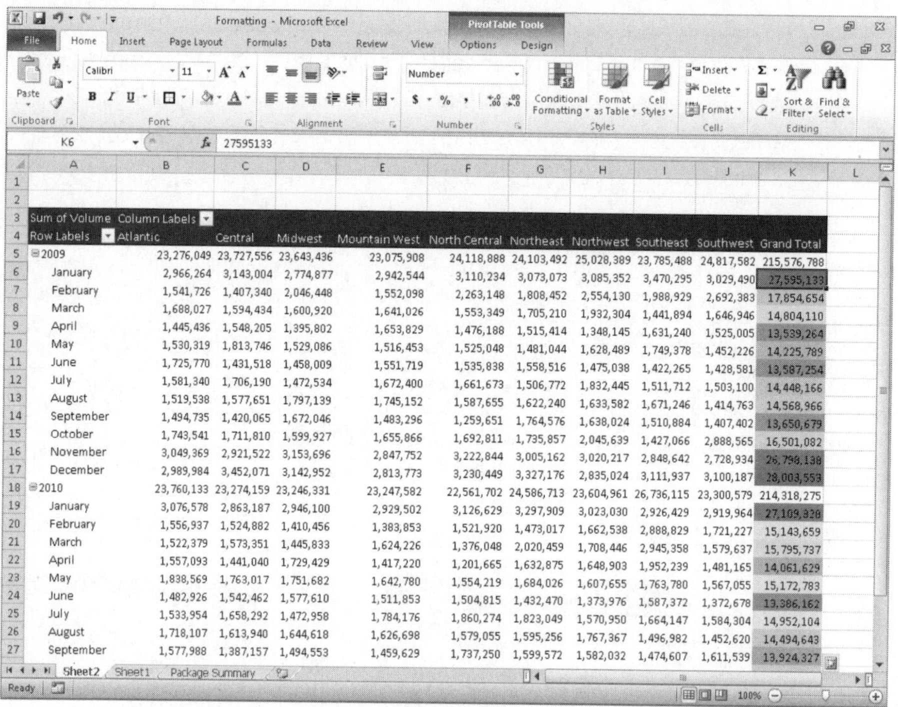

CLEAN UP Save the Formatting workbook, and then close it.

Creating PivotTables from External Data

Although most of the time you will create PivotTables from data stored in Excel worksheets, you can also bring data from outside sources into Excel. For example, you might need to work with data created in another spreadsheet program with a file format that Excel can't read directly. Fortunately, you can export the data from the original program into a text file, which Excel then translates into a worksheet.

Tip The data import technique shown here isn't exclusive to PivotTables. You can use this procedure to bring data into your worksheets for any purpose.

Spreadsheet programs store data in cells, so the goal of representing spreadsheet data in a text file is to indicate where the contents of one cell end and those of the next cell begin. The character that marks the end of a cell is a *delimiter*, in that it marks the end (or "limit") of a cell. The most common cell delimiter is the comma, so the delimited sequence *15, 18, 24, 28* represents data in four cells. The problem with using commas to delimit financial data is that larger values—such as *52,802*—can be written by using commas as thousands markers. To avoid confusion when importing a text file, the most commonly used delimiter for financial data is the Tab character.

To import data from a text file, on the Data tab, in the Get External Data group, click From Text to display the Import Text File dialog box.

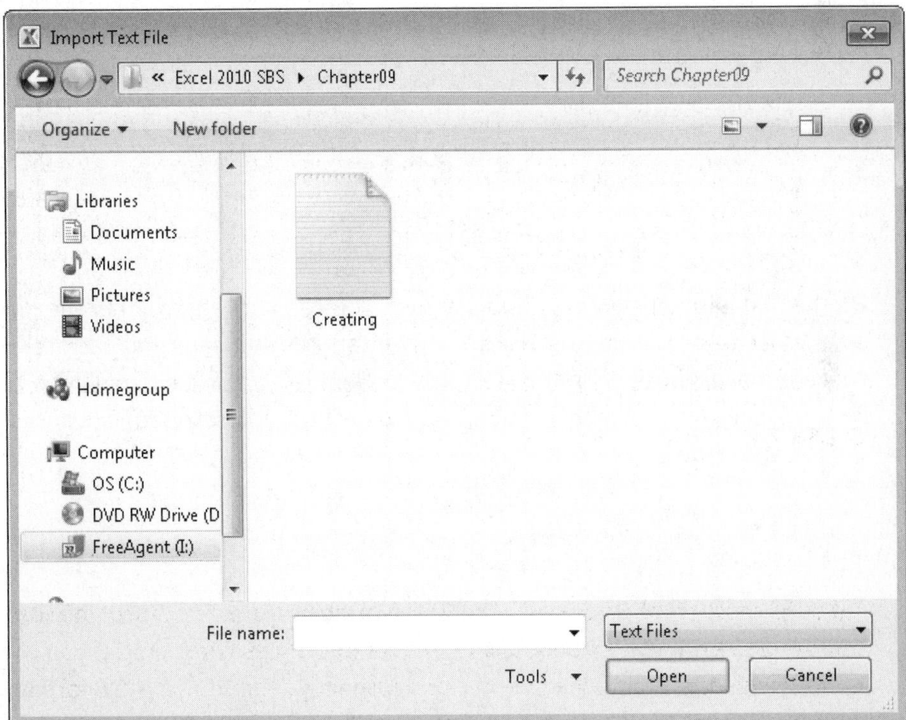

From within the Import Text File dialog box, browse to the directory that contains the text file you want to import. Double-clicking the file launches the Text Import wizard.

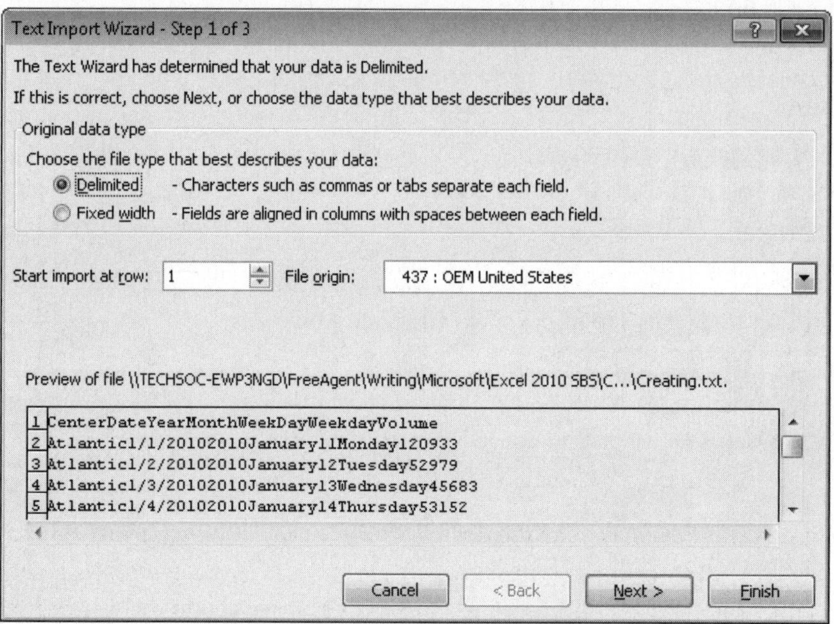

On the first page of the Text Import wizard, you can indicate whether the data file you are importing is Delimited or Fixed Width; Fixed Width means that each cell value will fall within a specific position in the file. Clicking Next to accept the default choice, Delimited (which Excel assigns after examining the data source you selected), advances you to the next wizard page.

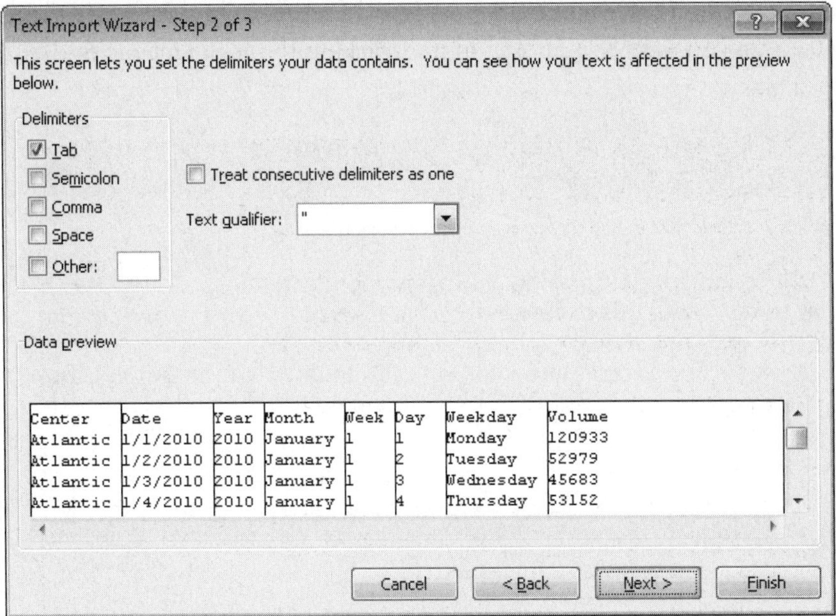

On this page, you can choose the delimiter for the file (in this case, Excel detected tabs in the file and selected the Tab check box for you) and gives you a preview of what the text file will look like when imported. Clicking Next advances you to the final wizard page.

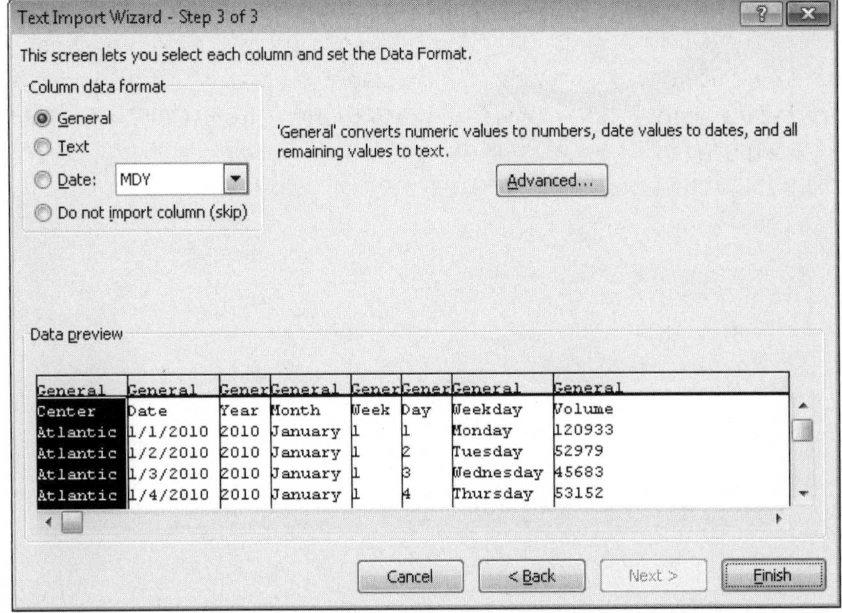

On this page, you can change the data type and formatting of the columns in your data. Because you'll assign number styles and PivotTable Quick Styles after you create the PivotTable, you can click Finish to import the data into your worksheet. After the data is in Excel, you can work with it normally.

In this exercise, you'll import data into Excel from a text file and then create a PivotTable based on that data.

SET UP You need the Creating_start text file located in your Chapter09 practice file folder to complete this exercise.

1. Create a new Excel workbook. On the **Data** tab, click the **Get External Data** button, and then click **From Text**.

   The Import Text File dialog box opens.

2. Navigate to the **Chapter09** practice file folder, and then double-click **Creating_start.txt**.

   The Text Import wizard starts.

3. Verify that the **Delimited** option is selected, and then click **Next**.

   The next Text Import Wizard page opens.

4. In the **Delimiters** area, verify that the **Tab** check box is selected and also verify that the data displayed in the **Data preview** area reflects the structure you expect.

5. Click **Finish**.

   Clicking Finish skips page 3 of the wizard, which has commands you can use to assign specific data types to each column. Excel assigns data types for you, so you don't need to do so. After you click Finish, the Import Data dialog box opens.

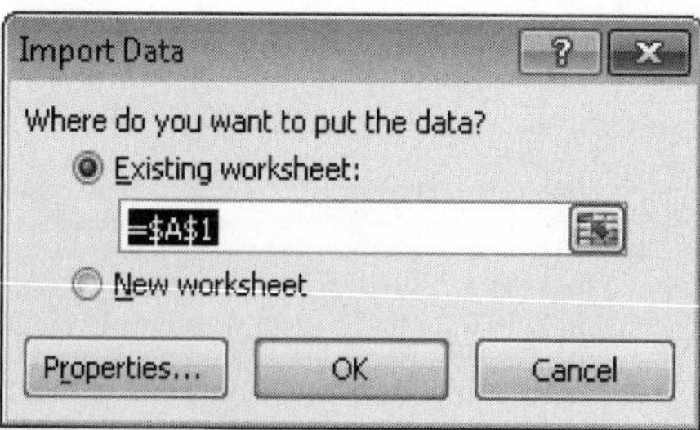

6. Verify that the **Existing worksheet** option is selected, and then click **OK**.

   Excel imports the data into your workbook.

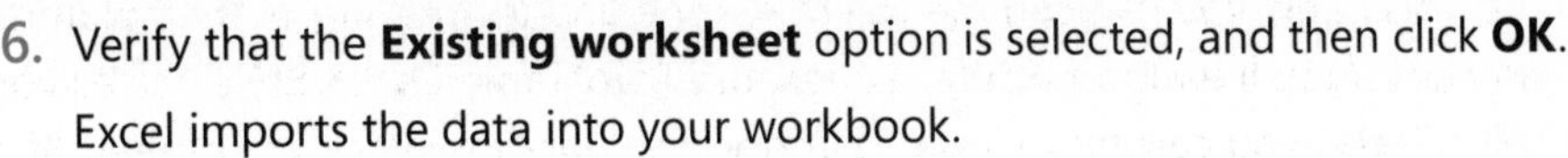

7. On the **Home** tab, in the **Styles** group, click **Format as Table**, and then click the first table style.

   The Format As Table dialog box opens.

8. Verify that the **My table has headers** check box is selected and that the range **=$A$1:$H$6571** appears in the **Where is the data for your table?** box, and then click **OK**.

   A confirmation dialog box opens.

9. Click **Yes** to confirm you want to create the Excel table and break its link to the external data source.

   Excel creates an Excel table from your imported data.

10. On the **Insert** tab, in the **Tables** group, click **PivotTable**.

    The Create PivotTable dialog box opens.

11. Verify that the **Select a table or range** option is selected, that **Table1** appears in the **Table/Range** field, and that the **New Worksheet** option is selected.

12. Click **OK**.

    Excel creates the PivotTable on a new worksheet.

13. In the **PivotTable Field List** task pane, drag the **Volume** field header to the **Values** area.

14. Drag the **Weekday** field header to the **Column Labels** area.

15. Drag the **Center** field header to the **Row Labels** data area.

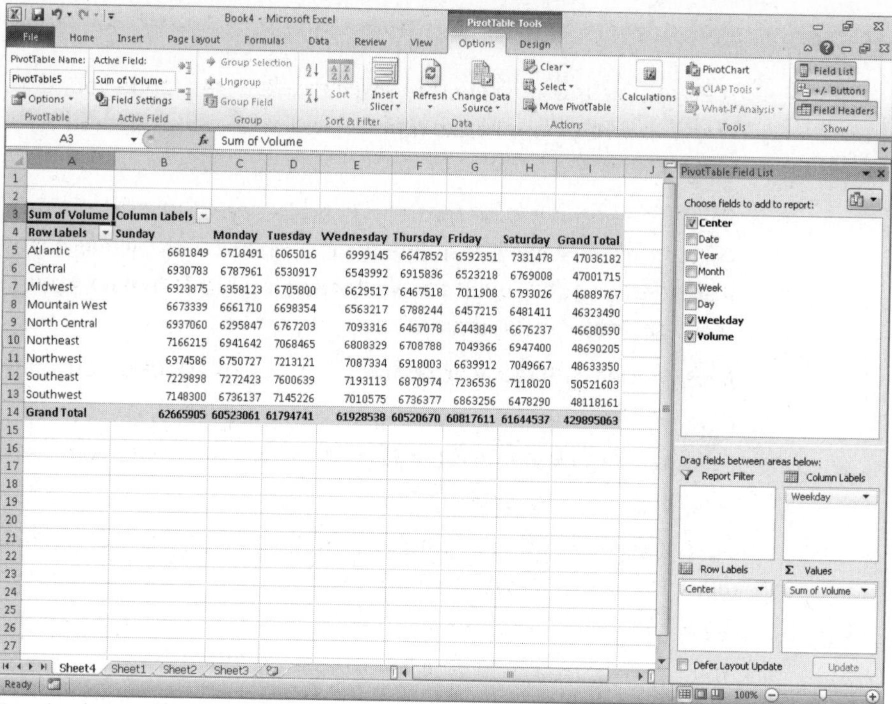

16. On the Quick Access Toolbar, click the **Save** button.

    The Save As dialog box opens.

17. Browse to the **Chapter09** folder.
18. In the **File name** field, type **ImportedData**.
19. Click **Save**.

    Excel saves your file.

CLEAN UP Close the Imported Data workbook. If you're not continuing directly to the next chapter, exit Excel.

Key Points

- A PivotTable is a versatile tool you can use to rearrange your data dynamically, enabling you to emphasize different aspects of your data without creating new worksheets.
- PivotTable data must be formatted as a list. By using a data table as the PivotTable data source, you can streamline the creation process by referring to the table name instead of being required to select the entire range that contains the data you want to summarize.
- Excel comes with many attractive styles for PivotTables; you'll probably find one you like.
- With the PivotTable Field List task pane, you can create your PivotTable by using a straightforward, compact tool.
- Just as you can limit the data shown in a static worksheet, you can use filters to limit the data shown in a PivotTable.
- Excel 2010 includes two new types of filters, search filters and Slicers, that you can use to limit the data in your PivotTables.
- If you have data in a compatible format, such as a text file, you can import that data into Excel and create a PivotTable from it.

Chapter at a Glance

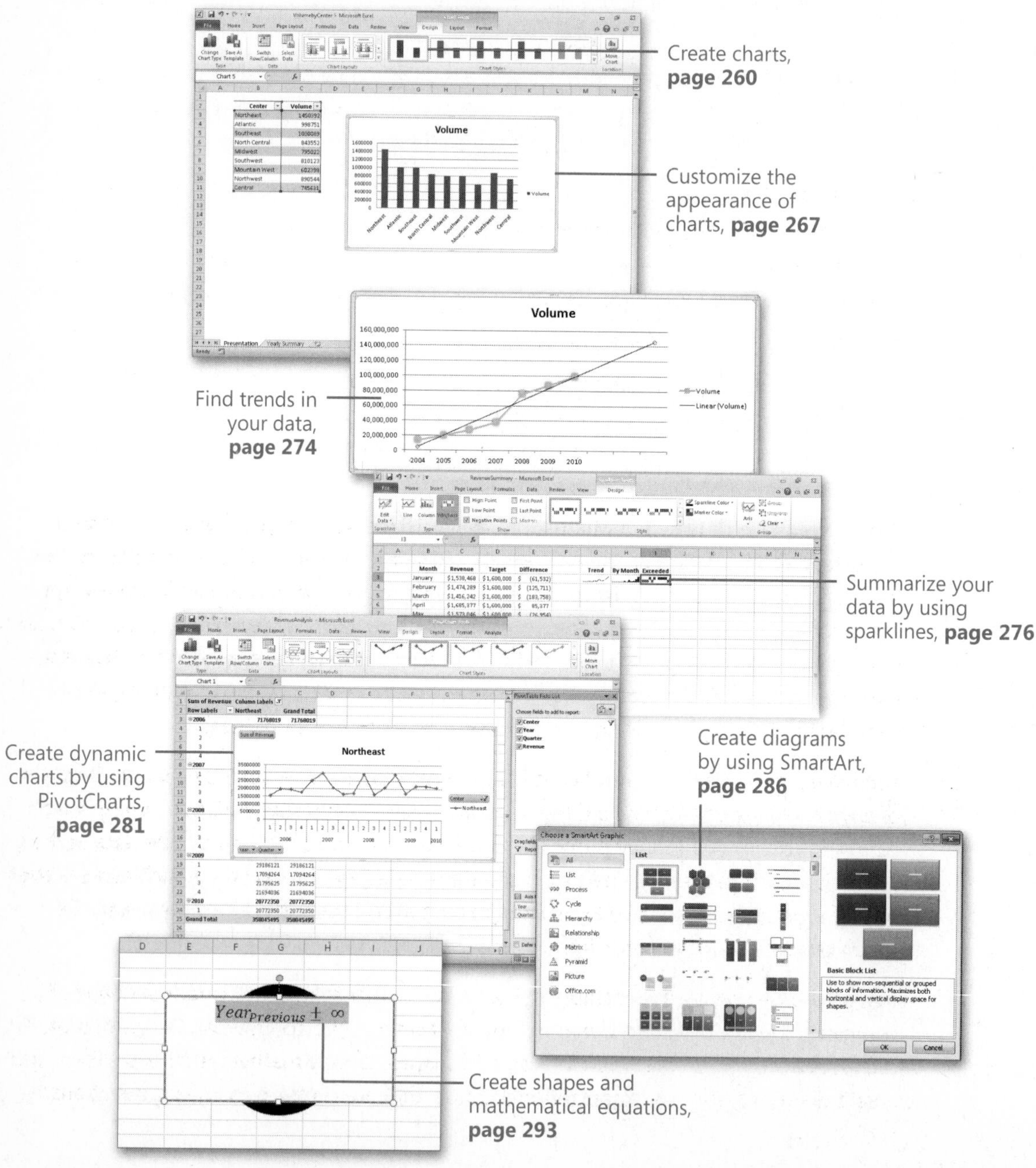
Create charts, page 260
Customize the appearance of charts, page 267
Find trends in your data, page 274
Summarize your data by using sparklines, page 276
Create dynamic charts by using PivotCharts, page 281
Create diagrams by using SmartArt, page 286
Create shapes and mathematical equations, page 293
Volume
Northeast
Choose a SmartArt Graphic
Basic Block List

10 Creating Charts and Graphics

In this chapter, you will learn how to

- ✔ Create charts.
- ✔ Customize the appearance of charts.
- ✔ Find trends in your data.
- ✔ Summarize your data by using sparklines.
- ✔ Create dynamic charts by using PivotCharts.
- ✔ Create diagrams by using SmartArt.
- ✔ Create shapes and mathematical equations.

When you enter data into a Microsoft Excel 2010 worksheet, you create a record of important events, whether they are individual sales, sales for an hour of a day, or the price of a product. What a list of values in cells can't communicate easily, however, is the overall trends in the data. The best way to communicate trends in a large collection of data is by creating a chart, which summarizes data visually. In addition to the standard charts, with Excel 2010 you can create compact charts called sparklines, which summarize a data series using a graph contained within a single cell.

You have a great deal of control over your charts' appearance—you can change the color of any chart element, choose a different chart type to better summarize the underlying data, and change the display properties of text and numbers in a chart. If the data in the worksheet used to create a chart represents a progression through time, such as sales over several months, you can have Excel extrapolate future sales and add a trendline to the graph representing that prediction.

Just as you can create a PivotTable dynamic view to reorganize your data dynamically, you can create a PivotChart dynamic view that reflects the contents and organization of the associated PivotTable. You can also add shapes, display mathematical equations, and create diagrams, such as organizational charts, that are useful in many organizations.

In this chapter, you'll learn how to create a chart and customize its elements, find trends in your overall data, summarize data using sparklines, create dynamic charts, and create and format shapes, diagrams, and shapes containing mathematical equations.

Practice Files Before you can complete the exercises in this chapter, you need to copy the book's practice files to your computer. The practice files you'll use to complete the exercises in this chapter are in the Chapter10 practice file folder. A complete list of practice files is provided in "Using the Practice Files" at the beginning of this book.

Creating Charts

To create a chart, select the data you want to summarize visually and then, on the Insert tab, in the Charts group, click the type of chart you want to create to have Excel display the available chart subtypes.

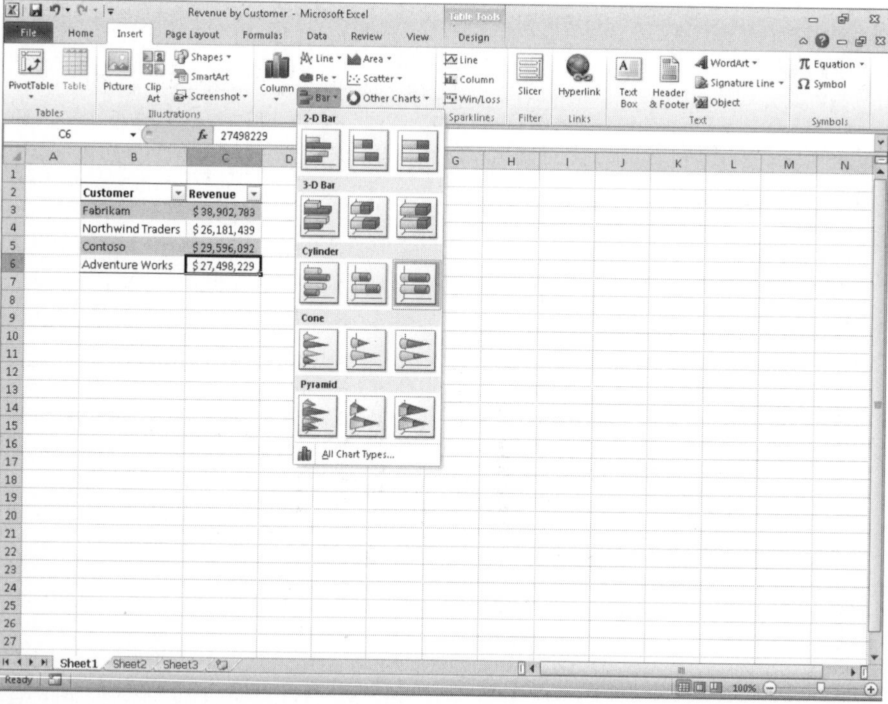

Troubleshooting The appearance of buttons and groups on the ribbon changes depending on the width of the program window. For information about changing the appearance of the ribbon to match our screen images, see "Modifying the Display of the Ribbon" at the beginning of this book.

When you click a chart subtype, Excel creates the chart by using the default layout and color scheme defined in your workbook's theme.

Keyboard Shortcut Press F11 to create a chart of the default type. Unless you or another user changed the default, Excel creates a column chart.

See Also To see a complete list of keyboard shortcuts, see "Keyboard Shortcuts" at the end of this book.

If Excel doesn't plot your data the way you want it to, you can change the axis on which Excel plots a data column. The most common reason for incorrect data plotting is that the column to be plotted on the horizontal axis contains numerical data instead of textual data. For example, if your data includes a Year column and a Volume column, instead of plotting volume data for each consecutive year along the horizontal axis, Excel plots both of those columns in the body of the chart and creates a sequential series to provide values for the horizontal axis.

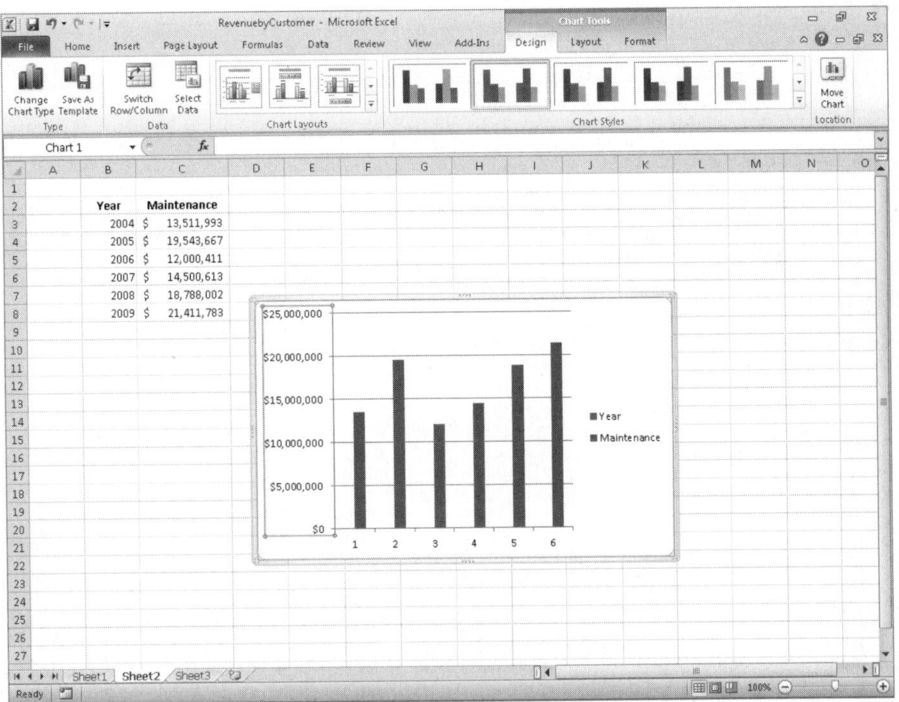

You can change which data Excel applies to the vertical axis (also known as the *y-axis*) and the horizontal axis (also known as the *x-axis*). To make that change, select the chart and then, on the Design tab, in the Data group, click Select Data to display the Select Data Source dialog box.

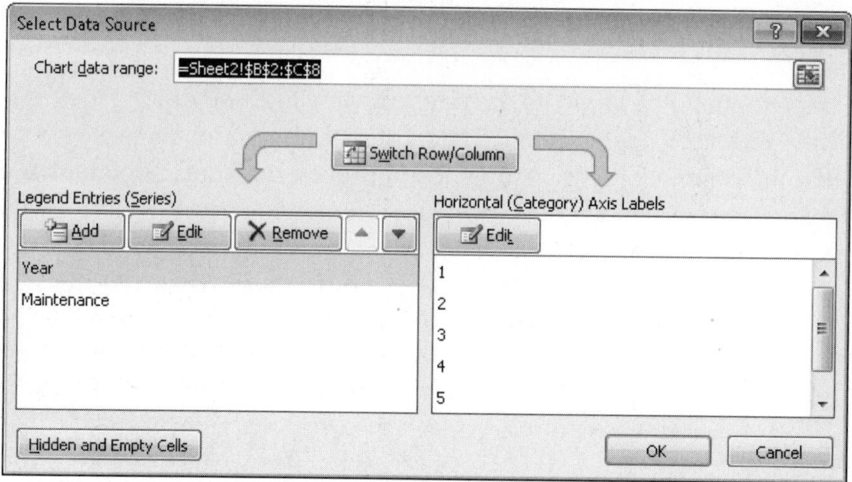

The Year column doesn't belong in the Legend Entries (Series) pane, which corresponds to a column chart's vertical axis. To remove a column from an axis, select the column's name, and then click Remove. To add the column to the Horizontal (Category) Axis Labels pane, click that pane's Edit button to display the Axis Labels dialog box.

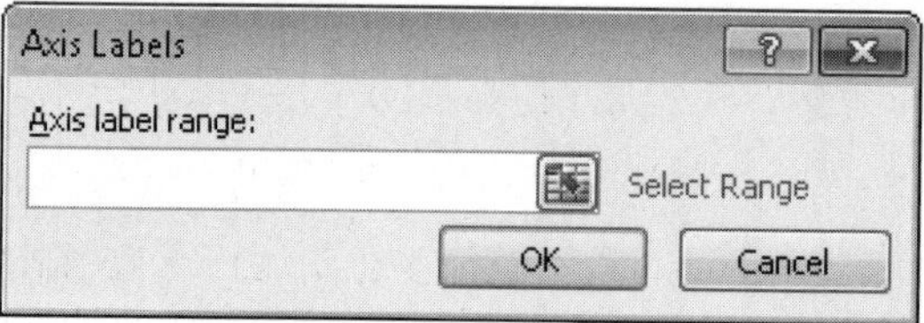

In the Axis Labels dialog box, click the Collapse Dialog button at the right edge of the Axis Label Range field, select the cells to provide the values for the horizontal axis (not including the column header, if any), click the Expand Dialog button, and then click OK. Click OK again to close the Select Data Source dialog box and revise your chart.

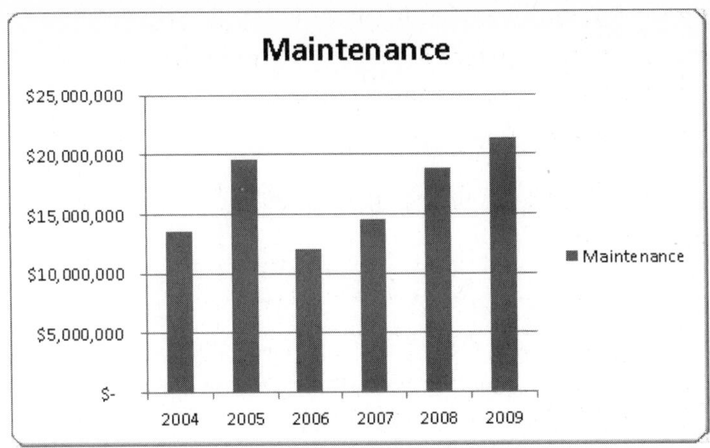

After you create your chart, you can change its size to reflect whether the chart should dominate its worksheet or take on a role as another informative element on the worksheet. For example, Gary Schare, the chief executive officer of Consolidated Messenger, could create a workbook that summarizes the performance of each of his company's business units. In that case, he would display the chart and data for each business unit on the same worksheet, so he would want to make his charts small.

To resize a chart, select the chart, and then drag one of the handles on the chart's edges. Handles in the middle of the edges enable you to resize the chart in one direction. Dragging a handle on the left or right edge enables you to make the chart narrower or wider, whereas dragging the handles on the chart's top and bottom edges enable you to make the chart shorter or taller. Dragging a corner handle enables you to change the chart's height and width at the same time; holding down the Shift key as you drag the corner handle changes the chart's size without changing its proportions.

Just as you can control a chart's size, you can also control its location. To move a chart within a worksheet, drag the chart to the desired location. If you want to move the chart to a new worksheet, click the chart and then, on the Design contextual tab, in the Location group, click Move Chart to display the Move Chart dialog box.

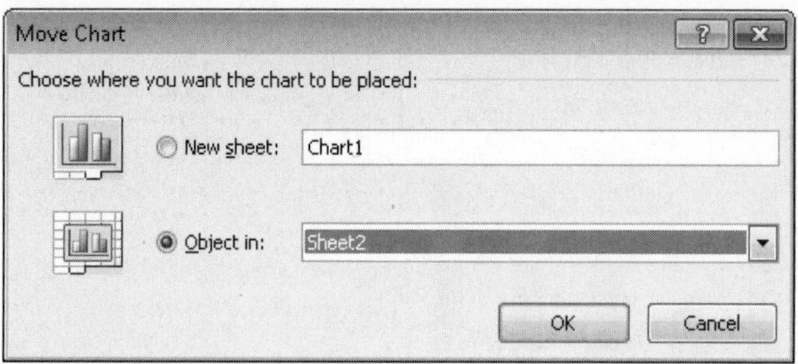

To move the chart to a new chart sheet, select the New Sheet option and type the new sheet's name in the accompanying field. Selecting the New Sheet option creates a chart sheet that contains only your chart. You can still resize the chart on that sheet, but when Excel creates the new chart sheet, the chart takes up the full sheet.

To move the chart to an existing worksheet, select the Object In option and then, in the Object In list, click the worksheet to which you want to move the chart.

In this exercise, you'll create a chart, change how the chart plots your data, move your chart within a worksheet, and move your chart to its own chart sheet.

SET UP You need the YearlyPackageVolume_start workbook located in your Chapter10 practice file folder to complete this exercise. Start Excel, open the YearlyPackageVolume_start workbook, and save it as *YearlyPackageVolume*. Then follow the steps.

1. On the **Data** worksheet, click any cell in the Excel table.

2. On the **Insert** tab, in the **Charts** group, click **Bar** and then, in the **2D Bar** group, click the first chart subtype. (The chart subtype is named *Clustered Bar*).

   Excel creates the chart, with both the Year and Volume data series plotted in the body of the chart.

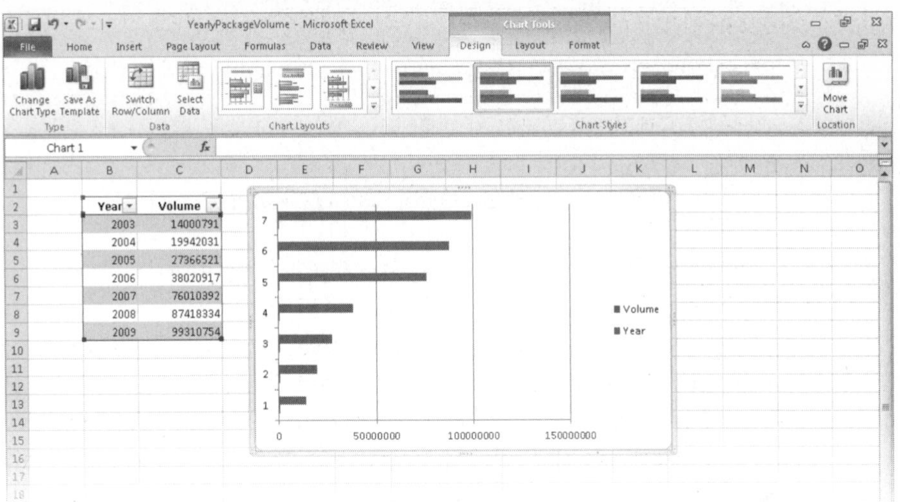

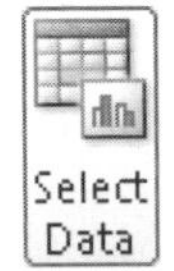

3. On the **Design** tab, in the **Data** group, click **Select Data**.

   The Select Data Source dialog box opens.

4. In the **Legend Entries (Series)** area, click **Year**.
5. Click **Remove**.

   The Year series disappears.

6. In the **Horizontal (Category) Axis Labels** area, click **Edit**.

   The Axis Labels dialog box opens.

7. Select cells **B3:B9**, and then click **OK**.

   The Axis Labels dialog box closes, and the Select Data Source dialog box reappears with the years in the Horizontal (Category) Axis Labels area.

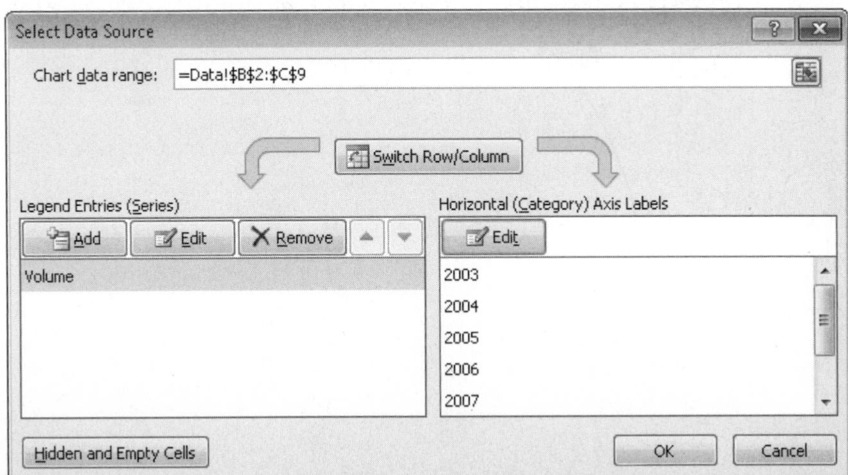

8. Click **OK**.

   Excel redraws your chart, using the years as the values for the horizontal axis.

9. Move the mouse pointer over the body of the chart.

   The mouse pointer changes to a four-headed arrow.

10. Drag the chart up and to the left so that it covers the Excel table.

11. On the **Design** tab, in the **Location** group, click **Move Chart**.

   The Move Chart dialog box opens.

12. Click **New sheet**, type **Volume Chart** in the sheet name box, and then click **OK**.

   Your chart appears on a chart sheet named Volume Chart.

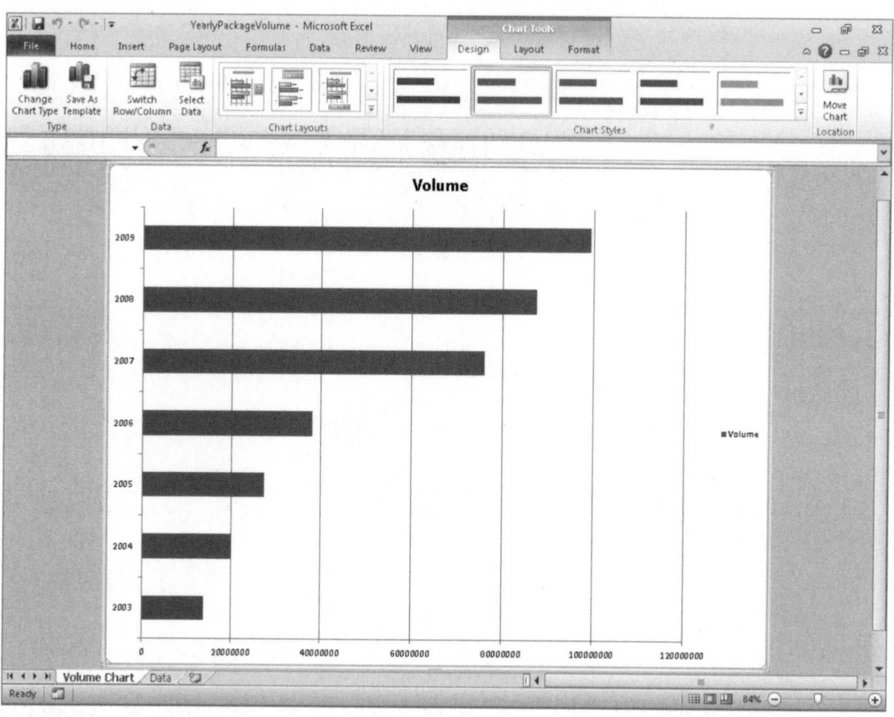

CLEAN UP Save the YearlyPackageVolume workbook, and then close it.

Customizing the Appearance of Charts

If you want to change a chart's appearance, select the chart and then, on the Design tab, click a style in the Chart Styles gallery. The gallery contains far more chart styles than are shown on the ribbon—to select a new look for your chart, click the More button at the gallery's lower-right corner, and then click the design you want.

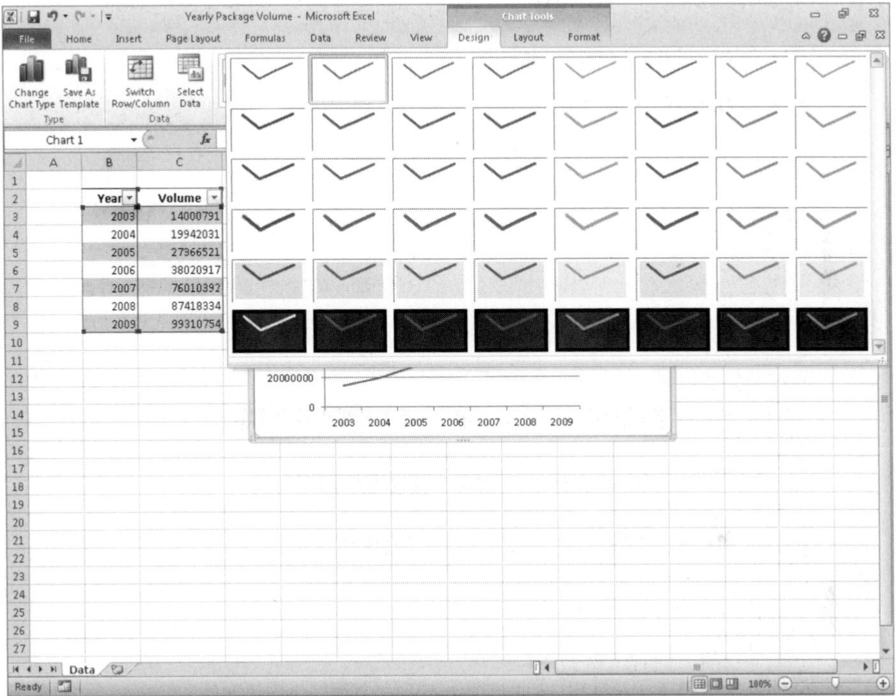

Tip The styles in the Chart Styles gallery are tied to your workbook's theme. If you change your workbook's theme, Excel changes your chart's appearance to reflect the new theme's colors.

When you create a chart by using the tools in the Insert tab's Charts group, Excel creates an attractive chart that focuses on the data. In most cases, the chart has a title, legend (list of data series displayed in the chart), horizontal lines in the body of the chart to make it easier to discern individual values, and axis labels. If you want to create a chart that has more or different elements, such as additional data labels for each data point plotted on your chart, you can do so by selecting the chart and then, on the Design tab, in the Chart Layouts group, clicking the layout you want.

If you don't find the exact chart layout you like, you can use the tools on the Layout contextual tab to control each element's appearance and placement.

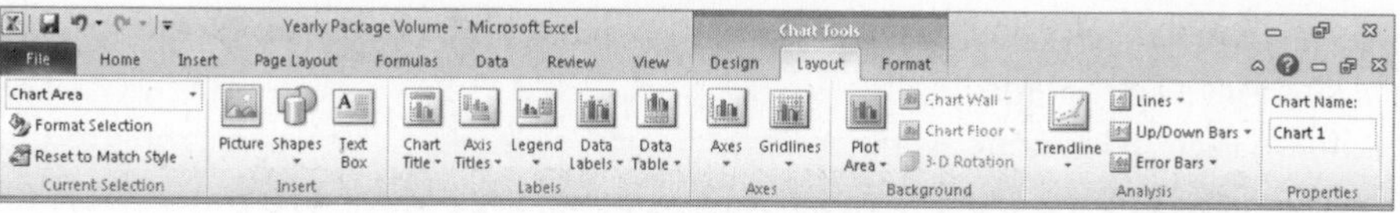

In the Axes group, clicking Gridlines enables you to determine whether the chart displays horizontal and vertical gridlines and, if it does, at what value intervals they should appear.

In addition to changing your chart's layout, you can control the appearance of each element within the chart. To select a chart element to format, click that element. For example, if you want to change the formatting of the data series named Volume in the column chart you created in the previous exercise, clicking any column in the series selects the entire series. Any formatting changes you make then apply to every point in the entire series. If you want to change a single data point, select the entire series, and then click the chart element (for example, a column) that represents the data point you want to change. For example, you can highlight the column representing the year 2008 in the chart you created in the previous exercise.

You can display a list of the selectable chart elements by selecting the chart and then, on the Format tab, in the Current Selection group, clicking the Chart Elements arrow. Then just click the desired chart element to select it.

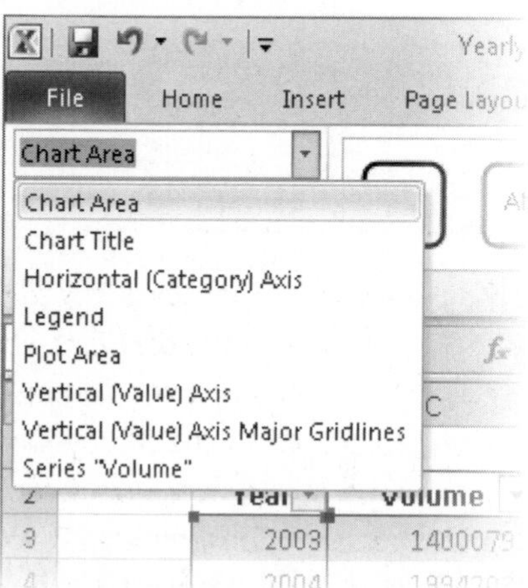

After you select the chart element, you can drag one of the element's handles to resize the element or drag the element to another location within the chart. To change the chart element's format, use the tools and dialog box launchers in the Format tab's Shape Styles, Word Art Styles, Arrange, and Size groups to change the element's appearance. You can also select the chart element and then, on the Format tab, in the Current Selection group, click Format Selection to display a Format dialog box that enables you to change the chart element's appearance.

If you think you want to apply the same set of changes to charts you'll create in the future, you can save your chart as a chart template. When you select the data you want to summarize visually and apply the chart template, you'll create consistently formatted charts in a minimum of steps. To save a chart as a chart template, select the chart you want to use as a template and then, on the Design tab, in the Type group, click Save Template. Use the controls in the dialog box that appears to name and save your template. Then, to create a chart based on that template, select the data you want to summarize and then, on the Insert tab, in the Charts group, click any chart type, and then click All Chart Types to display the Create Charts dialog box. Under Choose A Chart Type, click Templates, and then click the template you want to use.

Tip You can apply a template to an existing chart by selecting the chart and then, on the Design tab, in the Type group, clicking Change Chart Type to display the Change Chart Type dialog box. Click Templates, and then click the template you want to use.

In this exercise, you'll change a chart's layout, apply a new Chart Style, change the number format of the values on the vertical axis, save the chart as a chart template, and apply the template to another chart.

SET UP You need the VolumeByCenter_start workbook located in your Chapter10 practice file folder to complete this exercise. Open the VolumeByCenter_start workbook, and save it as *VolumeByCenter*. Then follow the steps.

1. On the **Presentation** worksheet, select the chart.

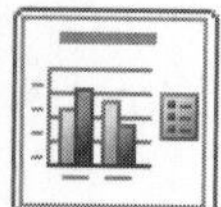

2. On the **Design** tab, in the **Chart Layouts** group, click the first chart layout (its screen tip says the layout name is *Layout 1*).

   Excel changes the chart's layout.

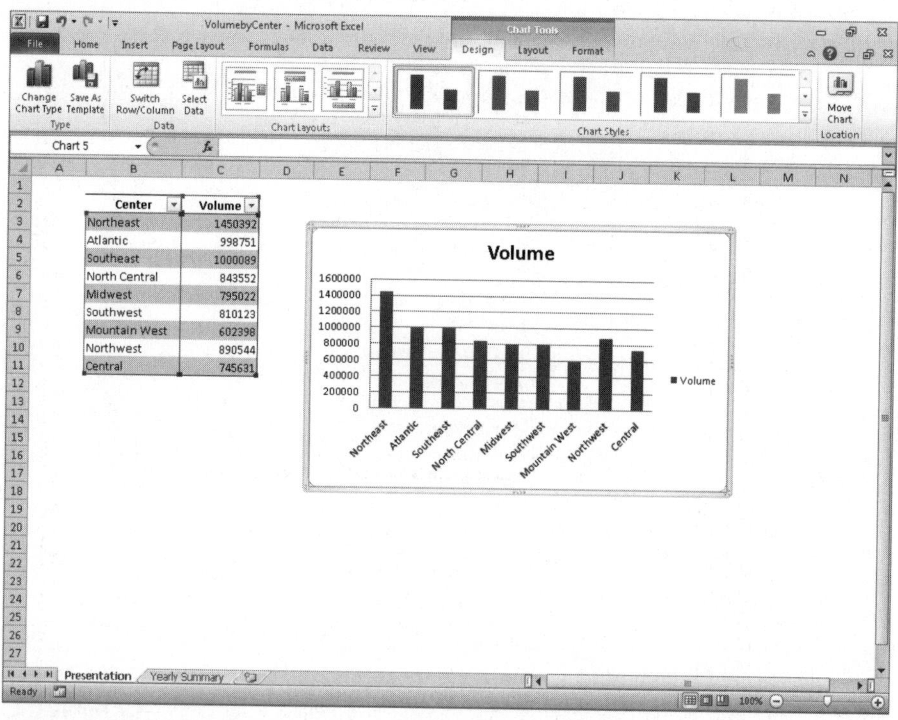

3. On the **Design** contextual tab, in the **Chart Styles** group, click the **More** button.

   The Chart Styles gallery expands.

4. Click **Style 7** (it's the second-from-the-right style on the top row of the gallery).

   Excel changes the chart's style.

5. Right-click the values on the vertical axis, and then click **Format Axis**.

   The Format Axis dialog box opens.

6. In the left pane, click **Number**.

   The Format Axis dialog box displays the Number page.

7. In the **Category** list, click **Number**.

   The Format Axis dialog box displays the Number style's options.

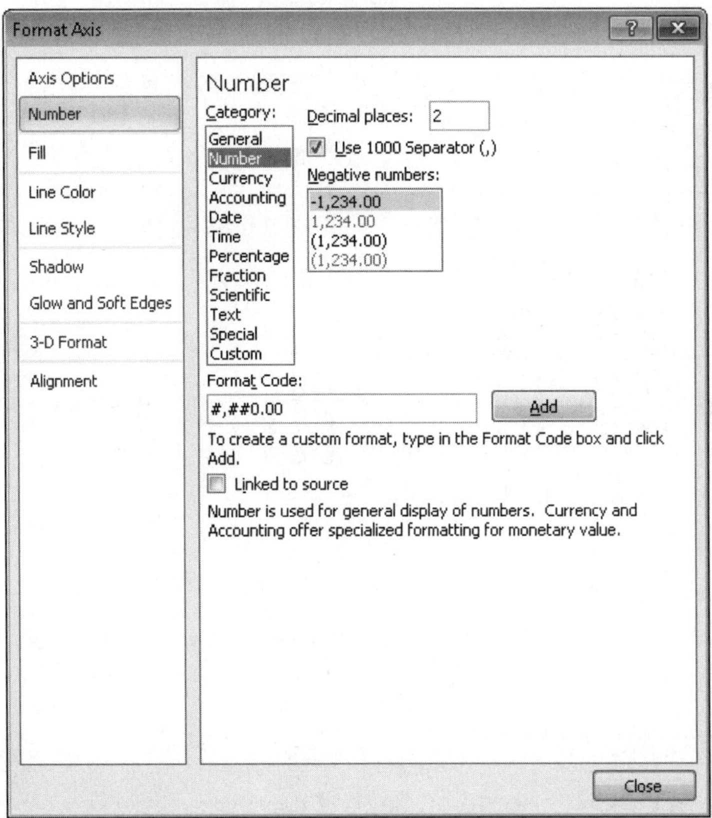

8. In the **Decimal places** field, type **0**.
9. If necessary, select the **Use 1000 Separator (,)** check box.
10. Click **Close**.

Excel changes the format of the values on the vertical axis.

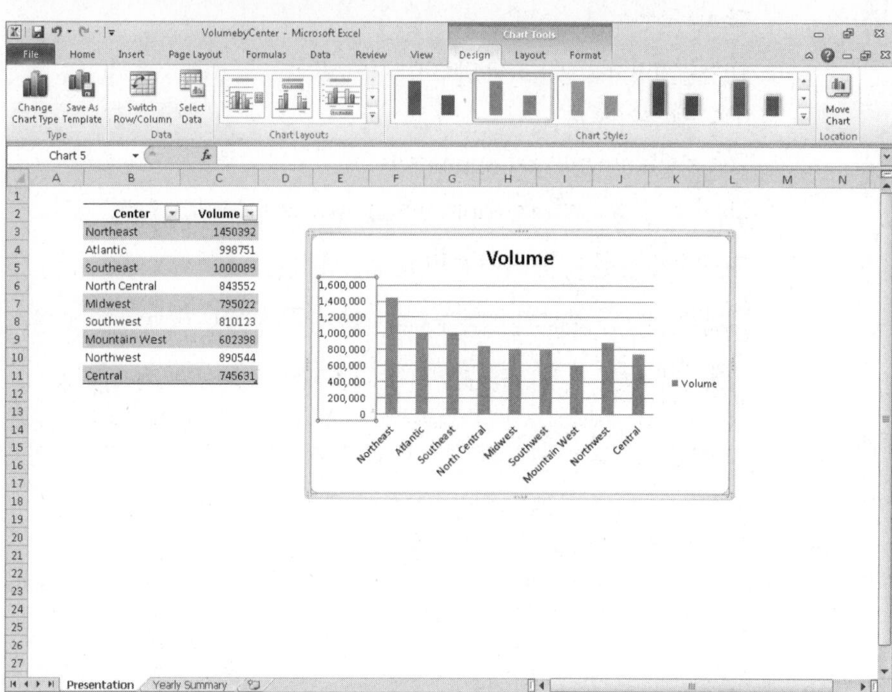

11. On the **Design** contextual tab, in the **Type** group, click **Save As Template**.

    The Save Chart Template dialog box opens.

12. In the **File name** field, type **Cool Blue**.

13. Click **Save**.

    Excel saves your template.

14. On the tab bar, click the **Yearly Summary** sheet tab.

    The Yearly Summary worksheet appears.

15. Select the chart and then, on the **Design** tab, in the **Type** group, click **Change Chart Type**.

    The Change Chart Type dialog box opens.

16. Click **Templates**.

    The My Templates list appears.

17. Click the **Cool Blue** custom template, and then click **OK**.

    Excel applies the template to your chart.

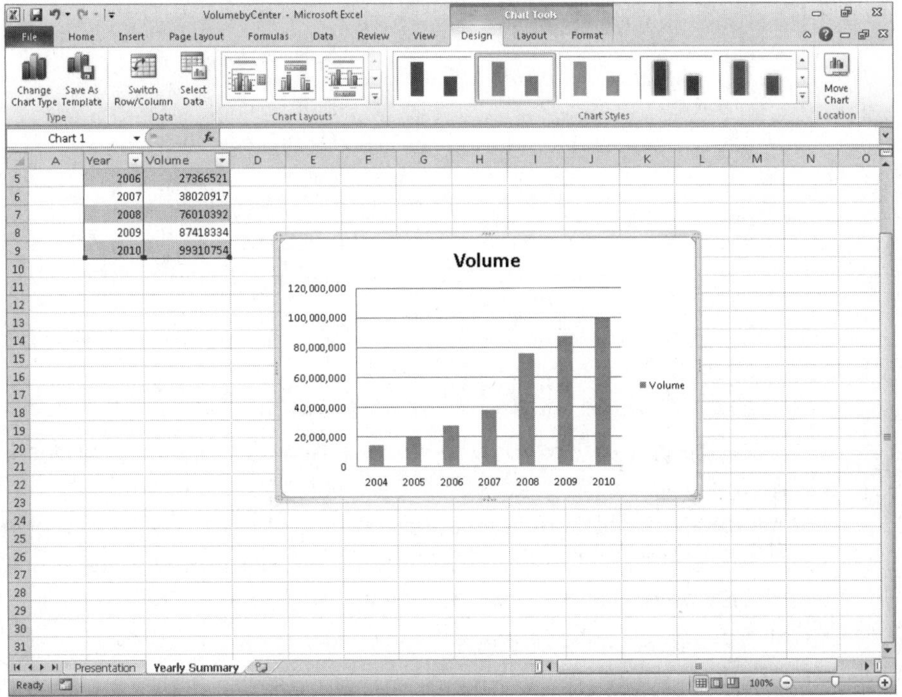

CLEAN UP Save the VolumeByCenter workbook, and then close it.

Finding Trends in Your Data

You can use the data in Excel workbooks to discover how your business has performed in the past, but you can also have Excel 2010 make its best guess, for example, as to future shipping revenues if the current trend continues. As an example, consider a graph that shows the fleet maintenance costs for the years 2004 through 2009 for Consolidated Messenger.

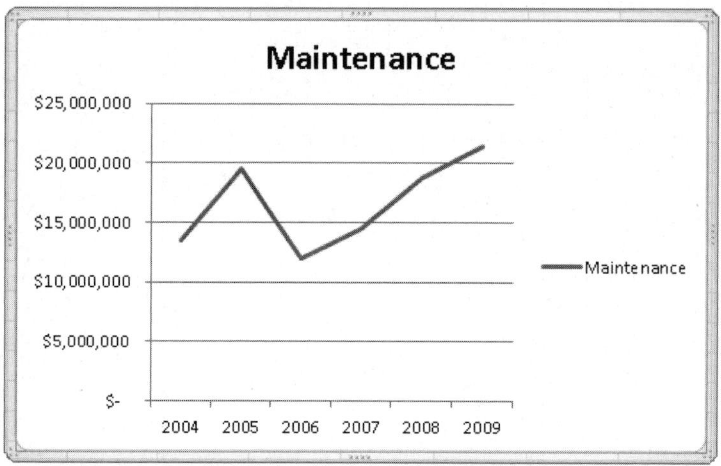

The total has increased from 2004 to 2009, but the growth hasn't been uniform, so guessing how much maintenance costs would increase if the overall trend continued would require difficult mathematical computations. Fortunately, Excel knows that math. To have Excel project future values in the maintenance costs data series, click the chart and then, on the Layout tab, in the Analysis group, click Trendline. Click More Trendline Options to display the Format Trendline dialog box.

With the Trendline Options page of the Format Trendline dialog box, you can choose the data distribution that Excel should expect when it makes its projection. The right choice for most business data is Linear—the other distributions (such as Exponential, Logarithmic, and Polynomial) are used for scientific and operations research applications.

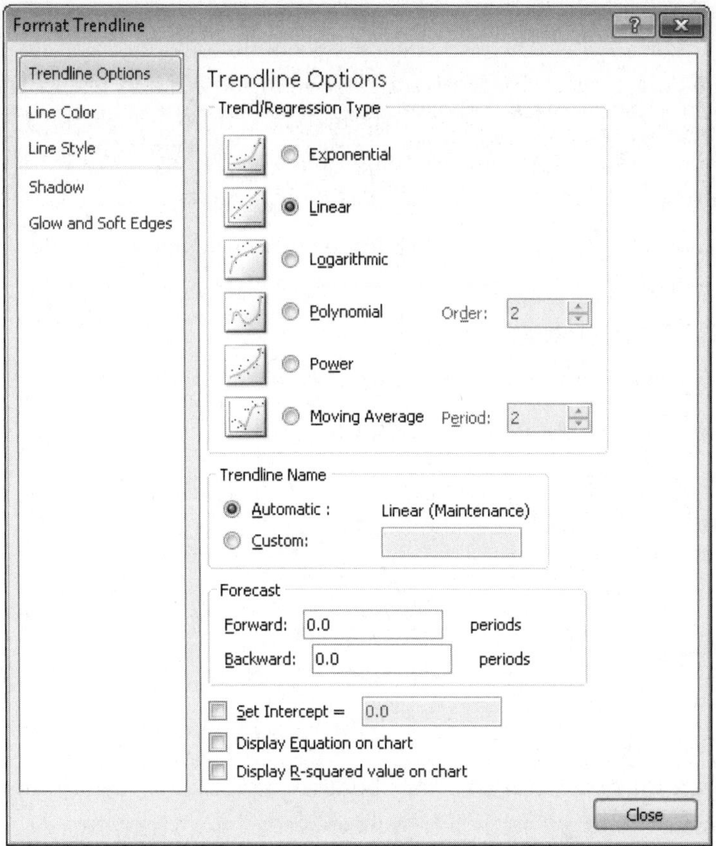

Tip If you don't know which distribution to choose, use Linear. The other distributions are used for scientific and engineering applications and you will know, or be told by a colleague, when to use them.

After you pick the distribution type, you need to tell Excel how far ahead to project the data trend. The horizontal axis of the chart used in this example shows revenues by year from 2004 to 2009. To tell Excel how far in the future to look, type a number in the Forecast area's Forward box. In this case, to look ahead one year, type *1* in the Forward box, and then click OK to add the trendline to the chart.

Tip When you click the Trendline button in the Analysis group, one of the options Excel displays is Linear Forecast Trendline, which adds a trendline with a two-period forecast.

As with other chart elements, you can double-click the trendline to open a formatting dialog box and change the line's appearance.

In this exercise, you'll add a trendline to a chart.

SET UP You need the FutureVolumes_start workbook located in your Chapter10 practice file folder to complete this exercise. Open the FutureVolumes_start workbook, and save it as *FutureVolumes*. Then follow the steps.

1. Select the chart.

2. On the **Layout** contextual tab, in the **Analysis** group, click **Trendline**, and then click **More Trendline Options**.

   The Format Trendline dialog box opens.
3. If necessary, in the **Trend/Regression Type** area, click **Linear**.
4. In the **Forecast** area, in the **Forward** field, type **3**.
5. Click **Close**.

   Excel adds the trendline to the chart.

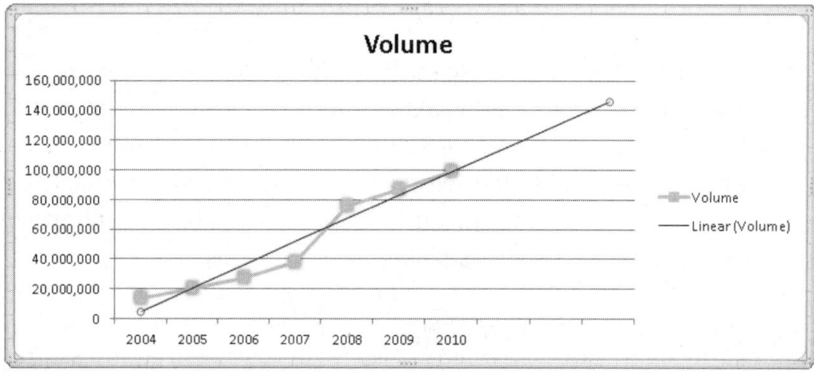

CLEAN UP Save the FutureVolumes workbook, and then close it.

Summarizing Your Data by Using Sparklines

You can create charts in Excel workbooks to summarize your data visually, by using legends, labels, and colors to highlight aspects of your data. It is possible to create very small charts to summarize your data in an overview worksheet, but you can also use sparklines, which are new in Excel 2010, to create compact, informative charts that provide valuable context for your data.

Edward Tufte introduced sparklines in his book *Beautiful Evidence* (Graphics Press, 2006), with the goal of creating charts that imparted their information in approximately the same space as a word of printed text. In Excel 2010, a sparkline occupies a single cell, which makes it ideal for use in summary worksheets. As an example, suppose Lori Penor wanted to summarize the monthly revenue data for one of Consolidated Messenger's local branches.

	A	B	C	D	E	F
1						
2		**Month**	**Revenue**	**Target**	**Difference**	
3		January	$1,538,468	$1,600,000	$ (61,532)	
4		February	$1,474,289	$1,600,000	$ (125,711)	
5		March	$1,416,242	$1,600,000	$ (183,758)	
6		April	$1,685,377	$1,600,000	$ 85,377	
7		May	$1,573,046	$1,600,000	$ (26,954)	
8		June	$1,979,077	$1,600,000	$ 379,077	
9		July	$1,600,000	$1,600,000	$ -	
10		August	$2,417,226	$1,600,000	$ 817,226	
11		September	$1,872,026	$1,600,000	$ 272,026	
12		October	$2,097,478	$1,600,000	$ 497,478	
13		November	$2,876,025	$2,750,000	$ 126,025	
14		December	$3,825,430	$4,000,000	$ (174,570)	
15						

Lori can create three types of sparklines: line, column, and win/loss. The line and column sparklines are compact versions of the standard line and column charts. The win/loss sparkline indicates whether a cell value is positive (a win), negative (a loss), or zero (a tie). To create a line sparkline, you select the data you want to summarize and then, on the Insert tab, in the Sparklines group, click the Line button. When you do, Excel 2010 displays the Create Sparklines dialog box.

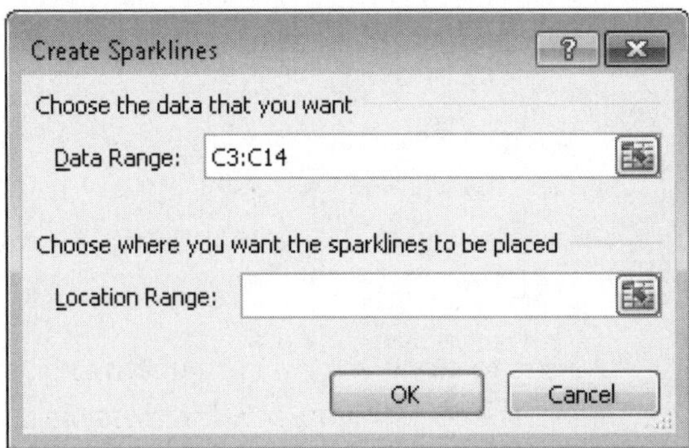

The data range you selected appears in the Data Range box. If the data range is not correct, you can click the Collapse Dialog button to the right of the Data Range box, select the correct cells, and then click the Expand Dialog button. Then, in the Location Range box, type the address of the cell into which you want to place your sparkline. When you click OK, Excel creates a line sparkline in the cell you specified.

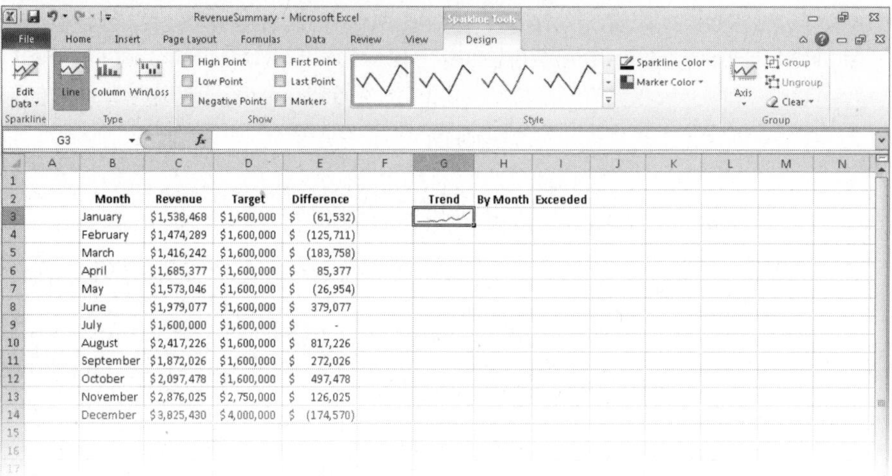

You follow the same basic procedure to create a column sparkline, except that instead of clicking the Line button in the Insert tab's Sparklines group, you click the Column button. To create a win/loss sparkline, you need to ensure that your data contains, or could contain, both positive and negative values. If you measured monthly revenue for Consolidated Messenger, every value would be positive and the win/loss sparkline would impart no meaningful information. Comparing revenue to revenue targets, however, could result in positive, negative, or tie values, which can be meaningfully summarized by using a win/loss sparkline.

To create a win/loss sparkline, follow the same data selection process and click the Win/Loss button.

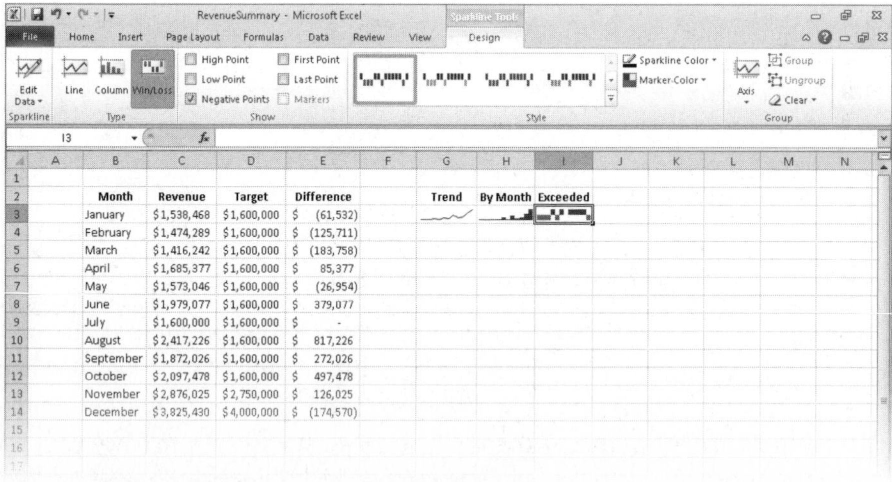

Months in which Consolidated Messenger's branch exceeded its revenue target appear in the top half of the cell in blue, months in which the branch fell short of its target appear in the bottom half of the cell in red, and the month in which the revenue was exactly the same as the target is blank.

After you create a sparkline, you can change its appearance. Because a sparkline takes up the entire interior of a single cell, resizing that cell's row or column resizes the sparkline. You can also change a sparkline's formatting. When you click a sparkline, Excel displays the Sparkline Tools Design contextual tab.

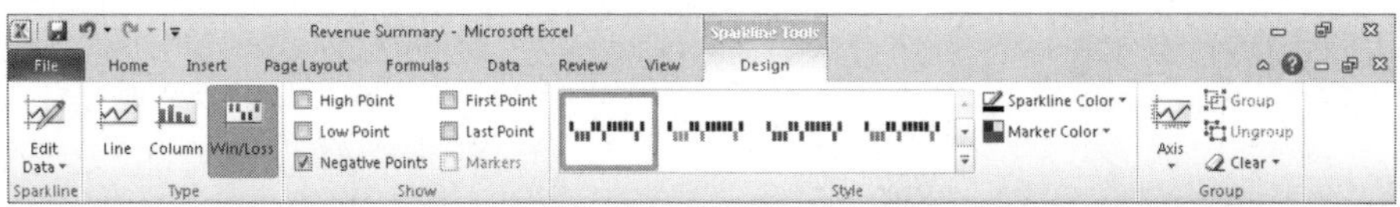

You can use the tools on the Design contextual tab to select a new style; show or hide value markers; change the color of your sparkline or the markers; edit the data used to create the sparkline; modify the labels on the sparkline's axes; or group, ungroup, or clear sparklines. You can't delete a sparkline by clicking its cell and then pressing the Delete or Backspace key—you must click the cell and then, on the Design contextual tab of the ribbon, click the Clear button.

Tip Remember that sparklines work best when displayed in compact form. If you find yourself adding markers and labels to a sparkline, you might consider using a regular chart to take advantage of its wider range of formatting and customization options.

In this exercise, you'll create a line, column, and win/loss sparkline, change the sparkline's formatting, and clear a sparkline from a cell.

SET UP You need the RevenueSummary_start workbook located in your Chapter10 practice file folder to complete this exercise. Open the RevenueSummary_start workbook, and save it as *RevenueSummary*. Then follow the steps.

1. Select the cell range **C3:C14**.

2. On the **Insert** tab, in the **Sparklines** group, click **Line**.

   The Create Sparklines dialog box opens.

3. Verify that **C3:C14** appears in the **Data Range** box. Then, in the **Location Range** box, type G3 and click **OK**.

   Excel 2010 creates a line sparkline in cell G3.

4. Select the cell range **C3:C14**.

5. On the **Insert** tab, in the **Sparklines** group, click **Column**.

   The Create Sparklines dialog box opens.

6. Verify that **C3:C14** appears in the **Data Range** box. Then, in the **Location Range** box, type **H3** and click **OK**.

   Excel creates a column sparkline in cell H3.

7. Drag the right edge of the column H header to the right until the cell's width is approximately doubled.

   Excel displays more details in the sparkline.

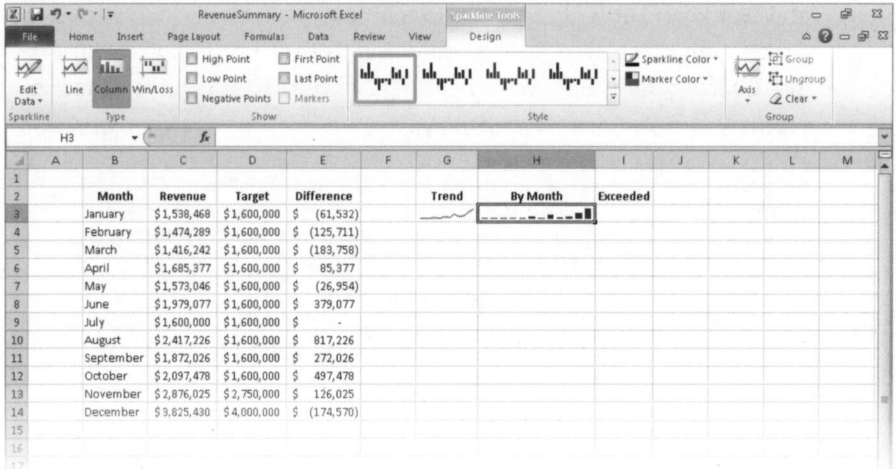

Month	Revenue	Target	Difference	Trend	By Month	Exceeded
January	$1,538,468	$1,600,000	$ (61,532)			
February	$1,474,289	$1,600,000	$ (125,711)			
March	$1,416,242	$1,600,000	$ (183,758)			
April	$1,685,377	$1,600,000	$ 85,377			
May	$1,573,046	$1,600,000	$ (26,954)			
June	$1,979,077	$1,600,000	$ 379,077			
July	$1,600,000	$1,600,000	$ -			
August	$2,417,226	$1,600,000	$ 817,226			
September	$1,872,026	$1,600,000	$ 272,026			
October	$2,097,478	$1,600,000	$ 497,478			
November	$2,876,025	$2,750,000	$ 126,025			
December	$3,825,430	$4,000,000	$ (174,570)			

8. Select the cell range **E3:E14**.

9. On the **Insert** tab, in the **Sparklines** group, click **Win/Loss**.

   The Create Sparklines dialog box opens.

10. Verify that **E3:E14** appears in the **Data Range** box. Then, in the **Location Range** box, type **I3** and click **OK**.

    Excel creates a win/loss sparkline in cell I3.

11. With cell I3 still selected, on the **Design** contextual tab, in the **Style** gallery, click the right-most sparkline style.

    Excel changes the win/loss sparkline's appearance.

12. Click cell **G3** and then, on the **Design** contextual tab, in the **Group** group, click the **Clear** button.

    The sparkline disappears.

CLEAN UP Save the RevenueSummary workbook, and then close it.

Creating Dynamic Charts by Using PivotCharts

Just as you can create PivotTables that you can reorganize on the fly to emphasize different aspects of the data in a list, you can also create dynamic charts, or PivotCharts, to reflect the contents and organization of a PivotTable.

Creating a PivotChart is fairly straightforward. Just click any cell in a list or Excel table you would use to create a PivotTable, and then click the Insert tab. In the Tables group, in the PivotTable list, click PivotChart to create the chart. To create a PivotChart from an existing PivotTable, click a cell in the PivotTable, display the Insert tab and then, in the Charts group, click the type of chart you want to create. After you complete either of these procedures, Excel displays a new PivotChart in your workbook.

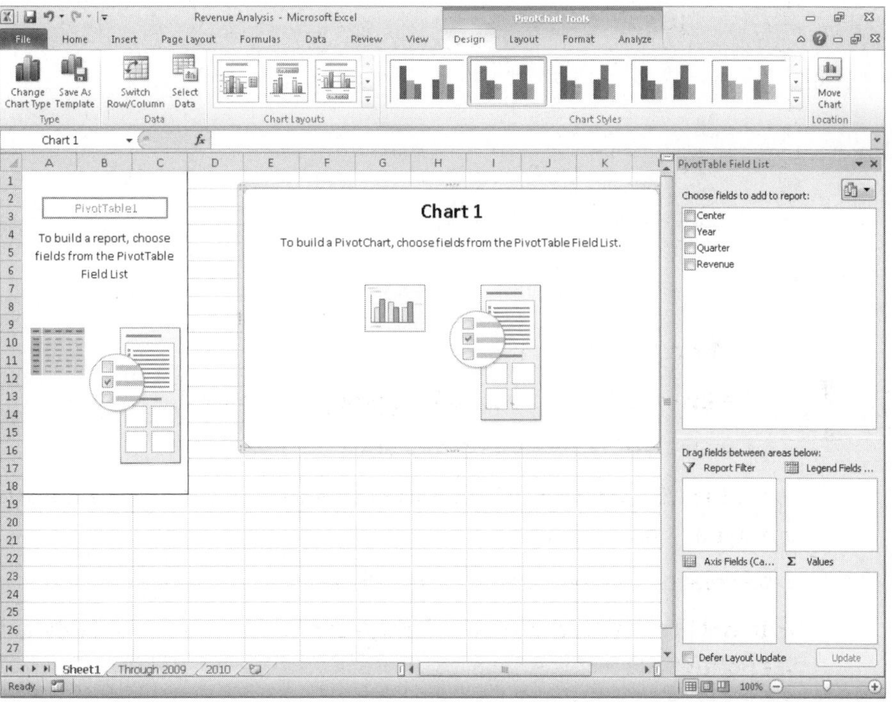

Any changes to the PivotTable on which the PivotChart is based are reflected in the PivotChart. For example, if the data in an underlying data set changes, clicking the Refresh button in the Data group on the Analyze contextual tab will change the PivotChart to reflect the new data. Also, if you filter the contents of a PivotTable, the filter will be reflected in the PivotChart. For instance, if you click 2006 in the Year list of a revenue analysis PivotTable and then click OK, both the PivotTable and the PivotChart will show only revenues from 2006.

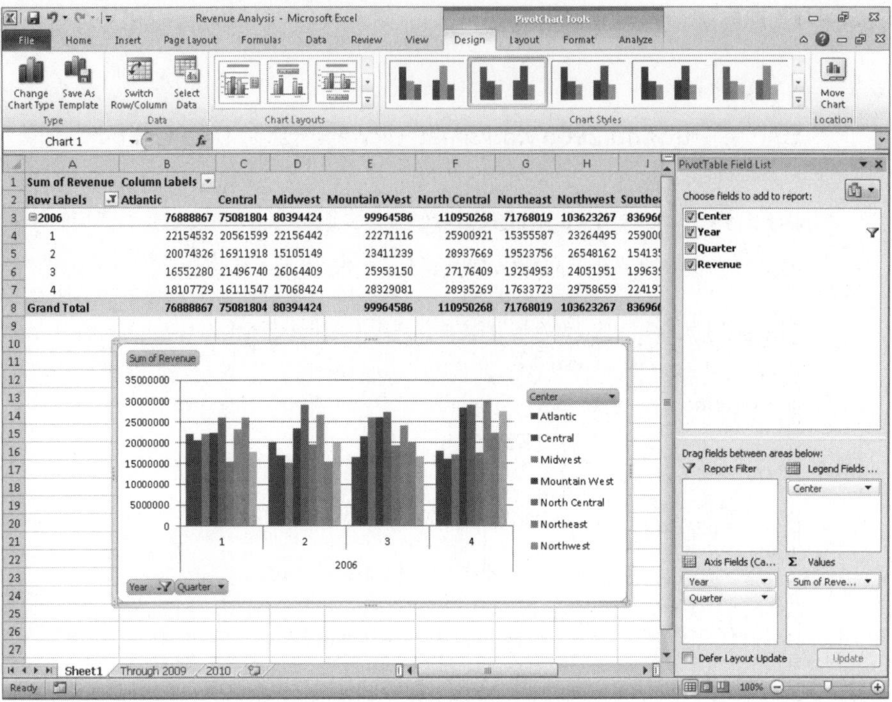

See Also For more information on manipulating PivotTables, see "Filtering, Showing, and Hiding PivotTable Data" in Chapter 9, "Creating Dynamic Worksheets by Using PivotTables."

A PivotChart has tools with which you can filter the data in the PivotChart and PivotTable. Clicking the Year arrow, clicking (All) in the list that appears, and then clicking OK will restore the PivotChart to its original configuration.

If you ever want to change the chart type of an existing chart, you can do so by selecting the chart and then, on the Design tab, in the Type group, clicking Change Chart Type to display the Change Chart Type dialog box. When you select the type you want and click OK, Excel re-creates your chart.

Important If your data is the wrong type to be represented by the chart type you select, Excel displays an error message.

In this exercise, you'll create a PivotTable and associated PivotChart, change the underlying data and update the PivotChart to reflect that change, change the PivotChart's type, and then filter a PivotTable and PivotChart.

SET UP You need the RevenueAnalysis_start workbook located in your Chapter10 practice file folder to complete this exercise. Open the RevenueAnalysis_start workbook, and save it as *RevenueAnalysis*. Then follow the steps.

1. On the **Through 2009** worksheet, click any cell in the Excel table.

2. On the **Insert** tab, in the **Tables** group, click the **PivotTable** arrow and then, in the list that appears, click **PivotChart**.

   The Create PivotTable With PivotChart dialog box opens.

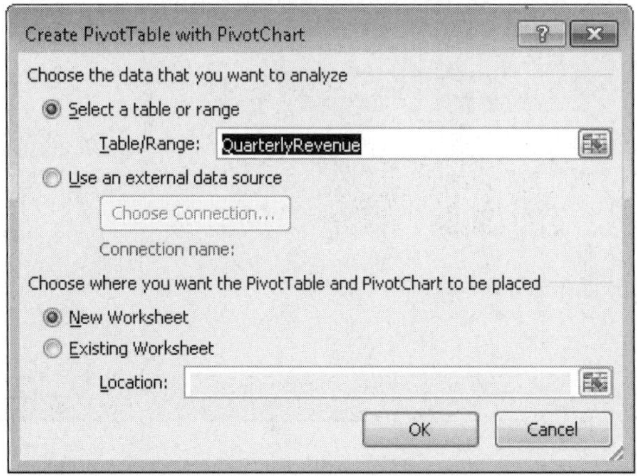

3. Verify that the QuarterlyRevenue table appears in the **Table/Range** field and that the **New Worksheet** option is selected.
4. Click **OK**.

   Excel creates the PivotTable and associated PivotChart.

5. In the **PivotTable Field List** task pane, drag the **Center** field header from the **Choose fields to add to report** area to the **Legend Fields** area.
6. Drag the **Year** field header from the **Choose fields to add to report** area to the **Axis Fields** area.
7. Drag the **Quarter** field header from the **Choose fields to add to report** area to the **Axis Fields** area, positioning it below the **Year** field header.
8. Drag the **Revenue** field header from the **Choose fields to add to report** area to the **Values** area.

   Excel updates the PivotChart to reflect the field placements.

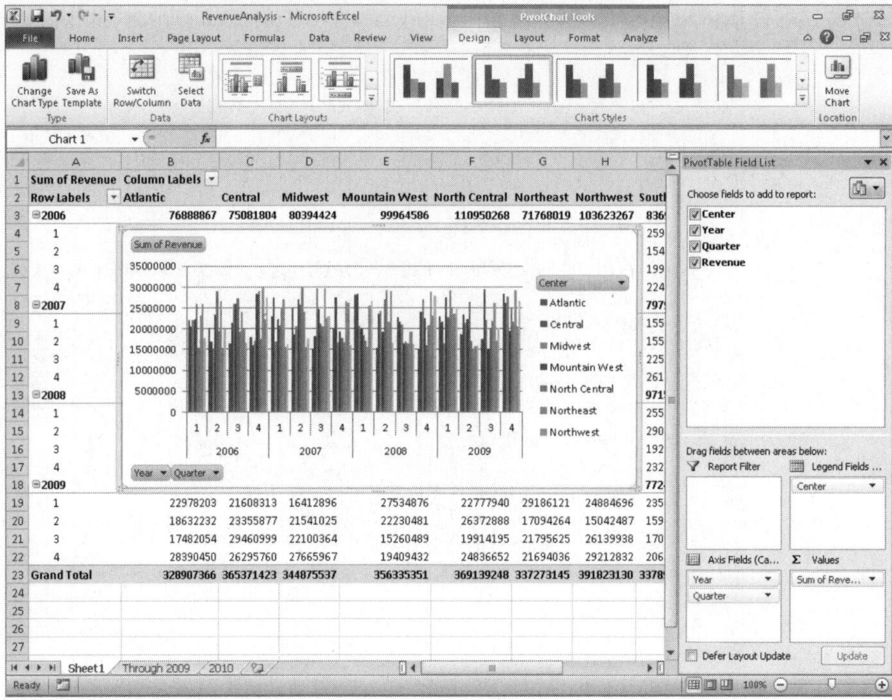

9. Click the **2010** sheet tab.

   The 2010 worksheet appears.

10. Select the data in cells **B2:E10**, and then press Ctrl+C.

    Excel copies the data to the Microsoft Office Clipboard.

11. On the tab bar, click the **Through 2009** sheet tab.

    The Through 2009 worksheet appears.

12. Select cell **B147**, and then press Ctrl+V.

    Excel pastes the data into the worksheet and includes it in the Excel table.

13. Click the tab of the worksheet that contains the PivotTable and the PivotChart.

    The PivotChart appears.

14. Select the PivotChart and then, on the **Analyze** contextual tab, in the **Data** group, click **Refresh**.

    Excel adds the new table data to your PivotChart.

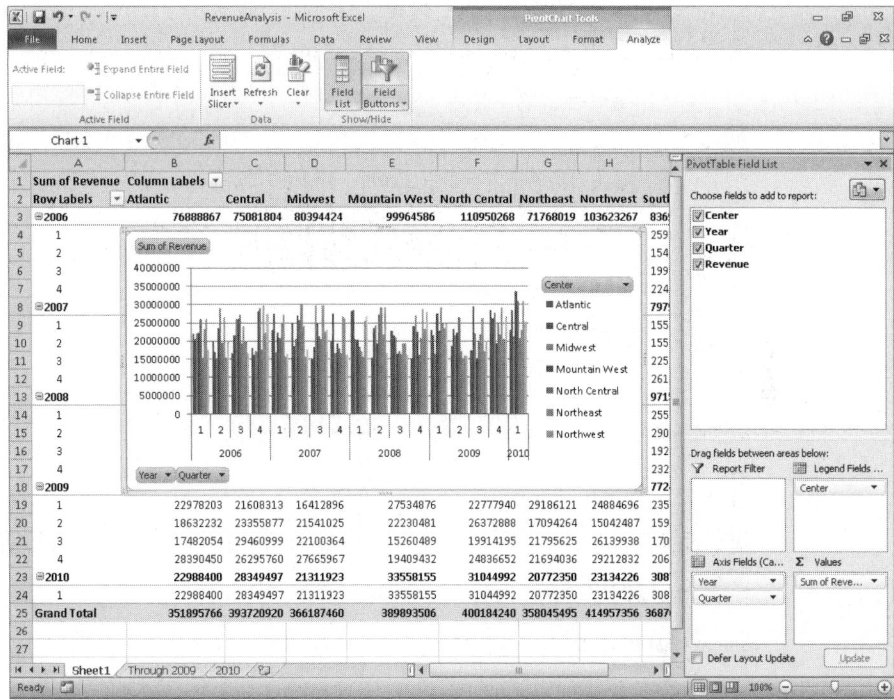

15. On the **Design** contextual tab, in the **Type** group, click **Change Chart Type**.

    The Change Chart Type dialog box opens.

16. Click **Line**, and then click the first Line chart subtype.

17. Click **OK**.

    Excel changes your PivotChart to a line chart.

18. In the **PivotTable Field List** task pane, in the **Choose fields to add to report** area, point to the **Center** field header.

19. Click the filter arrow that appears and then, in the filter menu, clear the **Select All** check box.

    Excel removes the check boxes from the filter list items.

20. Select the **Northeast** check box, and then click **OK**.

    Excel filters the PivotChart.

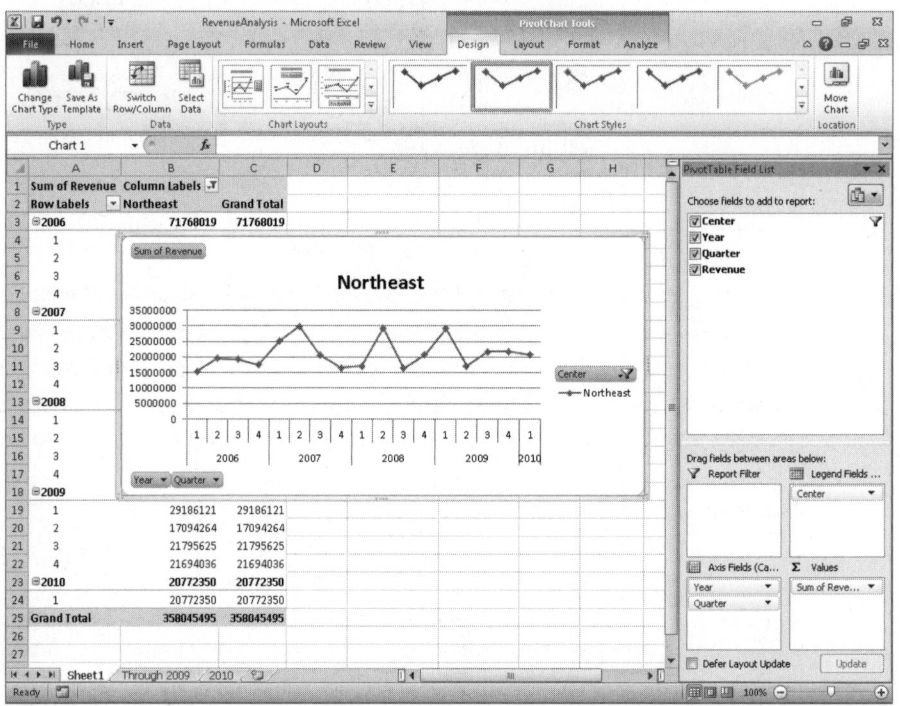

 **CLEAN UP** Save the RevenueAnalysis workbook, and then close it.

Creating Diagrams by Using SmartArt

As an international delivery company, Consolidated Messenger's business processes are quite complex. Many times, chief operating officer Lori Penor summarizes the company's processes for the board of directors by creating diagrams. Excel has just the tool she needs to create those diagrams: SmartArt. To create a SmartArt graphic, on the Insert tab, in the Illustrations group, click SmartArt to display the Choose A SmartArt Graphic dialog box.

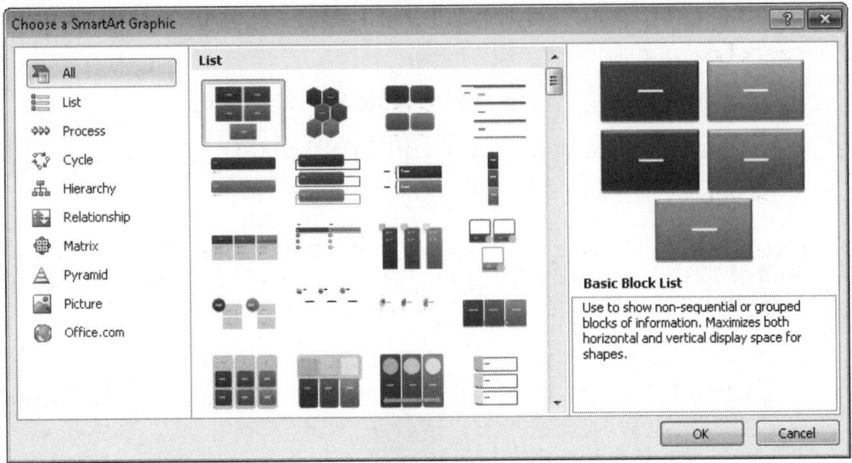

Clicking one of the buttons in the Choose A SmartArt Graphic dialog box selects the type of diagram the button represents and causes a description of the diagram type to appear in the rightmost pane of the dialog box. Clicking All displays every available SmartArt graphic type. The following table lists the nine types of diagrams you can create by using the Choose A SmartArt Graphic dialog box.

Diagram	Description
List	Shows a series of items that typically require a large amount of text to explain
Process	Shows a progression of sequential steps through a task, process, or workflow
Cycle	Shows a process with a continuous cycle or relationships of core elements
Hierarchy	Shows hierarchical relationships, such as those within a company
Relationship	Shows the relationships between two or more items
Matrix	Shows the relationship of components to a whole by using quadrants
Pyramid	Shows proportional, foundation-based, or hierarchical relationships such as a series of skills
Picture	Shows one or more images with captions
Office.com	Shows diagrams available from Office.com

Tip Some of the diagram types can be used to illustrate several types of relationships. Be sure to examine all your options before you decide on the type of diagram to use to illustrate your point.

After you click the button representing the type of diagram you want to create, clicking OK adds the diagram to your worksheet.

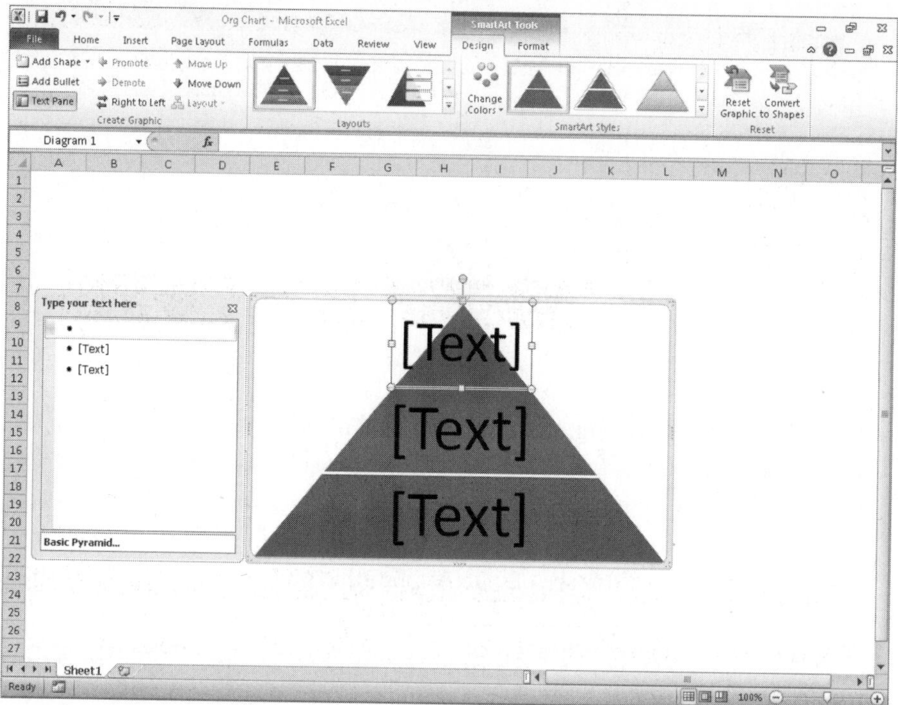

While the diagram is selected, Excel displays the SmartArt Tools Design and Format contextual tabs. You can use the tools on the Design contextual tab to change the graphic's layout, style, or color scheme. The Design contextual tab also contains the Create Graphic group, which is home to tools you can use to add a shape to the SmartArt graphic, add text to the graphic, and promote or demote shapes within the graphic.

As an example, consider a process diagram that describes how Consolidated Messenger handles a package within one of the company's regional distribution centers.

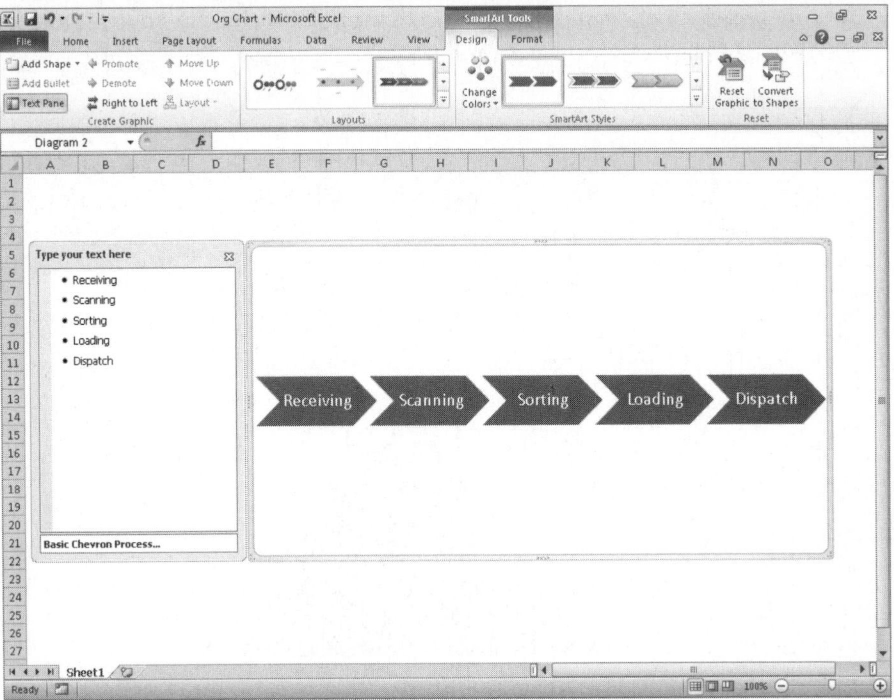

The Text Pane, located to the left of the SmartArt graphic, enables you to add text to a shape without having to click and type within the shape. If you enter the process steps in the wrong order, you can move a shape by right-clicking the shape you want to move and then clicking Cut on the shortcut menu that appears. To paste the shape back into the graphic, right-click the shape to the left of where you want the pasted shape to appear, and then click Paste. For example, if you have a five-step process and accidentally switch the second and third steps, you can move the third step to the second position by right-clicking the third step, clicking Cut, right-clicking the first shape, and then clicking Paste.

If you want to add a shape to a SmartArt graphic, to add a step to a process, for instance, click a shape next to the position you want the new shape to occupy and then, on the Design contextual tab, in the Create Graphic group, click Add Shape, and then click the option that represents where you want the new shape to appear in relation to the selected shape.

Tip The options that appear when you click Add Shape depend on the type of SmartArt graphic you created and which graphic element is selected. For an organizational chart, the options are Add Shape After, Add Shape Before, Add Shape Above, Add Shape Below, and Add Assistant.

You can edit the graphic's elements by using the buttons on the Format contextual tab as well as by right-clicking the shape and then clicking Format Shape to display the Format Shape dialog box. If you have selected the text in a shape, you can use the tools in the Font group on the Home tab to change the text's appearance.

Tip The controls in the Format Shape dialog box enable you to change the shape's fill color, borders, shadow, 3-D appearance, and text box properties.

In this exercise, you'll create an organization chart, fill in the shapes, delete a shape, add a shape, change the layout of the diagram without changing the information it embodies, and change the formatting of one of the diagram elements.

SET UP You need the OrgChart_start workbook located in your Chapter10 practice file folder to complete this exercise. Open the OrgChart_start workbook, and save it as *OrgChart*. Then follow the steps.

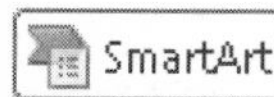

1. On the **Insert** tab, in the **Illustrations** group, click **SmartArt**.

   The Choose A SmartArt Graphic dialog box opens.

2. Click **Hierarchy**.

   The Hierarchy graphic subtypes appear.

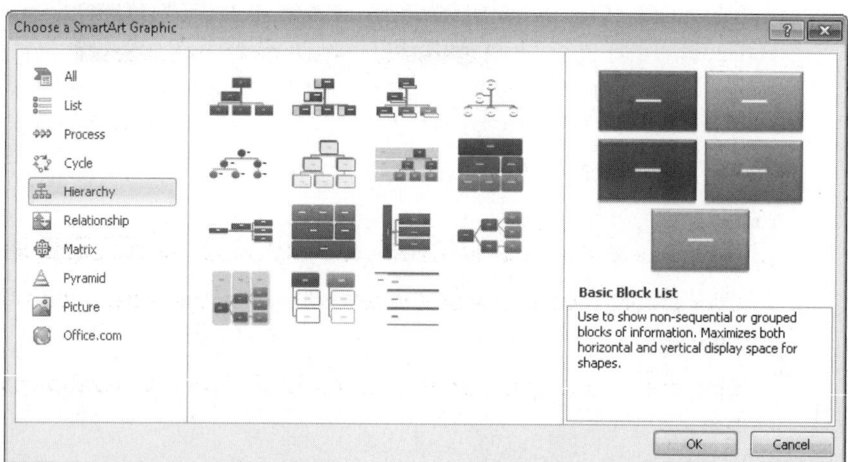

3. Click the first subtype (**Organization Chart**), and then click **OK**.

   Excel creates the organization chart graphic.

4. In the **Type your text here** pane, in the first text box, type **CEO**, and then press the Down Arrow key.

   The value *CEO* appears in the shape at the top level of the organization chart.

5. In the SmartArt diagram, right-click the assistant box, located below and to the left of the CEO shape, and then click **Cut**.

   Excel removes the shape and moves the shapes on the third level of the organization chart to the second level.

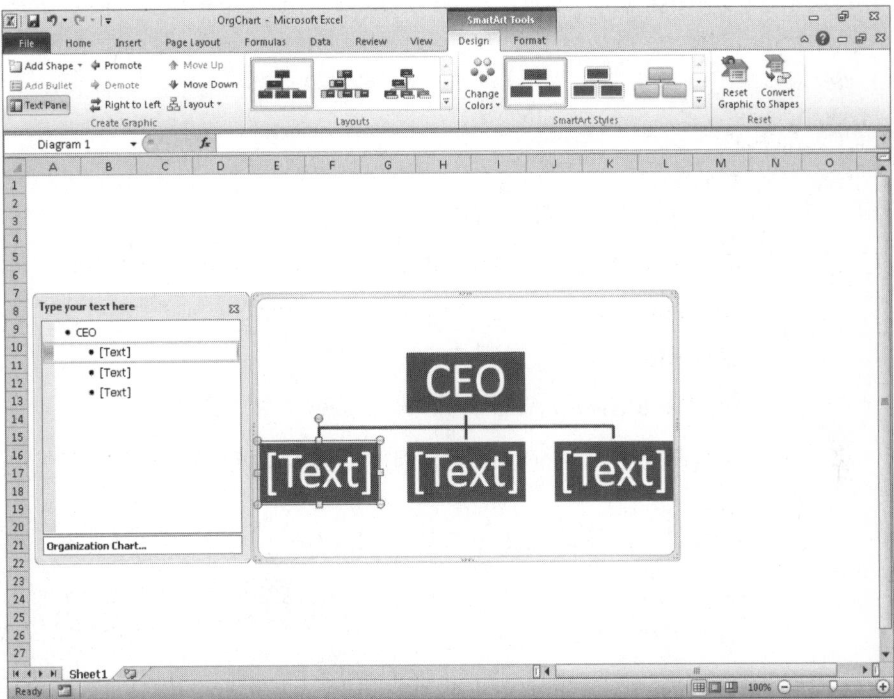

6. Click the leftmost shape on the second level of the organization chart, and then type **COO**.

7. Click the middle shape on the second level of the organization chart, and then type **CIO**.

8. Click the rightmost shape on the second level of the organization chart, and then type **CFO**.

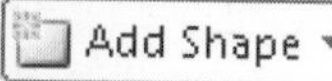

9. Click the CFO shape. On the **Design** contextual tab, in the **Create Graphic** group, in the **Add Shape** list, click **Add Shape Below**.

   A new shape appears below the CFO shape.

10. In the new shape, type **Comptroller**.

11. On the **Design** contextual tab, in the **Layouts** group, click the second layout from the left on the second line of layouts.

    Excel applies the new layout to your organization chart.

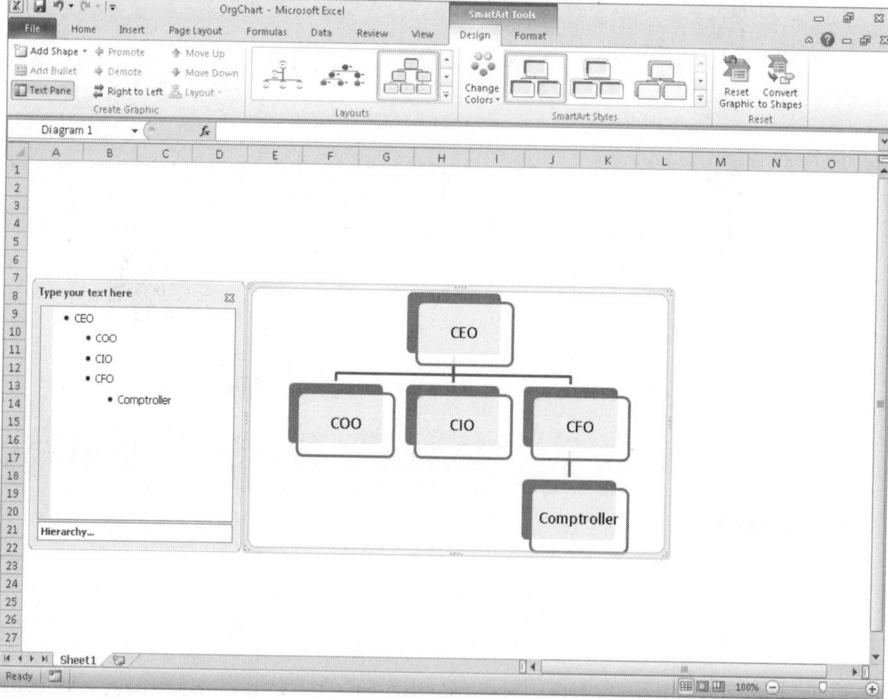

12. Right-click the Comptroller shape, and then click **Format Shape**.

    The Format Shape dialog box opens.

13. If necessary, click the **Fill** category.

    Excel displays the fill options.

14. Verify that the **Solid fill** option is selected, click the **Color** button and then, in the **Standard** color area of the color picker, click the red square.
15. Click **Close**.

    Excel changes the shape's fill to red.

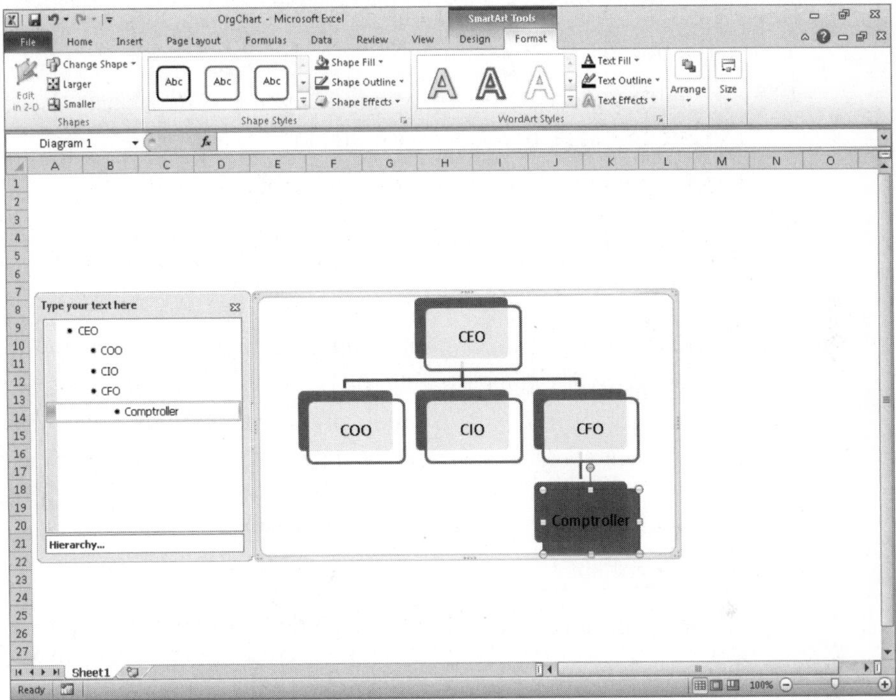

CLEAN UP Save the OrgChart workbook, and then close it.

Creating Shapes and Mathematical Equations

With Excel, you can analyze your worksheet data in many ways, including summarizing your data and business processes visually by using charts and SmartArt. You can also augment your worksheets by adding objects such as geometric shapes, lines, flowchart symbols, and banners.

To add a shape to your worksheet, click the Insert tab and then, in the Illustrations group, click the Shapes button to display the shapes available. When you click a shape in the gallery, your mouse pointer changes from a white arrow to a thin black crosshair. To draw your shape, click anywhere in the worksheet and drag the mouse pointer until your shape is the size you want. When you release the mouse button, your shape appears and Excel displays the Drawing Tools Format contextual tab on the ribbon.

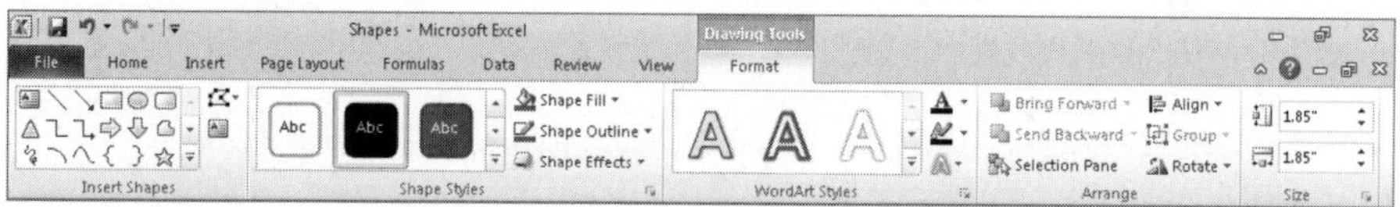

Tip Holding down the Shift key while you draw a shape keeps the shape's proportions constant. For example, clicking the Rectangle tool and then holding down the Shift key while you draw the shape causes you to draw a square.

You can resize a shape by clicking the shape and then dragging one of the resizing handles around the edge of the shape. Dragging a handle on a side of the shape lets you drag that side to a new position; dragging a handle on the corner of the shape lets you affect height and width simultaneously. If you hold down the Shift key while you drag a shape's corner, Excel keeps the shape's height and width in proportion as you drag the corner. To rotate a shape, select the shape and then drag the green circle at the top of the selection outline in a circle until the shape is in the orientation you want.

Tip You can assign your shape a specific height and width by clicking the shape and then, on the Format contextual tab, in the Size group, typing the values you want in the height and width boxes.

After you create a shape, you can use the controls on the Format contextual tab to change its formatting. To apply a pre-defined style, click the More button at the bottom right corner of the Shape Styles group's gallery and then click the style you want to apply. If none of the pre-defined styles are exactly what you want, you can use the Shape Fill, Shape Outline, and Shape Effects buttons' options to change those aspects of the shape's appearance.

Tip When you point to a formatting option, such as a style or option displayed in the Shape Fill, Shape Outline, or Shape Effects lists, Excel displays a live preview of how your shape would appear if you applied that formatting option. You can preview as many options as you like before committing to a change.

If you want to use a shape as a label or header in a worksheet, you can add text to the shape's interior. To do so, select the shape and begin typing; when you're done adding text, click outside the shape to deselect it. You can edit a shape's text by moving the mouse pointer over the text. When the mouse pointer is in position for you to edit the text, it will change from a white pointer with a four-pointed arrow to a black I-bar. You can then click the text to start editing it. If you want to change the text's appearance, you can use the commands on the Home tab or on the Mini Toolbar that appears when you select the text.

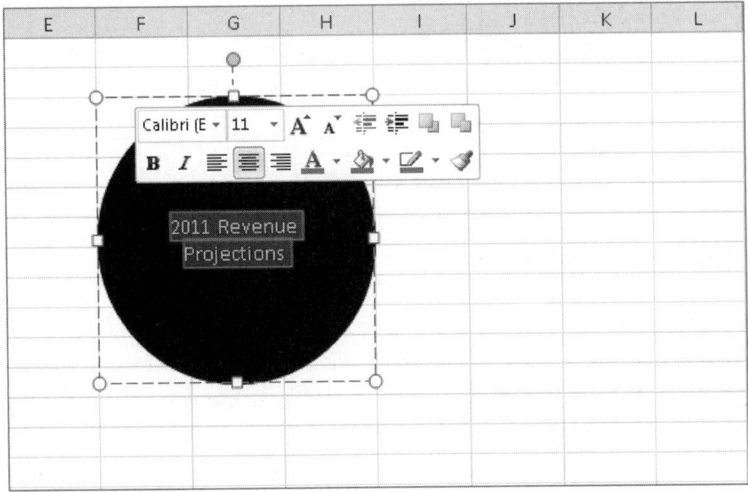

You can move a shape within your worksheet by dragging it to a new position. If your worksheet contains multiple shapes, you can align and distribute them within the worksheet. Aligning shapes horizontally means arranging them so they are lined up by their top edge, bottom edge, or center. Aligning them vertically means they have the same right edge, left edge, or center. To align a series of shapes, hold down the Ctrl key and click the shapes you want to align. Then, on the Format contextual tab, in the Arrange group, click Align, and then click the alignment option you want.

Distributing shapes moves the shapes so they have a consistent horizontal or vertical distance between them. To do so, select three or more shapes on a worksheet, click the Format contextual tab and then, in the Arrange group, click Align and then click either Distribute Horizontally or Distribute Vertically.

If you have multiple shapes on a worksheet, you will find that Excel arranges them from front to back, placing newer shapes in front of older shapes.

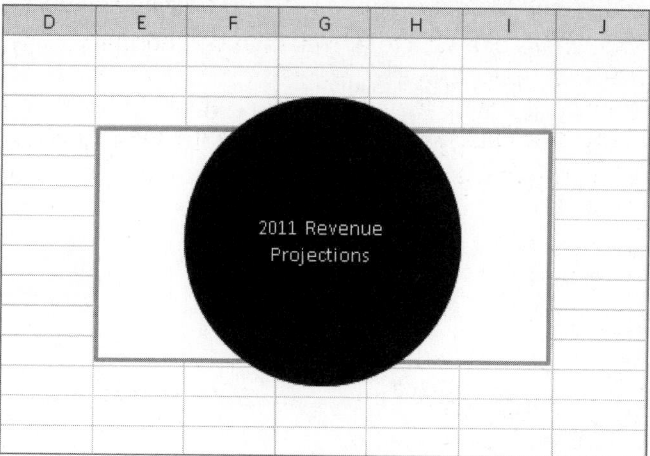

To change the order of the shapes, select the shape in the back, click the Format contextual tab, and then, in the Arrange group, click Bring Forward. When you do, Excel moves the back shape in front of the front shape. Clicking Send Backward has the opposite effect, moving the selected shape one layer back in the order. If you click the Bring Forward button's arrow, you can choose to bring a shape all the way to the front of the order; similarly, by clicking the Send Backward button's arrow, you can choose to send a shape to the back of the order.

One other way to work with shapes in Excel is to add mathematical equations to their interior. As an example, a business analyst might evaluate Consolidated Messenger's financial performance using a ratio that can be expressed using an equation. To add an equation to a shape, click the shape and then, on the Insert tab, in the Symbols group, click Equation, and then click the Equation Tools Design contextual tab on the ribbon to display the new interface for editing equations.

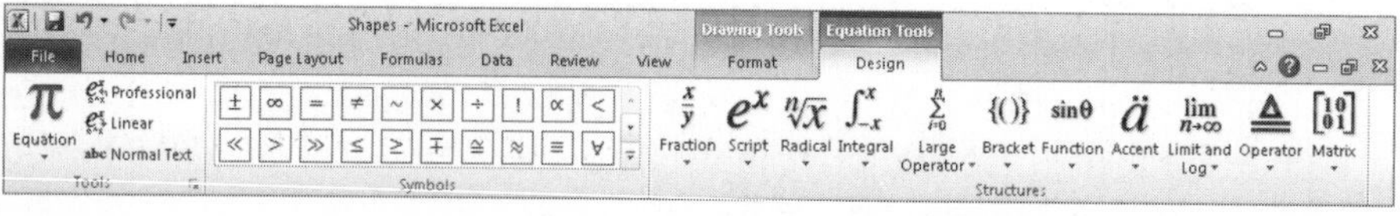

Tip Clicking the Equation button's arrow displays a list of common equations, such as the Pythagorean Theorem, that you can add with a single click.

Click any of the controls in the Structures group to begin creating an equation of that type. You can fill in the details of a structure by adding text normally or by adding symbols from the gallery in the Symbols group.

In this exercise, you'll create a circle and a rectangle, change the shapes' formatting, reorder the shapes, align the shapes, add text to the circle, and then add an equation to the rectangle.

SET UP You need the Shapes_start workbook located in your Chapter10 practice file folder to complete this exercise. Open the Shapes_start workbook, and save it as *Shapes*. Then follow the steps.

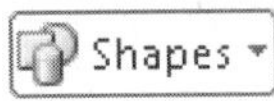

1. On the **Insert** tab, in the **Illustrations** group, click the **Shapes** button, and then click the oval.

   The mouse pointer changes to a thin black crosshair.

2. Starting near cell **C3**, hold down the Shift key and drag the mouse pointer to approximately cell **E9**.

   Excel draws a circle.

3. On the **Format** contextual tab, in the **Shapes Styles** group's gallery, click the second style.

   Excel formats the shape with white text and a black background.

4. On the **Insert** tab, in the **Illustrations** group, click the **Shapes** button, and then click the rectangle shape.

   The mouse pointer changes to a thin black crosshair.

5. Starting near cell **G3**, drag the mouse pointer to cell **K9**.

   Excel draws a rectangle.

6. On the **Format** contextual tab, in the **Shapes Styles** group's gallery, click the first style.

   Excel formats the shape with black text, an orange border, and a white background.

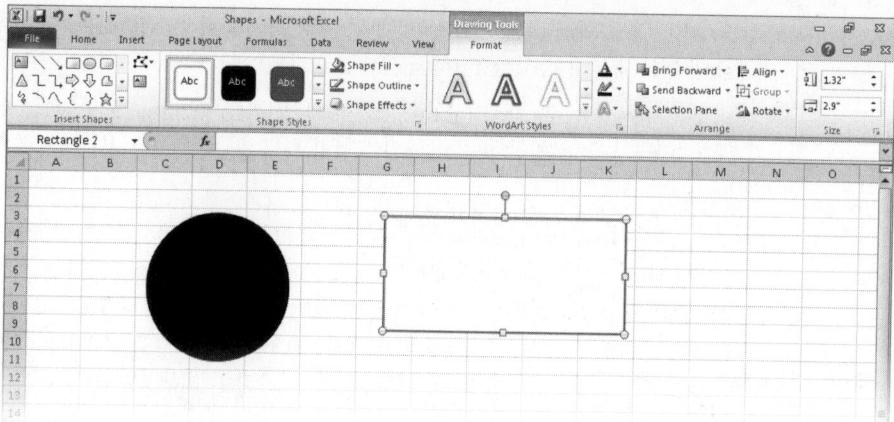

7. Click the circle and type **2011 Revenue Projections**. Then, on the **Home** tab, in the **Alignment** group, click the **Middle Align** button.

   The text is centered vertically within the circle.

8. On the **Home** tab, in the **Alignment** group, click the **Center** button.

   The text is centered horizontally within the circle.

Align

9. Hold down Ctrl and click the circle and the rectangle. Then, on the **Format** contextual tab, in the **Arrange** group, click the **Align** button and then click **Align Center**.

   Excel centers the shapes horizontally.

10. Without releasing the selection, on the **Format** contextual tab, in the **Arrange** group, click the **Align** button and then click **Align Middle**.

    Excel centers the shapes vertically.

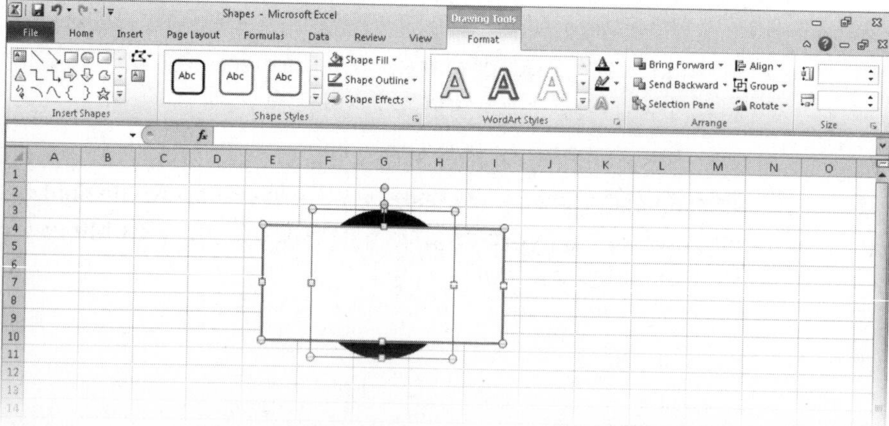

11. Click any spot on the worksheet outside of the circle and rectangle to release the selection, and then click the rectangle.
12. On the **Format** contextual tab, in the **Arrange** group, click **Send Backward**.

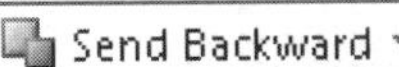

Excel moves the rectangle behind the circle.

13. Press Ctrl+Z to undo the last action.

Excel moves the rectangle in front of the circle.

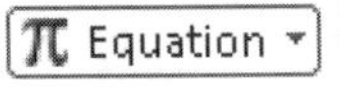

14. Click anywhere on the worksheet except on the circle or the rectangle. Click the rectangle and then, on the **Insert** tab, in the **Symbols** group, click **Equation**.

The text *Type Equation Here* appears in the rectangle.

15. On the **Equation Tools Design** contextual tab, in the **Structures** group, click the **Script** button, and then click the **Subscript** structure (the second from the left in the top row).

The Subscript structure's outline appears in the rectangle.

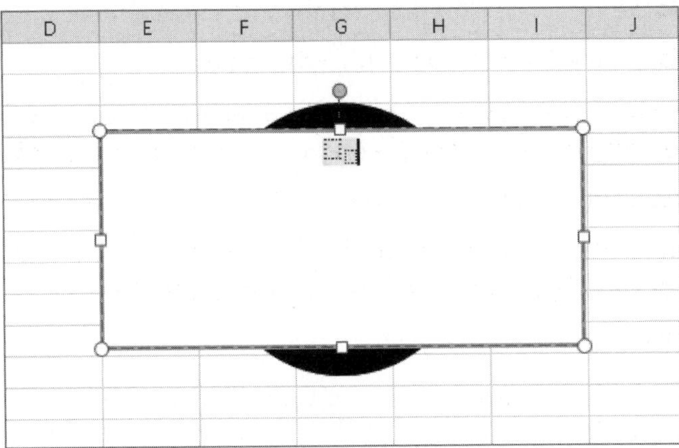

16. Click the left box of the structure and type **Year**.
17. Click the right box of the structure and type **Previous**.
18. Press the Right Arrow key once to move the cursor to the right of the word *Previous* and then, in the **Symbols** group's gallery, click the **Plus Minus** symbol (the first symbol on the top row).

19. In the **Symbols** group's gallery, click the **Infinity** symbol (the second symbol on the top row).

20. Select all of the text in the rectangle and then, on the **Home** tab, in the **Font** group, click the **Increase Font Size** button four times.

    Excel increases the equation text's font size.

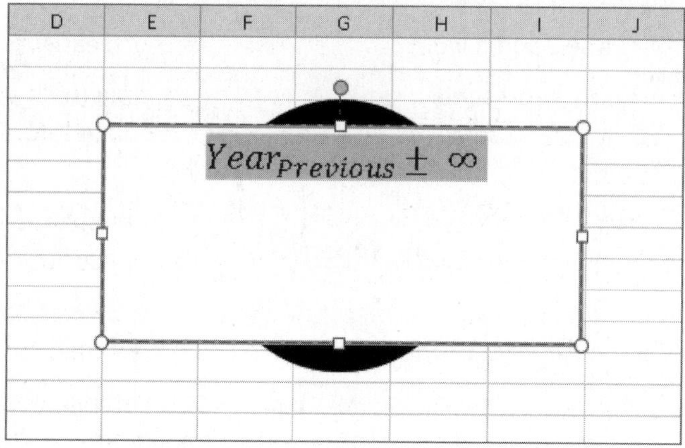

CLEAN UP Save the Shapes workbook, and then close it. If you're not continuing directly to the next chapter, exit Excel.

Key Points

- You can use charts to summarize large sets of data in an easy-to-follow visual format.
- You're not stuck with the chart you create; if you want to change it, you can.
- If you format many of your charts the same way, creating a chart template can save you a lot of work in the future.
- Adding chart labels and a legend makes your chart much easier to follow.
- If your chart data represents a series of events over time (such as monthly or yearly sales), you can use trendline analysis to extrapolate future events based on the past data.
- With sparklines, which are new in Excel 2010, you can summarize your data in a compact space, providing valuable context for values in your worksheets.
- With a PivotChart, you can rearrange your chart on the fly, emphasizing different aspects of the same data without having to create a new chart for each view.
- With Excel, you can quickly create and modify common business and organizational diagrams, such as organization charts and process diagrams.
- You can create and modify shapes to enhance your workbook's visual impact.
- The improved equation editing capabilities help Excel 2010 users communicate their thinking to their colleagues.

Chapter at a Glance

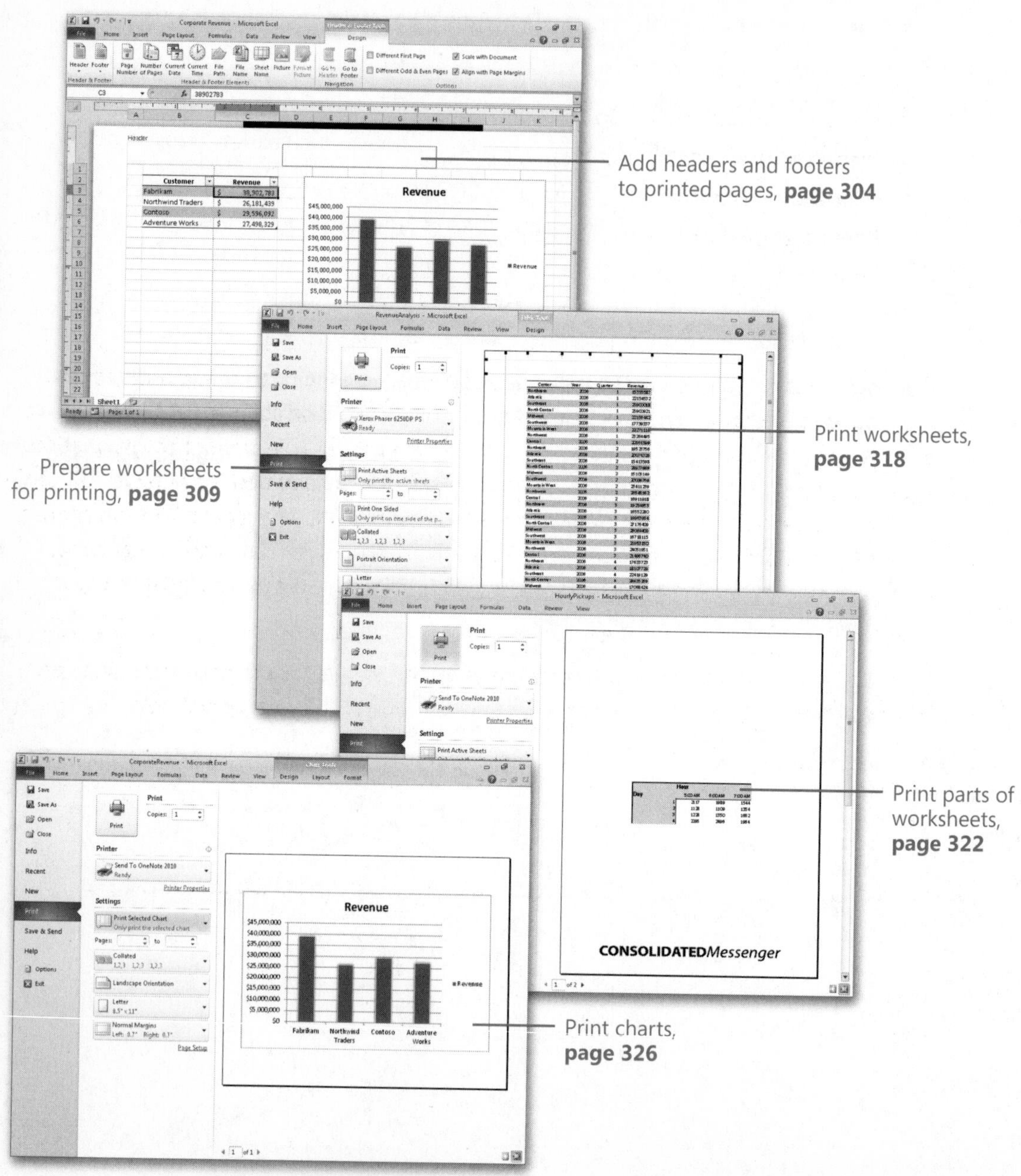

11 Printing

In this chapter, you will learn how to

- ✔ Add headers and footers to printed pages.
- ✔ Prepare worksheets for printing.
- ✔ Print worksheets.
- ✔ Print parts of worksheets.
- ✔ Print charts.

Microsoft Excel 2010 gives you a wide range of tools with which to create and manipulate your data. By using filters, by sorting, and by creating PivotTables and charts, you can change your worksheets so that they convey the greatest possible amount of information. After you configure your worksheet so that it shows your data to best advantage, you can print your Excel documents to use in a presentation or include in a report. You can choose to print all or part of any of your worksheets, change how your data and charts appear on the printed page, and even suppress any error messages that might appear in your worksheets.

In this chapter, you'll learn how to prepare your worksheets for printing, print all or part of a worksheet, print charts, and add headers and footers to your worksheets.

> **Practice Files** Before you can complete the exercises in this chapter, you need to copy the book's practice files to your computer. The practice files you'll use to complete the exercises in this chapter are in the Chapter11 practice file folder. A complete list of practice files is provided in "Using the Practice Files" at the beginning of this book.

Adding Headers and Footers to Printed Pages

If you want to ensure that the same information appears at the top or bottom of every printed page, you can do so by using headers or footers. A *header* is a section that appears at the top of every printed page; a *footer* is a section that appears at the bottom of every printed page. To create a header or footer in Excel, you display the Insert tab and then, in the Text group, click Header & Footer to display the Header & Footer Tools Design contextual tab.

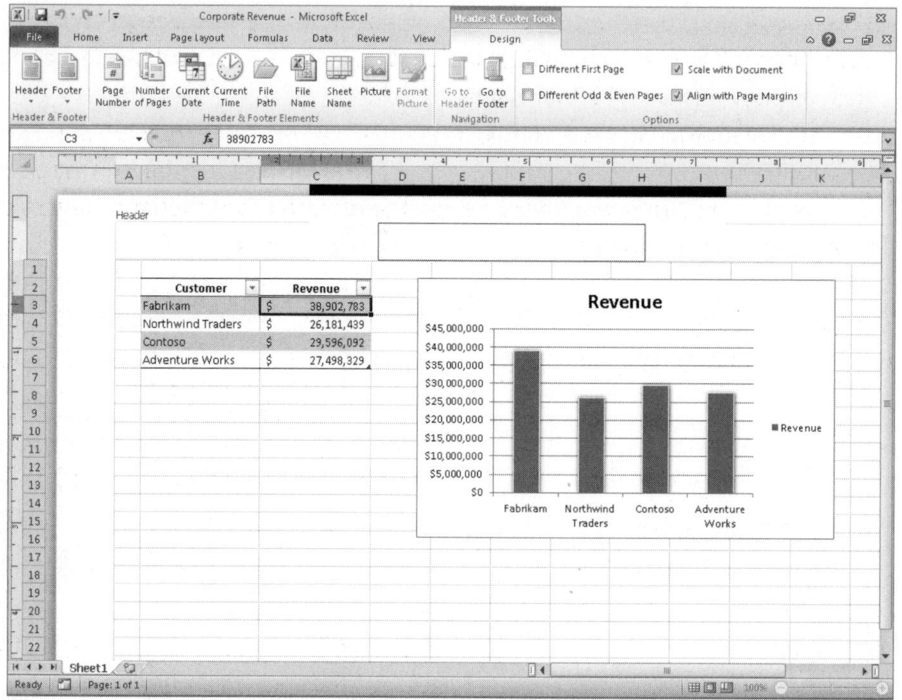

Troubleshooting The appearance of buttons and groups on the ribbon changes depending on the width of the program window. For information about changing the appearance of the ribbon to match our screen images, see "Modifying the Display of the Ribbon" at the beginning of this book.

When you display your workbook's headers and footers, Excel displays the workbook in Page Layout view. Page Layout view shows you exactly how your workbook will look when printed, while still enabling you to edit your file, a capability not provided by Print Preview. You can also switch to Page Layout view by displaying the View tab and then, in the Workbook Views group, clicking Page Layout.

See Also For information about editing your workbook in Print Preview mode, see the "Previewing Worksheets Before Printing" section later in this chapter.

Excel divides its headers and footers into left, middle, and right sections. When you point to an editable header or footer section, Excel highlights the section to indicate that clicking the left mouse button will open that header or footer section for editing.

Tip If you have a chart selected when you click the Header & Footer button on the Insert tab, Excel displays the Header/Footer page of the Page Setup dialog box instead of opening a header or footer section for editing.

When you click a header or footer section, Excel displays the Design contextual tab on the ribbon. The Design contextual tab contains several standard headers and footers, such as page numbers by themselves or followed by the name of the workbook. To add an Auto Header to your workbook, display the Design contextual tab and then, in the Header & Footer group, click Header. Then click the header you want to apply. The list of headers that appears will vary depending on the properties and contents of your worksheet and workbook.

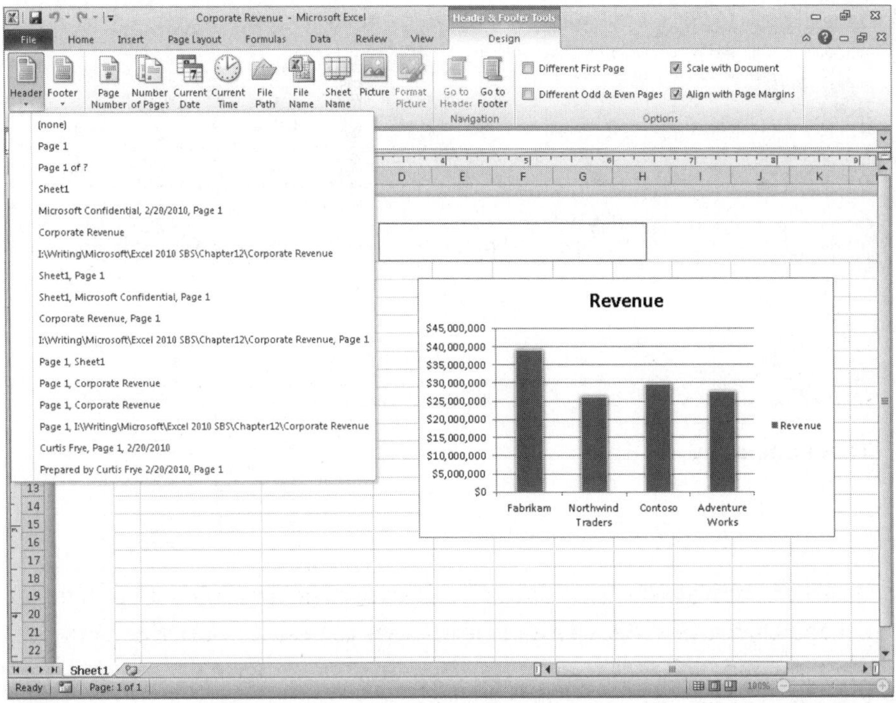

You can also create custom headers by typing your own text or by using the commands in the Header & Footer Elements group to insert a date, time, worksheet name, or page number. You can also add a graphic, such as a company logo, to a worksheet. By adding graphics, you can identify the worksheet as referring to your company and help reinforce your company's identity if you include the worksheet in a printed report distributed outside your company. After you insert a graphic into a header or footer, the Format Picture button in the Header & Footer Elements group will become available. Clicking that button opens a dialog box with tools for editing your graphic.

In this exercise, you'll create a custom header for a workbook. You'll add a graphic to the footer and then edit the graphic by using the Format Picture dialog box.

SET UP You need the RevenueByCustomer_start workbook and the ConsolidatedMessenger image located in your Chapter11 practice file folder to complete this exercise. Start Excel, open the RevenueByCustomer_start workbook, and save it as *RevenueByCustomer*. Then follow the steps.

1. On the **Insert** tab, in the **Text** group, click **Header & Footer**.

   Excel displays your workbook in Page Layout view.

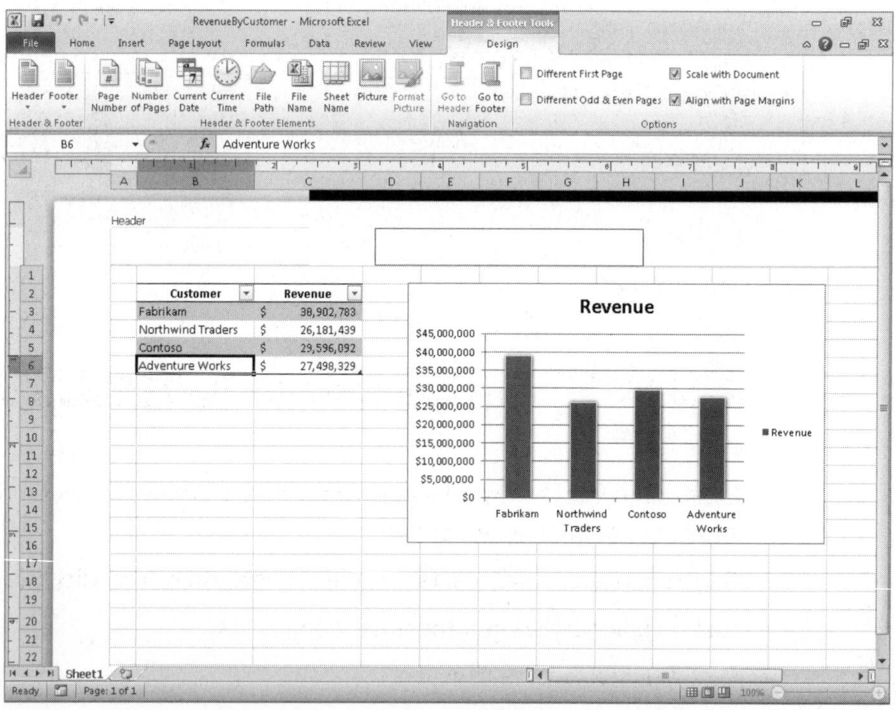

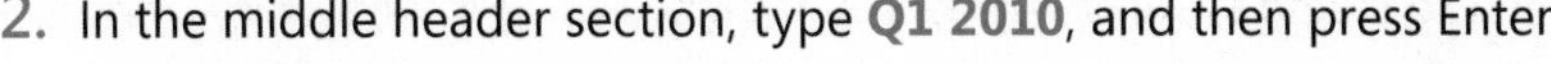

2. In the middle header section, type **Q1 2010**, and then press Enter.

3. On the **Design** contextual tab, in the **Header & Footer Elements** group, click **File Name**.

   Excel adds the *&[File]* code to the header.

4. To the right of the *&[File]* code, type a comma, and then press the Spacebar.

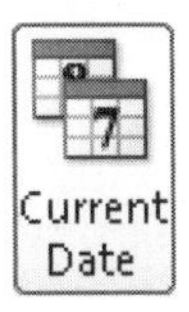

5. On the **Design** contextual tab, in the **Header & Footer Elements** group, click **Current Date**.

   Excel changes the contents of the middle header section to *&[File], &[Date]*.

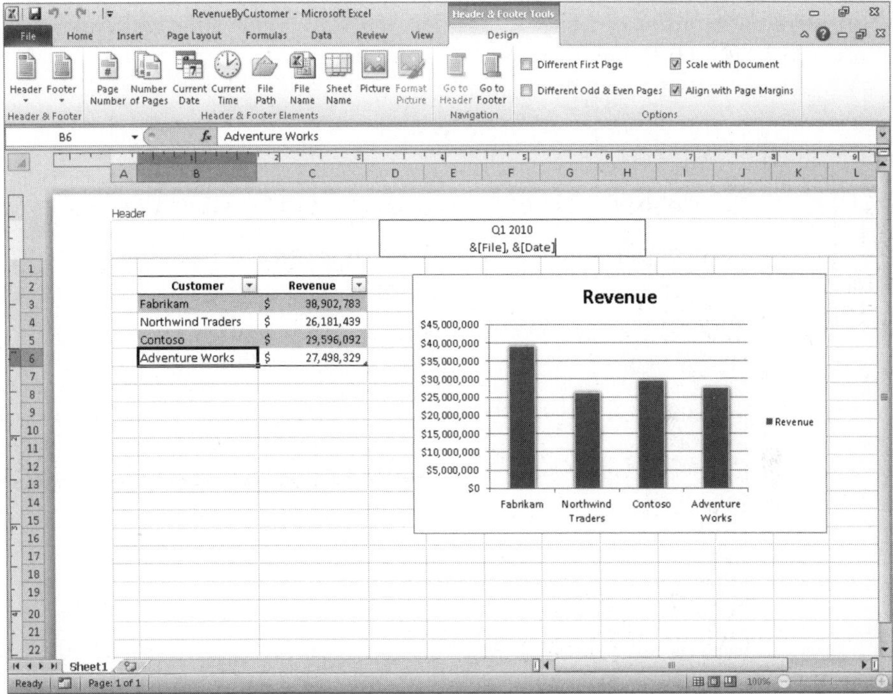

6. Press Tab.

   Excel highlights the right header section; the workbook name and current date appear in the middle header section.

7. On the **Design** contextual tab, in the **Navigation** group, click **Go to Footer**.

   Excel highlights the right footer section.

8. Click the middle footer section.

9. On the **Design** contextual tab, in the **Header & Footer Elements** group, click **Picture**.

   The Insert Picture dialog box opens.

10. Navigate to the **Chapter11** folder, and then double-click **ConsolidatedMessenger.png**.

    The code *&[Picture]* appears in the middle footer section.

11. Click any worksheet cell above the footer.

    Excel displays the worksheet as it will be printed.

12. Click the image in the footer and then, on the **Design** contextual tab, click **Format Picture**.

    The Format Picture dialog box opens.

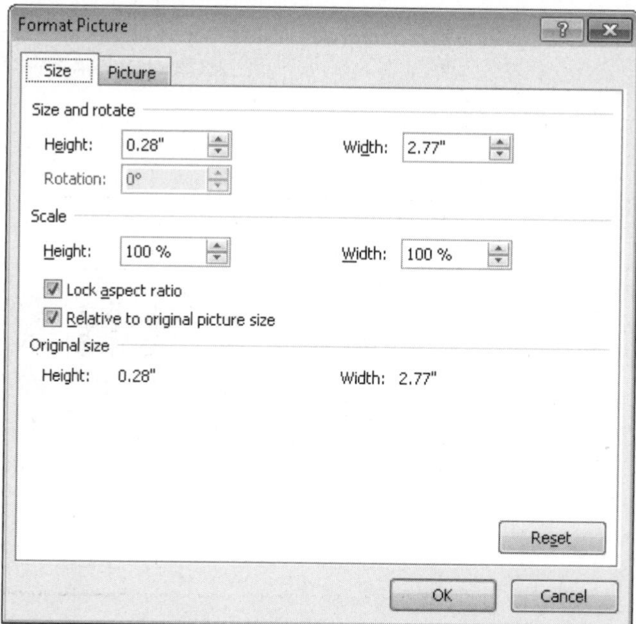

13. Click the **Size** tab if the **Size** page is not already displayed.

14. In the **Scale** area of the dialog box, in the **Height** field, type **80%**, and then press Enter.

    The Format Picture dialog box closes.

15. Click any worksheet cell above the footer.

    Excel displays the newly formatted picture.

 **CLEAN UP** Save the RevenueByCustomer workbook, and then close it.

Preparing Worksheets for Printing

When you are ready to print your workbook, you can change the workbook's properties to ensure that your worksheets display all your information and that printing is centered on the page. In Excel, all of these printing functions are gathered together in one place: the Backstage view. To preview your workbook in the Backstage view, click the File tab and then click Print.

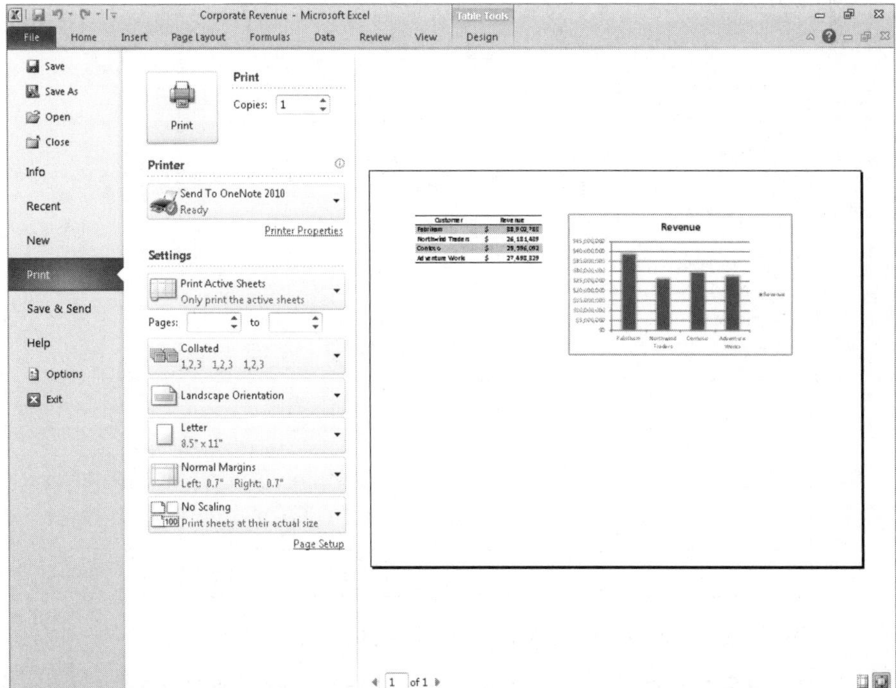

Keyboard Shortcut Press Ctrl+P to preview your worksheet in the Backstage view.

See Also For more information about keyboard shortcuts, see "Keyboard Shortcuts" at the end of this book.

Excel comes with three margin settings: Normal, Wide, and Narrow. Excel applies the Normal setting by default, but you can select any of the three options by displaying the workbook in the Backstage view and then, in the Settings area, clicking the Margins button and clicking the desired setting. If you want finer control over your margins, click the Margins button and then Custom Margins to display the Margins page of the Page Setup dialog box.

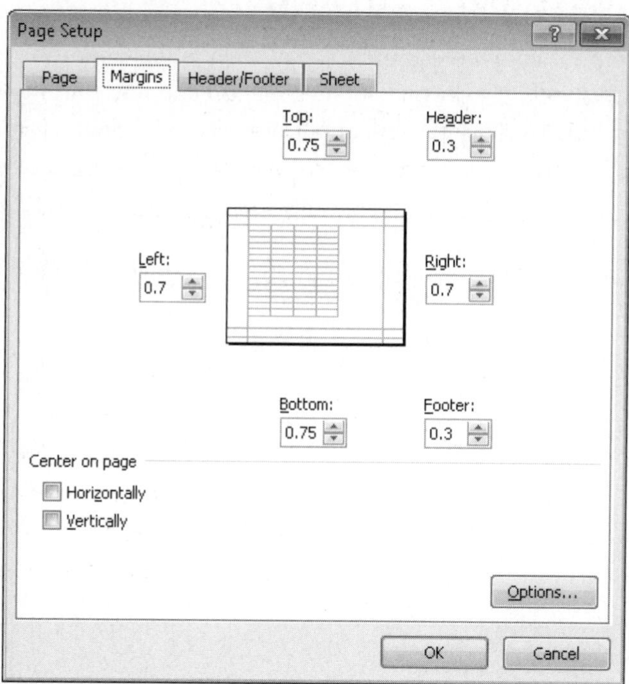

If you want to display a worksheet's margins while you have its workbook open in the Backstage view, click the Show Margins button near the bottom-right corner of the Backstage view window.

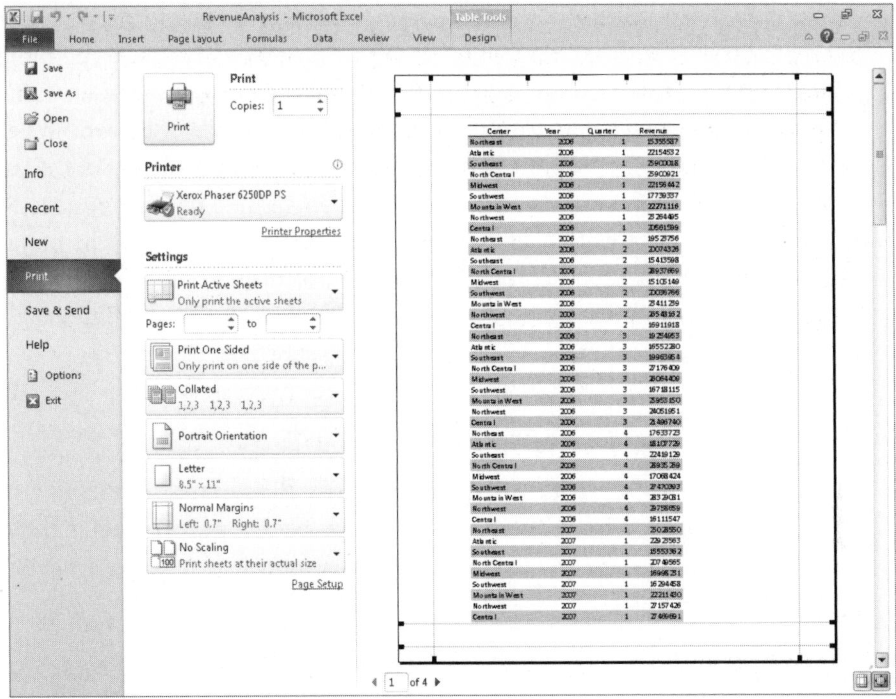

You can drag each margin line to change the corresponding margin's position, increasing or decreasing the amount of space allocated to each worksheet section. Do bear in mind that increasing the size of the header or footer reduces the size of the worksheet body, meaning that fewer rows can be printed on a page.

Another issue with printing worksheets is that the data in worksheets tends to be wider horizontally than a standard sheet of paper. You can use the commands in the Backstage view to change the alignment of the rows and columns on the page. When the columns parallel the long edge of a piece of paper, the page is laid out in portrait mode; when the columns parallel the short edge of a piece of paper, it is in landscape mode.

Changing between portrait and landscape mode can result in a better fit, but you might find that not all of your data will fit on a single printed page. This is where the options available on the Scaling button in the Backstage view come to the rescue. With the Scaling button's options, you can perform three tasks: reduce the size of the worksheet's contents until the worksheet can be printed on a single page, reduce the size of the worksheet's contents until all of the worksheet's columns fit on a single page, or reduce the size of the worksheet's contents until all of the worksheet's rows fit on a single page. You can make the same changes (and more) by using the controls in the Page Setup dialog box. To display the Page Setup dialog box, click the Page Layout tab, and then click the Page Setup dialog box launcher.

Previewing Worksheets Before Printing

You can view your worksheet as it will be printed by clicking the File tab and then clicking Print in the left pane. When you do, Excel displays the active worksheet in the Backstage view, which includes a preview of the printed worksheet.

When Excel displays your worksheet in the Backstage view, it shows the active worksheet as it will be printed with its current settings. At the bottom of the Backstage view, Excel indicates how many pages the worksheet will require when printed and the number of the page you are viewing.

Tip When you display a workbook in the Backstage view, you can see the next printed page by pressing the Page Down key; to move to the previous page, press the Page Up key. You can also use the Previous and Next arrows at the bottom of the Backstage view, type a page number in the Current Page box, or scroll through the pages by using the vertical scroll bar at the right edge of the Backstage view.

Changing Page Breaks in a Worksheet

Another way to affect how your worksheet will appear on the printed page is to change where Excel assigns its page breaks. A page break is the point at which Excel prints all subsequent data on a new sheet of paper. You can make these changes indirectly by modifying a worksheet's margins, but you can do so directly by displaying your document in Page Break Preview mode. To display your worksheet in Page Break Preview mode, on the View tab, in the Workbook Views group, click Page Break Preview.

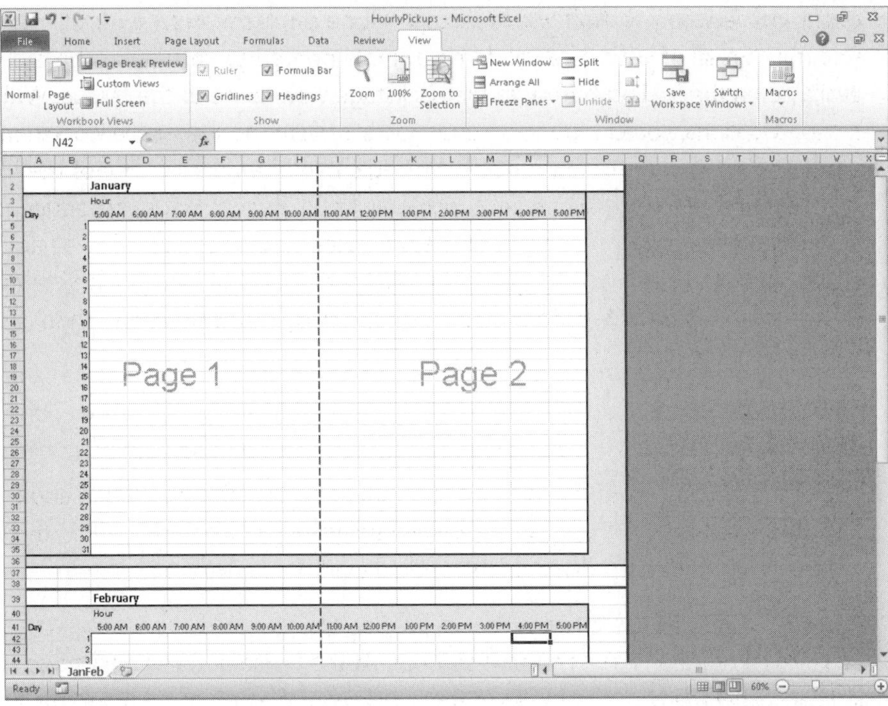

The blue lines in the window represent the page breaks. If you want to set a page break manually, you can do so by displaying your worksheet in Page Break Preview mode, right-clicking the row header of the row below where you want the new page to start, and clicking Insert Page Break. In other words, if you right-click the row header of row 15 and click Insert Page Break, row 14 will be the last row on the first printed page, and row 15 will be the first row on the second printed page. The same technique applies to columns: If you right-click the column H column header and click Insert Page Break, column G will be the last column on the first printed page, and column H will be the first column on the second printed page.

You can also add page breaks without displaying your workbook in Page Break Preview mode. To add a page break while your workbook is open in Normal view, click a row or column header and then, on the Page Layout tab, in the Page Setup area, click Breaks, and then click Insert Page Break. Items in the Breaks list also enable you to delete a page break or to reset all of the page breaks in your worksheets.

Important Be sure to click a row header or column header when you want to insert a single page break. If you view a workbook in Page Break Preview mode, right-click a cell within the body of a worksheet, and then click Insert Page Break, Excel creates both a vertical page break to the left of the selected cell and a horizontal page break above the selected cell.

To move a page break, drag the line representing the break to its new position. Excel will change the worksheet's properties so that the area you defined will be printed on a single page.

Changing the Page Printing Order for Worksheets

When you view a document in Page Break Preview mode, Excel indicates the order in which the pages will be printed with light gray words on the worksheet pages. (These indicators appear only in Page Break Preview mode; they don't show up when the document is printed.) You can change the order in which the pages are printed by displaying the Page Layout tab, clicking the Page Setup dialog box launcher, and displaying the Sheet page of the Page Setup dialog box.

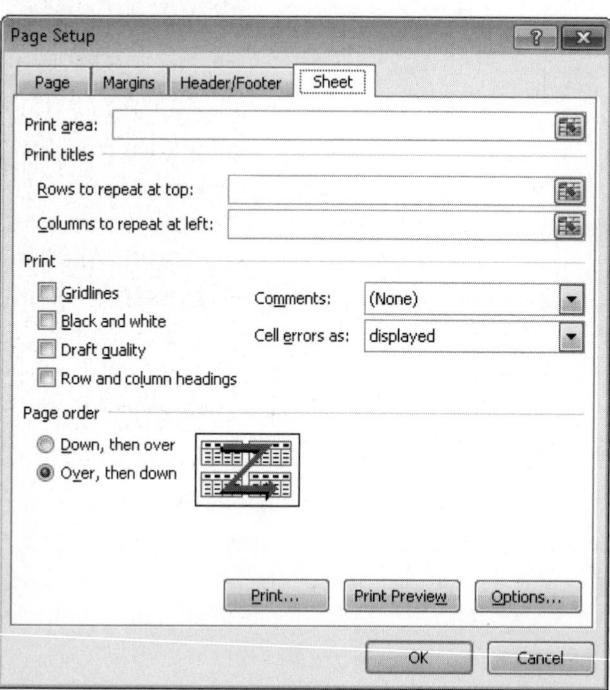

In the Page Order area, selecting the Over, Then Down option changes the order in which the worksheets will be printed from the default Down, Then Over. You might want to change the printing order to keep certain information together on consecutive printed pages. For example, suppose you have a worksheet that is designed to hold hourly package pickup information; the columns represent hours of the day, and the rows represent days of the month. If you want to print out consecutive days for each hour, you use Down, Then Over. In a typical configuration, pages 1 and 2 would enable you to see the 5:00 A.M. to 11:00 A.M. pickups for the months of January and February, pages 3 and 4 would enable you to see the 12:00 P.M. to 5:00 P.M. pickups for those months, and so on.

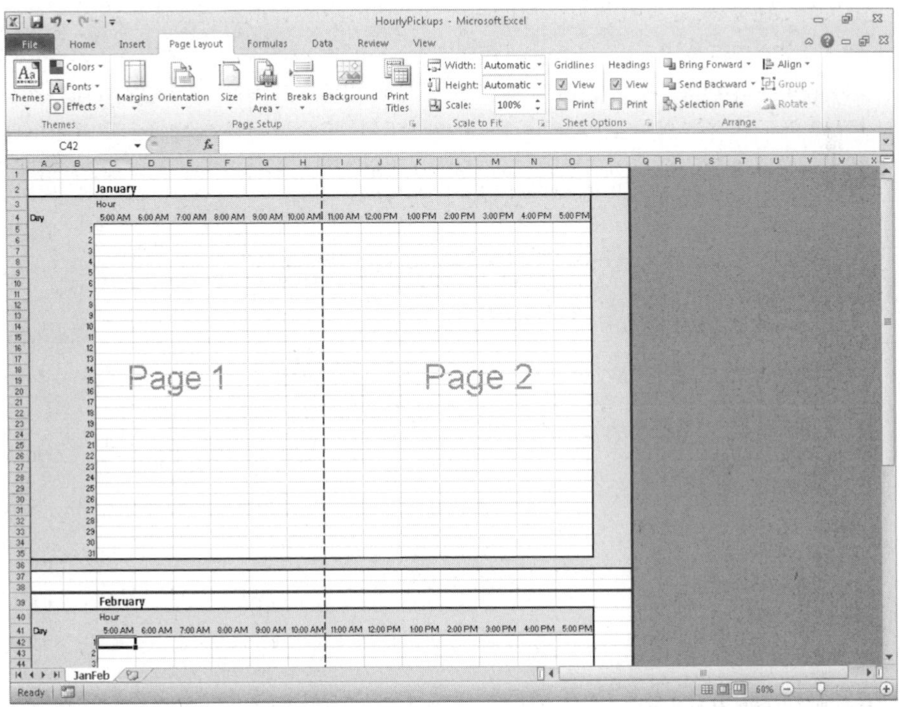

Changing the print order to Over, Then Down for the previous example could print consecutive hours for each day. Pages 1 and 2 would enable you to see the 5:00 A.M. to 5:00 P.M. pickups for January, and pages 3 and 4 would enable you to see the same pickups for February.

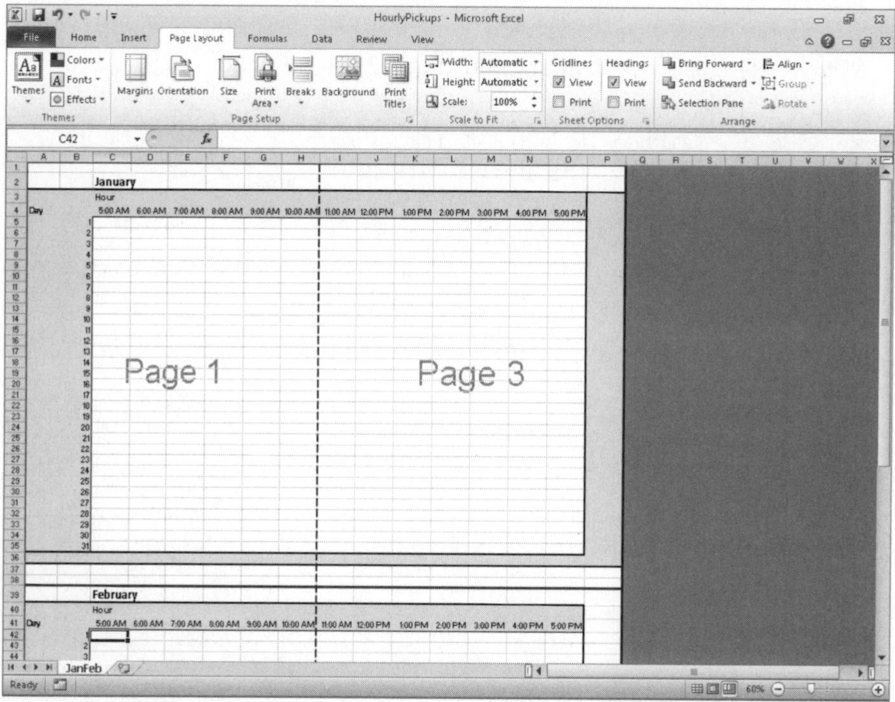

In this exercise, you'll preview a worksheet before printing, change a worksheet's margins, change a worksheet's orientation, reduce a worksheet's size, add a page break, and change the page printing order.

SET UP You need the PickupsByHour_start workbook located in your Chapter11 practice file folder to complete this exercise. Open the PickupsByHour_start workbook, and save it as *PickupsByHour*. Then follow the steps.

1. While displaying the **JanFeb** worksheet, click the **File** tab and then click **Print**.

   The workbook appears in the Backstage view.

2. In the Backstage view, click the **Orientation** button, and then click **Landscape Orientation**.

   Excel reorients the worksheet.

3. In the Backstage view, click the **Scaling** button, and then click **Custom Scaling Options**.

   The Page page of the Page Setup dialog box opens.

4. In the **Adjust to** field, type **80%**, and then press Enter.

   Excel resizes your worksheet.

5. On the ribbon, click the **Page Layout** tab.

   Excel displays the JanFeb worksheet and the Page Layout tab.

6. Click the row header for row **38**.

   Excel highlights row 38.

7. On the **Page Layout** tab, in the **Page Setup** group, click **Breaks**, and then click **Insert Page Break**.

   Excel sets a horizontal page break above row 38.

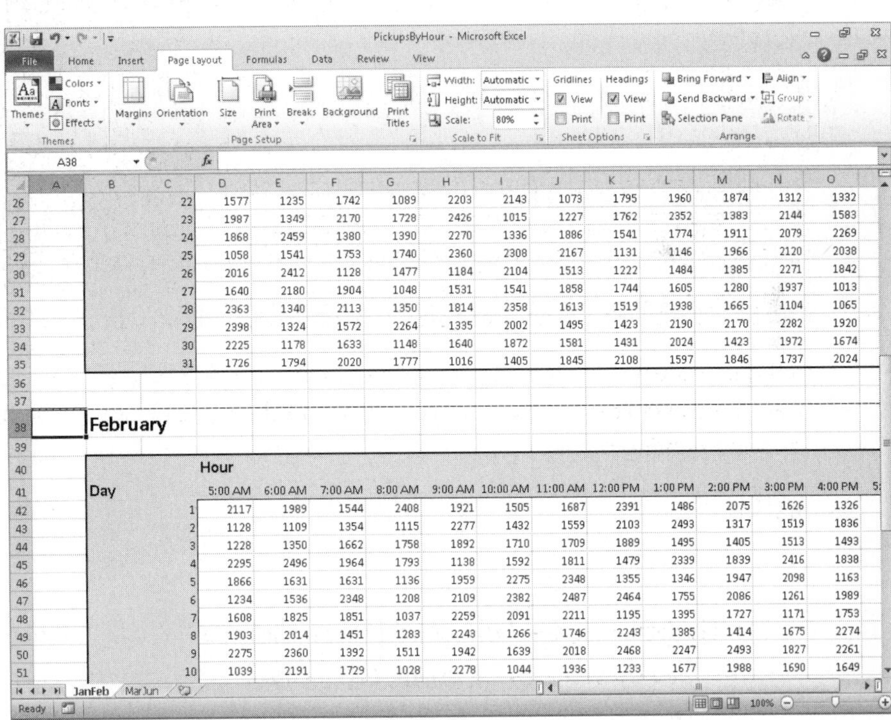

8. On the tab bar, click the **MarJun** sheet tab.

   The MarJun worksheet appears.

9. On the **Page Layout** tab, in the **Page Setup** group, click **Margins**, and then click **Wide**.

   Excel applies wide margins to the worksheet.

10. On the **Page Layout** tab, click the **Page Setup** dialog box launcher.

    The Page Setup dialog box opens.

11. If necessary, click the **Sheet** tab.

    The Sheet page is displayed.

12. In the **Page order** area, click **Over, then down**.

13. Click **OK**.

14. If desired, click the **File** tab, point to **Print**, and then click the **Print** button.

    Excel prints your worksheet.

CLEAN UP Save the PickupsByHour workbook, and then close it.

Printing Worksheets

When you're ready to print a worksheet, all you have to do is click the File tab, click Print, and then click the Print button. If you want a little more say in how Excel prints your worksheet, you can use the commands on the Print page of the Backstage view to determine how Excel prints your worksheet. For example, you can choose the printer to which you want to send this job, print multiple copies of the worksheet, and select whether the copies are collated (all pages of a document are printed together) or not (multiple copies of the same page are printed together).

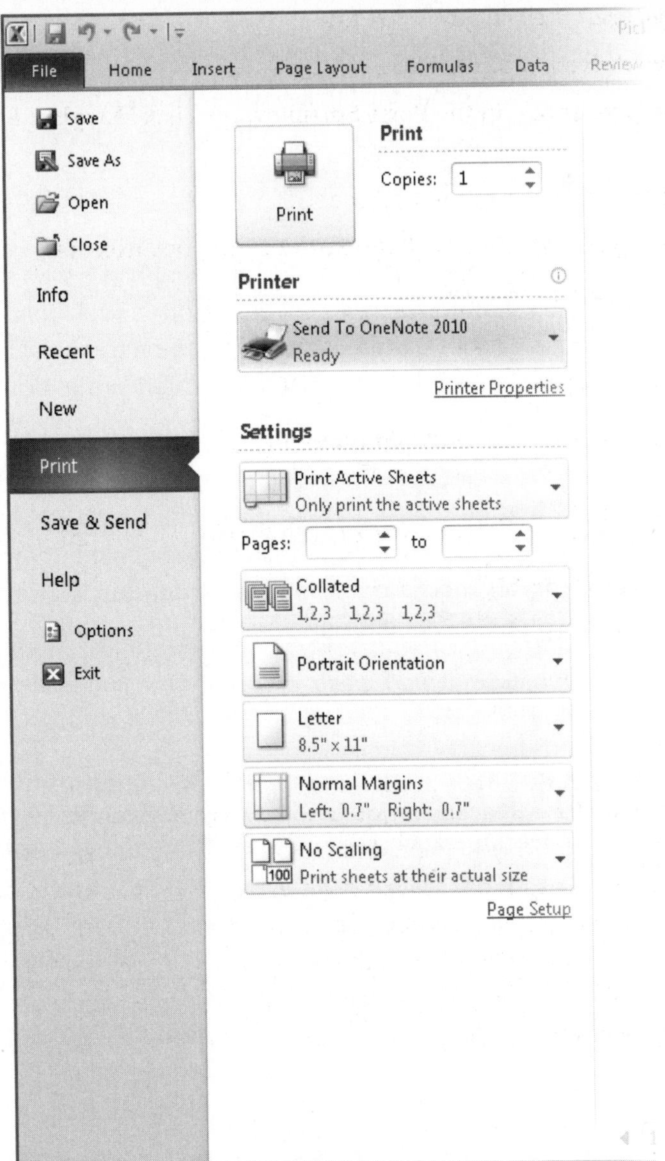
File
Home
Insert
Page Layout
Formulas
Data
Save
Save As
Open
Close
Info
Recent
New
Print
Save & Send
Help
Options
Exit
Print
Copies: 1
Print
Printer
Send To OneNote 2010
Ready
Printer Properties
Settings
Print Active Sheets
Only print the active sheets
Pages: to
Collated
1,2,3 1,2,3 1,2,3
Portrait Orientation
Letter
8.5" x 11"
Normal Margins
Left: 0.7" Right: 0.7"
No Scaling
Print sheets at their actual size
Page Setup

If you want to print more than one worksheet from the active workbook, but not every worksheet in the workbook, you can select the worksheets to print from the tab bar. To select the worksheets to print, hold down the Ctrl key while you click the sheet tabs of the worksheets you want to print. Then click the File tab, click Print, and click the Print button.

Tip The worksheets you select for printing do not need to be next to one another in the workbook.

One helpful option on the Sheet page of the Page Setup dialog box is the Cell Errors As box, which enables you to select how Excel will print any errors in your worksheet. You can print an error as it normally appears in the worksheet, print a blank cell in place of the error, or choose one of two other indicators that are not standard error messages.

After you prepare your workbook for printing, you can specify which elements to print by displaying the Print page of the Backstage view and then clicking the Print What button, which displays Print Active Sheets by default. To print the entire worksheet, verify that the Print What button displays Print Active Sheets, and then click the Print button. To print every worksheet in the active workbook, click the Print What button, click the Print Entire Workbook option, and then click the Print button.

In this exercise, you'll print nonadjacent worksheets in your workbook and suppress errors in the printed worksheet.

SET UP You need the SummaryByCustomer_start workbook located in your Chapter11 practice file folder to complete this exercise. Open the SummaryByCustomer_start workbook, and save it as *SummaryByCustomer*. Then follow the steps.

1. If necessary, display the **Summary** worksheet.
2. On the **Page Layout** tab, click the **Page Setup** dialog box launcher.

   The Page Setup dialog box opens.
3. Click the **Sheet** tab.

   The Sheet page is displayed.

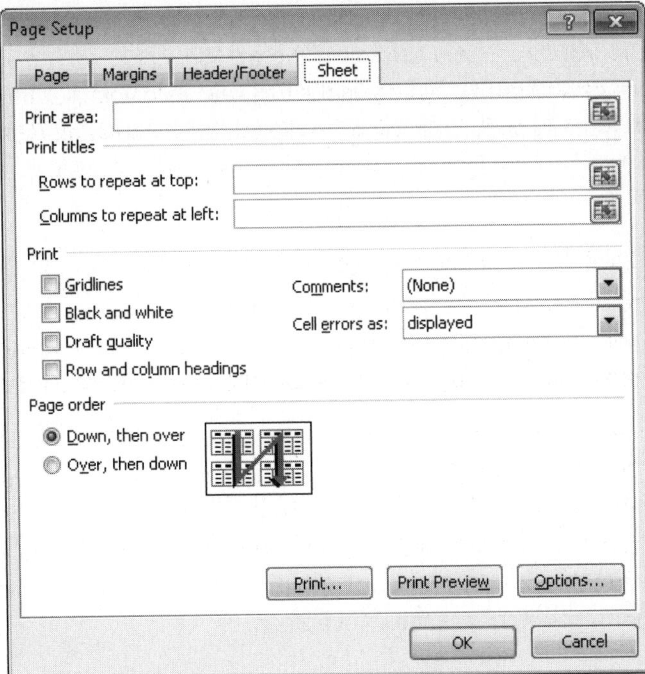

4. In the **Cell errors as** list, click **<blank>**.
5. Click **OK**.
6. Hold down the Ctrl key and then, on the tab bar, click the **Northwind** sheet tab.

   Excel selects the Summary and Northwind worksheets.
7. Click the **File** tab, and then click **Print**.

   The Print page of the Backstage view is displayed.
8. In the **Settings** area, verify that the **Print Active Sheets** option is selected.
9. Click any ribbon tab to cancel printing, or click the **Print** button if you want to print the worksheets.

CLEAN UP Save the SummaryByCustomer workbook, and then close it.

Printing Parts of Worksheets

Excel gives you a great deal of control over what your worksheets look like when you print them, but you also have a lot of control over which parts of your worksheets will be printed. For example, you can use the commands available on the Print page of the Backstage view to choose which pages of a multipage worksheet you want to print.

In the Settings area of the Print page of the Backstage view, you can fill in the page numbers you want to print in the Pages From and To boxes.

Tip You can also use the Page Break Preview window to determine which pages to print, and if the pages aren't in an order you like, you can use the commands on the Sheet page of the Page Setup dialog box to change the order in which they will be printed.

Another way you can modify how a worksheet will be printed is to have Excel fit the entire worksheet on a specified number of pages. For example, you can have Excel resize a worksheet so that it will fit on a single printed page. Fitting a worksheet onto a single page is a handy tool when you need to add a sales or other summary to a report and don't want to spread important information across more than one page.

To have Excel fit a worksheet on a set number of pages, display the Page Layout tab and use the controls in the Scale To Fit group. In the Width and Height lists, you can select how many pages wide or tall you want your printout to be.

If you want to print a portion of a worksheet instead of the entire worksheet, you can define the area or areas you want to have printed. To identify the area of the worksheet you want to print, select the cells with the data you want to print and, on the Page Layout tab, in the Page Setup group, click Print Area and then click Set Print Area. Excel marks the area with a dotted line around the border of the selected cells and prints only the cells you selected. To remove the selection, click Print Area, and then click Clear Print Area.

Tip You can include noncontiguous groups of cells in the area to be printed by holding down the Ctrl key as you select the cells.

After you define a print area, you can use the Page Setup dialog box to position the print area on the page. Specifically, you can have Excel center the print area on the page by selecting the Horizontally and Vertically check boxes in the Center On Page area of the Margins page.

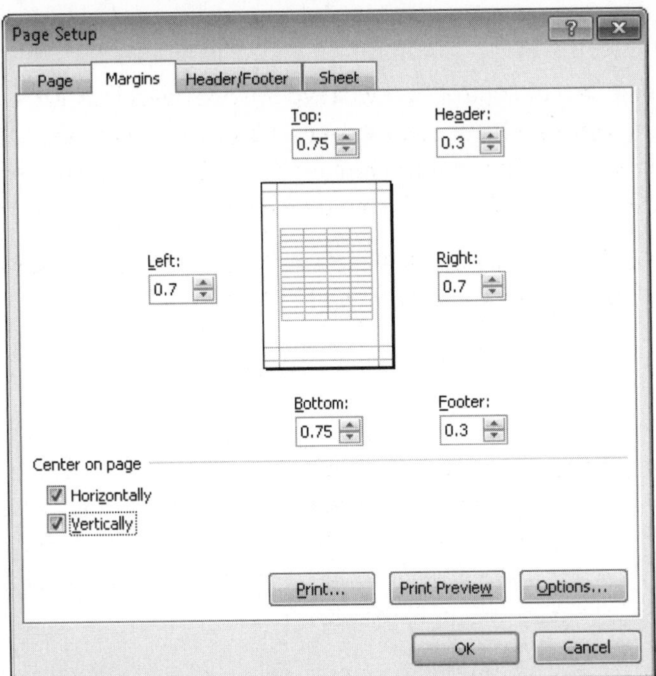

If the contents of a worksheet will take up more than one printed page, you can have Excel repeat one or more rows at the top of the page or columns at the left of the page. For example, if you want to print a lengthy worksheet containing the mailing addresses of customers signed up to receive your company's monthly newsletter, you could repeat the column headings Name, Address, City, and so forth at the top of the page. To repeat rows at the top of each printed page, on the Page Layout tab, in the Page Setup group, click Print Titles. Excel will display the Sheet page of the Page Setup dialog box.

On the Sheet page of the Page Setup dialog box, you can use the commands in the Print Titles area to select the rows or columns to repeat. To choose rows to repeat at the top of the page, click the Collapse Dialog button next to the Rows To Repeat At Top box, select the rows, and then click the Expand Dialog button. The rows you selected appear in the Rows To Repeat At Top box.

Similarly, to have a set of columns appear at the left of every printed page, click the Collapse Dialog button next to the Columns To Repeat At Left box, select the columns, and then click the Expand Dialog button. When you're done, click OK to accept the settings.

In this exercise, you'll select certain pages of a worksheet to print, have Excel fit your printed worksheet on a set number of pages, define a multi-region print area, center the printed material on the page, and repeat columns at the left edge of each printed page.

SET UP You need the HourlyPickups_start workbook located in your Chapter11 practice file folder to complete this exercise. Open the HourlyPickups_start workbook, and save it as *HourlyPickups*. Then follow the steps.

1. On the **Page Layout** tab, in the **Page Setup** group, click **Print Titles**.

   The Page Setup dialog box opens, displaying the Sheet page.

2. At the right edge of the **Columns to repeat at left** field, click the **Collapse Dialog** button.

   The dialog box collapses.

3. Select the column header of column **A**, and drag to select the column header of column **B**, too.

   The reference *$A:$B* appears in the Columns To Repeat At Left field.

4. At the right edge of the **Columns to repeat at left** field, click the **Expand Dialog** button.

   The dialog box expands.

5. Click **Print Preview**.

   Excel displays your worksheet in the Backstage view, which includes a preview of how your worksheet will appear when printed.

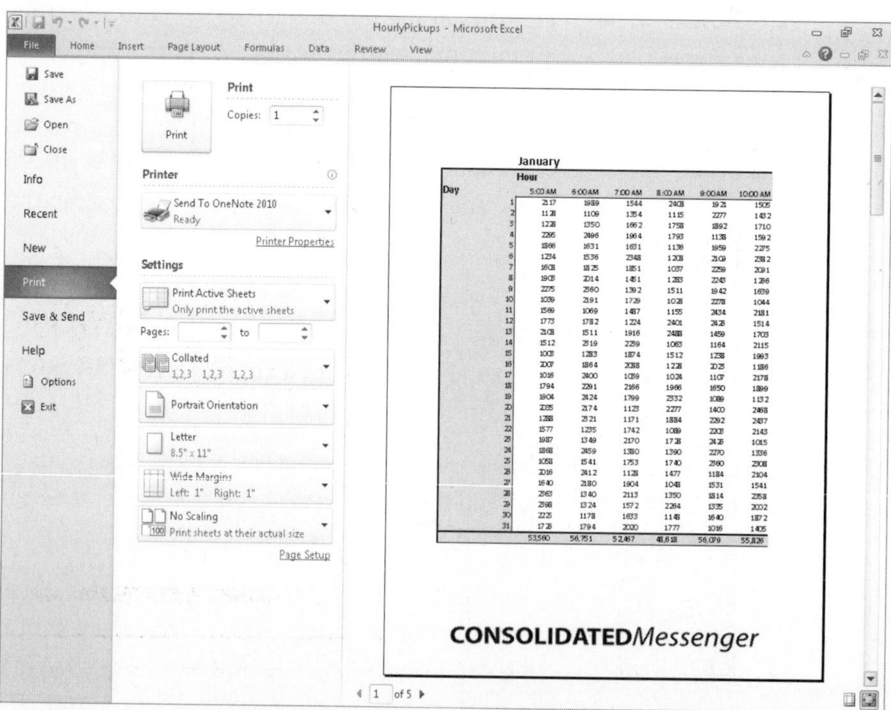

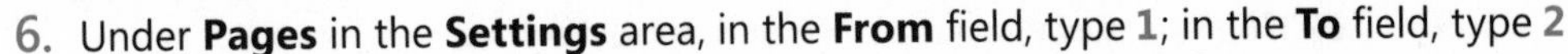

6. Under **Pages** in the **Settings** area, in the **From** field, type 1; in the **To** field, type 2.

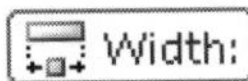

7. On the ribbon, click the **Page Layout** tab; in the **Scale to Fit** group, click the **Width** arrow and then, in the list that appears, click **1 page**.

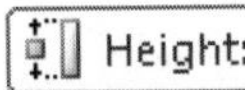

8. Click the **Height** arrow and then, in the list that appears, click **2 pages**.

   Excel resizes your worksheet so that it will fit on two printed pages. The new scaling and size values appear in the Scale To Fit group on the Page Layout tab.

9. Select the cell range **A1:E8**, hold down the Ctrl key, and then select the cell range **A38:E45**.

10. On the **Page Layout** tab, in the **Page Setup** group, click **Print Area**, and then click **Set Print Area**.

11. Click the **Page Setup** dialog box launcher.

    The Page Setup dialog box opens.

12. On the **Margins** page of the dialog box, in the **Center on page** area, select the **Horizontally** and **Vertically** check boxes.

13. Click **Print Preview**.

    Excel displays your worksheet in the Backstage view.

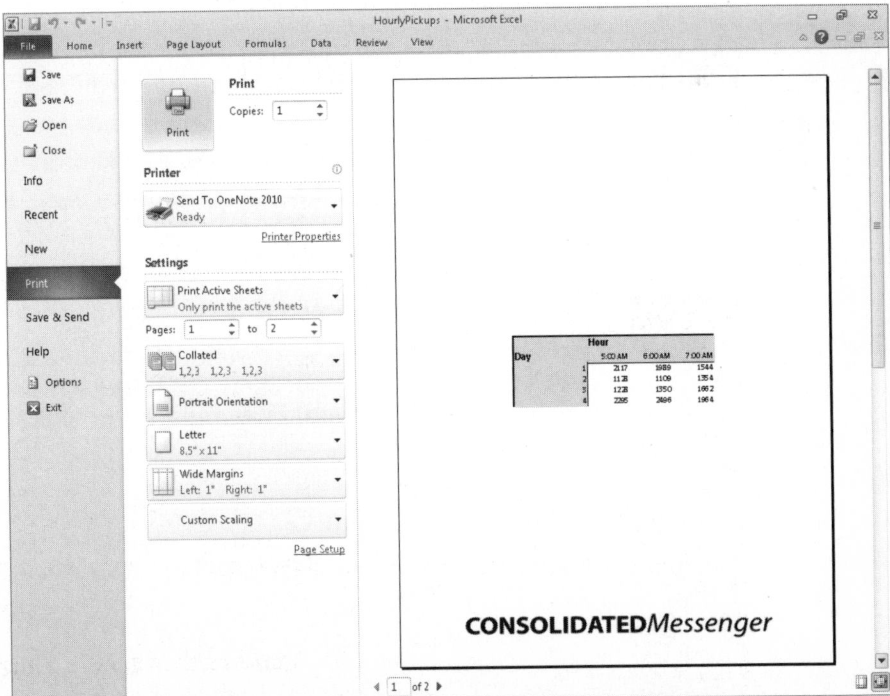

14. On the ribbon, click the **Page Layout** tab.

    Excel displays your worksheet in Normal view.

15. In the **Page Setup** group, click **Print Area**, and then click **Clear Print Area**.

    Excel removes the print areas defined for the JanFeb worksheet.

CLEAN UP Save the HourlyPickups workbook, and then close it.

Printing Charts

With charts, which are graphic representations of your Excel data, you can communicate lots of information with a single picture. Depending on your data and the type of chart you make, you can show trends across time, indicate the revenue share for various departments in a company for a month, or project future sales using trendline analysis. After you create a chart, you can print it to include in a report or use in a presentation.

If you embed a chart in a worksheet, however, the chart will probably obscure some of your data unless you move the chart to a second page in the worksheet. That's one way to handle printing a chart or the underlying worksheet, but there are other ways that don't involve changing the layout of your worksheets.

To print a chart, click the chart, click the File tab, and then click Print to display the Print page in the Backstage view. In the Settings area, Print Selected Chart will be the only option available. If you click anywhere on the worksheet outside the chart, the Print What area opens with the Print Active Sheets option selected, meaning that the chart and underlying worksheet are printed as they appear on the screen. When you're ready to print the chart, click the Print button.

In this exercise, you'll print a chart.

SET UP You need the CorporateRevenue_start workbook located in your Chapter11 practice file folder to complete this exercise. Open the CorporateRevenue_start workbook, and save it as *CorporateRevenue*. Then follow the steps.

1. Select the chart.
2. Click the **File** tab, and then click **Print**.

   The Print page of the Backstage view is displayed.

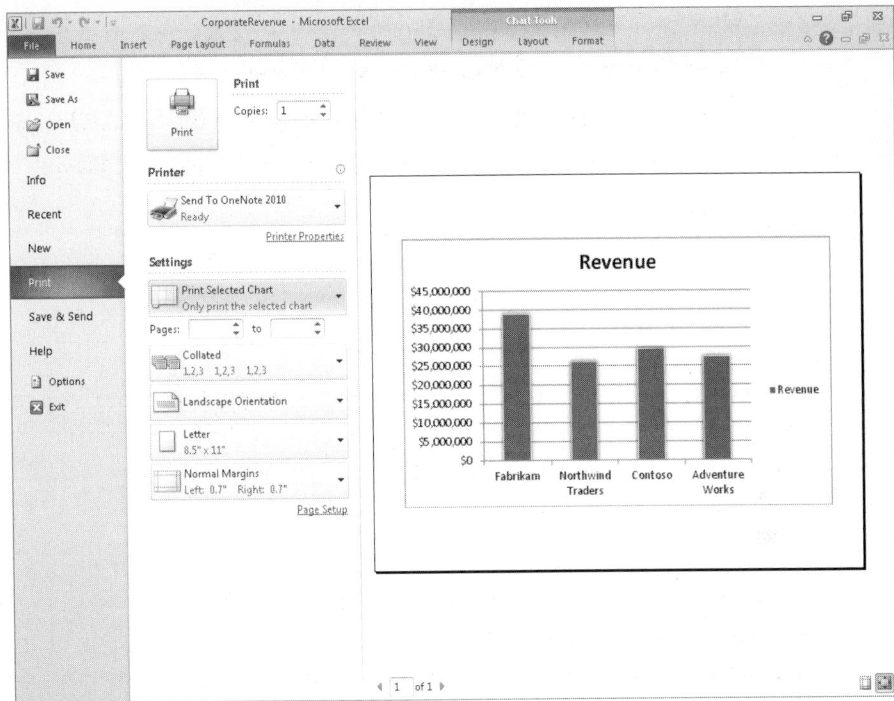

3. Verify that the **Print Selected Chart** option is selected, and then click **Print** (or click any tab on the ribbon to exit the Backstage view if you don't want to print the chart).

CLEAN UP Close the CorporateRevenue workbook. If you're not continuing directly to the next chapter, exit Excel.

Key Points

- Through the new Backstage view, Excel gives you complete control over how your worksheets appear on the printed page. Don't be afraid to experiment until you find a look you like.
- Displaying a worksheet in the Backstage view enables you to see what your worksheet will look like on paper before you print, which is a useful feature, especially if you're using an expensive color printer.
- You can preview where the page breaks will fall when you print a worksheet, and you can change them if you want.
- Don't forget that you can have Excel avoid printing error codes! You can repeat rows or columns in a printed worksheet.
- If you want to print a chart without printing the rest of the accompanying worksheet, be sure to select the chart before you start the printing procedure.

Chapter at a Glance

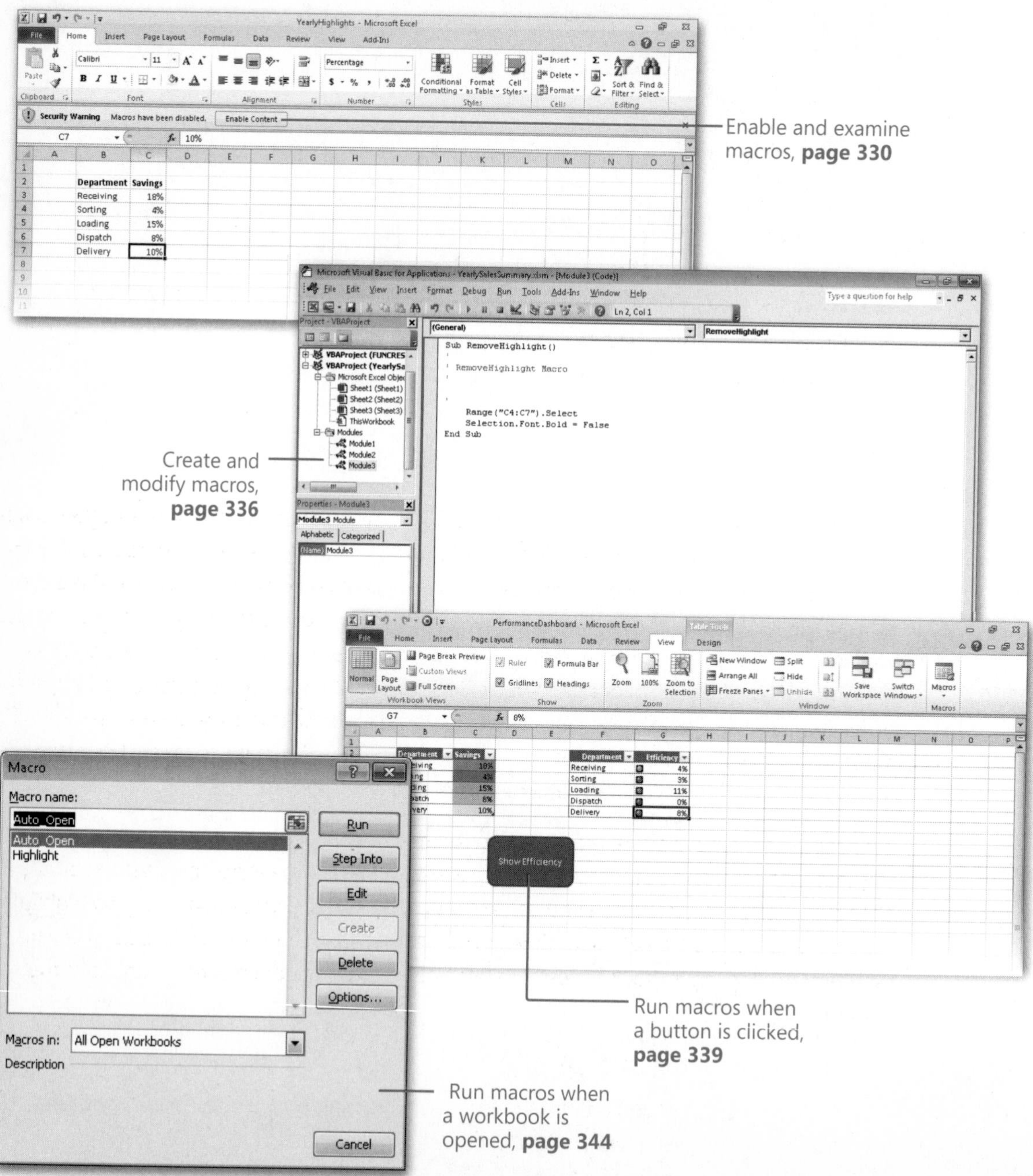

12 Automating Repetitive Tasks by Using Macros

In this chapter, you will learn how to

- ✔ Enable and examine macros.
- ✔ Create and modify macros.
- ✔ Run macros when a button is clicked.
- ✔ Run macros when a workbook is opened.

Many tasks you perform in Microsoft Excel 2010 are done once (for example, entering sales data for a particular day or adding formulas to a worksheet) or can be repeated quickly by using tools in Excel (for example, changing the format of a cell range). However, there are probably one or two tasks you perform frequently that require a lot of steps to accomplish. For example, you might have several cells in a worksheet that contain important data you use quite often in presentations to your colleagues. Instead of going through a lengthy series of steps to highlight the cells with the important information, you can create a macro, which is a recorded series of actions, to perform the steps for you. After you have created a macro, you can run, edit, or delete it as needed.

In Excel, you run and edit macros by using the items available in the Macros group on the View tab. You can make your macros easier to access by creating new buttons on the Quick Access Toolbar, to which you can assign your macros. If you run a macro to highlight specific cells in a worksheet every time you show that worksheet to a colleague, you can save time by adding a Quick Access Toolbar button that runs the macro to highlight the cells for you.

Another handy feature of Excel macros is that you can create macros that run when a workbook is opened. For example, you might want to ensure that no cells in a worksheet are highlighted when the worksheet opens. You can create a macro that removes any special formatting from your worksheet cells when its workbook opens, enabling you to emphasize the data you want as you present the information to your colleagues.

In this chapter, you'll learn how to open, run, create, and modify macros; create Quick Access Toolbar buttons and shapes that enable you to run macros with a single mouse click; define macro security settings; and run a macro when a workbook is opened.

Practice Files Before you can complete the exercises in this chapter, you need to copy the book's practice files to your computer. The practice files you'll use to complete the exercises in this chapter are in the Chapter12 practice file folder. A complete list of practice files is provided in "Using the Practice Files" at the beginning of this book.

Enabling and Examining Macros

It's possible for unscrupulous programmers to write viruses and other harmful programs by using the Microsoft Visual Basic for Applications (VBA) programming language, so you need to be sure that you don't run macros from unknown sources. In addition to running protective software such as Windows Defender, you can also change your Excel macro security settings to control when macros can be run. After you're sure a macro is safe, you open it in the Visual Basic Editor to examine its code.

Macro Security in Excel 2010

In versions of Excel prior to Excel 2007, you could define macro security levels to determine which macros, if any, your workbooks would be allowed to run, but there was no workbook type in which all macros were disallowed. Excel 2010 has several file types you can use to control whether a workbook will allow macros to be run. The following table summarizes the macro-related file types.

Extension	Description
.xlsx	Regular Excel 2010 workbook; macros are *disabled*
.xlsm	Regular Excel 2010 workbook; macros are *enabled*
.xltx	Excel 2010 template workbook; macros are *disabled*
.xltm	Excel 2010 template workbook; macros are *enabled*

When you open a macro-enabled workbook, the Excel program-level security settings might prevent the workbook from running the macro code. When that happens, Excel displays a security warning on the Message Bar.

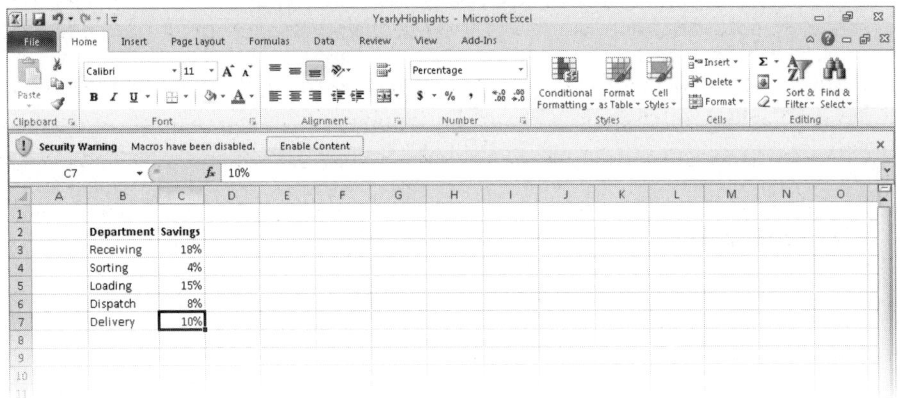

Troubleshooting The appearance of buttons and groups on the ribbon changes depending on the width of the program window. For information about changing the appearance of the ribbon to match our screen images, see "Modifying the Display of the Ribbon" at the beginning of this book.

Clicking the Enable Content button lets the workbook use its macros. Always take the time to verify the workbook's source and consider whether you expected the workbook to contain macros before you enable the content. If you decide not to enable the macros in a workbook, click the Close button at the right edge of the Message Bar.

You can change your program-level security settings to make them more or less restrictive; to do so, click the File tab, click Options, and then, in the Excel Options dialog box, click the Trust Center category. On the page that appears, click the Trust Center Settings button to display the Trust Center dialog box.

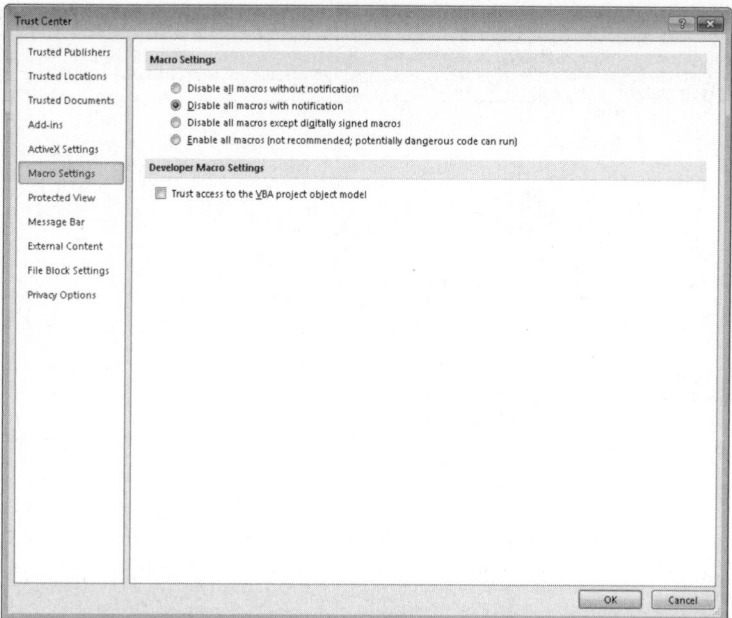

The Excel default macro security level is Disable All Macros With Notification, which means that Excel displays a warning on the Message Bar but allows you to enable the macros manually. Selecting the Disable All Macros Without Notification option does exactly what the label says. If Consolidated Messenger's company policy is to disallow all macros in all Excel workbooks, its employees would select the Disable All Macros Without Notification option.

Important Because it is possible to write macros that act as viruses, potentially causing harm to your computer and spreading copies of themselves to other computers, you should never choose the Enable All Macros security setting, even if you have virus-checking software installed on your computer.

Examining Macros

The best way to get an idea of how macros work is to examine an existing macro. To do that, display the View tab. In the Macros group, click the Macros button, and then click View Macros.

Tip In the Macro dialog box, you can display the macros available in other workbooks by clicking the Macros In box and selecting a workbook by name or selecting All Open Workbooks to display every macro in any open workbook. If you select either of those choices, the macro names that are displayed include the name of the workbook in which the macro is stored. Clicking This Workbook displays the macros in the active workbook.

The Macro dialog box displays a list of macros in your workbook. To view the code behind a macro, you click the macro's name and then click Edit to open the Visual Basic Editor.

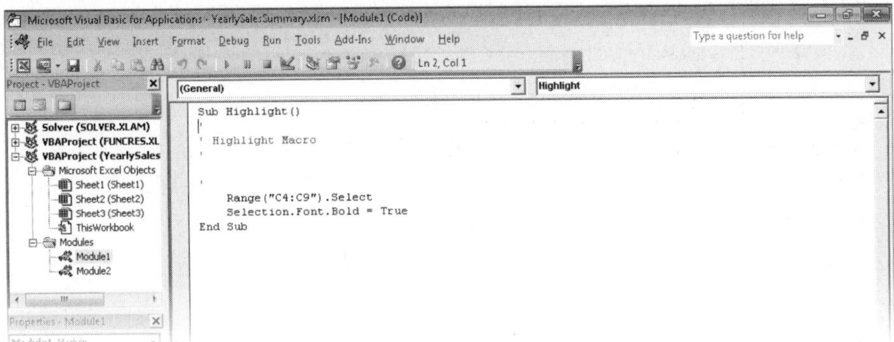

Keyboard Shortcut You can also open and close the Visual Basic Editor by pressing Alt+F11.

See Also To see a complete list of keyboard shortcuts, see "Keyboard Shortcuts" at the end of this book.

Excel macros are recorded by using VBA. Consider, for example, the code for a macro that selects the cell range C4:C9 and changes the cells' formatting to bold. The first line of the macro identifies the cell range to be selected (in this case, cells C4:C9). After the macro selects the cells, the next line of the macro changes the formatting of the selected cells to bold, which has the same result as clicking a cell and then clicking the Bold button in the Font group on the Home tab.

To see how the macro works, you can open the Macro dialog box, click the name of the macro you want to examine, and then click Step Into. The Visual Basic Editor opens, with a highlight around the instruction that will be executed next.

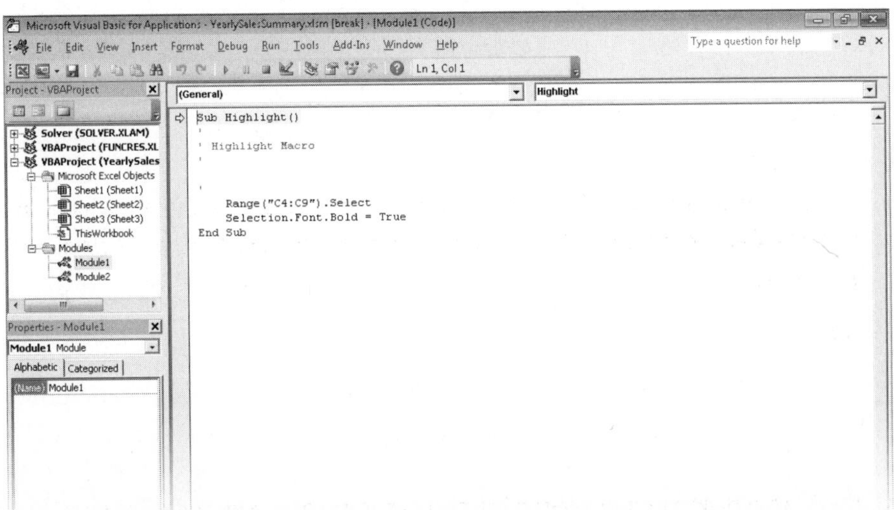

To execute an instruction, press F8. The highlight moves to the next instruction, and your worksheet then changes to reflect the action that resulted from executing the preceding instruction.

You can run a macro without stopping after each instruction by opening the Macro dialog box, clicking the macro to run, and then clicking Run. You'll usually run the macro this way; after all, the point of using macros is to save time.

In this exercise, you'll examine a macro in the Visual Basic Editor, move through the first part of the macro one step at a time, and then run the entire macro without stopping.

SET UP You need the VolumeHighlights_start workbook located in your Chapter12 practice file folder to complete this exercise. Start Excel, open the VolumeHighlights_start workbook, click the Enable Content button on the Message Bar (if necessary), and save the workbook as *VolumeHighlights*. Then follow the steps.

1. On the **View** tab, in the **Macros** group, click the **Macros** arrow and then, in the list that appears, click **View Macros**.

   The Macro dialog box opens.

   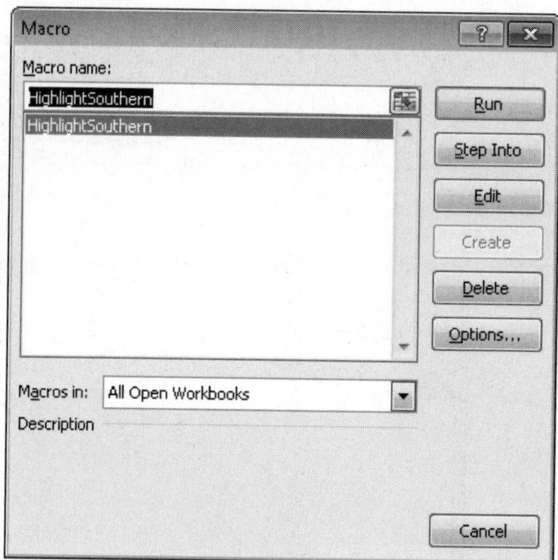

2. Click the **HighlightSouthern** macro, and then, to display the macro code, click **Edit**.

   The Visual Basic Editor opens, with the code for the HighlightSouthern macro displayed in the Module1 (Code) window.

3. In the Visual Basic Editor window, click the **Close** button.

   The Visual Basic Editor closes, and Excel displays the VolumeHighlights workbook.

4. In the **Macros** list, click **View Macros**.

   The Macro dialog box opens.

5. Click the **HighlightSouthern** macro, and then click **Step Into**.

   The macro appears in the Visual Basic Editor, with the first macro instruction highlighted.

6. Press the F8 key.

   Excel highlights the next instruction.

7. Press F8 again.

   The macro selects the Atlantic row in the table.

8. Press F8 twice.

   The macro changes the Atlantic row's text color to red.

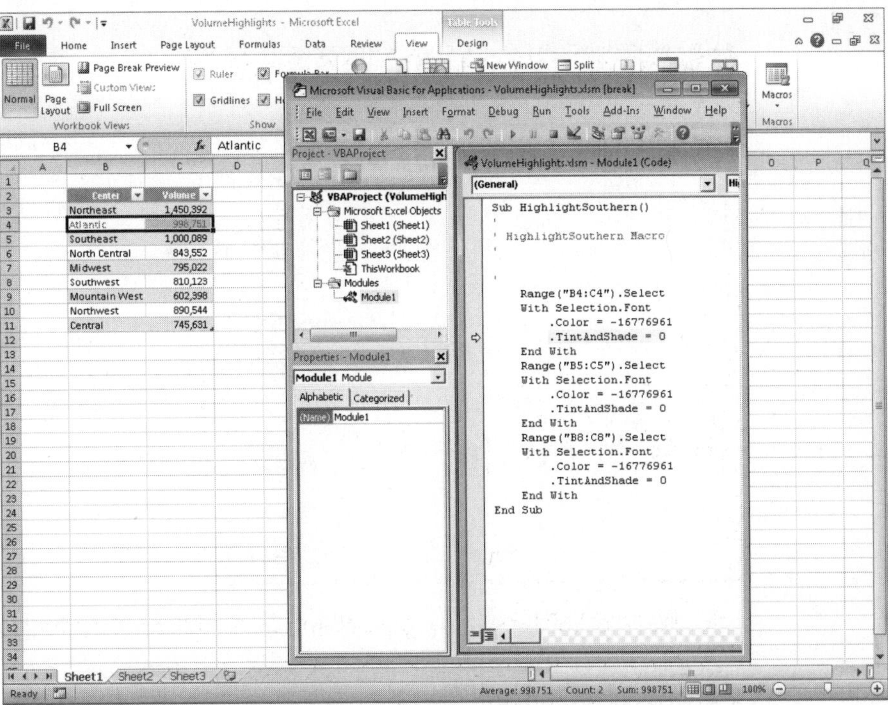

9. Click the Visual Basic Editor **Close** button.

   A warning dialog box opens, indicating that closing the Visual Basic Editor will stop the debugger.

10. Click **OK**.

    The Visual Basic Editor closes.

11. In the **Macros** list, click **View Macros**.

    The Macro dialog box opens.

12. Click the **HighlightSouthern** macro.

13. Click **Run**.

    The Macro dialog box closes, and Excel runs the entire macro.

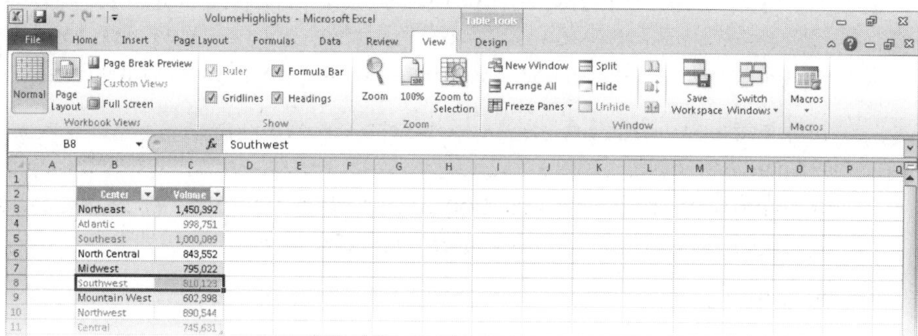

14. On the Quick Access Toolbar, click the **Save** button.

    Excel saves your work.

CLEAN UP Close the VolumeHighlights workbook.

Creating and Modifying Macros

The first step of creating a macro is to plan the process you want to automate. Computers today are quite fast, so adding an extra step that doesn't affect the outcome of a process doesn't slow you down noticeably, but leaving out a step means you will need to re-record your macro. After you plan your process, you can create a macro by clicking the View tab and then, in the Macros group, clicking the Macros arrow. In the list that appears, click Record Macro. When you do, the Record Macro dialog box opens.

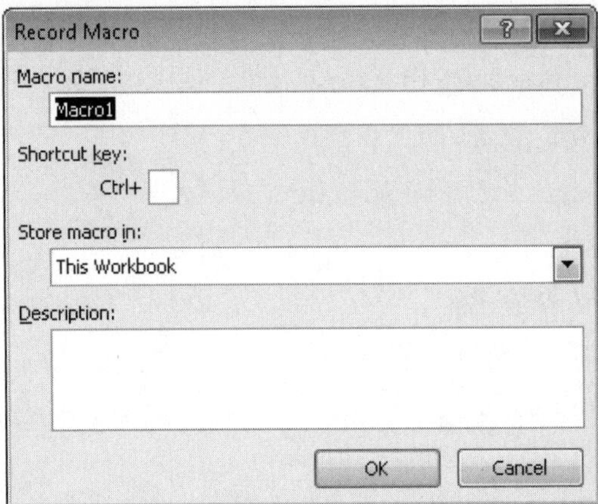

After you type the name of your macro in the Macro Name box, click OK. You can now perform the actions you want Excel to repeat later; when you're done, in the Macros list, click Stop Recording to add your macro to the list of macros available in your workbook.

To modify an existing macro, you can simply delete the macro and re-record it. Or if you just need to make a quick change, you can open it in the Visual Basic Editor and add to or change the macro's instructions. To delete a macro, open the Macro dialog box, click the macro you want to delete, and then click Delete.

See Also For more information about using the Visual Basic Editor, press Alt+F11 to display the Visual Basic Editor, and then press F1 to display the Visual Basic Help dialog box.

In this exercise, you'll record, edit, save, and run a macro that removes the bold formatting from selected cells.

SET UP You need the YearlySalesSummary_start workbook located in your Chapter12 practice file folder to complete this exercise. Open the YearlySalesSummary_start workbook, click the Enable Content button on the Message Bar (if necessary), and save the workbook as *YearlySalesSummary*. Then follow the steps.

1. On the **View** tab, in the **Macros** group, click the **Macros** arrow and then, in the list that appears, click **Record Macro**.

   The Record Macro dialog box opens.

2. In the **Macro name** box, delete the existing name, and then type **RemoveHighlight**.
3. Click **OK**.

   The Record Macro dialog box closes.

4. Select the cell range **C4:C7**.

   The text in these cells is currently bold.

5. On the **Home** tab, in the **Font** group, click the **Bold** button.

6. On the **View** tab, in the **Macros** list, click **Stop Recording**.

   Excel stops recording the macro.

7. In the **Macros** list, click **View Macros**.

   The Macro dialog box opens.

8. In the **Macro name** area, click **RemoveHighlight**, and then click **Edit**.

   The Visual Basic Editor starts.

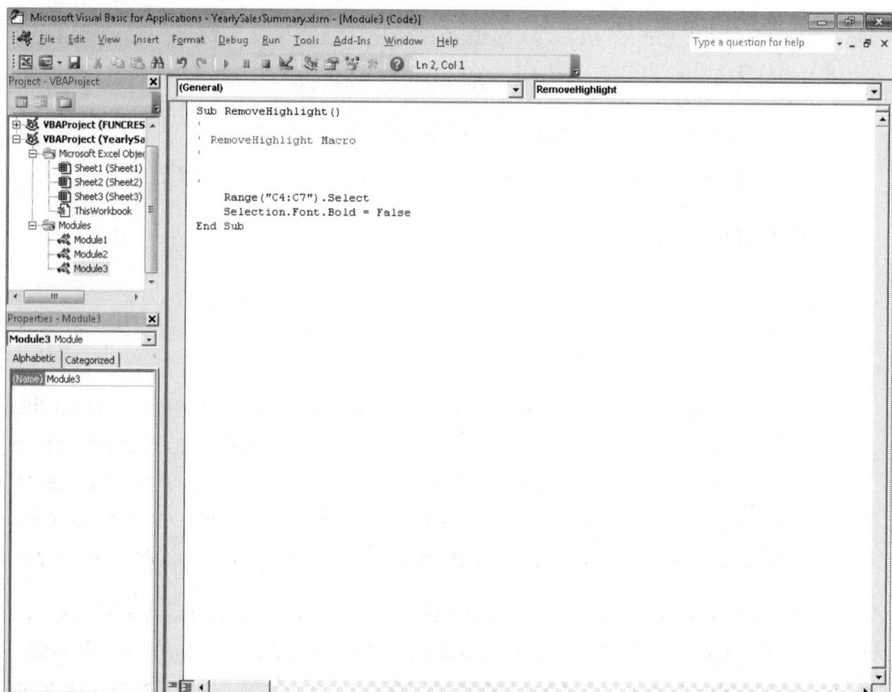

9. Edit the line of code that currently reads **Range("C4:C7").Select** so that it reads **Range("C3:C9").Select**.

This macro statement selects the cell range C3:C9, not the incorrect range C4:C7.

10. On the **Standard** toolbar of the Visual Basic Editor, click the **Save** button to save your change.

11. On the title bar of the Visual Basic Editor window, click the **Close** button.

    The Visual Basic Editor closes.

12. Select cells **C3:C9**, format them as bold, and then click cell **C9**.

    Excel formats the cells' contents in bold and then removes the highlight from cells C3:C9.

13. In the **Macros** list, click **View Macros**.

    The Macro dialog box opens.

14. Click **RemoveHighlight**, and then click **Run**.

    The bold formatting is removed from cells C3:C9.

15. On the Quick Access Toolbar, click the **Save** button.

    Excel saves your workbook.

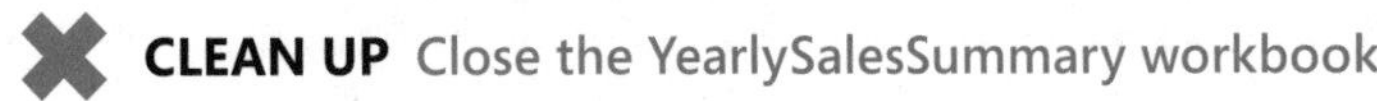

CLEAN UP Close the YearlySalesSummary workbook.

Running Macros When a Button Is Clicked

The ribbon enables you to discover the commands built into Excel quickly. However, it can take a few seconds to display the View tab, open the Macro dialog box, select the macro you want to run, and click the Run button. When you're in the middle of a presentation, taking even those few seconds can reduce your momentum and force you to regain your audience's attention. Excel offers several ways for you to make your macros more accessible.

If you want to display the Macro dialog box quickly, you can add the View Macros button to the Quick Access Toolbar. To do so, click the Customize Quick Access Toolbar button at the right edge of the Quick Access Toolbar, and then click More Commands to display the Customize The Quick Access Toolbar page of the Excel Options dialog box.

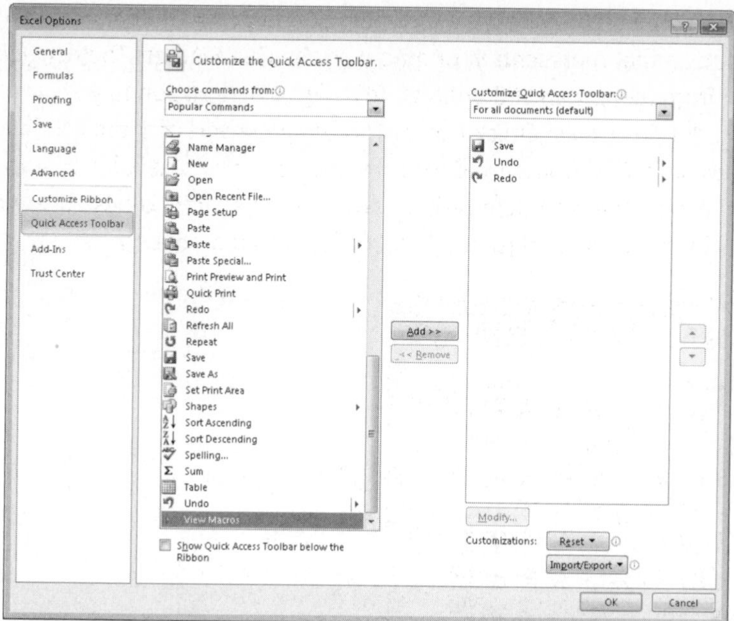

See Also For more information about customizing the Quick Access Toolbar, see "Customizing the Excel 2010 Program Window" in Chapter 1, "Setting Up a Workbook."

When you display the Popular Commands command group, you'll see that the last item in the command pane is View Macros. When you click the View Macros item, click the Add button, and then click OK, Excel adds the command to the Quick Access Toolbar and closes the Excel Options dialog box. Clicking the View Macros button on the Quick Access Toolbar displays the Macro dialog box, which saves a significant amount of time compared to displaying the View tab and moving the mouse to the far right edge of the ribbon.

If you prefer to run a macro without having to display the Macro dialog box, you can do so by adding a button representing the macro to the Quick Access Toolbar. Clicking that button runs the macro immediately, which is very handy when you create a macro for a task you perform frequently. To add a button representing a macro to the Quick Access Toolbar, click the Customize Quick Access Toolbar button at the right edge of the Quick Access Toolbar, and then click More Commands to display the Customize The Quick Access Toolbar page of the Excel Options dialog box. From there, in the Choose Commands From list, click Macros. Click the macro you want represented on the Quick Access Toolbar, click Add, and then click OK.

If you add more than one macro button to the Quick Access Toolbar or if you want to change the button that represents your macro on the Quick Access Toolbar, you can select a new button from more than 160 options. To assign a new button to your macro, click the macro item in the Customize Quick Access Toolbar pane and click the Modify button to display your choices. Click the symbol you want, type a new text value to appear when a user points to the button, and then click OK twice (the first time to close the Modify Button dialog box and the second to close the Excel Options dialog box).

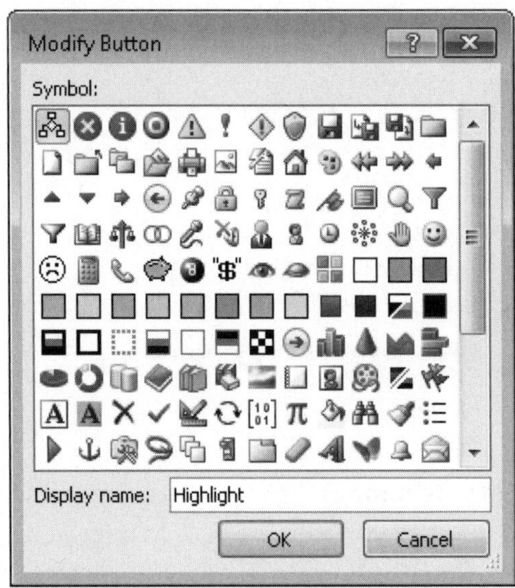

Finally, you can have Excel run a macro when you click a shape in your workbook. Assigning macros to shapes enables you to create "buttons" that are graphically richer than those available on the Quick Access Toolbar. If you're so inclined, you can even create custom button layouts that represent other objects, such as a remote control. To run a macro when you click a shape, right-click the shape, and then click Assign Macro on the shortcut menu that opens. In the Assign Macro dialog box, click the macro you want to run when you click the shape, and then click OK.

Important When you assign a macro to run when you click a shape, don't change the name of the macro that appears in the Assign Macro dialog box. The name that appears refers to the object and what the object should do when it is clicked; changing the macro name breaks that connection and prevents Excel from running the macro.

In this exercise, you'll add the View Macros button to the Quick Access Toolbar, add a macro button to the Quick Access Toolbar, assign a macro to a workbook shape, and then run the macros.

SET UP You need the PerformanceDashboard_start workbook located in your Chapter12 practice file folder to complete this exercise. Open the PerformanceDashboard_start workbook, click the Enable Content button on the Message Bar (if necessary), and save the workbook as *PerformanceDashboard*. Then follow the steps.

1. On the Quick Access Toolbar, click the **Customize Quick Access Toolbar** button, and then click **More Commands**.

   The Customize The Quick Access Toolbar page of the Excel Options dialog box opens, displaying the Popular Commands category in the Choose Commands From pane.

2. In the list of available commands, click **View Macros**.
3. Click **Add**.

   The View Macros command appears in the Customize Quick Access Toolbar pane.

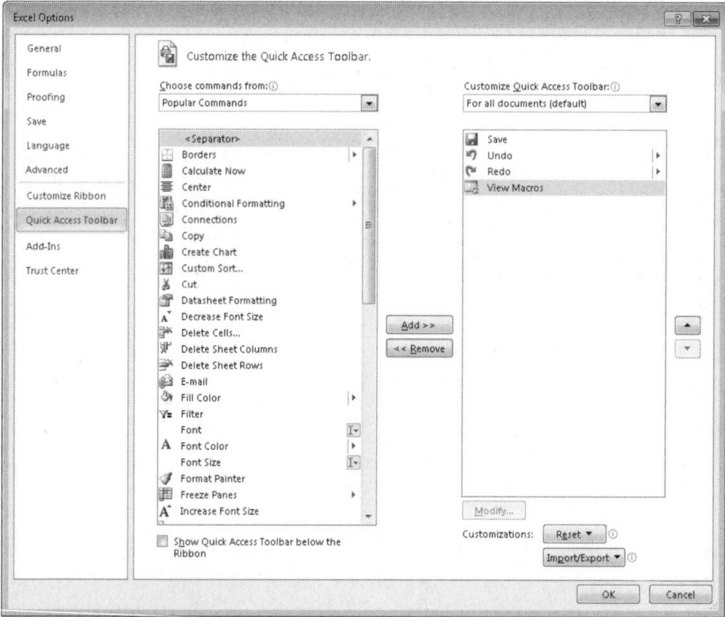

4. In the **Choose commands from** list, click **Macros**.

   The available macros appear in the pane below.

5. In the **Choose commands from** pane, click **SavingsHighlight**.

   Troubleshooting If macros in the workbook are not enabled, the SavingsHighlight macro will not appear in the list.

6. Click **Add**.

   The SavingsHighlight macro appears in the Customize Quick Access Toolbar pane.

7. In the **Customize Quick Access Toolbar** pane, click the **SavingsHighlight** command.

8. Click **Modify**.

   The Modify Button dialog box opens.

9. Click the blue button with the white circle inside it (the fourth button from the left on the top row).

10. Click **OK** twice to close the **Modify Button** dialog box and the **Excel Options** dialog box.

    The Excel Options dialog box closes, and the View Macros and SavingsHighlight buttons appear on the Quick Access Toolbar.

11. On the worksheet, right-click the **Show Efficiency** shape, and then click **Assign Macro**.

    The Assign Macro dialog box opens.

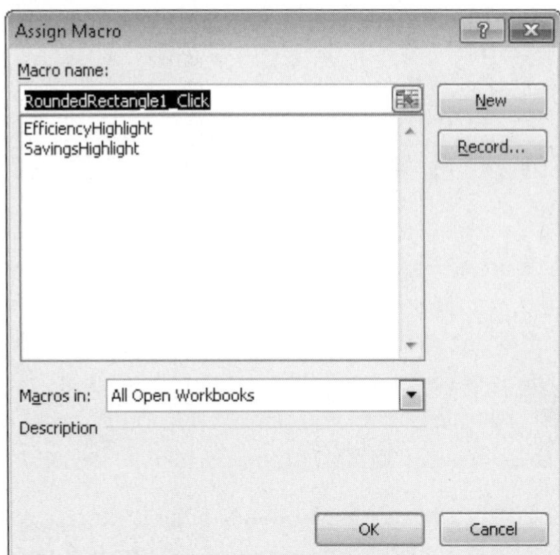

12. Click **EfficiencyHighlight**, and then click **OK**.

    The Assign Macro dialog box closes.

13. On the Quick Access Toolbar, click the **SavingsHighlight** button.

    Excel runs the macro, which applies a conditional format to the values in the Savings column of the table on the left.

14. Click the **Show Efficiency** shape.

    Excel runs the macro, which applies a conditional format to the values in the Efficiency column of the table on the right.

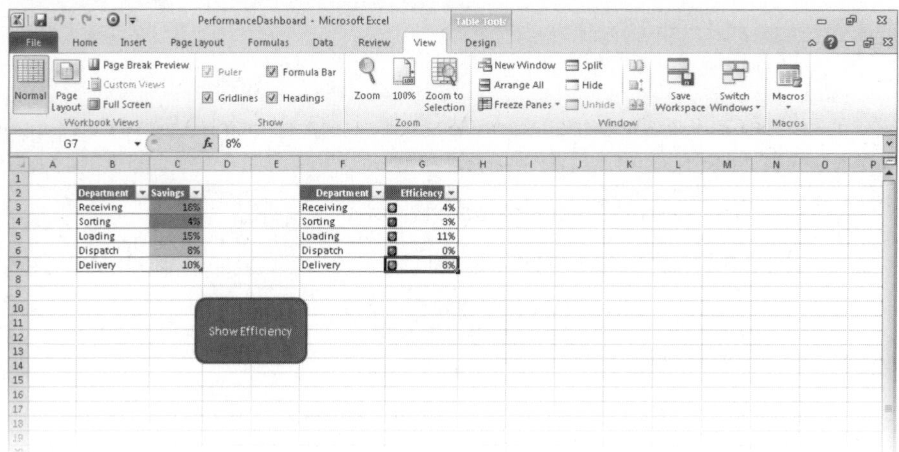

15. On the Quick Access Toolbar, click the **Save** button to save your work.

CLEAN UP Close the PerformanceDashboard workbook.

Running Macros When a Workbook Is Opened

One advantage of writing Excel macros in VBA is that you can have Excel run a macro whenever a workbook is opened. For example, if you use a worksheet for presentations, you can create macros that render the contents of selected cells in bold type, italic, or different typefaces to set the data apart from data in neighboring cells. If you close a workbook without removing that formatting, however, the contents of your workbook will still have that formatting applied when you open it. Although this is not a catastrophe, returning the workbook to its original formatting might take a few seconds to accomplish.

Instead of running a macro manually, or even from a toolbar button or a menu, you can have Excel run a macro whenever a workbook is opened. The trick of making that happen is in the name you give the macro. Whenever Excel finds a macro with the name Auto_Open, it runs the macro when the workbook to which it is attached is opened.

Tip If you have your macro security set to the Disable With Notification level, clicking the Options button that appears on the Message Bar, selecting the Enable This Content option, and then clicking OK allows the Auto_Open macro to run.

In this exercise, you'll create and test a macro that runs whenever someone opens the workbook to which it is attached.

SET UP You need the RunOnOpen_start workbook located in your Chapter12 practice file folder to complete this exercise. Open the RunOnOpen_start workbook, click the Enable Content button on the Message Bar (if necessary), and save the workbook as *RunOnOpen*. Then follow the steps.

1. On the **View** tab, in the **Macros** group, click the **Macros** arrow and then, in the list that appears, click **Record Macro**.

   The Record Macro dialog box opens.

2. In the **Macro name** box, delete the existing name, and then type **Auto_Open**.

3. Click **OK**.

   The Record Macro dialog box closes.

4. Select the cell range **B3:C11**.

5. On the **Home** tab, in the **Font** group, click the **Bold** button twice.

   The first click of the Bold button formats all the selected cells in bold; the second click removes the bold formatting from all the selected cells.

6. Click cell **C11** and then, in the **Macros** list, click **Stop Recording**.

   Excel stops recording your macro.

7. In the **Macros** list, click **View Macros**.

   The Macro dialog box opens.

8. Click **Highlight**, and then click **Run**.

   The contents of cells C4, C6, and C10 appear in bold type.

9. On the Quick Access Toolbar, click the **Save** button to save your work.

10. Click the **Close** button to close the **RunOnOpen** workbook.
11. Click the **File** tab and then, in the **Recent Documents** list, click **RunOnOpen.xlsm**. If a warning appears, click **Enable Content**, and then click **OK** to enable macros.

    RunOnOpen opens, and the contents of cells C4, C6, and C10 change immediately to regular type.

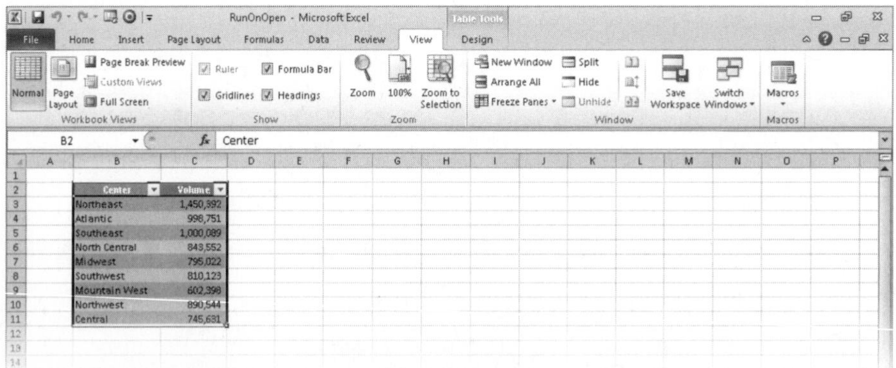

12. On the Quick Access Toolbar, click the **Save** button to save your work.

CLEAN UP Close the RunOnOpen workbook. If you're not continuing directly to the next chapter, exit Excel.

Key Points

- Macros are handy tools you can use to perform repetitive tasks quickly, such as inserting blocks of text.
- You don't have to be a programmer to use macros; you can record your actions and have Excel save them as a macro.
- Excel uses macro-enabled workbook types, which have the file extensions .xlsm (a macro-enabled workbook) and .xltm (a macro-enabled template workbook).
- If you're curious about what a macro looks like, you can display it in the Visual Basic Editor. If you know a little VBA, or if you just want to experiment, feel free to modify the macro code and see what happens.
- You can create Quick Access Toolbar buttons and shapes that, when clicked, run a macro.
- If you want a macro to run whenever you open a workbook, create a macro named Auto_Open.

Chapter at a Glance

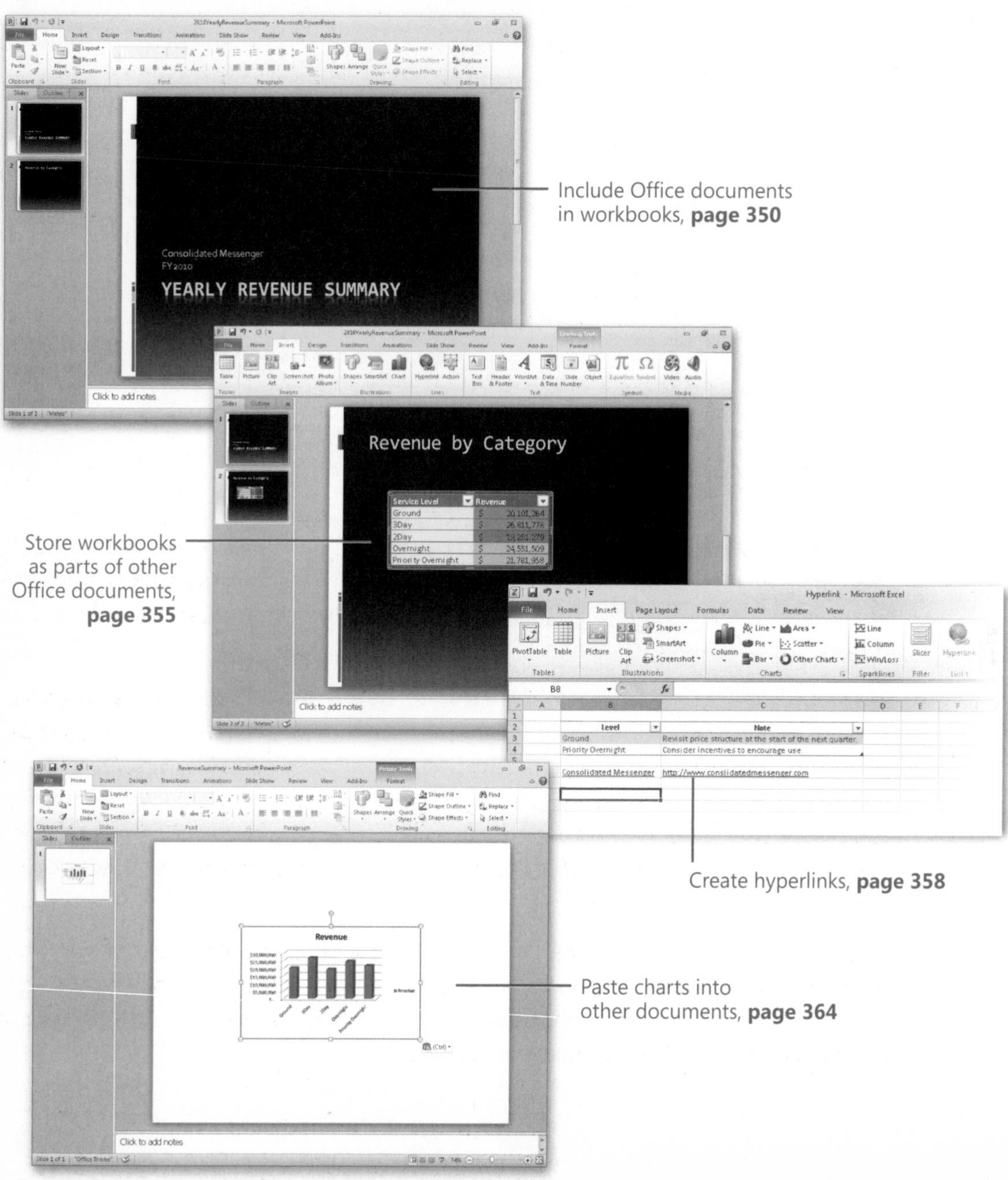
Include Office documents in workbooks, **page 350**
Store workbooks as parts of other Office documents, **page 355**
Create hyperlinks, **page 358**
Paste charts into other documents, **page 364**

13 Working with Other Microsoft Office Programs

In this chapter, you will learn how to

- ✔ Include Office documents in workbooks.
- ✔ Store workbooks as parts of other Office documents.
- ✔ Create hyperlinks.
- ✔ Paste charts into other documents.

By itself, Microsoft Excel 2010 provides a broad range of tools so that you can store, present, and summarize your financial data. When you use other Microsoft Office 2010 programs, you can extend your capabilities even further, creating databases, presentations, written reports, and custom Web pages through which you can organize and communicate your data in print and over networks.

All the Office programs interact with each other in many useful ways. For example, you can include a file created with another Office program in an Excel workbook. If you use Microsoft Word 2010 to write a quick note about why a customer's shipping expenditures decreased significantly in January, you can include the report in your workbook. Similarly, you can include your Excel workbooks in documents created with other Office programs. If you want to copy only part of a workbook, such as a chart, to another Office document, you can do that as well.

Excel integrates well with the Web. If you know of a Web-based resource that would be useful to someone who is viewing a document, you can create a hyperlink, or connection from a document to a place in the same file or to another file anywhere on a network or the Internet that the user's computer can reach.

In this chapter, you will learn how to include an Office 2010 document in a worksheet, store an Excel workbook as part of another Office document, create hyperlinks, and paste an Excel chart into another document.

> **Practice Files** Before you can complete the exercises in this chapter, you need to copy the book's practice files to your computer. The practice files you'll use to complete the exercises in this chapter are in the Chapter13 practice file folder. A complete list of practice files is provided in "Using the Practice Files" at the beginning of this book.

Including Office Documents in Workbooks

One benefit of working with Excel 2010 is that because it is part of Office 2010, it is possible to combine data from Excel and other Office programs to create informative documents and presentations. Just as you do when you combine data from more than one Excel document, when you combine information from another Office file with an Excel workbook, you can either paste the other Office document into the Excel workbook or create a link between the workbook and the other document.

There are two advantages to creating a link between your Excel workbook and the other file. The first benefit is that linking to the other file, as opposed to copying the entire file into your workbook, keeps your Excel workbook small. If the workbook is copied to another drive or computer, you can maintain the link by copying the linked file along with the Excel workbook or by re-creating the link if the linked file is on the same network as the Excel workbook. It is also possible to use the workbook if the linked file isn't available. The second benefit of linking to another file is that any changes in the file to which you link are reflected in your Excel workbook.

You create a link between an Excel workbook and another Office document by clicking the cell where you want the document to appear, clicking the Insert tab and then, in the Text group, clicking Object to display the Object dialog box. In the Object dialog box, click the Create From File tab.

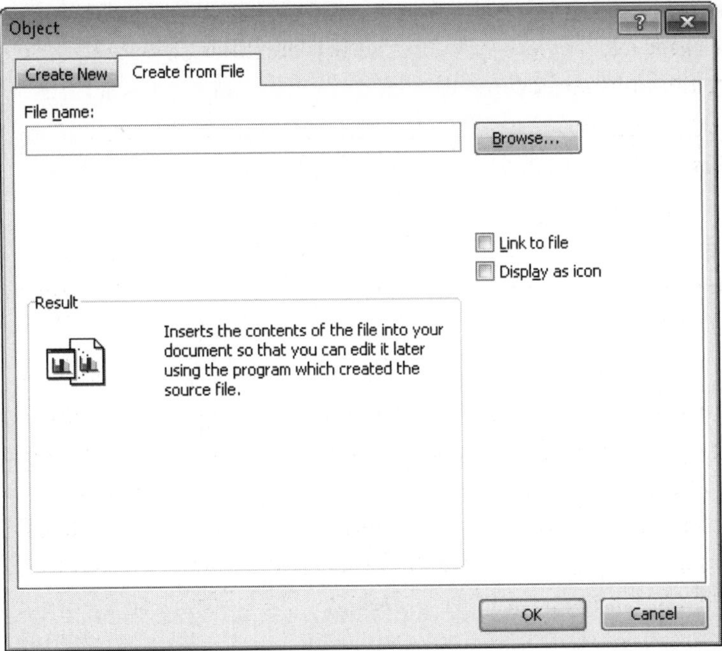

Clicking the Browse button on the Create From File page opens the Browse dialog box, from which you can browse to the folder containing the file you want to link to. After you locate the file, double-clicking it closes the Browse dialog box and adds the file's name and path to the File Name box of the Object dialog box. To create a link to the file, select the Link To File check box, and click OK. When you do, the file appears in your workbook near the active cell.

If you want to link a file to your workbook but don't want the file image to take up much space on the screen, you can also select the Display As Icon check box. After you select the file and click OK, the file will be represented by the same icon used to represent it in Windows. Double-clicking the icon displays the file.

After you have linked a file—for example, a Microsoft PowerPoint 2010 presentation—to your Excel workbook, you can edit the file by right-clicking its image or icon in your workbook and then, on the shortcut menu that appears, pointing to the appropriate Object command and clicking Edit. For a PowerPoint file, you point to Presentation Object. The file will open in its native application. When you finish editing the file, your changes appear in your workbook.

Tip The specific menu item you point to changes to reflect the program used to create the file to which you want to link. For a Word 2010 document, for example, the menu item you point to is Document Object.

In this exercise, you'll link a PowerPoint 2010 presentation showing a business summary to an Excel workbook and then edit the presentation from within Excel.

Important You must have PowerPoint 2010 installed on your computer to complete this exercise.

SET UP You need the SummaryPresentation_start workbook and the 2010YearlyRevenueSummary_start presentation located in your Chapter13 practice file folder to complete this exercise. Start Excel, open the SummaryPresentation_start workbook, and save it as *SummaryPresentation*. Then start PowerPoint, open the 2010YearlyRevenueSummary_start presentation, and save it as *2010YearlyRevenueSummary*. Close PowerPoint, and then follow the steps.

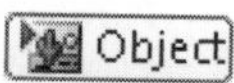

1. In the **SummaryPresentation** workbook, on the **Insert** tab, in the **Text** group, click **Object**.

   The Object dialog box opens.

2. Click the **Create from File** tab.

   The Create From File page is displayed.

3. Click **Browse**.

   The Browse dialog box opens.

4. Browse to the **2010YearlyRevenueSummary.pptx** presentation, and then click **Insert**.

   The Browse dialog box closes, and the full file path of the 2010YearlyRevenueSummary presentation appears in the File Name box.

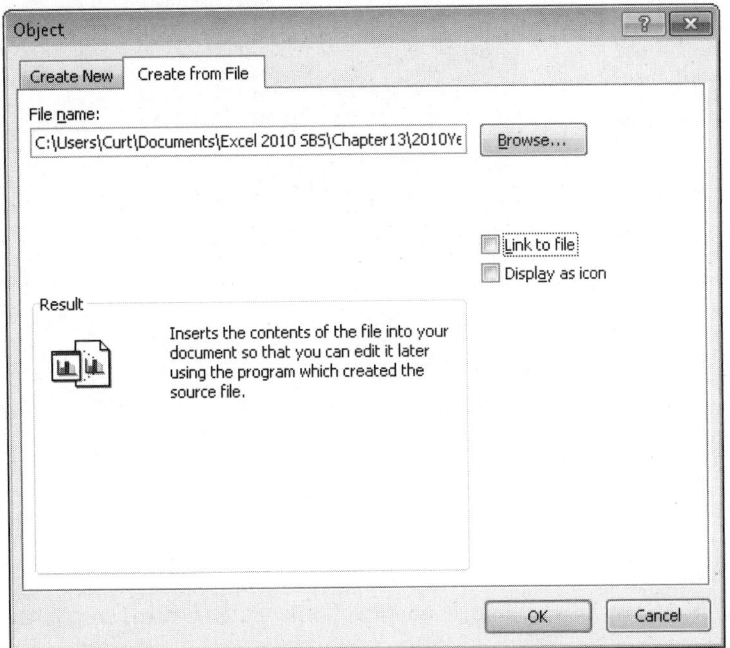

5. Select the **Link to file** check box, and then click **OK**.

   Excel creates a link from your workbook to the presentation.

6. Right-click the presentation, point to **Presentation Object**, and then click **Edit**.

   The presentation opens in a PowerPoint 2010 window.

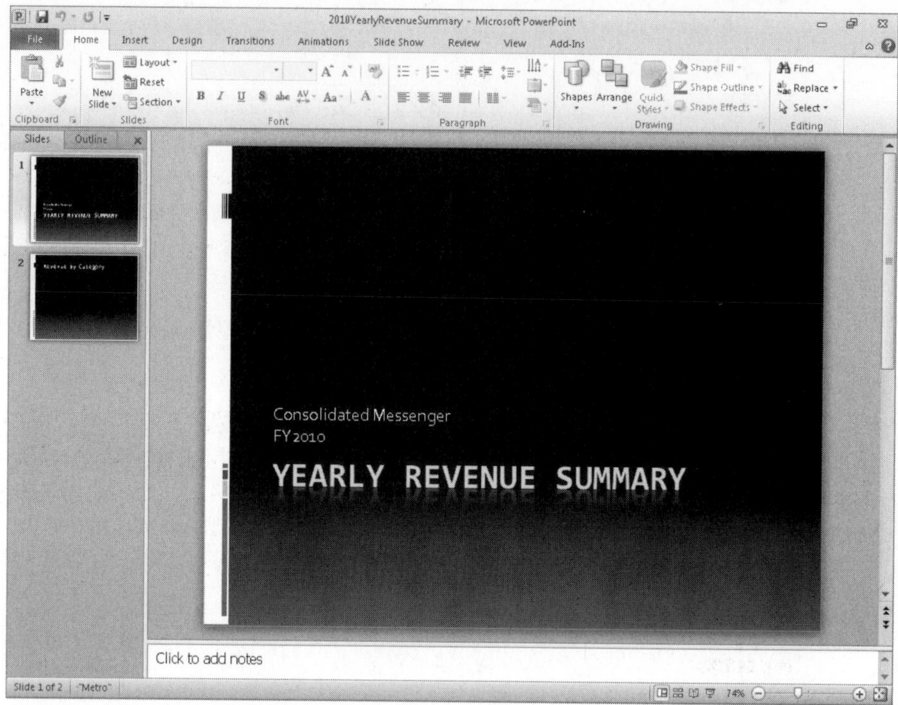

Troubleshooting The appearance of buttons and groups on the ribbon changes depending on the width of the program window. For information about changing the appearance of the ribbon to match our screen images, see "Modifying the Display of the Ribbon" at the beginning of this book.

7. Click **Consolidated Messenger FY2010**.

   The text box containing Consolidated Messenger FY2010 is activated.

8. Select the **FY2010** text, and then type **Calendar Year 2010**.
9. In PowerPoint, on the Quick Access Toolbar, click the **Save** button.

   PowerPoint saves your changes, and Excel updates the linked object's appearance to reflect the new text.

10. Click the **File** tab, and then click **Save**.

CLEAN UP Close the SummaryPresentation workbook and the 2010YearlyRevenueSummary presentation. If you don't plan to work through the next exercise immediately, exit PowerPoint.

Storing Workbooks as Parts of Other Office Documents

In the preceding section, you linked to another file from within your Excel workbook. The advantages of linking to a second file are that the size of your workbook is kept small and any changes in the second document will be reflected in your workbook. The disadvantage is that the second document must be copied with the workbook—or at least be on a network-accessible computer. If Excel can't find or access the second file where the link says it is located, Excel can't display it. You can still open your workbook, but you won't see the linked file's contents.

If file size isn't an issue and you want to ensure that the second document is always available, you can embed the file in your workbook. Embedding another file in an Excel workbook means that the entirety of the other file is saved as part of your workbook. Wherever your workbook goes, the embedded file goes along with it. Of course, the embedded version of the file is no longer connected to the original file, so changes in one aren't reflected in the other.

Important To view a linked or embedded file, you must have the program used to create it installed on the computer on which you open the workbook.

You can embed a file in an Excel workbook by following the procedure described in the preceding section but leaving the Link To File check box cleared.

It is also possible to embed your Excel workbooks in other Office documents. In PowerPoint, for example, you can embed an Excel file in a presentation by displaying the Insert tab in PowerPoint and then, in the Text group, clicking Object to display the Insert Object dialog box. Then in the Insert Object dialog box, select Create From File.

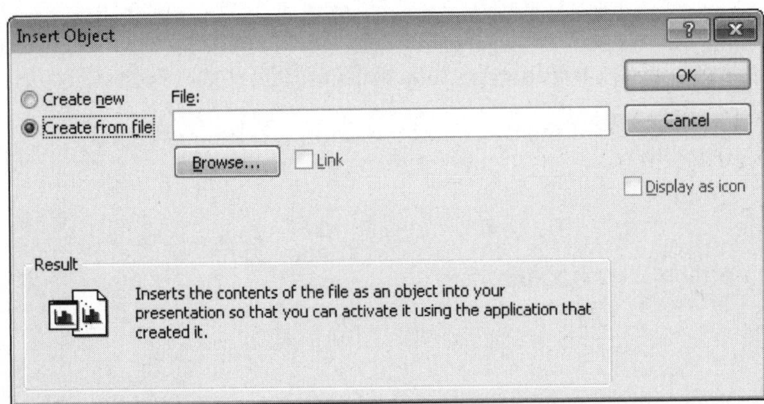

To identify the file you want to embed, click the Browse button and then, in the Browse dialog box that opens, navigate to the folder where the file is stored and double-click the file. The Browse dialog box closes, and the file path appears in the File box. Click OK to embed your workbook in the presentation.

If you want to embed a workbook in a file created with any other Office program but don't want the worksheet to take up much space on the screen, select the Display As Icon check box. After you select the file to embed and click OK, the file is represented by the same icon used to represent it in Windows. Double-clicking the icon opens the embedded document in its original application.

Troubleshooting If your Excel workbook's cells don't have a background fill color (that is, you have the No Fill option selected), PowerPoint treats the cells' backgrounds as if they were transparent. If you were to place cells with black text and no background fill over a dark background, you would not be able to see the text. To make your text visible, fill the cells with a very light gray color so the presentation's background doesn't show through.

To edit an embedded Excel workbook, right-click the workbook (or the icon representing it) and then, on the shortcut menu that appears, point to Worksheet Object and click Edit. The workbook opens for editing. After you finish making your changes, you can click anywhere outside the workbook to return to the presentation.

In this exercise, you'll embed an Excel workbook containing sales data in a PowerPoint presentation.

Important You must have PowerPoint 2010 installed on your computer to complete this exercise.

SET UP You need the 2010YearlyRevenueSummary presentation you created in the previous exercise, and the RevenueByServiceLevel_start workbook located in your Chapter13 practice file folder to complete this exercise. If you did not complete the previous exercise, you should do so now. Open the RevenueByServiceLevel_start workbook, and save it as *RevenueByServiceLevel*. Then, if necessary open the 2010YearlyRevenueSummary presentation. Then follow the steps.

1. In the **Slides** panel of the presentation window, click the second slide.

   The second slide appears.

2. On the **Insert** tab, in the **Text** group, click **Object**.

   The Insert Object dialog box opens.

3. Select **Create from file**.

   The Insert Object dialog box changes to allow you to enter a file name.

4. Click **Browse**.

   The Browse dialog box opens.

5. Browse to the **RevenueByServiceLevel** workbook and double-click it.

   The Browse dialog box closes, and the file's full path appears in the File box.

6. Click **OK**.

   The workbook appears in your presentation.

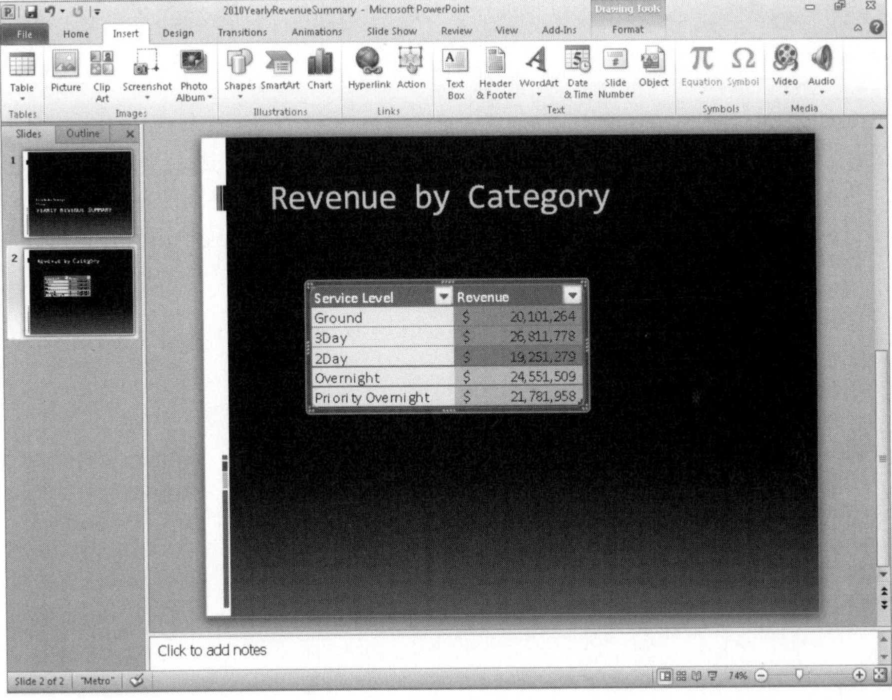

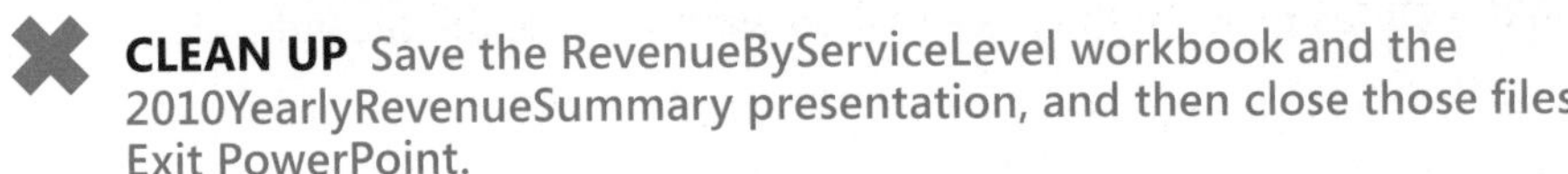

CLEAN UP Save the RevenueByServiceLevel workbook and the 2010YearlyRevenueSummary presentation, and then close those files. Exit PowerPoint.

Creating Hyperlinks

One of the characteristics of the Web is that documents published on Web pages can have references, or hyperlinks, to locations in the same document or to other Web documents. A hyperlink functions much like a link between two cells or between two files, but hyperlinks can reach any computer on the Web, not just those on a corporate network. Hyperlinks that haven't been clicked usually appear as underlined blue text, and hyperlinks that have been followed appear as underlined purple text, but those settings can be changed.

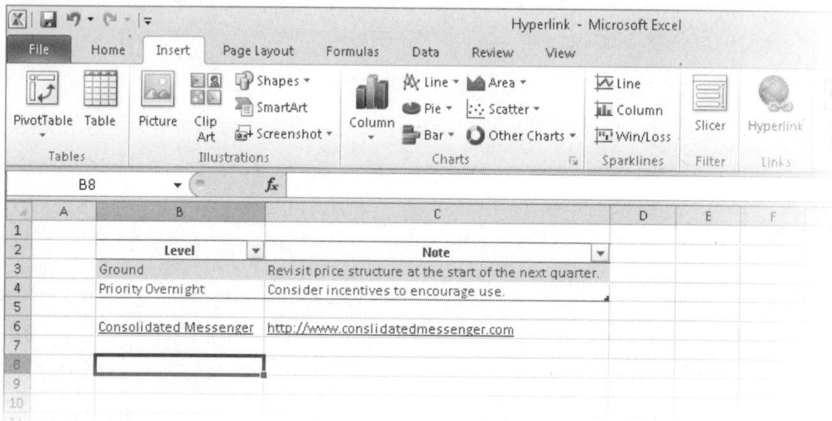

To create a hyperlink, click the cell in which you want to insert the hyperlink and then, on the Insert tab, click Hyperlink. The Insert Hyperlink dialog box opens.

Keyboard Shortcut You can also open the Insert Hyperlink dialog box by pressing Ctrl+K.

See Also For more information about keyboard shortcuts, see "Keyboard Shortcuts" at the end of this book.

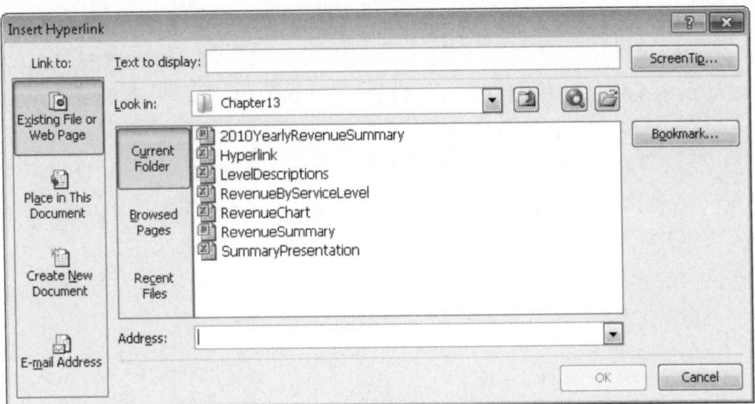

You can choose one of four types of targets, or destinations, for your hyperlink: an existing file or Web page, a place in the current document, a new document you create on the spot, or an e-mail address. By default, the Insert Hyperlink dialog box displays the tools to connect to an existing file or Web page.

To create a hyperlink to another file or Web page, you can use the Look In navigation tool to locate the file. If you recently opened the file or Web page to which you want to link, you can click either the Browsed Pages or the Recent Files button to display the Web pages or files in your History list.

If you want to create a hyperlink to another place in the current Excel workbook, you can click the Place In This Document button to display a list of available targets in the current workbook.

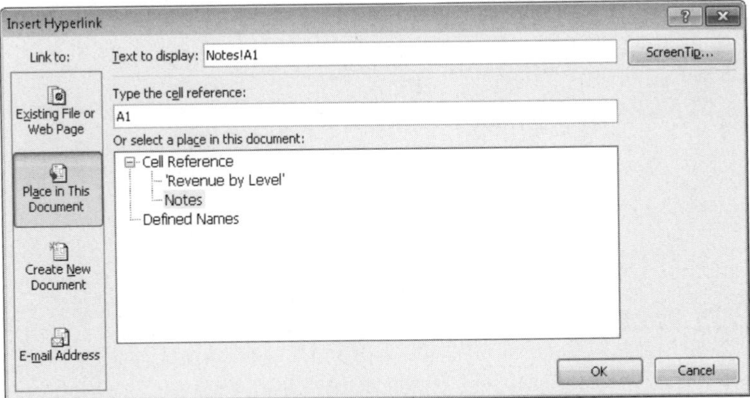

To select the worksheet to which you want to refer, you click the worksheet name in the Or Select A Place In This Document box. When you do, a reference with the name of the worksheet and cell A1 on that worksheet appears in the Text To Display box.

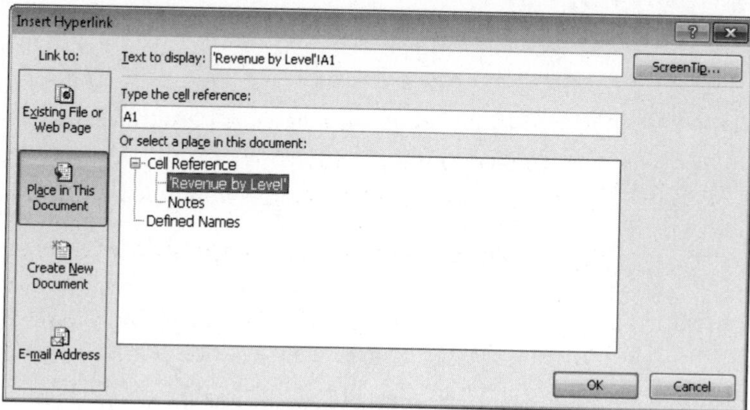

If you want to refer to a cell other than A1 on the selected worksheet, click the worksheet name in the Or Select A Place In This Document box, and then change the cell reference in the Type The Cell Reference box.

You can also create a hyperlink that generates an e-mail message to an address of your choice. To create this type of hyperlink, which is called a *mailto hyperlink*, click the E-mail Address button.

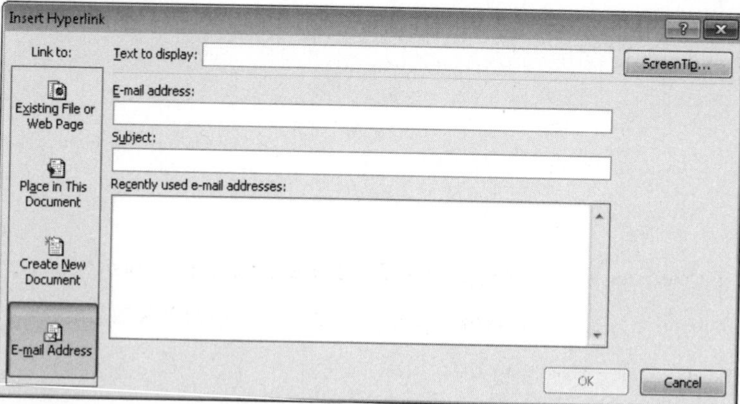

In the dialog box that opens, you can type the recipient's e-mail address in the E-mail Address box and the subject line for messages sent via this hyperlink in the Subject box.

Tip If you use Windows Mail, Microsoft Outlook, or Microsoft Outlook Express as your e-mail program, a list of recently used addresses will appear in the Recently Used E-Mail Addresses box. You can insert any of those addresses in the E-mail Address box by clicking the address.

Clicking a mailto hyperlink causes the user's default e-mail program to open and create a new e-mail message. The e-mail message is addressed to the address you entered in the E-mail Address box, and the subject is set to the text you typed in the Subject box.

Regardless of the type of hyperlink you create, you can specify the text you want to represent the hyperlink in your worksheet. You type that text in the Text To Display box. When you click OK, the text you type there appears in your worksheet, formatted as a hyperlink.

Tip If you leave the Text To Display box empty, the actual link will appear in your worksheet.

To edit an existing hyperlink, click the cell containing the hyperlink and then, on the shortcut menu that appears, click Edit Hyperlink. You can also click Open Hyperlink to go to the target document or create a new e-mail message, or click Remove Hyperlink to delete the hyperlink.

Tip If you delete a hyperlink from a cell, the text from the Text To Display box remains in the cell, but it no longer functions as a hyperlink.

In this exercise, you'll create a hyperlink to another document and then a second hyperlink to a different location in the current workbook.

SET UP You need the Hyperlink_start and LevelDescriptions_start workbooks located in your Chapter13 practice file folder to complete this exercise. Open the Hyperlink_start workbook and save it as *Hyperlink*, and then open the LevelDescriptions_start workbook and save it as *LevelDescriptions*. Then follow the steps.

1. In the **Hyperlink** workbook, on the **Revenue by Level** worksheet, click cell **B9**.

2. On the **Insert** tab, in the **Links** group, click the **Hyperlink** button.

   The Insert Hyperlink dialog box opens.
3. If necessary, click the **Existing File or Web Page** button.

4. If necessary, use the controls to the right of the **Look in** box to navigate to the **Chapter13** practice file folder.

   The files in the target folder appear in the Insert Hyperlink dialog box.

5. In the file list, click the **LevelDescriptions** workbook, and then click **OK**.

   The workbook's full path appears in the Text To Display box and the Address box.

6. In the **Text to display** box, edit the value so that it reads **LevelDescriptions**.

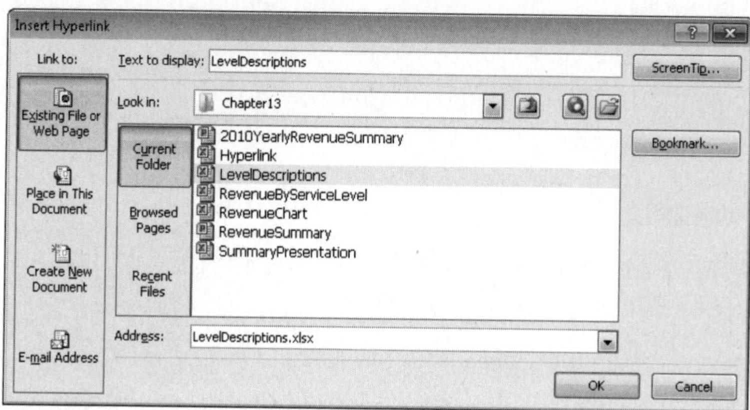

7. Click **OK**.

8. Click the hyperlink in cell **B9**.

   The LevelDescriptions workbook appears.

9. In the **LevelDescriptions** workbook, click the **File** tab, and then click **Close**.

   The LevelDescriptions workbook closes.

10. Right-click cell **B11**, and then click **Hyperlink**.

    The Insert Hyperlink dialog box opens.

11. In the **Link to** pane, click **Place in This Document**.

    The document elements to which you can link appear in the dialog box.

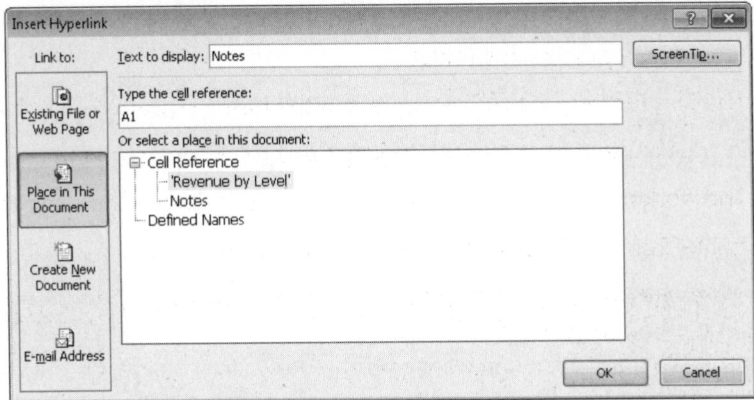

12. In the **Or select a place in this document** pane, click **Notes**.
13. Click **OK**.

    The Insert Hyperlink dialog box closes, and Excel creates a hyperlink in cell B11.
14. Right-click cell **B11**, and then click **Edit Hyperlink**.

    The Edit Hyperlink dialog box opens.
15. Edit the **Text to display** box's value so it reads **Revenue Notes**.
16. Click **OK**.

    The Edit Hyperlink dialog box closes, and the text in cell B11 changes to *Revenue Notes*.

17. On the Quick Access Toolbar, click the **Save** button to save your work.

CLEAN UP Close the Hyperlink and LevelDescriptions workbooks.

Pasting Charts into Other Documents

One more way to include objects from one workbook in another Office document is to copy the object you want to share and then paste it into its new location. You can copy Excel charts to Word documents and PowerPoint presentations to reuse your data without inserting a worksheet into the file and re-creating your chart in that new location.

When you want to copy the current appearance of the chart to another document without creating a link back to the chart, you right-click the chart and click Copy on the shortcut menu that appears to copy the chart to the Microsoft Office Clipboard. Then, in the document into which you want to paste the chart's image, on the Home tab of the ribbon, in the Clipboard group, click the Paste button's arrow to display the palette of paste options available. The last option on the right, Picture, pastes an image of the chart in its current state.

In this exercise, you'll copy a chart containing sales information to the Clipboard and paste an image of the chart into a PowerPoint presentation.

Important You must have PowerPoint installed on your computer to complete this exercise.

SET UP You need the RevenueChart_start workbook and the RevenueSummary_start presentation located in your Chapter13 practice file folder to complete this exercise. Open the RevenueChart_start workbook and save it as *RevenueChart*. Then open the RevenueSummary_start presentation and save it as *RevenueSummary*. Then follow the steps.

1. In the **RevenueChart** workbook, right-click the chart, and then click **Copy**.

   Excel copies the chart to the Clipboard.
2. Display the **RevenueSummary** presentation, which contains a single, blank slide.

3. Right-click a blank spot in the visible slide, and then, in the **Paste Options** area of the shortcut menu, click the **Picture** icon.

   The chart appears as a static image.

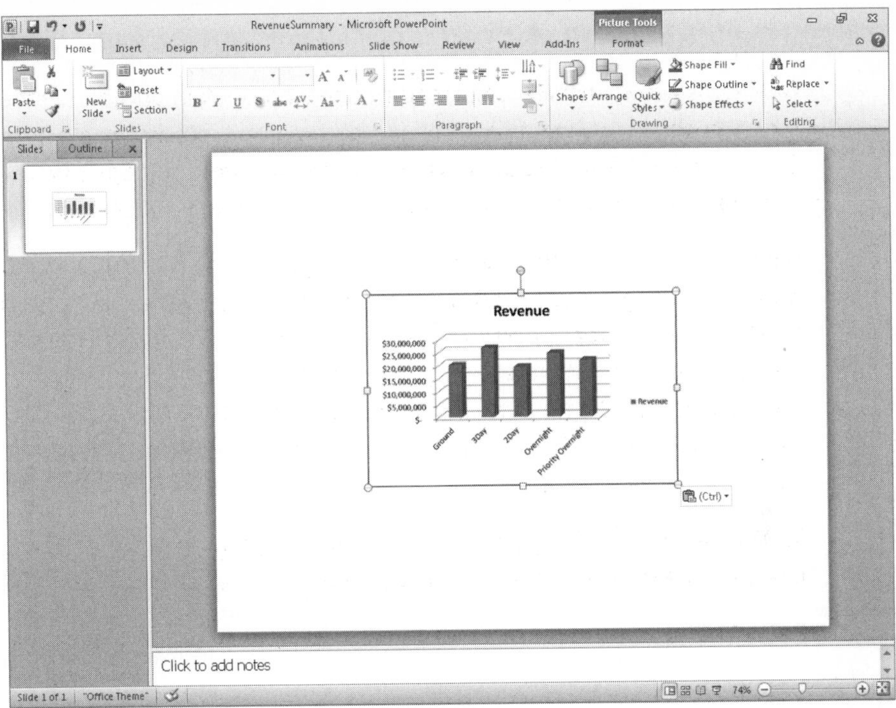

CLEAN UP Save the RevenueChart workbook and the RevenueSummary presentation, and exit PowerPoint. If you are not continuing directly to the next chapter, exit Excel.

Key Points

- Excel is a versatile program. You can exchange data between Excel and other Office programs in just a few steps.
- One benefit of Excel is that, because it is part of Microsoft Office 2010, you can embed Excel worksheets in other Office documents and embed other Office documents (such as PowerPoint presentations) in Excel workbooks.
- Excel works smoothly with the Web; adding hyperlinks to Web pages, other documents, or specific locations in the current workbook is possible through the Insert Hyperlink dialog box.
- After you create a hyperlink, you can edit it to reflect changes in the target site's design and layout.
- Excel is the easiest Microsoft Office system program in which to create charts. After you create a chart in Excel, you can paste it directly into another Office document.

Chapter at a Glance

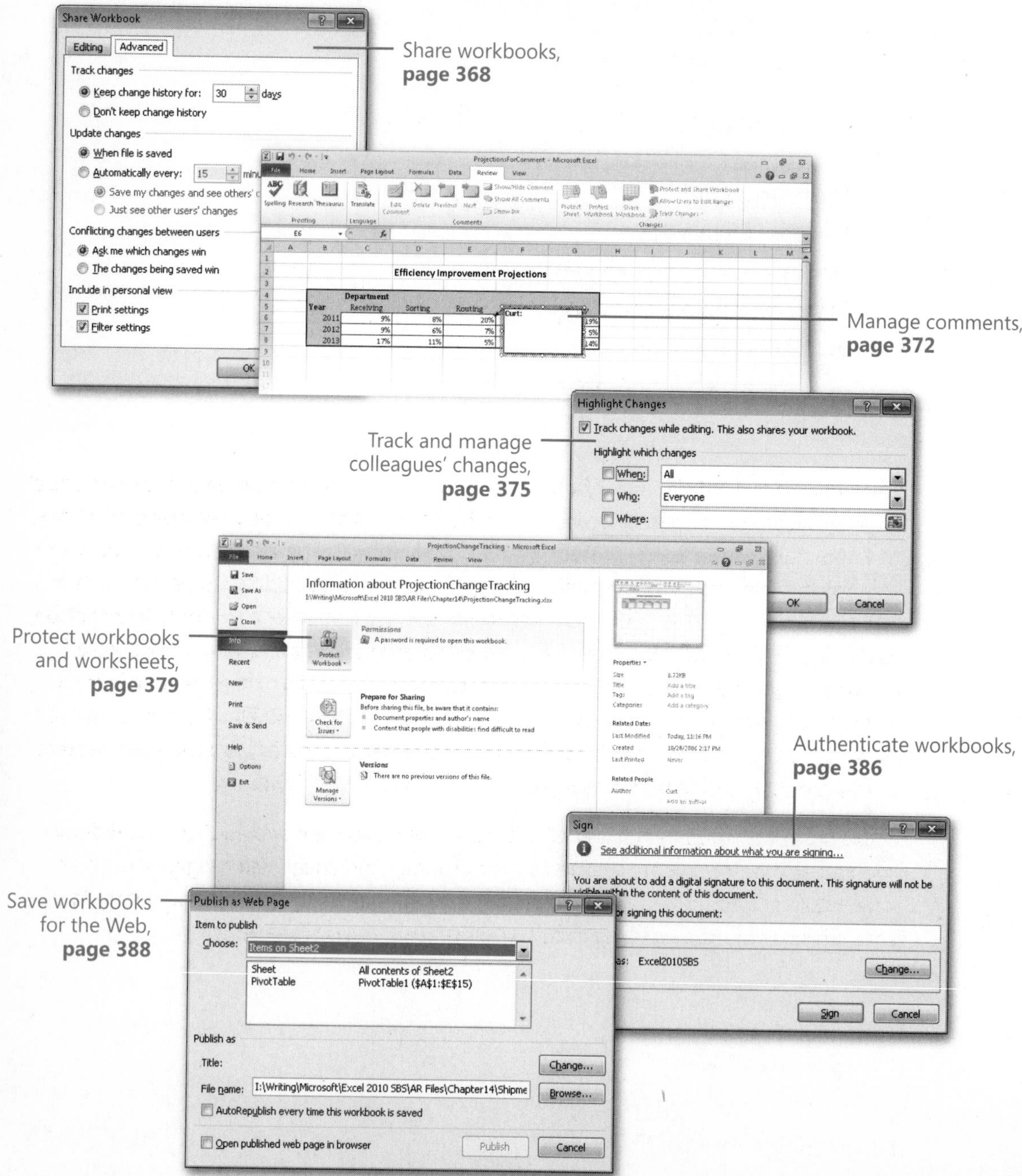

Share workbooks, page 368
Manage comments, page 372
Track and manage colleagues' changes, page 375
Protect workbooks and worksheets, page 379
Authenticate workbooks, page 386
Save workbooks for the Web, page 388

14 Collaborating with Colleagues

In this chapter, you will learn how to

- ✔ Share workbooks.
- ✔ Manage comments.
- ✔ Track and manage colleagues' changes.
- ✔ Protect workbooks and worksheets.
- ✔ Authenticate workbooks.
- ✔ Save workbooks for the Web.

Even though one individual might be responsible for managing an organization's financial data and related information, many people have input when making revenue projections. You and your colleagues can enhance the Microsoft Excel 2010 workbook data you share by adding comments that offer insight into the information the data represents, such as why revenue was so strong during a particular month or whether a service level might be discontinued. If the workbook in which those projections and comments will be stored is available on a network or an intranet, you can allow more than one user to access the workbook at a time by turning on workbook sharing. When a workbook has been shared with your colleagues, you can have the workbook mark and record any changes made to it. You can then decide which changes to keep and which to reject.

If you prefer to limit the number of colleagues who can view and edit your workbooks, you can add password protection to a workbook, worksheet, cell range, or even an individual cell. Adding password protection prevents changes to critical elements of your workbooks. You can also hide formulas used to calculate values.

If you work in an environment in which you and your colleagues, both inside and outside your organization, exchange files frequently, you can use a digital signature to help verify that your workbooks and any macros they contain are from a trusted source.

Finally, if you want to display information on a Web site, you can do so by saving a workbook as a Web page. Your colleagues won't be able to edit the workbook, but they will be able to view it and comment by e-mail or phone.

In this chapter, you'll learn how to share a workbook, manage comments in workbook cells, track and manage changes made by colleagues, protect workbooks and worksheets, digitally sign your workbooks, and save your workbooks for the Web.

Practice Files Before you can complete the exercises in this chapter, you need to copy the book's practice files to your computer. The practice files you'll use to complete the exercises in this chapter are in the Chapter14 practice file folder. A complete list of practice files is provided in "Using the Practice Files" at the beginning of this book.

Sharing Workbooks

To enable several users to edit a workbook simultaneously, you must turn on workbook sharing. Workbook sharing is perfect for an enterprise such as Consolidated Messenger, whose employees need to look up customer information, shipment numbers, and details on mistaken deliveries.

To turn on workbook sharing, on the Review tab, in the Changes group, click Share Workbook. On the Editing page of the Share Workbook dialog box, turn on workbook sharing by selecting the Allow Changes By More Than One User At The Same Time check box. You can then set the sharing options for the active workbook by clicking the Advanced tab.

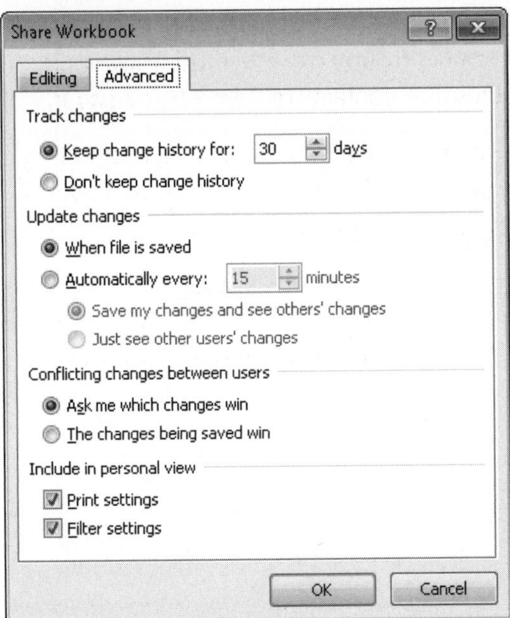

Important You can't share a workbook that contains an Excel table. To share the workbook, convert the Excel table to a regular cell range by clicking the Excel table, clicking the Design tab and then, in the Tools group, clicking Convert To Range. Click Yes in the dialog box that opens to confirm the change.

On the Advanced page of the Share Workbook dialog box, two settings are of particular interest. The first determines whether Excel should maintain a history of changes made to the workbook and, if so, for how many days it should keep the history. The default setting is for the program to retain a record of all changes made in the past 30 days, but you can enter any number of days you like. If you revisit your workbook on a regular basis, maintaining a list of all changes for the past 180 days might not be unreasonable. For a workbook that changes less frequently, a history reaching back 365 days (one year) could meet your tracking and auditing needs. Excel deletes the record of any changes made earlier than the time you set.

Tip You should find out whether your organization has an information retention policy that would affect the amount of time you should keep your workbooks' change histories.

The other important setting on this page deals with how Excel decides which of two conflicting changes in a cell should be applied. For example, a service level's price might change, and two of your colleagues might type in what they think the new price should be. Selecting the Ask Me Which Changes Win option enables you to decide whether to keep the original price or the changed price.

There are two main ways to share a workbook with your colleagues: you can make it available over your organization's network, and you can send a copy of the file to your colleagues via e-mail. Every organization's network is different, so you should check with your network administrators to determine the best way to share a file. Similarly, although the specific command to attach a file to an e-mail message is different in every e-mail program, the most common method of attaching a file is to create a new e-mail message and then click the Attach button, as in Microsoft Outlook 2010.

In this exercise, you'll turn on workbook sharing and then attach the file to an Outlook 2010 e-mail message.

Important You must have Outlook 2010 installed on your computer to follow this procedure exactly.

SET UP You need the CostProjections_start workbook located in your Chapter14 practice file folder to complete this exercise. Start Excel, open the CostProjections_start workbook, and save it as *CostProjections*. Then start Outlook, and follow the steps.

1. In Excel, on the **Review** tab, in the **Changes** group, click **Share Workbook**.

   The Share Workbook dialog box opens.

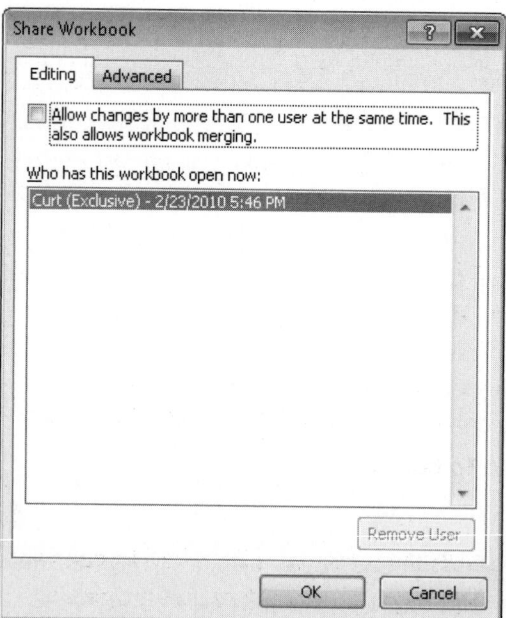

2. Select the **Allow changes by more than one user at the same time** check box.

Tip Workbook merging is the process of bringing changes from several copies of a shared workbook into the source workbook. For more information on the topic, press F1 to display the Excel Help dialog box, search for workbook merging, and click the Merge Copies Of A Shared Workbook link.

3. Click **OK**.

   A message box appears, indicating that you must save the workbook for the action to take effect.

4. Click **OK**.

   Excel saves and shares the workbook.

5. Click the **File** tab, click **Save & Send**, and then click **Send Using E-mail**.

6. Click **Send as Attachment**.

   A new e-mail message opens with the CostProjections workbook attached.

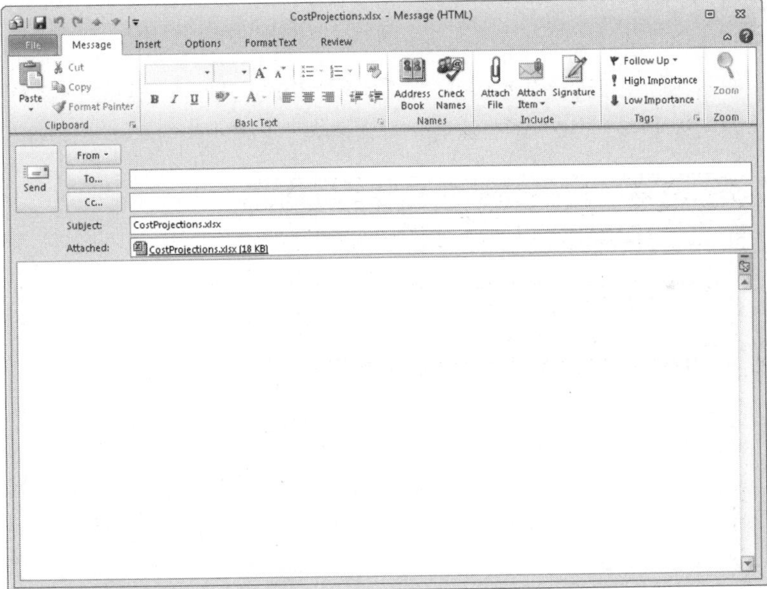

7. Type an address in the **To** box.

8. Click **Send**.

   Your e-mail program sends the message. If Excel had to open your e-mail program to send the message, the program would close at this point.

CLEAN UP Close the CostProjections workbook.

Saving a Workbook for Secure Electronic Distribution

You can create a secure, read-only copy of a workbook for electronic distribution by saving it as a Portable Document Format (PDF) or XML Paper Specification (XPS) file. The controls you use to do so are available on the Save & Send page of the Backstage view.

Tip You can also save a workbook as a PDF or XPS document by clicking the File tab and clicking Save As. Then, in the Save As dialog box, in the Save As Type list, select either PDF or XPS to create a file of the desired type.

To save a workbook as a PDF or XPS file:

1. Click the File tab, click Save & Send, click Create PDF/XPS Document, and then click the Create PDF/XPS button.
2. In the Publish As PDF Or XPS dialog box, select the file format you want.
3. If you plan to distribute the file online but not print it, click Minimum Size.
4. If you want to specify what portion of the workbook or types of content to publish, click the Options button, make your selections, and then click OK.
5. Click Publish.

Managing Comments

Excel makes it easy for you and your colleagues to insert comments in workbook cells, adding insights that go beyond the cell data. For example, if a regional processing center's package volume is exceptionally high on a particular day, the center's manager can add a comment to the cell in which shipments are recorded for that day, noting that two very large bulk shipments accounted for the disparity.

When you add a comment to a cell, a flag appears in the upper-right corner of the cell. When you point to a cell that contains a comment, the comment appears in a box next to the cell, along with the user name of the user who was logged on to the computer on which the comment was created.

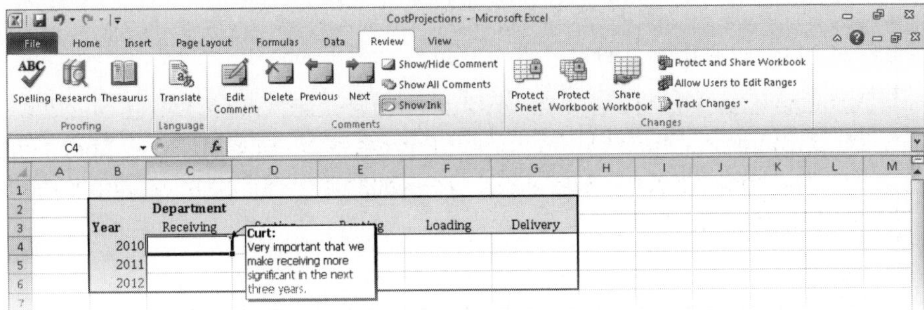

Important Note that the name attributed to a comment might not be the same as the name of the person who actually created it. Access controls, such as those that require users to enter account names and passwords when they access a computer, can help track the person who made a comment or change.

You can add a comment to a cell by clicking the cell, clicking the Review tab, and then clicking New Comment. When you do, the comment flag appears in the cell, and a comment box appears next to the cell. You can type the comment in the box and, when you're done, click another cell to close the box. When you point to the cell that contains the comment, the comment appears next to the cell.

If you want a comment to be shown the entire time the workbook is open, click the cell that contains the comment, click the Review tab and then, in the Comments group, click Show/Hide Comment. You can hide the comment by clicking the same button when the comment appears in the workbook, and delete the comment by clicking the Review tab and then, in the Comments group, clicking Delete. Or you can open the comment for editing by clicking Edit Comment in the Comments group.

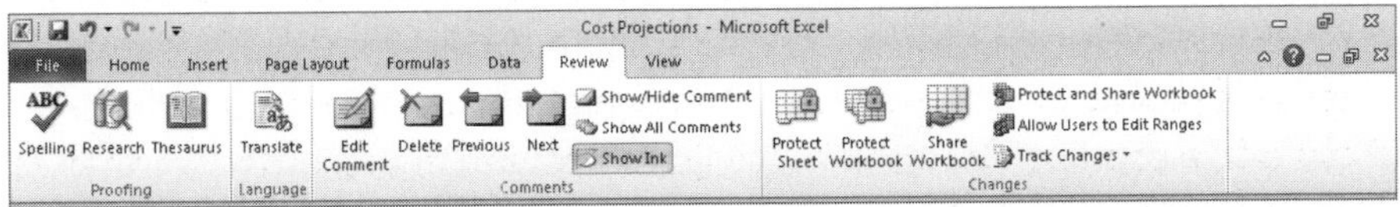

Troubleshooting The appearance of buttons and groups on the ribbon changes depending on the width of the program window. For information about changing the appearance of the ribbon to match our screen images, see "Modifying the Display of the Ribbon" at the beginning of this book.

Important When someone other than the original user edits a comment, that person's input is marked with the new user's name and is added to the original comment.

You can control whether a cell displays just the comment indicator or the indicator and the comment itself by clicking a cell that contains a comment and then, on the Review tab, clicking the Show/Hide Comment button. Clicking the Show/Hide Comment button again reverses your action. If you've just begun to review a worksheet and want to display all of the comments on the sheet, display the Review tab and click the Show All Comments button. To move through the worksheet's comments one at a time, click the Previous or Next button.

In this exercise, you'll add comments to two cells. You will then highlight the cells that contain comments, review a comment, and delete that comment.

SET UP You need the ProjectionsForComment_start workbook located in your Chapter14 practice file folder to complete this exercise. Open the ProjectionsForComment_start workbook, and save it as *ProjectionsForComment*. Then follow the steps.

1. Click cell **E6**.

2. On the **Review** tab, in the **Comments** group, click **New Comment**.

   A red comment flag appears in cell E6, and a comment box appears next to the cell.

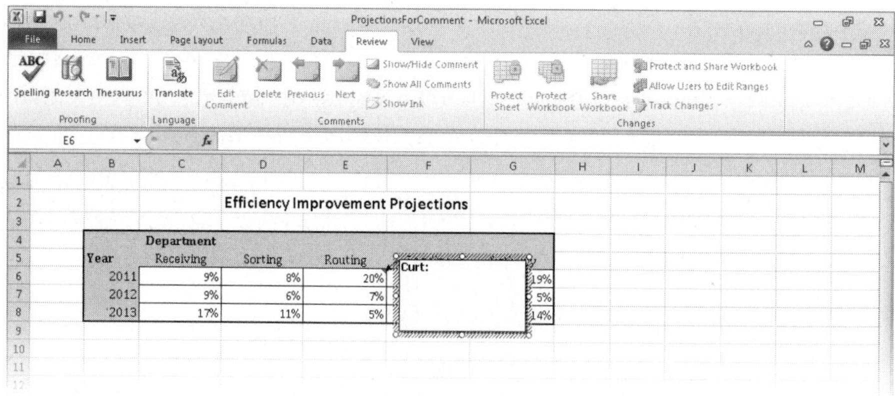

3. In the comment box, type **Seems optimistic; move some improvement to the next year?**
4. Click any cell outside the comment box.

   The comment box disappears.
5. Click cell **G7**.
6. On the **Review** tab, in the **Comments** group, click **New Comment**.

   A red comment flag appears in cell G7, and a comment box appears next to the cell.

7. In the comment box, type **Should see more increase as we integrate new processes**.
8. Click any cell outside the comment box.

   The comment box disappears.
9. Click cell **G7**.

10. On the **Review** tab, in the **Comments** group, click **Delete**.

    Excel deletes the comment.

CLEAN UP Save the ProjectionsForComment workbook, and then close it.

Tracking and Managing Colleagues' Changes

Whenever you collaborate with your colleagues to produce or edit a document, you should consider tracking the changes each user makes. When you turn on change tracking, any changes made to the workbook are highlighted in a color assigned to the user who made the changes. One benefit of tracking changes is that if you have a question about a change, you can quickly identify who made the change and verify that it is correct. In Excel, you can turn on change tracking in a workbook by clicking the Review tab and then, in the Changes group, clicking Track Changes and then Highlight Changes.

In the Highlight Changes dialog box that opens, select the Track Changes While Editing check box. Selecting this check box saves your workbook, turns on change tracking, and also shares your workbook, enabling more than one user to access the workbook simultaneously.

You can use the commands in the Highlight Changes dialog box to choose which changes to track. Clearing the When, Who, and Where check boxes makes Excel track all changes, whereas selecting a check box and using the commands to specify a time frame, users, or areas of the workbook limits which changes are highlighted. Each user's changes are displayed in a unique color. When you point to a cell that contains a change, the date and time when the change was made and the name of the user who made it appear as a ScreenTip.

After you and your colleagues finish modifying a workbook, anyone with permission to open the workbook can decide which changes to accept and which changes to reject. To start the process, click the Review tab. In the Changes group, click Track Changes, and then click Accept Or Reject Changes. After you clear the message box that indicates Excel will save your workbook, the Select Changes To Accept Or Reject dialog box opens. From the When list, you can choose which changes to review. The default choice is Not Yet Reviewed, but you can also click Since Date to open a dialog box in which you can enter the starting date of changes you want to review. To review all changes in your workbook, clear the When, Who, and Where check boxes.

Tip After you and your colleagues have finished making changes, you should turn off workbook sharing to help ensure that you are the only person able to review the changes and decide which to accept.

When you are ready to accept or reject changes, click OK. The Accept Or Reject Changes dialog box opens and displays the first change, which is described in the body of the dialog box. Clicking the Accept button finalizes the change; clicking the Reject button removes the change, restores the cell to its previous value, and erases any record of the change. Clicking Accept All or Reject All finalizes all changes or restores all cells to their original values, but you should choose one of those options only if you are absolutely certain you are doing the right thing.

Important Clicking the Undo button on the Quick Access Toolbar or pressing Ctrl+Z will not undo the operation.

You can create an itemized record of all changes made since the last time you saved the workbook by adding a History worksheet to your workbook. To add a History worksheet, click Track Changes in the Changes group, and then click Highlight Changes to open the Highlight Changes dialog box. Select the List Changes On A New Sheet check box. When you click OK, a new worksheet named History opens in your workbook. Excel will delete the History worksheet the next time you save your workbook.

In this exercise, you'll turn on change tracking in a workbook, make changes to the workbook, accept the changes, and create a History worksheet.

SET UP You need the ProjectionChangeTracking_start workbook located in your Chapter14 practice file folder to complete this exercise. Open the ProjectionChangeTracking_start workbook, and save it as *ProjectionChangeTracking*. Then follow the steps.

1. On the **Review** tab, in the **Changes** group, click **Track Changes**, and then click **Highlight Changes**.

   The Highlight Changes dialog box opens.

2. Select the **Track changes while editing** check box to activate the **Highlight which changes** area, and clear the **When** check box.

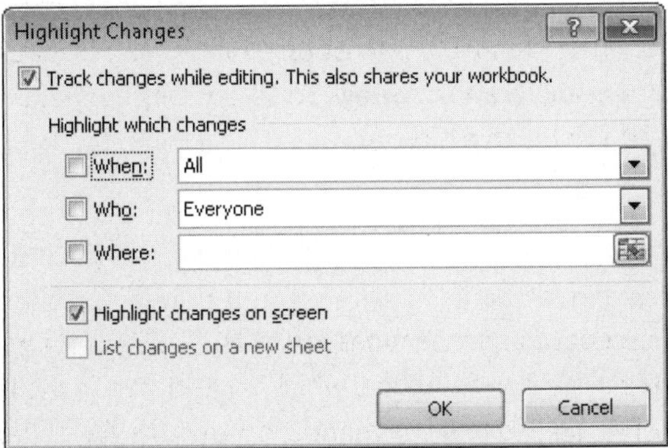

3. Click **OK**.

   A message box appears, indicating that Excel will save the workbook.

4. Click **OK**.

   The message box closes. Excel saves the workbook and begins tracking changes.

5. In cell **E6**, type **16%**, and then press Enter.

   A blue flag appears in the upper-left corner of cell E6.

6. In cell **E7**, type **14%**, and then press Enter.

   A blue flag appears in the upper-left corner of cell E7.

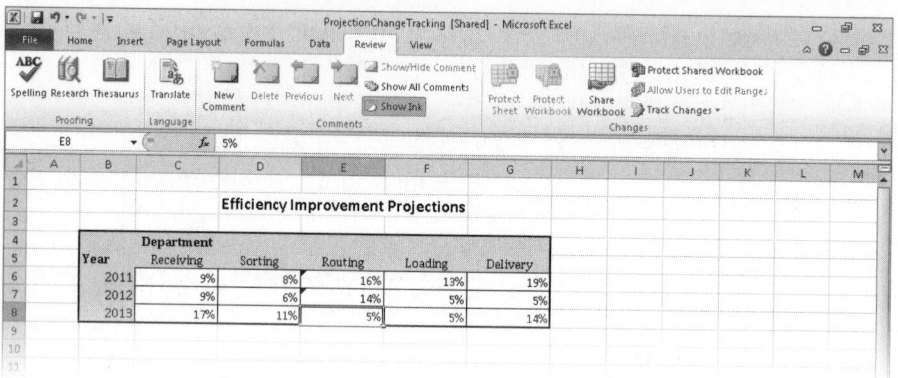

7. On the Quick Access Toolbar, click the **Save** button to save your work.
8. On the **Review** tab, in the **Changes** group, click **Track Changes**, and then click **Highlight Changes**.

   The Highlight Changes dialog box opens.
9. Select the **List changes on a new sheet** check box, clear the **When** check box, and then click **OK**.

   Excel creates and displays a worksheet named *History*, which contains a list of all changes made since the last time a user accepted or rejected changes.

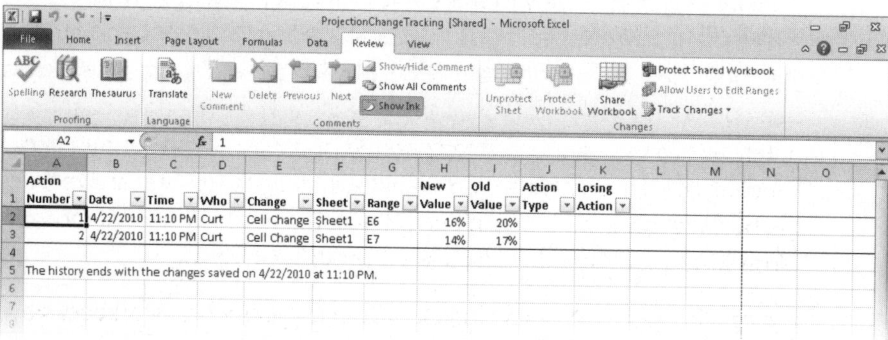

10. Click the **Sheet1** sheet tab.

    The Sheet1 worksheet opens.
11. On the **Review** tab, in the **Changes** group, click **Track Changes**, and then click **Accept/Reject Changes**.

    The Select Changes To Accept Or Reject dialog box opens.
12. Click **OK**.

    The Accept Or Reject Changes dialog box displays the first change.

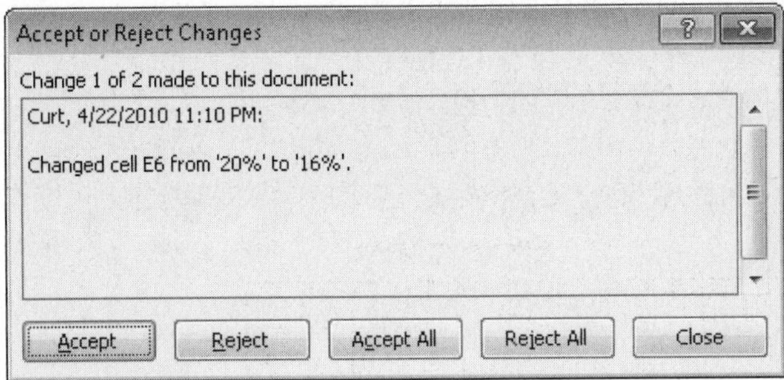

13. Click **Accept**.

    Excel keeps the change and then displays the next change.

14. Click **Accept**.

    Excel keeps the change and deletes the History worksheet. The Accept Or Reject Changes dialog box closes.

 **CLEAN UP** Save the ProjectionChangeTracking workbook, and then close it.

Protecting Workbooks and Worksheets

Excel gives you the ability to share your workbooks over the Web, over a corporate intranet, or by copying files for other users to take on business trips. An important part of sharing files, however, is ensuring that only those users you want to have access to the files can open or modify them. For example, Consolidated Messenger might have a series of computers available in a processing center so supervisors can look up package volumes and handling efficiency information. Although those computers are vital tools for managing the business process, it doesn't help the company to have unauthorized personnel, even those with good intentions, accessing critical workbooks.

You can limit access to your workbooks or elements within workbooks by setting passwords. When you set a password for an Excel workbook, any users who want to access the protected workbook must enter the workbook's password in a dialog box that opens when they try to open the file. If users don't know the password, they cannot open the workbook.

To set a password for a workbook, open the workbook to be protected, and click the File tab to display the workbook in the Backstage view. Then, on the Info page of the Backstage view, click the Protect Workbook button and then click Encrypt With Password. The Encrypt Document dialog box opens, with a Password box in which you can type your password. After you click OK, the Confirm Password dialog box opens, in which you can verify the password required to open the workbook. After you have confirmed the password, click OK. Now the Info page of the Backstage view indicates that users must enter a password to open the file.

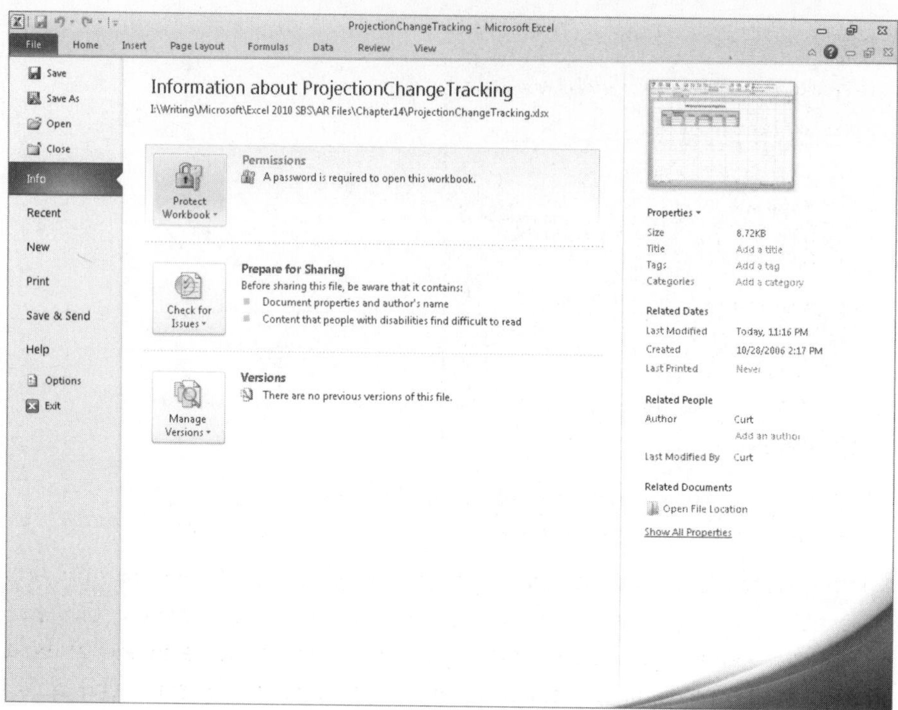

To remove the passwords from a workbook, repeat these steps, but delete the passwords from the Encrypt Document dialog box and save the file.

Tip The best passwords are long strings of random characters, but random characters are hard to remember. One good method of creating hard-to-guess passwords is to base your password on a longer phrase. For example, "I learned about passwords in Chapter 14 of *Microsoft Excel 2010 Step by Step*" could translate to the password *IlapiC14oME2SbS*. In any event, avoid dictionary words in English or any other language, because they can be found easily by password-guessing programs available on the Internet; include both uppercase and lowercase letters; and use characters other than letters or numbers if possible.

If you want to allow anyone to open a workbook but want to prevent unauthorized users from editing a worksheet, you can protect a worksheet by displaying that worksheet, clicking the Review tab and then, in the Changes group, clicking Protect Sheet to open the Protect Sheet dialog box.

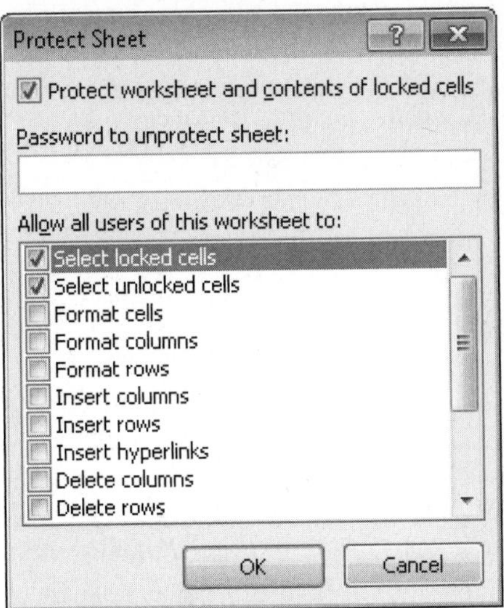

In the Protect Sheet dialog box, you select the Protect Worksheet And Contents Of Locked Cells check box to protect the sheet. You can also set a password that a user must type in before protection can be turned off again and choose which elements of the worksheet a user can change while protection is turned on. To enable a user to change a worksheet element without entering the password, select the check box next to that element's name.

The check box at the top of the worksheet mentions locked cells. A locked cell is a cell that can't be changed when worksheet protection is turned on. You can lock or unlock a cell by right-clicking the cell and clicking Format Cells on the shortcut menu that appears. In the Format Cells dialog box, you click the Protection tab and select the Locked check box.

When worksheet protection is turned on, selecting the Locked check box prevents unauthorized users from changing the contents or formatting of the locked cell, whereas selecting the Hidden check box hides the formulas in the cell. You might want to hide the formula in a cell if you draw sensitive data, such as customer contact information, from another workbook and don't want casual users to see the name of the workbook in a formula.

Finally, you can password-protect a cell range. For example, you might want to let users enter values in most worksheet cells but also want to protect the cells with formulas that perform calculations based on those values. To password-protect a range of cells, select the cells to protect, click the Review tab and then, in the Changes group, click Allow Users To Edit Ranges. The Allow Users To Edit Ranges dialog box opens.

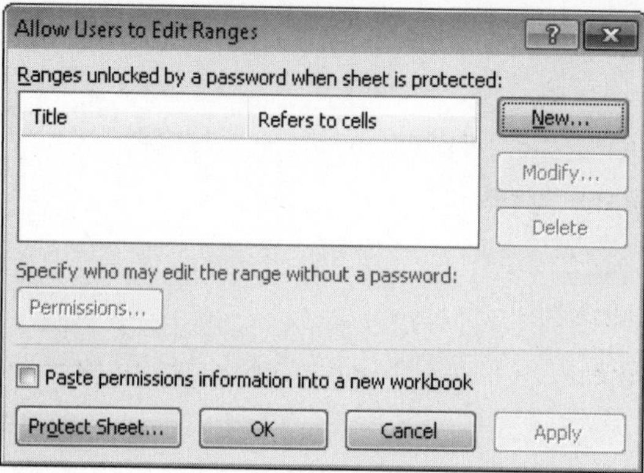

To create a protected range, click the New button to display the New Range dialog box. Type a name for the range in the Title box, and then type a password in the Range Password box. When you click OK, Excel asks you to confirm the password; after you do, click OK in the Confirm Password dialog box and again in the Allow Users To Edit Ranges dialog box to protect the range. Now, whenever users try to edit a cell in the protected range, they are prompted for a password.

Tip Remember that a range of cells can mean just one cell!

In this exercise, you'll password-protect a workbook, a worksheet, and a range of cells. You will also hide the formula in a cell.

SET UP You need the SecureInfo_start workbook located in your Chapter14 practice file folder to complete this exercise. Open the SecureInfo_start workbook, and save it as *SecureInfo*. Then follow the steps.

1. Click the **File** tab, and then, if necessary, click **Info**.

   The Info page of the Backstage view is displayed.

2. Click the **Protect Workbook** button, and then click **Encrypt with Password**.

   The Encrypt Document dialog box opens.

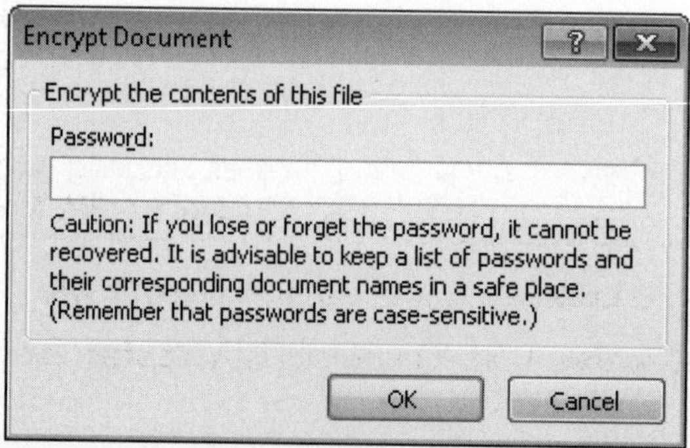

3. Type **work14pro** in the **Password** box.
4. Click **OK**.

   The Confirm Password dialog box opens.
5. In the **Reenter password** box, type **work14pro**.
6. Click **OK**.

   The Confirm Password dialog box closes.
7. Click the **Review** tab of the ribbon and, if necessary, click the **Performance** sheet tab.

   The Performance worksheet opens.
8. Right-click cell **B8**, and then click **Format Cells**.

   The Format Cells dialog box opens.
9. Click the **Protection** tab.

   The Protection page is displayed.

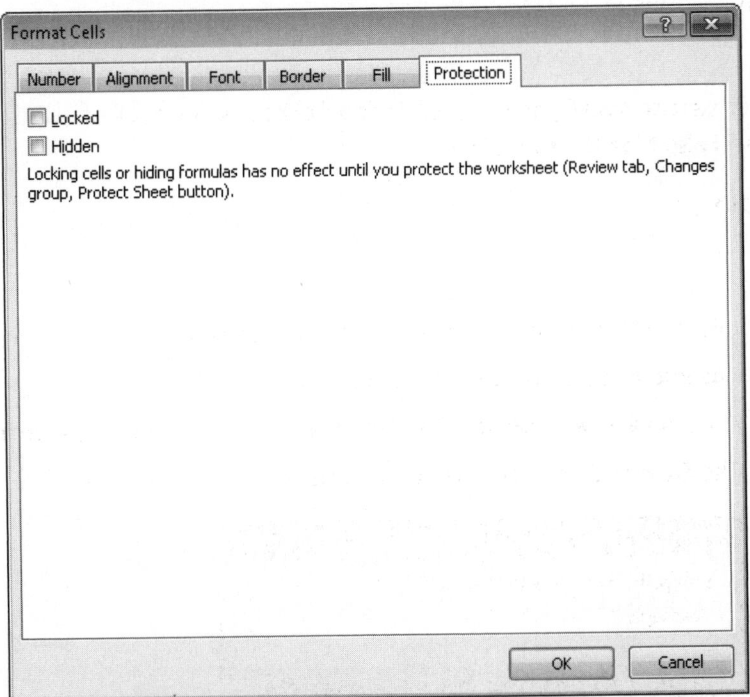

10. Select the **Hidden** and **Locked** check boxes, and then click **OK**.

    Excel formats cell B8 so that it won't display its formula after you protect the worksheet.

11. On the **Review** tab, in the **Changes** group, click **Protect Sheet**.

    The Protect Sheet dialog box opens.

12. In the **Password to unprotect sheet** box, type **prot300pswd**.
13. Clear the **Select locked cells** and **Select unlocked cells** check boxes, and then click **OK**.

    The Confirm Password dialog box opens.

14. In the **Reenter password to proceed** box, type **prot300pswd**, and then click **OK**.
15. Click the **Weights** sheet tab.

    The Weights worksheet opens.

16. Select the cell range **B2:C7**.
17. On the **Review** tab, in the **Changes** group, click **Allow Users to Edit Ranges**.

    The Allow Users To Edit Ranges dialog box opens.

18. Click **New**.

    The New Range dialog box opens, with the range B2:C7 displayed in the Refers To Cells box.

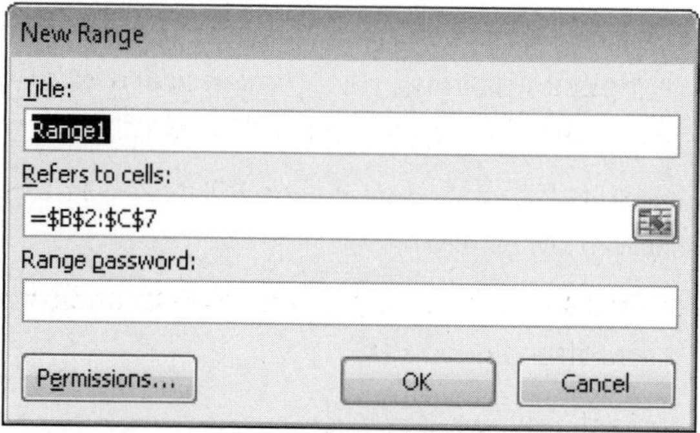

19. In the **Title** box, type **AllWeights**.
20. In the **Range password** box, type **work14pro**, and then click **OK**.
21. In the **Confirm Password** dialog box, reenter the password **work14pro**.

    The range appears in the Allow Users To Edit Ranges box.

22. Click **Protect Sheet**.

    The Protect Sheet dialog box opens.

23. In the **Password to unprotect sheet** box, type **work14pro**, and then click **OK**.
24. In the **Confirm Password** dialog box, reenter the password **work14pro**, and then click **OK**.

CLEAN UP Save the SecureInfo workbook, and then close it.

Finalizing a Workbook

Distributing a workbook to other users carries many risks, not the least of which is the possibility that the workbook might contain private information you don't want to share with users outside your organization. With Excel, you can inspect a workbook for information you might not want to distribute to other people, and create a read-only final version that prevents other people from making changes to the workbook content.

Using the Document Inspector, you can quickly locate comments and annotations, document properties and personal information, custom XML data, headers and footers, hidden rows and columns, hidden worksheets, and invisible content. You can then easily remove any hidden or personal information that the Document Inspector finds.

To inspect and remove hidden or personal information, follow these steps:

1. Save the file.
2. Click the File tab, and then, on the Info page of the Backstage view, click Check for Issues, and then click Inspect Document.
3. In the Document Inspector window, clear the check box of any content type you want to remain in the document, and click Inspect.
4. In the inspection results list, click the Remove All button to the right of any category of data you want to remove.

Marking a workbook as final sets the status property to Final and turns off data entry, editing commands, and proofreading marks.

To mark a workbook as final, follow these steps:

1. Click the File tab, and then, on the Info page of the Backstage view, click Protect Workbook, and then click Mark as Final.
2. In the message box indicating that the file will be marked as final and then saved, click OK.
3. In the message box indicating that the file has been marked as final, click OK.

To restore functionality to a workbook that has been marked as final, click the File tab and then, on the Info page of the Backstage view, click Protect Workbook, and then click Mark As Final to change its status.

Authenticating Workbooks

The unfortunate reality of exchanging files over networks, especially over the Internet, is that you need to be sure you know the origin of the files you're working with. One way an organization can guard against files with viruses or substitute data is to authenticate every workbook using a digital signature. A digital signature is a character string created by combining a user's unique secret digital signature file mathematically with the contents of the workbook, which programs such as Excel can recognize and use to verify the identity of the user who signed the file. A good analogy for a digital signature is a wax seal, which was used for thousands of years to verify the integrity and origin of a document.

Tip The technical details of and procedure for managing digital certificates are beyond the scope of this book, but your network administrator should be able to create a digital certificate for you. You can also directly purchase a digital signature from a third party, which can usually be renewed annually for a small fee. For the purposes of this book, you'll use the selfcert.exe Microsoft Office accessory program to generate a certificate with which to perform the exercise at the end of this topic. This type of certificate is useful for certifying a document as part of a demonstration, but other users will not accept it as a valid certificate to verify that the contents of the document haven't changed since it was signed.

To create a digital certificate that you can use as a demonstration, open the Start menu, click All Programs, click Microsoft Office, click Microsoft Office 2010 Tools, and then click Digital Certificate For VBA Projects. In the Create Digital Certificate dialog box, type a name for your certificate and click OK to have the program create your trial certificate. Then, in Excel, click the File tab and on the Info page of the Backstage view, click Protect Workbook and then click Add A Digital Signature. In the Sign dialog box, type your purpose for signing the document, and then click Sign to sign your workbook.

Tip After you click Add A Digital Signature, Excel displays a dialog box, indicating that you can buy digital signatures from third-party providers. To get information about those services, click the Signature Services From The Office Marketplace button. To bypass the message, click OK; to prevent the dialog box from appearing again, select the Don't Show This Message Again check box, and then click OK.

If you have several certificates from which to choose, and the desired certificate doesn't appear in the Sign dialog box, you can click Change to display the Select Certificate dialog box. In the Select Certificate dialog box, click the certificate with which you want to sign the workbook, and then click OK. The Select Certificate dialog box closes, and the certificate with which you signed the workbook appears in the Sign dialog box. As before, click Sign to sign your document by using the digital certificate.

In this exercise, you'll create a digital certificate and digitally sign a workbook by using the certificate.

SET UP You need the ProjectionsSigned_start workbook located in your Chapter14 practice file folder to complete this exercise. Open the ProjectionsSigned_start workbook, and save it as *ProjectionsSigned*. Then follow the steps.

1. On the **Start** menu, click **All Programs**, click **Microsoft Office**, click **Microsoft Office 2010 Tools**, and then click **Digital Certificate for VBA Projects**.

   The Create Digital Certificate dialog box opens.

2. In the **Your certificate's name** box, type **Excel2010SBS**, and then click **OK**.

   A message box indicates that the program created your certificate successfully.

3. Click **OK**.

   The message box closes.

4. Click the **File** tab and then, if necessary, click **Info**. Click **Protect Workbook** and then click **Add a Digital Signature**.

   A message box appears, offering the opportunity to view signature services on Office Marketplace.

5. Click **OK**.

   The message box closes, and the Sign dialog box opens.

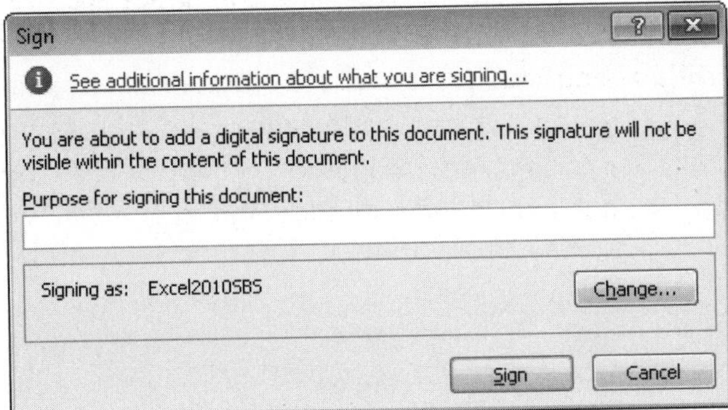

6. In the **Purpose for signing this document** box, type **Testing**.

7. Verify that the **Excel2010SBS** certificate appears in the **Signing as** area of the dialog box, and then click **Sign**.

   The Signature Confirmation dialog box opens.

8. Click **OK**.

   The Signatures task pane opens and the workbook is marked as final. If you edit the workbook, it will invalidate the digital signature, which is based on the workbook's contents at the time you signed it.

CLEAN UP Save the ProjectionsSigned workbook, and then close it.

Saving Workbooks for the Web

With Excel, you can save your workbooks as Web documents, so you and your colleagues can view workbooks over the Internet or an organization's intranet. For a document to be viewable on the Web, it must be saved as a Hypertext Markup Language (HTML) file. HTML files, which end with either the *.htm* or the *.html* extension, include tags that tell a Web browser such as Windows Internet Explorer how to display the contents of the file.

For example, you might want to set the data labels in a workbook apart from the rest of the data by having the labels displayed with bold text. The coding in an HTML file that indicates text to be displayed as bold text is *<b>...</b>*, where the ellipsis between the tags is replaced by the text to be displayed. So the following HTML fragment would be displayed as **Excel** in a Web page:

```
<b>Excel</b>
```

You can create HTML files in Excel by clicking the File tab and clicking Save As to display the Save As dialog box. To save a workbook as an HTML file, click the Save As Type arrow and then click Web Page. Then, in the Save As dialog box, select the Entire Workbook option, type a name for the file in the File Name box, and click Save to have Excel create an HTML document for each sheet in the workbook.

Tip If the only sheet in your workbook that contains data is the one displayed when you save the workbook as a Web page, Excel only saves that worksheet as a Web page.

After you save an Excel workbook as a set of HTML documents, you can open it in your Web browser. To open the Excel file, start Internet Explorer, and then click Open on the File menu to display the Open dialog box. In the Open dialog box, click the Browse button to open the Windows Internet Explorer dialog box. You can use the commands in that dialog box to identify the file you want to open.

When you double-click the file you want to open, the Windows Internet Explorer dialog box closes and the file's name and path appear in the Open box. To display the Excel workbook, click OK, and the workbook appears in Internet Explorer. You can move among the workbook's worksheets by clicking the sheet tabs in the lower-left corner of the page.

Saving a workbook to an organization's intranet site enables you to share data with your colleagues. For example, Consolidated Messenger's chief operating officer, Lori Penor, could save a daily report on package misdeliveries to her team's intranet so that everyone could examine what happened, where the problem occurred, and how to fix the problem. It's also possible to save a workbook as a Web file that retains a link to the original workbook. Whenever someone updates the workbook, Excel updates the Web files to reflect the new content.

To publish a workbook to the Web, click the File tab, click Save As and then, in the Save As Type list, click Web Page. When you do, Excel displays the Publish button; clicking the Publish button displays the Publish As Web Page dialog box.

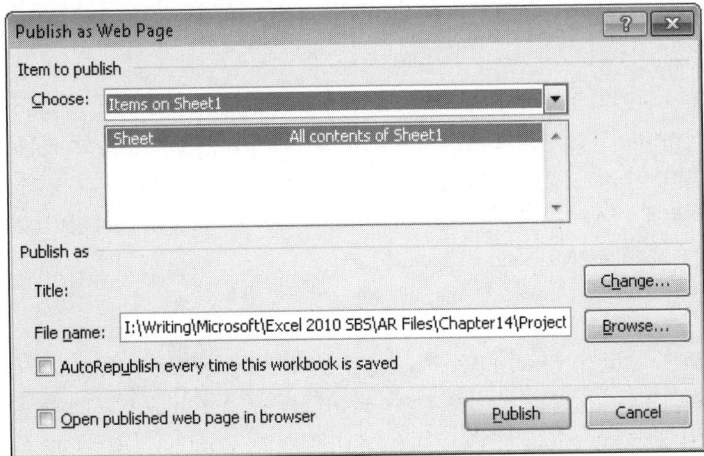

You can use the options in the Publish As Web Page dialog box to select which elements of your workbook you want to publish to the Web. Clicking the Choose arrow displays a list of publishable items, including the option to publish the entire workbook, items on specific sheets, or a range of cells. To have Excel update the Web page whenever someone updates the source workbook, select the AutoRepublish Every Time This Workbook Is Saved check box. You can also specify which text appears on the Web page's title bar. To do so, click the Change button, type the page title in the Set Title dialog box, and click OK. When you save a workbook that has AutoRepublish turned on, Excel displays a dialog box indicating that the changes will update the associated Web file.

Important When you save a PivotTable to the Web, the PivotTable doesn't retain its interactivity. Instead, Excel publishes a static image of the PivotTable's current configuration.

In this exercise, you'll save a workbook as a Web page and then publish a worksheet's PivotTable to the Web.

SET UP You need the ShipmentSummary_start workbook located in your Chapter14 practice file folder to complete this exercise. Open the ShipmentSummary_start workbook, and save it as *ShipmentSummary*. Then follow the steps.

1. Click the **File** tab, and then click **Save As**.

   The Save As dialog box opens.

2. In the **File name** box, type **ShipmentSummaryWeb**.
3. In the **Save as type** list, click **Web Page**.

   The Save As dialog box changes to reflect the Web Page file type.

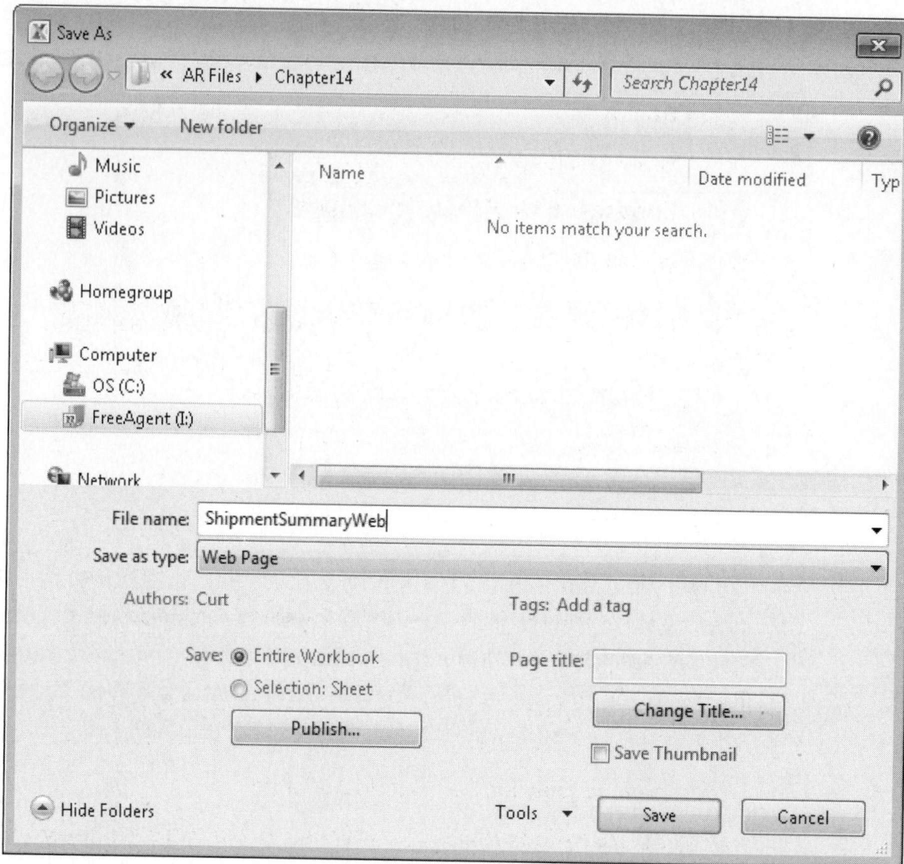

4. Click **Save**.

   A warning message box appears, indicating that the workbook might contain elements that can't be saved in a Web page.
5. Click **Yes** to save the workbook as a Web file.

   The message box closes, and Excel saves the workbook as a Web page.
6. Click the **File** tab, and then click **Close**.
7. Click the **File** tab, click **Recent**, and then, in the list of recently viewed files, click **ShipmentSummary**.

   The ShipmentSummary workbook opens.

8. Click the **File** tab, and then click **Save As**.

   The Save As dialog box opens.

9. In the **File name** box, type **ShipmentSummaryPublish**.
10. In the **Save as type** list, click **Web Page**.

    The Save As dialog box changes to reflect the Web Page file type.

11. Click **Publish**.

    The Publish As Web Page dialog box opens.

12. In the **Choose** list, click **Items on Sheet2**.

    The available items on Sheet2 appear.

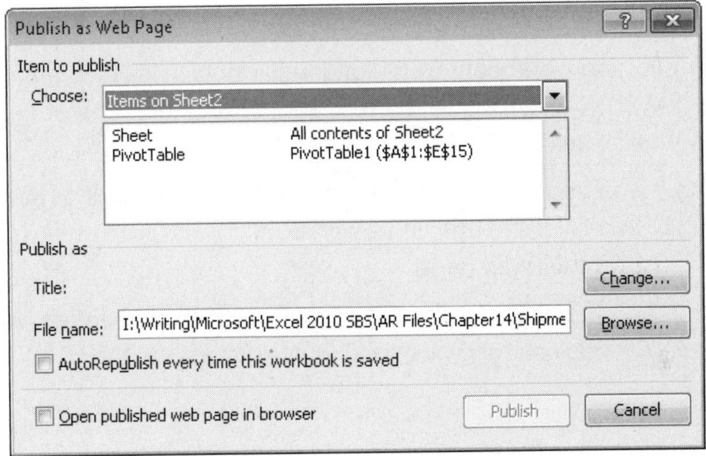

13. In the **Item to publish** list, click **PivotTable**.
14. Select the **AutoRepublish every time this workbook is saved** check box.
15. Click **Publish**.

    Excel publishes the PivotTable to a Web page. Excel will update the contents of the Web page whenever a user saves the ShipmentSummary workbook.

CLEAN UP Save the ShipmentSummary workbook, and then close it. Exit Excel.

Key Points

- Sharing a workbook enables more than one user to view and edit the data at one time, which is useful in group projects in which each member has a distinct area of responsibility.
- Sending files by e-mail is a very efficient means of collaborating with colleagues.
- Adding comments to cells is a quick way to let your colleagues know what you're thinking without taking up valuable space in a cell.
- Tracking changes is vital when you share responsibility for a workbook with several other people.
- When your workbook's data is too important to leave lying around in the open, use passwords to protect all or part of the file!
- Authenticating workbooks with digital signatures helps to identify the source of your files, so you won't have to guess about the origins of that next attachment in your e-mail inbox.
- Saving a workbook as a Web-accessible HTML document is as easy as saving it as a regular Excel file, and opening a workbook saved for the Web is just as easy as opening any other Web page.
- Use the AutoRepublish facility to update Excel files on the Web. Whenever anyone changes the original workbook, Excel writes the edits to the HTML version of the file.

Glossary

3-D reference A pattern for referring to the workbook, worksheet, and cell from which a value should be read.

absolute reference A cell reference, such as =$B$3, that doesn't change when you copy a formula containing the reference to another cell.

active cell The cell that is currently selected and open for editing.

add-in A supplemental program that can be used to extend Excel's functions.

alignment The manner in which a cell's contents are arranged within that cell (for example, centered).

arguments The specific data a function requires to calculate a value.

aspect ratio The relationship between a graphic's height and its width.

auditing The process of examining a worksheet for errors.

AutoComplete The Excel functionality that completes data entry for a cell based on similar values in other cells in the same column.

AutoFill The Excel functionality that extends a series of values based on the contents of a single cell. See also *Fill Series*.

AutoFilter An Excel tool you can use to create filters.

AutoRepublish An Excel technology that maintains a link between a Web document and the worksheet on which the Web document is based, and updates the Web document whenever the original worksheet is saved.

Backstage view A new view in Excel 2010, accessed by clicking the File tab, that gathers workbook management tasks into a single location.

browser A program with which users view Web documents.

cell The box at the intersection of a row and a column.

cell range A group of cells.

cell reference The letter and number combination, such as C16, that identifies the row and column intersection of a cell.

chart A visual summary of worksheet data, also called a graph.

column Cells that are on the same vertical line in a worksheet.

conditional format A format that is applied only when cell contents meet certain criteria.

conditional formula A formula that calculates a value using one of two different expressions, depending on whether a third expression is true or false.

data bar A horizontal line within a cell that indicates the relative magnitude of the cell's value.

data consolidation Summarizing data from a set of similar cell ranges.

dependent A cell with a formula that uses the value from a particular cell. See also *precedent*.

embed To save a file as part of another file, as opposed to linking one file to another. See also *link*.

error code A brief message that appears in a worksheet cell, describing a problem with a formula or a function.

Excel table An Excel object with which you can store and refer to data based on the name of the table and the names of its columns and rows.

Extensible Markup Language (XML) A content-marking system with which you store data about the contents of a document in that document.

field A column of data used to create a PivotTable.

fill handle The square at the lower-right corner of a cell that can be dragged to indicate other cells that should hold values in the series defined by the active cell.

FillSeries The ability to extend a series of values based on the contents of two cells, where the first cell has the starting value for the series and the second cell shows the increment. See also *AutoFill.*

filter A rule that Excel uses to determine which worksheet rows to display.

format A predefined set of characteristics that can be applied to cell contents.

formula An expression used to calculate a value.

Formula AutoComplete The Excel functionality with which you can enter a formula quickly by selecting functions, named ranges, and table references that appear when you begin to type the formula into a cell.

formula bar The area just above the worksheet grid that displays the active cell's formula and within which you can edit the formula.

function A predefined formula.

Goal Seek An analysis tool that finds the value for a selected cell that would produce a given result from a calculation.

graph A visual summary of worksheet data, also called a chart.

header An area of the worksheet that appears above the contents of the worksheet grid when you print the worksheet or view it in Layout View.

HTML See *Hypertext Markup Language.*

hyperlink A reference to a file on the Web.

Hypertext Markup Language (HTML) A document-formatting system that tells a Web browser such as Windows Internet Explorer how to display the contents of a file.

icon set A conditional format that uses distinct visual indicators to designate how a value compares to a set of criteria.

landscape mode A display and printing mode whereby columns run parallel to the short edge of a sheet of paper.

link A formula that has a cell show the value from another cell.

live preview A feature of Excel that displays the result of an operation, such as pasting data or applying a cell style, without implementing the change until you complete the operation.

locked cell A cell that cannot be modified if its worksheet is protected.

macro A series of recorded automated actions that can be replayed.

mailto hyperlink A special type of hyperlink with which a user creates an e-mail message to a particular e-mail address.

Merge And Center An operation that combines a contiguous group of cells into a single cell. Selecting a merged cell and clicking the Merge And Center button splits the merged cells into the original group of separate cells.

named range A group of related cells defined by a single name.

Paste Options A button that appears after you paste an item from the Microsoft Office Clipboard into your workbook, and which provides options for how the item appears in the workbook.

Pick from List The Excel functionality that allows you to enter a value into a cell by choosing the value from the set of values already entered into cells in the same column.

pivot To reorganize the contents of a PivotTable.

PivotChart A chart that is linked to a PivotTable and that can be reorganized dynamically to emphasize different aspects of the underlying data.

PivotTable A dynamic worksheet that can be reorganized by a user.

portrait mode A display and printing mode whereby columns run parallel to the long edge of a sheet of paper.

precedent A cell that is used in a formula.

primary key A field or group of fields with values that distinguish a row of data from all other rows.

property A file detail, such as an author name or project code, that helps identify the file.

Quick Access Toolbar A customizable toolbar that contains a set of commands that are independent of the tab on the ribbon that is currently displayed.

range A group of related cells.

refresh To update the contents of one document when the contents of another document are changed.

relative reference A cell reference in a formula, such as =B3, that refers to a cell that is a specific distance away from the cell that contains the formula. For example, if the formula =B3 were in cell C3, copying the formula to cell C4 would cause the formula to change to =B4. See also *absolute reference*.

ribbon The tab-based user interface introduced in Microsoft Office 2007.

row Cells that are on the same horizontal line in a worksheet.

scenario An alternative data set with which you view the impact of specific changes on your worksheet.

search filter A filter in which you type a string of characters and have Excel display every value within an Excel table, data set, or PivotTable that contains that character string.

sharing Making a workbook available for more than one user to open and modify simultaneously.

sheet tab The indicator for selecting a worksheet, located at the bottom of the workbook window.

Slicer An Excel tool with which you can filter an Excel table, data list, or PivotTable while indicating which items are displayed and which are hidden.

Solver An Excel add-in that finds the optimal value for one cell by varying the results of other cells.

sort To reorder the contents of a worksheet based on a criterion.

sparkline A compact chart that summarizes data visually within a single worksheet cell.

subtotal A partial total for related data in a worksheet.

template A workbook used as a pattern for creating other workbooks.

theme A predefined format that can be applied to a worksheet.

tracer arrow An arrow that indicates the formulas to which a cell contributes its value (a dependent arrow) or the cells from which a formula derives its value (a precedent arrow).

trendline A projection of future data (such as sales) based on past performance.

validation rule A test that data must pass to be entered into a cell without generating a warning message.

watch Display of a cell's contents in a separate window even when the cell is not visible in the Excel workbook.

what-if analysis Analysis of the contents of a worksheet to determine the impact that specific changes have on your calculations.

workbook The basic Excel document, consisting of one or more worksheets.

worksheet A page in an Excel workbook.

workspace An Excel file type (.xlw) that allows you to open several files at once.

XML See *Extensible Markup Language*.

Keyboard Shortcuts

This list of shortcuts is a comprehensive list derived from Microsoft Excel 2010 Help. Some of the shortcuts might not be available in every version of Excel 2010.

Ctrl Combination Shortcut Keys

Key	Description
Ctrl+Shift+(	Unhides any hidden rows within the selection.
Ctrl+Shift+&	Applies the outline border to the selected cells.
Ctrl+Shift+_	Removes the outline border from the selected cells.
Ctrl+Shift+~	Applies the General number format.
Ctrl+Shift+$	Applies the Currency format with two decimal places (negative numbers in parentheses).
Ctrl+Shift+%	Applies the Percentage format with no decimal places.
Ctrl+Shift+^	Applies the Scientific number format with two decimal places.
Ctrl+Shift+#	Applies the Date format with the day, month, and year.
Ctrl+Shift+@	Applies the Time format with the hour and minute, and A.M. or P.M.
Ctrl+Shift+!	Applies the Number format with two decimal places, thousands separator, and minus sign (-) for negative values.
Ctrl+Shift+*	Selects the current region around the active cell (the data area enclosed by blank rows and blank columns). In a PivotTable, it selects the entire PivotTable report.
Ctrl+Shift+:	Enters the current time.
Ctrl+Shift+"	Copies the value from the cell above the active cell into the cell or the formula bar.
Ctrl+Shift+Plus (+)	Displays the Insert dialog box to insert blank cells.
Ctrl+Minus (-)	Displays the Delete dialog box to delete the selected cells.
Ctrl+;	Enters the current date.
Ctrl+`	Toggles between displaying cell values and displaying formulas in the worksheet.
Ctrl+'	Copies a formula from the cell above the active cell into the cell or the formula bar.
Ctrl+1	Displays the Format Cells dialog box.

(continued)

Key	Description
Ctrl+2	Toggles to apply or remove bold formatting.
Ctrl+3	Toggles to apply or remove italic formatting.
Ctrl+4	Toggles to apply or remove underlining.
Ctrl+5	Toggles to apply or remove strikethrough.
Ctrl+6	Toggles between hiding and displaying objects.
Ctrl+8	Toggles to display or hide the outline symbols.
Ctrl+9	Hides the selected rows.
Ctrl+0	Hides the selected columns.
Ctrl+A	Selects the entire worksheet. If the worksheet contains data, Ctrl+A selects the current region. Pressing Ctrl+A a second time selects the entire worksheet. When the insertion point is to the right of a function name in a formula, displays the Function Arguments dialog box.
Ctrl+Shift+A	Inserts the argument names and parentheses when the insertion point is to the right of a function name in a formula.
Ctrl+B	Toggles to apply or remove bold formatting.
Ctrl+C	Copies the selected cells.
Ctrl+D	Uses the Fill Down command to copy the contents and format of the topmost cell of a selected range into the cells below.
Ctrl+F	Displays the Find And Replace dialog box, with the Find page active. Shift+F5 also displays this page, whereas Shift+F4 repeats the last Find action.
Ctrl+Shift+F	Opens the Format Cells dialog box with the Font page active.
Ctrl+G	Displays the Go To dialog box. F5 also displays this dialog box.
Ctrl+H	Displays the Find And Replace dialog box, with the Replace page active.
Ctrl+I	Toggles to apply or remove italic formatting.
Ctrl+K	Displays the Insert Hyperlink dialog box for new hyperlinks or the Edit Hyperlink dialog box for selected existing hyperlinks.
Ctrl+L	Displays the Create Table dialog box.
Ctrl+N	Creates a new, blank workbook.
Ctrl+O	Displays the Open dialog box to open or find a file.
Ctrl+Shift+O	Selects all cells that contain comments.
Ctrl+P	Displays the Print page in the Backstage view.
Ctrl+Shift+P	Opens the Format Cells dialog box with the Font page active.
Ctrl+R	Uses the Fill Right command to copy the contents and format of the leftmost cell of a selected range into the cells to the right.
Ctrl+S	Saves the active file with its current file name, location, and file format.

Key	Description
Ctrl+T	Displays the Create Table dialog box.
Ctrl+U	Toggles to apply or remove underlining.
Ctrl+Shift+U	Toggles between expanding and collapsing the formula bar.
Ctrl+V	Inserts the contents of the Microsoft Office Clipboard at the insertion point and replaces any selection. Available only after you have cut or copied an object, text, or cell contents.
Ctrl+Alt+V	Displays the Paste Special dialog box. Available only after you have cut or copied an object, text, or cell contents on a worksheet or in another program.
Ctrl+W	Closes the selected workbook window.
Ctrl+X	Cuts the selected cells.
Ctrl+Y	Repeats the last command or action, if possible.
Ctrl+Z	Uses the Undo command to reverse the last command or to delete the last entry that you typed.

Tip The Ctrl combinations Ctrl+E, Ctrl+J, Ctrl+M, and Ctrl+Q are currently unassigned to any shortcuts.

Function Keys

Key	Description
F1	Displays the Excel Help task pane.
Ctrl+F1	Displays or hides the ribbon.
Alt+F1	Creates an embedded chart of the data in the current range.
Alt+Shift+F1	Inserts a new worksheet.
F2	Opens the active cell for editing and positions the insertion point at the end of the cell contents. It also moves the insertion point into the formula bar when editing in a cell is turned off.
Ctrl+F2	Displays the print preview area on the Print page in the Backstage view.
Shift+F2	Adds a cell comment or opens an existing comment for editing.
F3	Displays the Paste Name dialog box. Available only if there are existing names in the workbook.
Shift+F3	Displays the Insert Function dialog box.
F4	Repeats the last command or action, if possible.
Ctrl+F4	Closes the selected workbook window.
Alt+F4	Closes Excel.
F5	Displays the Go To dialog box.

(continued)

Key	Description
Ctrl+F5	Restores the window size of the selected workbook window.
F6	Switches between the worksheet, ribbon, task pane, and Zoom controls. In a worksheet that has been split, F6 includes the split panes when switching between panes and the ribbon area.
Ctrl+F6	Switches to the next workbook window when more than one workbook window is open.
Shift+F6	Switches between the worksheet, Zoom controls, task pane, and ribbon.
F7	Displays the Spelling dialog box to check spelling in the active worksheet or selected range.
Ctrl+F7	Performs the Move command on the workbook window when it is not maximized. Use the arrow keys to move the window, and when finished press Enter or Esc to cancel.
F8	Turns extend mode on or off. In extend mode, *Extended Selection* appears in the status line, and the arrow keys extend the selection.
Ctrl+F8	Performs the Size command (on the Control menu for the workbook window) when a workbook is not maximized.
Alt+F8	Displays the Macro dialog box to create, run, edit, or delete a macro.
Shift+F8	Enables you to add a nonadjacent cell or range to a selection of cells by using the arrow keys.
F9	Calculates all worksheets in all open workbooks.
Ctrl+F9	Minimizes a workbook window to an icon.
Shift+F9	Calculates the active worksheet.
Ctrl+Alt+F9	Calculates all worksheets in all open workbooks, regardless of whether they have changed since the last calculation.
Ctrl+Alt+Shift+F9	Rechecks dependent formulas, and then calculates all cells in all open workbooks, including cells not marked as needing to be calculated.
F10	Turns key tips on or off. (Pressing Alt does the same thing.)
Ctrl+F10	Maximizes or restores the selected workbook window.
Shift+F10	Displays the shortcut menu for a selected item.
Alt+Shift+F10	Displays the menu or message for an Error Checking button.
F11	Creates a chart of the data in the current range in a separate Chart sheet.
Alt+F11	Opens the Microsoft Visual Basic Editor, in which you can create a macro by using Visual Basic for Applications (VBA).
Shift+F11	Inserts a new worksheet.
F12	Displays the Save As dialog box.

Other Useful Shortcut Keys

Key	Description
Arrow keys	Moves one cell up, down, left, or right in a worksheet.
Ctrl+Arrow key	Moves to the edge of the current data region (range of cells that contains data and that is bounded by empty cells or datasheet borders) in a worksheet.
Shift+Arrow key	Extends the selection of cells by one cell.
Ctrl+Shift+Arrow key	Extends the selection of cells to the last nonblank cell in the same column or row as the active cell, or if the next cell is blank, extends the selection to the next nonblank cell.
Left Arrow or Right Arrow	Selects the tab to the left or right when the ribbon is selected. When a submenu is open or selected, these arrow keys switch between the main menu and the submenu.
Down Arrow or Up Arrow	Selects the next or previous command when a menu or submenu is open. When a ribbon tab is selected, these keys navigate up or down the tab group. In a dialog box, arrow keys move between options in an open drop-down list, or between options in a group of options.
Down Arrow or Alt+Down Arrow	Opens a selected drop-down list.
Backspace	Deletes one character to the left in the formula bar. Also clears the content of the active cell. In cell editing mode, deletes the character to the left of the insertion point.
Delete	Removes the cell contents (data and formulas) from selected cells without affecting cell formats or comments. In cell editing mode, deletes the character to the right of the insertion point.
End	Turns End mode on. In End mode, you can press an arrow key to move to the next nonblank cell in the same column or row as the active cell. If the cells are blank, pressing End followed by an arrow key moves to the last cell in the row or column. End also selects the last command on the menu when a menu or submenu is visible.
Ctrl+End	Moves to the last cell on a worksheet, to the lowest used row of the rightmost used column. If the cursor is in the formula bar, Ctrl+End moves the cursor to the end of the text.
Ctrl+Shift+End	Extends the selection of cells to the last used cell on the worksheet (lower-right corner). If the cursor is in the formula bar, Ctrl+Shift+End selects all text in the formula bar from the cursor position to the end—this does not affect the height of the formula bar.

(continued)

Key	Description
Enter	Completes a cell entry from the cell or the formula bar, and selects the cell below (by default). In a data form, moves to the first field in the next record. Opens a selected menu (press F10 to activate the menu bar) or performs the action for a selected command. In a dialog box, performs the action for the default command button in the dialog box (the button with the bold outline, often the OK button).
Alt+Enter	Starts a new line in the same cell.
Ctrl+Enter	Fills the selected cell range with the current entry.
Shift+Enter	Completes a cell entry and selects the cell above.
Esc	Cancels an entry in the cell or formula bar. Closes an open menu or submenu, dialog box, or message window. Also closes full screen mode when this mode has been applied, and returns to normal screen mode to display the ribbon and status bar again.
Home	Moves to the beginning of a row in a worksheet. Moves to the cell in the upper-left corner of the window when Scroll Lock is turned on. Selects the first command on the menu when a menu or submenu is visible.
Ctrl+Home	Moves to the beginning of a worksheet.
Ctrl+Shift+Home	Extends the selection of cells to the beginning of the worksheet.
Page Down	Moves one screen down in a worksheet.
Alt+Page Down	Moves one screen to the right in a worksheet.
Ctrl+Page Down	Moves to the next sheet in a workbook.
Ctrl+Shift+Page Down	Selects the current and next sheet in a workbook.
Page Up	Moves one screen up in a worksheet.
Alt+Page Up	Moves one screen to the left in a worksheet.
Ctrl+Page Up	Moves to the previous sheet in a workbook.
Ctrl+Shift+Page Up	Selects the current and previous sheet in a workbook.
Spacebar	In a dialog box, performs the action for the selected button, or selects or clears a check box.
Ctrl+Spacebar	Selects an entire column in a worksheet.
Shift+Spacebar	Selects an entire row in a worksheet.
Ctrl+Shift+Spacebar	Selects the entire worksheet. If the worksheet contains data, Ctrl+Shift+Spacebar selects the current region. Pressing Ctrl+Shift+Spacebar a second time selects the current region and its summary rows. Pressing Ctrl+Shift+Spacebar a third time selects the entire worksheet. When an object is selected, Ctrl+Shift+Spacebar selects all objects on a worksheet.

Key	Description
Alt+Spacebar	Displays the Control menu for the Excel window.
Tab	Moves one cell to the right in a worksheet. Moves between unlocked cells in a protected worksheet. Moves to the next option or option group in a dialog box.
Shift+Tab	Moves to the previous cell in a worksheet or the previous option in a dialog box.
Ctrl+Tab	Switches to the next page in a dialog box.
Ctrl+Shift+Tab	Switches to the previous page in a dialog box.

Index

Symbols and Numbers

A

B

C

D

E

F

G

H

I

K

L

M

N

O

P

Q

S

T

U

X

Z

About the Author

Curtis Frye is a writer, speaker, and performer living in Portland, Oregon. He is the sole or lead author of more than 20 books, including *Microsoft Excel 2010 Plain & Simple*, *Microsoft Access 2010 Plain & Simple*, and *Excel 2007 Pocket Guide*. In addition to his writing, Curt presents keynote addresses on Excel and motivational topics.